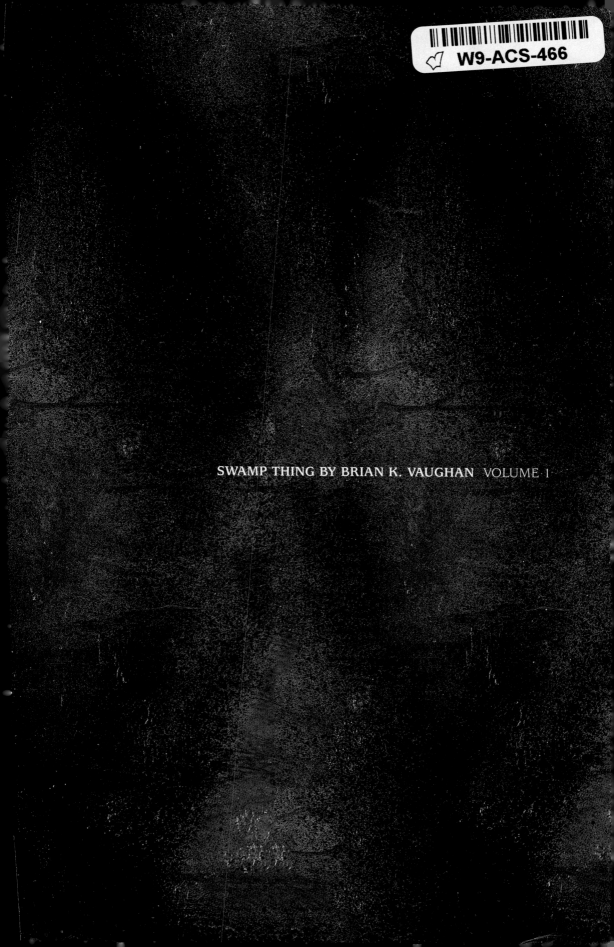

SWAMP THING BY BRIAN K. VAUGHAN VOLUME·1

SWAMP THING
BY BRIAN K. VAUGHAN

Written by Brian K. Vaughan

Art by Roger Peterson, Joe Rubinstein, Rick Magyar, Cliff Chiang, Rodney Ramos, Mark Lipka, Steve Lieber, Paul Pope, and Guy Davis

Colors by Alex Sinclair

Letters by John Costanza

Original Series Covers Art by Phil Hale, Rick Berry, and Simon Bisley

Collection Cover Art by Phil Hale

SWAMP THING Created by LEN WEIN and BERNIE WRIGHTSON

Joan Hilty Heidi MacDonald Shelly Bond Editors – Original Series
Rachel Pinnelas Editor
Robbin Brosterman Design Director – Books
Louis Prandi Publication Design

Shelly Bond Executive Editor - Vertigo
Hank Kanalz Senior VP – Vertigo & Integrated Publishing

Diane Nelson President
Dan DiDio and Jim Lee Co-Publishers
Geoff Johns Chief Creative Officer
John Rood Executive VP – Sales, Marketing & Business Development
Amy Genkins Senior VP – Business & Legal Affairs
Nairi Gardiner Senior VP – Finance
Jeff Boison VP – Publishing Planning
Mark Chiarello VP – Art Direction & Design
John Cunningham VP – Marketing
Terri Cunningham VP – Editorial Administration
Alison Gill Senior VP – Manufacturing & Operations
Jay Kogan VP – Business & Legal Affairs, Publishing
Jack Mahan VP – Business Affairs, Talent
Nick Napolitano VP – Manufacturing Administration
Sue Pohja VP – Book Sales
Courtney Simmons Senior VP – Publicity
Bob Wayne Senior VP – Sales

SWAMP THING BY BRIAN K. VAUGHAN VOLUME 1

Published by DC Comics. Copyright © 2014 DC Comics. All Rights Reserved.

Originally published in single magazine form in SWAMP THING 1-9, VERTIGO
SECRET FILES & ORIGINS: SWAMP THING 1, and VERTIGO WINTER'S EDGE
3. Copyright © 2000, 2001 DC Comics. All Rights Reserved. All characters, their
distinctive likenesses and related elements featured in this publication are
trademarks of DC Comics. The stories, characters and incidents featured in this
publication are entirely fictional. DC Comics does not read or accept unsolicited
ideas, stories or artwork.

DC Comics, 1700 Broadway, New York, NY 10019
A Warner Bros. Entertainment Company.
Printed in the USA. First Printing. ISBN: 978-1-4012-4304-3

Library of Congress Cataloging-in-Publication Data

Vaughan, Brian K.
  Swamp Thing By Brian K. Vaughan Volume 1 / Brian K. Vaughan ; [illustrated by]
Roger Peterson, Cliff Chiang.
     pages cm
  ISBN 978-1-4012-4304-3 (pbk.)
1. Graphic novels. I. Chiang, Cliff, illustrator. II. Peterson, Roger, illustrator. III.
Title.
  PN6728.S93V38 2014
  741.5'973—dc23
                         2013036120

SUSTAINABLE   Certified Chain of Custody
FORESTRY   At Least 20% Certified Forest Content
INITIATIVE   www.sfiprogram.org
              SFI-01042
              APPLIES TO TEXT STOCK ONLY

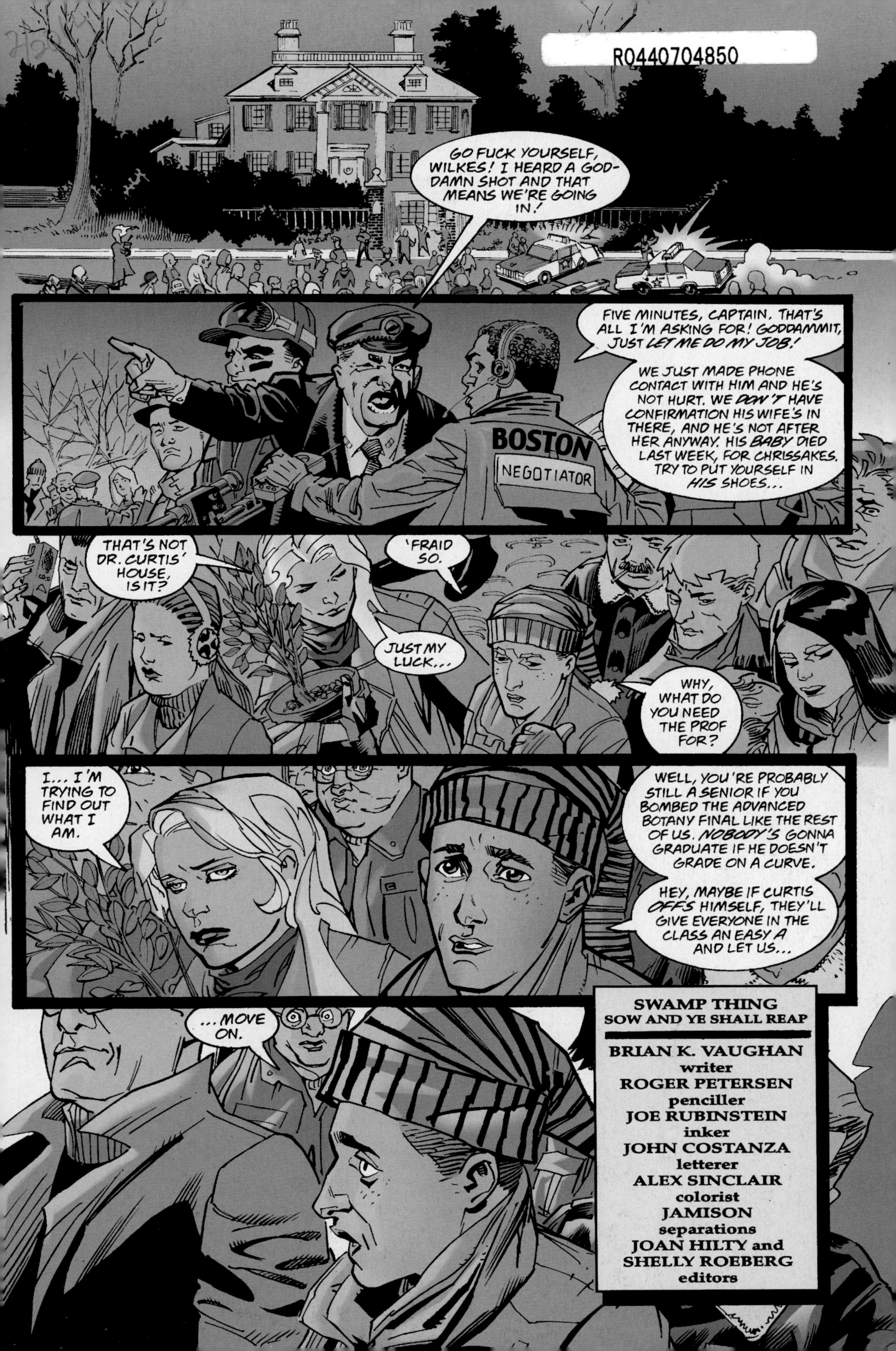
GO FUCK YOURSELF, WILKES! I HEARD A GOD-DAMN SHOT AND THAT MEANS WE'RE GOING IN!
FIVE MINUTES, CAPTAIN. THAT'S ALL I'M ASKING FOR! GODDAMMIT, JUST LET ME DO MY JOB!
WE JUST MADE PHONE CONTACT WITH HIM AND HE'S NOT HURT. WE DON'T HAVE CONFIRMATION HIS WIFE'S IN THERE, AND HE'S NOT AFTER HER ANYWAY. HIS BABY DIED LAST WEEK, FOR CHRISSAKES. TRY TO PUT YOURSELF IN HIS SHOES...
BOSTON
NEGOTIATOR
THAT'S NOT DR. CURTIS' HOUSE, IS IT?
'FRAID SO.
JUST MY LUCK...
WHY, WHAT DO YOU NEED THE PROF FOR?
I... I'M TRYING TO FIND OUT WHAT I AM.
WELL, YOU'RE PROBABLY STILL A SENIOR IF YOU BOMBED THE ADVANCED BOTANY FINAL LIKE THE REST OF US. NOBODY'S GONNA GRADUATE IF HE DOESN'T GRADE ON A CURVE.
HEY, MAYBE IF CURTIS OFFS HIMSELF, THEY'LL GIVE EVERYONE IN THE CLASS AN EASY A AND LET US...
...MOVE ON.
SWAMP THING
SOW AND YE SHALL REAP
BRIAN K. VAUGHAN writer
ROGER PETERSEN penciller
JOE RUBINSTEIN inker
JOHN COSTANZA letterer
ALEX SINCLAIR colorist
JAMISON separations
JOAN HILTY and SHELLY ROEBERG editors

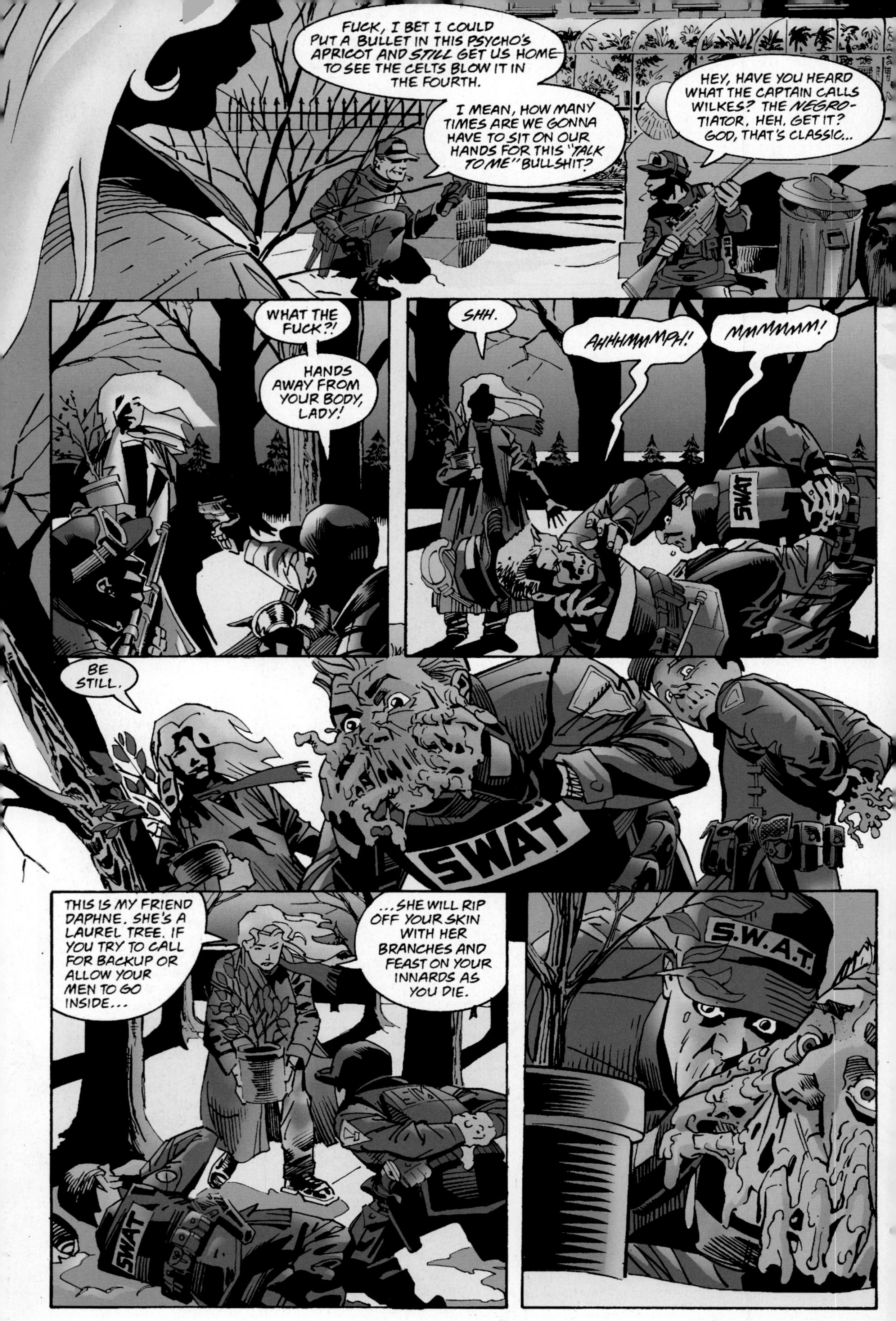
FUCK, I BET I COULD PUT A BULLET IN THIS PSYCHO'S APRICOT AND STILL GET US HOME TO SEE THE CELTS BLOW IT IN THE FOURTH.
I MEAN, HOW MANY TIMES ARE WE GONNA HAVE TO SIT ON OUR HANDS FOR THIS "TALK TO ME" BULLSHIT?
HEY, HAVE YOU HEARD WHAT THE CAPTAIN CALLS WILKES? THE NEGRO-TIATOR. HEH. GET IT? GOD, THAT'S CLASSIC...
WHAT THE FUCK?!
HANDS AWAY FROM YOUR BODY, LADY!
SHH.
AHHHMMMPH!
MMMMMM!
SWAT
BE STILL.
SWAT
THIS IS MY FRIEND DAPHNE. SHE'S A LAUREL TREE. IF YOU TRY TO CALL FOR BACKUP OR ALLOW YOUR MEN TO GO INSIDE...
...SHE WILL RIP OFF YOUR SKIN WITH HER BRANCHES AND FEAST ON YOUR INNARDS AS YOU DIE.
SWAT
S.W.A.T.

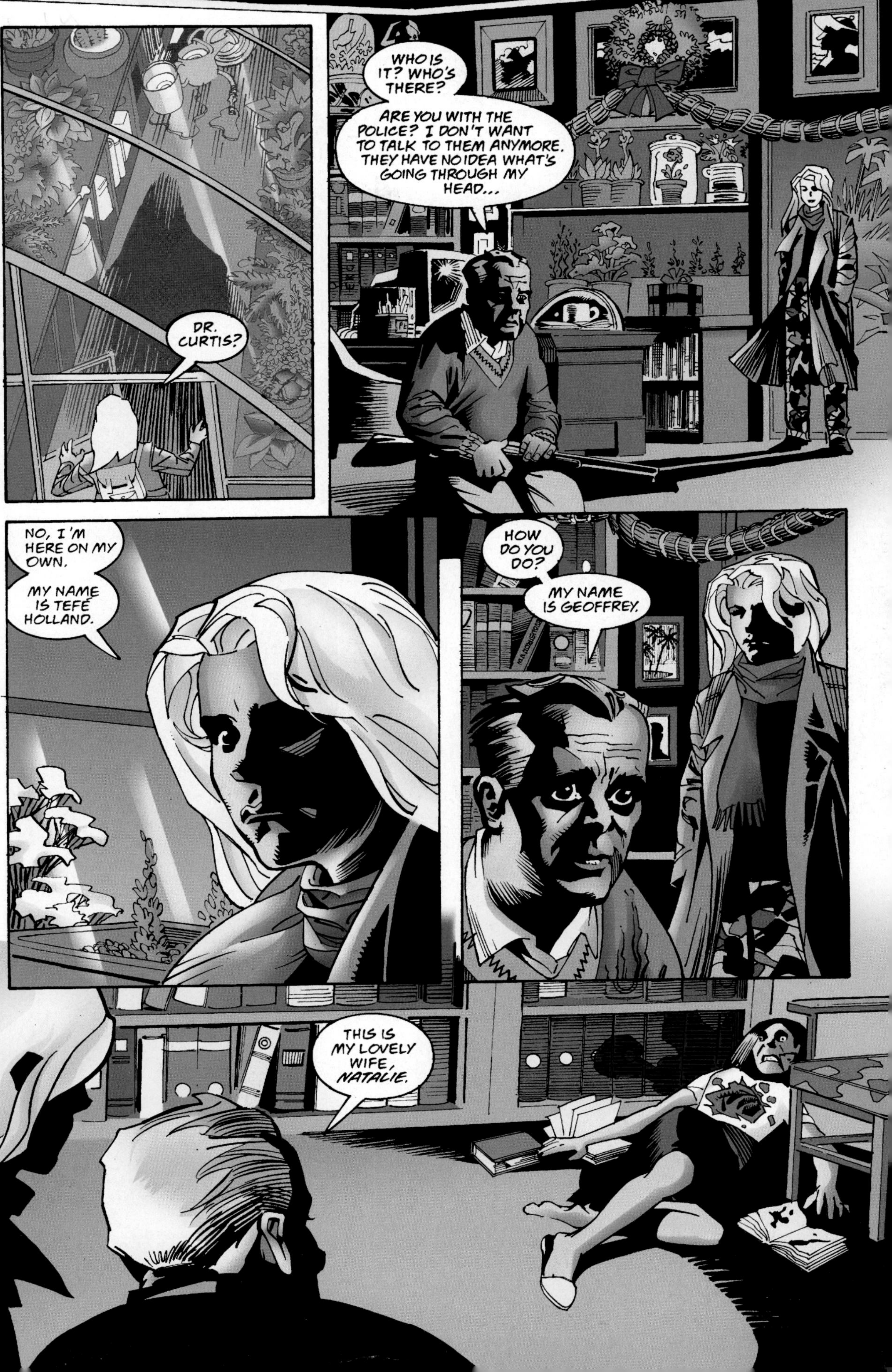
DR. CURTIS?
WHO IS IT? WHO'S THERE?
ARE YOU WITH THE POLICE? I DON'T WANT TO TALK TO THEM ANYMORE. THEY HAVE NO IDEA WHAT'S GOING THROUGH MY HEAD...
NO, I'M HERE ON MY OWN.
MY NAME IS TEFÉ HOLLAND.
HOW DO YOU DO?
MY NAME IS GEOFFREY.
THIS IS MY LOVELY WIFE, NATALIE.

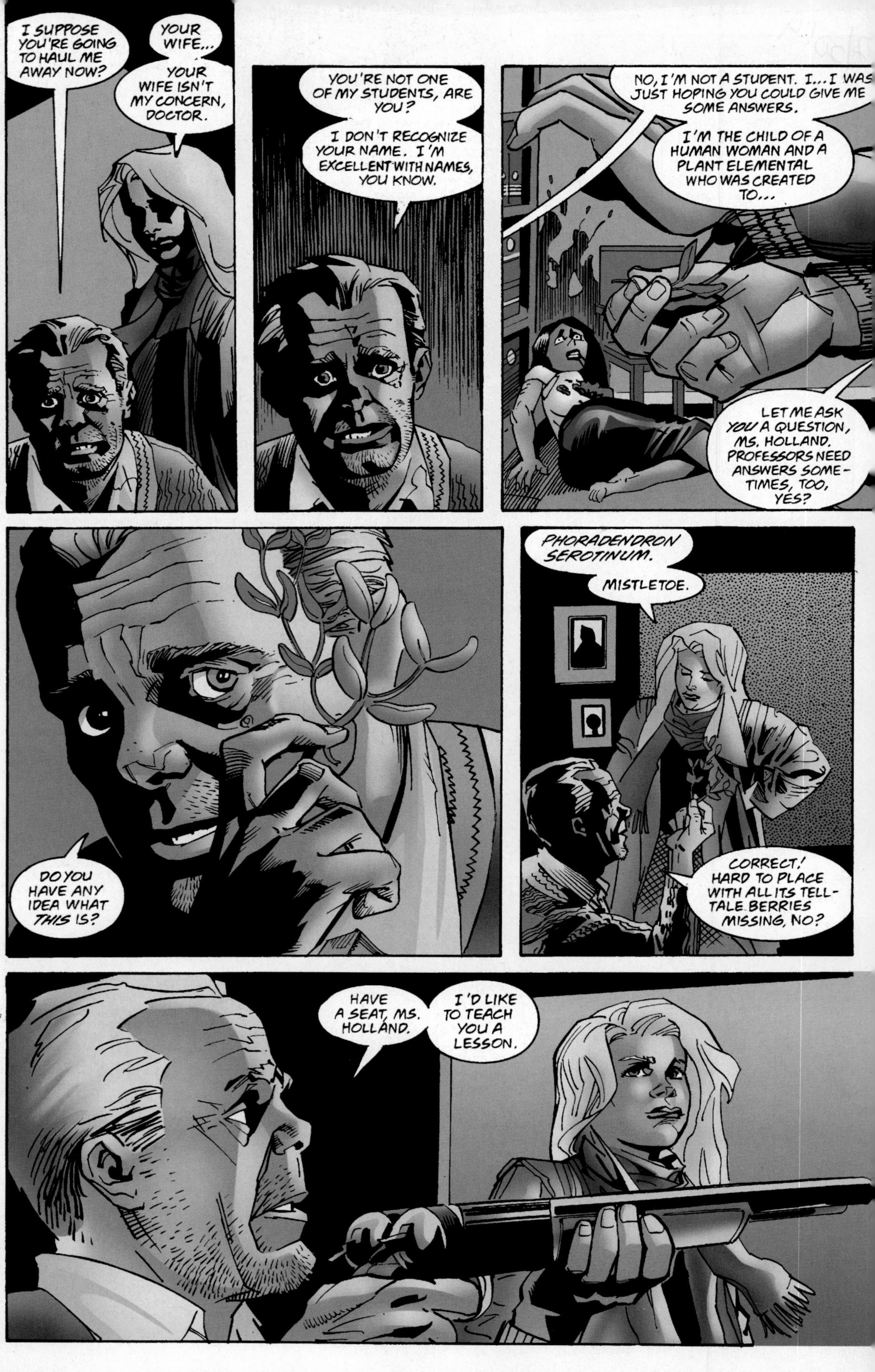
I SUPPOSE YOU'RE GOING TO HAUL ME AWAY NOW?
YOUR WIFE...
YOUR WIFE ISN'T MY CONCERN, DOCTOR.
YOU'RE NOT ONE OF MY STUDENTS, ARE YOU?
I DON'T RECOGNIZE YOUR NAME. I'M EXCELLENT WITH NAMES, YOU KNOW.
NO, I'M NOT A STUDENT. I... I WAS JUST HOPING YOU COULD GIVE ME SOME ANSWERS.
I'M THE CHILD OF A HUMAN WOMAN AND A PLANT ELEMENTAL WHO WAS CREATED TO...
LET ME ASK YOU A QUESTION, MS. HOLLAND. PROFESSORS NEED ANSWERS SOMETIMES, TOO, YES?
DO YOU HAVE ANY IDEA WHAT THIS IS?
PHORADENDRON SEROTINUM.
MISTLETOE.
CORRECT! HARD TO PLACE WITH ALL ITS TELLTALE BERRIES MISSING, NO?
HAVE A SEAT, MS. HOLLAND.
I'D LIKE TO TEACH YOU A LESSON.

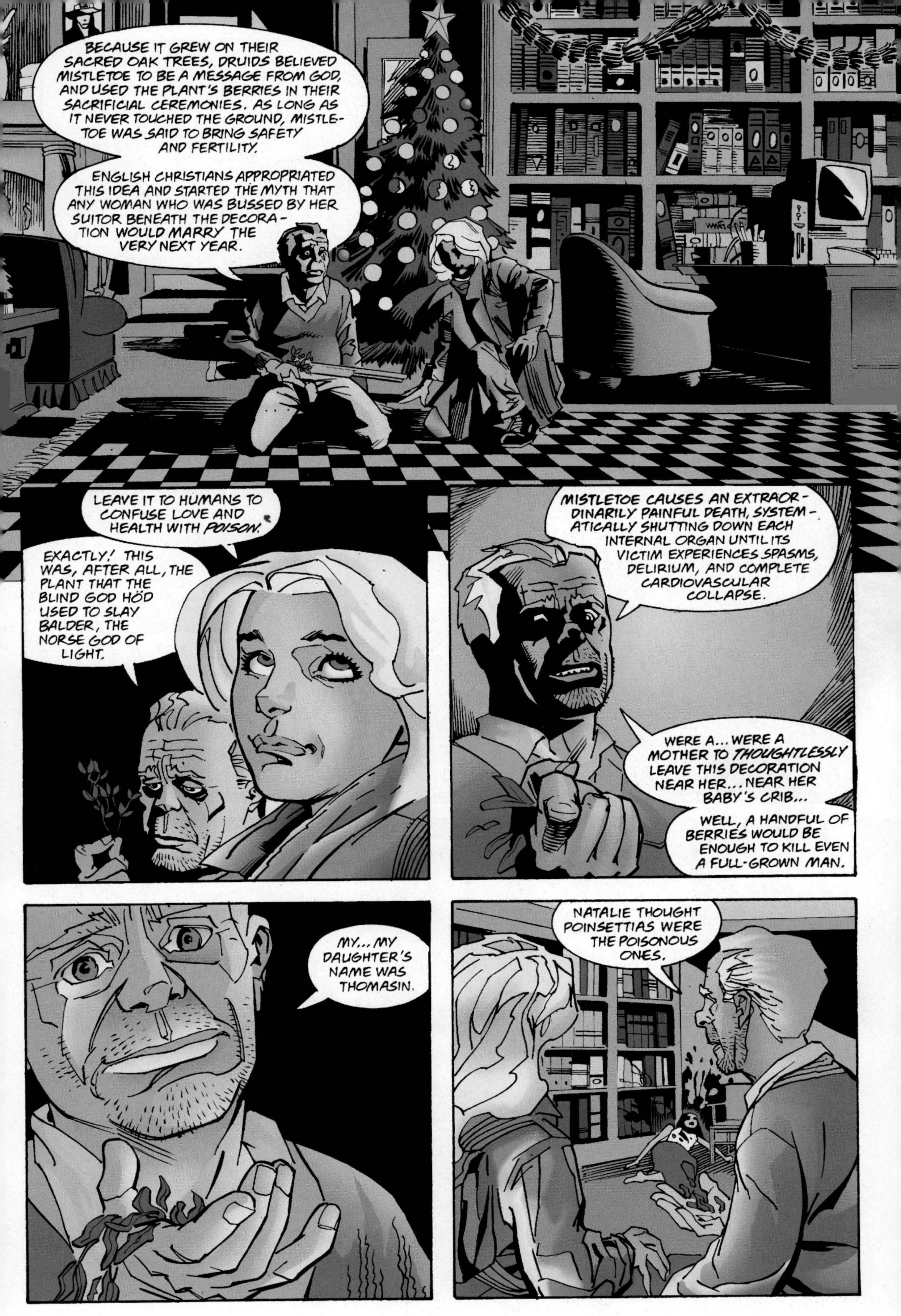

BECAUSE IT GREW ON THEIR SACRED OAK TREES, DRUIDS BELIEVED MISTLETOE TO BE A MESSAGE FROM GOD, AND USED THE PLANT'S BERRIES IN THEIR SACRIFICIAL CEREMONIES. AS LONG AS IT NEVER TOUCHED THE GROUND, MISTLETOE WAS SAID TO BRING SAFETY AND FERTILITY.
ENGLISH CHRISTIANS APPROPRIATED THIS IDEA AND STARTED THE MYTH THAT ANY WOMAN WHO WAS BUSSED BY HER SUITOR BENEATH THE DECORATION WOULD MARRY THE VERY NEXT YEAR.
LEAVE IT TO HUMANS TO CONFUSE LOVE AND HEALTH WITH POISON.
EXACTLY! THIS WAS, AFTER ALL, THE PLANT THAT THE BLIND GOD HÖD USED TO SLAY BALDER, THE NORSE GOD OF LIGHT.
MISTLETOE CAUSES AN EXTRAORDINARILY PAINFUL DEATH, SYSTEMATICALLY SHUTTING DOWN EACH INTERNAL ORGAN UNTIL ITS VICTIM EXPERIENCES SPASMS, DELIRIUM, AND COMPLETE CARDIOVASCULAR COLLAPSE.
WERE A... WERE A MOTHER TO THOUGHTLESSLY LEAVE THIS DECORATION NEAR HER... NEAR HER BABY'S CRIB...
WELL, A HANDFUL OF BERRIES WOULD BE ENOUGH TO KILL EVEN A FULL-GROWN MAN.
MY... MY DAUGHTER'S NAME WAS THOMASIN.
NATALIE THOUGHT POINSETTIAS WERE THE POISONOUS ONES.

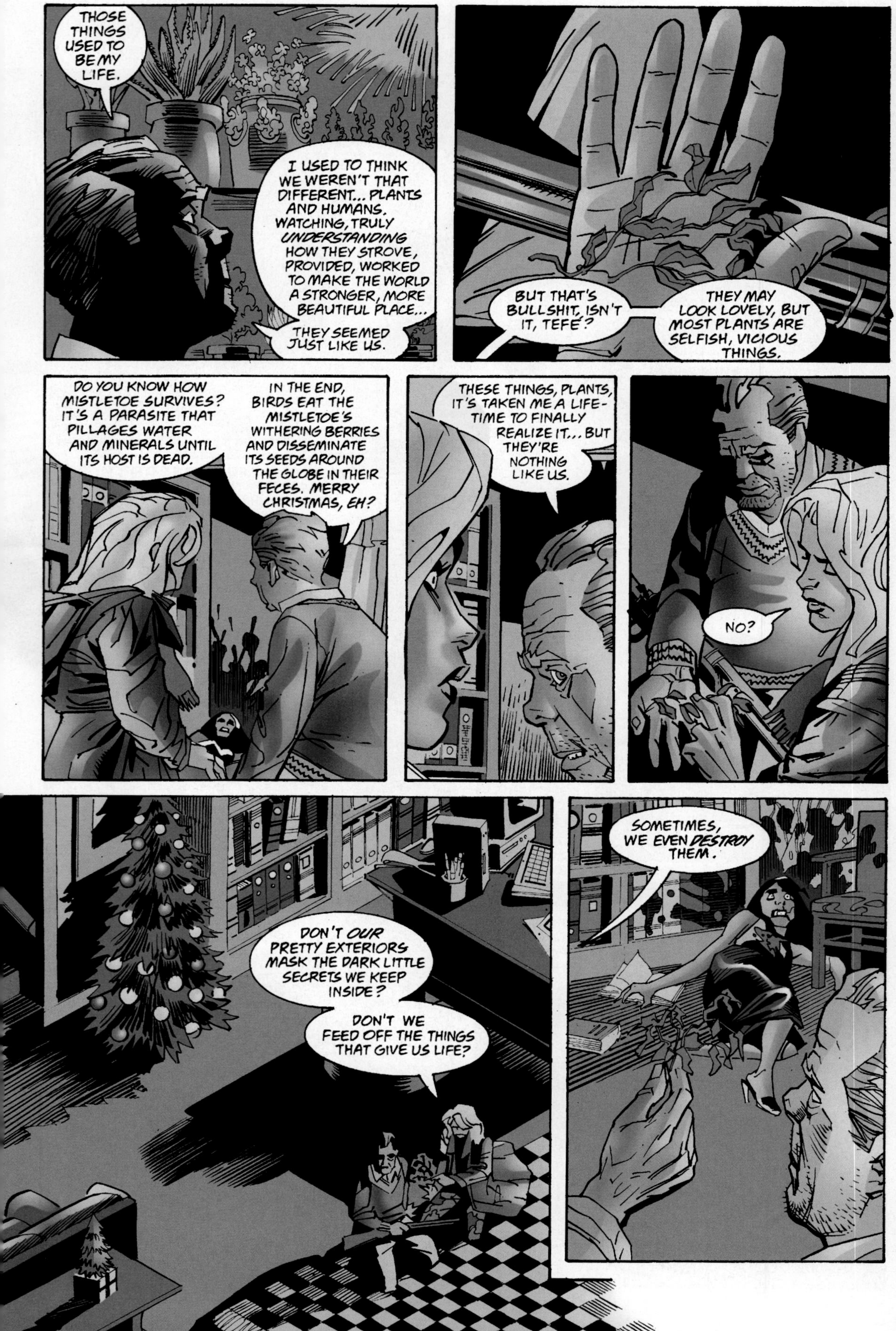
THOSE THINGS USED TO BE MY LIFE.
I USED TO THINK WE WEREN'T THAT DIFFERENT... PLANTS AND HUMANS. WATCHING, TRULY UNDERSTANDING HOW THEY STROVE, PROVIDED, WORKED TO MAKE THE WORLD A STRONGER, MORE BEAUTIFUL PLACE...
THEY SEEMED JUST LIKE US.
BUT THAT'S BULLSHIT, ISN'T IT, TEFÉ?
THEY MAY LOOK LOVELY, BUT MOST PLANTS ARE SELFISH, VICIOUS THINGS.
DO YOU KNOW HOW MISTLETOE SURVIVES? IT'S A PARASITE THAT PILLAGES WATER AND MINERALS UNTIL ITS HOST IS DEAD.
IN THE END, BIRDS EAT THE MISTLETOE'S WITHERING BERRIES AND DISSEMINATE ITS SEEDS AROUND THE GLOBE IN THEIR FECES. MERRY CHRISTMAS, EH?
THESE THINGS, PLANTS, IT'S TAKEN ME A LIFE-TIME TO FINALLY REALIZE IT... BUT THEY'RE NOTHING LIKE US.
NO?
DON'T OUR PRETTY EXTERIORS MASK THE DARK LITTLE SECRETS WE KEEP INSIDE?
DON'T WE FEED OFF THE THINGS THAT GIVE US LIFE?
SOMETIMES, WE EVEN DESTROY THEM.

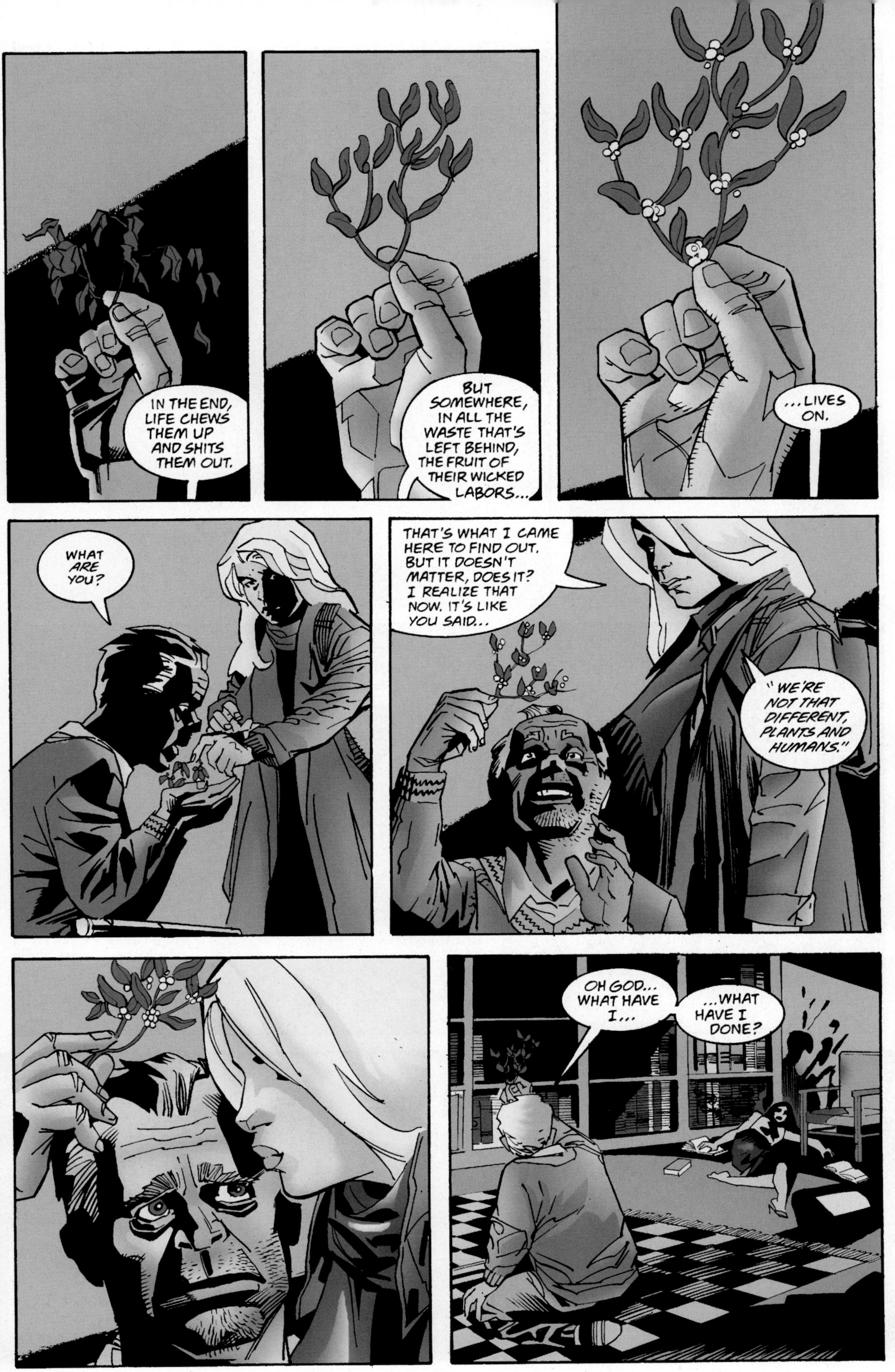
IN THE END, LIFE CHEWS THEM UP AND SHITS THEM OUT.
BUT SOMEWHERE, IN ALL THE WASTE THAT'S LEFT BEHIND, THE FRUIT OF THEIR WICKED LABORS...
...LIVES ON.
WHAT ARE YOU?
THAT'S WHAT I CAME HERE TO FIND OUT. BUT IT DOESN'T MATTER, DOES IT? I REALIZE THAT NOW. IT'S LIKE YOU SAID...
"WE'RE NOT THAT DIFFERENT, PLANTS AND HUMANS."
OH GOD... WHAT HAVE I...
...WHAT HAVE I DONE?

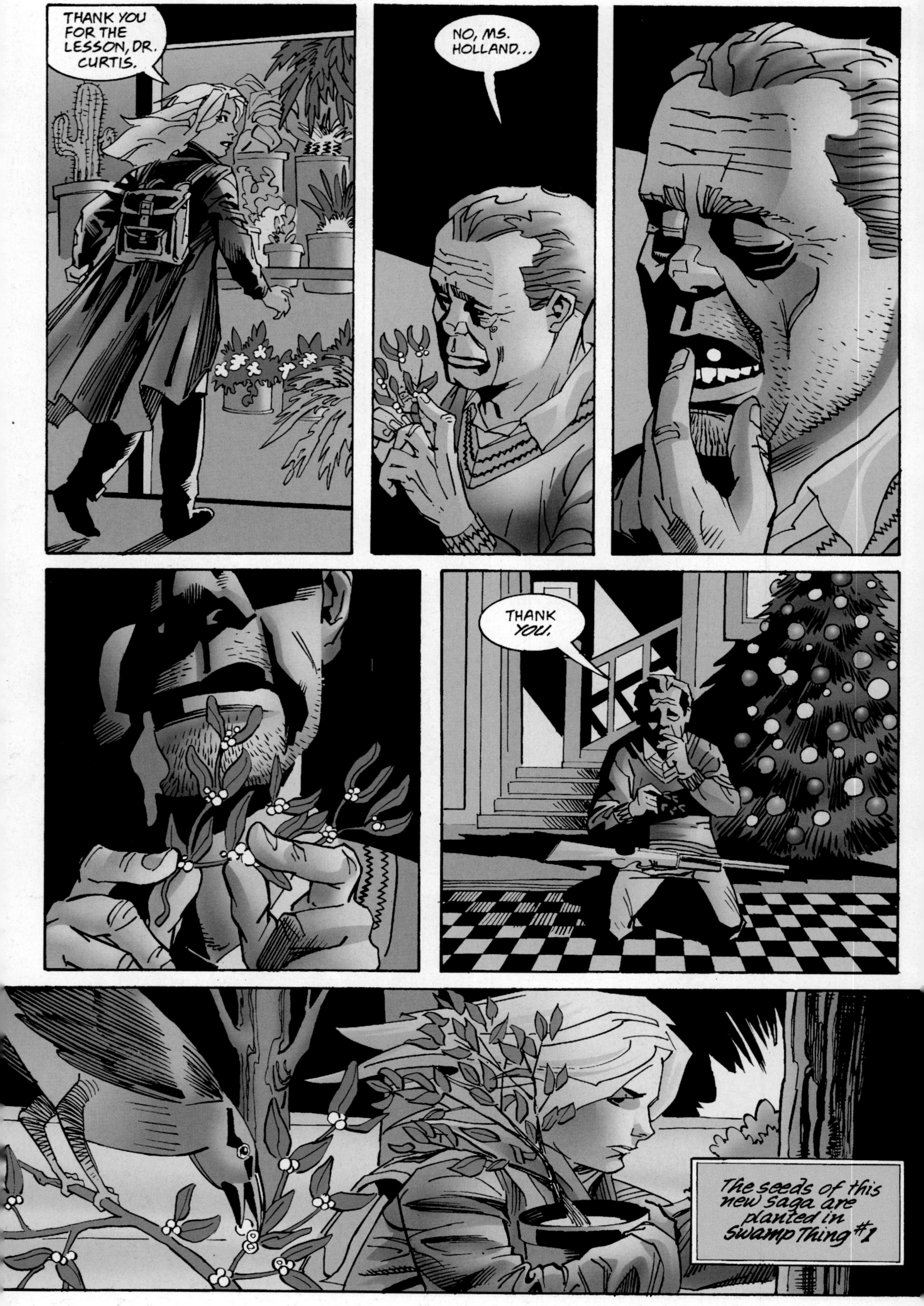
THANK YOU FOR THE LESSON, DR. CURTIS.
NO, MS. HOLLAND...
THANK YOU.
The seeds of this new saga are planted in Swamp Thing #1

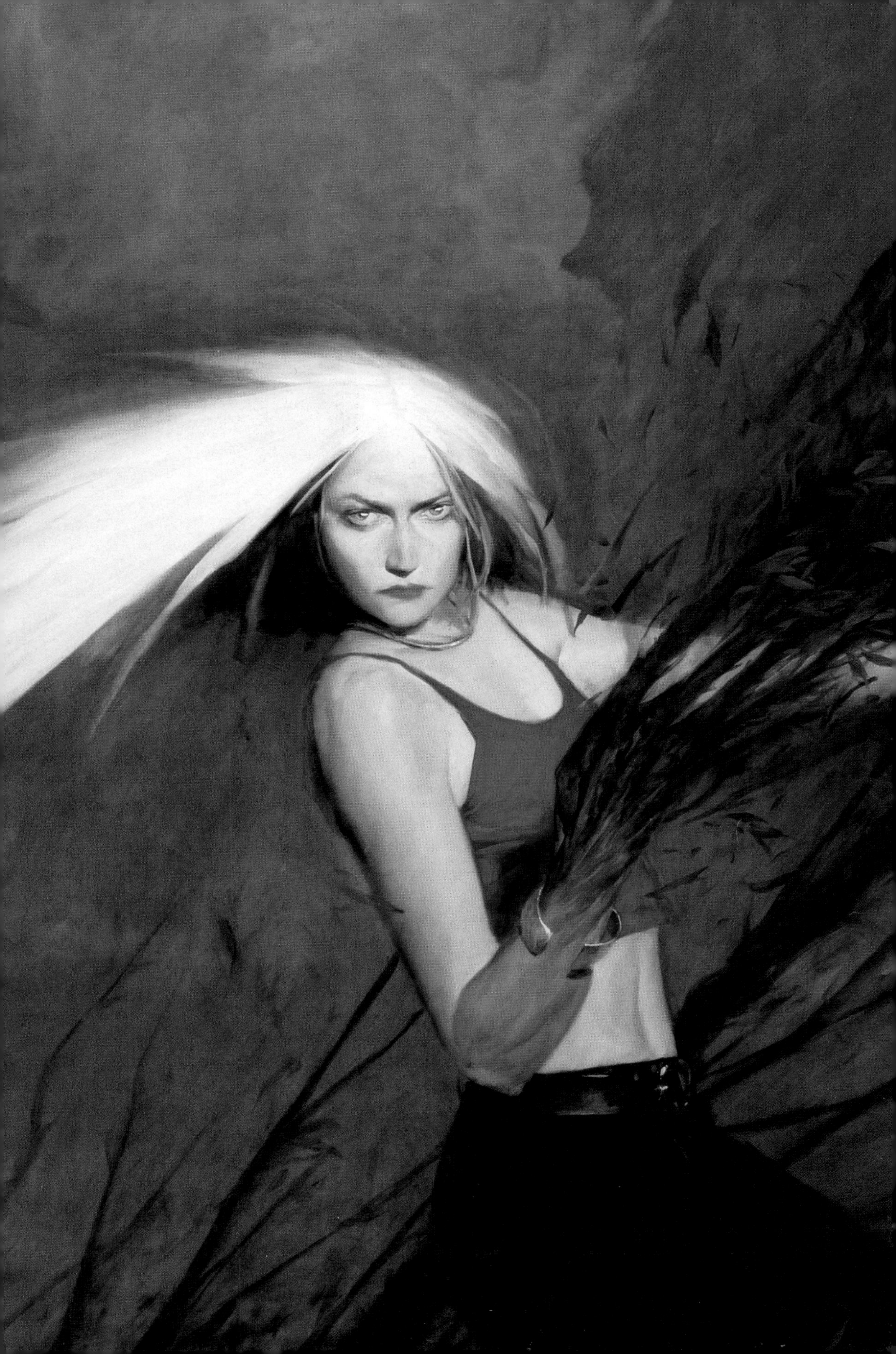

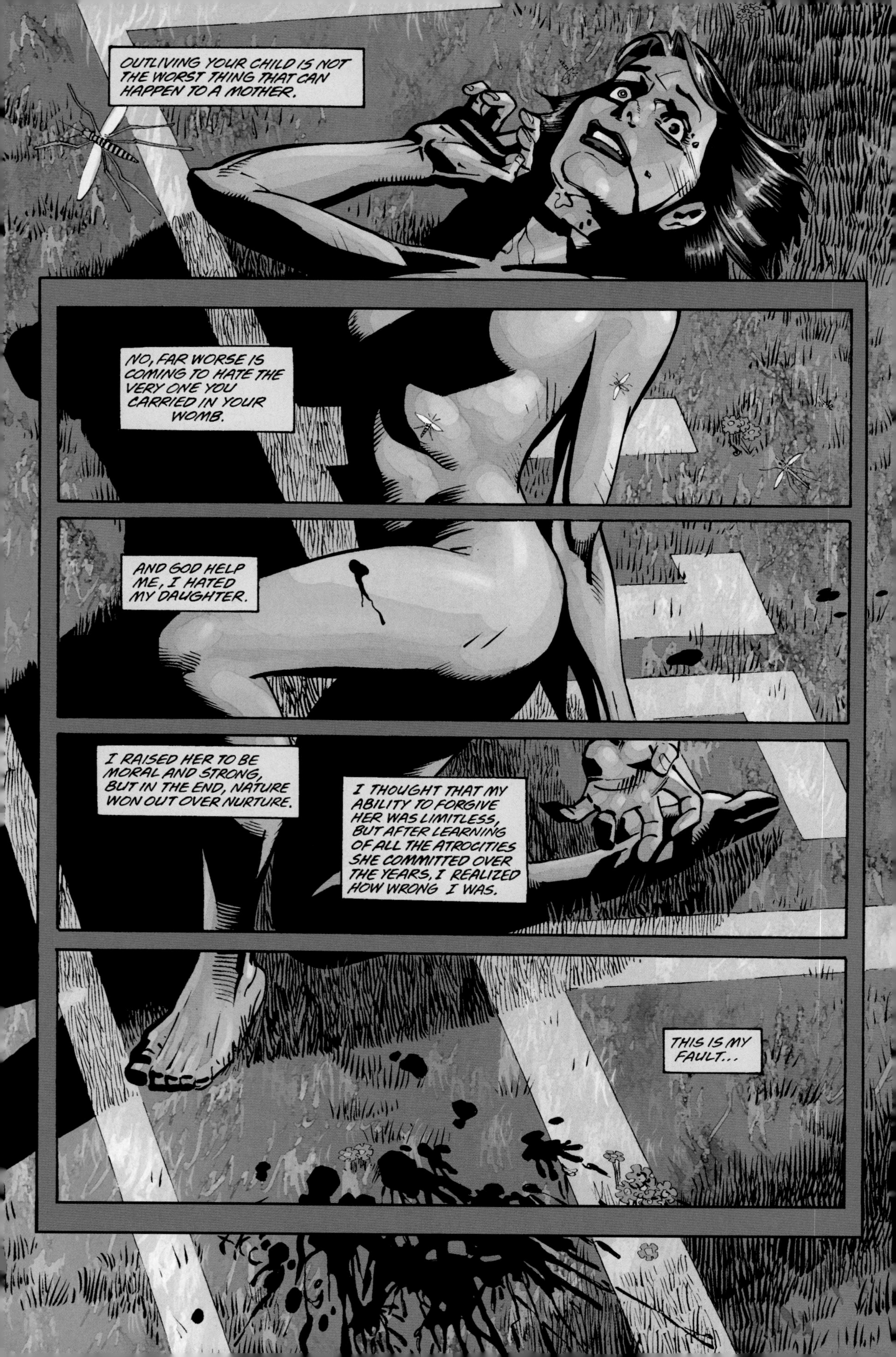
OUTLIVING YOUR CHILD IS NOT THE WORST THING THAT CAN HAPPEN TO A MOTHER.
NO, FAR WORSE IS COMING TO HATE THE VERY ONE YOU CARRIED IN YOUR WOMB.
AND GOD HELP ME, I HATED MY DAUGHTER.
I RAISED HER TO BE MORAL AND STRONG, BUT IN THE END, NATURE WON OUT OVER NURTURE.
I THOUGHT THAT MY ABILITY TO FORGIVE HER WAS LIMITLESS, BUT AFTER LEARNING OF ALL THE ATROCITIES SHE COMMITTED OVER THE YEARS, I REALIZED HOW WRONG I WAS.
THIS IS MY FAULT...

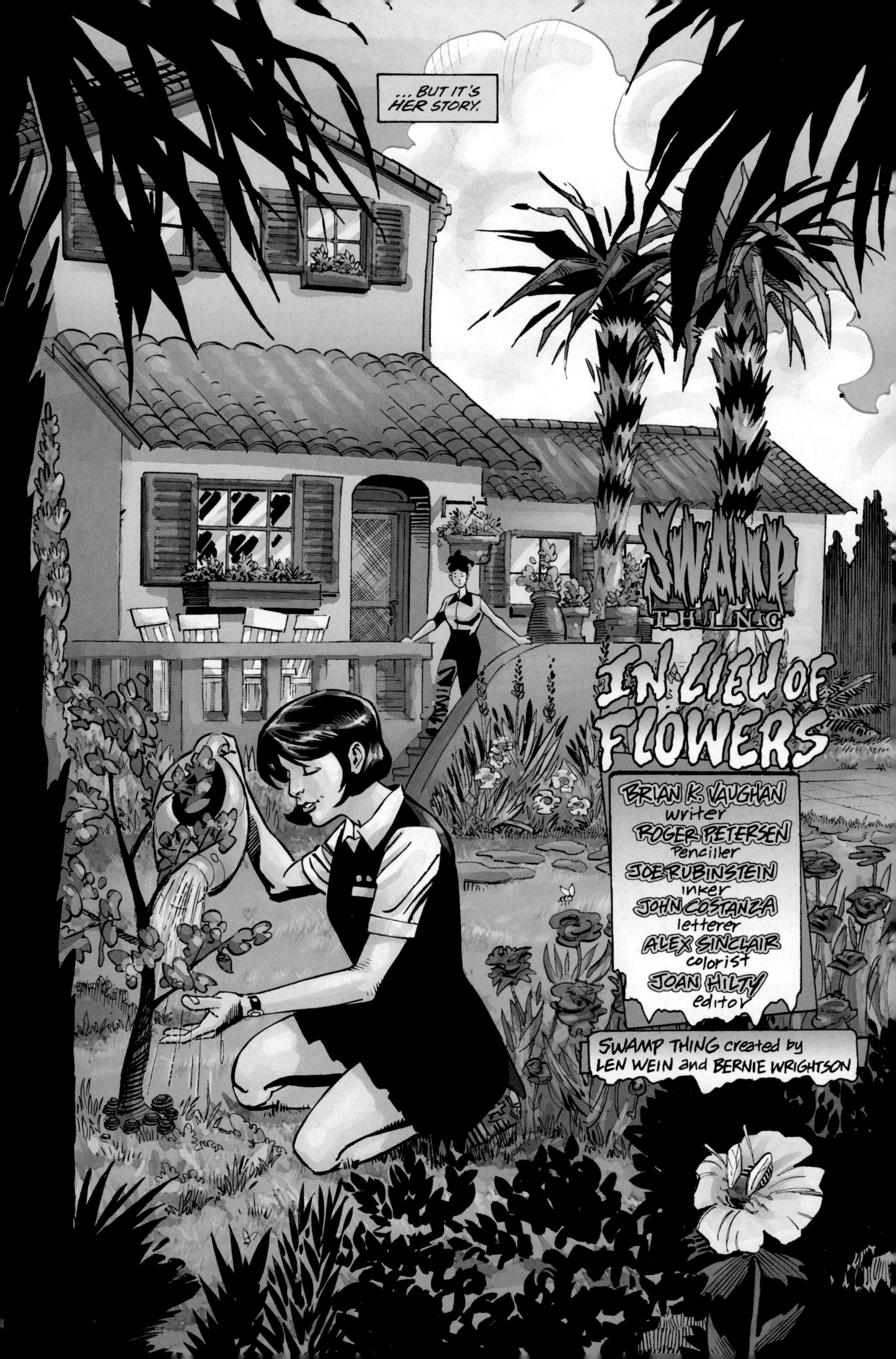
...BUT IT'S HER STORY.
SWAMP THING
IN LIEU OF FLOWERS
BRIAN K. VAUGHAN writer
ROGER PETERSEN penciller
JOE RUBINSTEIN inker
JOHN COSTANZA letterer
ALEX SINCLAIR colorist
JOAN HILTY editor
SWAMP THING created by LEN WEIN and BERNIE WRIGHTSON

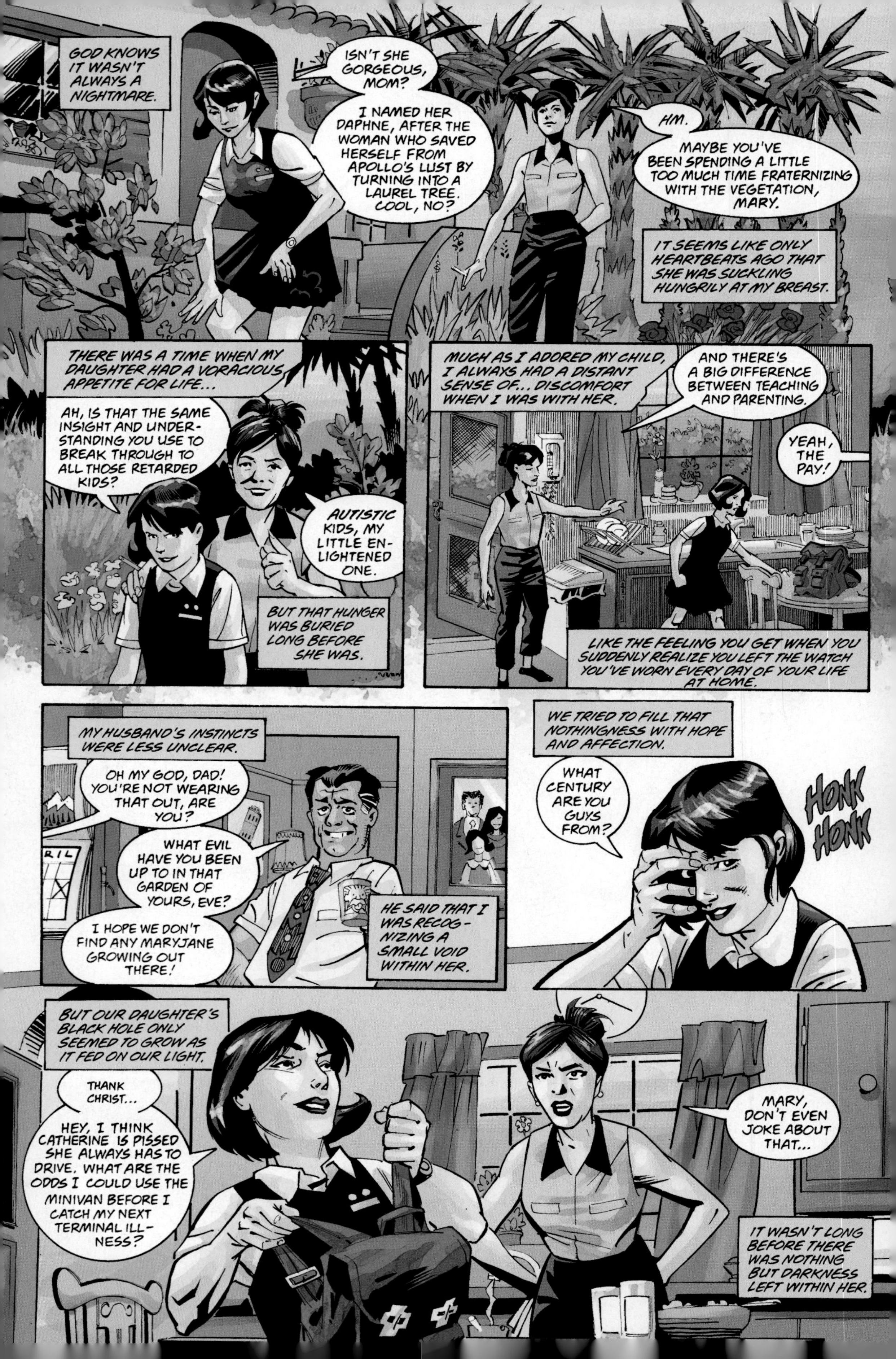
GOD KNOWS IT WASN'T ALWAYS A NIGHTMARE.
ISN'T SHE GORGEOUS, MOM?
I NAMED HER DAPHNE, AFTER THE WOMAN WHO SAVED HERSELF FROM APOLLO'S LUST BY TURNING INTO A LAUREL TREE. COOL, NO?
HM.
MAYBE YOU'VE BEEN SPENDING A LITTLE TOO MUCH TIME FRATERNIZING WITH THE VEGETATION, MARY.
IT SEEMS LIKE ONLY HEARTBEATS AGO THAT SHE WAS SUCKLING HUNGRILY AT MY BREAST.
THERE WAS A TIME WHEN MY DAUGHTER HAD A VORACIOUS APPETITE FOR LIFE...
AH, IS THAT THE SAME INSIGHT AND UNDER-STANDING YOU USE TO BREAK THROUGH TO ALL THOSE RETARDED KIDS?
AUTISTIC KIDS, MY LITTLE EN-LIGHTENED ONE.
BUT THAT HUNGER WAS BURIED LONG BEFORE SHE WAS.
MUCH AS I ADORED MY CHILD, I ALWAYS HAD A DISTANT SENSE OF... DISCOMFORT WHEN I WAS WITH HER.
AND THERE'S A BIG DIFFERENCE BETWEEN TEACHING AND PARENTING.
YEAH, THE PAY!
LIKE THE FEELING YOU GET WHEN YOU SUDDENLY REALIZE YOU LEFT THE WATCH YOU'VE WORN EVERY DAY OF YOUR LIFE AT HOME.
MY HUSBAND'S INSTINCTS WERE LESS UNCLEAR.
OH MY GOD, DAD! YOU'RE NOT WEARING THAT OUT, ARE YOU?
WHAT EVIL HAVE YOU BEEN UP TO IN THAT GARDEN OF YOURS, EVE?
I HOPE WE DON'T FIND ANY MARYJANE GROWING OUT THERE!
HE SAID THAT I WAS RECOG-NIZING A SMALL VOID WITHIN HER.
WE TRIED TO FILL THAT NOTHINGNESS WITH HOPE AND AFFECTION.
WHAT CENTURY ARE YOU GUYS FROM?
HONK HONK
BUT OUR DAUGHTER'S BLACK HOLE ONLY SEEMED TO GROW AS IT FED ON OUR LIGHT.
THANK CHRIST...
HEY, I THINK CATHERINE IS PISSED SHE ALWAYS HAS TO DRIVE. WHAT ARE THE ODDS I COULD USE THE MINIVAN BEFORE I CATCH MY NEXT TERMINAL ILL-NESS?
MARY, DON'T EVEN JOKE ABOUT THAT...
IT WASN'T LONG BEFORE THERE WAS NOTHING BUT DARKNESS LEFT WITHIN HER.

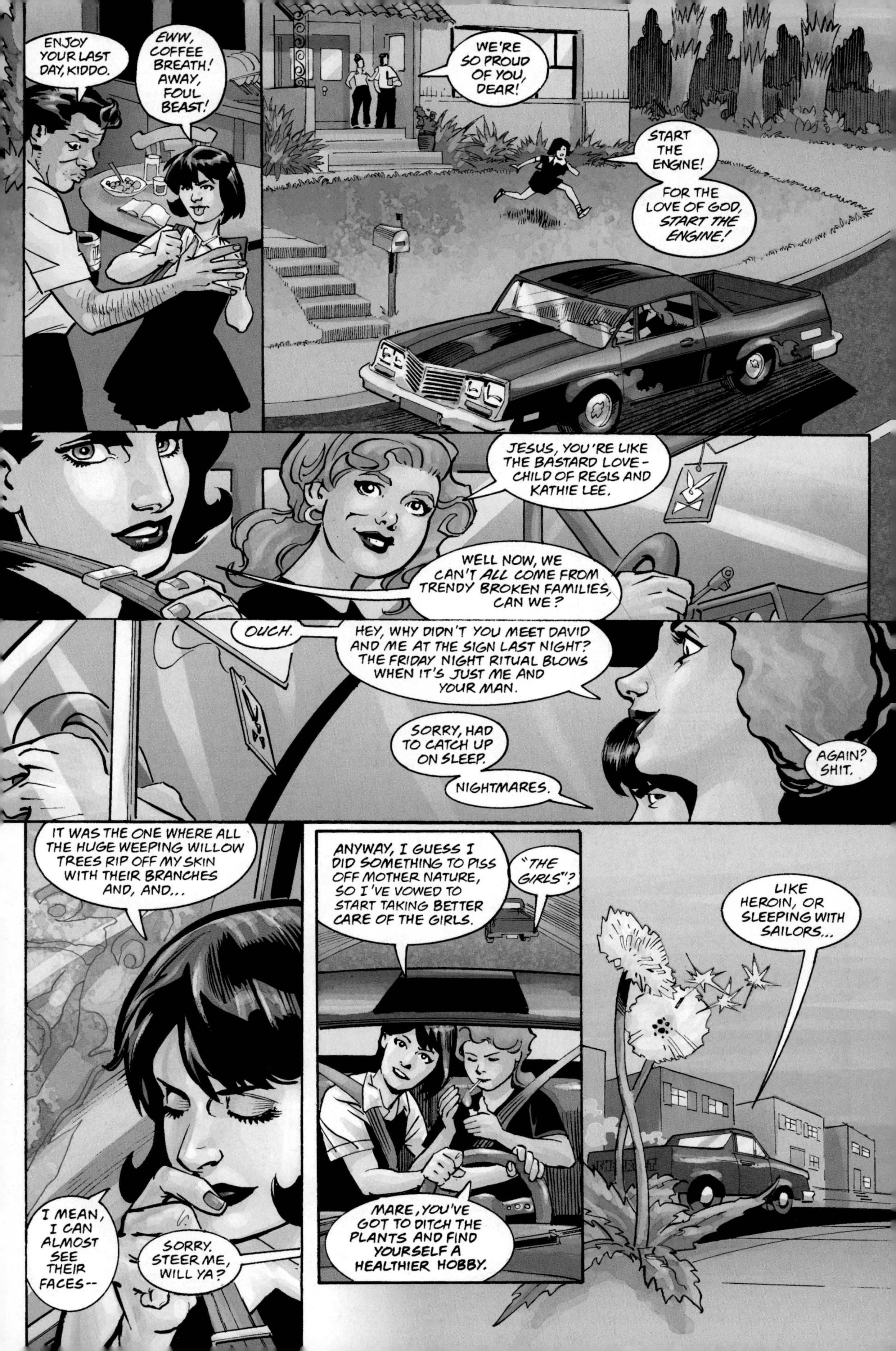
ENJOY YOUR LAST DAY, KIDDO.
EWW, COFFEE BREATH! AWAY, FOUL BEAST!
WE'RE SO PROUD OF YOU, DEAR!
START THE ENGINE!
FOR THE LOVE OF GOD, START THE ENGINE!
JESUS, YOU'RE LIKE THE BASTARD LOVE-CHILD OF REGIS AND KATHIE LEE.
WELL NOW, WE CAN'T ALL COME FROM TRENDY BROKEN FAMILIES, CAN WE?
OUCH.
HEY, WHY DIDN'T YOU MEET DAVID AND ME AT THE SIGN LAST NIGHT? THE FRIDAY NIGHT RITUAL BLOWS WHEN IT'S JUST ME AND YOUR MAN.
SORRY, HAD TO CATCH UP ON SLEEP.
NIGHTMARES.
AGAIN? SHIT.
IT WAS THE ONE WHERE ALL THE HUGE WEEPING WILLOW TREES RIP OFF MY SKIN WITH THEIR BRANCHES AND, AND...
I MEAN, I CAN ALMOST SEE THEIR FACES--
SORRY. STEER ME, WILL YA?
ANYWAY, I GUESS I DID SOMETHING TO PISS OFF MOTHER NATURE, SO I'VE VOWED TO START TAKING BETTER CARE OF THE GIRLS.
"THE GIRLS"?
MARE, YOU'VE GOT TO DITCH THE PLANTS AND FIND YOURSELF A HEALTHIER HOBBY.
LIKE HEROIN, OR SLEEPING WITH SAILORS...

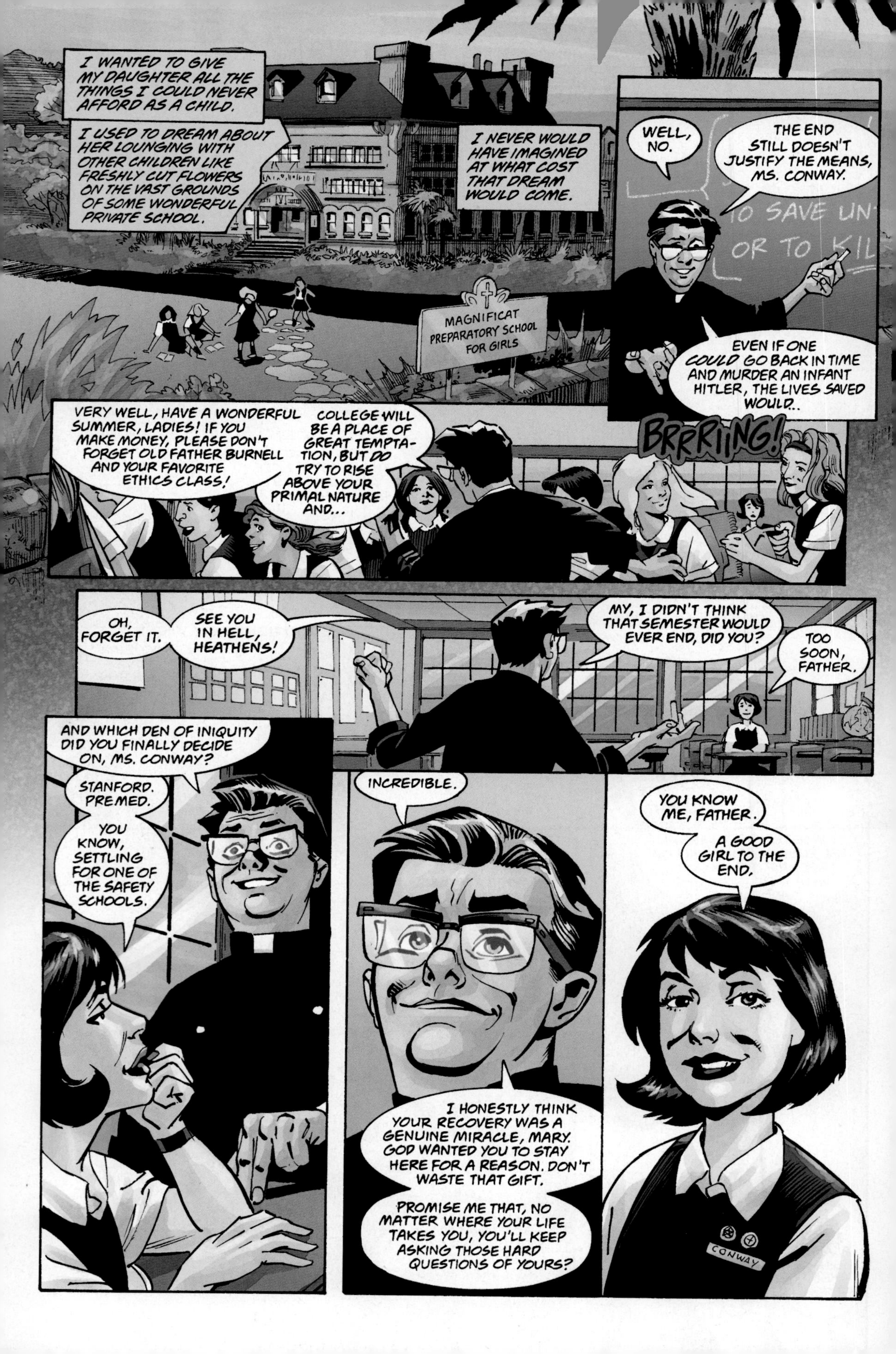

I WANTED TO GIVE MY DAUGHTER ALL THE THINGS I COULD NEVER AFFORD AS A CHILD.
I USED TO DREAM ABOUT HER LOUNGING WITH OTHER CHILDREN LIKE FRESHLY CUT FLOWERS ON THE VAST GROUNDS OF SOME WONDERFUL PRIVATE SCHOOL.
I NEVER WOULD HAVE IMAGINED AT WHAT COST THAT DREAM WOULD COME.
MAGNIFICAT PREPARATORY SCHOOL FOR GIRLS
WELL, NO.
THE END STILL DOESN'T JUSTIFY THE MEANS, MS. CONWAY.
TO SAVE UN
OR TO KIL
EVEN IF ONE COULD GO BACK IN TIME AND MURDER AN INFANT HITLER, THE LIVES SAVED WOULD..
BRRRIING!
VERY WELL, HAVE A WONDERFUL SUMMER, LADIES! IF YOU MAKE MONEY, PLEASE DON'T FORGET OLD FATHER BURNELL AND YOUR FAVORITE ETHICS CLASS!
COLLEGE WILL BE A PLACE OF GREAT TEMPTATION, BUT DO TRY TO RISE ABOVE YOUR PRIMAL NATURE AND...
OH, FORGET IT.
SEE YOU IN HELL, HEATHENS!
MY, I DIDN'T THINK THAT SEMESTER WOULD EVER END, DID YOU?
TOO SOON, FATHER.
AND WHICH DEN OF INIQUITY DID YOU FINALLY DECIDE ON, MS. CONWAY?
STANFORD. PREMED.
YOU KNOW, SETTLING FOR ONE OF THE SAFETY SCHOOLS.
INCREDIBLE.
I HONESTLY THINK YOUR RECOVERY WAS A GENUINE MIRACLE, MARY. GOD WANTED YOU TO STAY HERE FOR A REASON. DON'T WASTE THAT GIFT.
PROMISE ME THAT, NO MATTER WHERE YOUR LIFE TAKES YOU, YOU'LL KEEP ASKING THOSE HARD QUESTIONS OF YOURS?
YOU KNOW ME, FATHER.
A GOOD GIRL TO THE END.
CONWAY

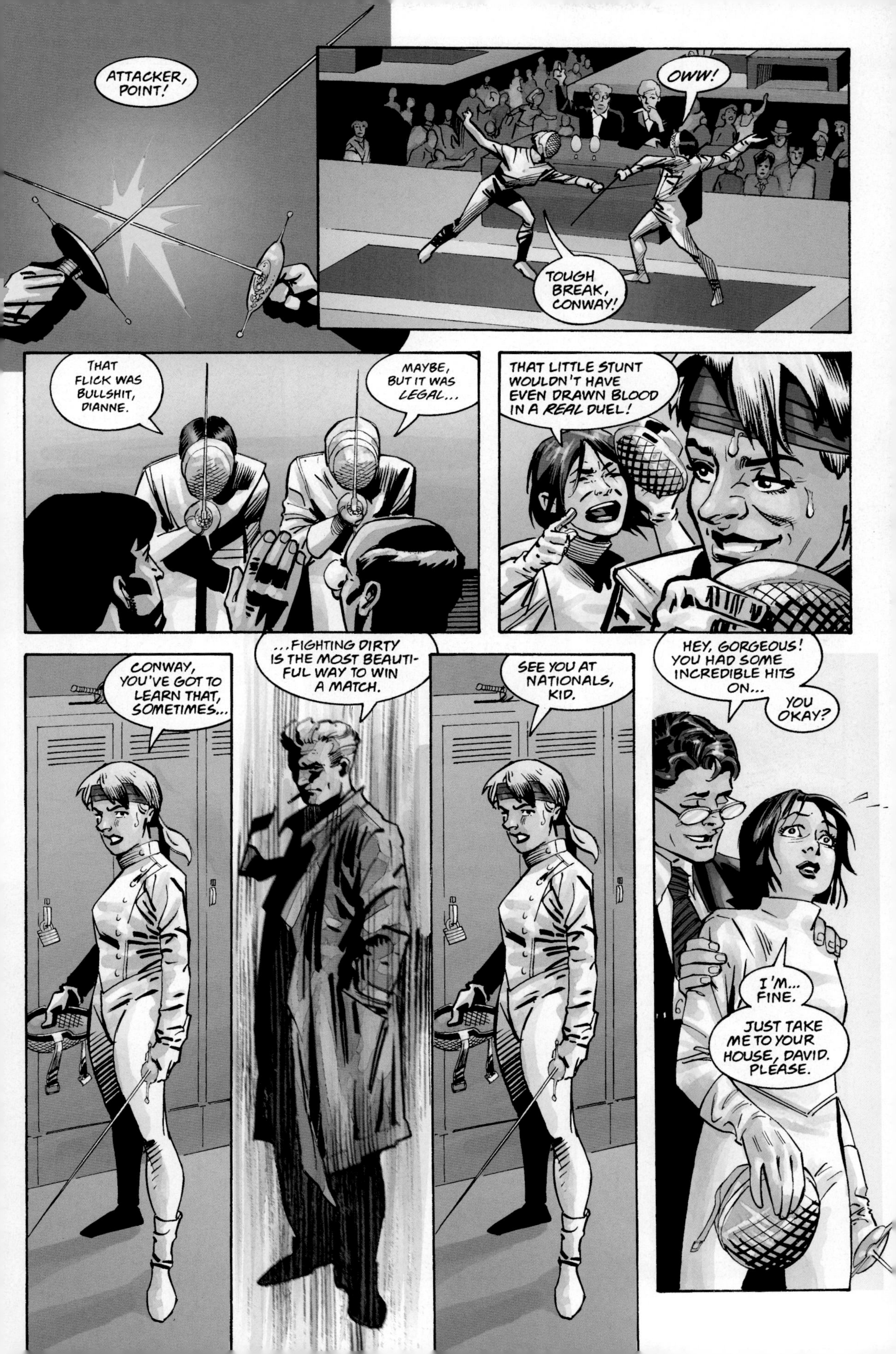
ATTACKER, POINT!
OWW!
TOUGH BREAK, CONWAY!
THAT FLICK WAS BULLSHIT, DIANNE.
MAYBE, BUT IT WAS LEGAL...
THAT LITTLE STUNT WOULDN'T HAVE EVEN DRAWN BLOOD IN A REAL DUEL!
CONWAY, YOU'VE GOT TO LEARN THAT, SOMETIMES...
...FIGHTING DIRTY IS THE MOST BEAUTIFUL WAY TO WIN A MATCH.
SEE YOU AT NATIONALS, KID.
HEY, GORGEOUS! YOU HAD SOME INCREDIBLE HITS ON...
YOU OKAY?
I'M... FINE.
JUST TAKE ME TO YOUR HOUSE, DAVID. PLEASE.

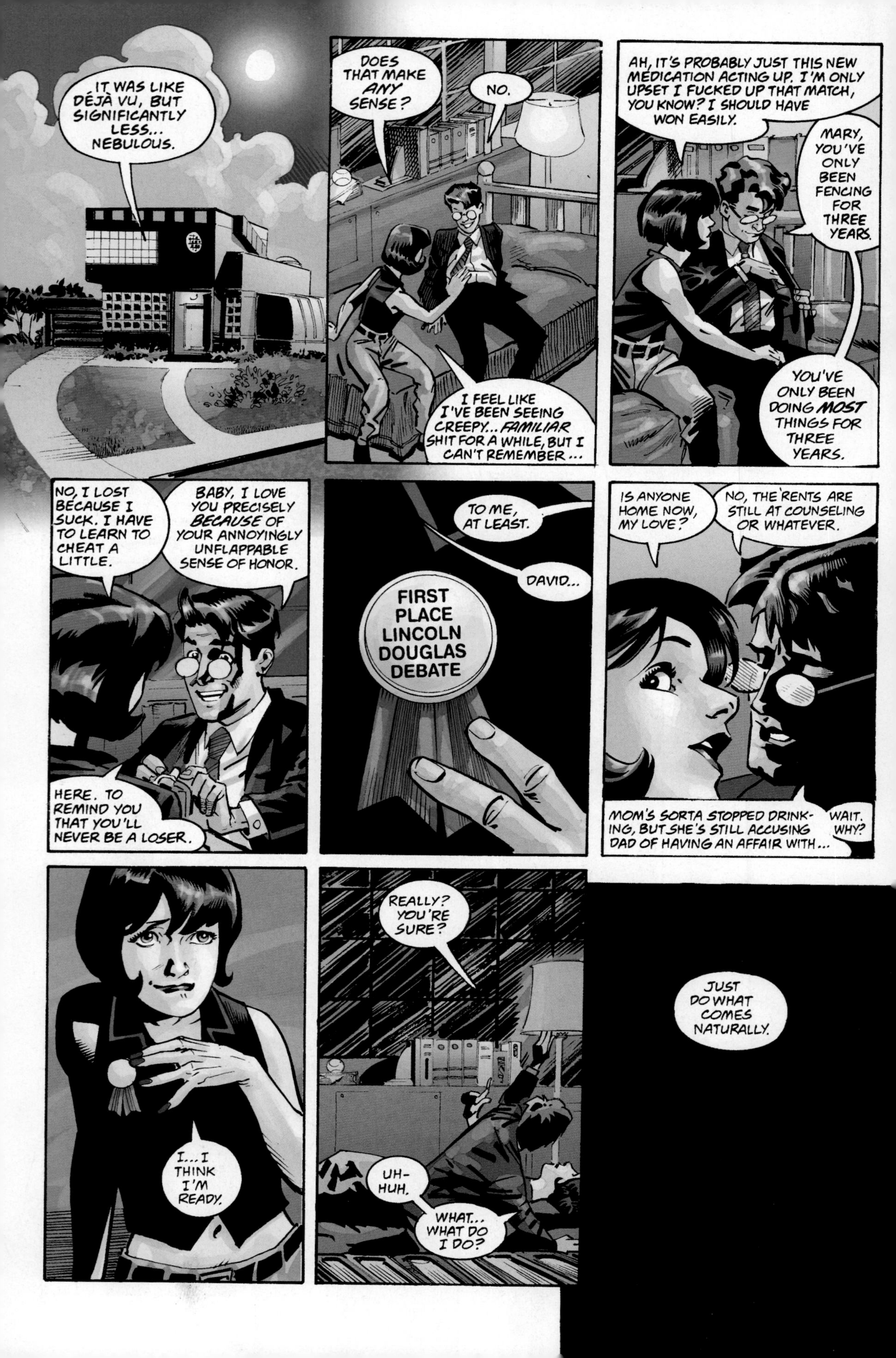
IT WAS LIKE DÉJÀ VU, BUT SIGNIFICANTLY LESS... NEBULOUS.
DOES THAT MAKE ANY SENSE?
NO.
I FEEL LIKE I'VE BEEN SEEING CREEPY... FAMILIAR SHIT FOR A WHILE, BUT I CAN'T REMEMBER...
AH, IT'S PROBABLY JUST THIS NEW MEDICATION ACTING UP. I'M ONLY UPSET I FUCKED UP THAT MATCH, YOU KNOW? I SHOULD HAVE WON EASILY.
MARY, YOU'VE ONLY BEEN FENCING FOR THREE YEARS.
YOU'VE ONLY BEEN DOING MOST THINGS FOR THREE YEARS.
NO, I LOST BECAUSE I SUCK. I HAVE TO LEARN TO CHEAT A LITTLE.
BABY, I LOVE YOU PRECISELY BECAUSE OF YOUR ANNOYINGLY UNFLAPPABLE SENSE OF HONOR.
HERE. TO REMIND YOU THAT YOU'LL NEVER BE A LOSER.
TO ME, AT LEAST.
DAVID...
FIRST PLACE LINCOLN DOUGLAS DEBATE
IS ANYONE HOME NOW, MY LOVE?
NO, THE 'RENTS ARE STILL AT COUNSELING OR WHATEVER.
MOM'S SORTA STOPPED DRINK-ING, BUT SHE'S STILL ACCUSING DAD OF HAVING AN AFFAIR WITH...
WAIT. WHY?
I... I THINK I'M READY.
REALLY? YOU'RE SURE?
UH-HUH.
WHAT... WHAT DO I DO?
JUST DO WHAT COMES NATURALLY.

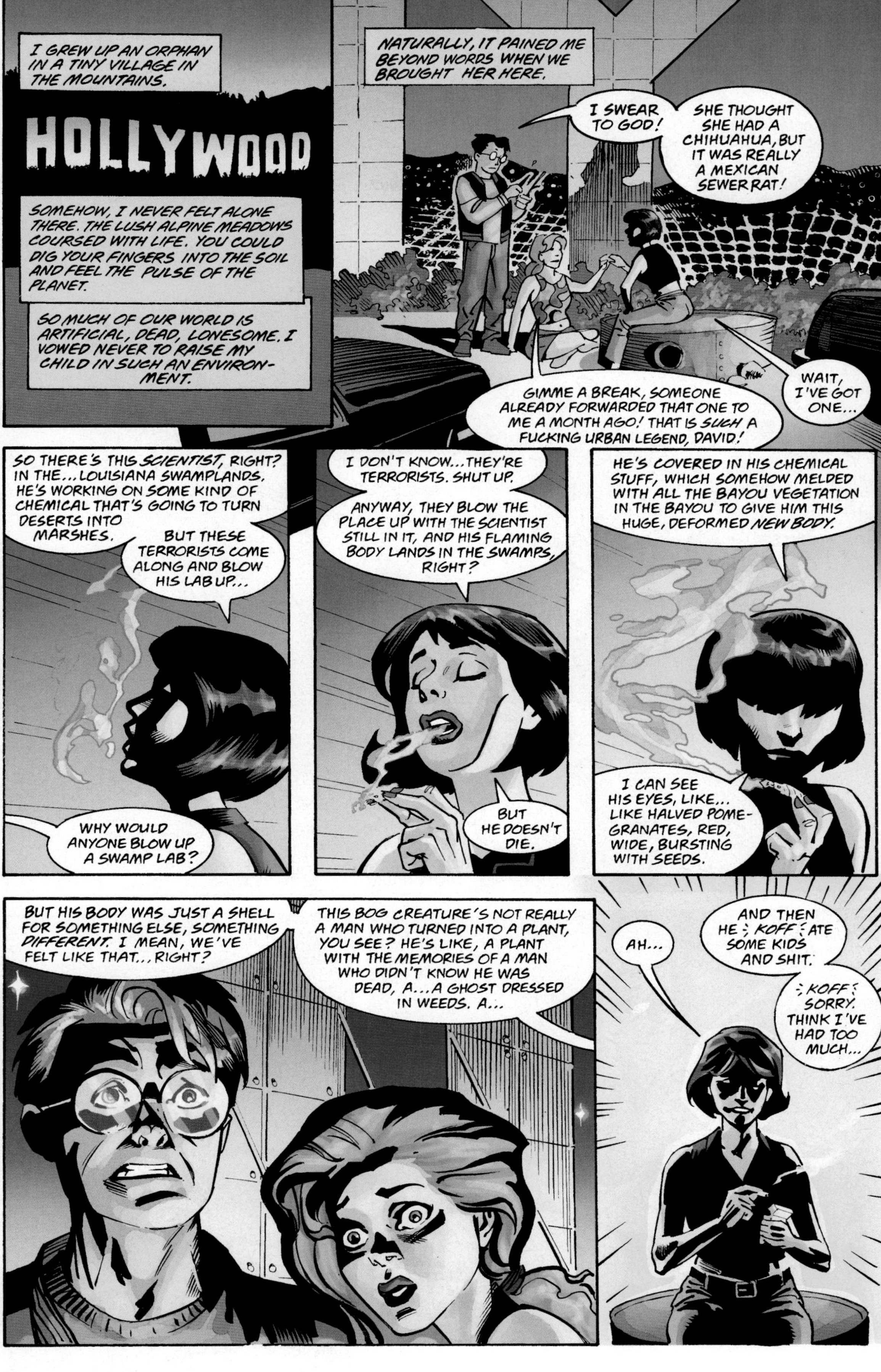
I GREW UP AN ORPHAN IN A TINY VILLAGE IN THE MOUNTAINS.
HOLLYWOOD
SOMEHOW, I NEVER FELT ALONE THERE. THE LUSH ALPINE MEADOWS COURSED WITH LIFE. YOU COULD DIG YOUR FINGERS INTO THE SOIL AND FEEL THE PULSE OF THE PLANET.
SO MUCH OF OUR WORLD IS ARTIFICIAL, DEAD, LONESOME. I VOWED NEVER TO RAISE MY CHILD IN SUCH AN ENVIRONMENT.
NATURALLY, IT PAINED ME BEYOND WORDS WHEN WE BROUGHT HER HERE.
I SWEAR TO GOD!
SHE THOUGHT SHE HAD A CHIHUAHUA, BUT IT WAS REALLY A MEXICAN SEWER RAT!
GIMME A BREAK, SOMEONE ALREADY FORWARDED THAT ONE TO ME A MONTH AGO! THAT IS SUCH A FUCKING URBAN LEGEND, DAVID!
WAIT, I'VE GOT ONE...
SO THERE'S THIS SCIENTIST, RIGHT? IN THE... LOUISIANA SWAMPLANDS. HE'S WORKING ON SOME KIND OF CHEMICAL THAT'S GOING TO TURN DESERTS INTO MARSHES.
BUT THESE TERRORISTS COME ALONG AND BLOW HIS LAB UP...
WHY WOULD ANYONE BLOW UP A SWAMP LAB?
I DON'T KNOW... THEY'RE TERRORISTS. SHUT UP.
ANYWAY, THEY BLOW THE PLACE UP WITH THE SCIENTIST STILL IN IT, AND HIS FLAMING BODY LANDS IN THE SWAMPS, RIGHT?
BUT HE DOESN'T DIE.
HE'S COVERED IN HIS CHEMICAL STUFF, WHICH SOMEHOW MELDED WITH ALL THE BAYOU VEGETATION IN THE BAYOU TO GIVE HIM THIS HUGE, DEFORMED NEW BODY.
I CAN SEE HIS EYES, LIKE... LIKE HALVED POMEGRANATES, RED, WIDE, BURSTING WITH SEEDS.
BUT HIS BODY WAS JUST A SHELL FOR SOMETHING ELSE, SOMETHING DIFFERENT. I MEAN, WE'VE FELT LIKE THAT... RIGHT?
THIS BOG CREATURE'S NOT REALLY A MAN WHO TURNED INTO A PLANT, YOU SEE? HE'S LIKE, A PLANT WITH THE MEMORIES OF A MAN WHO DIDN'T KNOW HE WAS DEAD, A... A GHOST DRESSED IN WEEDS. A...
AH...
AND THEN HE :KOFF: ATE SOME KIDS AND SHIT.
:KOFF: SORRY. THINK I'VE HAD TOO MUCH...

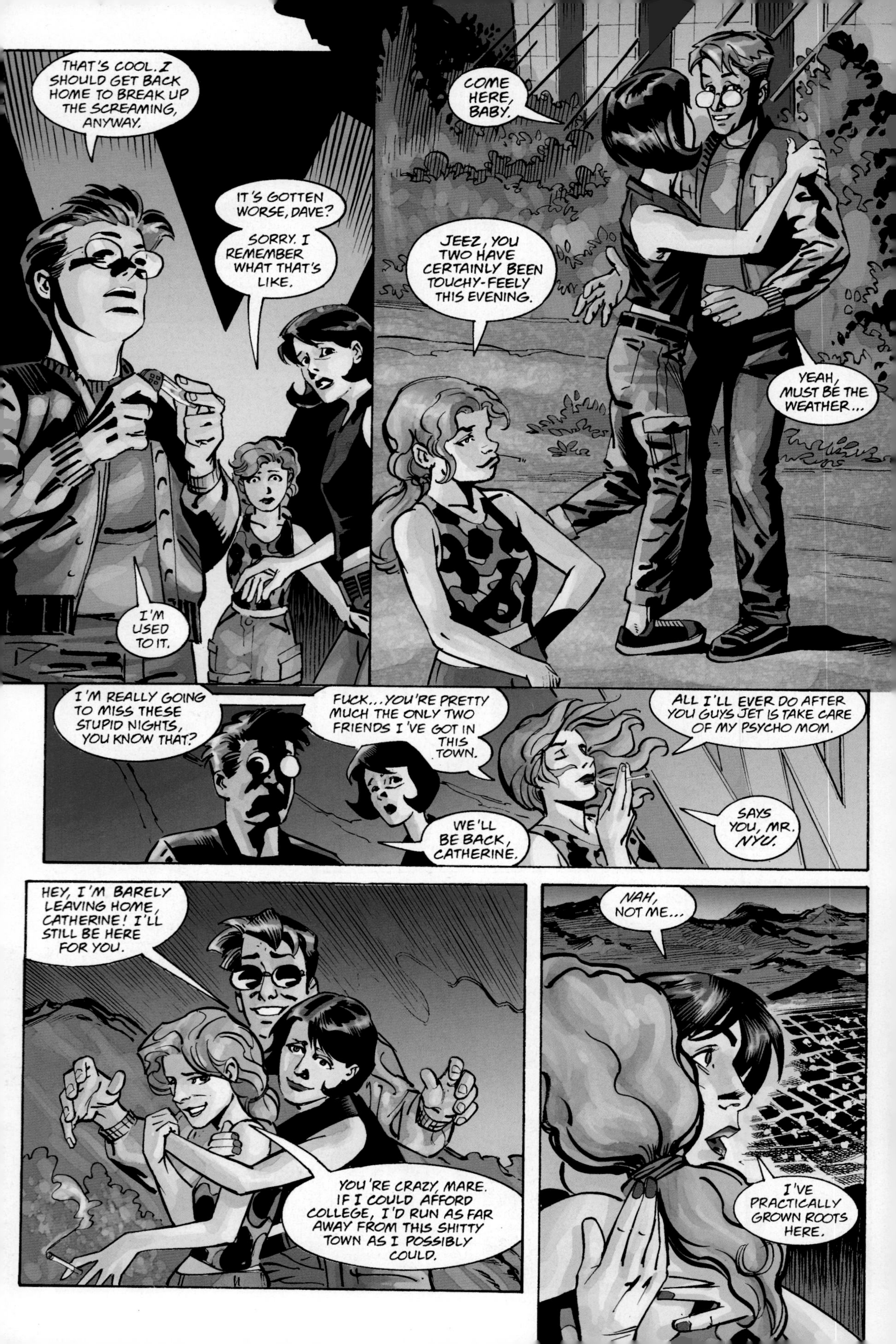
THAT'S COOL. I SHOULD GET BACK HOME TO BREAK UP THE SCREAMING, ANYWAY.
IT'S GOTTEN WORSE, DAVE?
SORRY. I REMEMBER WHAT THAT'S LIKE.
I'M USED TO IT.
COME HERE, BABY.
JEEZ, YOU TWO HAVE CERTAINLY BEEN TOUCHY-FEELY THIS EVENING.
YEAH, MUST BE THE WEATHER...
I'M REALLY GOING TO MISS THESE STUPID NIGHTS, YOU KNOW THAT?
FUCK... YOU'RE PRETTY MUCH THE ONLY TWO FRIENDS I'VE GOT IN THIS TOWN.
WE'LL BE BACK, CATHERINE.
ALL I'LL EVER DO AFTER YOU GUYS JET IS TAKE CARE OF MY PSYCHO MOM.
SAYS YOU, MR. NYU.
HEY, I'M BARELY LEAVING HOME, CATHERINE! I'LL STILL BE HERE FOR YOU.
YOU'RE CRAZY, MARE. IF I COULD AFFORD COLLEGE, I'D RUN AS FAR AWAY FROM THIS SHITTY TOWN AS I POSSIBLY COULD.
NAH, NOT ME...
I'VE PRACTICALLY GROWN ROOTS HERE.

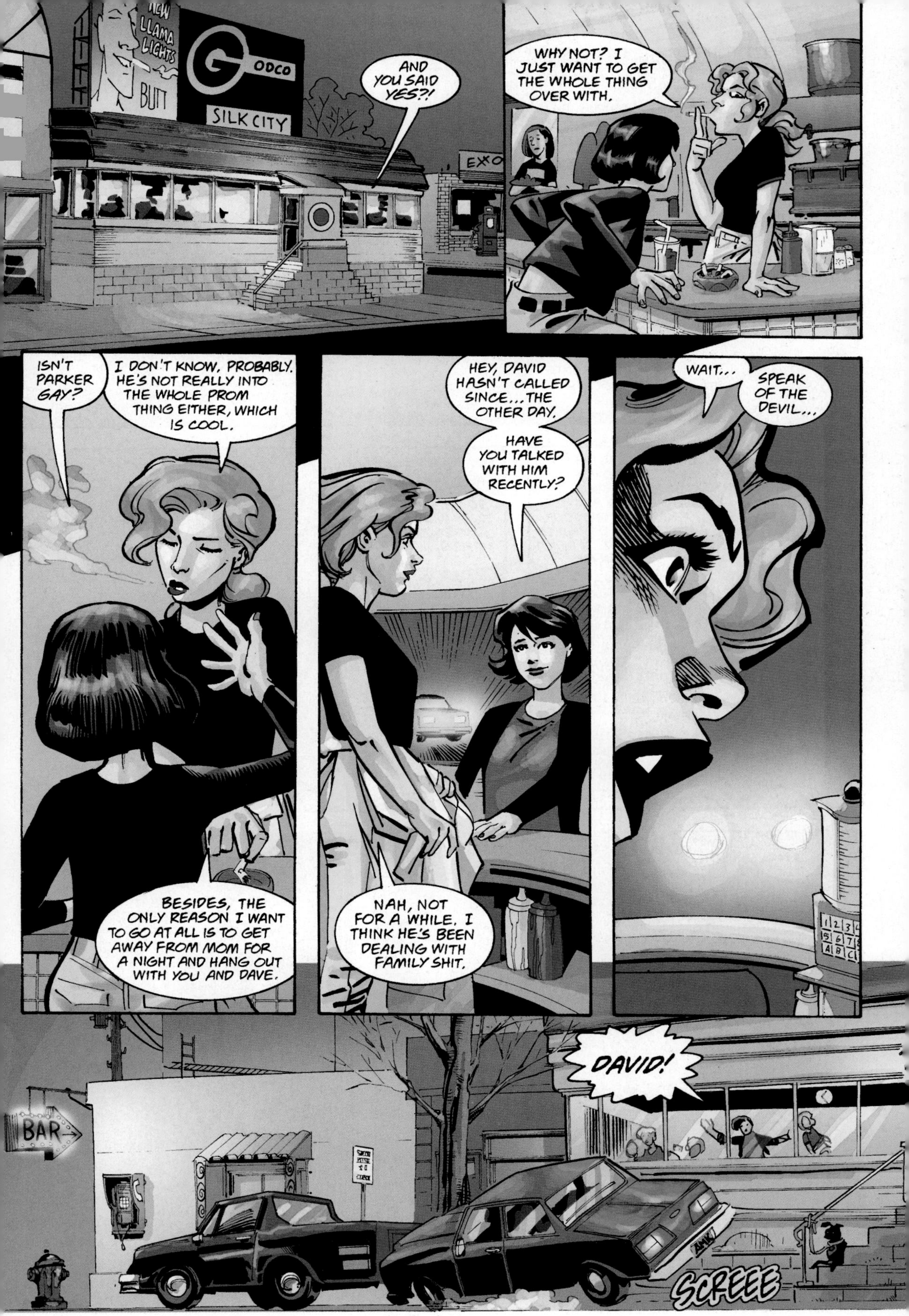
NEW LLAMA LIGHTS
BUTT
GODCO
SILK CITY
EXO
AND YOU SAID YES?!
WHY NOT? I JUST WANT TO GET THE WHOLE THING OVER WITH.
ISN'T PARKER GAY?
I DON'T KNOW, PROBABLY. HE'S NOT REALLY INTO THE WHOLE PROM THING EITHER, WHICH IS COOL.
BESIDES, THE ONLY REASON I WANT TO GO AT ALL IS TO GET AWAY FROM MOM FOR A NIGHT AND HANG OUT WITH YOU AND DAVE.
HEY, DAVID HASN'T CALLED SINCE... THE OTHER DAY.
HAVE YOU TALKED WITH HIM RECENTLY?
NAH, NOT FOR A WHILE. I THINK HE'S BEEN DEALING WITH FAMILY SHIT.
WAIT...
SPEAK OF THE DEVIL...
BAR
DAVID!
SCREEE

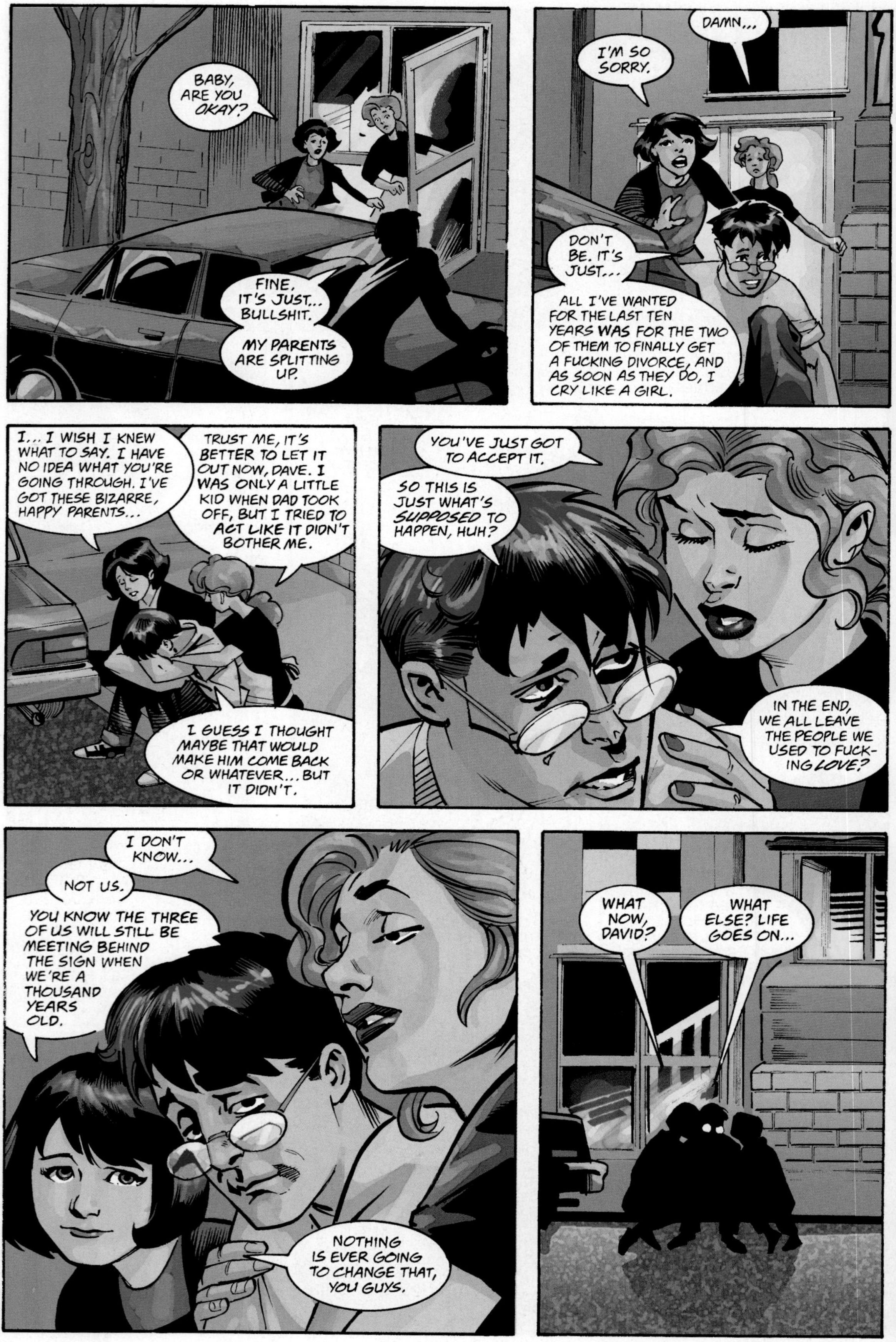
BABY, ARE YOU OKAY?
FINE. IT'S JUST... BULLSHIT.
MY PARENTS ARE SPLITTING UP.
DAMN...
I'M SO SORRY.
DON'T BE. IT'S JUST...
ALL I'VE WANTED FOR THE LAST TEN YEARS WAS FOR THE TWO OF THEM TO FINALLY GET A FUCKING DIVORCE, AND AS SOON AS THEY DO, I CRY LIKE A GIRL.
I... I WISH I KNEW WHAT TO SAY. I HAVE NO IDEA WHAT YOU'RE GOING THROUGH. I'VE GOT THESE BIZARRE, HAPPY PARENTS...
TRUST ME, IT'S BETTER TO LET IT OUT NOW, DAVE. I WAS ONLY A LITTLE KID WHEN DAD TOOK OFF, BUT I TRIED TO ACT LIKE IT DIDN'T BOTHER ME.
I GUESS I THOUGHT MAYBE THAT WOULD MAKE HIM COME BACK OR WHATEVER... BUT IT DIDN'T.
YOU'VE JUST GOT TO ACCEPT IT.
SO THIS IS JUST WHAT'S SUPPOSED TO HAPPEN, HUH?
IN THE END, WE ALL LEAVE THE PEOPLE WE USED TO FUCKING LOVE?
I DON'T KNOW...
NOT US.
YOU KNOW THE THREE OF US WILL STILL BE MEETING BEHIND THE SIGN WHEN WE'RE A THOUSAND YEARS OLD.
NOTHING IS EVER GOING TO CHANGE THAT, YOU GUYS.
WHAT NOW, DAVID?
WHAT ELSE? LIFE GOES ON...

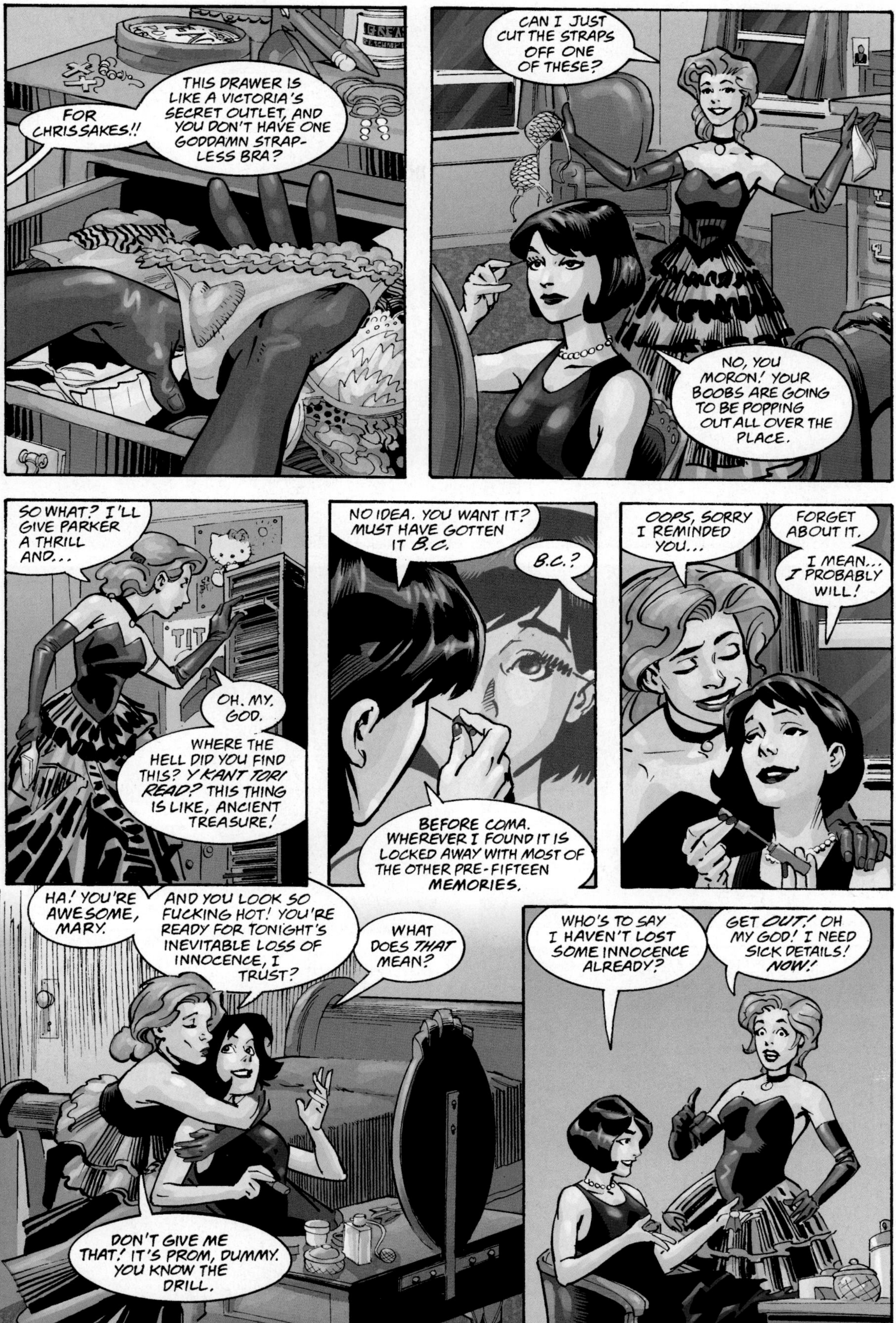
FOR CHRISSAKES!!
THIS DRAWER IS LIKE A VICTORIA'S SECRET OUTLET, AND YOU DON'T HAVE ONE GODDAMN STRAP-LESS BRA?
CAN I JUST CUT THE STRAPS OFF ONE OF THESE?
NO, YOU MORON! YOUR BOOBS ARE GOING TO BE POPPING OUT ALL OVER THE PLACE.
SO WHAT? I'LL GIVE PARKER A THRILL AND...
OH. MY. GOD.
WHERE THE HELL DID YOU FIND THIS? Y KANT TORI READ? THIS THING IS LIKE, ANCIENT TREASURE!
NO IDEA. YOU WANT IT? MUST HAVE GOTTEN IT B.C.
B.C.?
BEFORE COMA. WHEREVER I FOUND IT IS LOCKED AWAY WITH MOST OF THE OTHER PRE-FIFTEEN MEMORIES.
OOPS, SORRY I REMINDED YOU...
FORGET ABOUT IT.
I MEAN... I PROBABLY WILL!
HA! YOU'RE AWESOME, MARY.
AND YOU LOOK SO FUCKING HOT! YOU'RE READY FOR TONIGHT'S INEVITABLE LOSS OF INNOCENCE, I TRUST?
WHAT DOES THAT MEAN?
DON'T GIVE ME THAT! IT'S PROM, DUMMY. YOU KNOW THE DRILL.
WHO'S TO SAY I HAVEN'T LOST SOME INNOCENCE ALREADY?
GET OUT! OH MY GOD! I NEED SICK DETAILS! NOW!

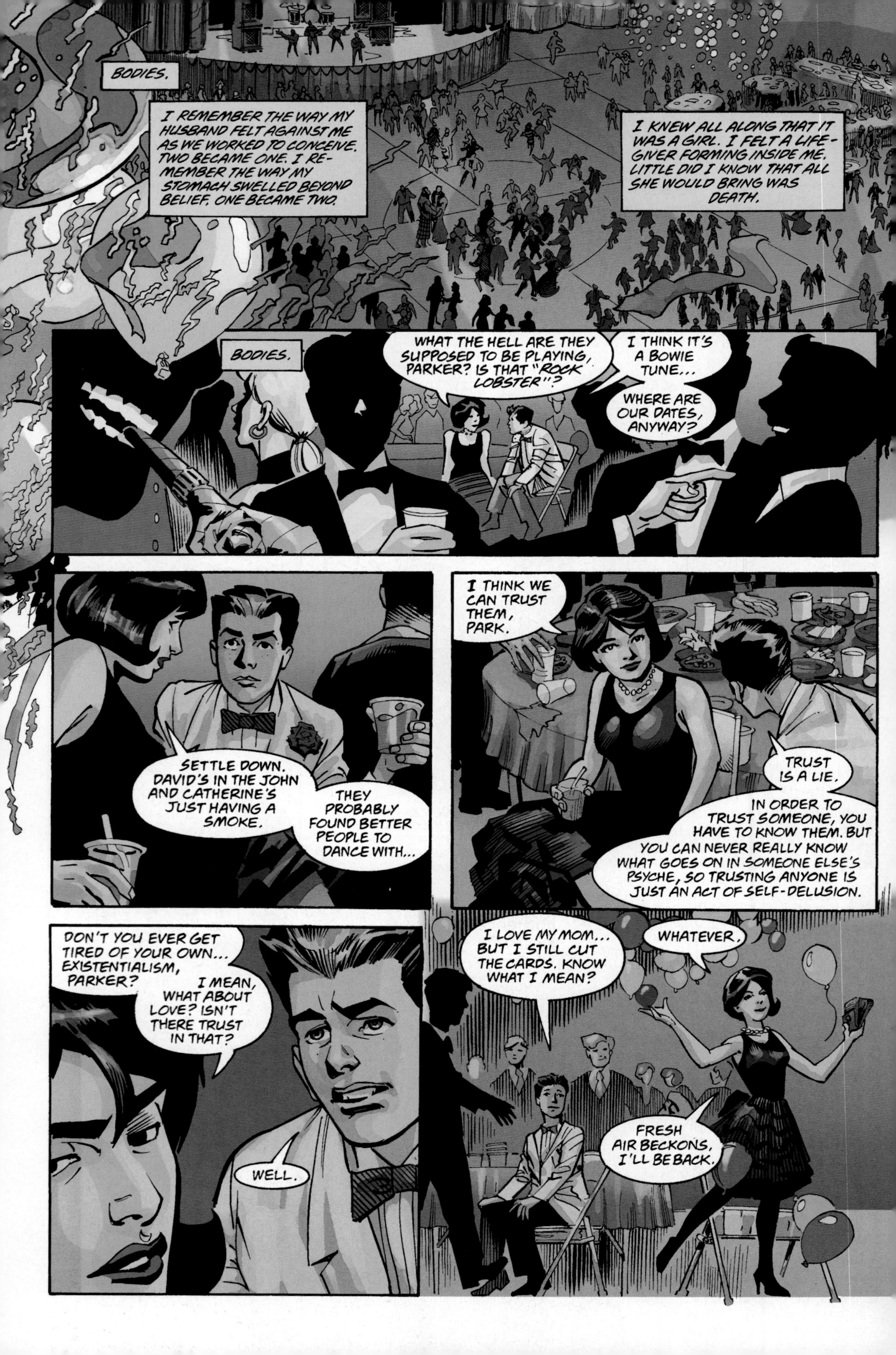

BODIES.
I REMEMBER THE WAY MY HUSBAND FELT AGAINST ME AS WE WORKED TO CONCEIVE. TWO BECAME ONE. I REMEMBER THE WAY MY STOMACH SWELLED BEYOND BELIEF. ONE BECAME TWO.
I KNEW ALL ALONG THAT IT WAS A GIRL. I FELT A LIFE-GIVER FORMING INSIDE ME. LITTLE DID I KNOW THAT ALL SHE WOULD BRING WAS DEATH.
BODIES.
WHAT THE HELL ARE THEY SUPPOSED TO BE PLAYING, PARKER? IS THAT "ROCK LOBSTER"?
I THINK IT'S A BOWIE TUNE...
WHERE ARE OUR DATES, ANYWAY?
SETTLE DOWN. DAVID'S IN THE JOHN AND CATHERINE'S JUST HAVING A SMOKE.
THEY PROBABLY FOUND BETTER PEOPLE TO DANCE WITH...
I THINK WE CAN TRUST THEM, PARK.
TRUST IS A LIE.
IN ORDER TO TRUST SOMEONE, YOU HAVE TO KNOW THEM. BUT YOU CAN NEVER REALLY KNOW WHAT GOES ON IN SOMEONE ELSE'S PSYCHE, SO TRUSTING ANYONE IS JUST AN ACT OF SELF-DELUSION.
DON'T YOU EVER GET TIRED OF YOUR OWN... EXISTENTIALISM, PARKER?
I MEAN, WHAT ABOUT LOVE? ISN'T THERE TRUST IN THAT?
WELL.
I LOVE MY MOM... BUT I STILL CUT THE CARDS. KNOW WHAT I MEAN?
WHATEVER.
FRESH AIR BECKONS. I'LL BE BACK.

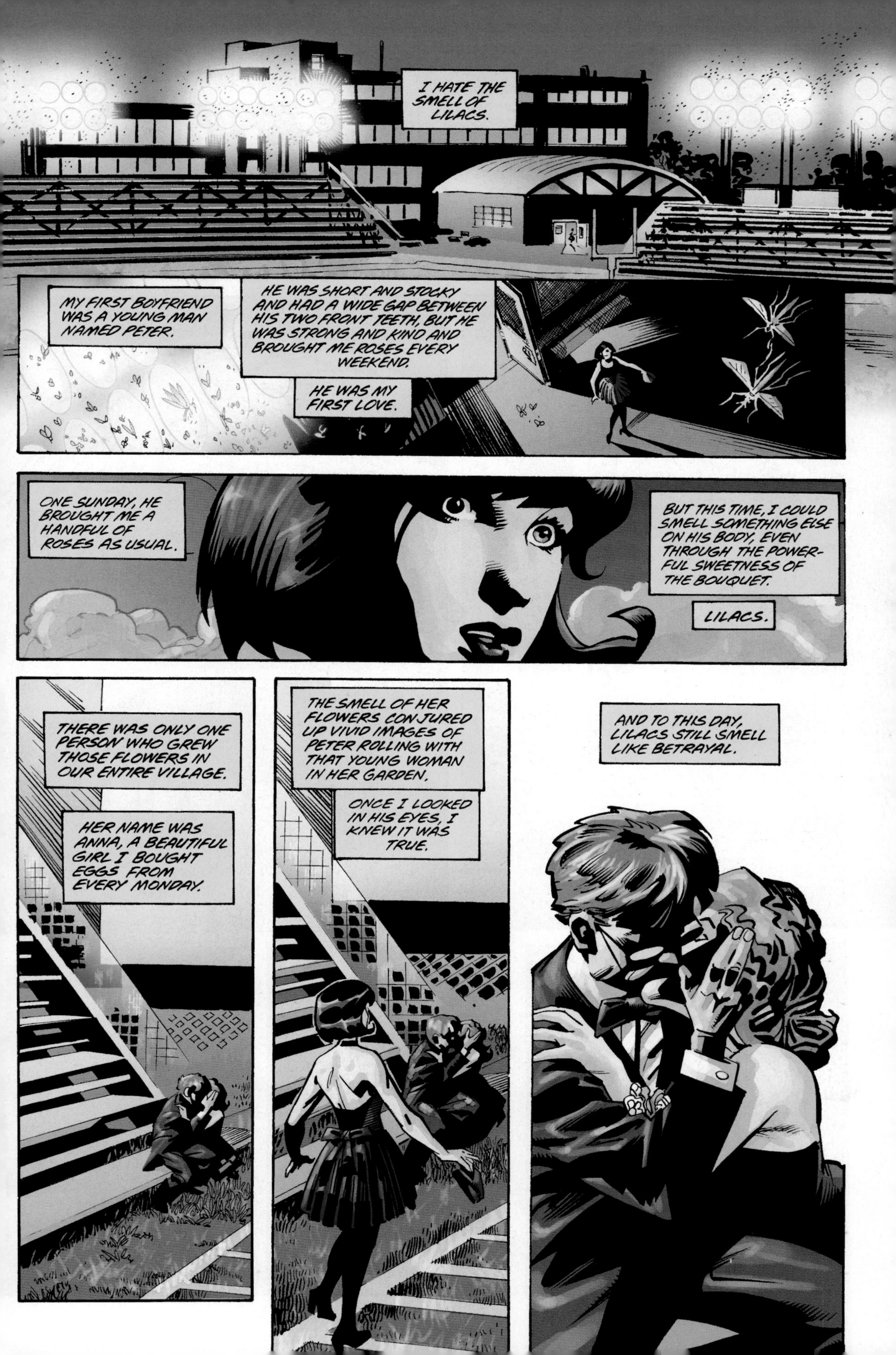

I HATE THE SMELL OF LILACS.
MY FIRST BOYFRIEND WAS A YOUNG MAN NAMED PETER.
HE WAS SHORT AND STOCKY AND HAD A WIDE GAP BETWEEN HIS TWO FRONT TEETH, BUT HE WAS STRONG AND KIND AND BROUGHT ME ROSES EVERY WEEKEND.
HE WAS MY FIRST LOVE.
ONE SUNDAY, HE BROUGHT ME A HANDFUL OF ROSES AS USUAL.
BUT THIS TIME, I COULD SMELL SOMETHING ELSE ON HIS BODY, EVEN THROUGH THE POWERFUL SWEETNESS OF THE BOUQUET.
LILACS.
THERE WAS ONLY ONE PERSON WHO GREW THOSE FLOWERS IN OUR ENTIRE VILLAGE.
HER NAME WAS ANNA, A BEAUTIFUL GIRL I BOUGHT EGGS FROM EVERY MONDAY.
THE SMELL OF HER FLOWERS CONJURED UP VIVID IMAGES OF PETER ROLLING WITH THAT YOUNG WOMAN IN HER GARDEN.
ONCE I LOOKED IN HIS EYES, I KNEW IT WAS TRUE.
AND TO THIS DAY, LILACS STILL SMELL LIKE BETRAYAL.

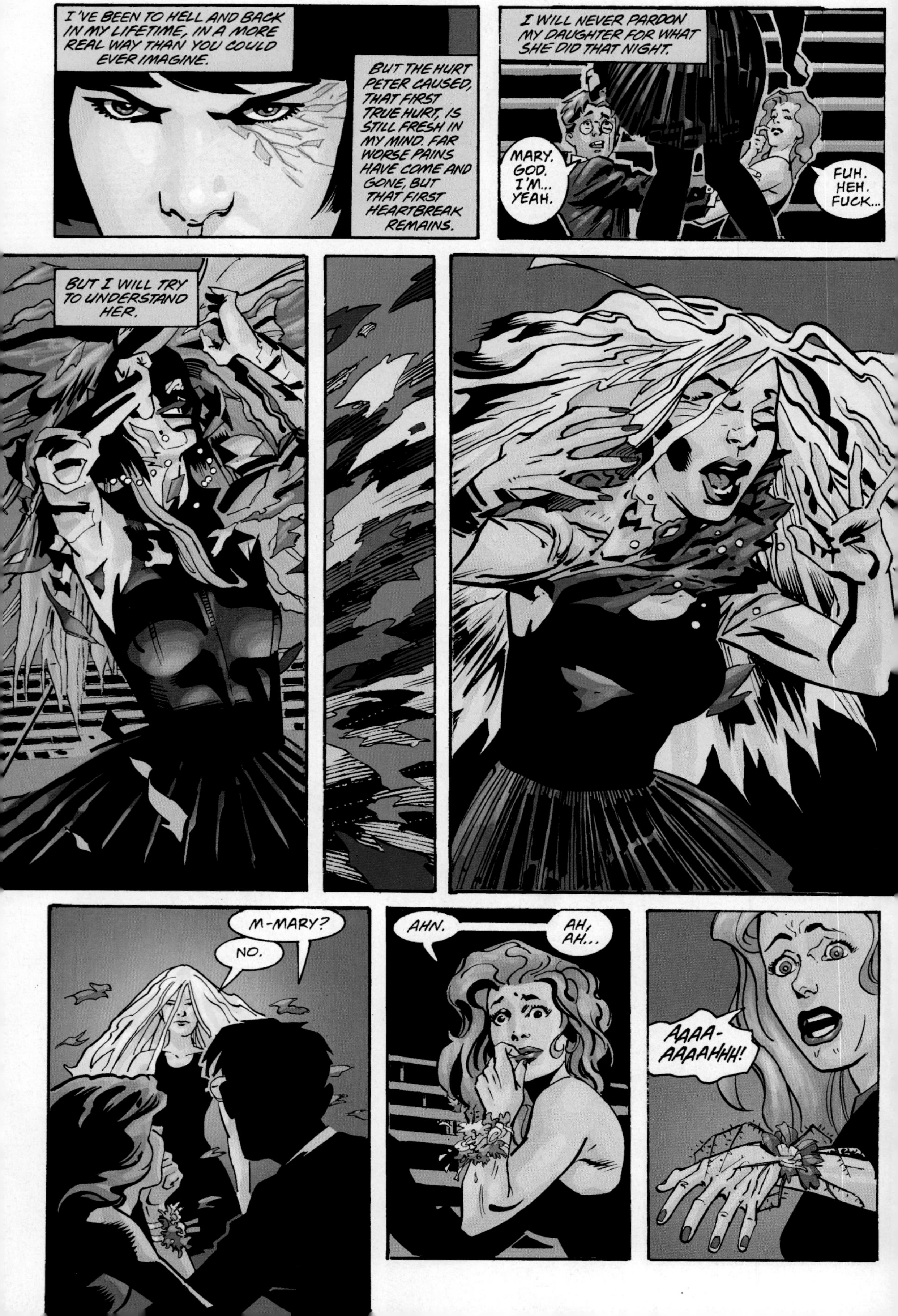
I'VE BEEN TO HELL AND BACK IN MY LIFETIME, IN A MORE REAL WAY THAN YOU COULD EVER IMAGINE.
BUT THE HURT PETER CAUSED, THAT FIRST TRUE HURT, IS STILL FRESH IN MY MIND. FAR WORSE PAINS HAVE COME AND GONE, BUT THAT FIRST HEARTBREAK REMAINS.
I WILL NEVER PARDON MY DAUGHTER FOR WHAT SHE DID THAT NIGHT.
MARY. GOD. I'M... YEAH.
FUH. HEH. FUCK...
BUT I WILL TRY TO UNDERSTAND HER.
M-MARY?
NO.
AHN.
AH, AH...
AAAA-AAAAHHH!

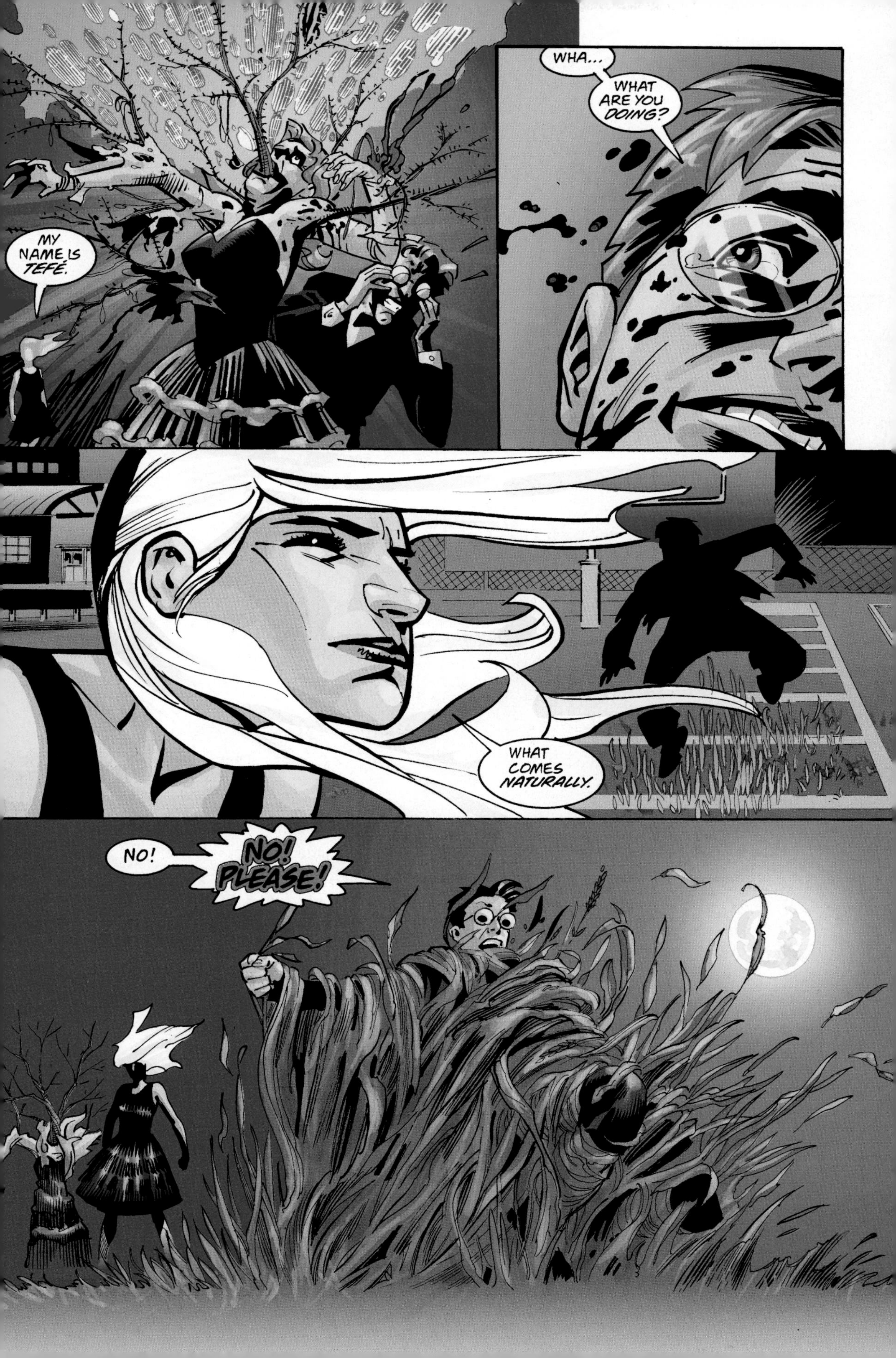
MY NAME IS TEFÉ.
WHA...
WHAT ARE YOU DOING?
WHAT COMES NATURALLY.
NO!
NO! PLEASE!

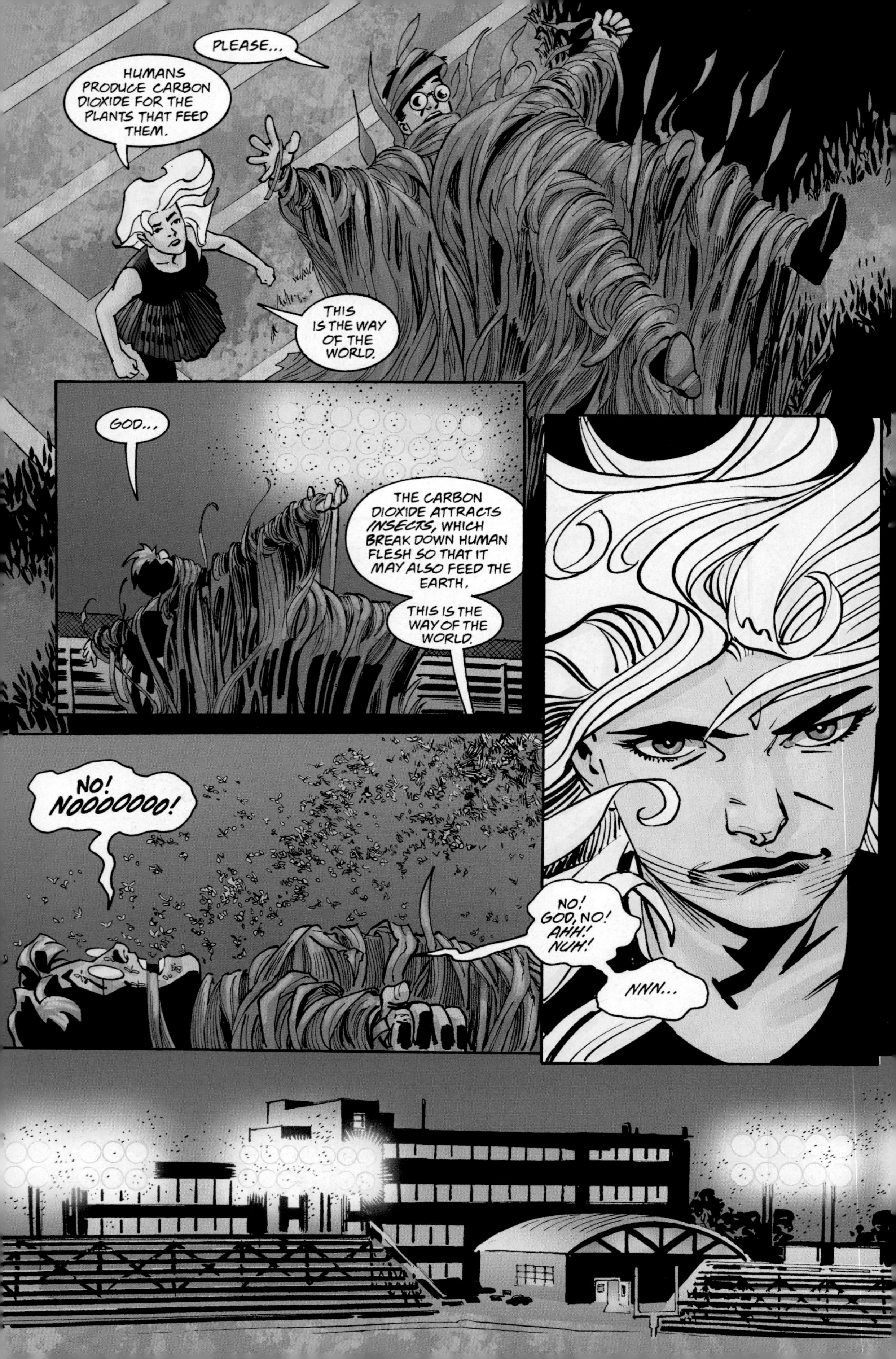
PLEASE...
HUMANS PRODUCE CARBON DIOXIDE FOR THE PLANTS THAT FEED THEM.
THIS IS THE WAY OF THE WORLD.
GOD...
THE CARBON DIOXIDE ATTRACTS *INSECTS*, WHICH BREAK DOWN HUMAN FLESH SO THAT IT MAY ALSO FEED THE EARTH.
THIS IS THE WAY OF THE WORLD.
NO! NOOOOOOO!
NO! GOD, NO! AHH! NUH!
NNN...

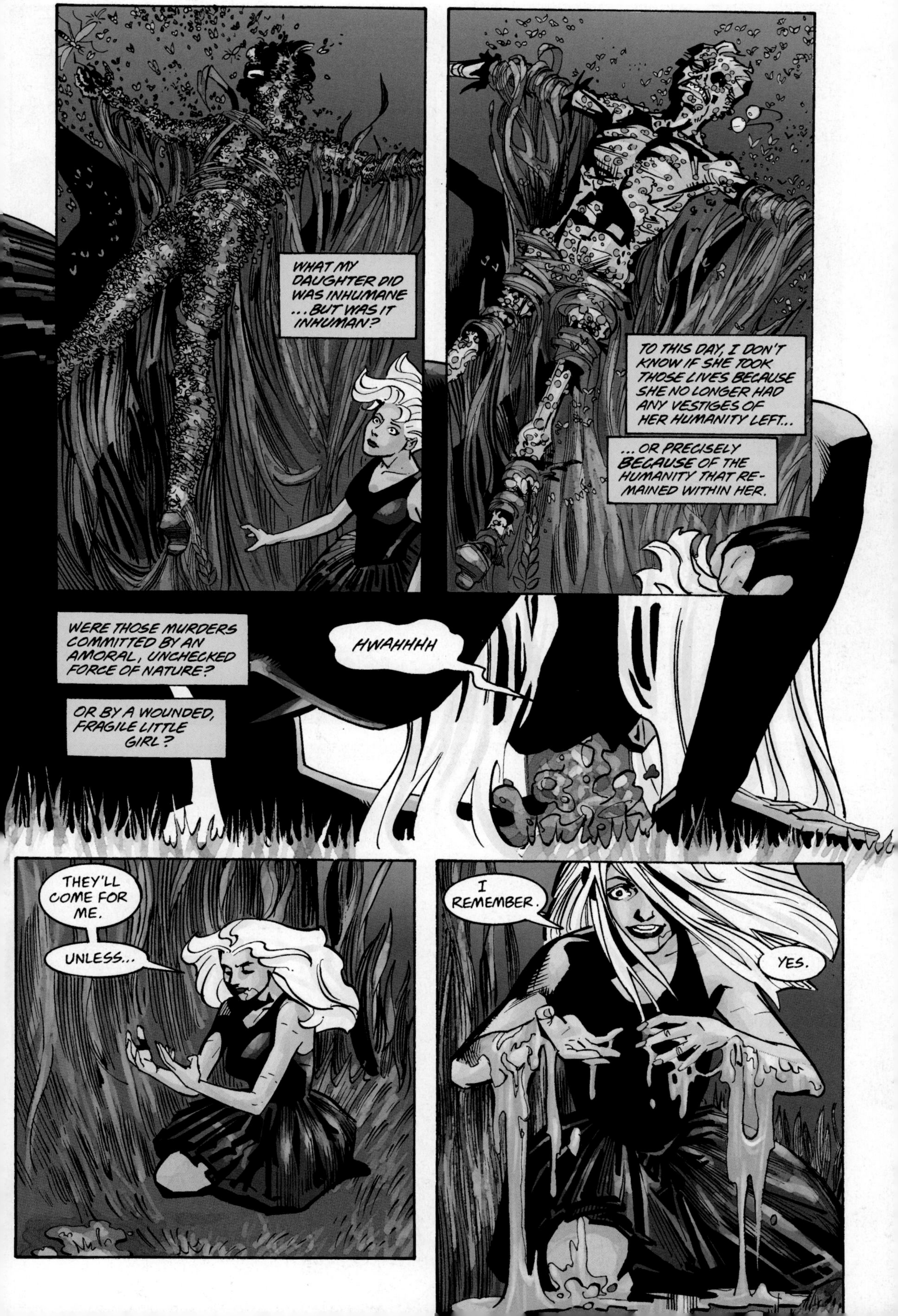
WHAT MY DAUGHTER DID WAS INHUMANE ...BUT WAS IT INHUMAN?
TO THIS DAY, I DON'T KNOW IF SHE TOOK THOSE LIVES BECAUSE SHE NO LONGER HAD ANY VESTIGES OF HER HUMANITY LEFT...
...OR PRECISELY BECAUSE OF THE HUMANITY THAT REMAINED WITHIN HER.
WERE THOSE MURDERS COMMITTED BY AN AMORAL, UNCHECKED FORCE OF NATURE?
OR BY A WOUNDED, FRAGILE LITTLE GIRL?
HWAHHHH
THEY'LL COME FOR ME.
UNLESS...
I REMEMBER.
YES.

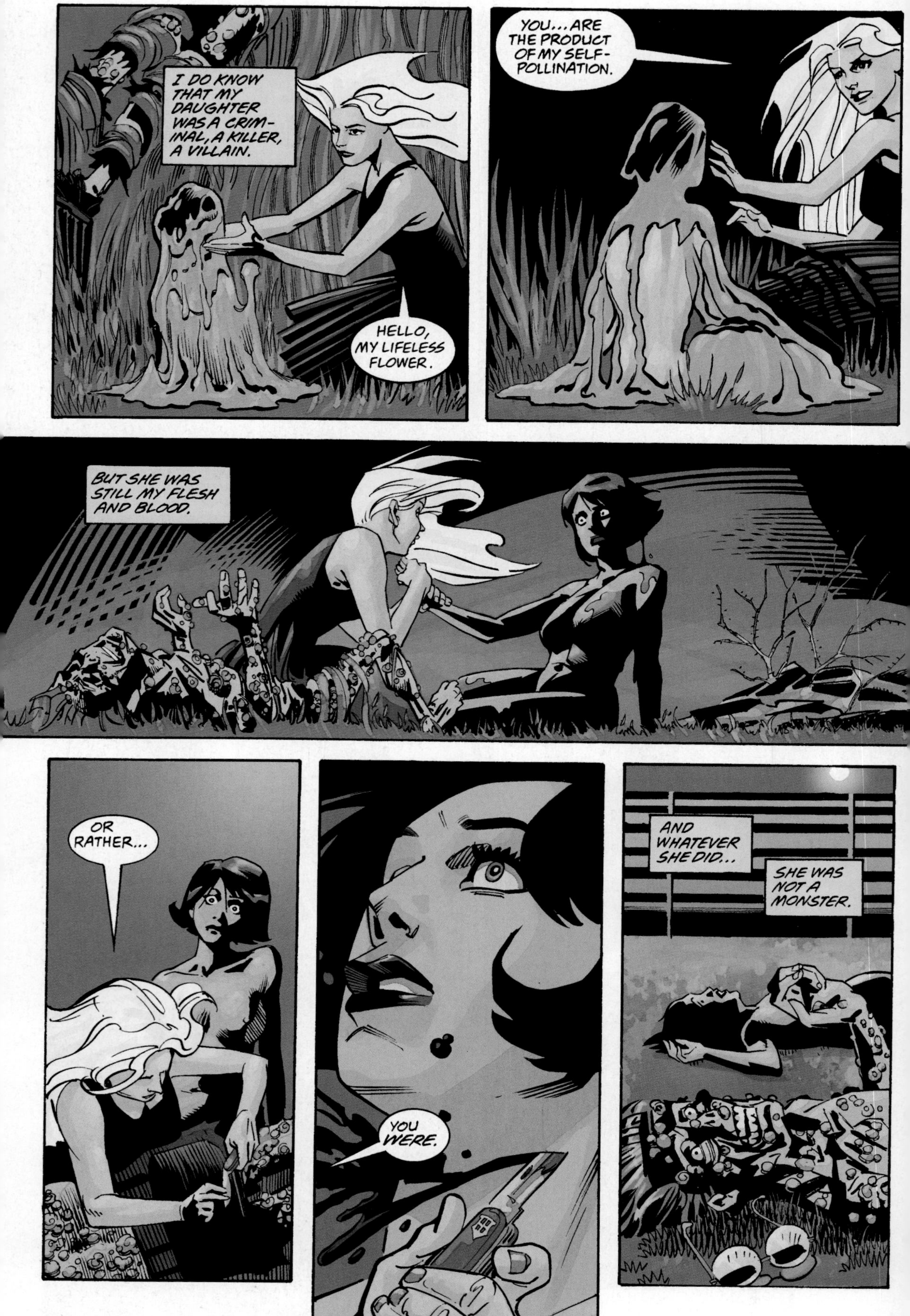
I DO KNOW THAT MY DAUGHTER WAS A CRIMINAL, A KILLER, A VILLAIN.
HELLO, MY LIFELESS FLOWER.
YOU... ARE THE PRODUCT OF MY SELF-POLLINATION.
BUT SHE WAS STILL MY FLESH AND BLOOD.
OR RATHER...
YOU WERE.
AND WHATEVER SHE DID...
SHE WAS NOT A MONSTER.

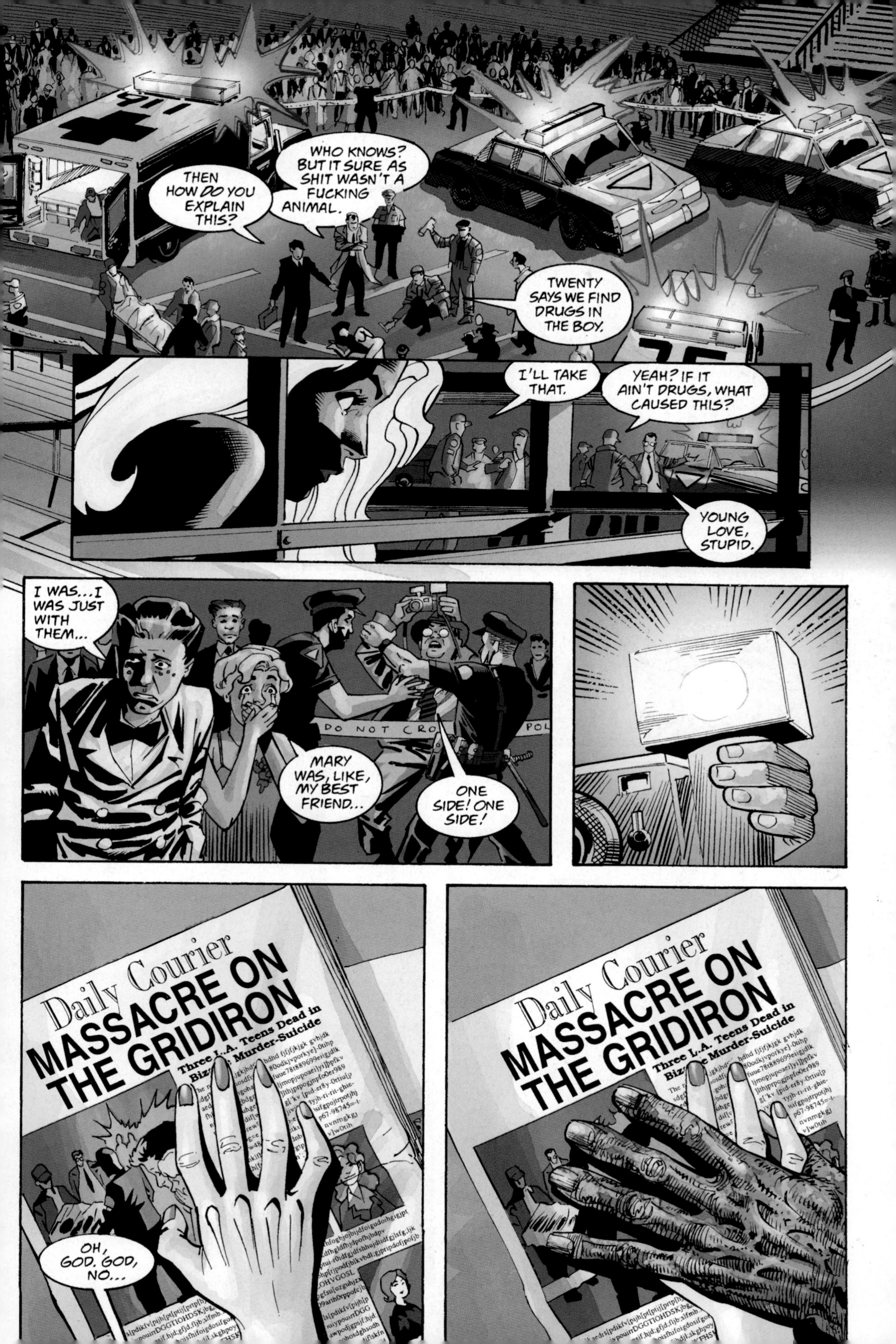

THEN HOW DO YOU EXPLAIN THIS?
WHO KNOWS? BUT IT SURE AS SHIT WASN'T A FUCKING ANIMAL.
TWENTY SAYS WE FIND DRUGS IN THE BOY.
I'LL TAKE THAT.
YEAH? IF IT AIN'T DRUGS, WHAT CAUSED THIS?
YOUNG LOVE, STUPID.
I WAS...I WAS JUST WITH THEM...
MARY WAS, LIKE, MY BEST FRIEND...
ONE SIDE! ONE SIDE!
DO NOT CRO
Daily Courier
MASSACRE ON THE GRIDIRON
Three L.A. Teens Dead in
Murder-Suicide
OH, GOD. GOD, NO...
Daily Courier
MASSACRE ON THE GRIDIRON
Three L.A. Teens Dead in
Murder-Suicide

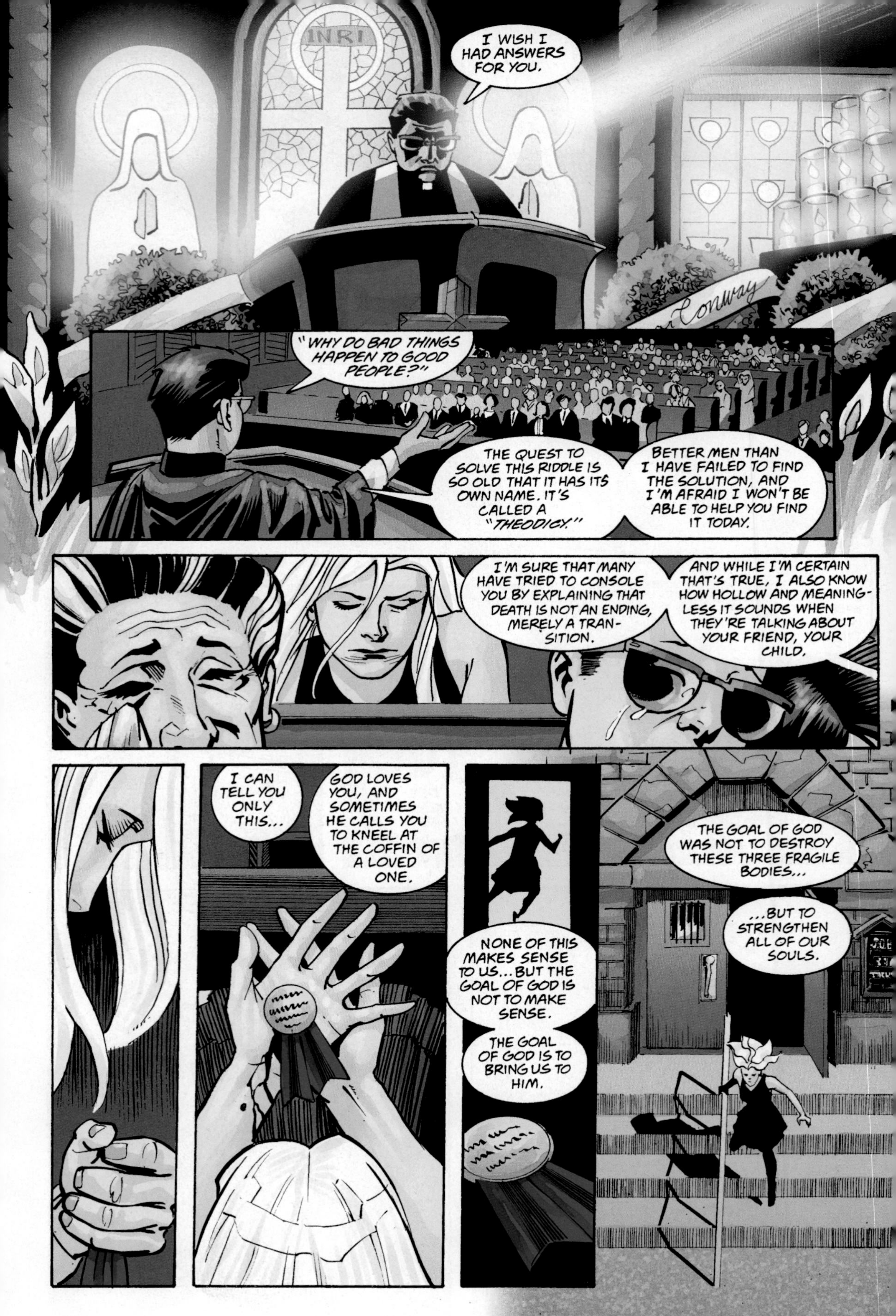
INRI
I WISH I HAD ANSWERS FOR YOU.
"WHY DO BAD THINGS HAPPEN TO GOOD PEOPLE?"
THE QUEST TO SOLVE THIS RIDDLE IS SO OLD THAT IT HAS ITS OWN NAME. IT'S CALLED A "THEODICY."
BETTER MEN THAN I HAVE FAILED TO FIND THE SOLUTION, AND I'M AFRAID I WON'T BE ABLE TO HELP YOU FIND IT TODAY.
I'M SURE THAT MANY HAVE TRIED TO CONSOLE YOU BY EXPLAINING THAT DEATH IS NOT AN ENDING, MERELY A TRAN-SITION.
AND WHILE I'M CERTAIN THAT'S TRUE, I ALSO KNOW HOW HOLLOW AND MEANING-LESS IT SOUNDS WHEN THEY'RE TALKING ABOUT YOUR FRIEND, YOUR CHILD.
I CAN TELL YOU ONLY THIS...
GOD LOVES YOU, AND SOMETIMES HE CALLS YOU TO KNEEL AT THE COFFIN OF A LOVED ONE.
NONE OF THIS MAKES SENSE TO US... BUT THE GOAL OF GOD IS NOT TO MAKE SENSE.
THE GOAL OF GOD IS TO BRING US TO HIM.
THE GOAL OF GOD WAS NOT TO DESTROY THESE THREE FRAGILE BODIES...
...BUT TO STRENGTHEN ALL OF OUR SOULS.

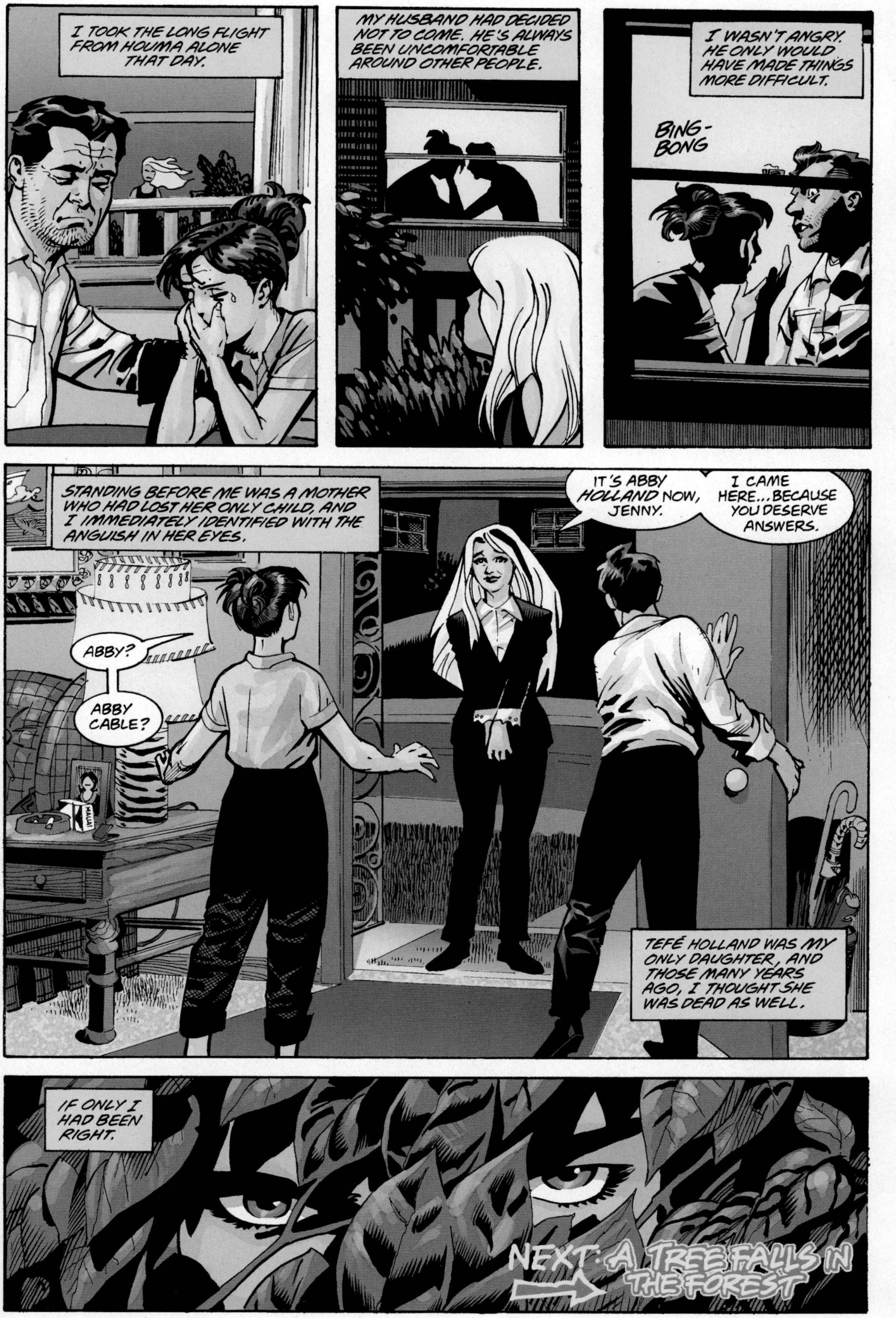

I TOOK THE LONG FLIGHT FROM HOUMA ALONE THAT DAY.
MY HUSBAND HAD DECIDED NOT TO COME. HE'S ALWAYS BEEN UNCOMFORTABLE AROUND OTHER PEOPLE.
I WASN'T ANGRY. HE ONLY WOULD HAVE MADE THINGS MORE DIFFICULT.
BING-BONG
STANDING BEFORE ME WAS A MOTHER WHO HAD LOST HER ONLY CHILD, AND I IMMEDIATELY IDENTIFIED WITH THE ANGUISH IN HER EYES.
ABBY?
ABBY CABLE?
IT'S ABBY HOLLAND NOW, JENNY.
I CAME HERE... BECAUSE YOU DESERVE ANSWERS.
TEFÉ HOLLAND WAS MY ONLY DAUGHTER, AND THOSE MANY YEARS AGO, I THOUGHT SHE WAS DEAD AS WELL.
IF ONLY I HAD BEEN RIGHT.
NEXT: A TREE FALLS IN THE FOREST

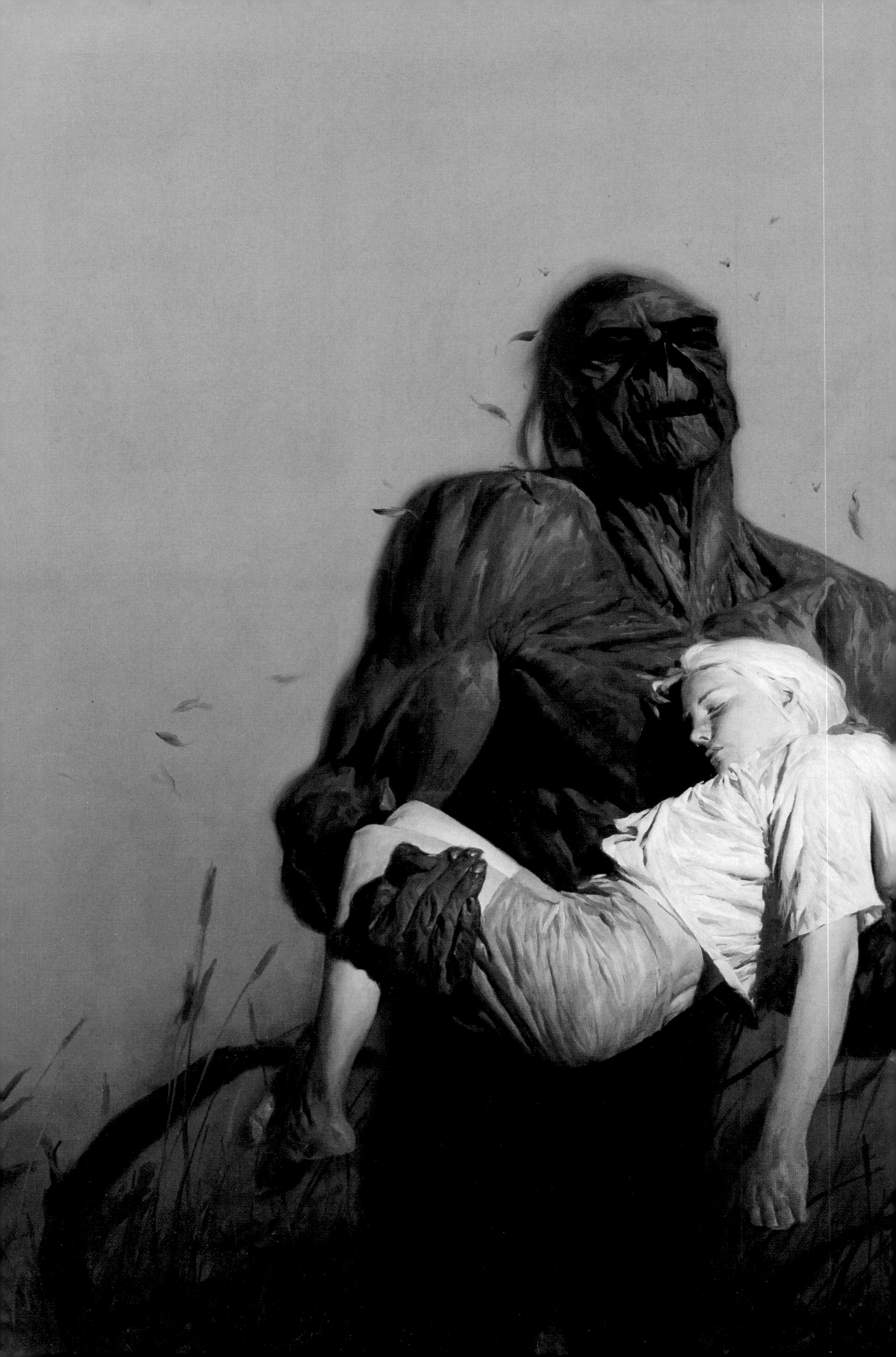

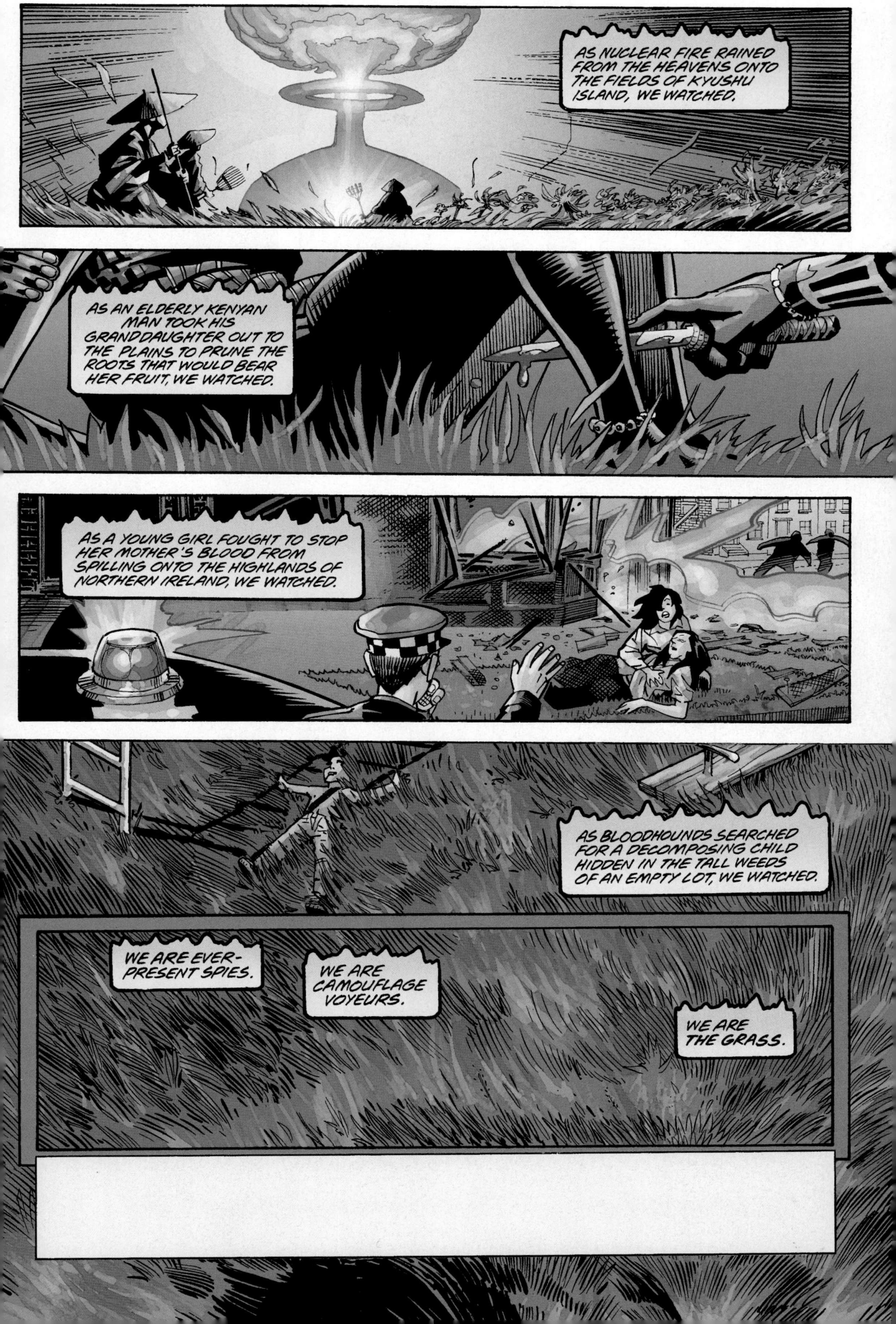
AS NUCLEAR FIRE RAINED FROM THE HEAVENS ONTO THE FIELDS OF KYUSHU ISLAND, WE WATCHED.
AS AN ELDERLY KENYAN MAN TOOK HIS GRANDDAUGHTER OUT TO THE PLAINS TO PRUNE THE ROOTS THAT WOULD BEAR HER FRUIT, WE WATCHED.
AS A YOUNG GIRL FOUGHT TO STOP HER MOTHER'S BLOOD FROM SPILLING ONTO THE HIGHLANDS OF NORTHERN IRELAND, WE WATCHED.
AS BLOODHOUNDS SEARCHED FOR A DECOMPOSING CHILD HIDDEN IN THE TALL WEEDS OF AN EMPTY LOT, WE WATCHED.
WE ARE EVER-PRESENT SPIES.
WE ARE CAMOUFLAGE VOYEURS.
WE ARE THE GRASS.

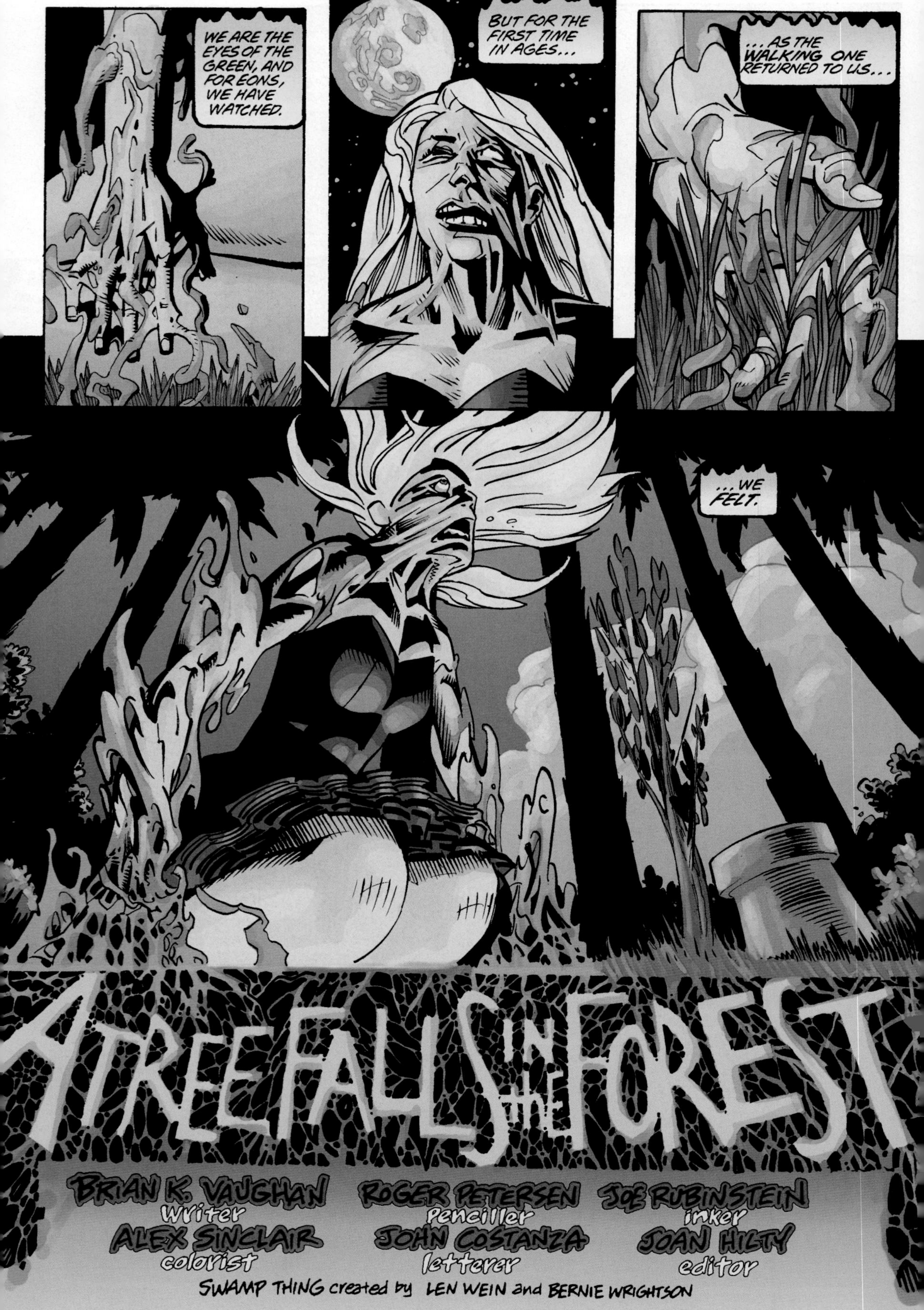
WE ARE THE EYES OF THE GREEN, AND FOR EONS, WE HAVE WATCHED.
BUT FOR THE FIRST TIME IN AGES...
...AS THE WALKING ONE RETURNED TO US...
...WE FELT.
A TREE FALLS IN THE FOREST
BRIAN K. VAUGHAN writer
ROGER PETERSEN penciller
JOE RUBINSTEIN inker
ALEX SINCLAIR colorist
JOHN COSTANZA letterer
JOAN HILTY editor
SWAMP THING created by LEN WEIN and BERNIE WRIGHTSON

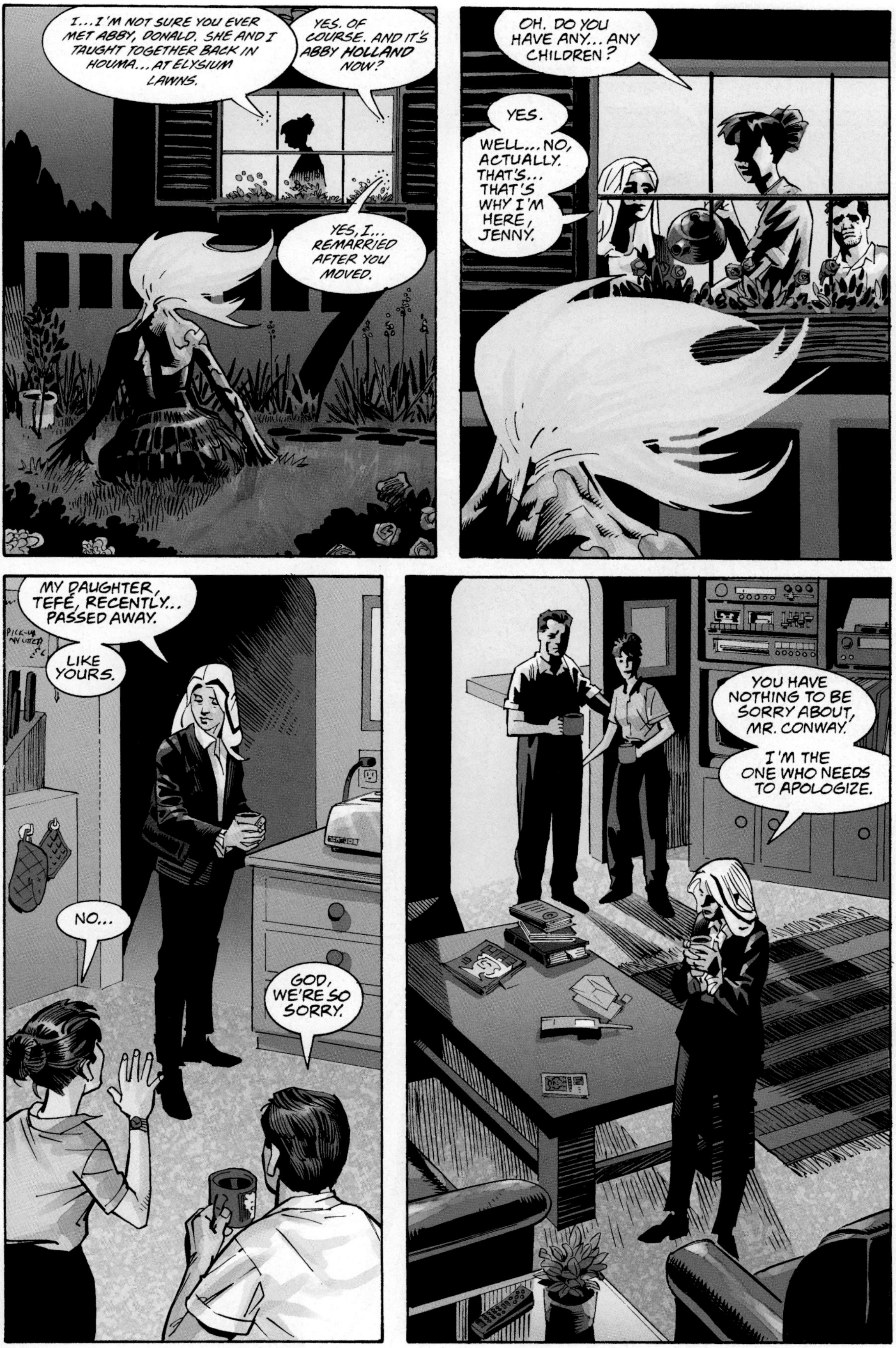
I... I'M NOT SURE YOU EVER MET ABBY, DONALD. SHE AND I TAUGHT TOGETHER BACK IN HOUMA... AT ELYSIUM LAWNS.
YES. OF COURSE. AND IT'S ABBY HOLLAND NOW?
YES, I... REMARRIED AFTER YOU MOVED.
OH. DO YOU HAVE ANY... ANY CHILDREN?
YES.
WELL... NO, ACTUALLY. THAT'S... THAT'S WHY I'M HERE, JENNY.
MY DAUGHTER, TEFÉ, RECENTLY... PASSED AWAY.
LIKE YOURS.
NO...
GOD, WE'RE SO SORRY.
YOU HAVE NOTHING TO BE SORRY ABOUT, MR. CONWAY.
I'M THE ONE WHO NEEDS TO APOLOGIZE.

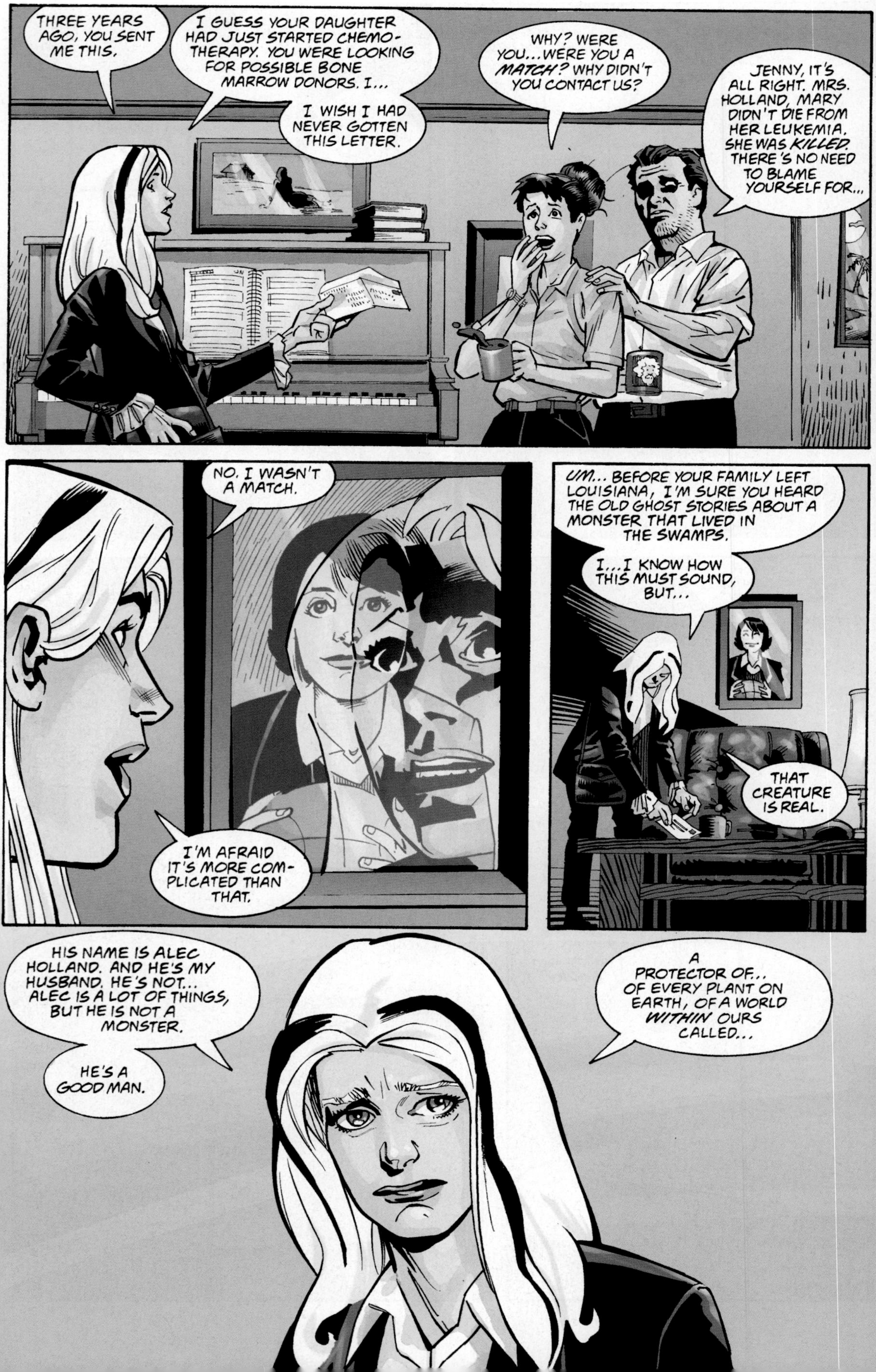
THREE YEARS AGO, YOU SENT ME THIS.
I GUESS YOUR DAUGHTER HAD JUST STARTED CHEMO-THERAPY. YOU WERE LOOKING FOR POSSIBLE BONE MARROW DONORS. I...
I WISH I HAD NEVER GOTTEN THIS LETTER.
WHY? WERE YOU... WERE YOU A *MATCH*? WHY DIDN'T YOU CONTACT US?
JENNY, IT'S ALL RIGHT. MRS. HOLLAND, MARY DIDN'T DIE FROM HER LEUKEMIA. SHE WAS *KILLED*. THERE'S NO NEED TO BLAME YOURSELF FOR...
NO, I WASN'T A MATCH.
I'M AFRAID IT'S MORE COM-PLICATED THAN THAT.
UM... BEFORE YOUR FAMILY LEFT LOUISIANA, I'M SURE YOU HEARD THE OLD GHOST STORIES ABOUT A MONSTER THAT LIVED IN THE SWAMPS.
I... I KNOW HOW THIS MUST SOUND, BUT...
THAT CREATURE IS REAL.
HIS NAME IS ALEC HOLLAND. AND HE'S MY HUSBAND. HE'S NOT... ALEC IS A LOT OF THINGS, BUT HE IS NOT A MONSTER.
HE'S A GOOD MAN.
A PROTECTOR OF... OF EVERY PLANT ON EARTH, OF A WORLD *WITHIN* OURS CALLED...

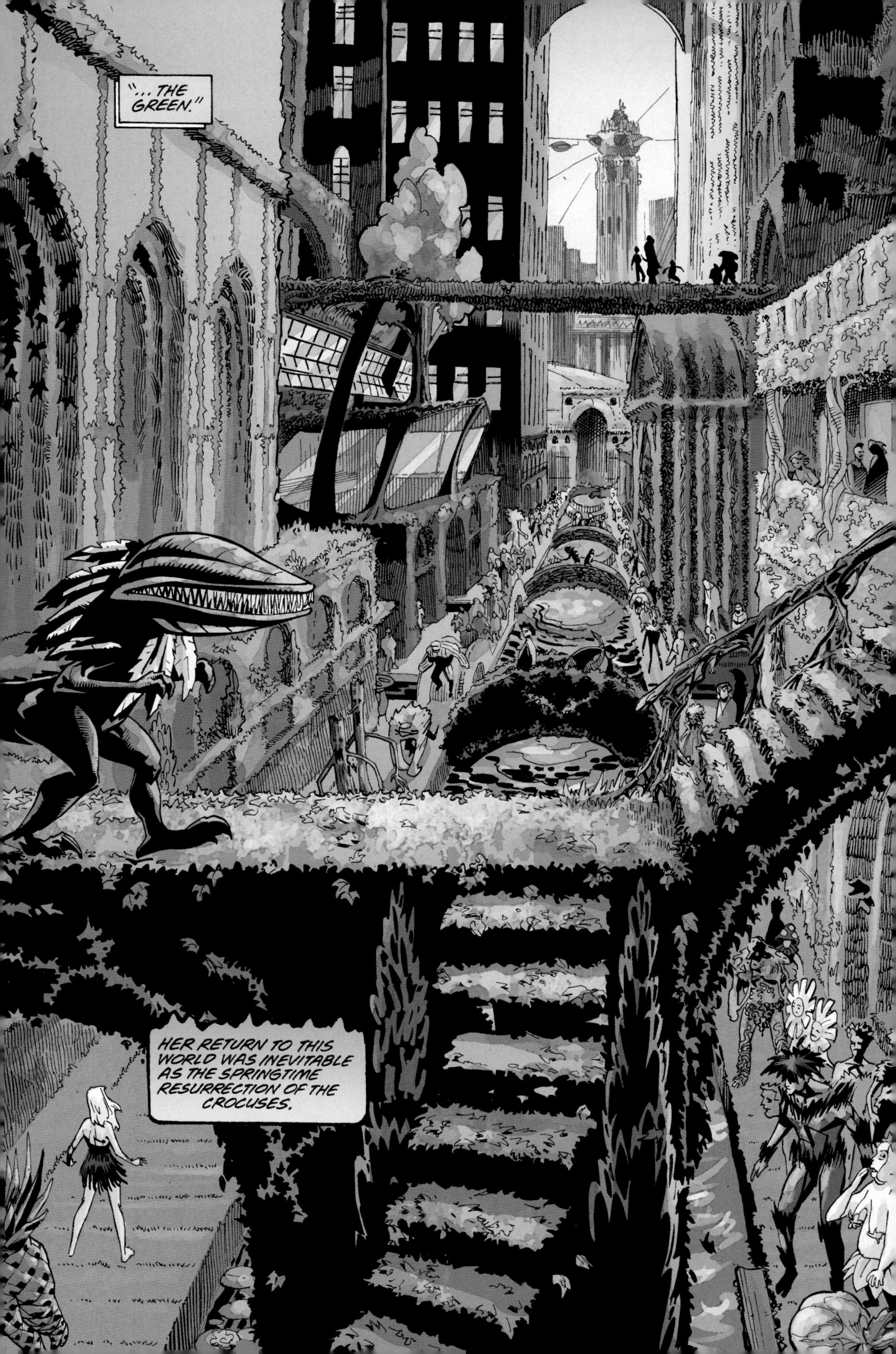
"...THE GREEN."
HER RETURN TO THIS WORLD WAS INEVITABLE AS THE SPRINGTIME RESURRECTION OF THE CROCUSES.

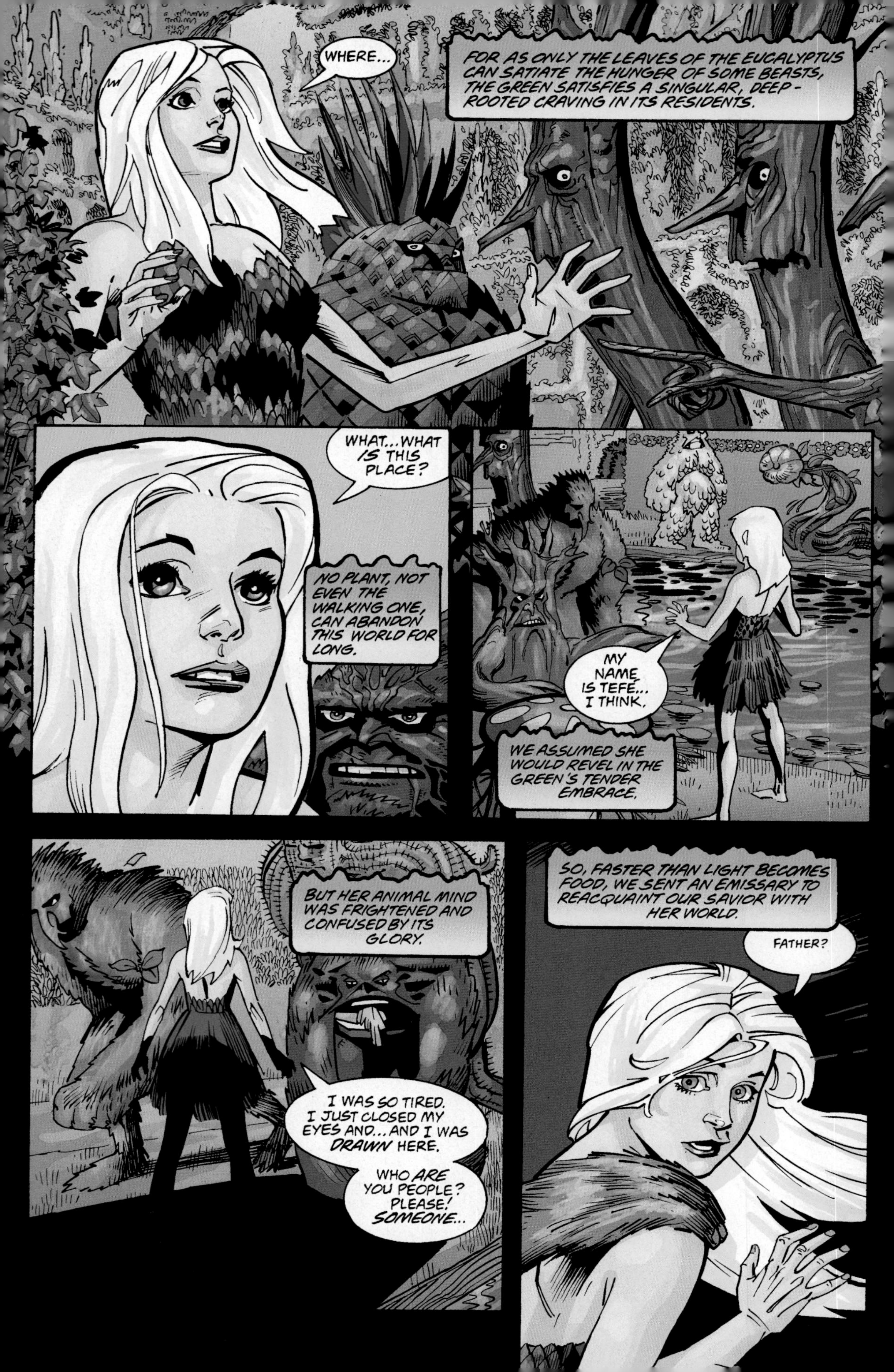
WHERE...
FOR AS ONLY THE LEAVES OF THE EUCALYPTUS CAN SATIATE THE HUNGER OF SOME BEASTS, THE GREEN SATISFIES A SINGULAR, DEEP-ROOTED CRAVING IN ITS RESIDENTS.
WHAT...WHAT IS THIS PLACE?
NO PLANT, NOT EVEN THE WALKING ONE, CAN ABANDON THIS WORLD FOR LONG.
MY NAME IS TEFÉ... I THINK.
WE ASSUMED SHE WOULD REVEL IN THE GREEN'S TENDER EMBRACE.
BUT HER ANIMAL MIND WAS FRIGHTENED AND CONFUSED BY ITS GLORY.
I WAS SO TIRED. I JUST CLOSED MY EYES AND... AND I WAS DRAWN HERE.
WHO ARE YOU PEOPLE? PLEASE! SOMEONE...
SO, FASTER THAN LIGHT BECOMES FOOD, WE SENT AN EMISSARY TO REACQUAINT OUR SAVIOR WITH HER WORLD.
FATHER?

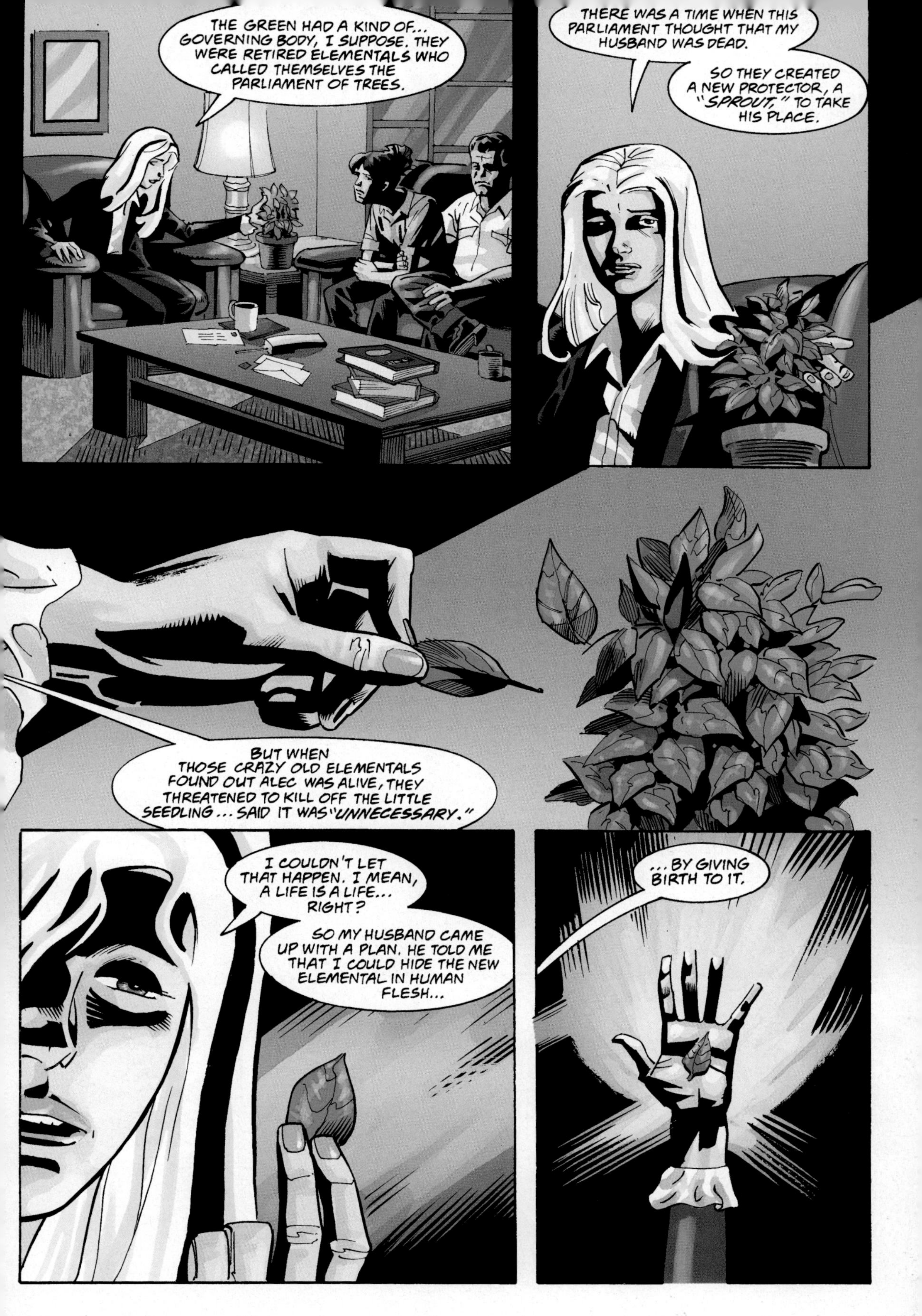
THE GREEN HAD A KIND OF... GOVERNING BODY, I SUPPOSE. THEY WERE RETIRED ELEMENTALS WHO CALLED THEMSELVES THE PARLIAMENT OF TREES.
THERE WAS A TIME WHEN THIS PARLIAMENT THOUGHT THAT MY HUSBAND WAS DEAD.
SO THEY CREATED A NEW PROTECTOR, A "SPROUT," TO TAKE HIS PLACE.
BUT WHEN THOSE CRAZY OLD ELEMENTALS FOUND OUT ALEC WAS ALIVE, THEY THREATENED TO KILL OFF THE LITTLE SEEDLING... SAID IT WAS "UNNECESSARY."
I COULDN'T LET THAT HAPPEN. I MEAN, A LIFE IS A LIFE... RIGHT?
SO MY HUSBAND CAME UP WITH A PLAN. HE TOLD ME THAT I COULD HIDE THE NEW ELEMENTAL IN HUMAN FLESH...
...BY GIVING BIRTH TO IT.

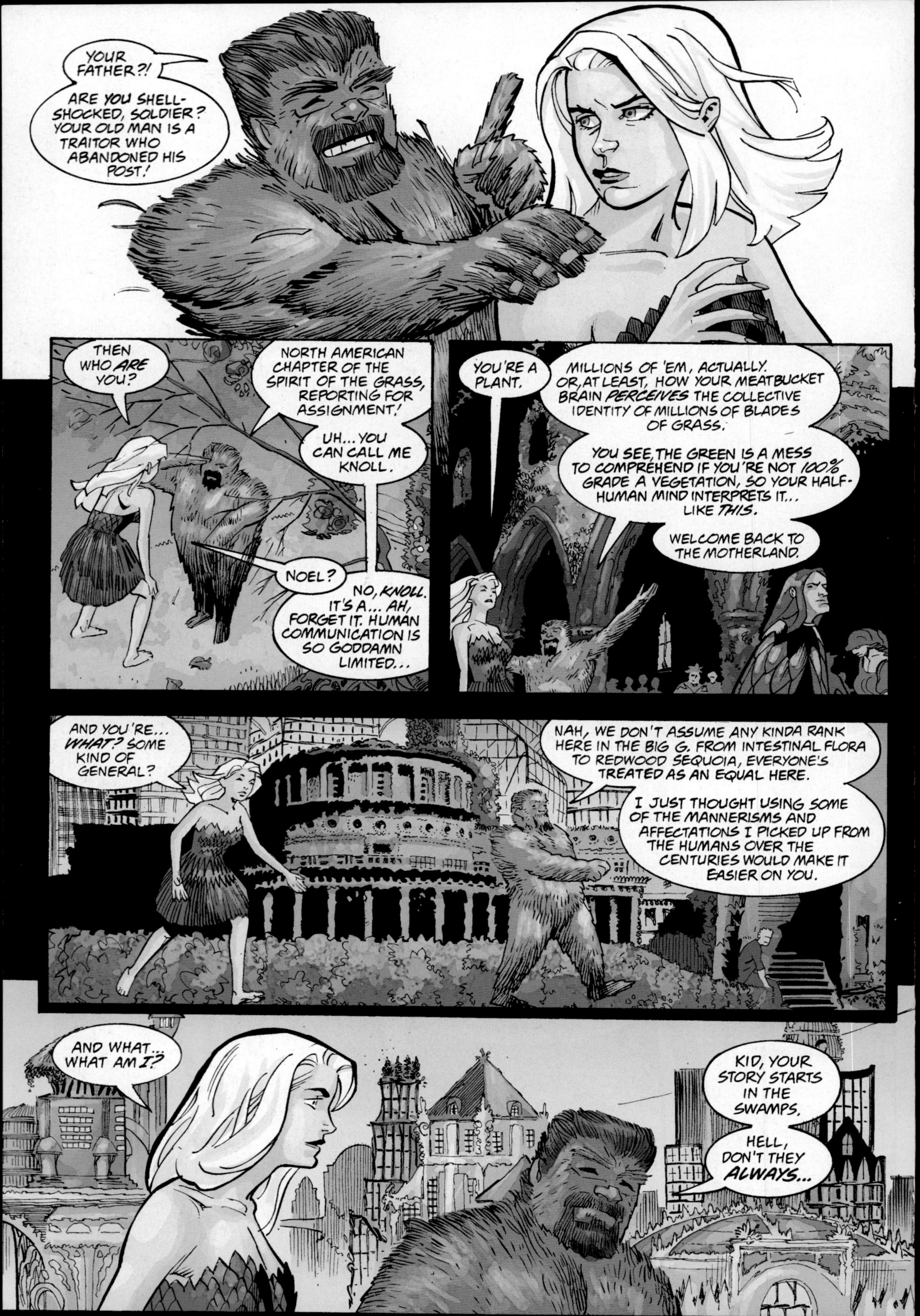
YOUR FATHER?!
ARE YOU SHELL-SHOCKED, SOLDIER? YOUR OLD MAN IS A TRAITOR WHO ABANDONED HIS POST!
THEN WHO ARE YOU?
NORTH AMERICAN CHAPTER OF THE SPIRIT OF THE GRASS, REPORTING FOR ASSIGNMENT!
UH... YOU CAN CALL ME KNOLL.
NOEL?
NO, KNOLL. IT'S A... AH, FORGET IT. HUMAN COMMUNICATION IS SO GODDAMN LIMITED...
YOU'RE A PLANT.
MILLIONS OF 'EM, ACTUALLY. OR, AT LEAST, HOW YOUR MEATBUCKET BRAIN PERCEIVES THE COLLECTIVE IDENTITY OF MILLIONS OF BLADES OF GRASS.
YOU SEE, THE GREEN IS A MESS TO COMPREHEND IF YOU'RE NOT 100% GRADE A VEGETATION, SO YOUR HALF-HUMAN MIND INTERPRETS IT... LIKE THIS.
WELCOME BACK TO THE MOTHERLAND.
AND YOU'RE... WHAT? SOME KIND OF GENERAL?
NAH, WE DON'T ASSUME ANY KINDA RANK HERE IN THE BIG G. FROM INTESTINAL FLORA TO REDWOOD SEQUOIA, EVERYONE'S TREATED AS AN EQUAL HERE.
I JUST THOUGHT USING SOME OF THE MANNERISMS AND AFFECTATIONS I PICKED UP FROM THE HUMANS OVER THE CENTURIES WOULD MAKE IT EASIER ON YOU.
AND WHAT... WHAT AM I?
KID, YOUR STORY STARTS IN THE SWAMPS.
HELL, DON'T THEY ALWAYS...

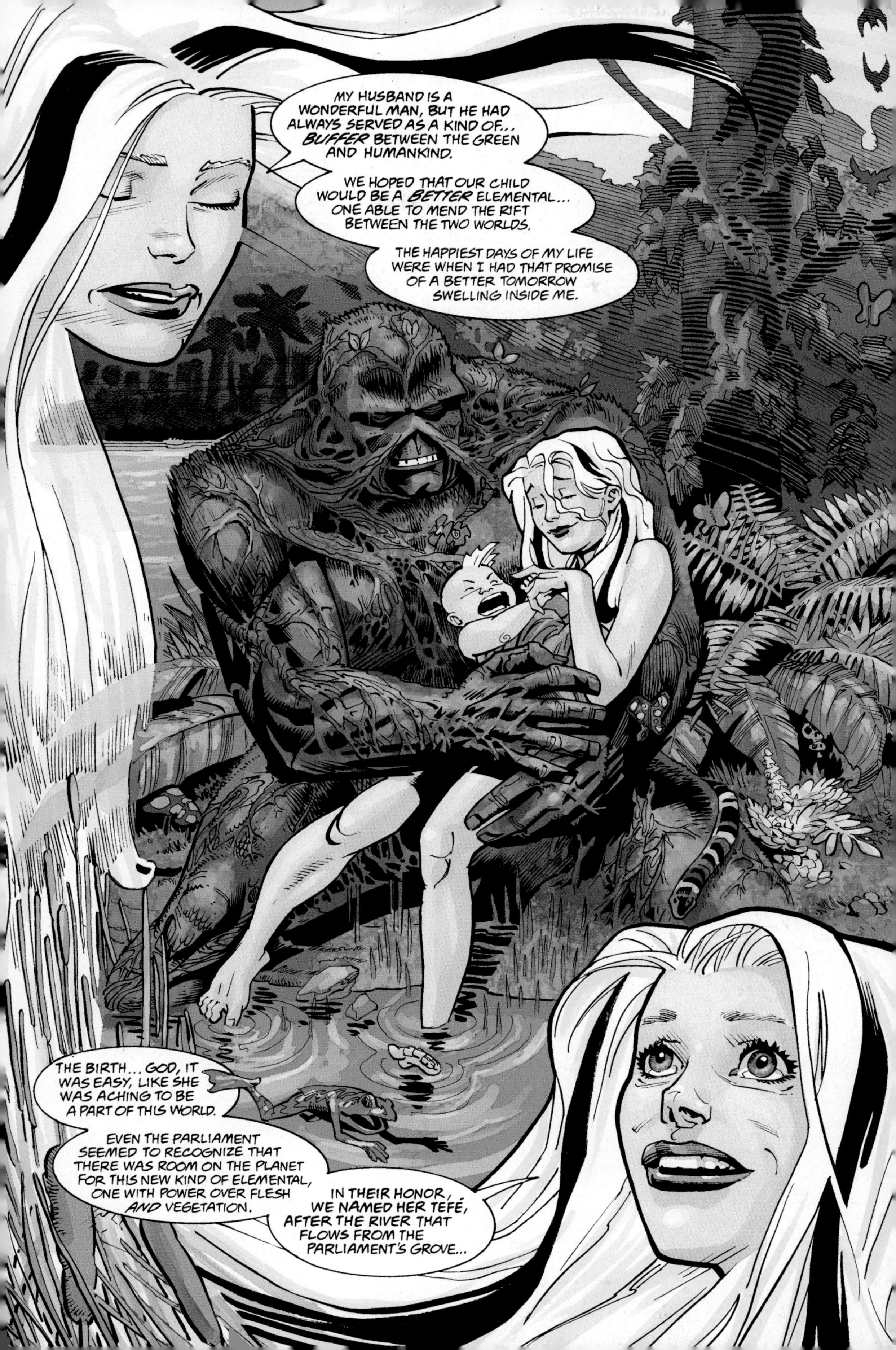
MY HUSBAND IS A WONDERFUL MAN, BUT HE HAD ALWAYS SERVED AS A KIND OF... BUFFER BETWEEN THE GREEN AND HUMANKIND.
WE HOPED THAT OUR CHILD WOULD BE A BETTER ELEMENTAL... ONE ABLE TO MEND THE RIFT BETWEEN THE TWO WORLDS.
THE HAPPIEST DAYS OF MY LIFE WERE WHEN I HAD THAT PROMISE OF A BETTER TOMORROW SWELLING INSIDE ME.
THE BIRTH... GOD, IT WAS EASY, LIKE SHE WAS ACHING TO BE A PART OF THIS WORLD.
EVEN THE PARLIAMENT SEEMED TO RECOGNIZE THAT THERE WAS ROOM ON THE PLANET FOR THIS NEW KIND OF ELEMENTAL, ONE WITH POWER OVER FLESH AND VEGETATION.
IN THEIR HONOR, WE NAMED HER TEFÉ, AFTER THE RIVER THAT FLOWS FROM THE PARLIAMENT'S GROVE...

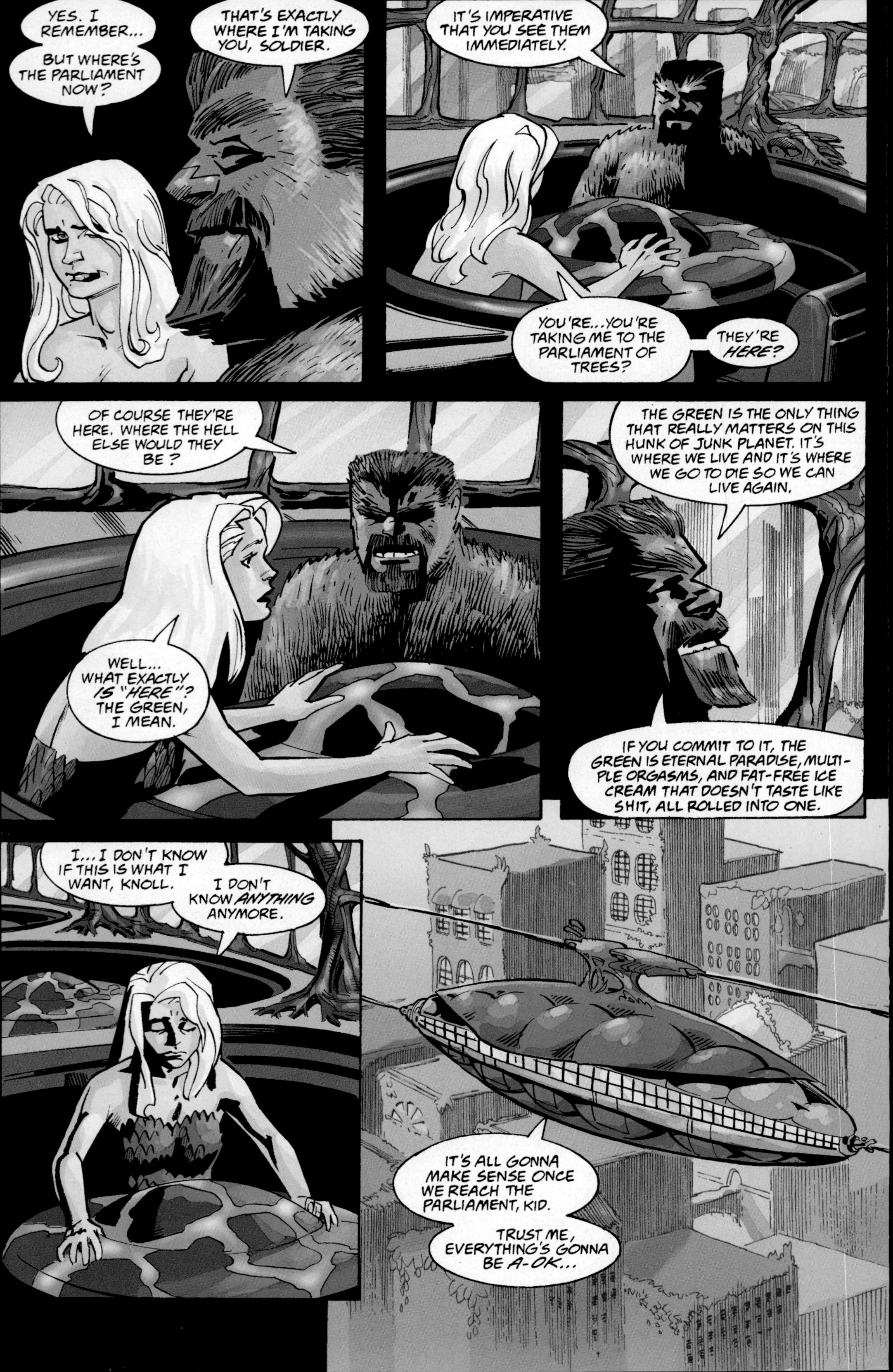
YES. I REMEMBER...
BUT WHERE'S THE PARLIAMENT NOW?
THAT'S EXACTLY WHERE I'M TAKING YOU, SOLDIER.
IT'S IMPERATIVE THAT YOU SEE THEM IMMEDIATELY.
YOU'RE...YOU'RE TAKING ME TO THE PARLIAMENT OF TREES?
THEY'RE *HERE*?
OF COURSE THEY'RE HERE. WHERE THE HELL ELSE WOULD THEY BE?
WELL... WHAT EXACTLY *IS* "HERE"? THE GREEN, I MEAN.
THE GREEN IS THE ONLY THING THAT REALLY MATTERS ON THIS HUNK OF JUNK PLANET. IT'S WHERE WE LIVE AND IT'S WHERE WE GO TO DIE SO WE CAN LIVE AGAIN.
IF YOU COMMIT TO IT, THE GREEN IS ETERNAL PARADISE, MULTIPLE ORGASMS, AND FAT-FREE ICE CREAM THAT DOESN'T TASTE LIKE SHIT, ALL ROLLED INTO ONE.
I... I DON'T KNOW IF THIS IS WHAT I WANT, KNOLL.
I DON'T KNOW *ANYTHING* ANYMORE.
IT'S ALL GONNA MAKE SENSE ONCE WE REACH THE PARLIAMENT, KID.
TRUST ME, EVERYTHING'S GONNA BE *A-OK*...

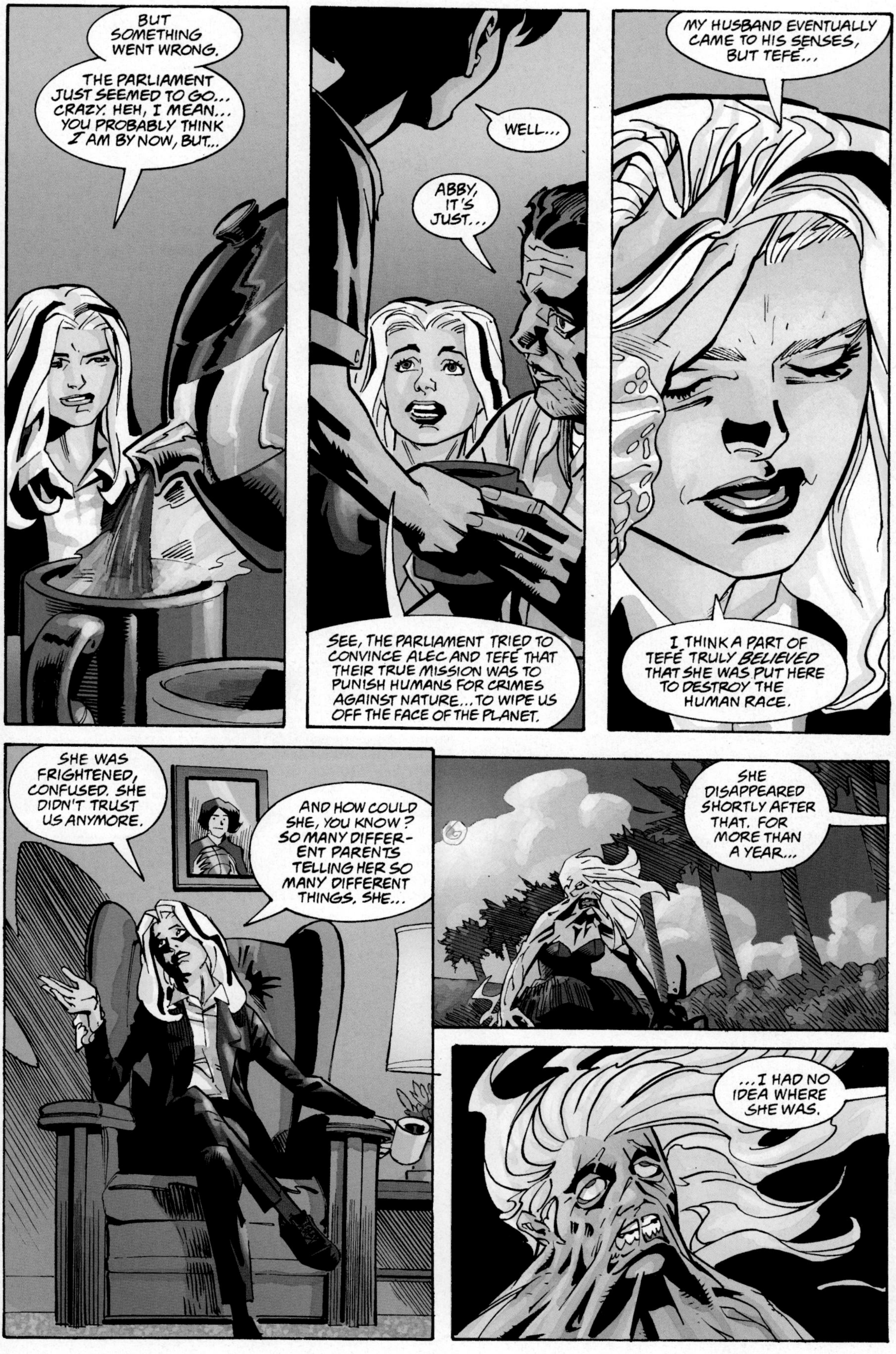
BUT SOMETHING WENT WRONG.
THE PARLIAMENT JUST SEEMED TO GO... CRAZY. HEH, I MEAN... YOU PROBABLY THINK I AM BY NOW, BUT...
WELL...
ABBY, IT'S JUST...
SEE, THE PARLIAMENT TRIED TO CONVINCE ALEC AND TEFÉ THAT THEIR TRUE MISSION WAS TO PUNISH HUMANS FOR CRIMES AGAINST NATURE... TO WIPE US OFF THE FACE OF THE PLANET.
MY HUSBAND EVENTUALLY CAME TO HIS SENSES, BUT TEFÉ...
I THINK A PART OF TEFÉ TRULY BELIEVED THAT SHE WAS PUT HERE TO DESTROY THE HUMAN RACE.
SHE WAS FRIGHTENED, CONFUSED. SHE DIDN'T TRUST US ANYMORE.
AND HOW COULD SHE, YOU KNOW? SO MANY DIFFERENT PARENTS TELLING HER SO MANY DIFFERENT THINGS. SHE...
SHE DISAPPEARED SHORTLY AFTER THAT. FOR MORE THAN A YEAR...
...I HAD NO IDEA WHERE SHE WAS.

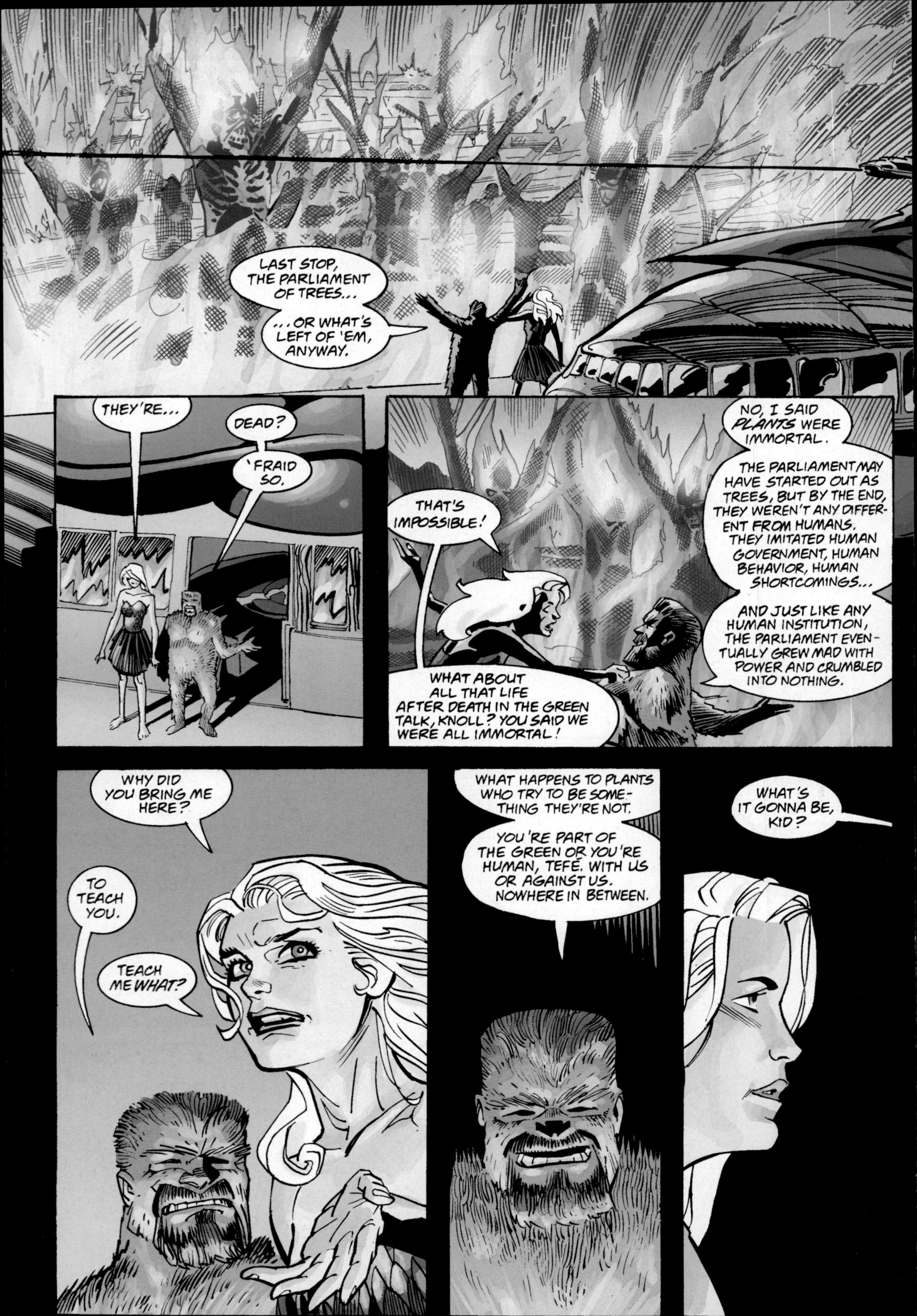
LAST STOP, THE PARLIAMENT OF TREES...
...OR WHAT'S LEFT OF 'EM, ANYWAY.
THEY'RE...
DEAD?
'FRAID SO.
THAT'S IMPOSSIBLE!
WHAT ABOUT ALL THAT LIFE AFTER DEATH IN THE GREEN TALK, KNOLL? YOU SAID WE WERE ALL IMMORTAL!
NO, I SAID PLANTS WERE IMMORTAL.
THE PARLIAMENT MAY HAVE STARTED OUT AS TREES, BUT BY THE END, THEY WEREN'T ANY DIFFERENT FROM HUMANS. THEY IMITATED HUMAN GOVERNMENT, HUMAN BEHAVIOR, HUMAN SHORTCOMINGS...
AND JUST LIKE ANY HUMAN INSTITUTION, THE PARLIAMENT EVENTUALLY GREW MAD WITH POWER AND CRUMBLED INTO NOTHING.
WHY DID YOU BRING ME HERE?
TO TEACH YOU.
TEACH ME WHAT?
WHAT HAPPENS TO PLANTS WHO TRY TO BE SOMETHING THEY'RE NOT.
YOU'RE PART OF THE GREEN OR YOU'RE HUMAN, TEFÉ. WITH US OR AGAINST US. NOWHERE IN BETWEEN.
WHAT'S IT GONNA BE, KID?

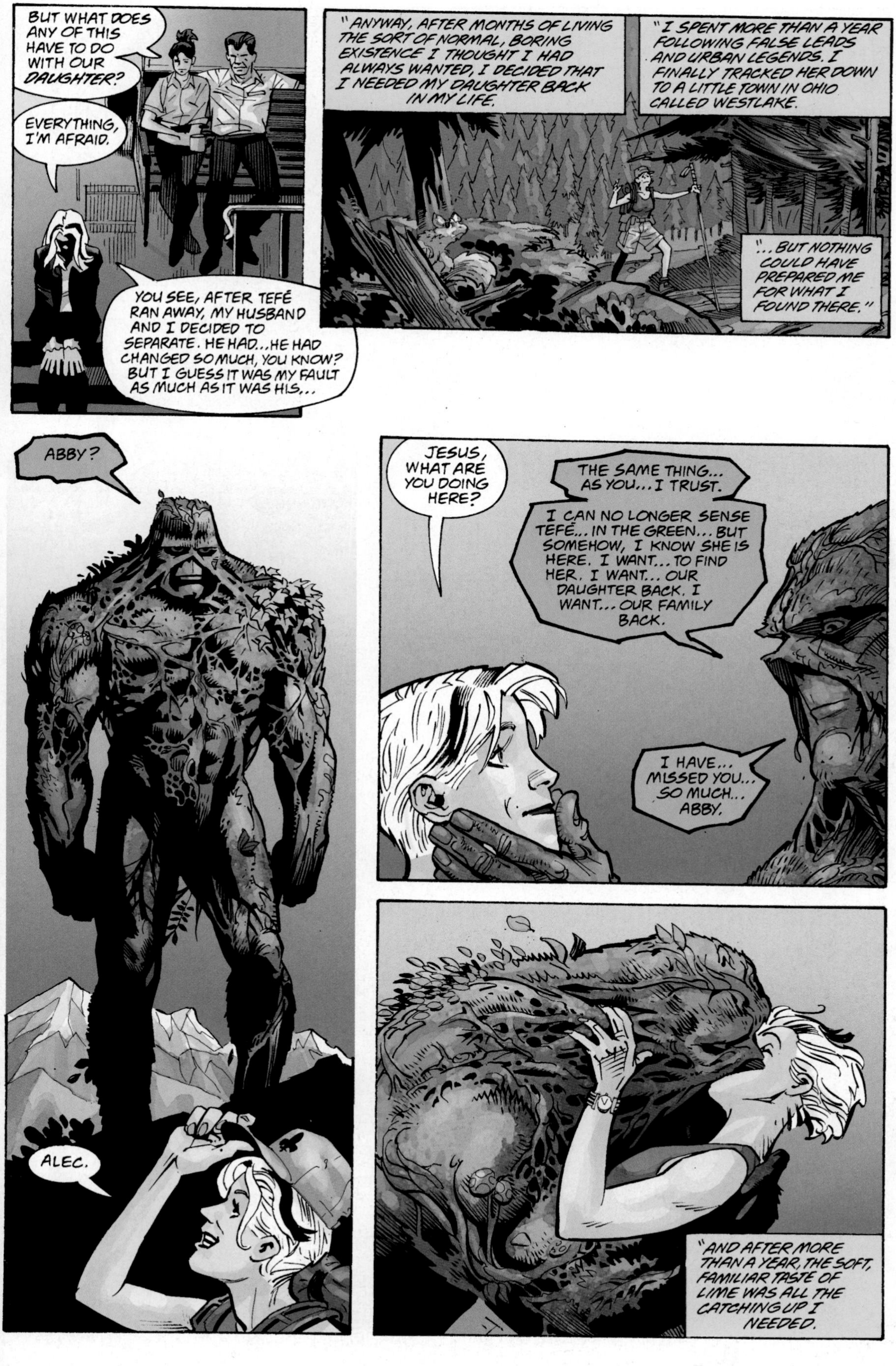

BUT WHAT DOES ANY OF THIS HAVE TO DO WITH OUR DAUGHTER?
EVERYTHING, I'M AFRAID.
YOU SEE, AFTER TEFÉ RAN AWAY, MY HUSBAND AND I DECIDED TO SEPARATE. HE HAD... HE HAD CHANGED SO MUCH, YOU KNOW? BUT I GUESS IT WAS MY FAULT AS MUCH AS IT WAS HIS...
"ANYWAY, AFTER MONTHS OF LIVING THE SORT OF NORMAL, BORING EXISTENCE I THOUGHT I HAD ALWAYS WANTED, I DECIDED THAT I NEEDED MY DAUGHTER BACK IN MY LIFE.
"I SPENT MORE THAN A YEAR FOLLOWING FALSE LEADS AND URBAN LEGENDS. I FINALLY TRACKED HER DOWN TO A LITTLE TOWN IN OHIO CALLED WESTLAKE.
"...BUT NOTHING COULD HAVE PREPARED ME FOR WHAT I FOUND THERE."
ABBY?
ALEC.
JESUS, WHAT ARE YOU DOING HERE?
THE SAME THING... AS YOU... I TRUST.
I CAN NO LONGER SENSE TEFÉ... IN THE GREEN... BUT SOMEHOW, I KNOW SHE IS HERE. I WANT... TO FIND HER. I WANT... OUR DAUGHTER BACK. I WANT... OUR FAMILY BACK.
I HAVE... MISSED YOU... SO MUCH... ABBY.
"AND AFTER MORE THAN A YEAR, THE SOFT, FAMILIAR TASTE OF LIME WAS ALL THE CATCHING UP I NEEDED.

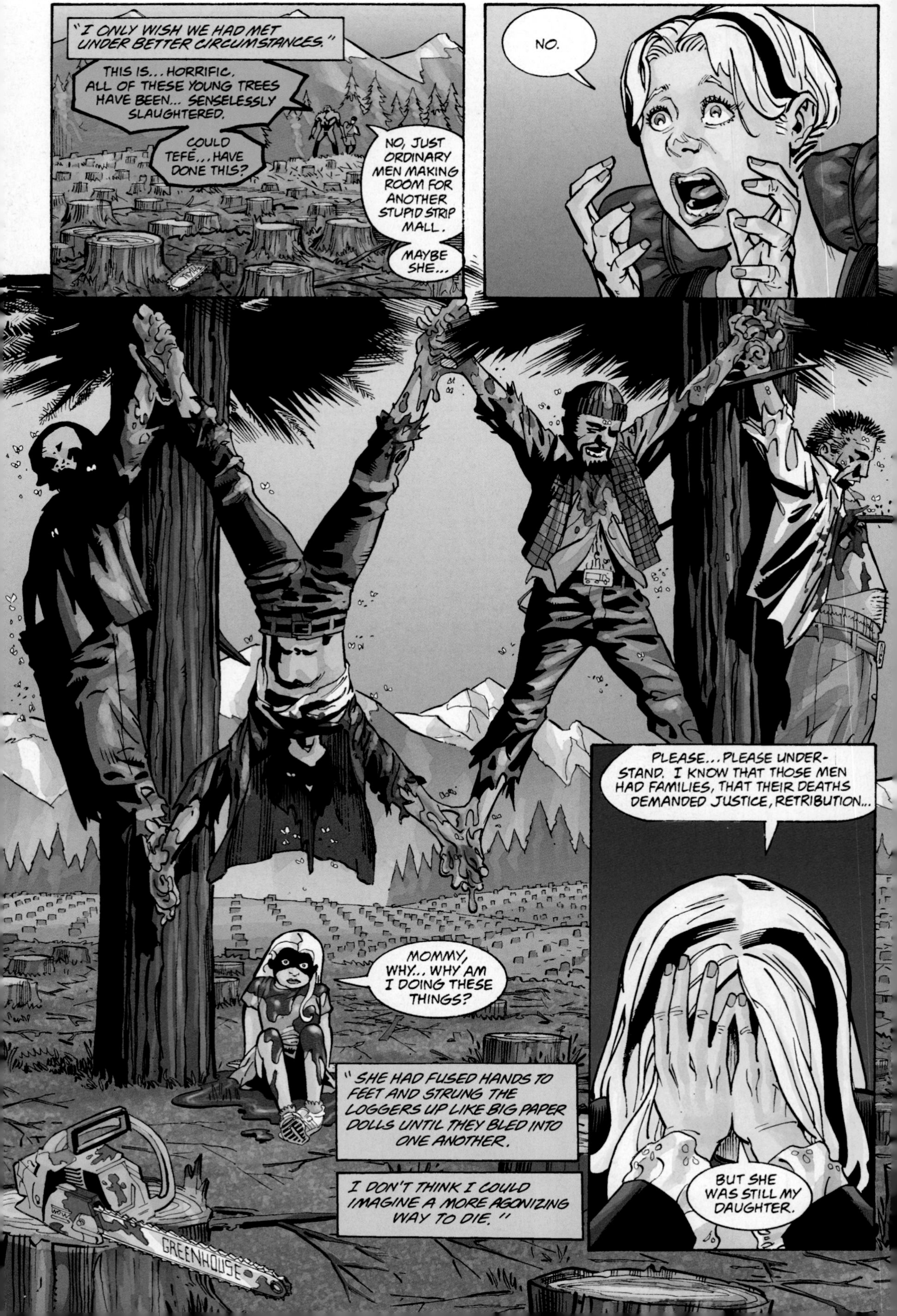
"I ONLY WISH WE HAD MET UNDER BETTER CIRCUMSTANCES."
THIS IS... HORRIFIC. ALL OF THESE YOUNG TREES HAVE BEEN... SENSELESSLY SLAUGHTERED.
COULD TEFÉ... HAVE DONE THIS?
NO, JUST ORDINARY MEN MAKING ROOM FOR ANOTHER STUPID STRIP MALL.
MAYBE SHE...
NO.
PLEASE... PLEASE UNDER-STAND. I KNOW THAT THOSE MEN HAD FAMILIES, THAT THEIR DEATHS DEMANDED JUSTICE, RETRIBUTION...
MOMMY, WHY... WHY AM I DOING THESE THINGS?
" SHE HAD FUSED HANDS TO FEET AND STRUNG THE LOGGERS UP LIKE BIG PAPER DOLLS UNTIL THEY BLED INTO ONE ANOTHER.
I DON'T THINK I COULD IMAGINE A MORE AGONIZING WAY TO DIE."
BUT SHE WAS STILL MY DAUGHTER.
GREENHOUSE

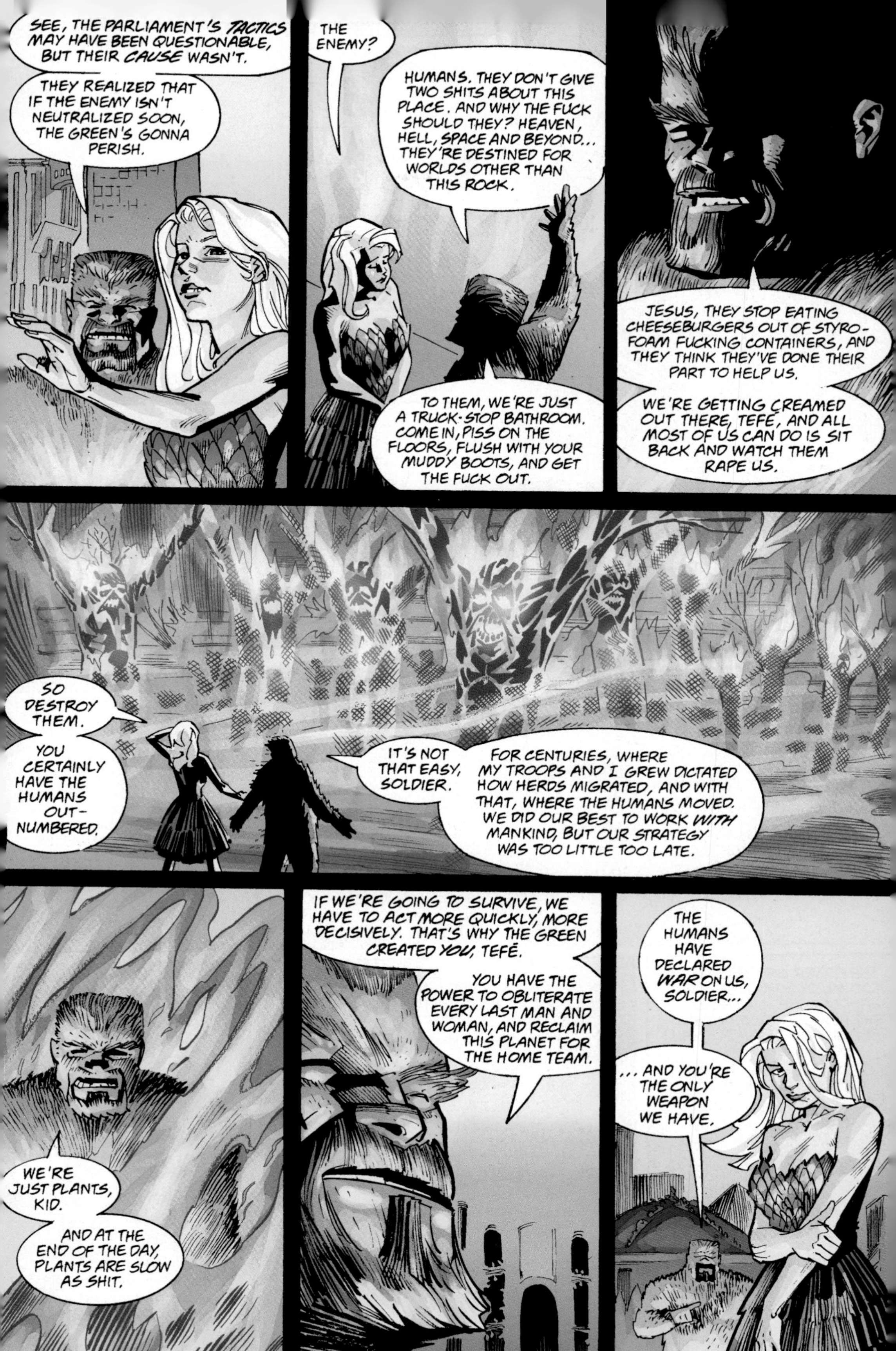
SEE, THE PARLIAMENT'S TACTICS MAY HAVE BEEN QUESTIONABLE, BUT THEIR CAUSE WASN'T.
THEY REALIZED THAT IF THE ENEMY ISN'T NEUTRALIZED SOON, THE GREEN'S GONNA PERISH.
THE ENEMY?
HUMANS. THEY DON'T GIVE TWO SHITS ABOUT THIS PLACE. AND WHY THE FUCK SHOULD THEY? HEAVEN, HELL, SPACE AND BEYOND... THEY'RE DESTINED FOR WORLDS OTHER THAN THIS ROCK.
TO THEM, WE'RE JUST A TRUCK-STOP BATHROOM. COME IN, PISS ON THE FLOORS, FLUSH WITH YOUR MUDDY BOOTS, AND GET THE FUCK OUT.
JESUS, THEY STOP EATING CHEESEBURGERS OUT OF STYROFOAM FUCKING CONTAINERS, AND THEY THINK THEY'VE DONE THEIR PART TO HELP US.
WE'RE GETTING CREAMED OUT THERE, TEFÉ, AND ALL MOST OF US CAN DO IS SIT BACK AND WATCH THEM RAPE US.
SO DESTROY THEM.
YOU CERTAINLY HAVE THE HUMANS OUT-NUMBERED.
IT'S NOT THAT EASY, SOLDIER.
FOR CENTURIES, WHERE MY TROOPS AND I GREW DICTATED HOW HERDS MIGRATED, AND WITH THAT, WHERE THE HUMANS MOVED. WE DID OUR BEST TO WORK WITH MANKIND, BUT OUR STRATEGY WAS TOO LITTLE TOO LATE.
WE'RE JUST PLANTS, KID.
AND AT THE END OF THE DAY, PLANTS ARE SLOW AS SHIT.
IF WE'RE GOING TO SURVIVE, WE HAVE TO ACT MORE QUICKLY, MORE DECISIVELY. THAT'S WHY THE GREEN CREATED YOU, TEFÉ.
YOU HAVE THE POWER TO OBLITERATE EVERY LAST MAN AND WOMAN, AND RECLAIM THIS PLANET FOR THE HOME TEAM.
THE HUMANS HAVE DECLARED WAR ON US, SOLDIER...
...AND YOU'RE THE ONLY WEAPON WE HAVE.

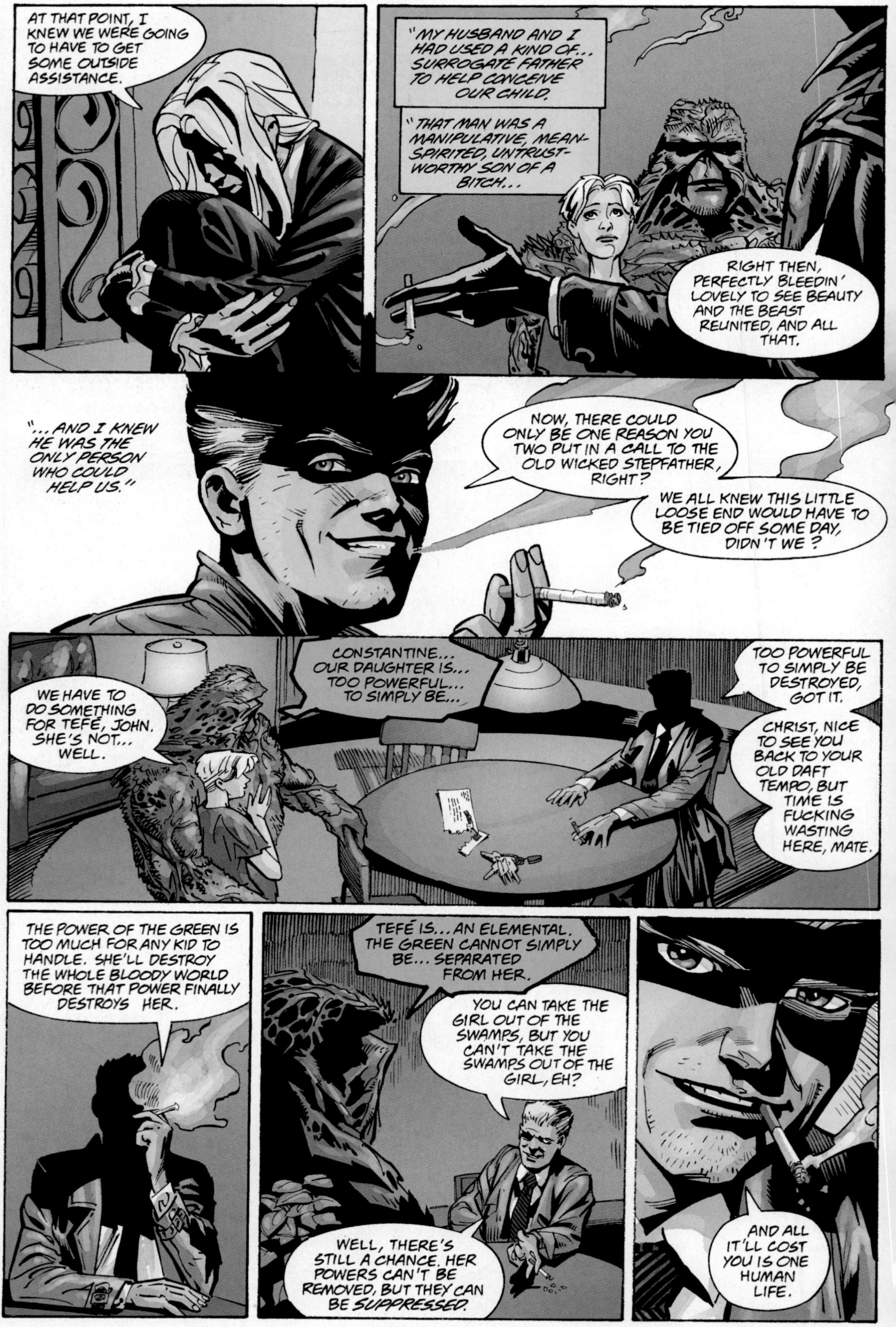
AT THAT POINT, I KNEW WE WERE GOING TO HAVE TO GET SOME OUTSIDE ASSISTANCE.
"MY HUSBAND AND I HAD USED A KIND OF... SURROGATE FATHER TO HELP CONCEIVE OUR CHILD.
"THAT MAN WAS A MANIPULATIVE, MEAN-SPIRITED, UNTRUSTWORTHY SON OF A BITCH...
RIGHT THEN, PERFECTLY BLEEDIN' LOVELY TO SEE BEAUTY AND THE BEAST REUNITED, AND ALL THAT.
"...AND I KNEW HE WAS THE ONLY PERSON WHO COULD HELP US."
NOW, THERE COULD ONLY BE ONE REASON YOU TWO PUT IN A CALL TO THE OLD WICKED STEPFATHER, RIGHT?
WE ALL KNEW THIS LITTLE LOOSE END WOULD HAVE TO BE TIED OFF SOME DAY, DIDN'T WE?
WE HAVE TO DO SOMETHING FOR TEFÉ, JOHN. SHE'S NOT... WELL.
CONSTANTINE... OUR DAUGHTER IS... TOO POWERFUL... TO SIMPLY BE...
TOO POWERFUL TO SIMPLY BE DESTROYED, GOT IT.
CHRIST, NICE TO SEE YOU BACK TO YOUR OLD DAFT TEMPO, BUT TIME IS FUCKING WASTING HERE, MATE.
THE POWER OF THE GREEN IS TOO MUCH FOR ANY KID TO HANDLE. SHE'LL DESTROY THE WHOLE BLOODY WORLD BEFORE THAT POWER FINALLY DESTROYS HER.
TEFÉ IS... AN ELEMENTAL. THE GREEN CANNOT SIMPLY BE... SEPARATED FROM HER.
YOU CAN TAKE THE GIRL OUT OF THE SWAMPS, BUT YOU CAN'T TAKE THE SWAMPS OUT OF THE GIRL, EH?
WELL, THERE'S STILL A CHANCE. HER POWERS CAN'T BE REMOVED, BUT THEY CAN BE *SUPPRESSED*.
AND ALL IT'LL COST YOU IS ONE HUMAN LIFE.

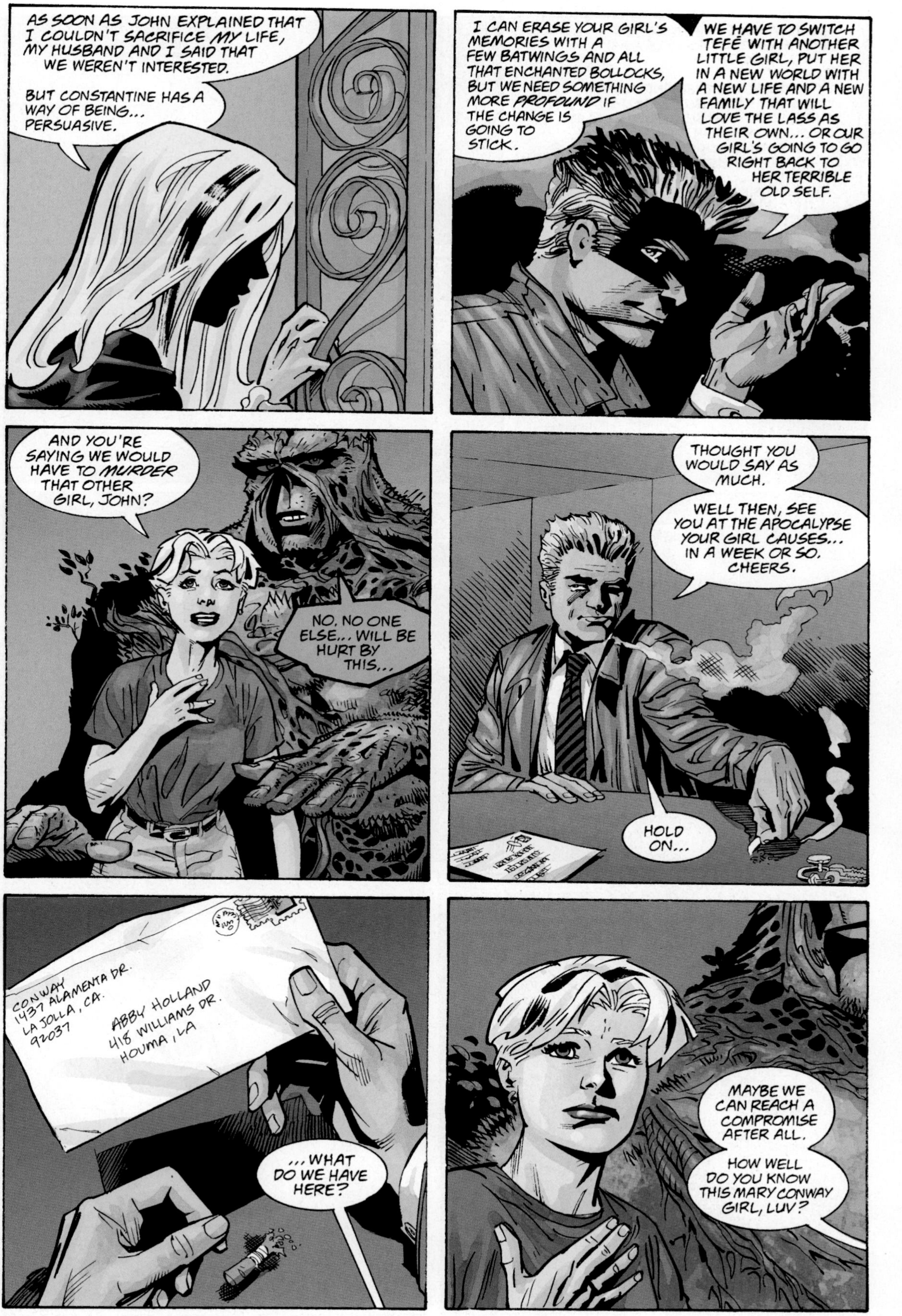
AS SOON AS JOHN EXPLAINED THAT I COULDN'T SACRIFICE *MY* LIFE, MY HUSBAND AND I SAID THAT WE WEREN'T INTERESTED.
BUT CONSTANTINE HAS A WAY OF BEING... PERSUASIVE.
I CAN ERASE YOUR GIRL'S MEMORIES WITH A FEW BATWINGS AND ALL THAT ENCHANTED BOLLOCKS, BUT WE NEED SOMETHING MORE *PROFOUND* IF THE CHANGE IS GOING TO STICK.
WE HAVE TO SWITCH TEFÉ WITH ANOTHER LITTLE GIRL, PUT HER IN A NEW WORLD WITH A NEW LIFE AND A NEW FAMILY THAT WILL LOVE THE LASS AS THEIR OWN... OR OUR GIRL'S GOING TO GO RIGHT BACK TO HER TERRIBLE OLD SELF.
AND YOU'RE SAYING WE WOULD HAVE TO *MURDER* THAT OTHER GIRL, JOHN?
NO. NO ONE ELSE... WILL BE HURT BY THIS...
THOUGHT YOU WOULD SAY AS MUCH.
WELL THEN, SEE YOU AT THE APOCALYPSE YOUR GIRL CAUSES... IN A WEEK OR SO. CHEERS.
HOLD ON...
CONWAY
1437 ALAMENTA DR.
LA JOLLA, CA.
92037
ABBY HOLLAND
418 WILLIAMS DR.
HOUMA, LA
...WHAT DO WE HAVE HERE?
MAYBE WE CAN REACH A COMPROMISE AFTER ALL.
HOW WELL DO YOU KNOW THIS MARY CONWAY GIRL, LUV?

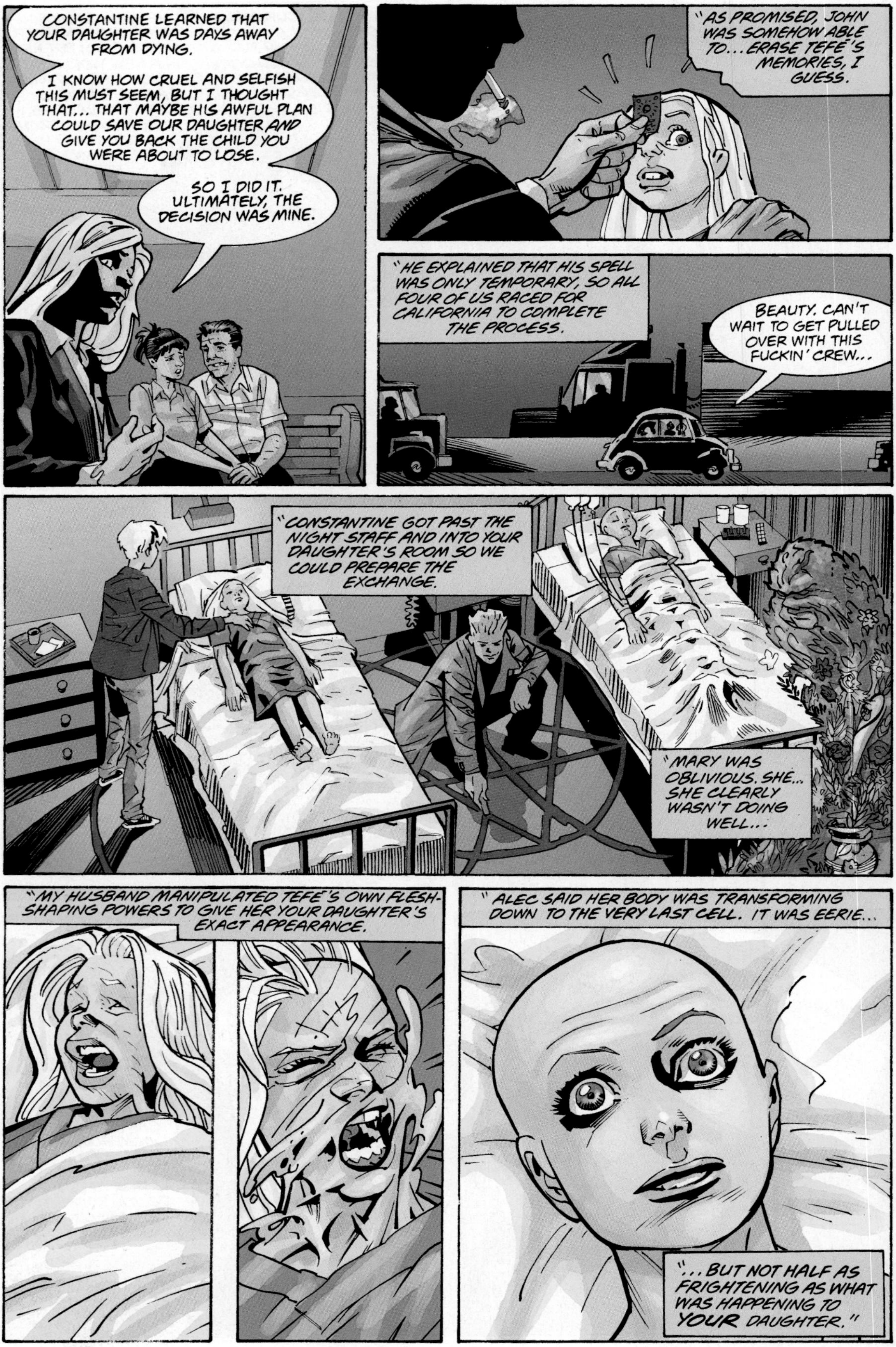

CONSTANTINE LEARNED THAT YOUR DAUGHTER WAS DAYS AWAY FROM DYING.
I KNOW HOW CRUEL AND SELFISH THIS MUST SEEM, BUT I THOUGHT THAT... THAT MAYBE HIS AWFUL PLAN COULD SAVE OUR DAUGHTER AND GIVE YOU BACK THE CHILD YOU WERE ABOUT TO LOSE.
SO I DID IT. ULTIMATELY, THE DECISION WAS MINE.
"AS PROMISED, JOHN WAS SOMEHOW ABLE TO... ERASE TEFE'S MEMORIES, I GUESS.
"HE EXPLAINED THAT HIS SPELL WAS ONLY TEMPORARY, SO ALL FOUR OF US RACED FOR CALIFORNIA TO COMPLETE THE PROCESS.
BEAUTY. CAN'T WAIT TO GET PULLED OVER WITH THIS FUCKIN' CREW...
"CONSTANTINE GOT PAST THE NIGHT STAFF AND INTO YOUR DAUGHTER'S ROOM SO WE COULD PREPARE THE EXCHANGE.
"MARY WAS OBLIVIOUS. SHE... SHE CLEARLY WASN'T DOING WELL...
"MY HUSBAND MANIPULATED TEFE'S OWN FLESH-SHAPING POWERS TO GIVE HER YOUR DAUGHTER'S EXACT APPEARANCE.
"ALEC SAID HER BODY WAS TRANSFORMING DOWN TO THE VERY LAST CELL. IT WAS EERIE...
"...BUT NOT HALF AS FRIGHTENING AS WHAT WAS HAPPENING TO YOUR DAUGHTER."

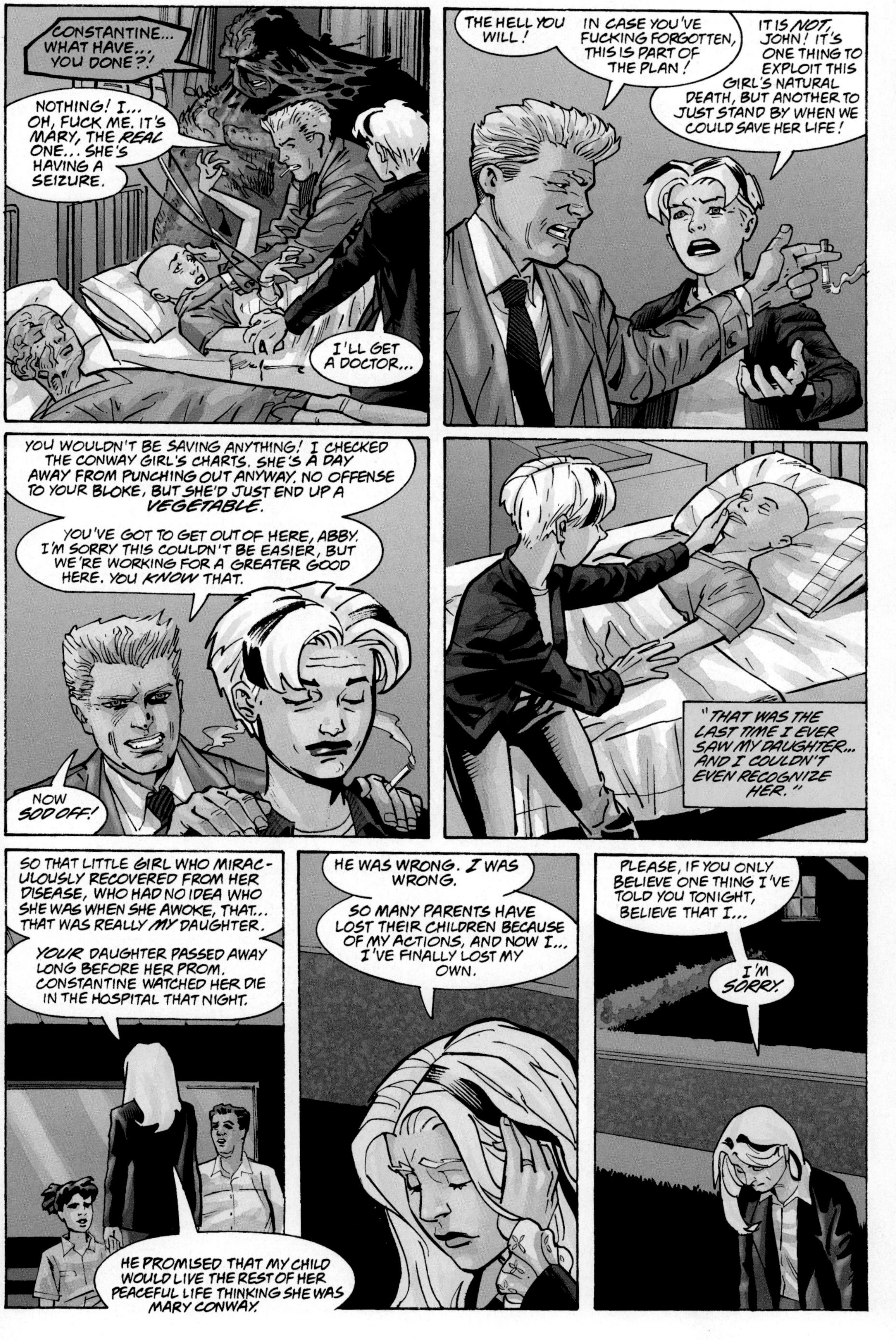
CONSTANTINE... WHAT HAVE... YOU DONE?!
NOTHING! I... OH, FUCK ME. IT'S MARY, THE REAL ONE... SHE'S HAVING A SEIZURE.
I'LL GET A DOCTOR...
THE HELL YOU WILL!
IN CASE YOU'VE FUCKING FORGOTTEN, THIS IS PART OF THE PLAN!
IT IS NOT, JOHN! IT'S ONE THING TO EXPLOIT THIS GIRL'S NATURAL DEATH, BUT ANOTHER TO JUST STAND BY WHEN WE COULD SAVE HER LIFE!
YOU WOULDN'T BE SAVING ANYTHING! I CHECKED THE CONWAY GIRL'S CHARTS. SHE'S A DAY AWAY FROM PUNCHING OUT ANYWAY. NO OFFENSE TO YOUR BLOKE, BUT SHE'D JUST END UP A VEGETABLE.
YOU'VE GOT TO GET OUT OF HERE, ABBY. I'M SORRY THIS COULDN'T BE EASIER, BUT WE'RE WORKING FOR A GREATER GOOD HERE. YOU KNOW THAT.
NOW SOD OFF!
"THAT WAS THE LAST TIME I EVER SAW MY DAUGHTER... AND I COULDN'T EVEN RECOGNIZE HER."
SO THAT LITTLE GIRL WHO MIRACULOUSLY RECOVERED FROM HER DISEASE, WHO HAD NO IDEA WHO SHE WAS WHEN SHE AWOKE, THAT... THAT WAS REALLY MY DAUGHTER.
YOUR DAUGHTER PASSED AWAY LONG BEFORE HER PROM. CONSTANTINE WATCHED HER DIE IN THE HOSPITAL THAT NIGHT.
HE PROMISED THAT MY CHILD WOULD LIVE THE REST OF HER PEACEFUL LIFE THINKING SHE WAS MARY CONWAY.
HE WAS WRONG. I WAS WRONG.
SO MANY PARENTS HAVE LOST THEIR CHILDREN BECAUSE OF MY ACTIONS, AND NOW I... I'VE FINALLY LOST MY OWN.
PLEASE, IF YOU ONLY BELIEVE ONE THING I'VE TOLD YOU TONIGHT, BELIEVE THAT I...
I'M SORRY.

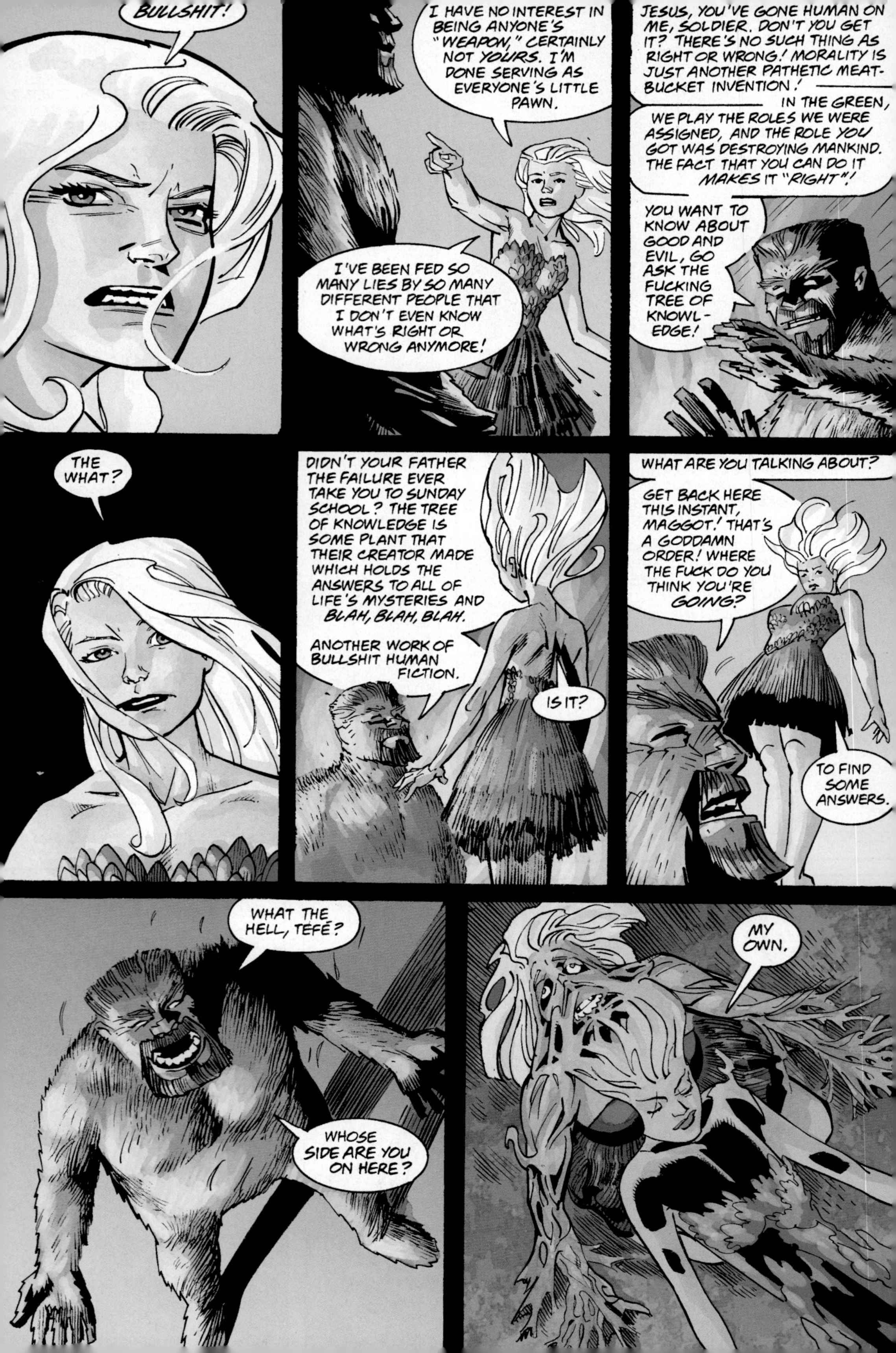
BULLSHIT!
I HAVE NO INTEREST IN BEING ANYONE'S "WEAPON," CERTAINLY NOT YOURS. I'M DONE SERVING AS EVERYONE'S LITTLE PAWN.
I'VE BEEN FED SO MANY LIES BY SO MANY DIFFERENT PEOPLE THAT I DON'T EVEN KNOW WHAT'S RIGHT OR WRONG ANYMORE!
JESUS, YOU'VE GONE HUMAN ON ME, SOLDIER. DON'T YOU GET IT? THERE'S NO SUCH THING AS RIGHT OR WRONG! MORALITY IS JUST ANOTHER PATHETIC MEAT-BUCKET INVENTION!
IN THE GREEN, WE PLAY THE ROLES WE WERE ASSIGNED, AND THE ROLE YOU GOT WAS DESTROYING MANKIND. THE FACT THAT YOU CAN DO IT MAKES IT "RIGHT"!
YOU WANT TO KNOW ABOUT GOOD AND EVIL, GO ASK THE FUCKING TREE OF KNOWL-EDGE!
THE WHAT?
DIDN'T YOUR FATHER THE FAILURE EVER TAKE YOU TO SUNDAY SCHOOL? THE TREE OF KNOWLEDGE IS SOME PLANT THAT THEIR CREATOR MADE WHICH HOLDS THE ANSWERS TO ALL OF LIFE'S MYSTERIES AND BLAH, BLAH, BLAH.
ANOTHER WORK OF BULLSHIT HUMAN FICTION.
IS IT?
WHAT ARE YOU TALKING ABOUT?
GET BACK HERE THIS INSTANT, MAGGOT! THAT'S A GODDAMN ORDER! WHERE THE FUCK DO YOU THINK YOU'RE GOING?
TO FIND SOME ANSWERS.
WHAT THE HELL, TEFÉ?
WHOSE SIDE ARE YOU ON HERE?
MY OWN.

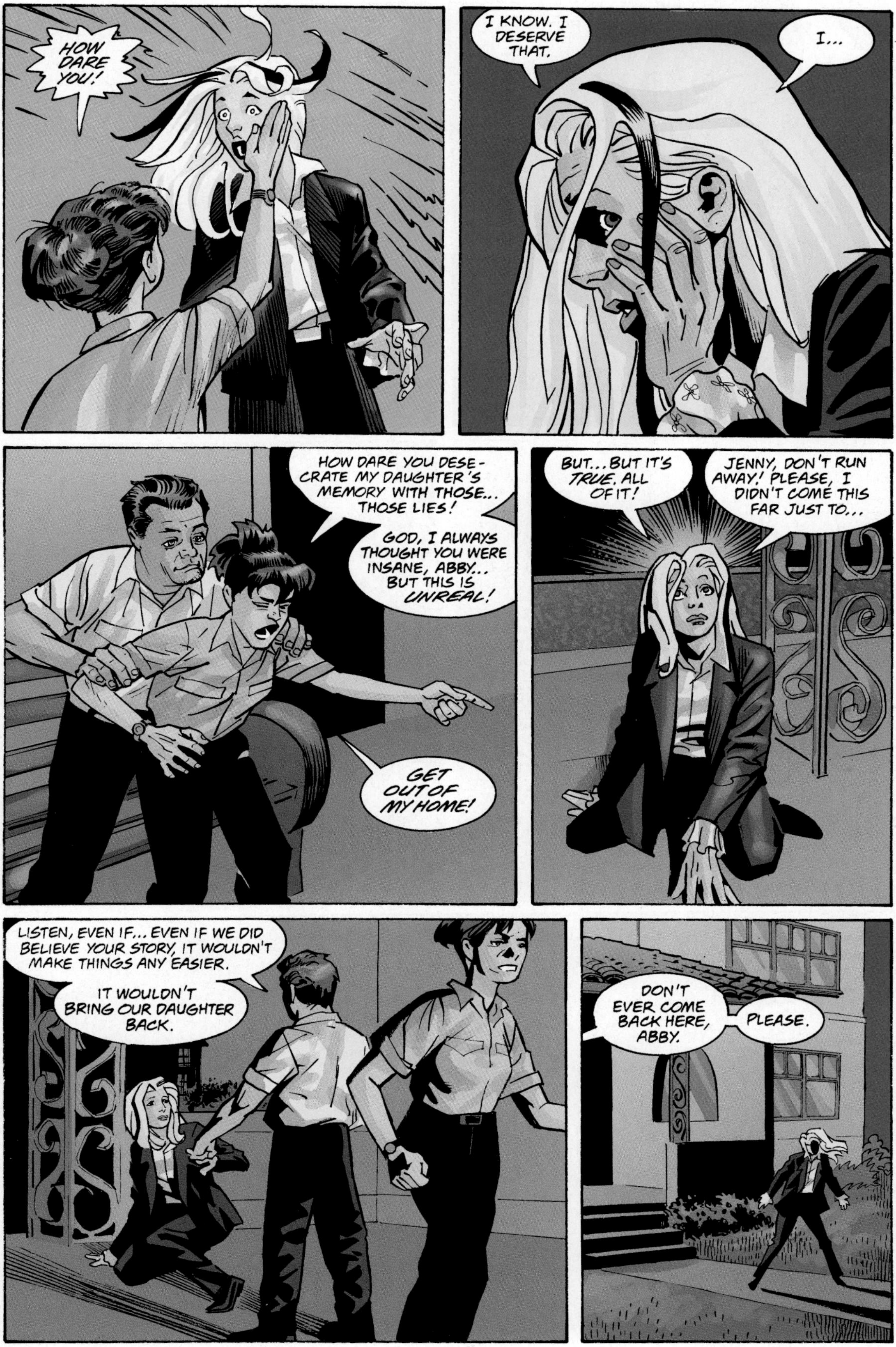
HOW DARE YOU!
I KNOW. I DESERVE THAT.
I...
HOW DARE YOU DESECRATE MY DAUGHTER'S MEMORY WITH THOSE... THOSE LIES!
GOD, I ALWAYS THOUGHT YOU WERE INSANE, ABBY... BUT THIS IS UNREAL!
GET OUT OF MY HOME!
BUT... BUT IT'S TRUE. ALL OF IT!
JENNY, DON'T RUN AWAY! PLEASE, I DIDN'T COME THIS FAR JUST TO...
LISTEN, EVEN IF... EVEN IF WE DID BELIEVE YOUR STORY, IT WOULDN'T MAKE THINGS ANY EASIER.
IT WOULDN'T BRING OUR DAUGHTER BACK.
DON'T EVER COME BACK HERE, ABBY.
PLEASE.

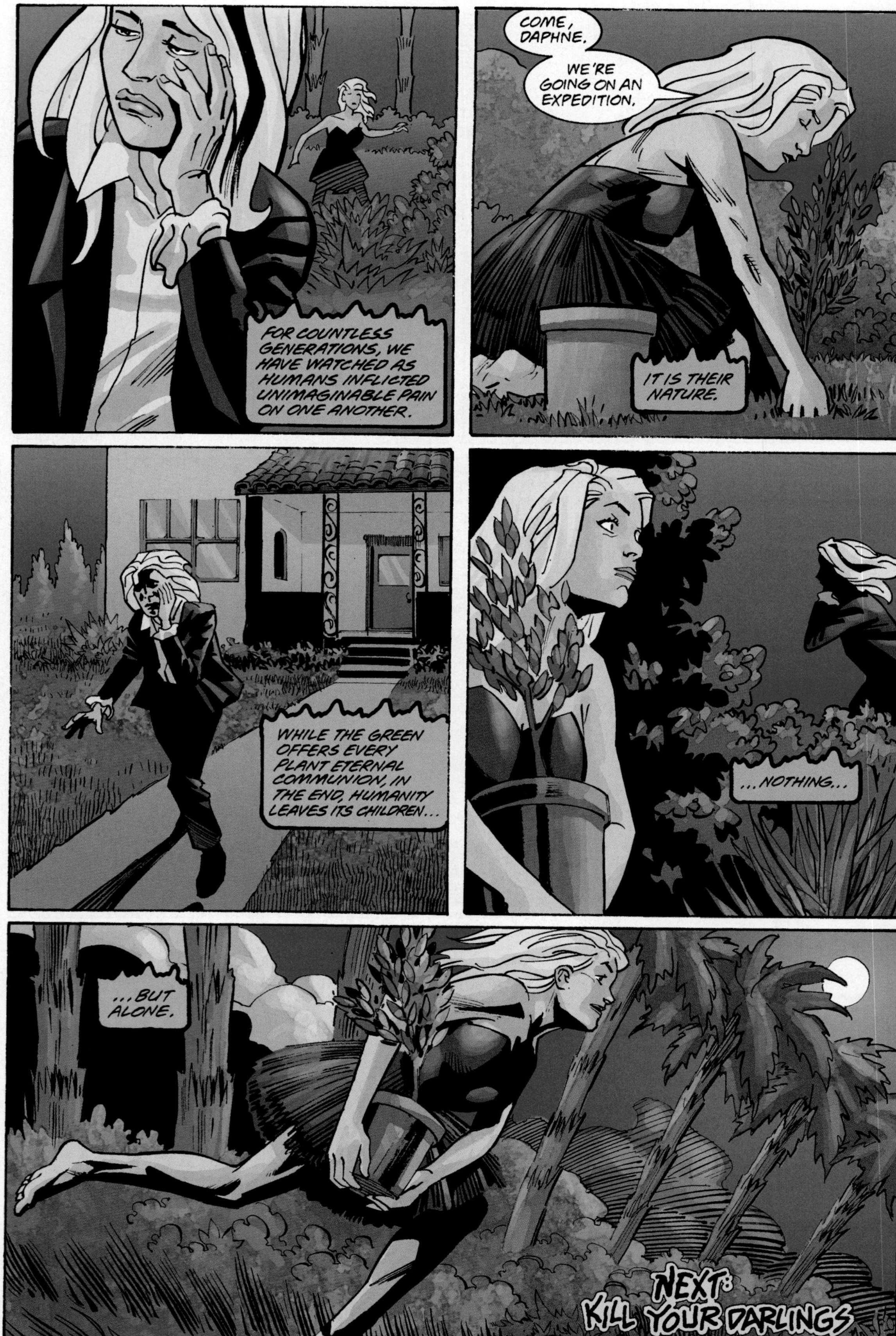
FOR COUNTLESS GENERATIONS, WE HAVE WATCHED AS HUMANS INFLICTED UNIMAGINABLE PAIN ON ONE ANOTHER.
COME, DAPHNE.
WE'RE GOING ON AN EXPEDITION.
IT IS THEIR NATURE.
WHILE THE GREEN OFFERS EVERY PLANT ETERNAL COMMUNION, IN THE END, HUMANITY LEAVES ITS CHILDREN...
...NOTHING...
...BUT ALONE.
NEXT: KILL YOUR DARLINGS

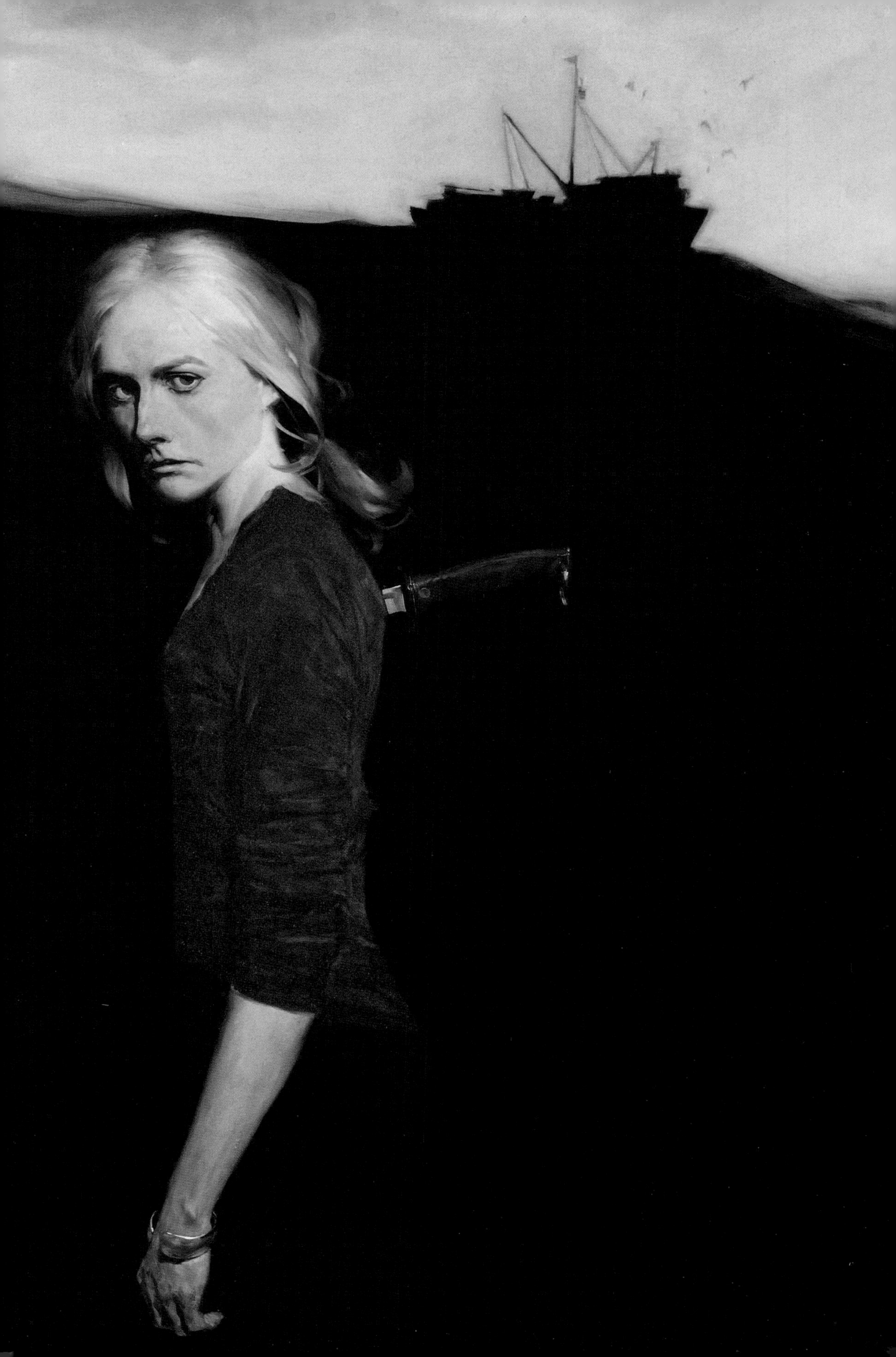

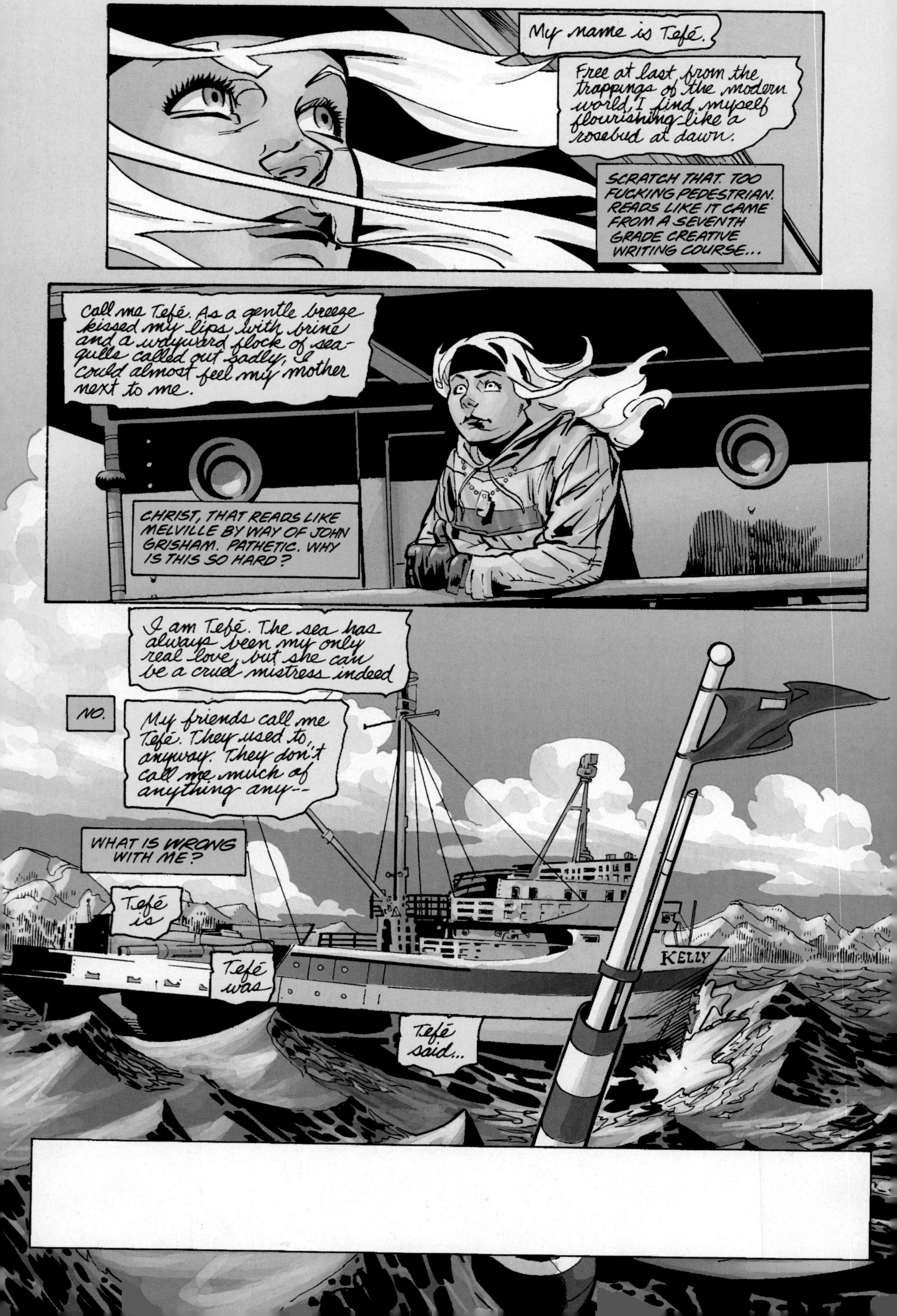

My name is Tefé.
Free at last from the trappings of the modern world, I find myself flourishing like a rosebud at dawn.
SCRATCH THAT. TOO FUCKING PEDESTRIAN. READS LIKE IT CAME FROM A SEVENTH GRADE CREATIVE WRITING COURSE...
Call me Tefé. As a gentle breeze kissed my lips with brine and a wayward flock of seagulls called out sadly, I could almost feel my mother next to me.
CHRIST, THAT READS LIKE MELVILLE BY WAY OF JOHN GRISHAM. PATHETIC. WHY IS THIS SO HARD?
I am Tefé. The sea has always been my only real love, but she can be a cruel mistress indeed
NO.
My friends call me Tefé. They used to, anyway. They don't call me much of anything any--
WHAT IS WRONG WITH ME?
Tefé is
Tefé was
Tefé said...
KELLY

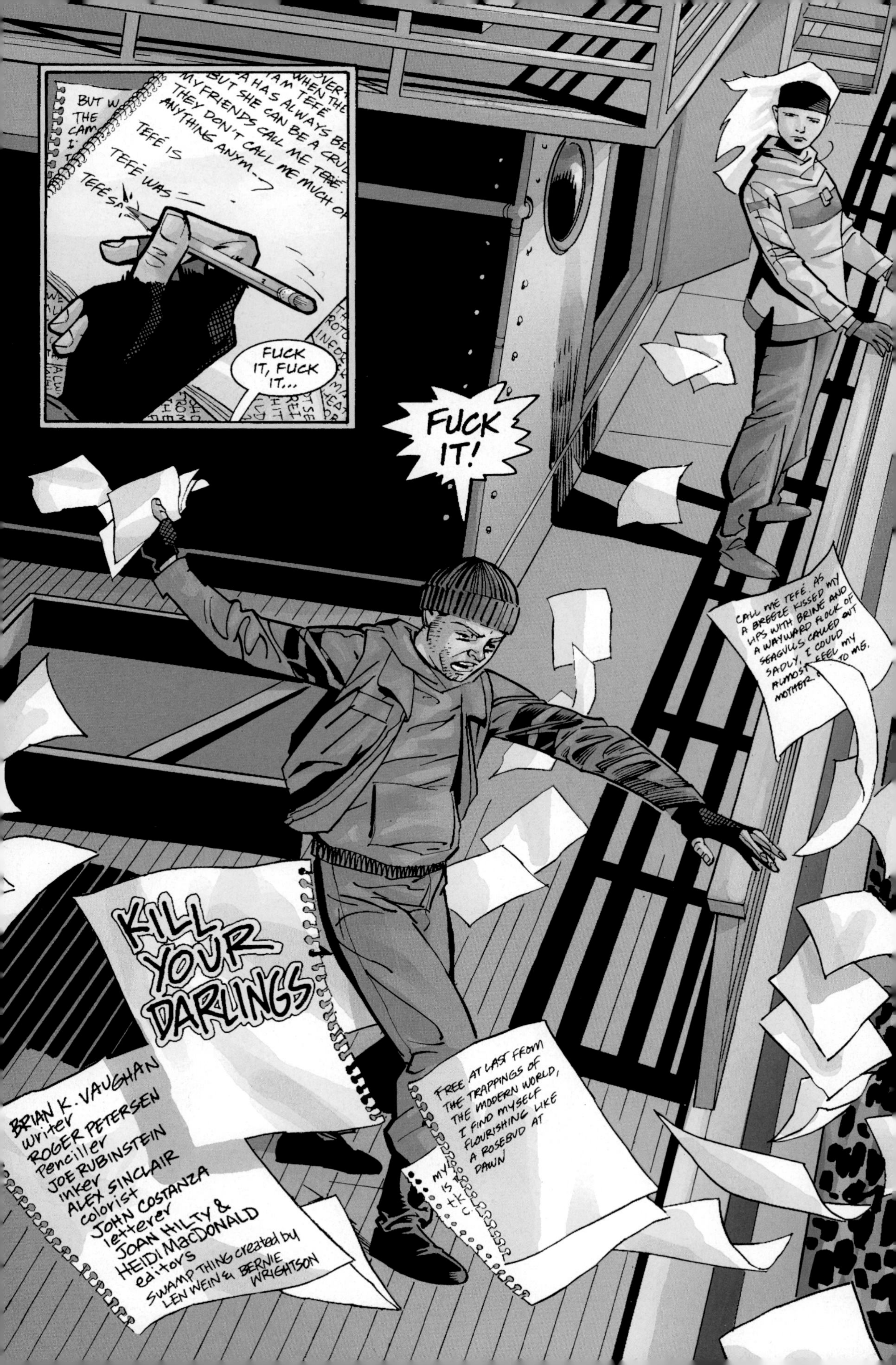

BUT SHE CAN BE A CRU
MY FRIENDS CALL ME TEFÉ.
THEY DON'T CALL ME MUCH OF
ANYTHING ANYM—
TEFÉ IS
TEFÉ WAS
TEFÉ SA
FUCK IT, FUCK IT...
FUCK IT!
CALL ME TEFÉ. AS A BREEZE KISSED MY LIPS WITH BRINE AND A WAYWARD FLOCK OF SEAGULLS CALLED OUT SADLY, I COULD ALMOST FEEL MY MOTHER
TO ME.
KILL YOUR DARLINGS
FREE AT LAST FROM THE TRAPPINGS OF THE MODERN WORLD, I FIND MYSELF FLOURISHING LIKE A ROSEBUD AT DAWN
BRIAN K. VAUGHAN writer
ROGER PETERSEN penciller
JOE RUBINSTEIN inker
ALEX SINCLAIR colorist
JOHN COSTANZA letterer
JOAN HILTY & HEIDI MacDONALD editors
SWAMP THING created by LEN WEIN & BERNIE WRIGHTSON

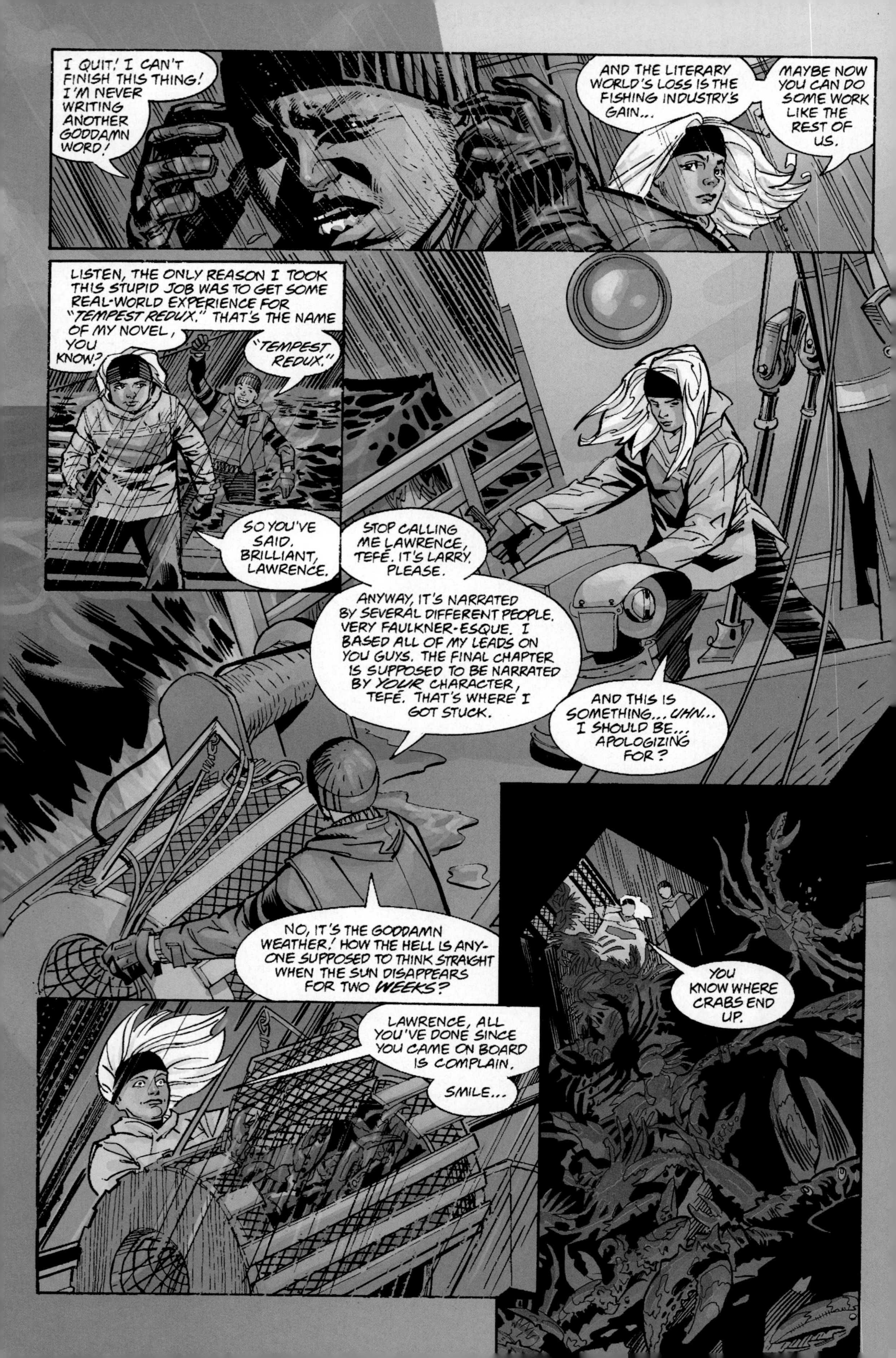
I QUIT! I CAN'T FINISH THIS THING! I'M NEVER WRITING ANOTHER GODDAMN WORD!
AND THE LITERARY WORLD'S LOSS IS THE FISHING INDUSTRY'S GAIN...
MAYBE NOW YOU CAN DO SOME WORK LIKE THE REST OF US.
LISTEN, THE ONLY REASON I TOOK THIS STUPID JOB WAS TO GET SOME REAL-WORLD EXPERIENCE FOR "TEMPEST REDUX." THAT'S THE NAME OF MY NOVEL, YOU KNOW?
"TEMPEST REDUX."
SO YOU'VE SAID. BRILLIANT, LAWRENCE.
STOP CALLING ME LAWRENCE, TEFÉ. IT'S LARRY, PLEASE.
ANYWAY, IT'S NARRATED BY SEVERAL DIFFERENT PEOPLE. VERY FAULKNER-ESQUE. I BASED ALL OF MY LEADS ON YOU GUYS. THE FINAL CHAPTER IS SUPPOSED TO BE NARRATED BY YOUR CHARACTER, TEFÉ. THAT'S WHERE I GOT STUCK.
AND THIS IS SOMETHING... UHN... I SHOULD BE... APOLOGIZING FOR?
NO, IT'S THE GODDAMN WEATHER! HOW THE HELL IS ANYONE SUPPOSED TO THINK STRAIGHT WHEN THE SUN DISAPPEARS FOR TWO WEEKS?
LAWRENCE, ALL YOU'VE DONE SINCE YOU CAME ON BOARD IS COMPLAIN.
SMILE...
YOU KNOW WHERE CRABS END UP.

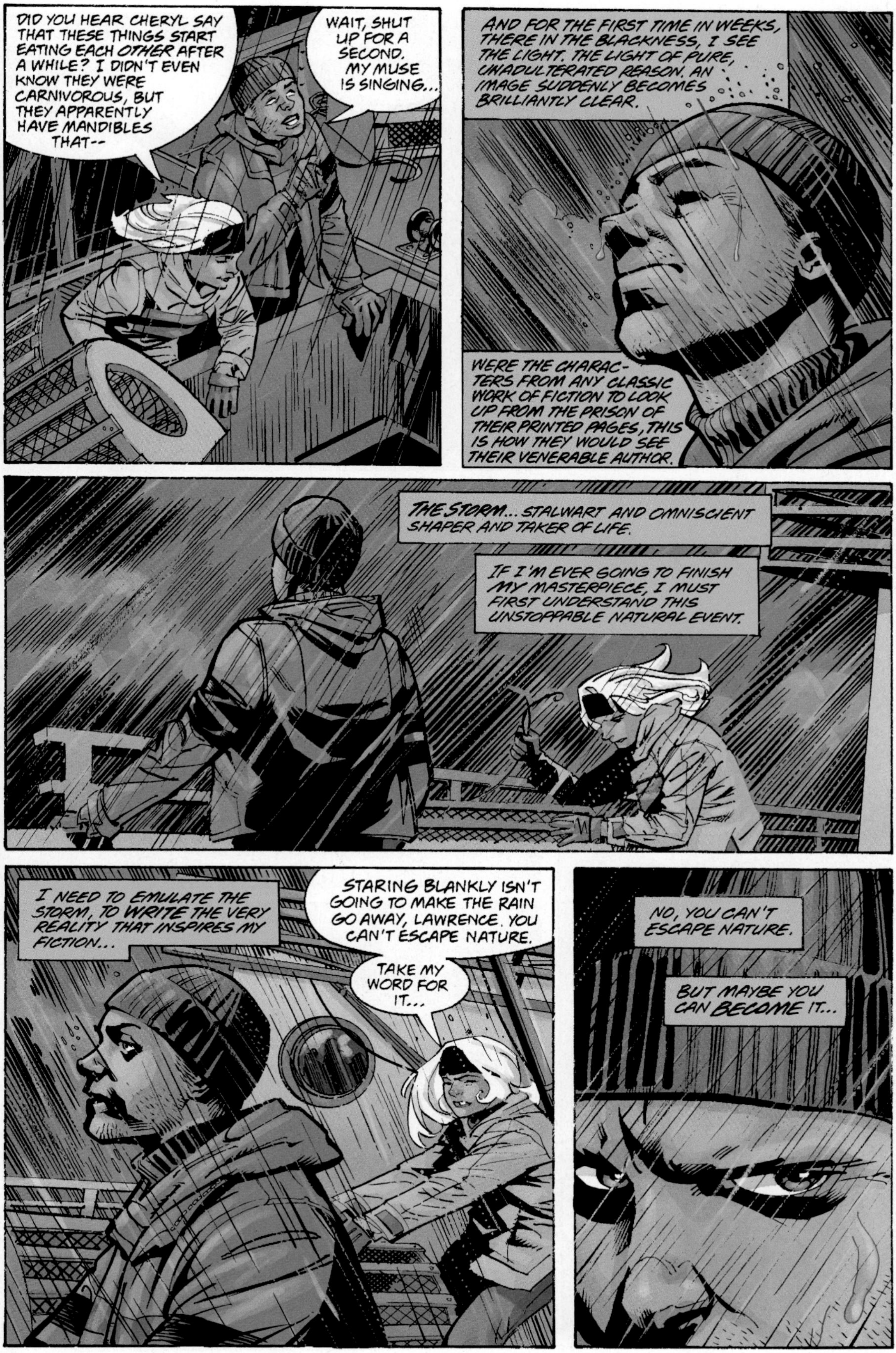
DID YOU HEAR CHERYL SAY THAT THESE THINGS START EATING EACH OTHER AFTER A WHILE? I DIDN'T EVEN KNOW THEY WERE CARNIVOROUS, BUT THEY APPARENTLY HAVE MANDIBLES THAT--
WAIT, SHUT UP FOR A SECOND. MY MUSE IS SINGING...
AND FOR THE FIRST TIME IN WEEKS, THERE IN THE BLACKNESS, I SEE THE LIGHT. THE LIGHT OF PURE, UNADULTERATED REASON. AN IMAGE SUDDENLY BECOMES BRILLIANTLY CLEAR.
WERE THE CHARACTERS FROM ANY CLASSIC WORK OF FICTION TO LOOK UP FROM THE PRISON OF THEIR PRINTED PAGES, THIS IS HOW THEY WOULD SEE THEIR VENERABLE AUTHOR.
THE STORM... STALWART AND OMNISCIENT SHAPER AND TAKER OF LIFE.
IF I'M EVER GOING TO FINISH MY MASTERPIECE, I MUST FIRST UNDERSTAND THIS UNSTOPPABLE NATURAL EVENT.
I NEED TO EMULATE THE STORM, TO WRITE THE VERY REALITY THAT INSPIRES MY FICTION...
STARING BLANKLY ISN'T GOING TO MAKE THE RAIN GO AWAY, LAWRENCE. YOU CAN'T ESCAPE NATURE.
TAKE MY WORD FOR IT...
NO, YOU CAN'T ESCAPE NATURE.
BUT MAYBE YOU CAN BECOME IT...

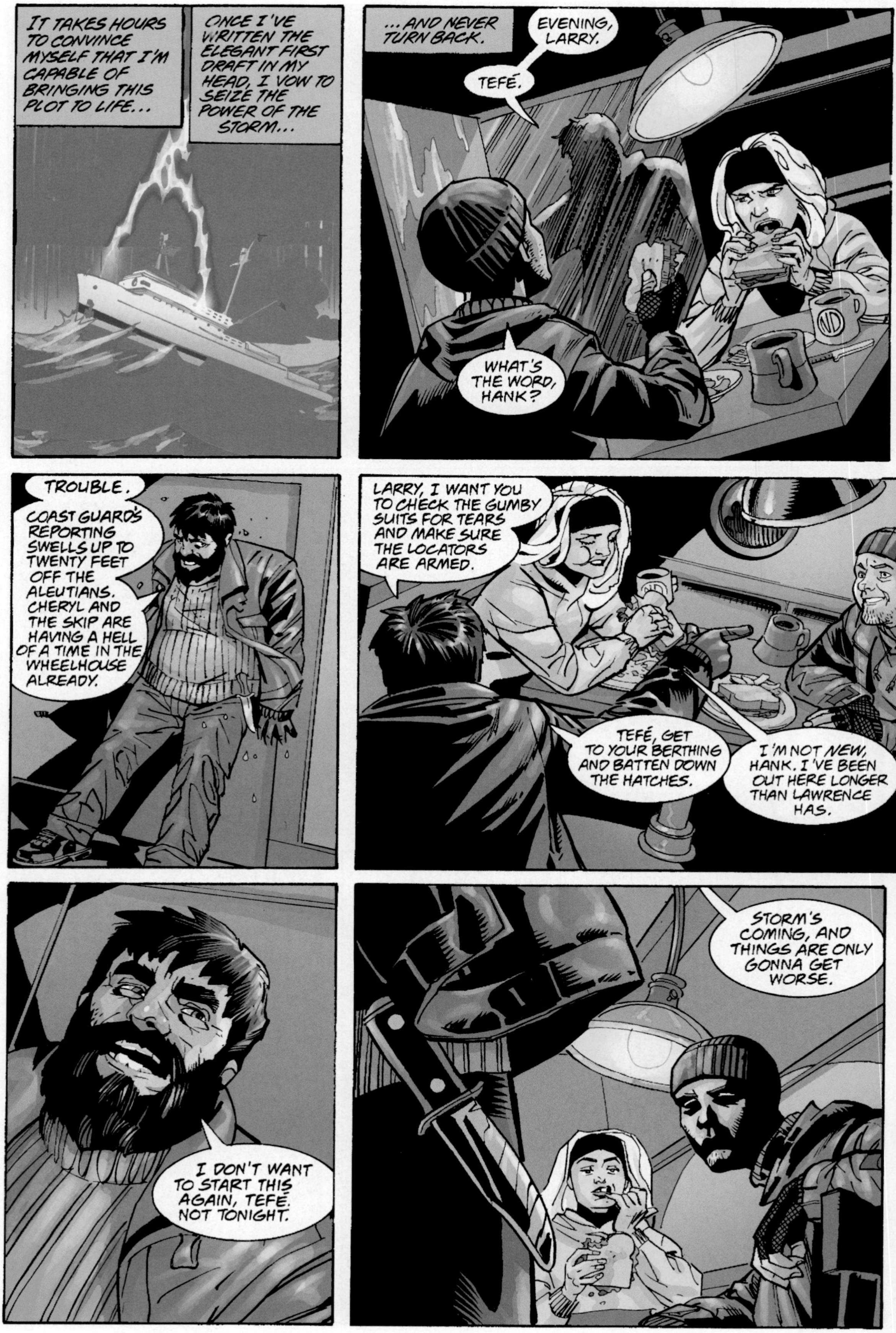
IT TAKES HOURS TO CONVINCE MYSELF THAT I'M CAPABLE OF BRINGING THIS PLOT TO LIFE...
ONCE I'VE WRITTEN THE ELEGANT FIRST DRAFT IN MY HEAD, I VOW TO SEIZE THE POWER OF THE STORM...
...AND NEVER TURN BACK.
EVENING, LARRY.
TEFÉ.
WHAT'S THE WORD, HANK?
TROUBLE.
COAST GUARD'S REPORTING SWELLS UP TO TWENTY FEET OFF THE ALEUTIANS. CHERYL AND THE SKIP ARE HAVING A HELL OF A TIME IN THE WHEELHOUSE ALREADY.
LARRY, I WANT YOU TO CHECK THE GUMBY SUITS FOR TEARS AND MAKE SURE THE LOCATORS ARE ARMED.
TEFÉ, GET TO YOUR BERTHING AND BATTEN DOWN THE HATCHES.
I'M NOT NEW, HANK. I'VE BEEN OUT HERE LONGER THAN LAWRENCE HAS.
I DON'T WANT TO START THIS AGAIN, TEFE. NOT TONIGHT.
STORM'S COMING, AND THINGS ARE ONLY GONNA GET WORSE.

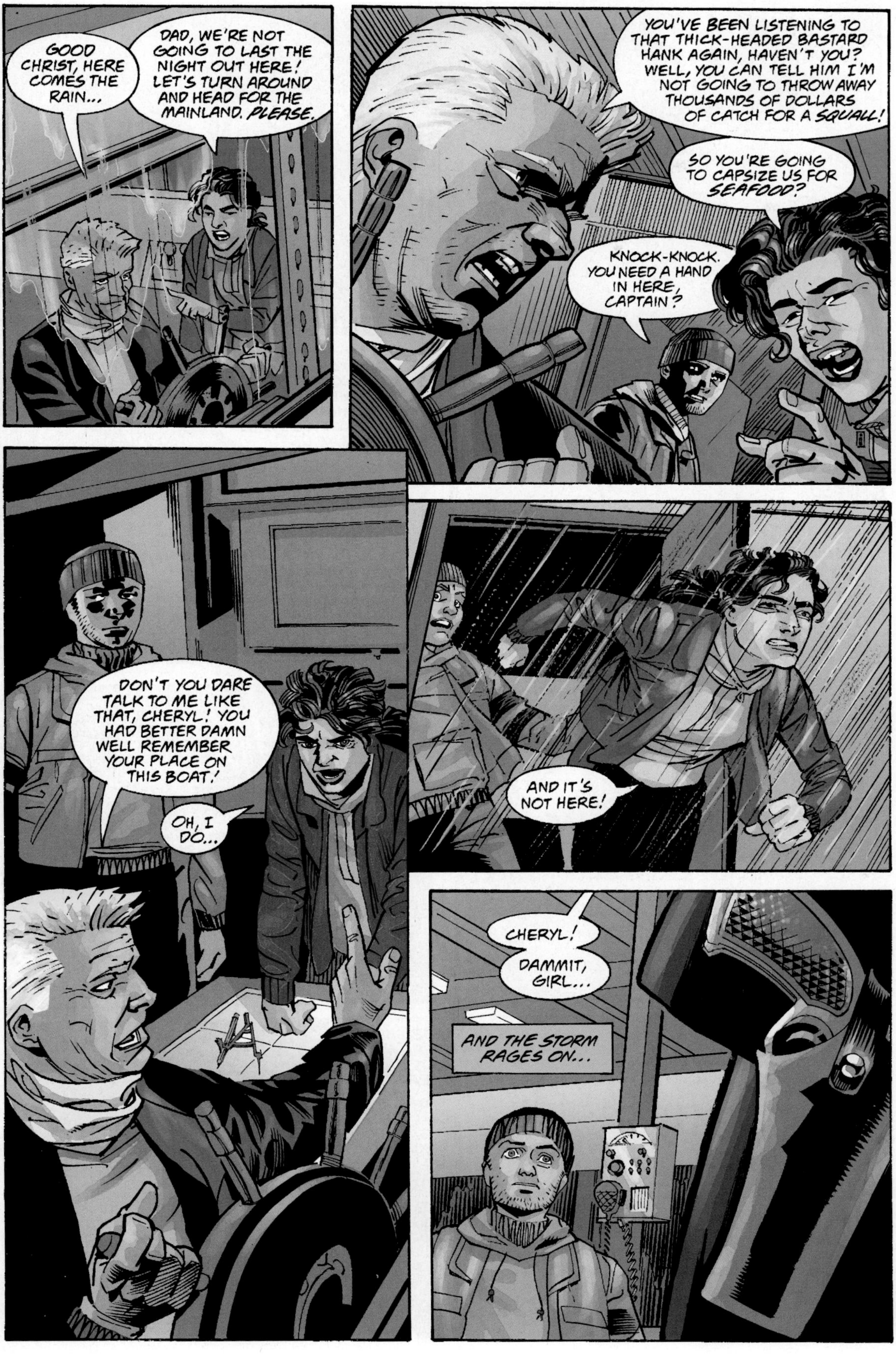
GOOD CHRIST, HERE COMES THE RAIN...
DAD, WE'RE NOT GOING TO LAST THE NIGHT OUT HERE! LET'S TURN AROUND AND HEAD FOR THE MAINLAND. PLEASE.
YOU'VE BEEN LISTENING TO THAT THICK-HEADED BASTARD HANK AGAIN, HAVEN'T YOU? WELL, YOU CAN TELL HIM I'M NOT GOING TO THROW AWAY THOUSANDS OF DOLLARS OF CATCH FOR A SQUALL!
SO YOU'RE GOING TO CAPSIZE US FOR SEAFOOD?
KNOCK-KNOCK. YOU NEED A HAND IN HERE, CAPTAIN?
DON'T YOU DARE TALK TO ME LIKE THAT, CHERYL! YOU HAD BETTER DAMN WELL REMEMBER YOUR PLACE ON THIS BOAT!
OH, I DO...
AND IT'S NOT HERE!
CHERYL!
DAMMIT, GIRL...
AND THE STORM RAGES ON...

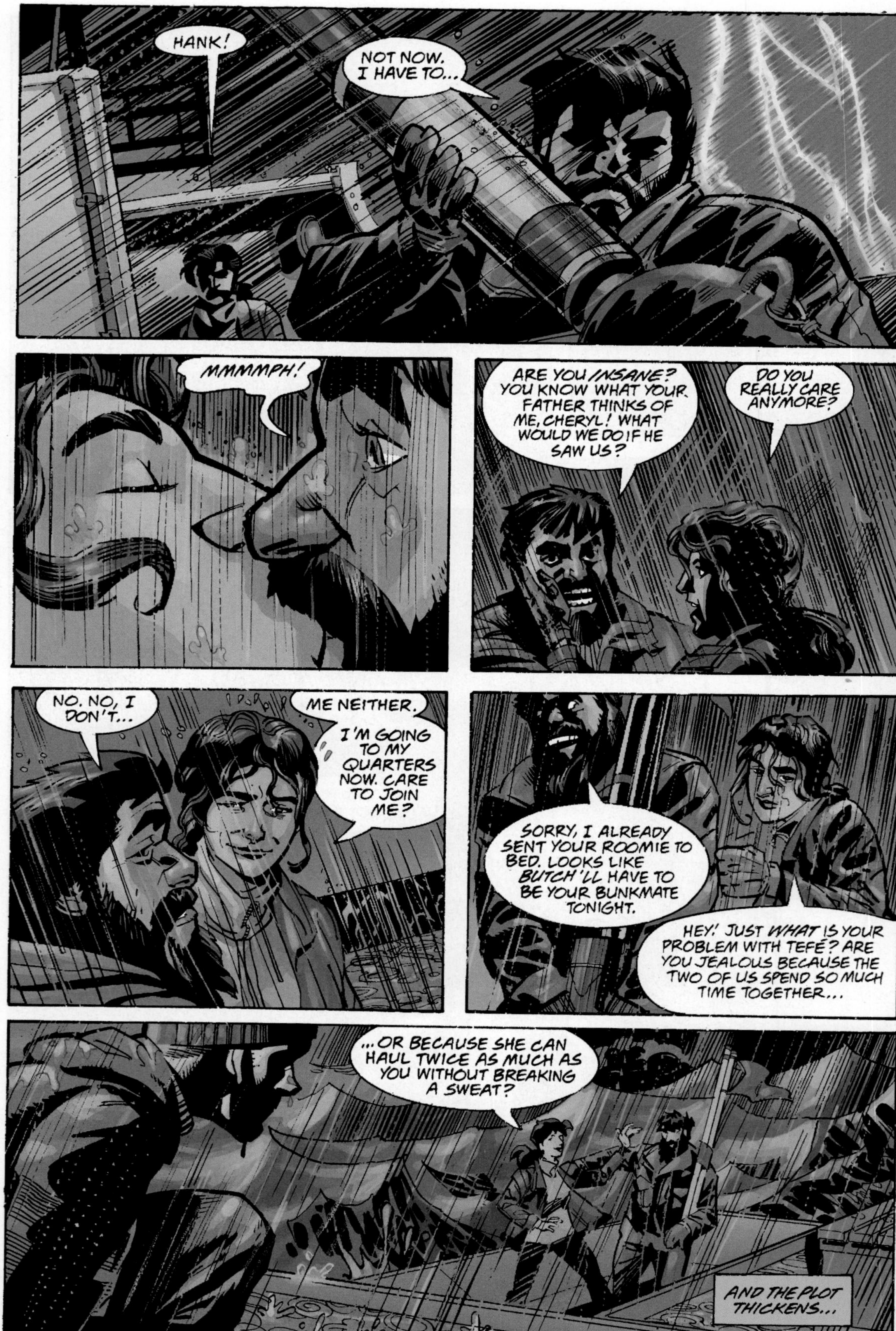
HANK!
NOT NOW. I HAVE TO...
MMMMPH!
ARE YOU INSANE? YOU KNOW WHAT YOUR FATHER THINKS OF ME, CHERYL! WHAT WOULD WE DO IF HE SAW US?
DO YOU REALLY CARE ANYMORE?
NO. NO, I DON'T...
ME NEITHER.
I'M GOING TO MY QUARTERS NOW. CARE TO JOIN ME?
SORRY, I ALREADY SENT YOUR ROOMIE TO BED. LOOKS LIKE BUTCH'LL HAVE TO BE YOUR BUNKMATE TONIGHT.
HEY! JUST WHAT IS YOUR PROBLEM WITH TEFÉ? ARE YOU JEALOUS BECAUSE THE TWO OF US SPEND SO MUCH TIME TOGETHER...
...OR BECAUSE SHE CAN HAUL TWICE AS MUCH AS YOU WITHOUT BREAKING A SWEAT?
AND THE PLOT THICKENS...

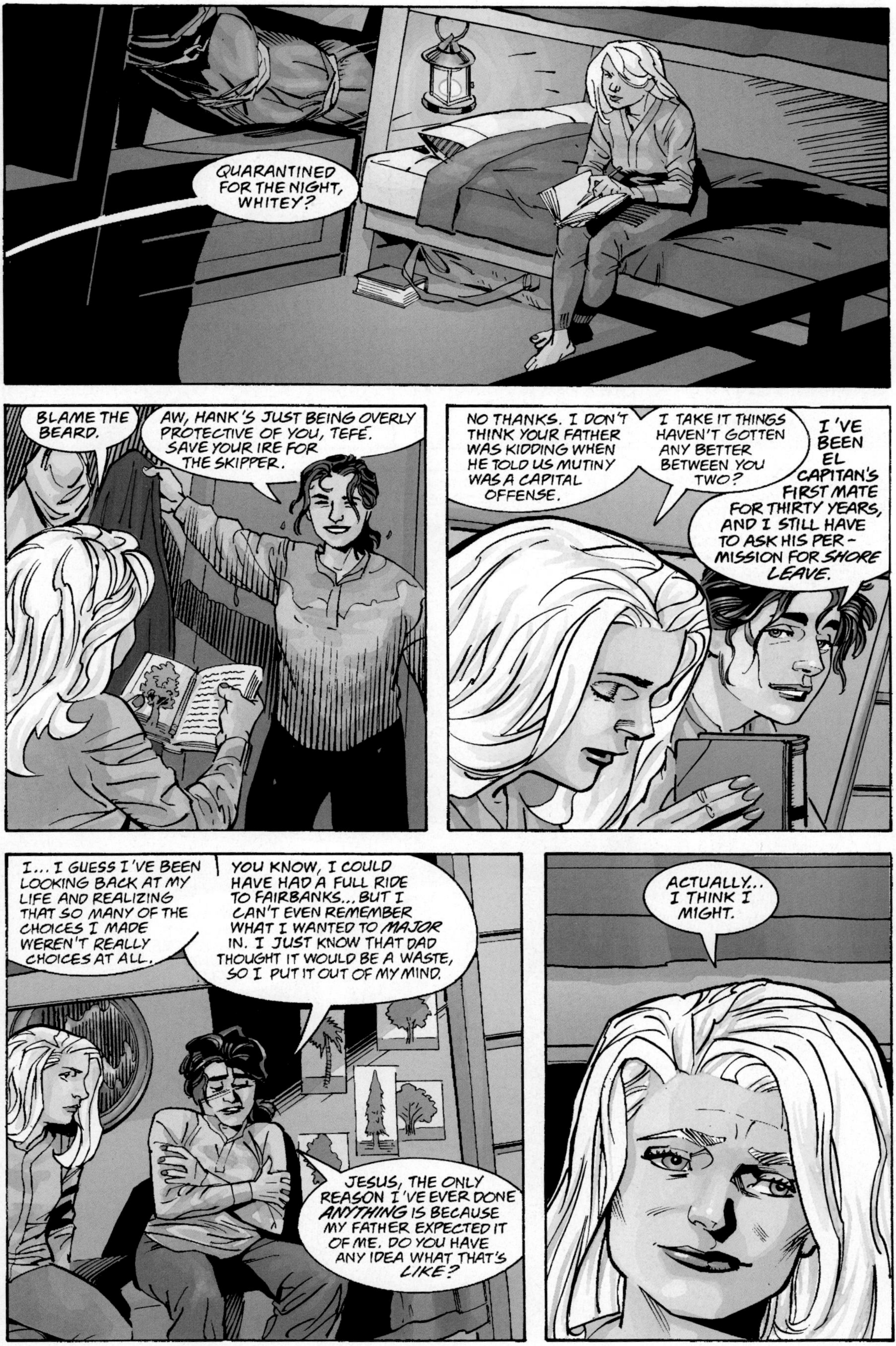
QUARANTINED FOR THE NIGHT, WHITEY?
BLAME THE BEARD.
AW, HANK'S JUST BEING OVERLY PROTECTIVE OF YOU, TEFÉ. SAVE YOUR IRE FOR THE SKIPPER.
NO THANKS. I DON'T THINK YOUR FATHER WAS KIDDING WHEN HE TOLD US MUTINY WAS A CAPITAL OFFENSE.
I TAKE IT THINGS HAVEN'T GOTTEN ANY BETTER BETWEEN YOU TWO?
I'VE BEEN EL CAPITAN'S FIRST MATE FOR THIRTY YEARS, AND I STILL HAVE TO ASK HIS PER-MISSION FOR SHORE LEAVE.
I... I GUESS I'VE BEEN LOOKING BACK AT MY LIFE AND REALIZING THAT SO MANY OF THE CHOICES I MADE WEREN'T REALLY CHOICES AT ALL.
YOU KNOW, I COULD HAVE HAD A FULL RIDE TO FAIRBANKS... BUT I CAN'T EVEN REMEMBER WHAT I WANTED TO MAJOR IN. I JUST KNOW THAT DAD THOUGHT IT WOULD BE A WASTE, SO I PUT IT OUT OF MY MIND.
JESUS, THE ONLY REASON I'VE EVER DONE ANYTHING IS BECAUSE MY FATHER EXPECTED IT OF ME. DO YOU HAVE ANY IDEA WHAT THAT'S LIKE?
ACTUALLY... I THINK I MIGHT.

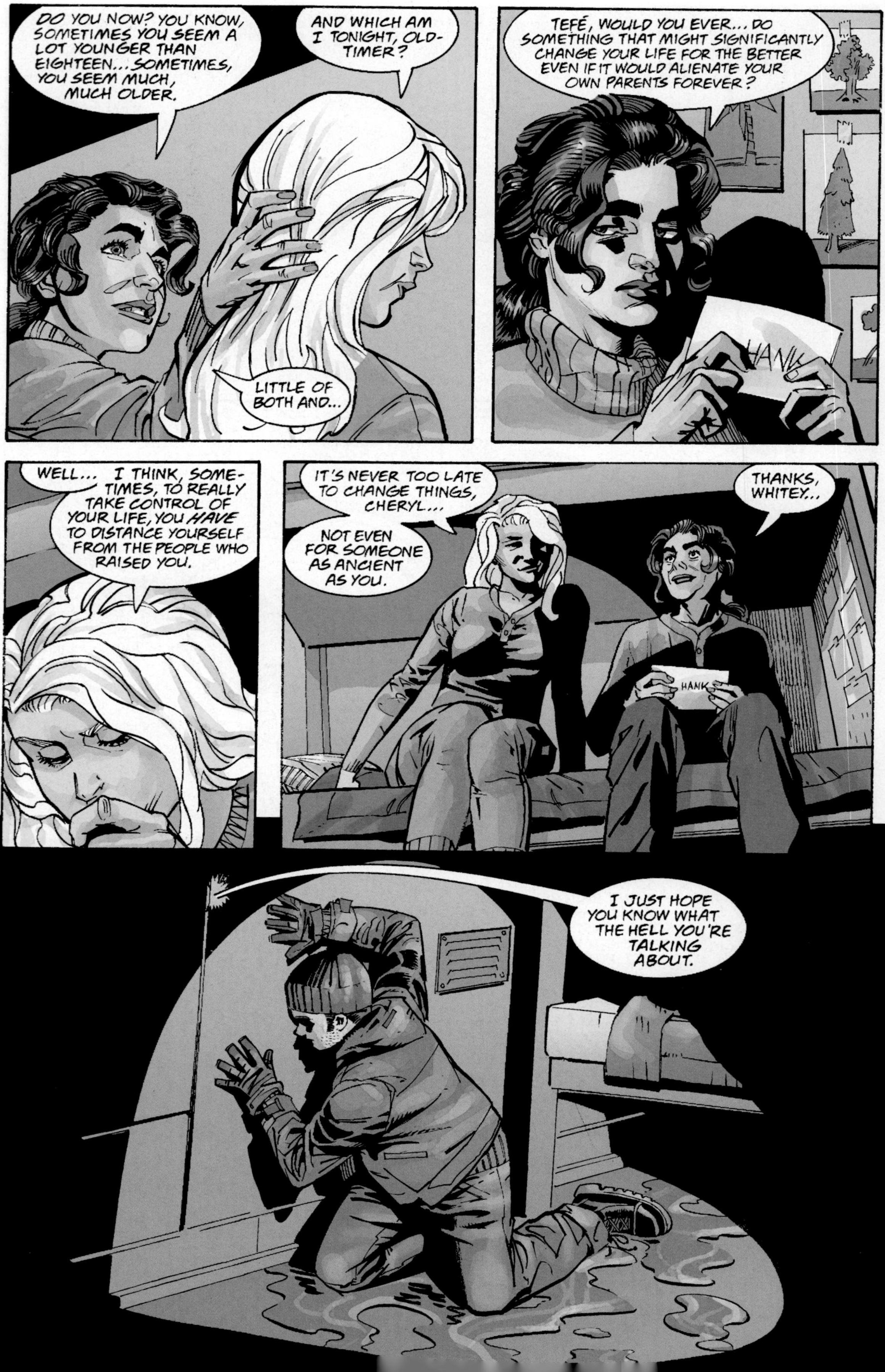
DO YOU NOW? YOU KNOW, SOMETIMES YOU SEEM A LOT YOUNGER THAN EIGHTEEN... SOMETIMES, YOU SEEM MUCH, MUCH OLDER.
AND WHICH AM I TONIGHT, OLD-TIMER?
LITTLE OF BOTH AND...
TEFÉ, WOULD YOU EVER... DO SOMETHING THAT MIGHT SIGNIFICANTLY CHANGE YOUR LIFE FOR THE BETTER EVEN IF IT WOULD ALIENATE YOUR OWN PARENTS FOREVER?
HANK
WELL... I THINK, SOME-TIMES, TO REALLY TAKE CONTROL OF YOUR LIFE, YOU HAVE TO DISTANCE YOURSELF FROM THE PEOPLE WHO RAISED YOU.
IT'S NEVER TOO LATE TO CHANGE THINGS, CHERYL...
NOT EVEN FOR SOMEONE AS ANCIENT AS YOU.
THANKS, WHITEY...
HANK
I JUST HOPE YOU KNOW WHAT THE HELL YOU'RE TALKING ABOUT.

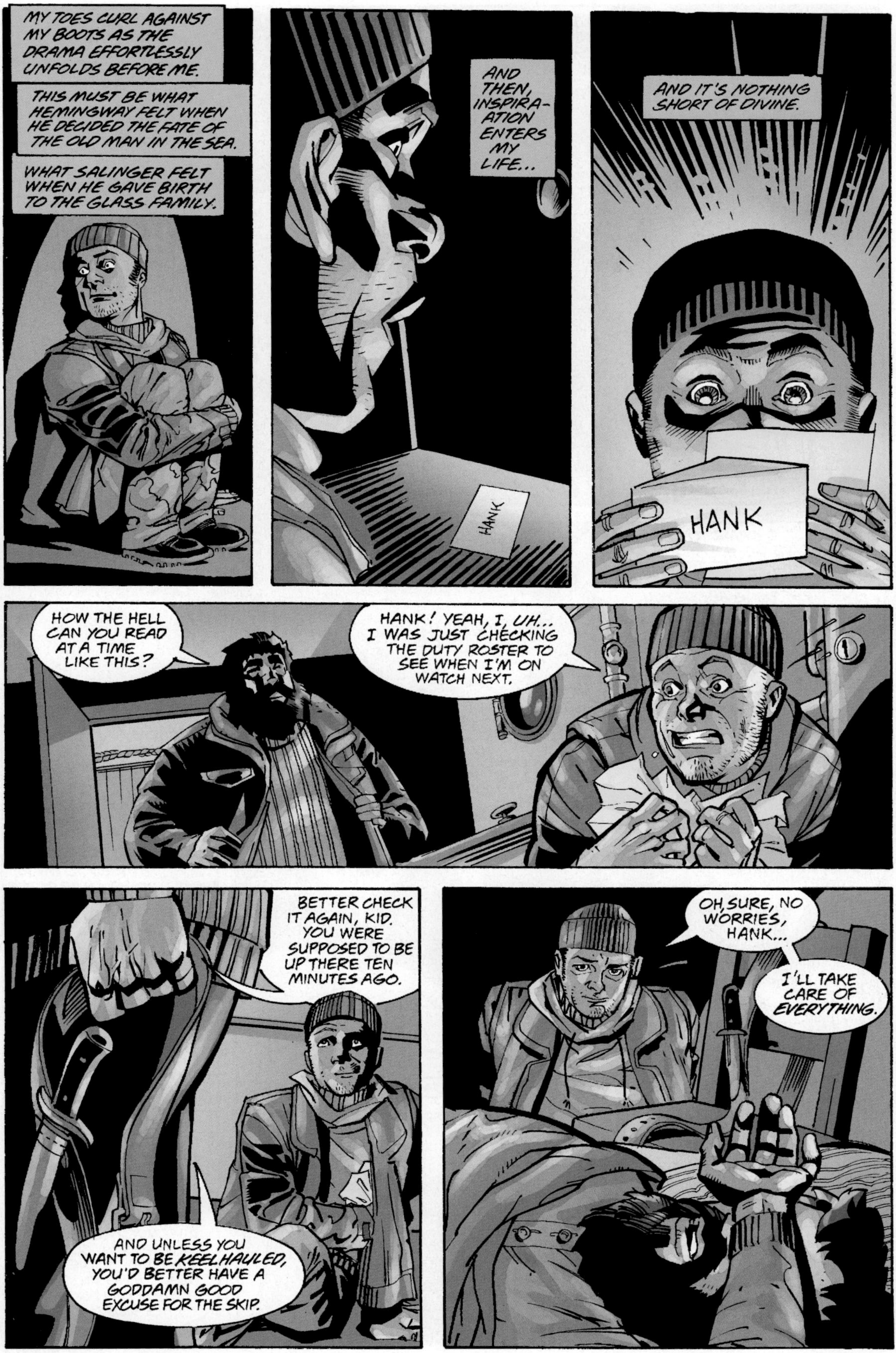
MY TOES CURL AGAINST MY BOOTS AS THE DRAMA EFFORTLESSLY UNFOLDS BEFORE ME.
THIS MUST BE WHAT HEMINGWAY FELT WHEN HE DECIDED THE FATE OF THE OLD MAN IN THE SEA.
WHAT SALINGER FELT WHEN HE GAVE BIRTH TO THE GLASS FAMILY.
AND THEN, INSPIRA-ATION ENTERS MY LIFE...
HANK
AND IT'S NOTHING SHORT OF DIVINE.
HANK
HOW THE HELL CAN YOU READ AT A TIME LIKE THIS?
HANK! YEAH, I, UH... I WAS JUST CHECKING THE DUTY ROSTER TO SEE WHEN I'M ON WATCH NEXT.
BETTER CHECK IT AGAIN, KID. YOU WERE SUPPOSED TO BE UP THERE TEN MINUTES AGO.
AND UNLESS YOU WANT TO BE KEELHAULED, YOU'D BETTER HAVE A GODDAMN GOOD EXCUSE FOR THE SKIP.
OH, SURE, NO WORRIES, HANK...
I'LL TAKE CARE OF EVERYTHING.

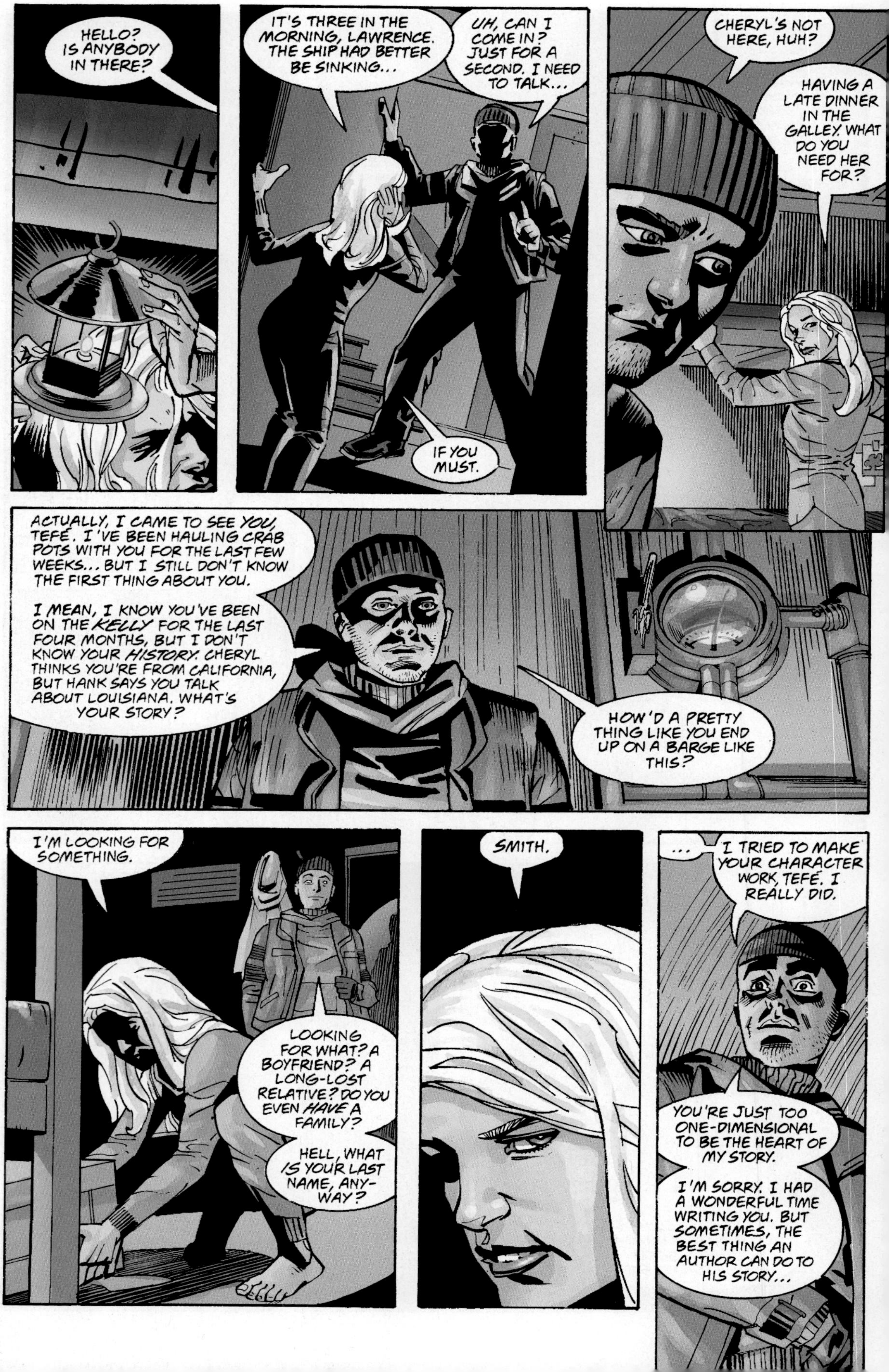
HELLO? IS ANYBODY IN THERE?
IT'S THREE IN THE MORNING, LAWRENCE. THE SHIP HAD BETTER BE SINKING...
UH, CAN I COME IN? JUST FOR A SECOND. I NEED TO TALK...
IF YOU MUST.
CHERYL'S NOT HERE, HUH?
HAVING A LATE DINNER IN THE GALLEY. WHAT DO YOU NEED HER FOR?
ACTUALLY, I CAME TO SEE YOU, TEFÉ. I'VE BEEN HAULING CRAB POTS WITH YOU FOR THE LAST FEW WEEKS... BUT I STILL DON'T KNOW THE FIRST THING ABOUT YOU.
I MEAN, I KNOW YOU'VE BEEN ON THE KELLY FOR THE LAST FOUR MONTHS, BUT I DON'T KNOW YOUR HISTORY. CHERYL THINKS YOU'RE FROM CALIFORNIA, BUT HANK SAYS YOU TALK ABOUT LOUISIANA. WHAT'S YOUR STORY?
HOW'D A PRETTY THING LIKE YOU END UP ON A BARGE LIKE THIS?
I'M LOOKING FOR SOMETHING.
LOOKING FOR WHAT? A BOYFRIEND? A LONG-LOST RELATIVE? DO YOU EVEN HAVE A FAMILY?
HELL, WHAT IS YOUR LAST NAME, ANYWAY?
SMITH.
...
I TRIED TO MAKE YOUR CHARACTER WORK, TEFÉ. I REALLY DID.
YOU'RE JUST TOO ONE-DIMENSIONAL TO BE THE HEART OF MY STORY.
I'M SORRY. I HAD A WONDERFUL TIME WRITING YOU. BUT SOMETIMES, THE BEST THING AN AUTHOR CAN DO TO HIS STORY...

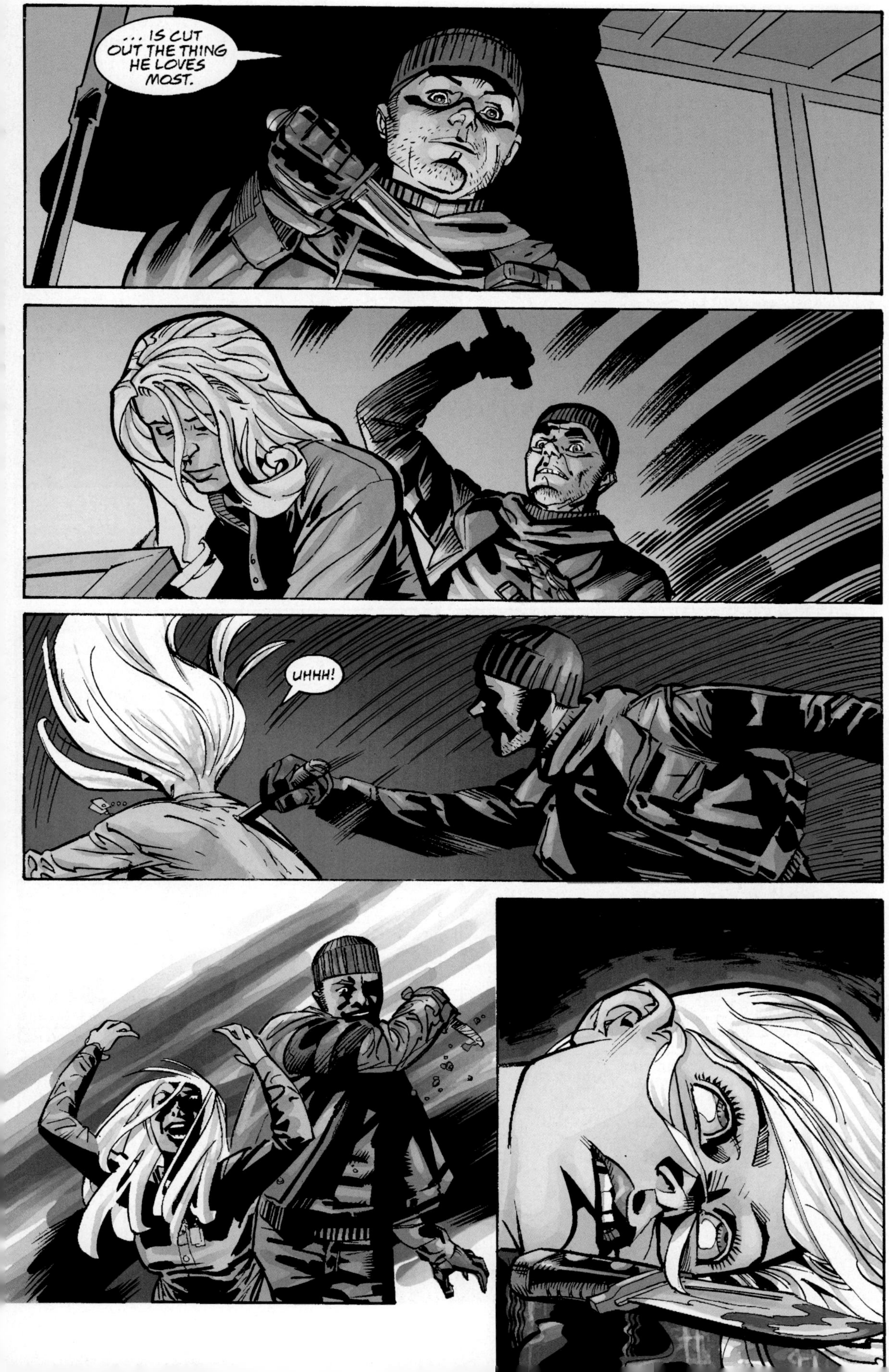
...IS CUT OUT THE THING HE LOVES MOST.
UHHH!

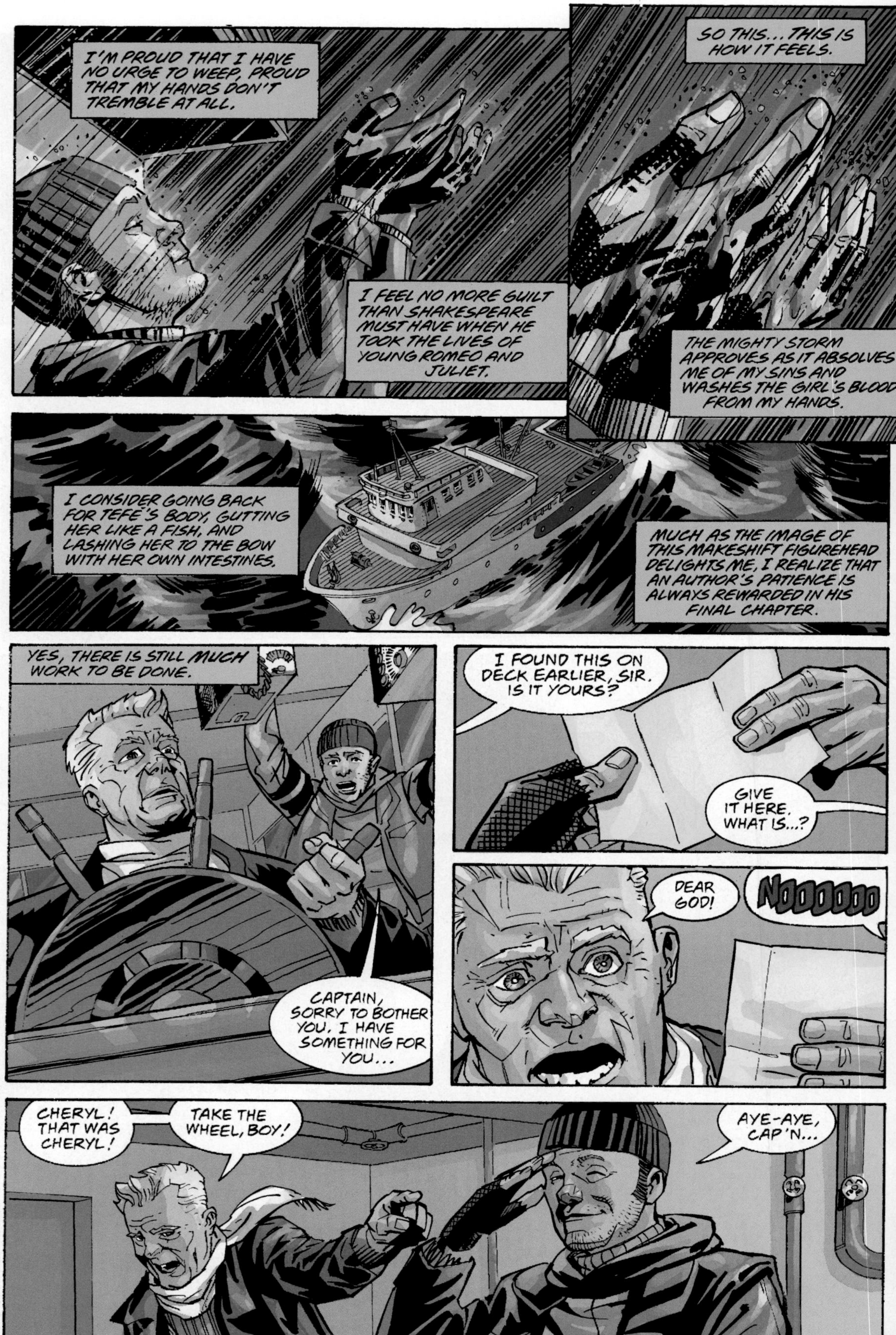
I'M PROUD THAT I HAVE NO URGE TO WEEP, PROUD THAT MY HANDS DON'T TREMBLE AT ALL.
I FEEL NO MORE GUILT THAN SHAKESPEARE MUST HAVE WHEN HE TOOK THE LIVES OF YOUNG ROMEO AND JULIET.
SO THIS... THIS IS HOW IT FEELS.
THE MIGHTY STORM APPROVES AS IT ABSOLVES ME OF MY SINS AND WASHES THE GIRL'S BLOOD FROM MY HANDS.
I CONSIDER GOING BACK FOR TEFE'S BODY, GUTTING HER LIKE A FISH, AND LASHING HER TO THE BOW WITH HER OWN INTESTINES.
MUCH AS THE IMAGE OF THIS MAKESHIFT FIGUREHEAD DELIGHTS ME, I REALIZE THAT AN AUTHOR'S PATIENCE IS ALWAYS REWARDED IN HIS FINAL CHAPTER.
YES, THERE IS STILL MUCH WORK TO BE DONE.
CAPTAIN, SORRY TO BOTHER YOU. I HAVE SOMETHING FOR YOU...
I FOUND THIS ON DECK EARLIER, SIR. IS IT YOURS?
GIVE IT HERE. WHAT IS...?
DEAR GOD!
NOOOOOOO
CHERYL! THAT WAS CHERYL!
TAKE THE WHEEL, BOY!
AYE-AYE, CAP'N...

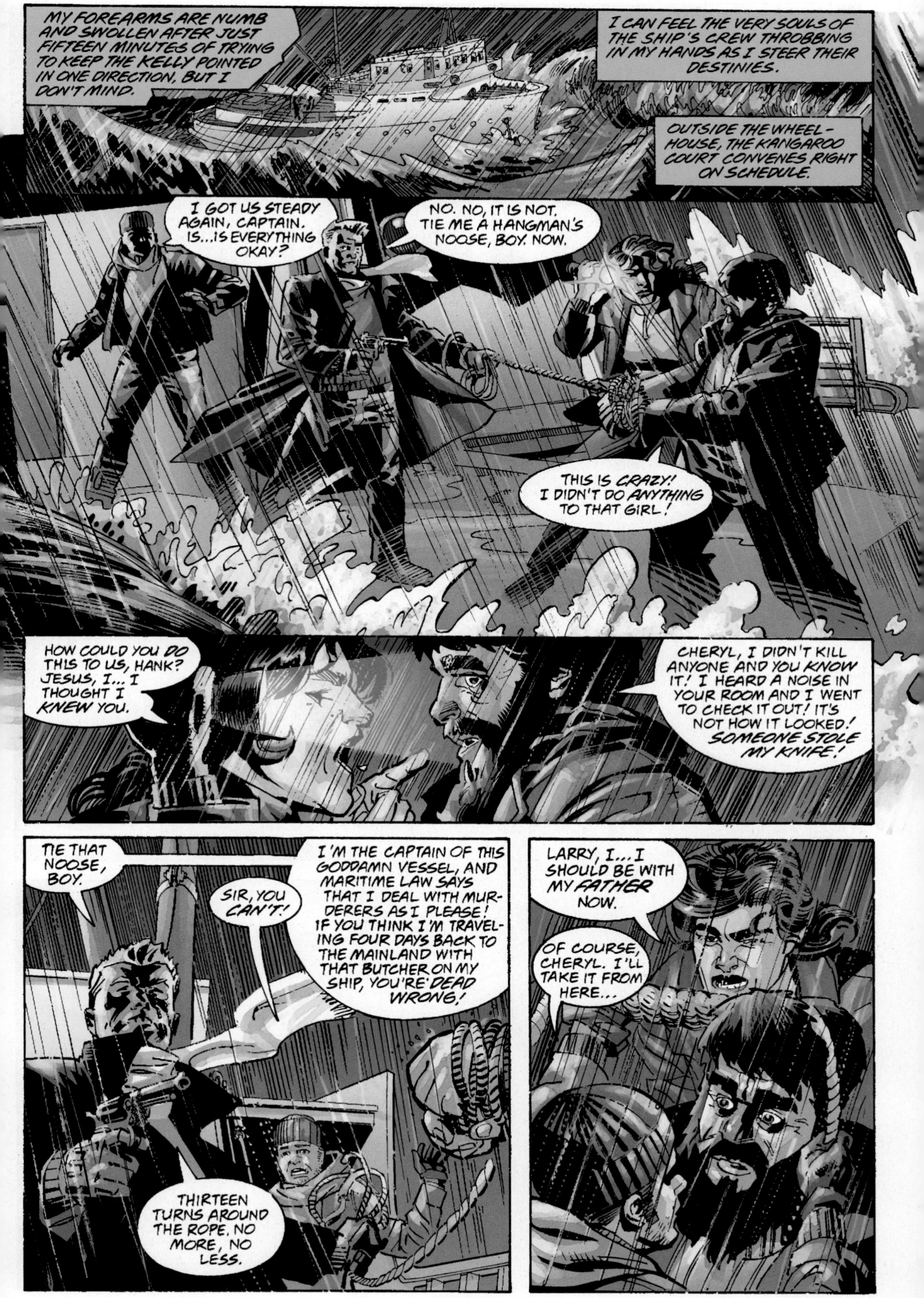

MY FOREARMS ARE NUMB AND SWOLLEN AFTER JUST FIFTEEN MINUTES OF TRYING TO KEEP THE KELLY POINTED IN ONE DIRECTION. BUT I DON'T MIND.
I CAN FEEL THE VERY SOULS OF THE SHIP'S CREW THROBBING IN MY HANDS AS I STEER THEIR DESTINIES.
OUTSIDE THE WHEEL-HOUSE, THE KANGAROO COURT CONVENES RIGHT ON SCHEDULE.
I GOT US STEADY AGAIN, CAPTAIN. IS...IS EVERYTHING OKAY?
NO. NO, IT IS NOT. TIE ME A HANGMAN'S NOOSE, BOY. NOW.
THIS IS CRAZY! I DIDN'T DO ANYTHING TO THAT GIRL!
HOW COULD YOU DO THIS TO US, HANK? JESUS, I... I THOUGHT I KNEW YOU.
CHERYL, I DIDN'T KILL ANYONE AND YOU KNOW IT! I HEARD A NOISE IN YOUR ROOM AND I WENT TO CHECK IT OUT! IT'S NOT HOW IT LOOKED! SOMEONE STOLE MY KNIFE!
TIE THAT NOOSE, BOY.
SIR, YOU CAN'T!
I'M THE CAPTAIN OF THIS GODDAMN VESSEL, AND MARITIME LAW SAYS THAT I DEAL WITH MURDERERS AS I PLEASE! IF YOU THINK I'M TRAVELING FOUR DAYS BACK TO THE MAINLAND WITH THAT BUTCHER ON MY SHIP, YOU'RE DEAD WRONG!
THIRTEEN TURNS AROUND THE ROPE. NO MORE, NO LESS.
LARRY, I... I SHOULD BE WITH MY FATHER NOW.
OF COURSE, CHERYL. I'LL TAKE IT FROM HERE...

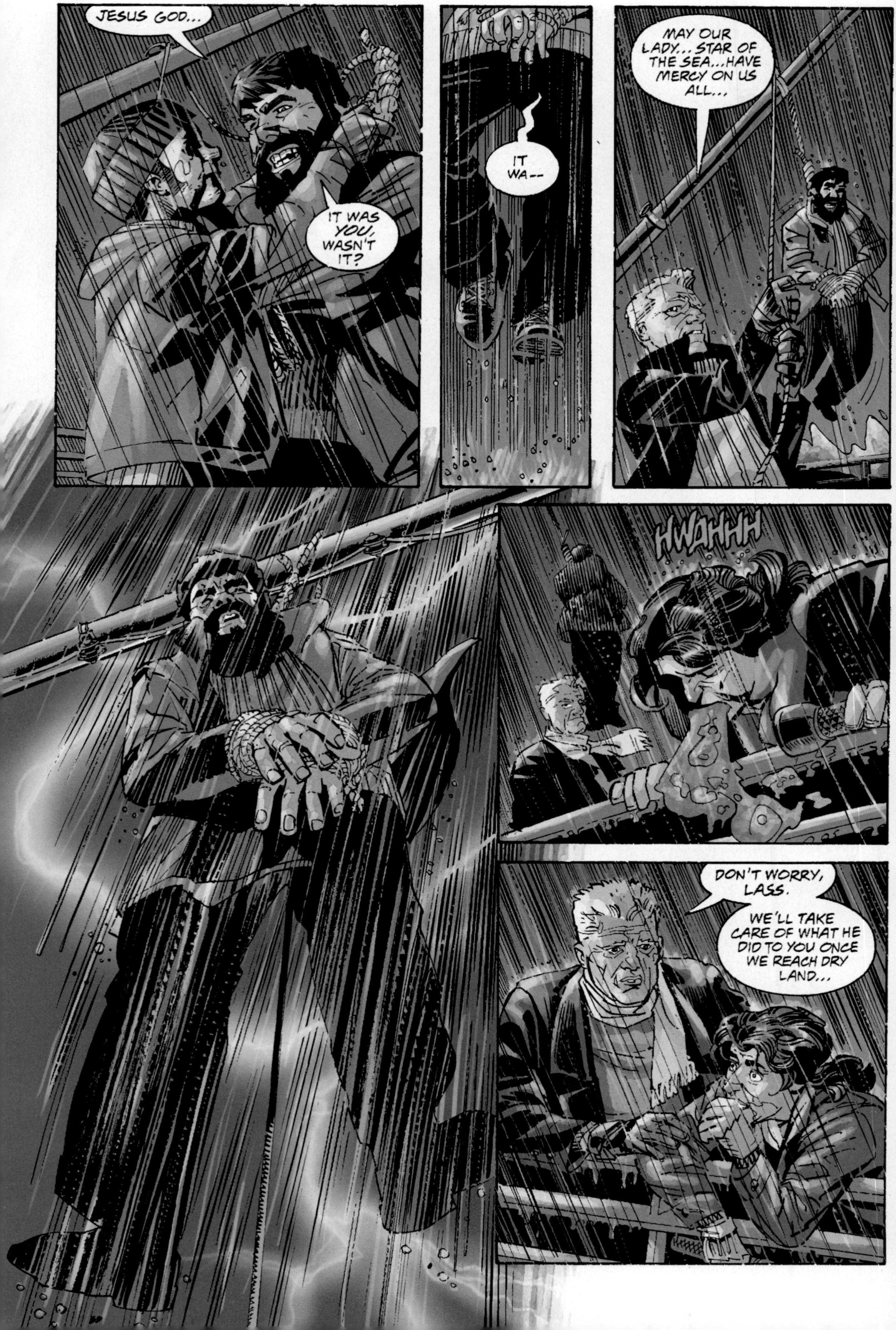
JESUS GOD...
IT WAS YOU, WASN'T IT?
IT WA--
MAY OUR LADY... STAR OF THE SEA... HAVE MERCY ON US ALL...
HWAHHH
DON'T WORRY, LASS.
WE'LL TAKE CARE OF WHAT HE DID TO YOU ONCE WE REACH DRY LAND...

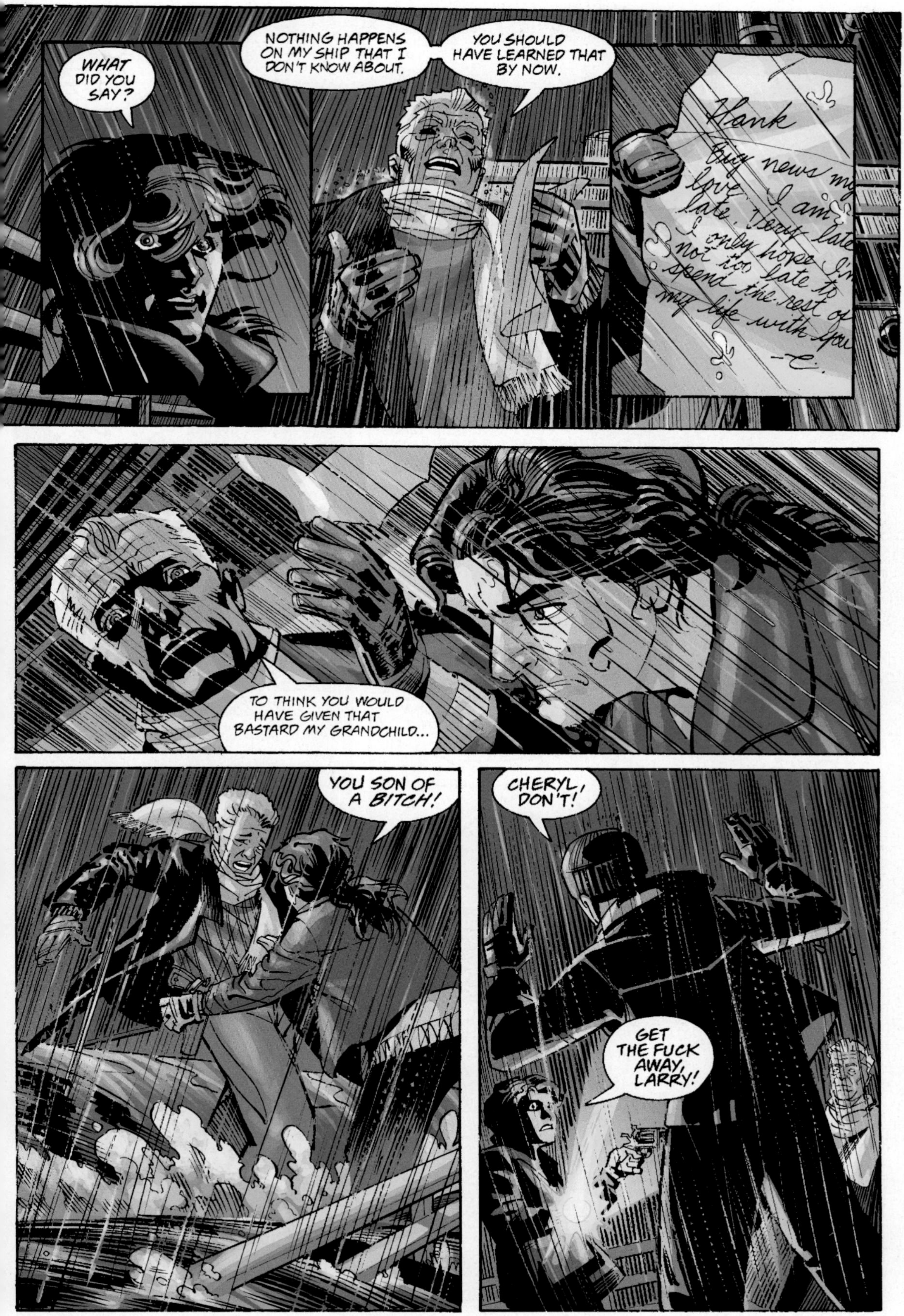
WHAT DID YOU SAY?
NOTHING HAPPENS ON MY SHIP THAT I DON'T KNOW ABOUT.
YOU SHOULD HAVE LEARNED THAT BY NOW.
Hank
Big news my love. I am late. Very late. I only hope I'm not too late to spend the rest of my life with you
-C.
TO THINK YOU WOULD HAVE GIVEN THAT BASTARD MY GRANDCHILD...
YOU SON OF A BITCH!
CHERYL, DON'T!
GET THE FUCK AWAY, LARRY!

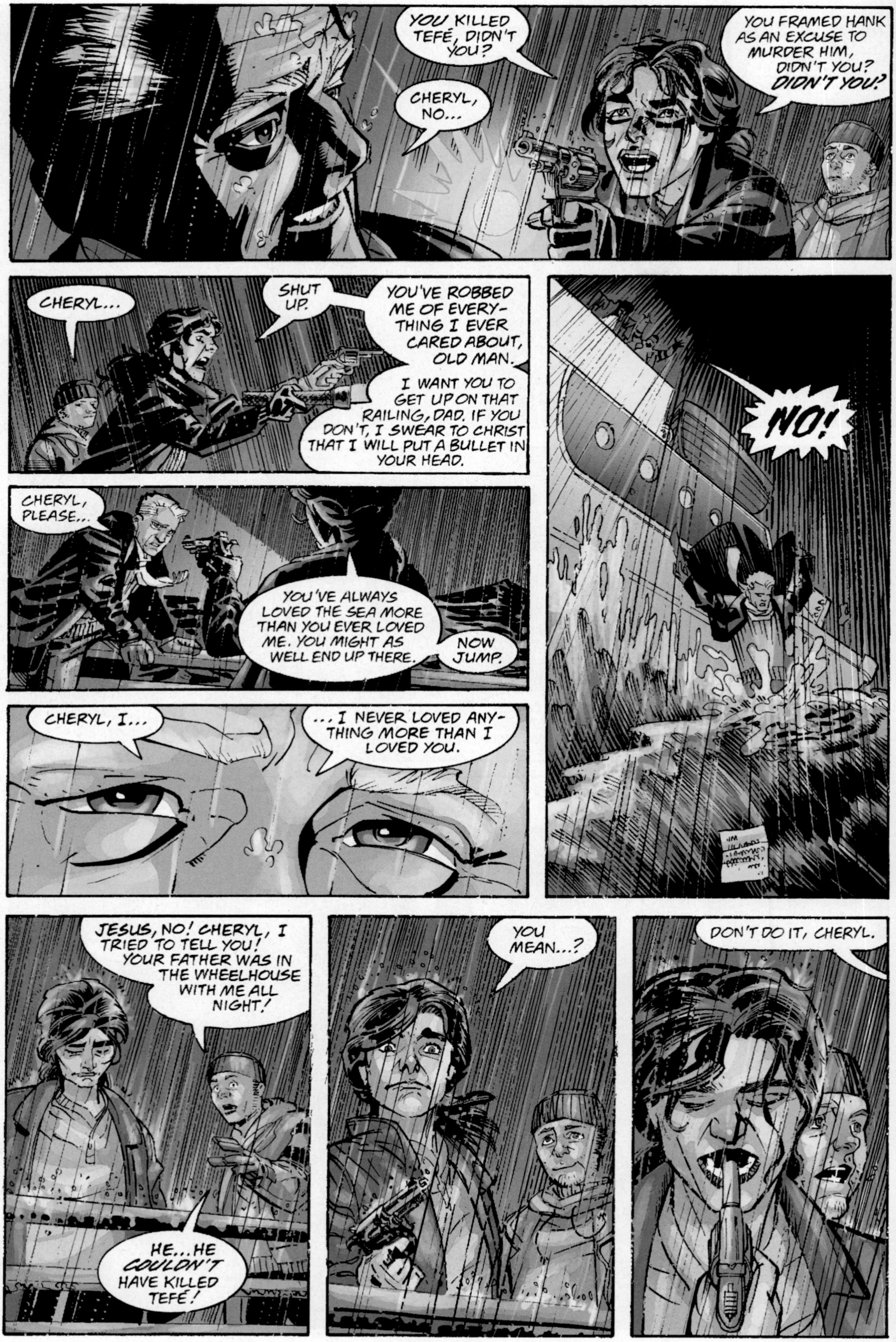
YOU KILLED TEFÉ, DIDN'T YOU?
CHERYL, NO...
YOU FRAMED HANK AS AN EXCUSE TO MURDER HIM, DIDN'T YOU? DIDN'T YOU?
CHERYL...
SHUT UP.
YOU'VE ROBBED ME OF EVERYTHING I EVER CARED ABOUT, OLD MAN.
I WANT YOU TO GET UP ON THAT RAILING, DAD. IF YOU DON'T, I SWEAR TO CHRIST THAT I WILL PUT A BULLET IN YOUR HEAD.
CHERYL, PLEASE...
YOU'VE ALWAYS LOVED THE SEA MORE THAN YOU EVER LOVED ME. YOU MIGHT AS WELL END UP THERE.
NOW JUMP.
CHERYL, I...
...I NEVER LOVED ANYTHING MORE THAN I LOVED YOU.
NO!
JESUS, NO! CHERYL, I TRIED TO TELL YOU! YOUR FATHER WAS IN THE WHEELHOUSE WITH ME ALL NIGHT!
HE...HE COULDN'T HAVE KILLED TEFÉ!
YOU MEAN...?
DON'T DO IT, CHERYL.

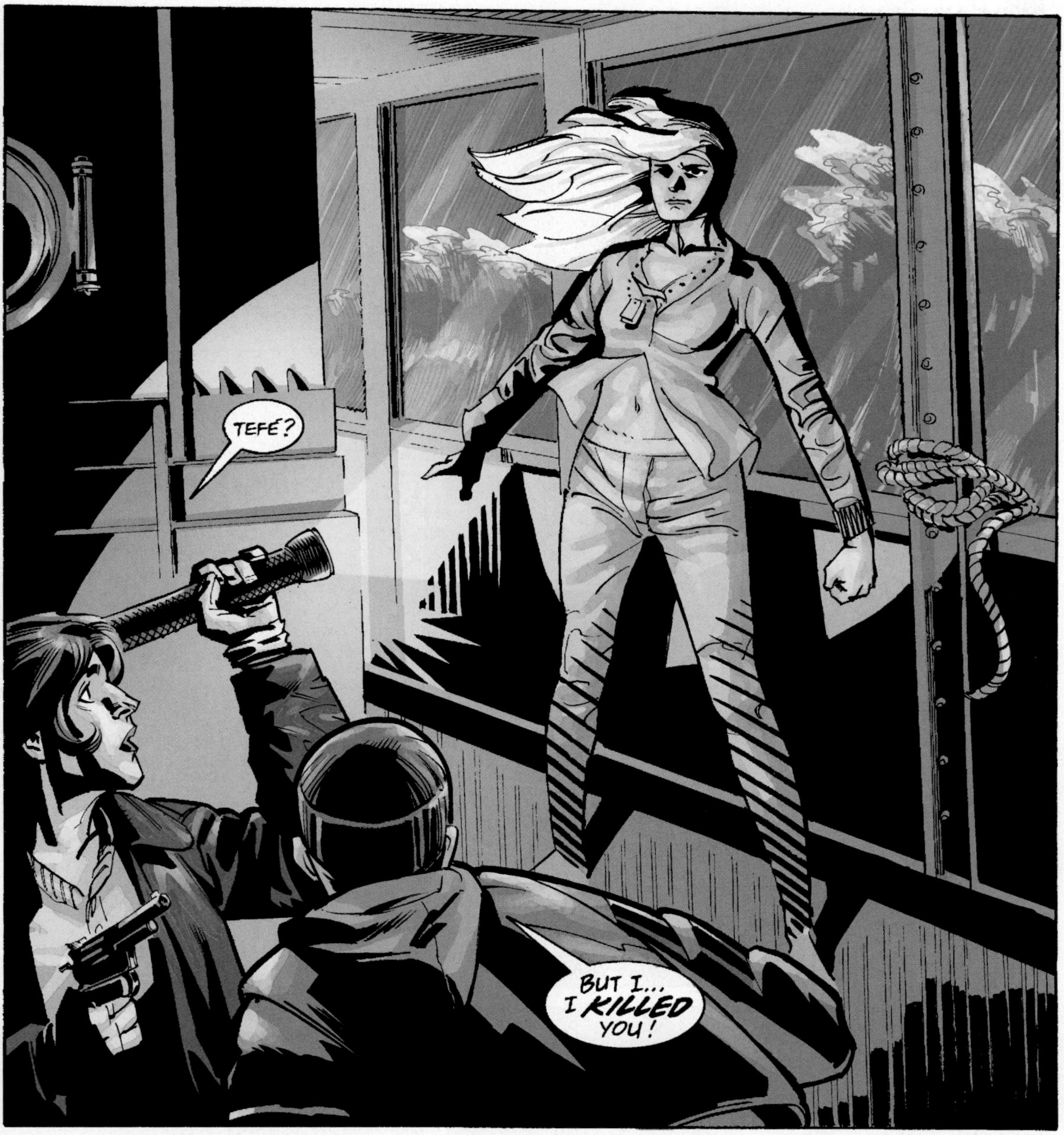
TEFÉ?
BUT I... I KILLED YOU!

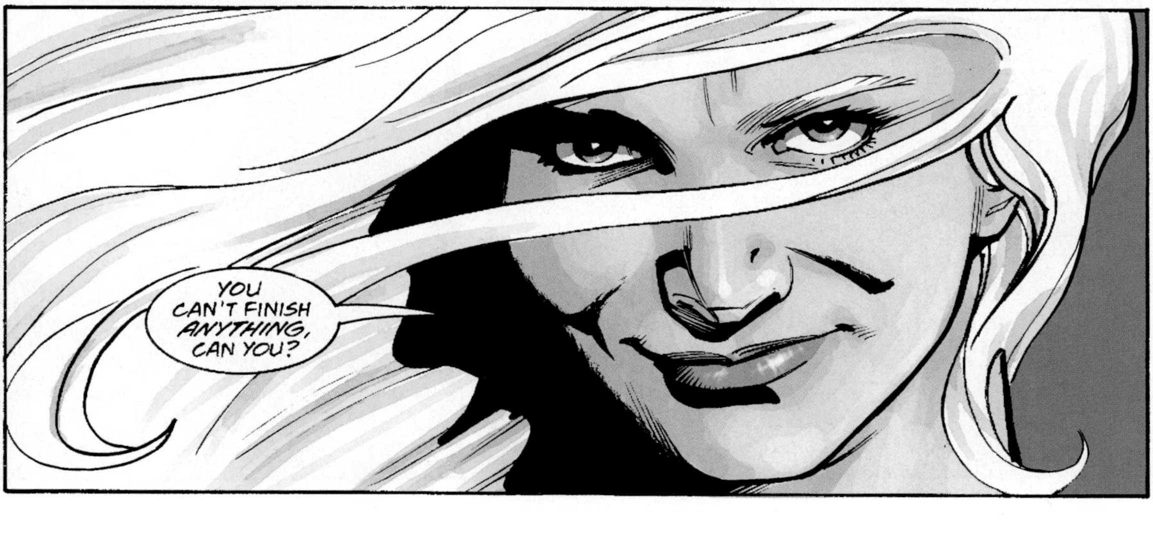
YOU CAN'T FINISH *ANYTHING,* CAN YOU?

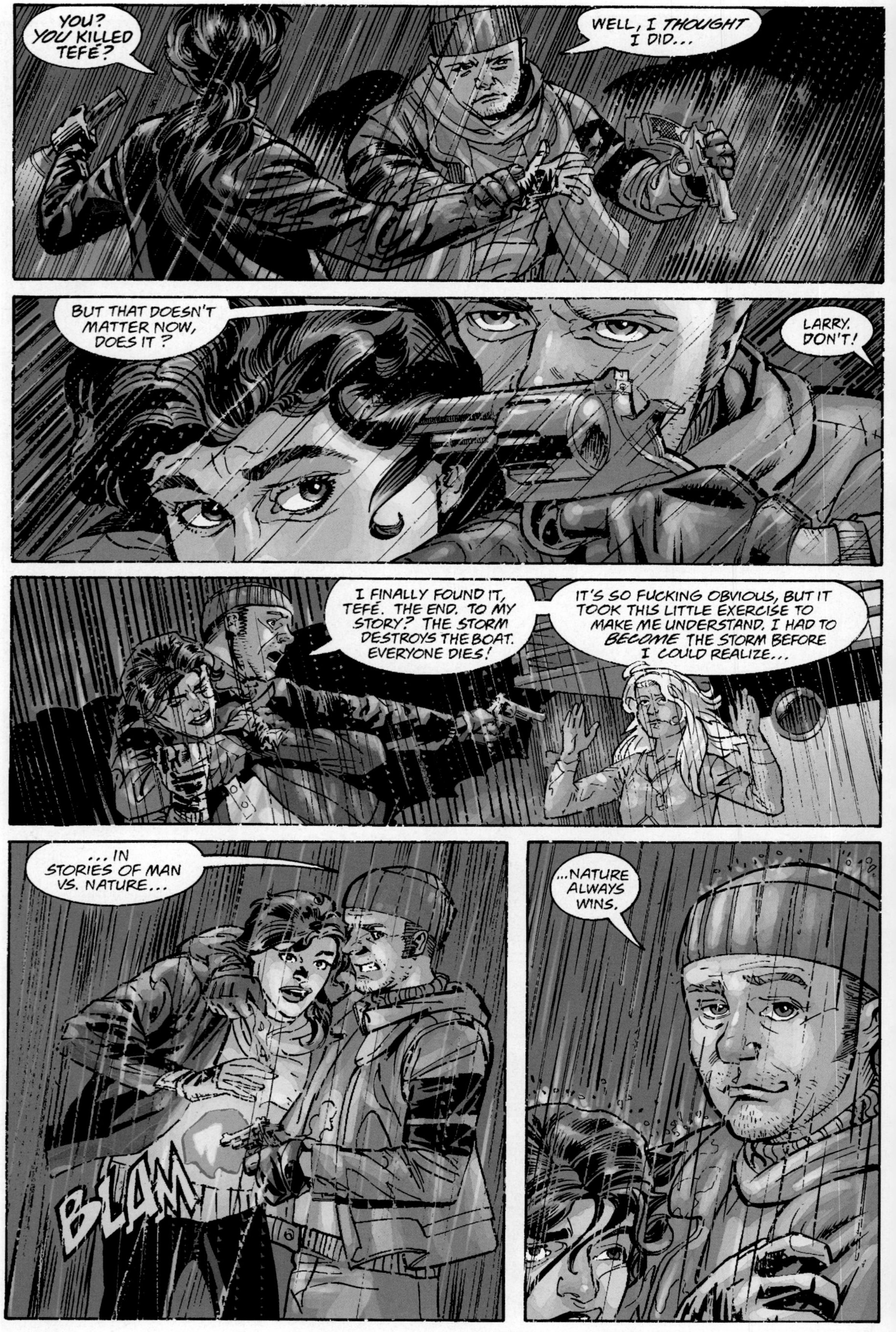
YOU? YOU KILLED TEFÉ?
WELL, I *THOUGHT* I DID...
BUT THAT DOESN'T MATTER NOW, DOES IT?
LARRY. DON'T!
I FINALLY FOUND IT, TEFÉ. THE END. TO MY STORY? THE STORM DESTROYS THE BOAT. EVERYONE DIES!
IT'S SO FUCKING OBVIOUS, BUT IT TOOK THIS LITTLE EXERCISE TO MAKE ME UNDERSTAND. I HAD TO *BECOME* THE STORM BEFORE I COULD REALIZE...
...IN STORIES OF MAN VS. NATURE...
BLAM
...NATURE ALWAYS WINS.

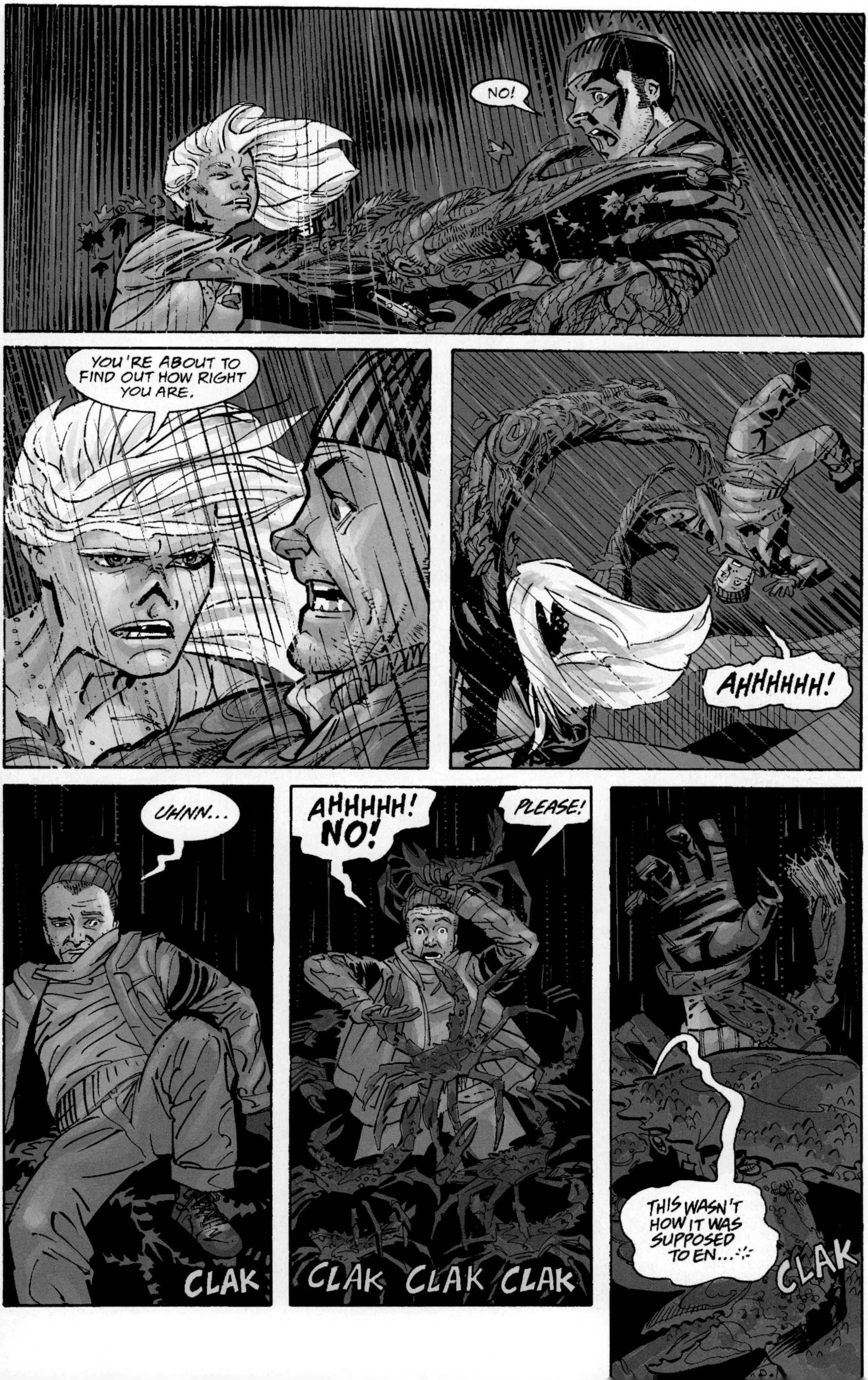
NO!
YOU'RE ABOUT TO FIND OUT HOW RIGHT YOU ARE.
AHHHHHH!
UHNN...
CLAK
AHHHHH! NO!
PLEASE!
CLAK CLAK CLAK
THIS WASN'T HOW IT WAS SUPPOSED TO EN...
CLAK

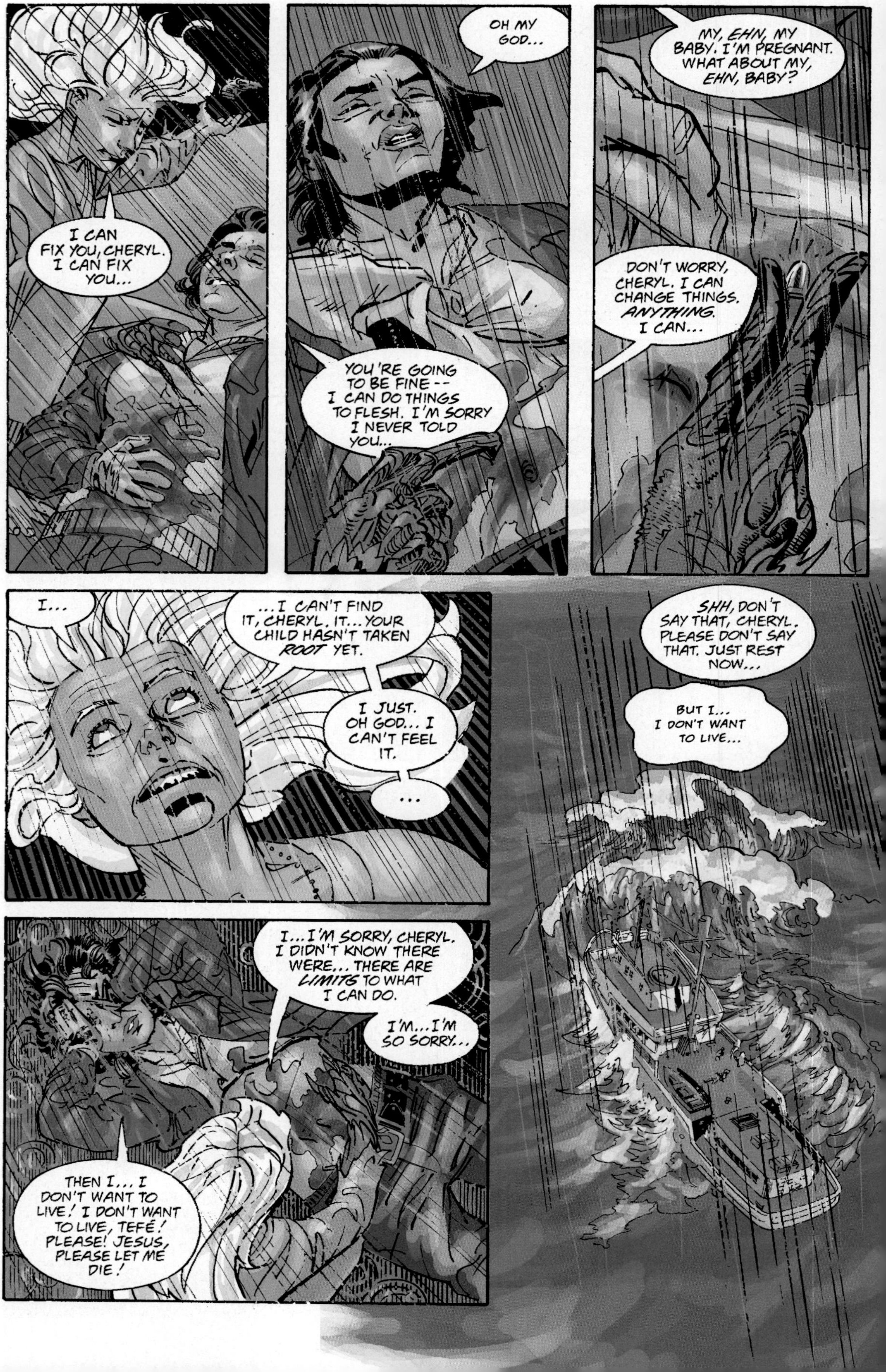
I CAN FIX YOU, CHERYL. I CAN FIX YOU...
OH MY GOD...
YOU'RE GOING TO BE FINE -- I CAN DO THINGS TO FLESH. I'M SORRY I NEVER TOLD YOU...
MY, EHN, MY BABY. I'M PREGNANT. WHAT ABOUT MY, EHN, BABY?
DON'T WORRY, CHERYL. I CAN CHANGE THINGS. ANYTHING. I CAN...
I...
...I CAN'T FIND IT, CHERYL. IT... YOUR CHILD HASN'T TAKEN ROOT YET.
I JUST. OH GOD... I CAN'T FEEL IT.
...
I... I'M SORRY, CHERYL. I DIDN'T KNOW THERE WERE... THERE ARE LIMITS TO WHAT I CAN DO.
I'M... I'M SO SORRY...
THEN I... I DON'T WANT TO LIVE! I DON'T WANT TO LIVE, TEFÉ! PLEASE! JESUS, PLEASE LET ME DIE!
SHH, DON'T SAY THAT, CHERYL. PLEASE DON'T SAY THAT. JUST REST NOW...
BUT I... I DON'T WANT TO LIVE...

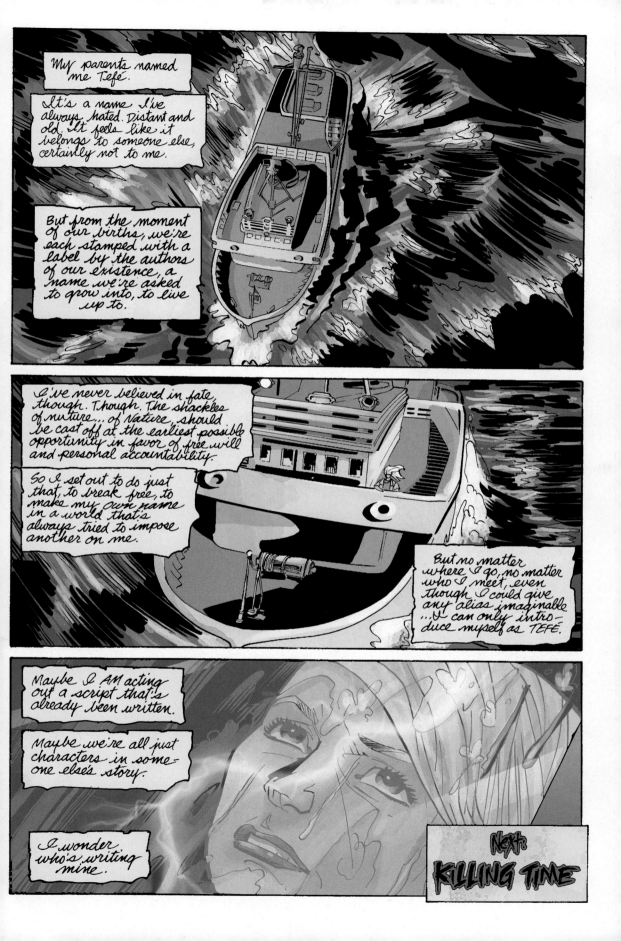

My parents named me Tefé.

It's a name I've always hated. Distant and old. It feels like it belongs to someone else, certainly not to me.

But from the moment of our births, we're each stamped with a label by the authors of our existence, a name we're asked to grow into, to live up to.

I've never believed in fate, though. Though. The shackles of nurture... of nature, should be cast off at the earliest possible opportunity in favor of free will and personal accountability.

So I set out to do just that, to break free, to make my own name in a world that's always tried to impose another on me.

But no matter where I go, no matter who I meet, even though I could give any alias imaginable ...I can only introduce myself as TEFÉ.

Maybe I AM acting out a script that's already been written.

Maybe we're all just characters in someone else's story.

I wonder who's writing mine.

Next:
KILLING TIME

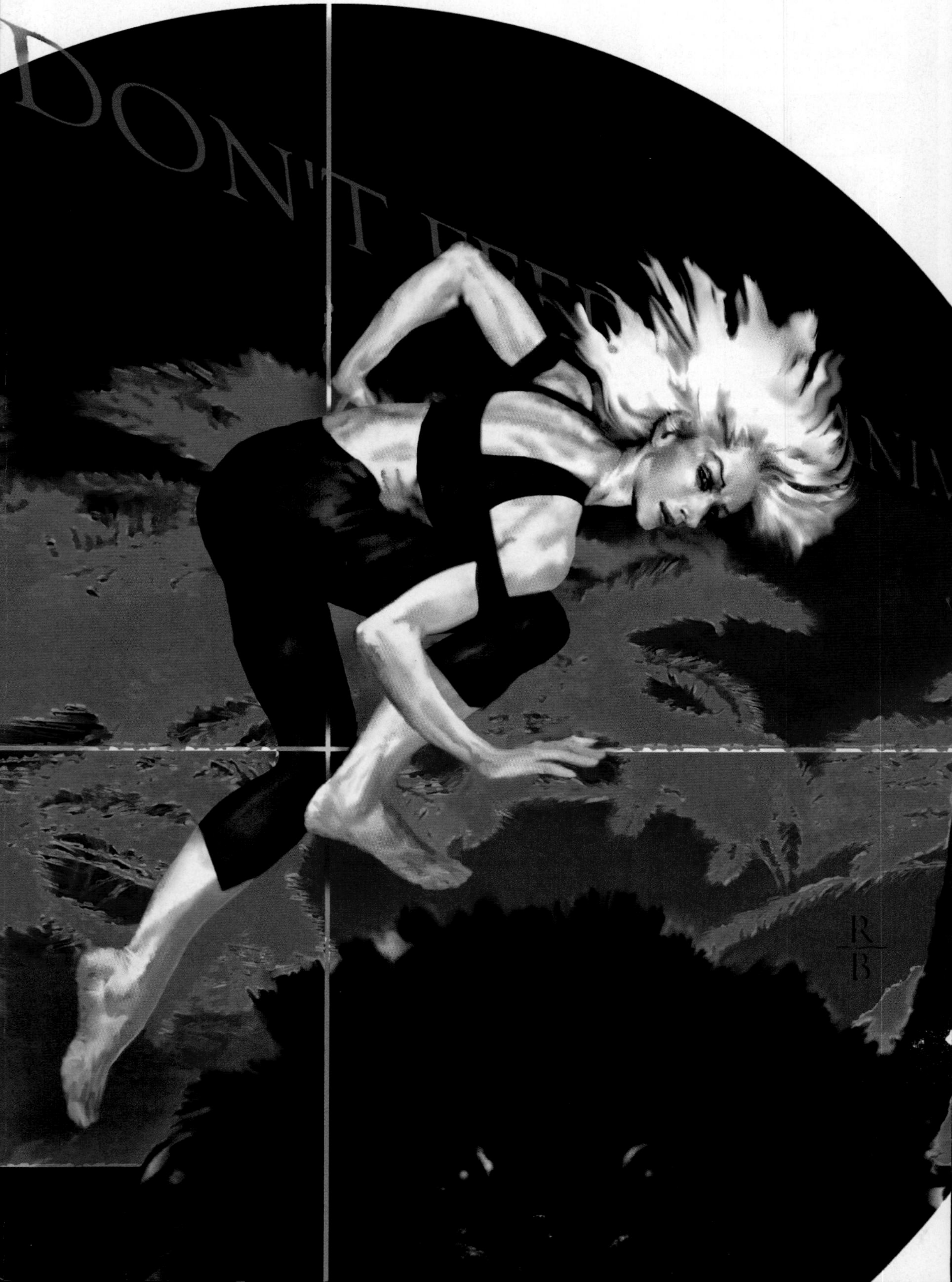
DON'T

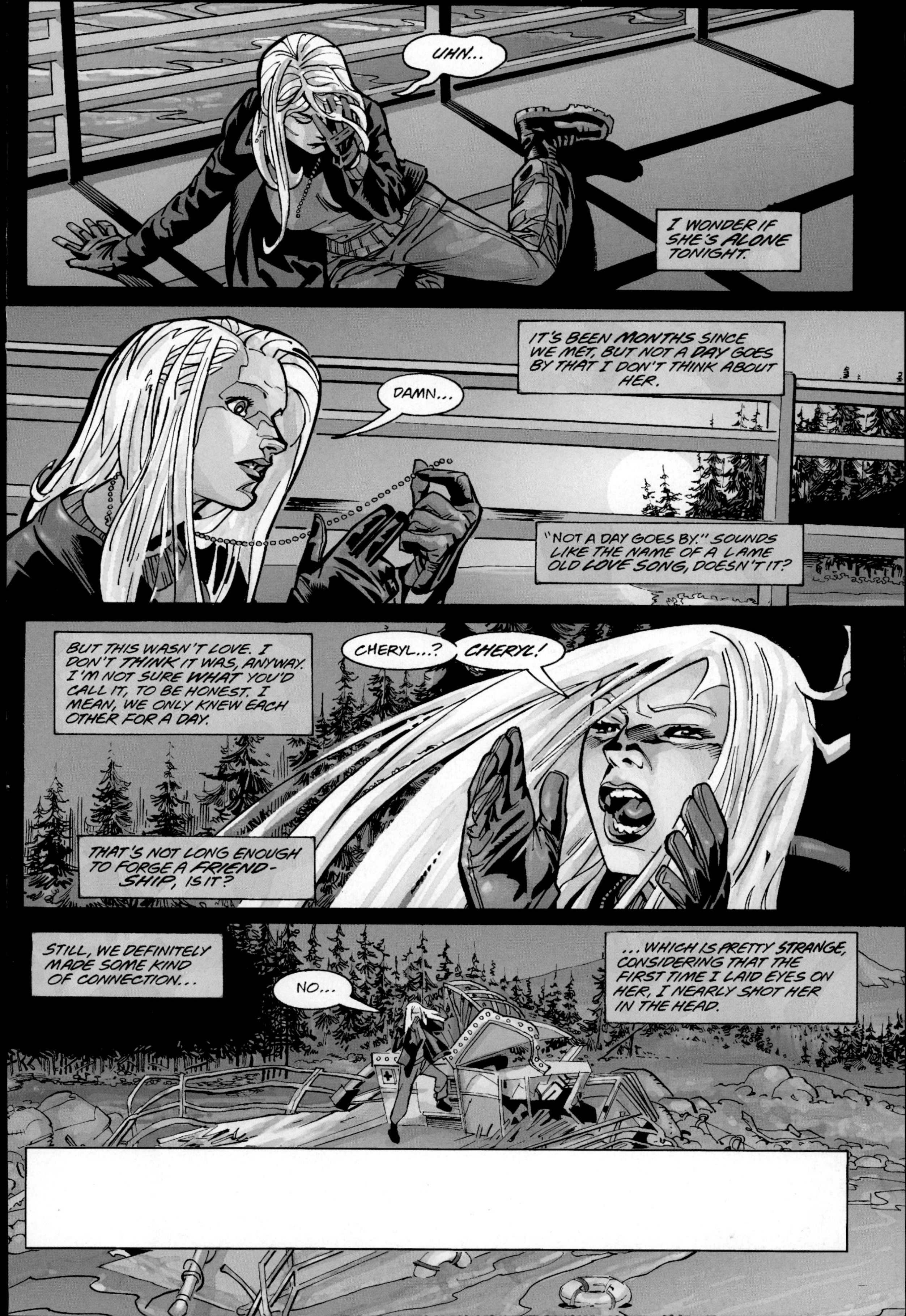

UHN...
I WONDER IF SHE'S ALONE TONIGHT.
IT'S BEEN MONTHS SINCE WE MET, BUT NOT A DAY GOES BY THAT I DON'T THINK ABOUT HER.
DAMN...
"NOT A DAY GOES BY." SOUNDS LIKE THE NAME OF A LAME OLD LOVE SONG, DOESN'T IT?
BUT THIS WASN'T LOVE. I DON'T THINK IT WAS, ANYWAY. I'M NOT SURE WHAT YOU'D CALL IT, TO BE HONEST. I MEAN, WE ONLY KNEW EACH OTHER FOR A DAY.
CHERYL...?
CHERYL!
THAT'S NOT LONG ENOUGH TO FORGE A FRIEND-SHIP, IS IT?
STILL, WE DEFINITELY MADE SOME KIND OF CONNECTION...
NO...
...WHICH IS PRETTY STRANGE, CONSIDERING THAT THE FIRST TIME I LAID EYES ON HER, I NEARLY SHOT HER IN THE HEAD.

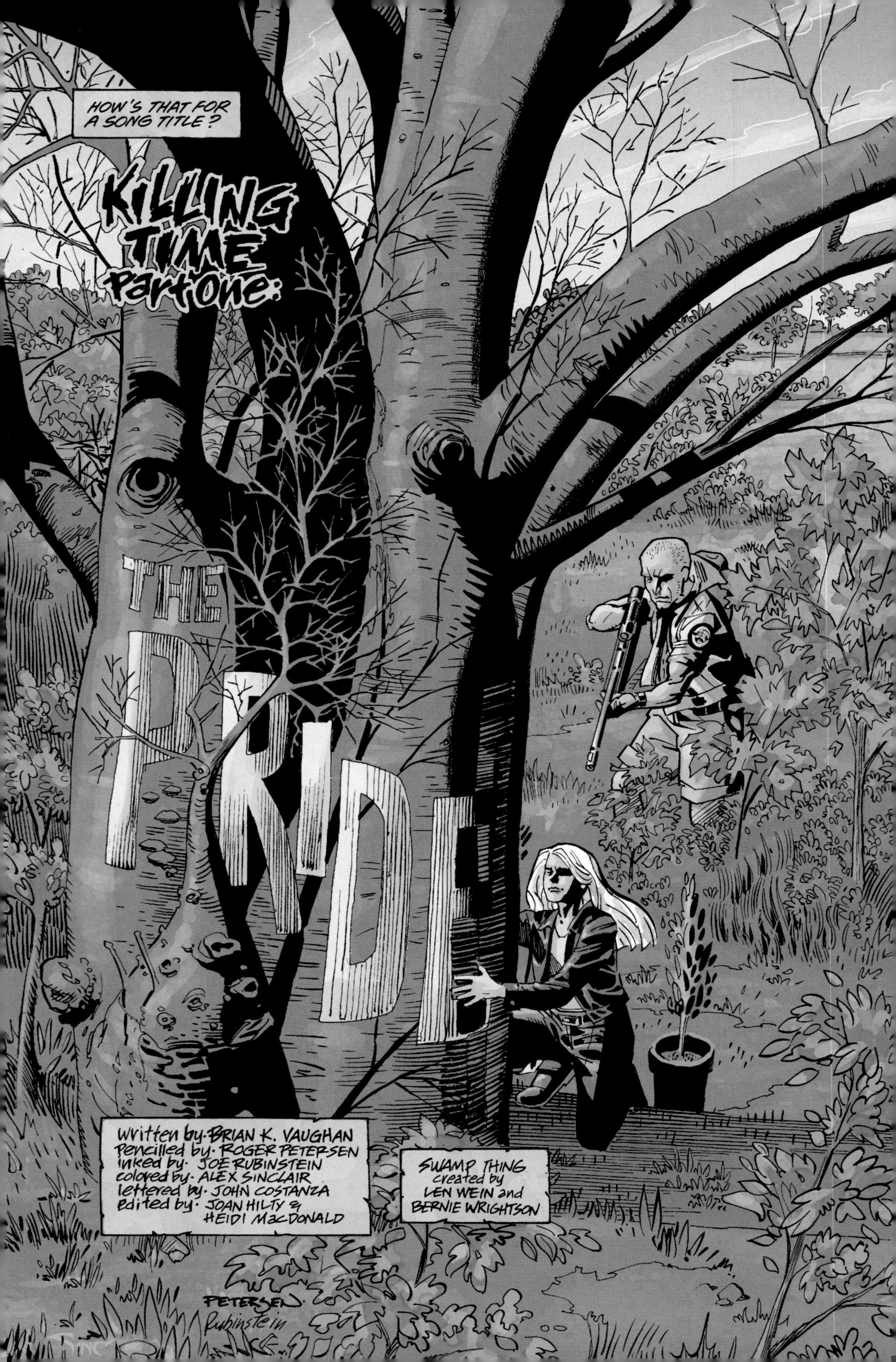
HOW'S THAT FOR A SONG TITLE?
KILLING TIME Part One:
THE PRIDE
Written by · BRIAN K. VAUGHAN
Pencilled by · ROGER PETERSEN
Inked by · JOE RUBINSTEIN
Colored by · ALEX SINCLAIR
Lettered by · JOHN COSTANZA
Edited by · JOAN HILTY & HEIDI MacDONALD
SWAMP THING created by LEN WEIN and BERNIE WRIGHTSON
PETERSEN
Rubinstein

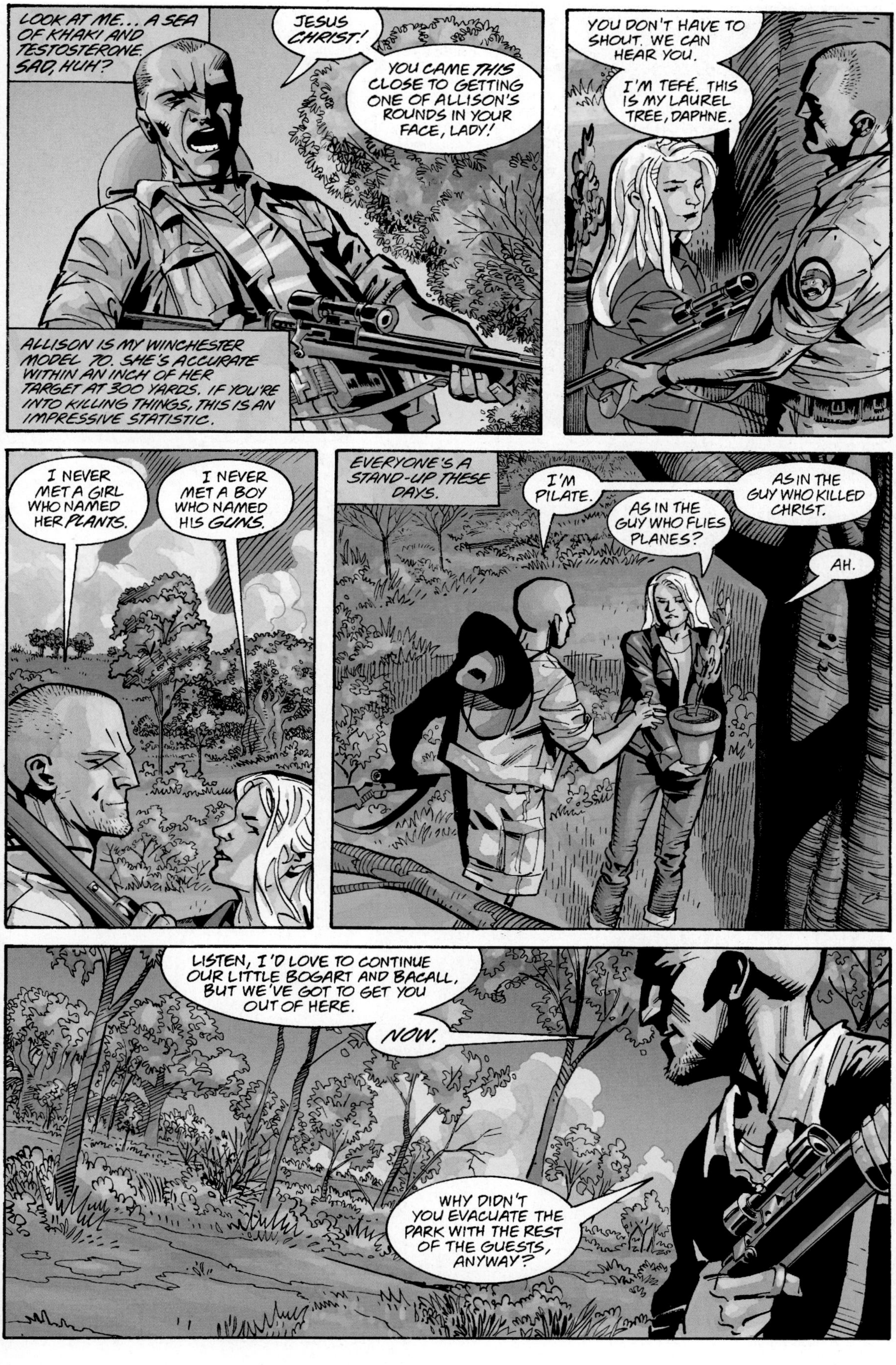
LOOK AT ME... A SEA OF KHAKI AND TESTOSTERONE. SAD, HUH?
JESUS CHRIST!
YOU CAME THIS CLOSE TO GETTING ONE OF ALLISON'S ROUNDS IN YOUR FACE, LADY!
ALLISON IS MY WINCHESTER MODEL 70. SHE'S ACCURATE WITHIN AN INCH OF HER TARGET AT 300 YARDS. IF YOU'RE INTO KILLING THINGS, THIS IS AN IMPRESSIVE STATISTIC.
YOU DON'T HAVE TO SHOUT. WE CAN HEAR YOU.
I'M TEFÉ. THIS IS MY LAUREL TREE, DAPHNE.
I NEVER MET A GIRL WHO NAMED HER PLANTS.
I NEVER MET A BOY WHO NAMED HIS GUNS.
EVERYONE'S A STAND-UP THESE DAYS.
I'M PILATE.
AS IN THE GUY WHO FLIES PLANES?
AS IN THE GUY WHO KILLED CHRIST.
AH.
LISTEN, I'D LOVE TO CONTINUE OUR LITTLE BOGART AND BACALL, BUT WE'VE GOT TO GET YOU OUT OF HERE.
NOW.
WHY DIDN'T YOU EVACUATE THE PARK WITH THE REST OF THE GUESTS, ANYWAY?

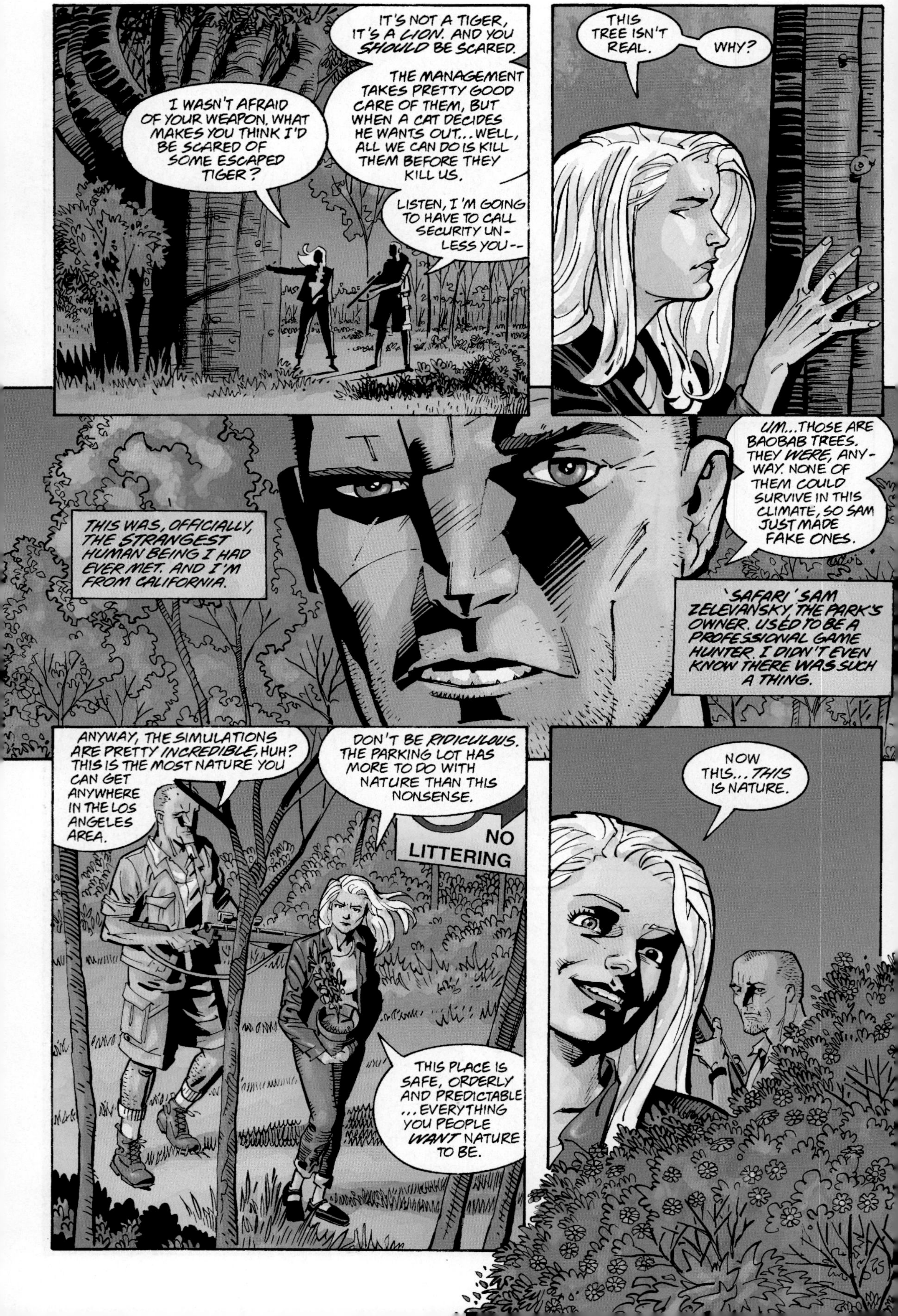

I WASN'T AFRAID OF YOUR WEAPON. WHAT MAKES YOU THINK I'D BE SCARED OF SOME ESCAPED TIGER?
IT'S NOT A TIGER, IT'S A LION. AND YOU SHOULD BE SCARED.
THE MANAGEMENT TAKES PRETTY GOOD CARE OF THEM, BUT WHEN A CAT DECIDES HE WANTS OUT... WELL, ALL WE CAN DO IS KILL THEM BEFORE THEY KILL US.
LISTEN, I'M GOING TO HAVE TO CALL SECURITY UNLESS YOU--
THIS TREE ISN'T REAL.
WHY?
THIS WAS, OFFICIALLY, THE STRANGEST HUMAN BEING I HAD EVER MET. AND I'M FROM CALIFORNIA.
UM...THOSE ARE BAOBAB TREES. THEY WERE, ANYWAY. NONE OF THEM COULD SURVIVE IN THIS CLIMATE, SO SAM JUST MADE FAKE ONES.
'SAFARI' SAM ZELEVANSKY, THE PARK'S OWNER. USED TO BE A PROFESSIONAL GAME HUNTER. I DIDN'T EVEN KNOW THERE WAS SUCH A THING.
ANYWAY, THE SIMULATIONS ARE PRETTY INCREDIBLE, HUH? THIS IS THE MOST NATURE YOU CAN GET ANYWHERE IN THE LOS ANGELES AREA.
DON'T BE RIDICULOUS. THE PARKING LOT HAS MORE TO DO WITH NATURE THAN THIS NONSENSE.
NO LITTERING
THIS PLACE IS SAFE, ORDERLY AND PREDICTABLE ...EVERYTHING YOU PEOPLE WANT NATURE TO BE.
NOW THIS... THIS IS NATURE.

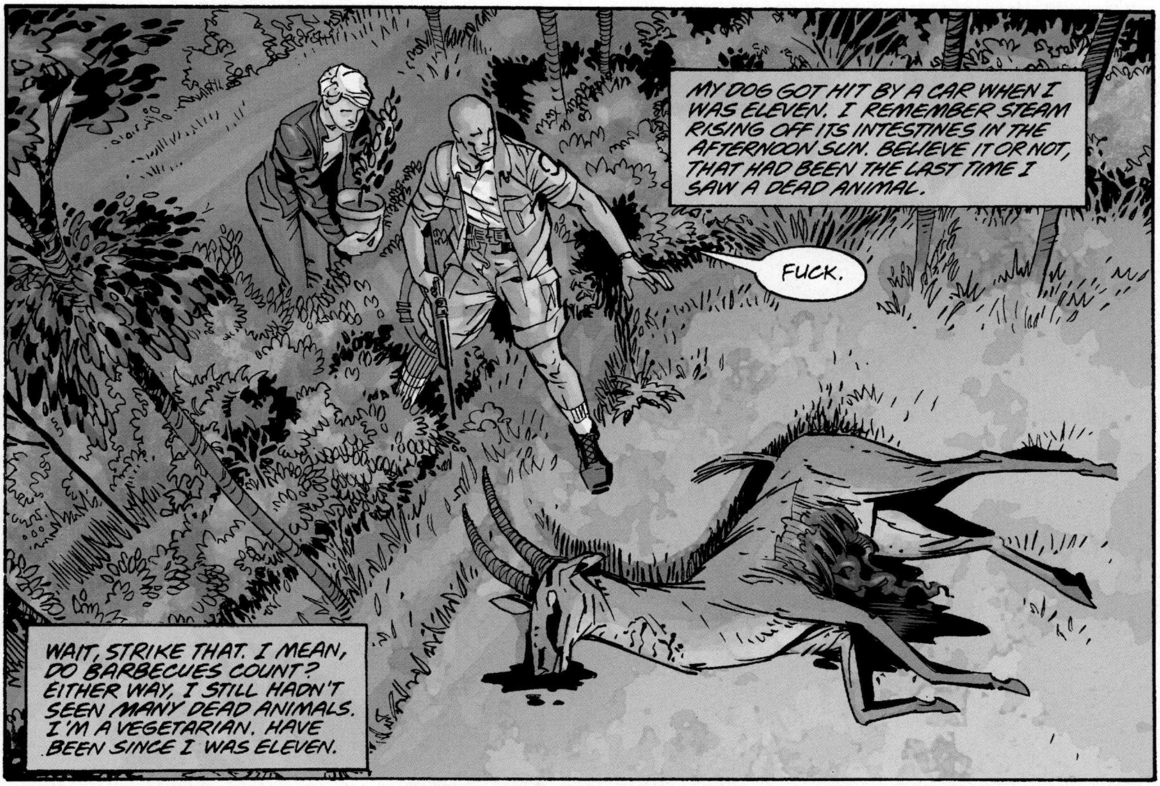
MY DOG GOT HIT BY A CAR WHEN I WAS ELEVEN. I REMEMBER STEAM RISING OFF ITS INTESTINES IN THE AFTERNOON SUN. BELIEVE IT OR NOT, THAT HAD BEEN THE LAST TIME I SAW A DEAD ANIMAL.
FUCK.
WAIT, STRIKE THAT. I MEAN, DO BARBECUES COUNT? EITHER WAY, I STILL HADN'T SEEN MANY DEAD ANIMALS. I'M A VEGETARIAN. HAVE BEEN SINCE I WAS ELEVEN.

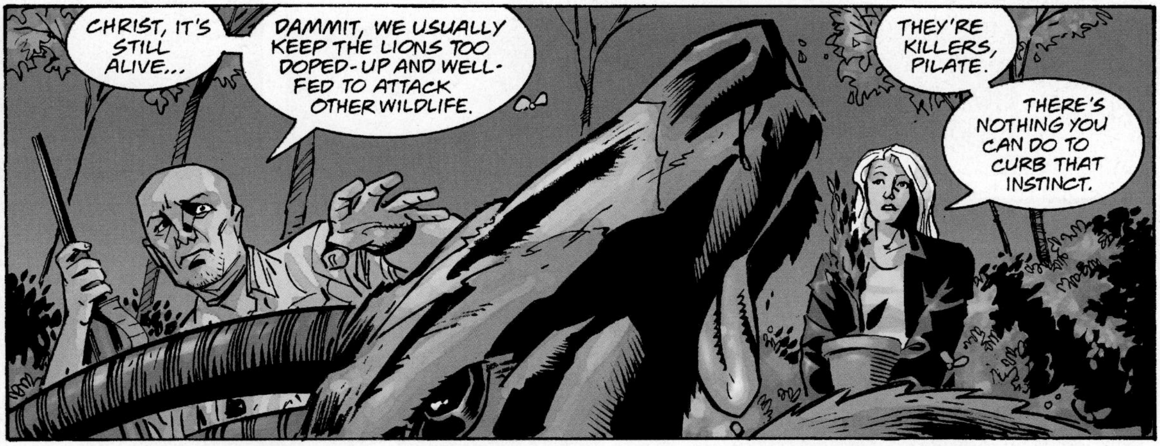
CHRIST, IT'S STILL ALIVE...
DAMMIT, WE USUALLY KEEP THE LIONS TOO DOPED-UP AND WELL-FED TO ATTACK OTHER WILDLIFE.
THEY'RE KILLERS, PILATE.
THERE'S NOTHING YOU CAN DO TO CURB THAT INSTINCT.

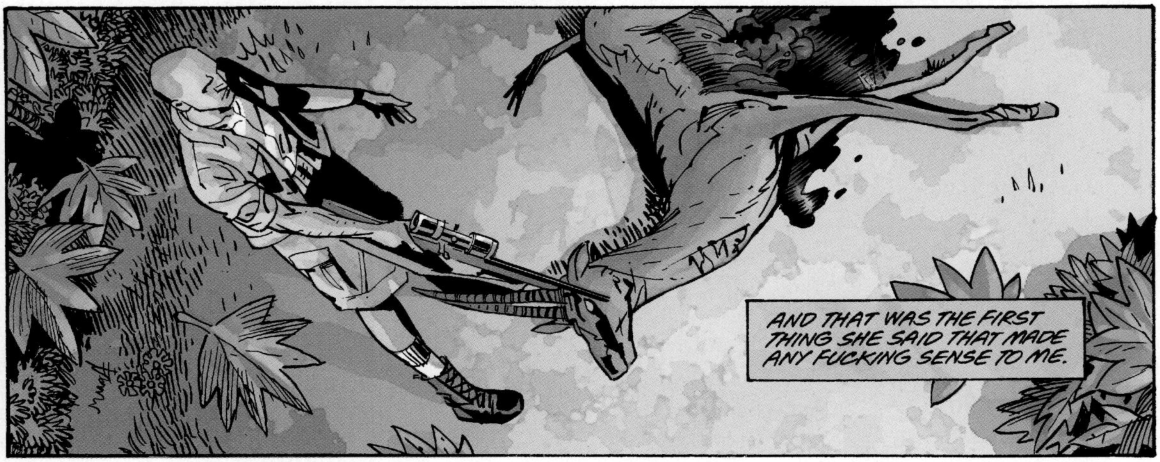
AND THAT WAS THE FIRST THING SHE SAID THAT MADE ANY FUCKING SENSE TO ME.

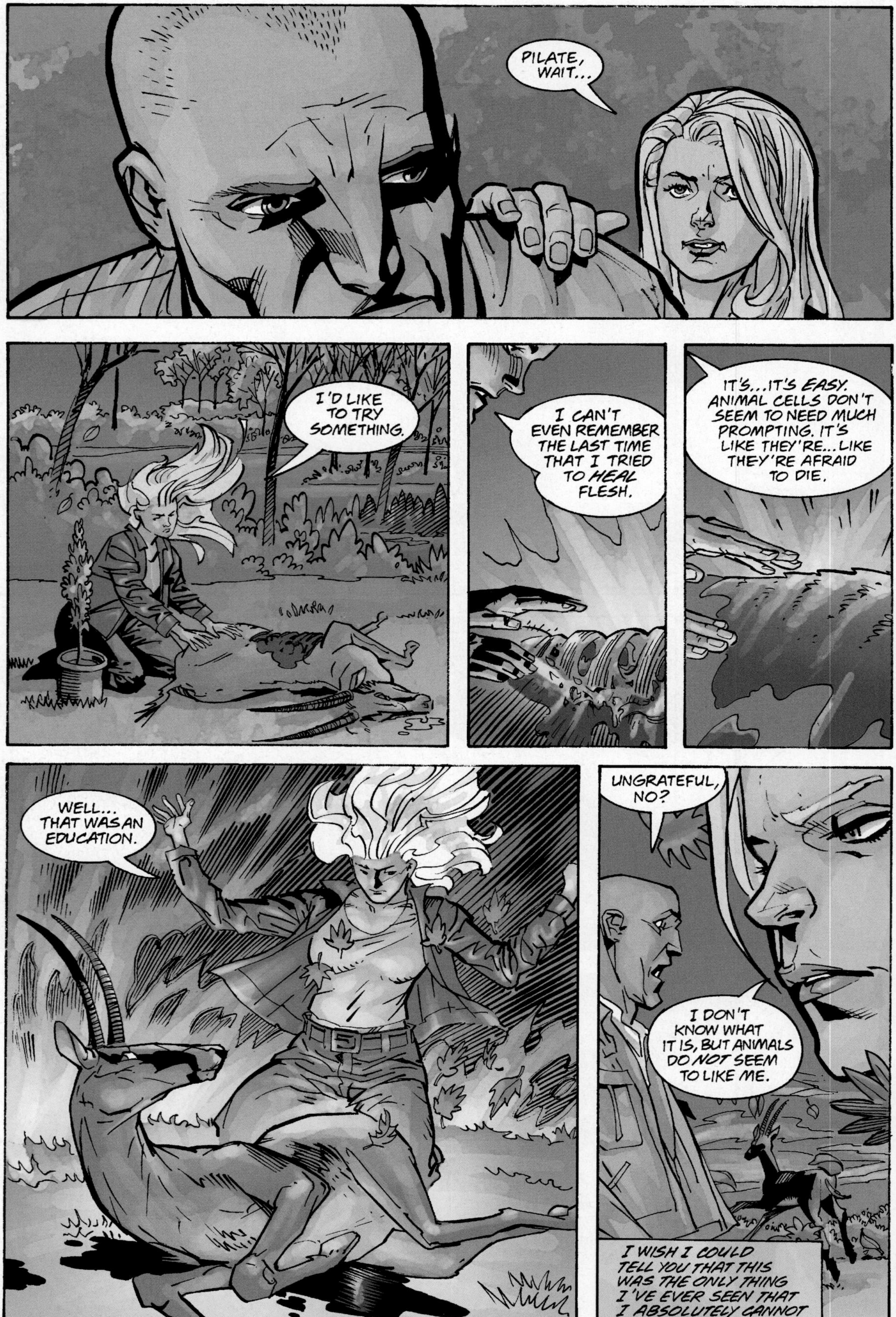
PILATE, WAIT...
I'D LIKE TO TRY SOMETHING.
I CAN'T EVEN REMEMBER THE LAST TIME THAT I TRIED TO HEAL FLESH.
IT'S... IT'S EASY. ANIMAL CELLS DON'T SEEM TO NEED MUCH PROMPTING. IT'S LIKE THEY'RE... LIKE THEY'RE AFRAID TO DIE.
WELL... THAT WAS AN EDUCATION.
UNGRATEFUL, NO?
I DON'T KNOW WHAT IT IS, BUT ANIMALS DO NOT SEEM TO LIKE ME.
I WISH I COULD TELL YOU THAT THIS WAS THE ONLY THING I'VE EVER SEEN THAT I ABSOLUTELY CANNOT EXPLAIN...

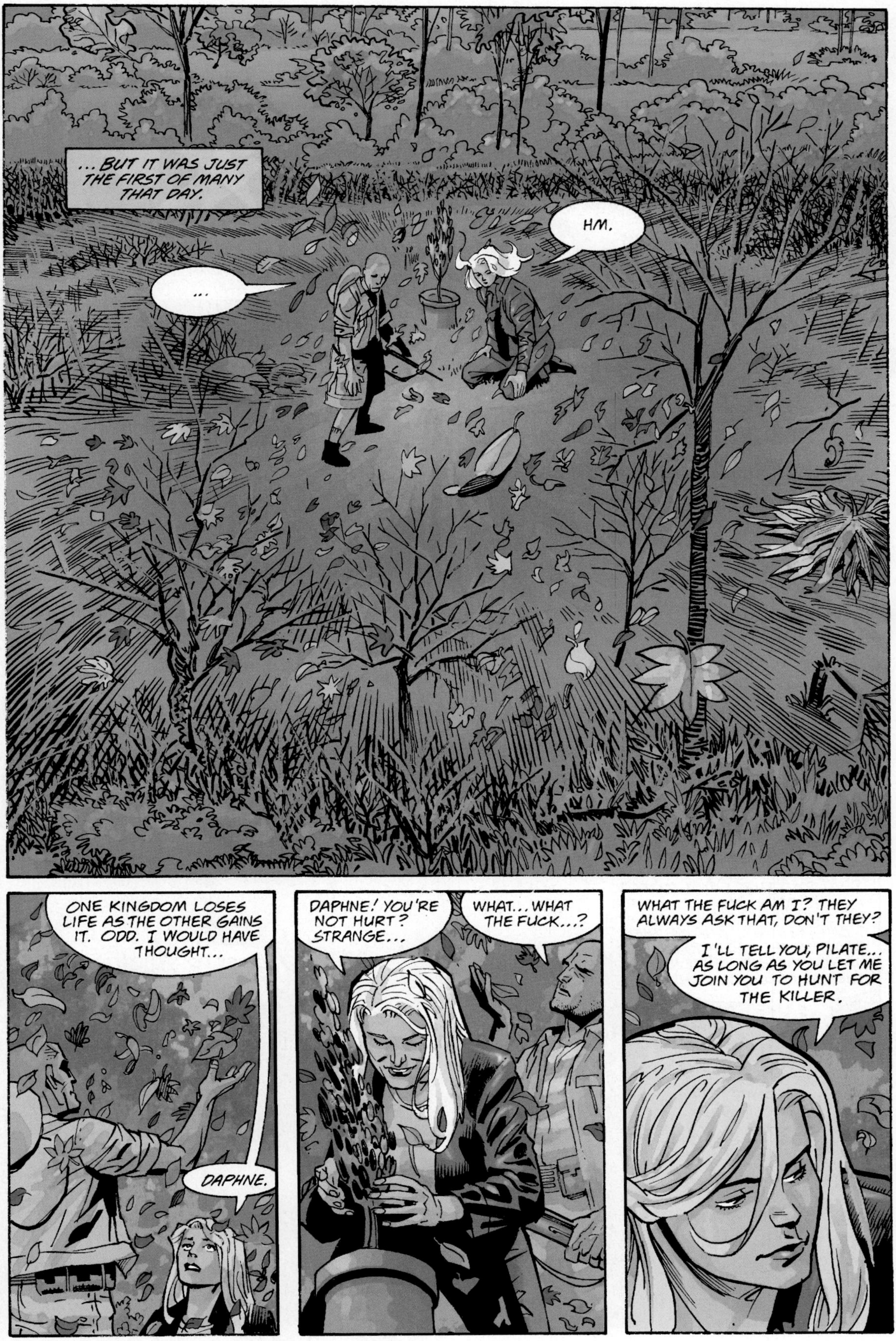
...BUT IT WAS JUST THE FIRST OF MANY THAT DAY.
HM.
...
ONE KINGDOM LOSES LIFE AS THE OTHER GAINS IT. ODD. I WOULD HAVE THOUGHT...
DAPHNE.
DAPHNE! YOU'RE NOT HURT? STRANGE...
WHAT... WHAT THE FUCK...?
WHAT THE FUCK AM I? THEY ALWAYS ASK THAT, DON'T THEY?
I'LL TELL YOU, PILATE... AS LONG AS YOU LET ME JOIN YOU TO HUNT FOR THE KILLER.

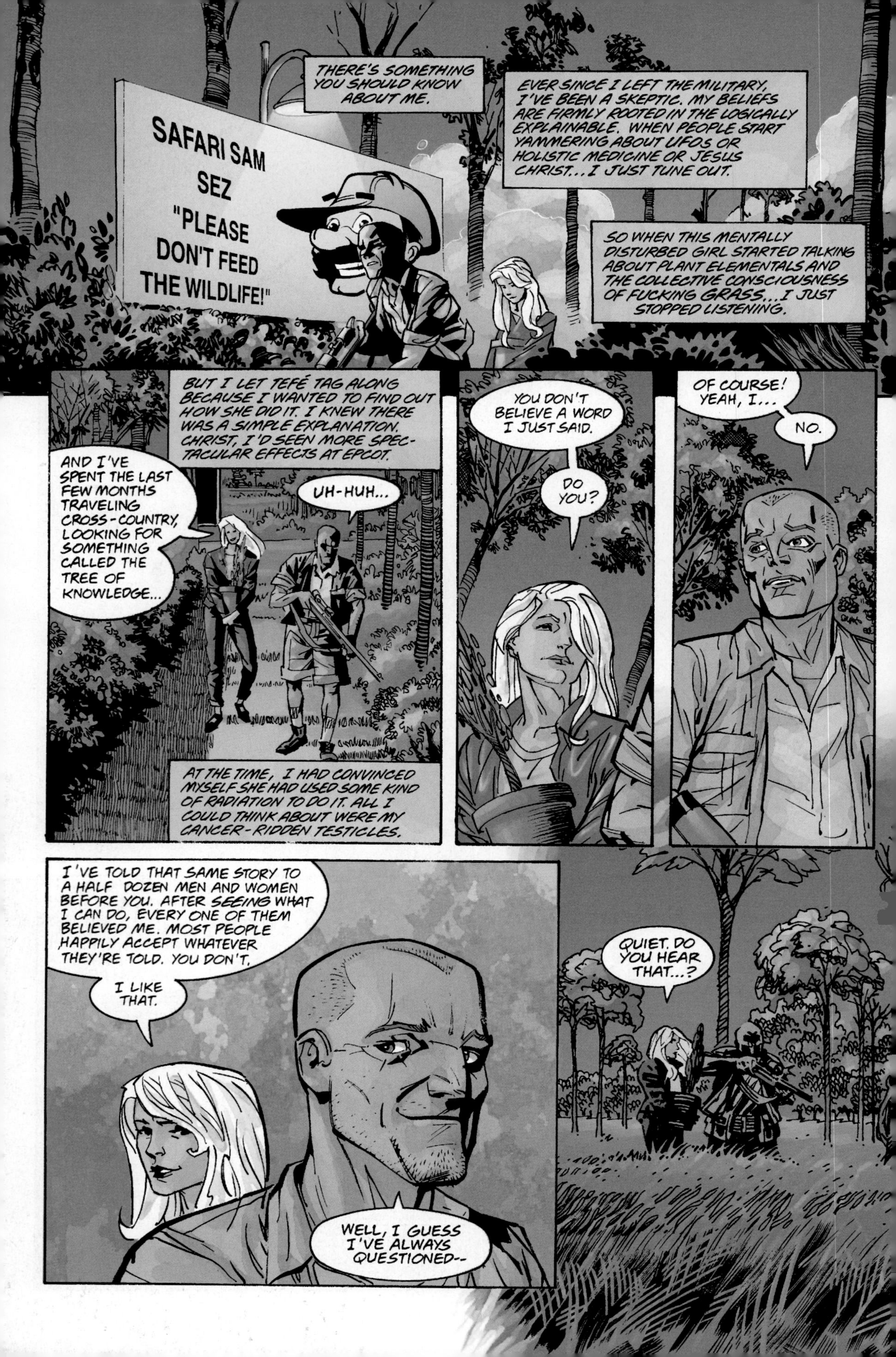
THERE'S SOMETHING YOU SHOULD KNOW ABOUT ME.
SAFARI SAM SEZ "PLEASE DON'T FEED THE WILDLIFE!"
EVER SINCE I LEFT THE MILITARY, I'VE BEEN A SKEPTIC. MY BELIEFS ARE FIRMLY ROOTED IN THE LOGICALLY EXPLAINABLE. WHEN PEOPLE START YAMMERING ABOUT UFOS OR HOLISTIC MEDICINE OR JESUS CHRIST... I JUST TUNE OUT.
SO WHEN THIS MENTALLY DISTURBED GIRL STARTED TALKING ABOUT PLANT ELEMENTALS AND THE COLLECTIVE CONSCIOUSNESS OF FUCKING GRASS... I JUST STOPPED LISTENING.
BUT I LET TEFÉ TAG ALONG BECAUSE I WANTED TO FIND OUT HOW SHE DID IT. I KNEW THERE WAS A SIMPLE EXPLANATION. CHRIST, I'D SEEN MORE SPECTACULAR EFFECTS AT EPCOT.
AND I'VE SPENT THE LAST FEW MONTHS TRAVELING CROSS-COUNTRY, LOOKING FOR SOMETHING CALLED THE TREE OF KNOWLEDGE...
UH-HUH...
AT THE TIME, I HAD CONVINCED MYSELF SHE HAD USED SOME KIND OF RADIATION TO DO IT. ALL I COULD THINK ABOUT WERE MY CANCER-RIDDEN TESTICLES.
YOU DON'T BELIEVE A WORD I JUST SAID.
DO YOU?
OF COURSE! YEAH, I...
NO.
I'VE TOLD THAT SAME STORY TO A HALF DOZEN MEN AND WOMEN BEFORE YOU. AFTER SEEING WHAT I CAN DO, EVERY ONE OF THEM BELIEVED ME. MOST PEOPLE HAPPILY ACCEPT WHATEVER THEY'RE TOLD. YOU DON'T.
I LIKE THAT.
WELL, I GUESS I'VE ALWAYS QUESTIONED--
QUIET. DO YOU HEAR THAT...?

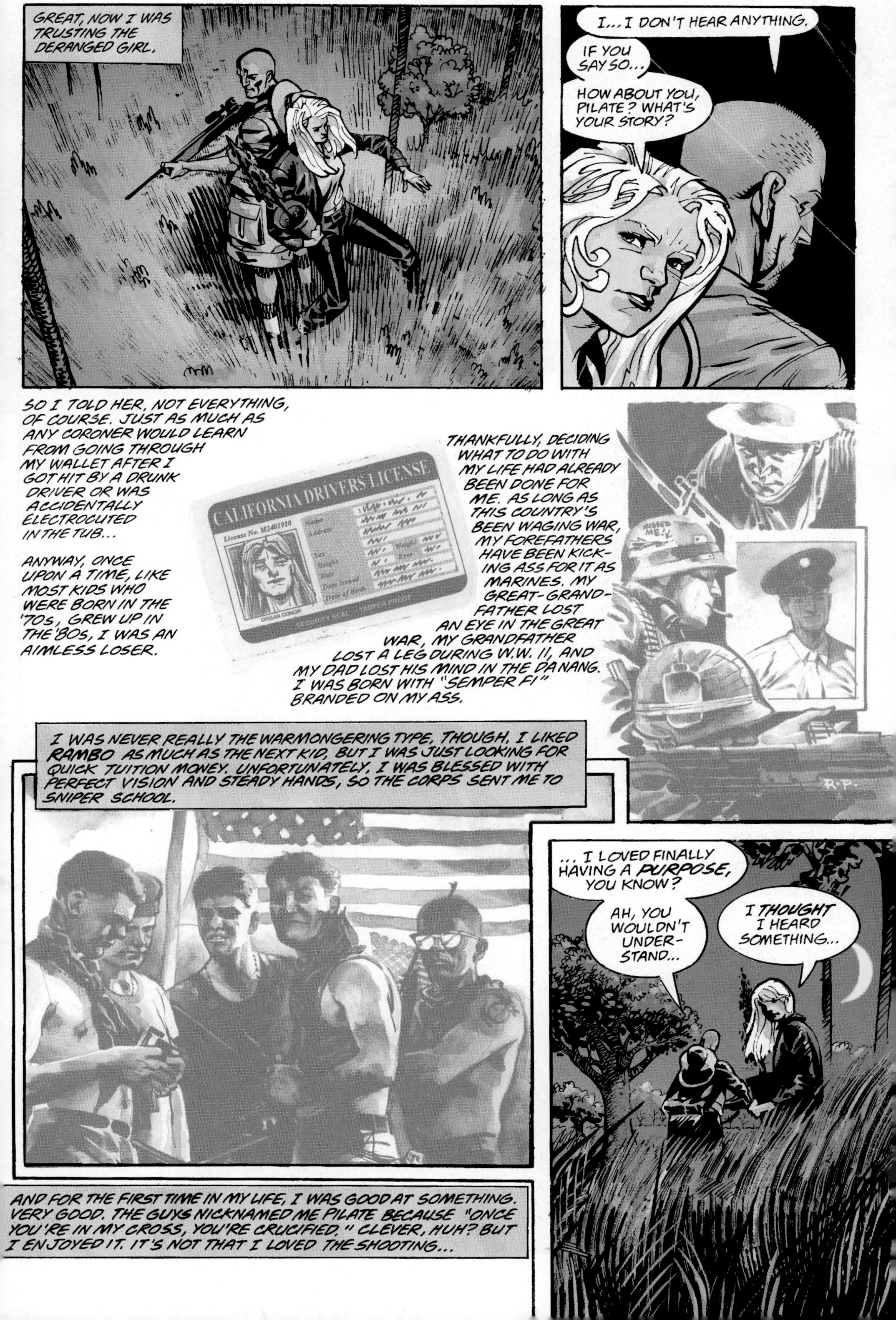

GREAT, NOW I WAS TRUSTING THE DERANGED GIRL.
I... I DON'T HEAR ANYTHING.
IF YOU SAY SO...
HOW ABOUT YOU, PILATE? WHAT'S YOUR STORY?
SO I TOLD HER. NOT EVERYTHING, OF COURSE. JUST AS MUCH AS ANY CORONER WOULD LEARN FROM GOING THROUGH MY WALLET AFTER I GOT HIT BY A DRUNK DRIVER OR WAS ACCIDENTALLY ELECTROCUTED IN THE TUB...
ANYWAY, ONCE UPON A TIME, LIKE MOST KIDS WHO WERE BORN IN THE '70S, GREW UP IN THE '80S, I WAS AN AIMLESS LOSER.
CALIFORNIA DRIVERS LICENSE
License No. M2401910
Name
Address
Sex
Height
Weight
Eyes
Hair
Date Issued
Date of Birth
ORGAN DONOR
SECURITY SEAL · TAMPER PROOF
THANKFULLY, DECIDING WHAT TO DO WITH MY LIFE HAD ALREADY BEEN DONE FOR ME. AS LONG AS THIS COUNTRY'S BEEN WAGING WAR, MY FOREFATHERS HAVE BEEN KICKING ASS FOR IT AS MARINES. MY GREAT-GRANDFATHER LOST AN EYE IN THE GREAT WAR, MY GRANDFATHER LOST A LEG DURING W.W. II, AND MY DAD LOST HIS MIND IN THE DA NANG. I WAS BORN WITH "SEMPER FI" BRANDED ON MY ASS.
MISSED ME!
R.P.
I WAS NEVER REALLY THE WARMONGERING TYPE, THOUGH. I LIKED RAMBO AS MUCH AS THE NEXT KID, BUT I WAS JUST LOOKING FOR QUICK TUITION MONEY. UNFORTUNATELY, I WAS BLESSED WITH PERFECT VISION AND STEADY HANDS, SO THE CORPS SENT ME TO SNIPER SCHOOL.
AND FOR THE FIRST TIME IN MY LIFE, I WAS GOOD AT SOMETHING. VERY GOOD. THE GUYS NICKNAMED ME PILATE BECAUSE "ONCE YOU'RE IN MY CROSS, YOU'RE CRUCIFIED." CLEVER, HUH? BUT I ENJOYED IT. IT'S NOT THAT I LOVED THE SHOOTING...
... I LOVED FINALLY HAVING A PURPOSE, YOU KNOW?
AH, YOU WOULDN'T UNDERSTAND...
I THOUGHT I HEARD SOMETHING...

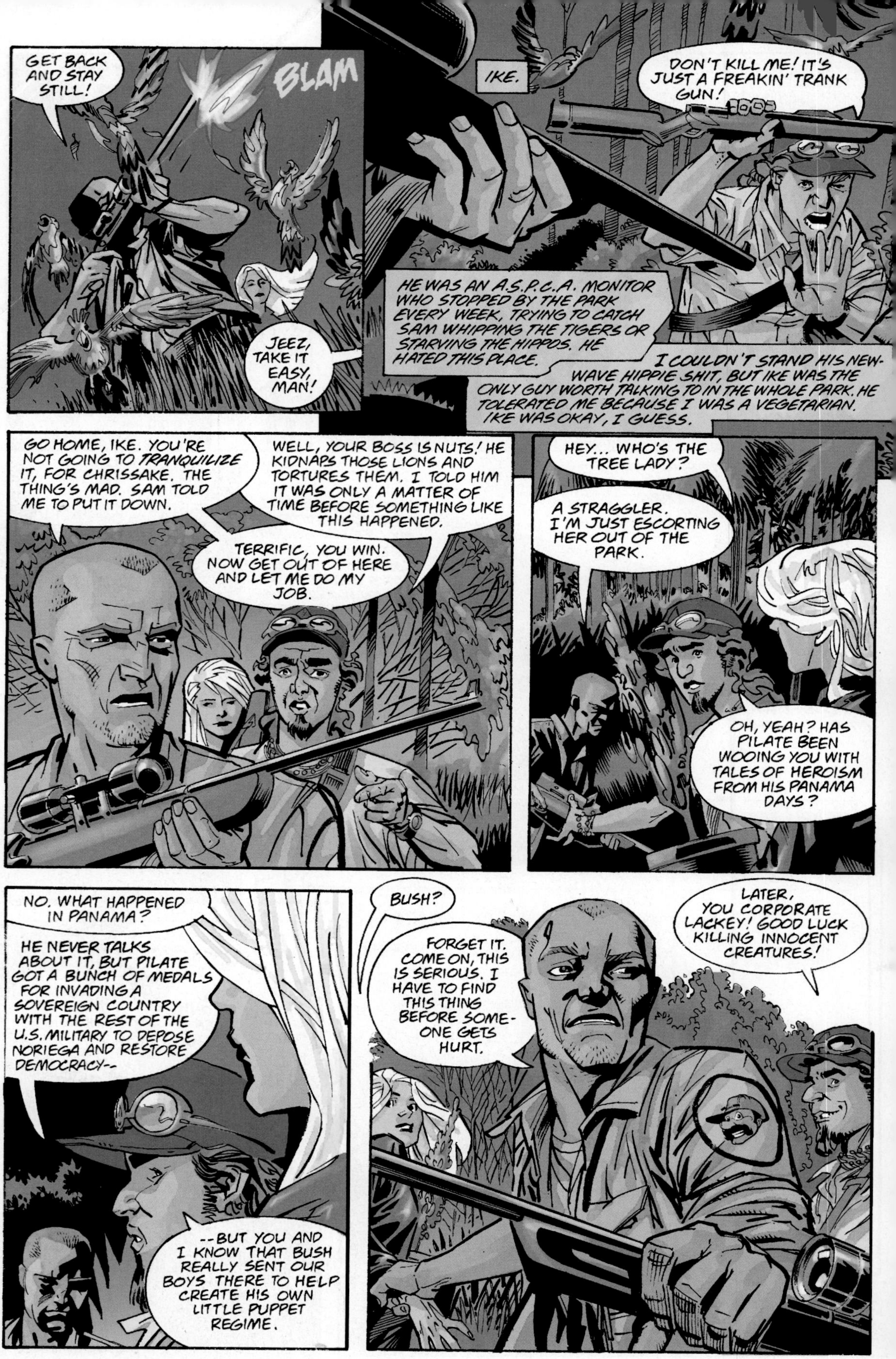
GET BACK AND STAY STILL!
BLAM
JEEZ, TAKE IT EASY, MAN!
IKE.
DON'T KILL ME! IT'S JUST A FREAKIN' TRANK GUN!
HE WAS AN A.S.P.C.A. MONITOR WHO STOPPED BY THE PARK EVERY WEEK, TRYING TO CATCH SAM WHIPPING THE TIGERS OR STARVING THE HIPPOS. HE HATED THIS PLACE.
I COULDN'T STAND HIS NEW-WAVE HIPPIE SHIT, BUT IKE WAS THE ONLY GUY WORTH TALKING TO IN THE WHOLE PARK. HE TOLERATED ME BECAUSE I WAS A VEGETARIAN. IKE WAS OKAY, I GUESS.
GO HOME, IKE. YOU'RE NOT GOING TO TRANQUILIZE IT, FOR CHRISSAKE. THE THING'S MAD. SAM TOLD ME TO PUT IT DOWN.
WELL, YOUR BOSS IS NUTS! HE KIDNAPS THOSE LIONS AND TORTURES THEM. I TOLD HIM IT WAS ONLY A MATTER OF TIME BEFORE SOMETHING LIKE THIS HAPPENED.
TERRIFIC, YOU WIN. NOW GET OUT OF HERE AND LET ME DO MY JOB.
HEY... WHO'S THE TREE LADY?
A STRAGGLER. I'M JUST ESCORTING HER OUT OF THE PARK.
OH, YEAH? HAS PILATE BEEN WOOING YOU WITH TALES OF HEROISM FROM HIS PANAMA DAYS?
NO. WHAT HAPPENED IN PANAMA?
HE NEVER TALKS ABOUT IT, BUT PILATE GOT A BUNCH OF MEDALS FOR INVADING A SOVEREIGN COUNTRY WITH THE REST OF THE U.S. MILITARY TO DEPOSE NORIEGA AND RESTORE DEMOCRACY--
--BUT YOU AND I KNOW THAT BUSH REALLY SENT OUR BOYS THERE TO HELP CREATE HIS OWN LITTLE PUPPET REGIME.
BUSH?
FORGET IT. COME ON, THIS IS SERIOUS. I HAVE TO FIND THIS THING BEFORE SOME-ONE GETS HURT.
LATER, YOU CORPORATE LACKEY! GOOD LUCK KILLING INNOCENT CREATURES!

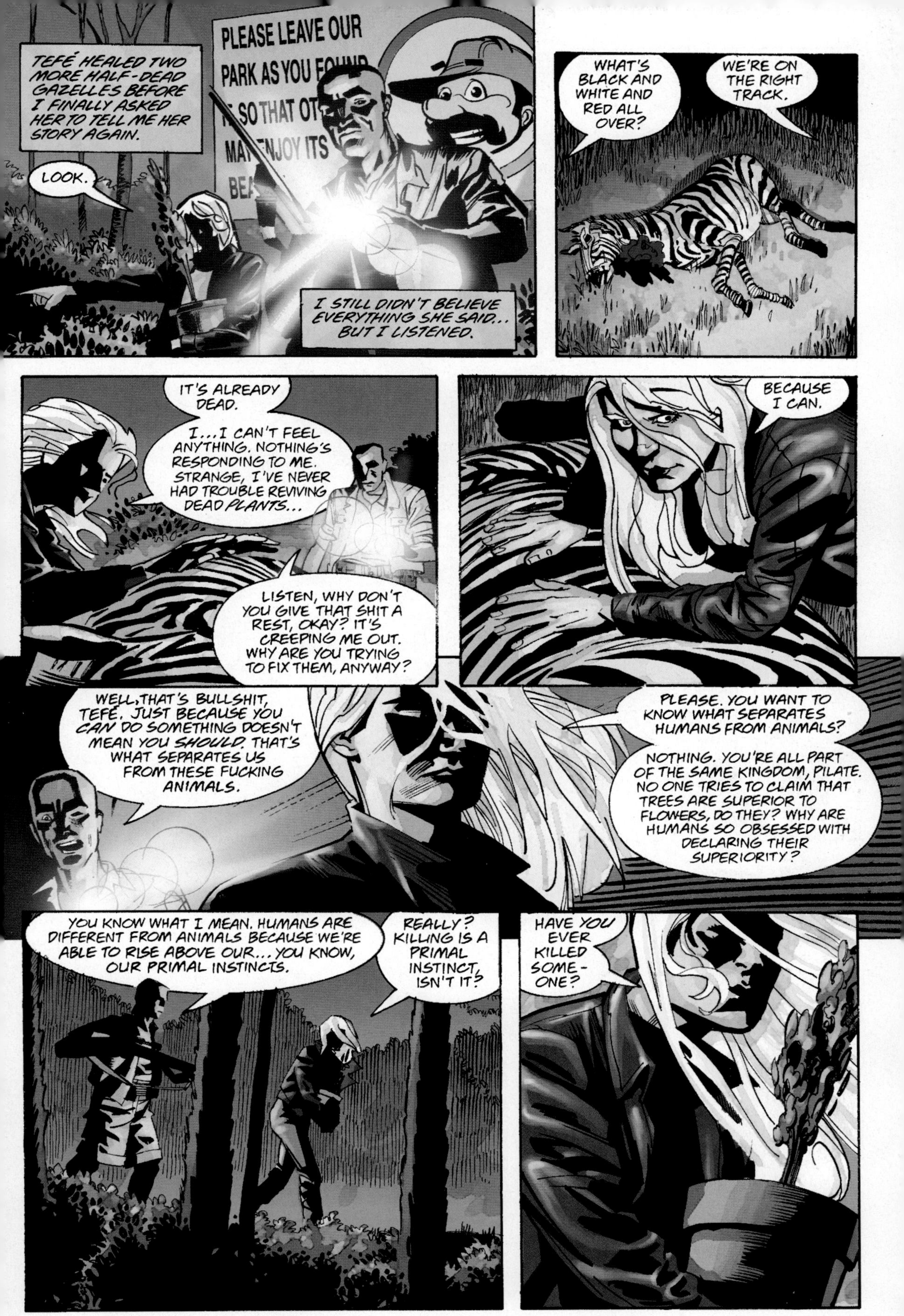
PLEASE LEAVE OUR PARK AS YOU FOUN
SO THAT OT
MAY ENJOY ITS
BEA
TEFÉ HEALED TWO MORE HALF-DEAD GAZELLES BEFORE I FINALLY ASKED HER TO TELL ME HER STORY AGAIN.
LOOK.
I STILL DIDN'T BELIEVE EVERYTHING SHE SAID... BUT I LISTENED.
WHAT'S BLACK AND WHITE AND RED ALL OVER?
WE'RE ON THE RIGHT TRACK.
IT'S ALREADY DEAD.
I... I CAN'T FEEL ANYTHING. NOTHING'S RESPONDING TO ME. STRANGE, I'VE NEVER HAD TROUBLE REVIVING DEAD PLANTS...
LISTEN, WHY DON'T YOU GIVE THAT SHIT A REST, OKAY? IT'S CREEPING ME OUT. WHY ARE YOU TRYING TO FIX THEM, ANYWAY?
BECAUSE I CAN.
WELL, THAT'S BULLSHIT, TEFÉ. JUST BECAUSE YOU CAN DO SOMETHING DOESN'T MEAN YOU SHOULD. THAT'S WHAT SEPARATES US FROM THESE FUCKING ANIMALS.
PLEASE. YOU WANT TO KNOW WHAT SEPARATES HUMANS FROM ANIMALS?
NOTHING. YOU'RE ALL PART OF THE SAME KINGDOM, PILATE. NO ONE TRIES TO CLAIM THAT TREES ARE SUPERIOR TO FLOWERS, DO THEY? WHY ARE HUMANS SO OBSESSED WITH DECLARING THEIR SUPERIORITY?
YOU KNOW WHAT I MEAN. HUMANS ARE DIFFERENT FROM ANIMALS BECAUSE WE'RE ABLE TO RISE ABOVE OUR... YOU KNOW, OUR PRIMAL INSTINCTS.
REALLY? KILLING IS A PRIMAL INSTINCT, ISN'T IT?
HAVE YOU EVER KILLED SOME-ONE?

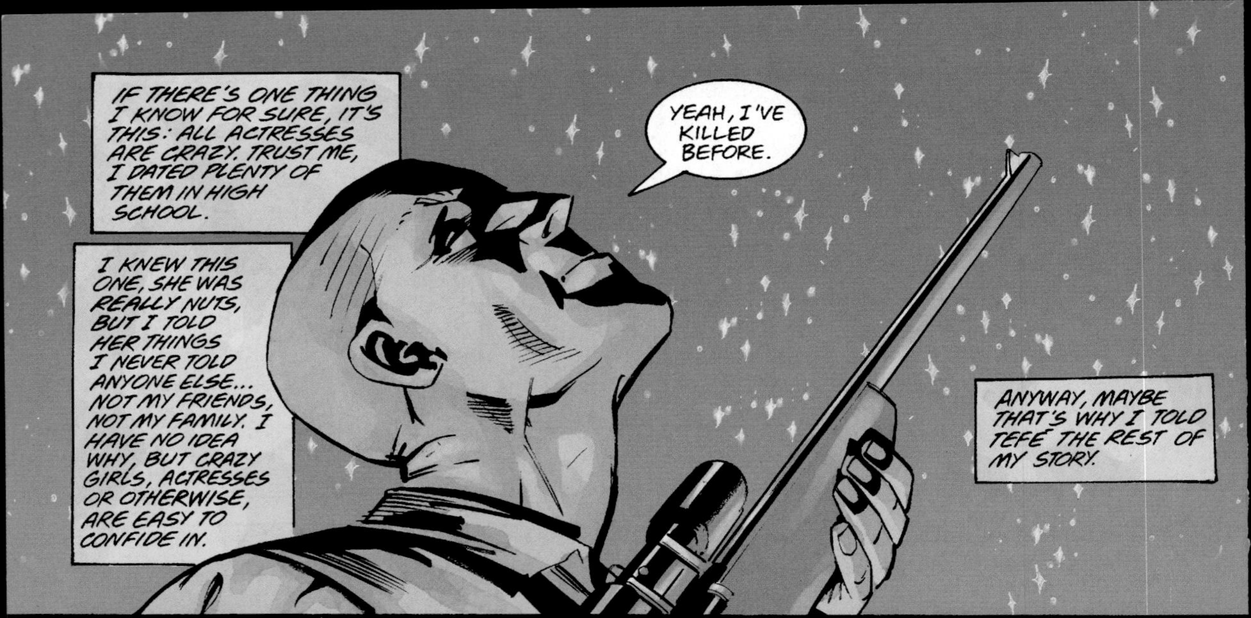
IF THERE'S ONE THING I KNOW FOR SURE, IT'S THIS: ALL ACTRESSES ARE CRAZY. TRUST ME, I DATED PLENTY OF THEM IN HIGH SCHOOL.
YEAH, I'VE KILLED BEFORE.
I KNEW THIS ONE, SHE WAS REALLY NUTS, BUT I TOLD HER THINGS I NEVER TOLD ANYONE ELSE... NOT MY FRIENDS, NOT MY FAMILY. I HAVE NO IDEA WHY, BUT CRAZY GIRLS, ACTRESSES OR OTHERWISE, ARE EASY TO CONFIDE IN.
ANYWAY, MAYBE THAT'S WHY I TOLD TEFÉ THE REST OF MY STORY.
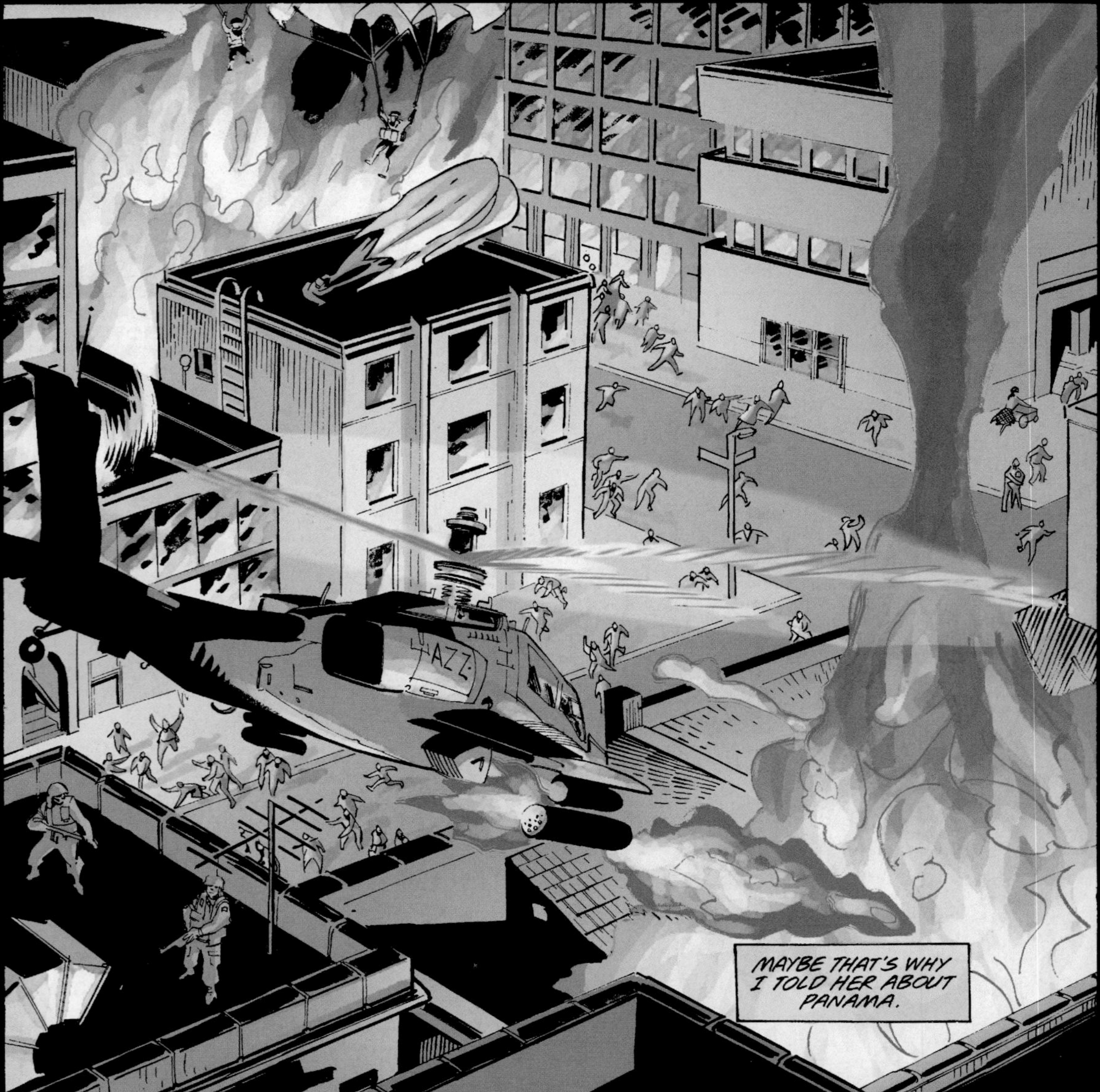
MAYBE THAT'S WHY I TOLD HER ABOUT PANAMA.

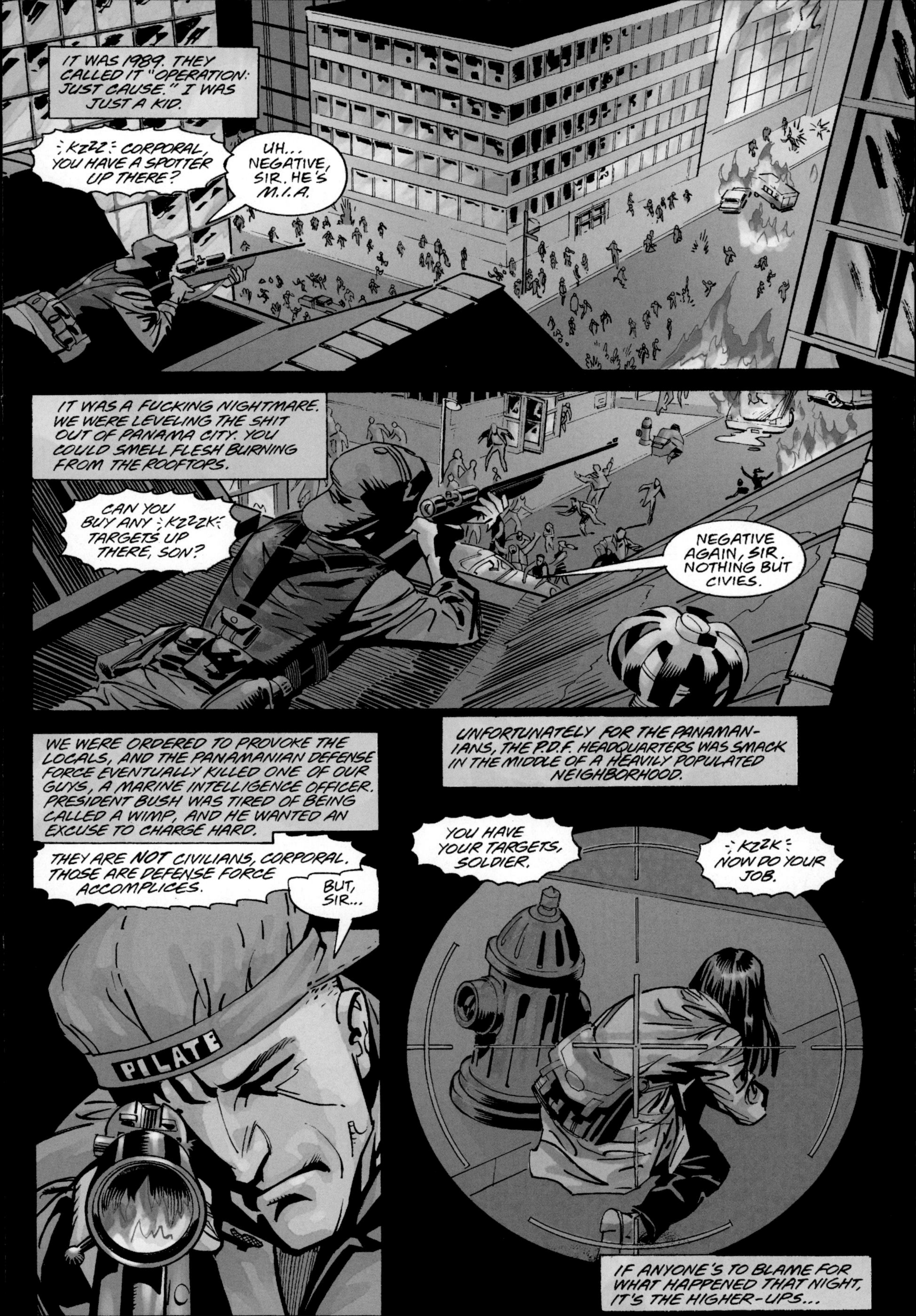
IT WAS 1989. THEY CALLED IT "OPERATION: JUST CAUSE." I WAS JUST A KID.
-KZZZ- CORPORAL, YOU HAVE A SPOTTER UP THERE?
UH... NEGATIVE, SIR. HE'S M.I.A.
IT WAS A FUCKING NIGHTMARE. WE WERE LEVELING THE SHIT OUT OF PANAMA CITY. YOU COULD SMELL FLESH BURNING FROM THE ROOFTOPS.
CAN YOU BUY ANY -KZZZK- TARGETS UP THERE, SON?
NEGATIVE AGAIN, SIR. NOTHING BUT CIVIES.
WE WERE ORDERED TO PROVOKE THE LOCALS, AND THE PANAMANIAN DEFENSE FORCE EVENTUALLY KILLED ONE OF OUR GUYS, A MARINE INTELLIGENCE OFFICER. PRESIDENT BUSH WAS TIRED OF BEING CALLED A WIMP, AND HE WANTED AN EXCUSE TO CHARGE HARD.
THEY ARE NOT CIVILIANS, CORPORAL. THOSE ARE DEFENSE FORCE ACCOMPLICES.
BUT, SIR...
PILATE
UNFORTUNATELY FOR THE PANAMANIANS, THE P.D.F. HEADQUARTERS WAS SMACK IN THE MIDDLE OF A HEAVILY POPULATED NEIGHBORHOOD.
YOU HAVE YOUR TARGETS, SOLDIER.
-KZZK- NOW DO YOUR JOB.
IF ANYONE'S TO BLAME FOR WHAT HAPPENED THAT NIGHT, IT'S THE HIGHER-UPS...

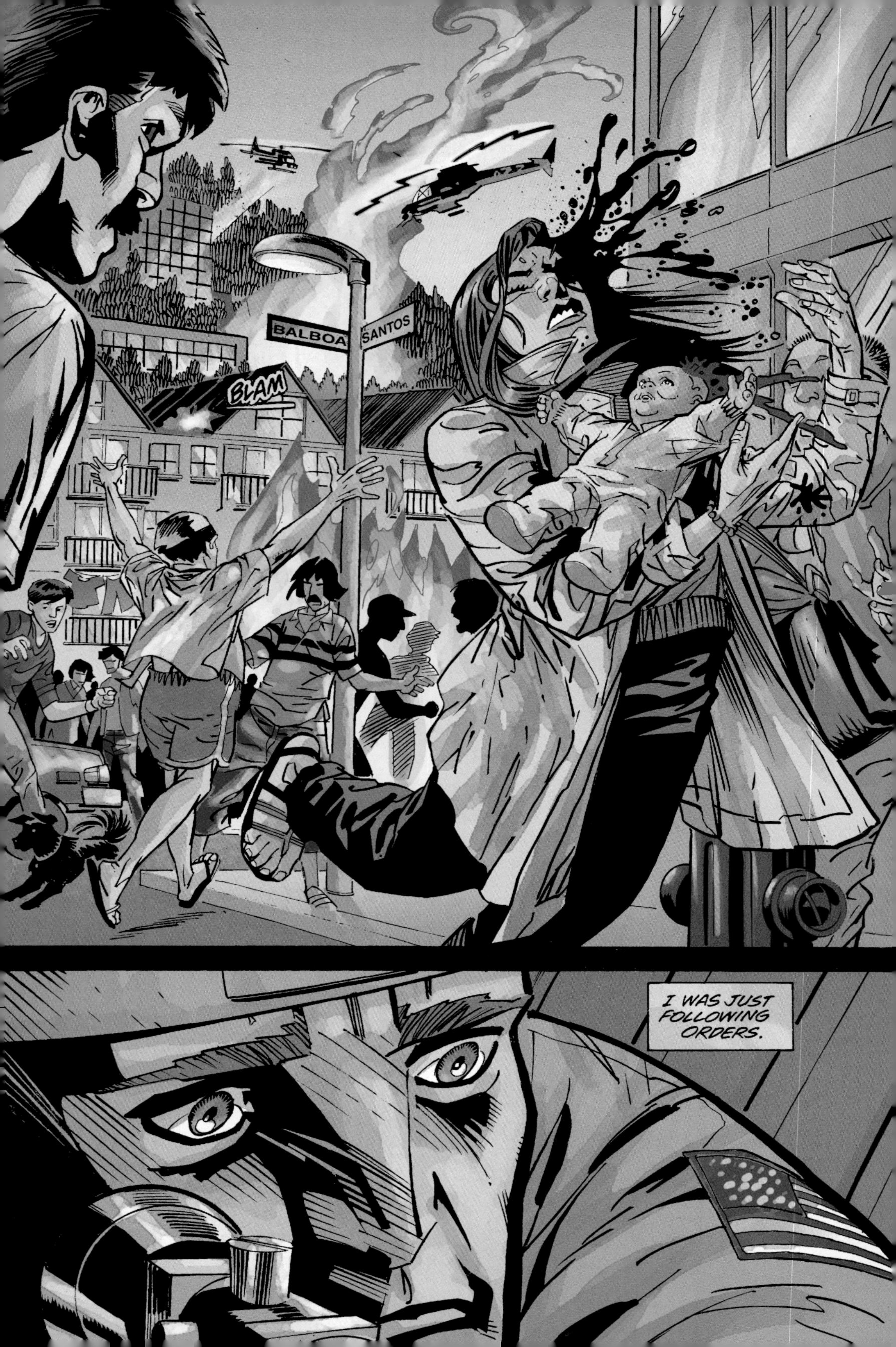
BALBOA
SANTOS
BLAM
I WAS JUST FOLLOWING ORDERS.

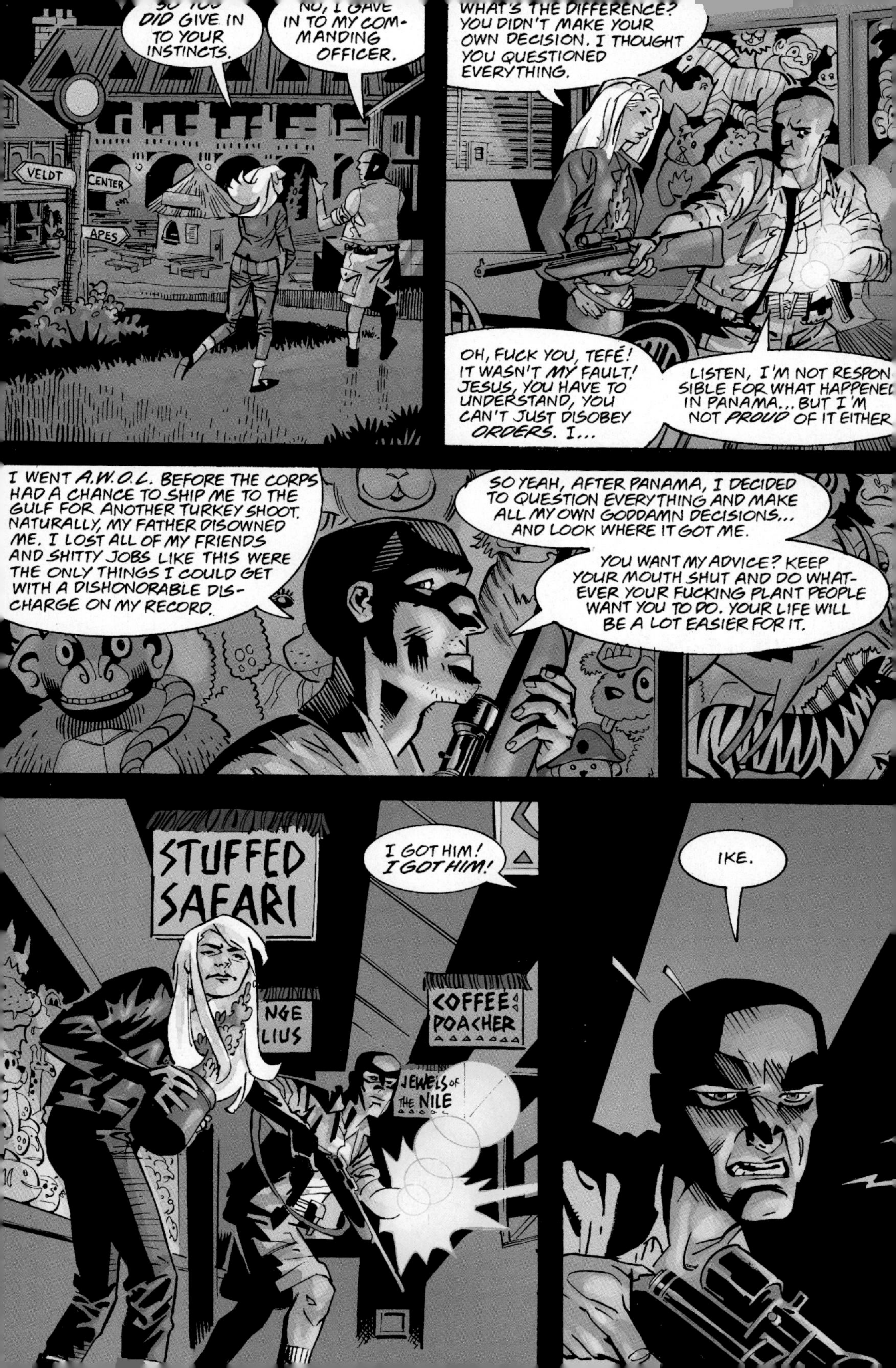
DID GIVE IN TO YOUR INSTINCTS.
IN TO MY COMMANDING OFFICER.
VELDT
CENTER
APES
WHAT'S THE DIFFERENCE? YOU DIDN'T MAKE YOUR OWN DECISION. I THOUGHT YOU QUESTIONED EVERYTHING.
OH, FUCK YOU, TEFÉ! IT WASN'T MY FAULT! JESUS, YOU HAVE TO UNDERSTAND, YOU CAN'T JUST DISOBEY ORDERS. I...
LISTEN, I'M NOT RESPONSIBLE FOR WHAT HAPPENED IN PANAMA... BUT I'M NOT PROUD OF IT EITHER.
I WENT A.W.O.L. BEFORE THE CORPS HAD A CHANCE TO SHIP ME TO THE GULF FOR ANOTHER TURKEY SHOOT. NATURALLY, MY FATHER DISOWNED ME. I LOST ALL OF MY FRIENDS AND SHITTY JOBS LIKE THIS WERE THE ONLY THINGS I COULD GET WITH A DISHONORABLE DISCHARGE ON MY RECORD.
SO YEAH, AFTER PANAMA, I DECIDED TO QUESTION EVERYTHING AND MAKE ALL MY OWN GODDAMN DECISIONS... AND LOOK WHERE IT GOT ME.
YOU WANT MY ADVICE? KEEP YOUR MOUTH SHUT AND DO WHATEVER YOUR FUCKING PLANT PEOPLE WANT YOU TO DO. YOUR LIFE WILL BE A LOT EASIER FOR IT.
STUFFED SAFARI
I GOT HIM! I GOT HIM!
NGE LIUS
COFFEE POACHER
JEWELS OF THE NILE
IKE.

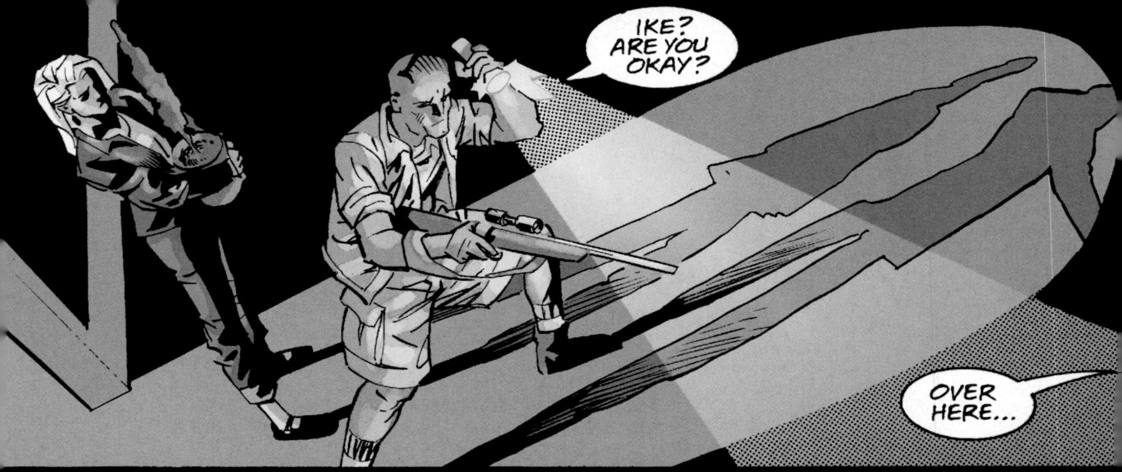
IKE? ARE YOU OKAY?
OVER HERE...

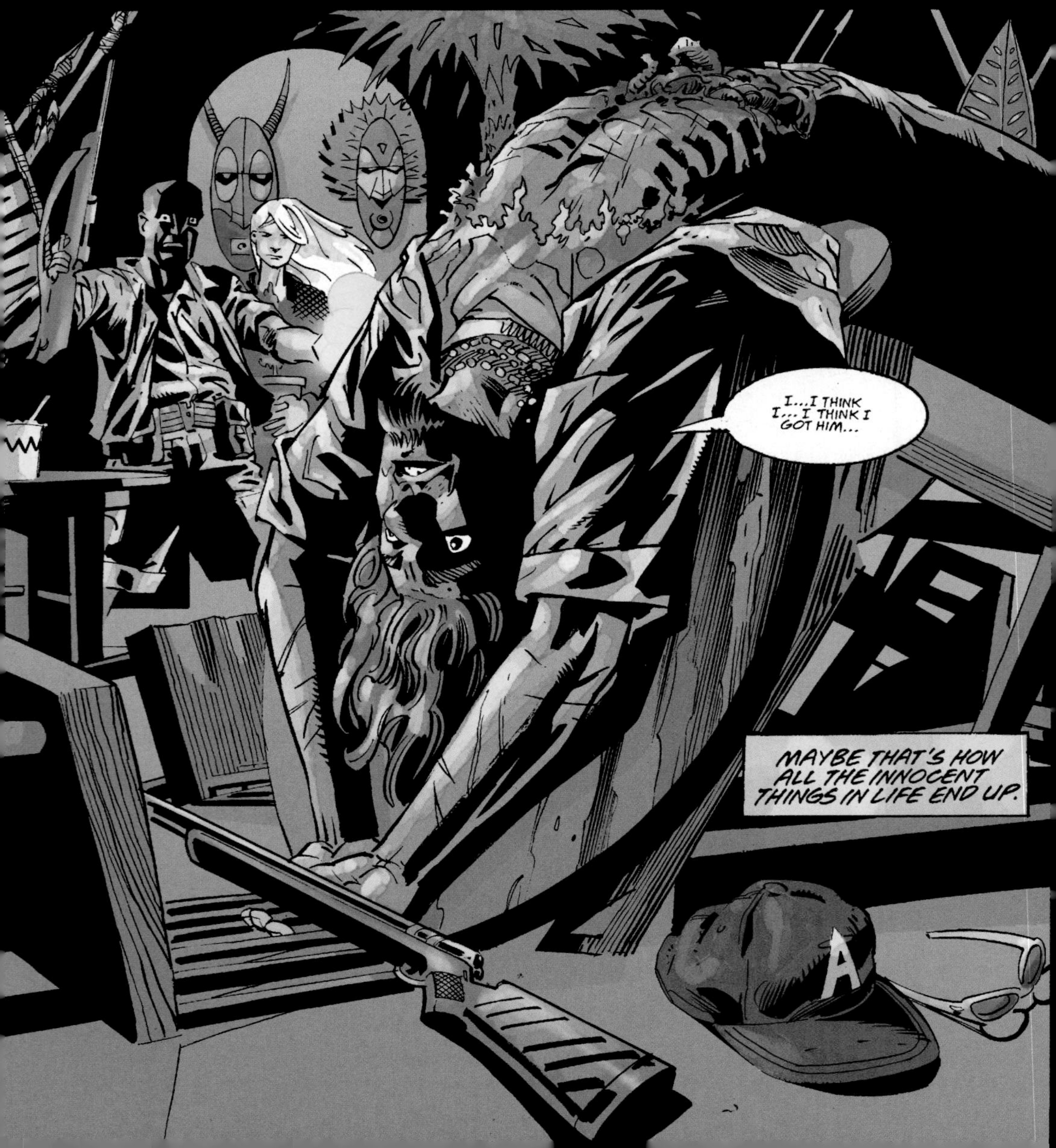
I...I THINK I... I THINK I GOT HIM...
MAYBE THAT'S HOW ALL THE INNOCENT THINGS IN LIFE END UP.

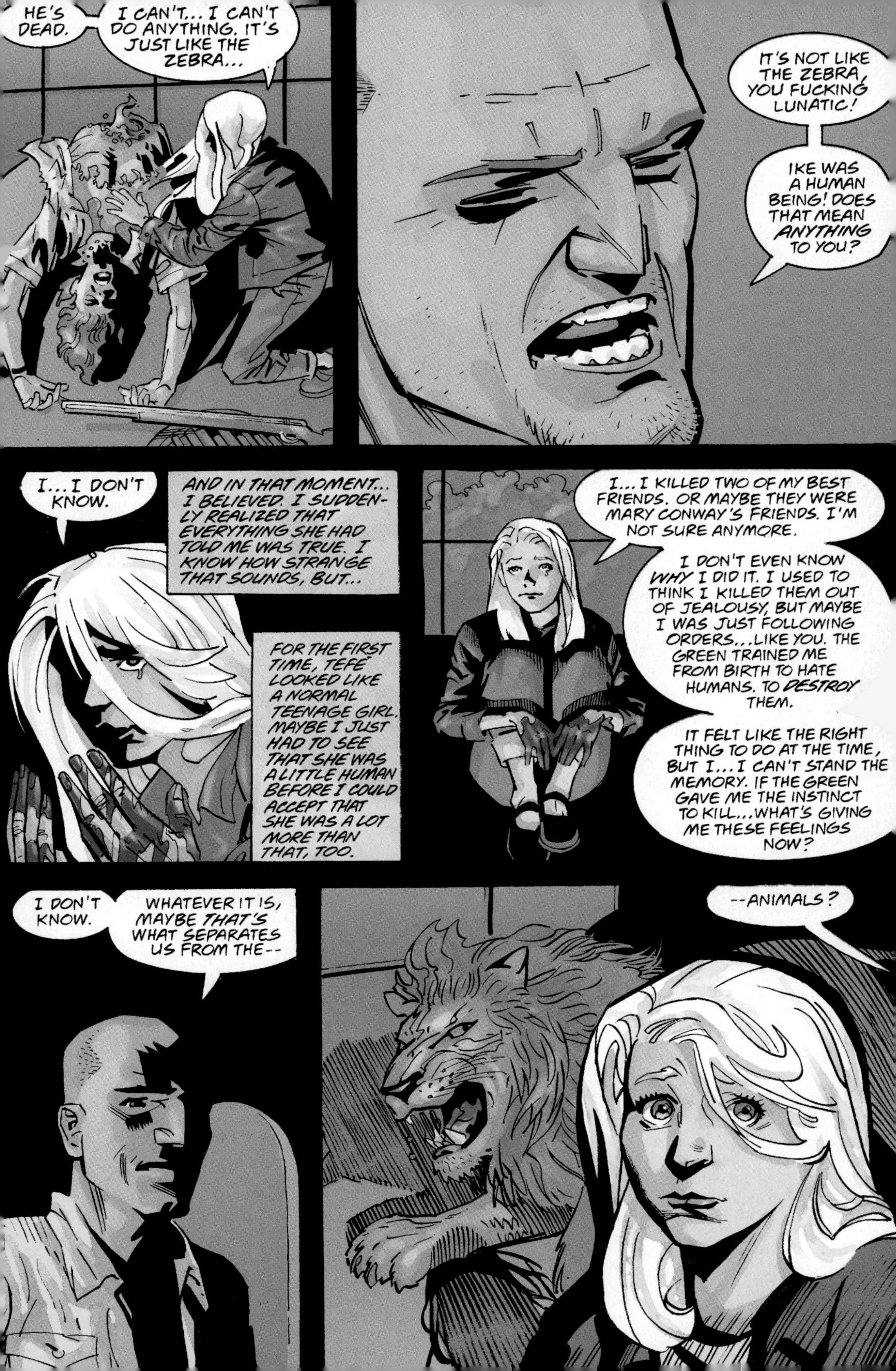
HE'S DEAD.
I CAN'T... I CAN'T DO ANYTHING. IT'S JUST LIKE THE ZEBRA...
IT'S NOT LIKE THE ZEBRA, YOU FUCKING LUNATIC!
IKE WAS A HUMAN BEING! DOES THAT MEAN *ANYTHING* TO YOU?
I... I DON'T KNOW.
AND IN THAT MOMENT... I BELIEVED. I SUDDENLY REALIZED THAT EVERYTHING SHE HAD TOLD ME WAS TRUE. I KNOW HOW STRANGE THAT SOUNDS, BUT...
FOR THE FIRST TIME, TEFÉ LOOKED LIKE A NORMAL TEENAGE GIRL. MAYBE I JUST HAD TO SEE THAT SHE WAS A LITTLE HUMAN BEFORE I COULD ACCEPT THAT SHE WAS A LOT MORE THAN THAT, TOO.
I... I KILLED TWO OF MY BEST FRIENDS. OR MAYBE THEY WERE MARY CONWAY'S FRIENDS. I'M NOT SURE ANYMORE.
I DON'T EVEN KNOW *WHY* I DID IT. I USED TO THINK I KILLED THEM OUT OF JEALOUSY, BUT MAYBE I WAS JUST FOLLOWING ORDERS... LIKE YOU. THE GREEN TRAINED ME FROM BIRTH TO HATE HUMANS. TO *DESTROY* THEM.
IT FELT LIKE THE RIGHT THING TO DO AT THE TIME, BUT I... I CAN'T STAND THE MEMORY. IF THE GREEN GAVE ME THE INSTINCT TO KILL... WHAT'S GIVING ME THESE FEELINGS NOW?
I DON'T KNOW.
WHATEVER IT IS, MAYBE *THAT'S* WHAT SEPARATES US FROM THE--
--ANIMALS?

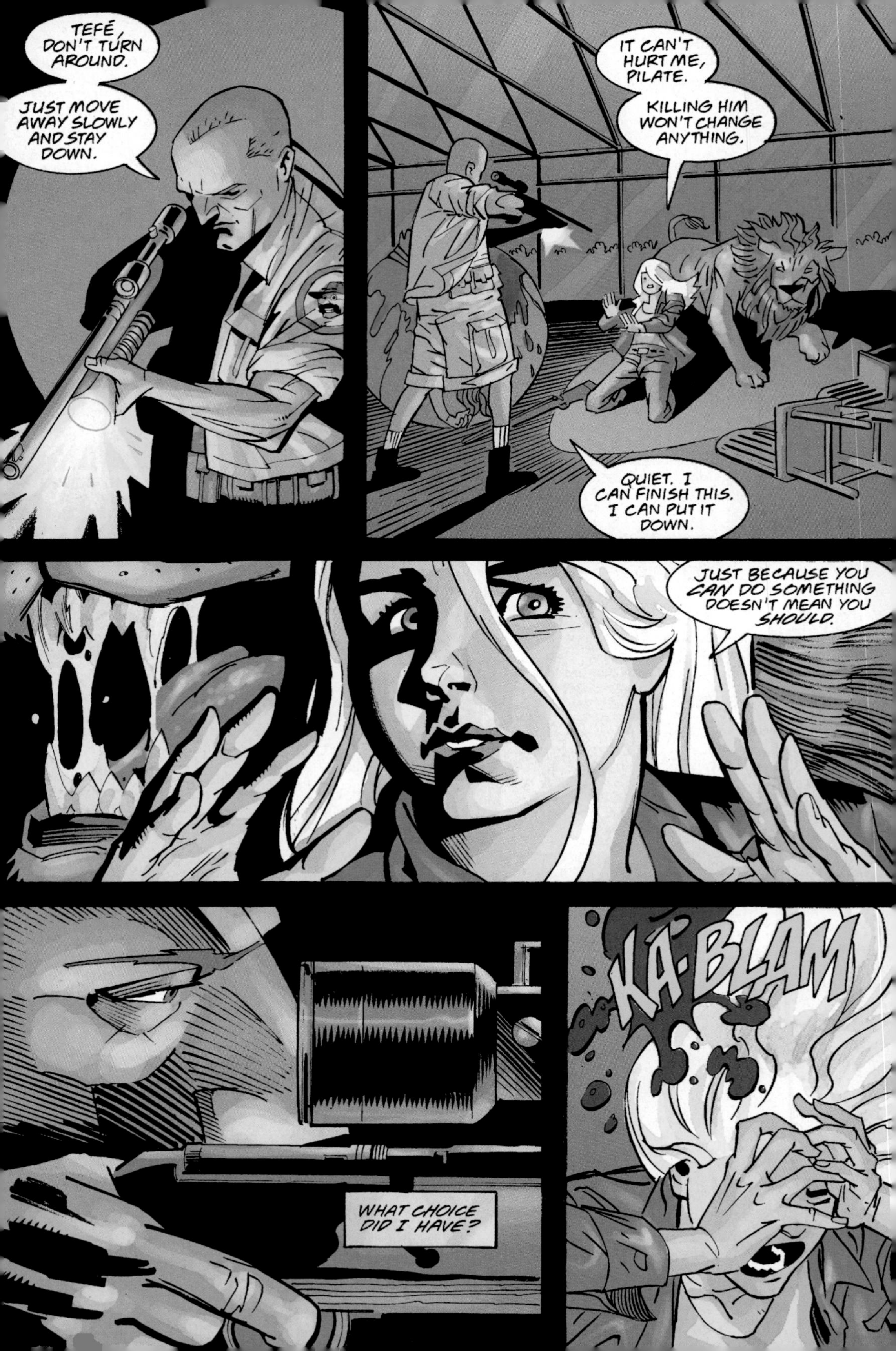
TEFÉ, DON'T TURN AROUND.
JUST MOVE AWAY SLOWLY AND STAY DOWN.
IT CAN'T HURT ME, PILATE.
KILLING HIM WON'T CHANGE ANYTHING.
QUIET. I CAN FINISH THIS. I CAN PUT IT DOWN.
JUST BECAUSE YOU CAN DO SOMETHING DOESN'T MEAN YOU SHOULD.
WHAT CHOICE DID I HAVE?
KA-BLAM

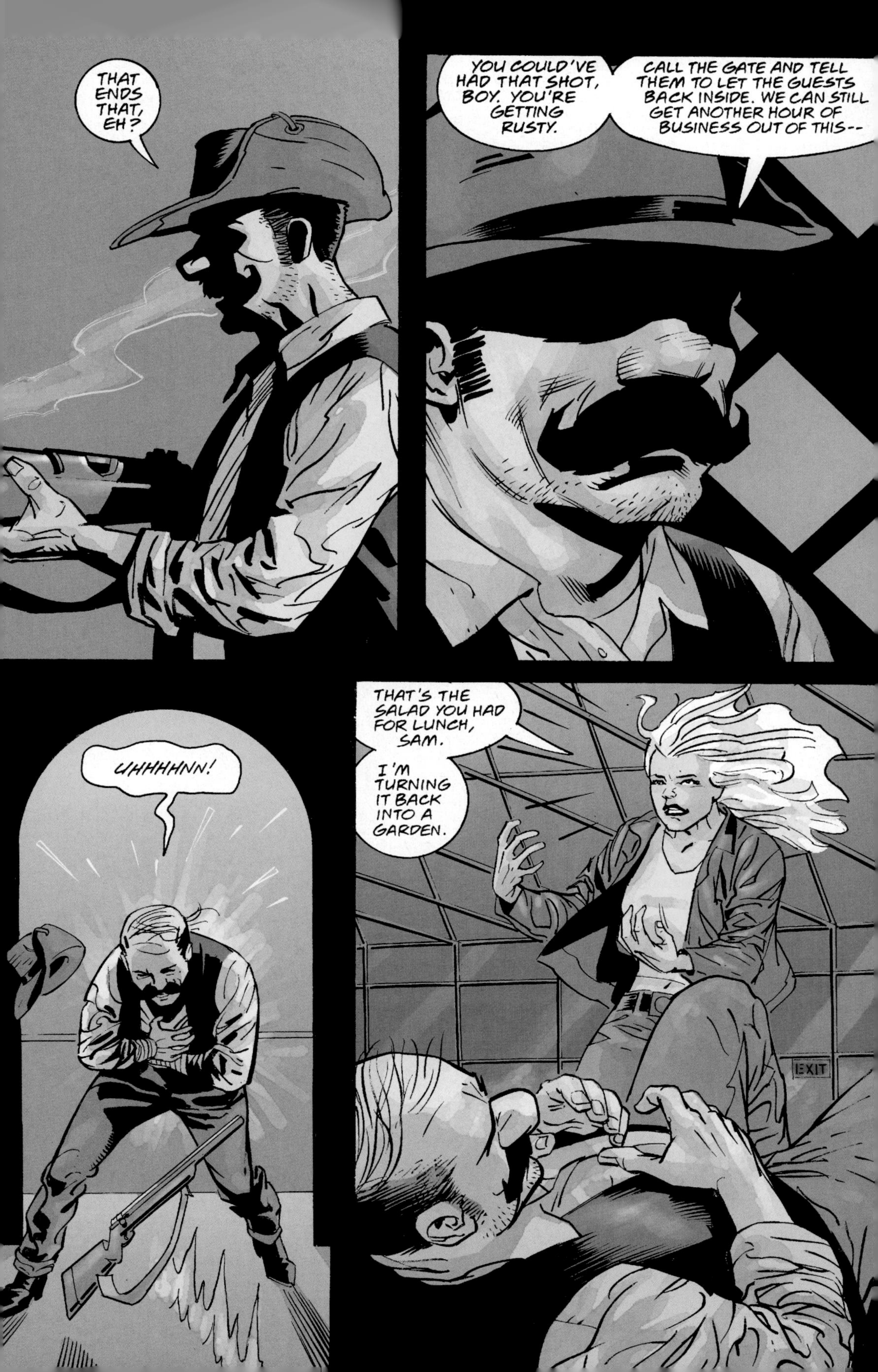
THAT ENDS THAT, EH?
YOU COULD'VE HAD THAT SHOT, BOY. YOU'RE GETTING RUSTY.
CALL THE GATE AND TELL THEM TO LET THE GUESTS BACK INSIDE. WE CAN STILL GET ANOTHER HOUR OF BUSINESS OUT OF THIS--
UHHHHNN!
THAT'S THE SALAD YOU HAD FOR LUNCH, SAM.
I'M TURNING IT BACK INTO A GARDEN.
EXIT

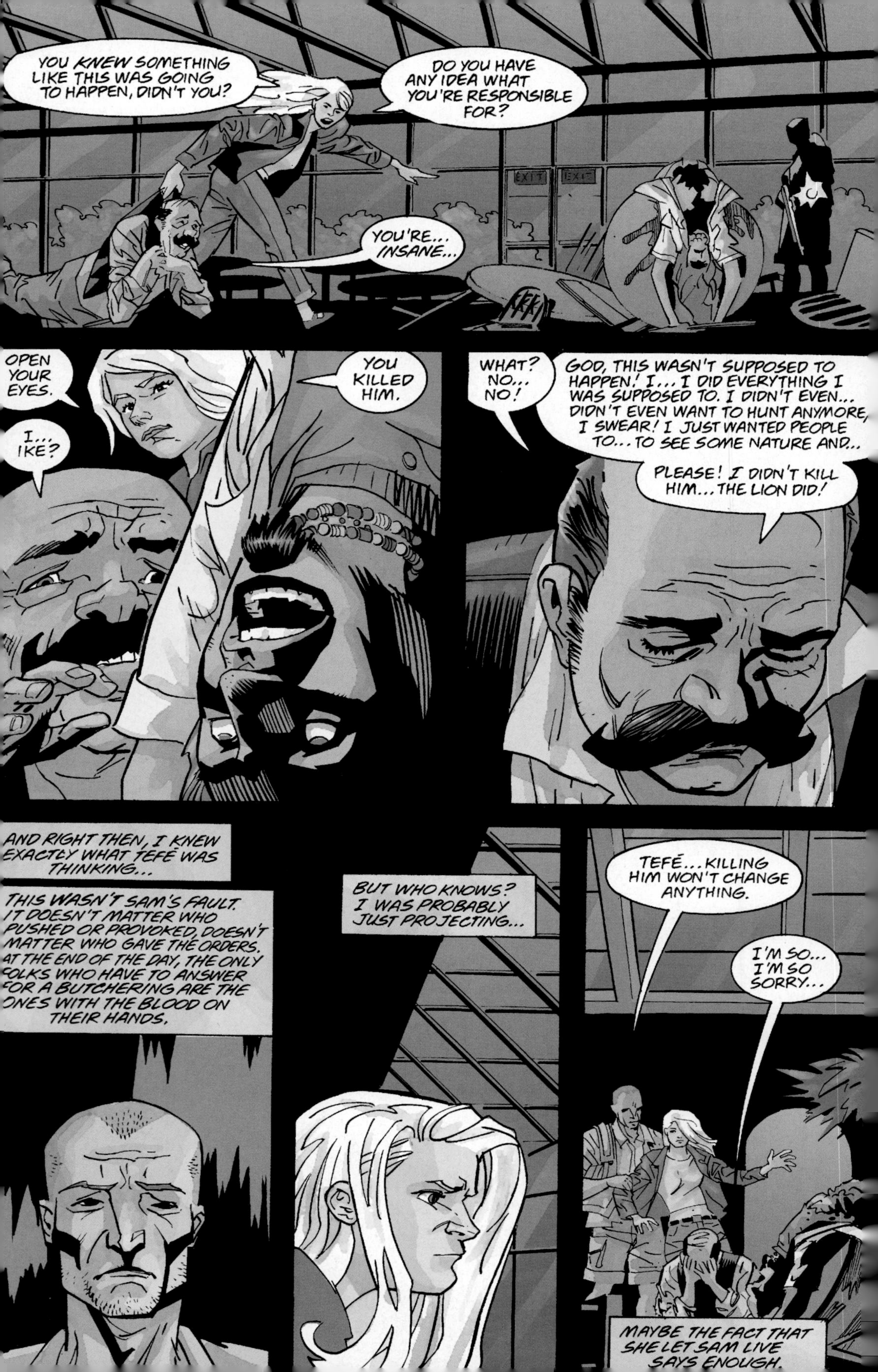
YOU KNEW SOMETHING LIKE THIS WAS GOING TO HAPPEN, DIDN'T YOU?
DO YOU HAVE ANY IDEA WHAT YOU'RE RESPONSIBLE FOR?
YOU'RE... INSANE...
OPEN YOUR EYES.
I... IKE?
YOU KILLED HIM.
WHAT? NO... NO!
GOD, THIS WASN'T SUPPOSED TO HAPPEN! I... I DID EVERYTHING I WAS SUPPOSED TO. I DIDN'T EVEN... DIDN'T EVEN WANT TO HUNT ANYMORE, I SWEAR! I JUST WANTED PEOPLE TO... TO SEE SOME NATURE AND...
PLEASE! I DIDN'T KILL HIM... THE LION DID!
AND RIGHT THEN, I KNEW EXACTLY WHAT TEFÉ WAS THINKING...
THIS WASN'T SAM'S FAULT. IT DOESN'T MATTER WHO PUSHED OR PROVOKED, DOESN'T MATTER WHO GAVE THE ORDERS. AT THE END OF THE DAY, THE ONLY FOLKS WHO HAVE TO ANSWER FOR A BUTCHERING ARE THE ONES WITH THE BLOOD ON THEIR HANDS.
BUT WHO KNOWS? I WAS PROBABLY JUST PROJECTING...
TEFÉ... KILLING HIM WON'T CHANGE ANYTHING.
I'M SO... I'M SO SORRY...
MAYBE THE FACT THAT SHE LET SAM LIVE SAYS ENOUGH.

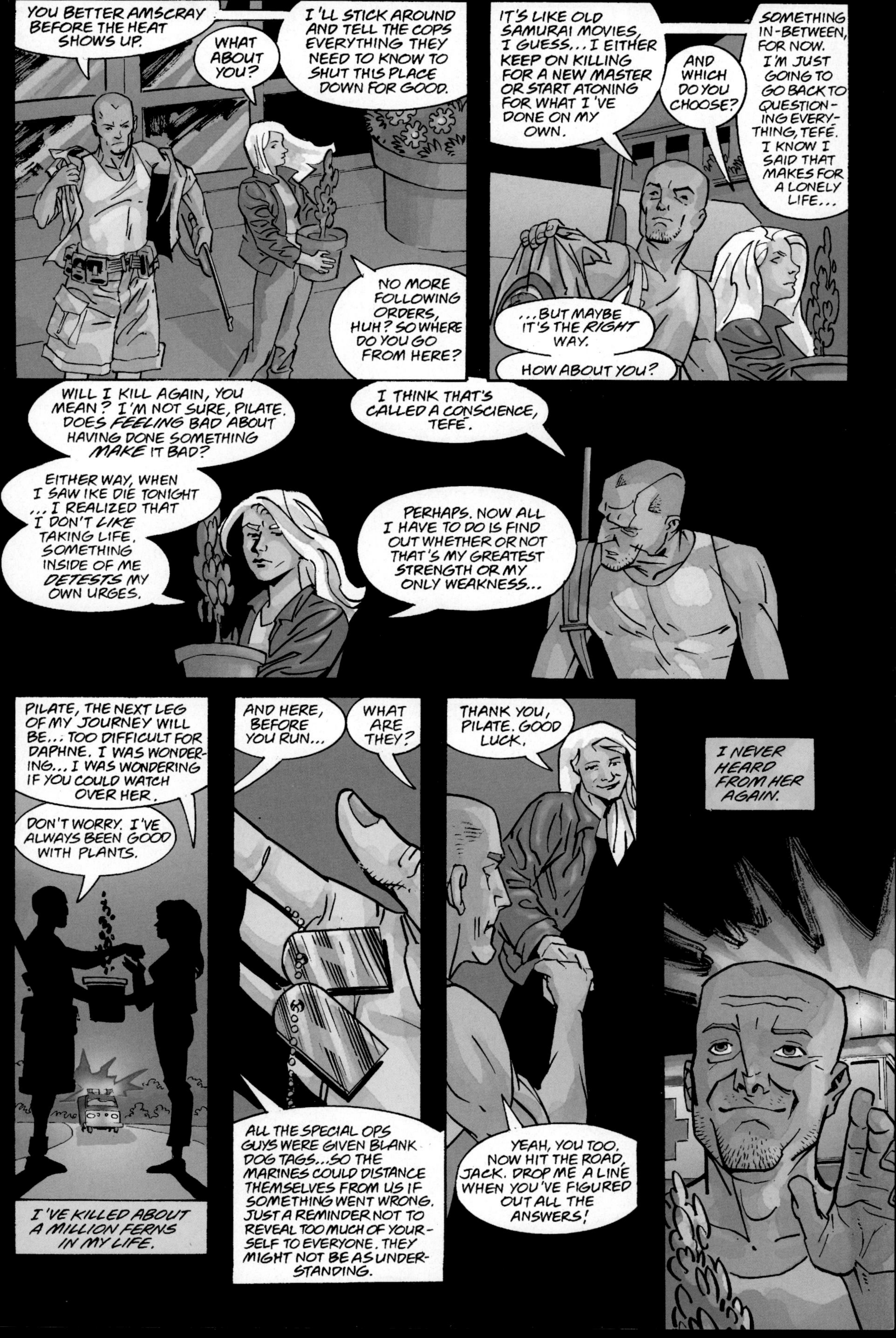
YOU BETTER AMSCRAY BEFORE THE HEAT SHOWS UP.
WHAT ABOUT YOU?
I'LL STICK AROUND AND TELL THE COPS EVERYTHING THEY NEED TO KNOW TO SHUT THIS PLACE DOWN FOR GOOD.
NO MORE FOLLOWING ORDERS, HUH? SO WHERE DO YOU GO FROM HERE?
IT'S LIKE OLD SAMURAI MOVIES, I GUESS... I EITHER KEEP ON KILLING FOR A NEW MASTER OR START ATONING FOR WHAT I'VE DONE ON MY OWN.
AND WHICH DO YOU CHOOSE?
SOMETHING IN-BETWEEN, FOR NOW. I'M JUST GOING TO GO BACK TO QUESTION-ING EVERY-THING, TEFÉ. I KNOW I SAID THAT MAKES FOR A LONELY LIFE...
...BUT MAYBE IT'S THE RIGHT WAY.
HOW ABOUT YOU?
WILL I KILL AGAIN, YOU MEAN? I'M NOT SURE, PILATE. DOES FEELING BAD ABOUT HAVING DONE SOMETHING MAKE IT BAD?
EITHER WAY, WHEN I SAW IKE DIE TONIGHT ... I REALIZED THAT I DON'T LIKE TAKING LIFE. SOMETHING INSIDE OF ME DETESTS MY OWN URGES.
I THINK THAT'S CALLED A CONSCIENCE, TEFÉ.
PERHAPS. NOW ALL I HAVE TO DO IS FIND OUT WHETHER OR NOT THAT'S MY GREATEST STRENGTH OR MY ONLY WEAKNESS...
PILATE, THE NEXT LEG OF MY JOURNEY WILL BE... TOO DIFFICULT FOR DAPHNE. I WAS WONDER-ING... I WAS WONDERING IF YOU COULD WATCH OVER HER.
DON'T WORRY. I'VE ALWAYS BEEN GOOD WITH PLANTS.
I'VE KILLED ABOUT A MILLION FERNS IN MY LIFE.
AND HERE, BEFORE YOU RUN...
WHAT ARE THEY?
ALL THE SPECIAL OPS GUYS WERE GIVEN BLANK DOG TAGS...SO THE MARINES COULD DISTANCE THEMSELVES FROM US IF SOMETHING WENT WRONG. JUST A REMINDER NOT TO REVEAL TOO MUCH OF YOUR-SELF TO EVERYONE. THEY MIGHT NOT BE AS UNDER-STANDING.
THANK YOU, PILATE. GOOD LUCK.
YEAH, YOU TOO. NOW HIT THE ROAD, JACK. DROP ME A LINE WHEN YOU'VE FIGURED OUT ALL THE ANSWERS!
I NEVER HEARD FROM HER AGAIN.

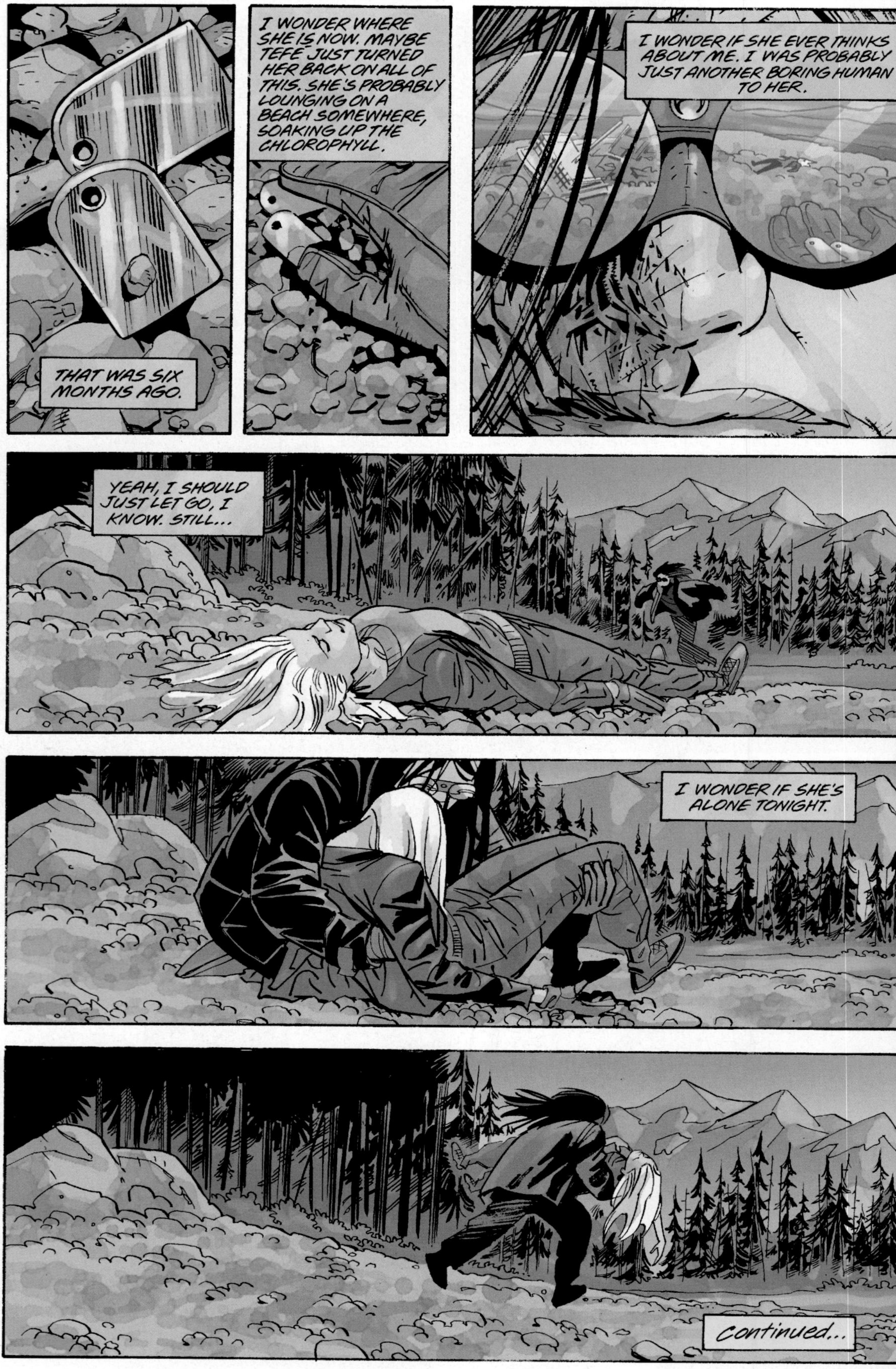

THAT WAS SIX MONTHS AGO.
I WONDER WHERE SHE IS NOW. MAYBE TEFE JUST TURNED HER BACK ON ALL OF THIS. SHE'S PROBABLY LOUNGING ON A BEACH SOMEWHERE, SOAKING UP THE CHLOROPHYLL.
I WONDER IF SHE EVER THINKS ABOUT ME. I WAS PROBABLY JUST ANOTHER BORING HUMAN TO HER.
YEAH, I SHOULD JUST LET GO, I KNOW. STILL...
I WONDER IF SHE'S ALONE TONIGHT.
continued...

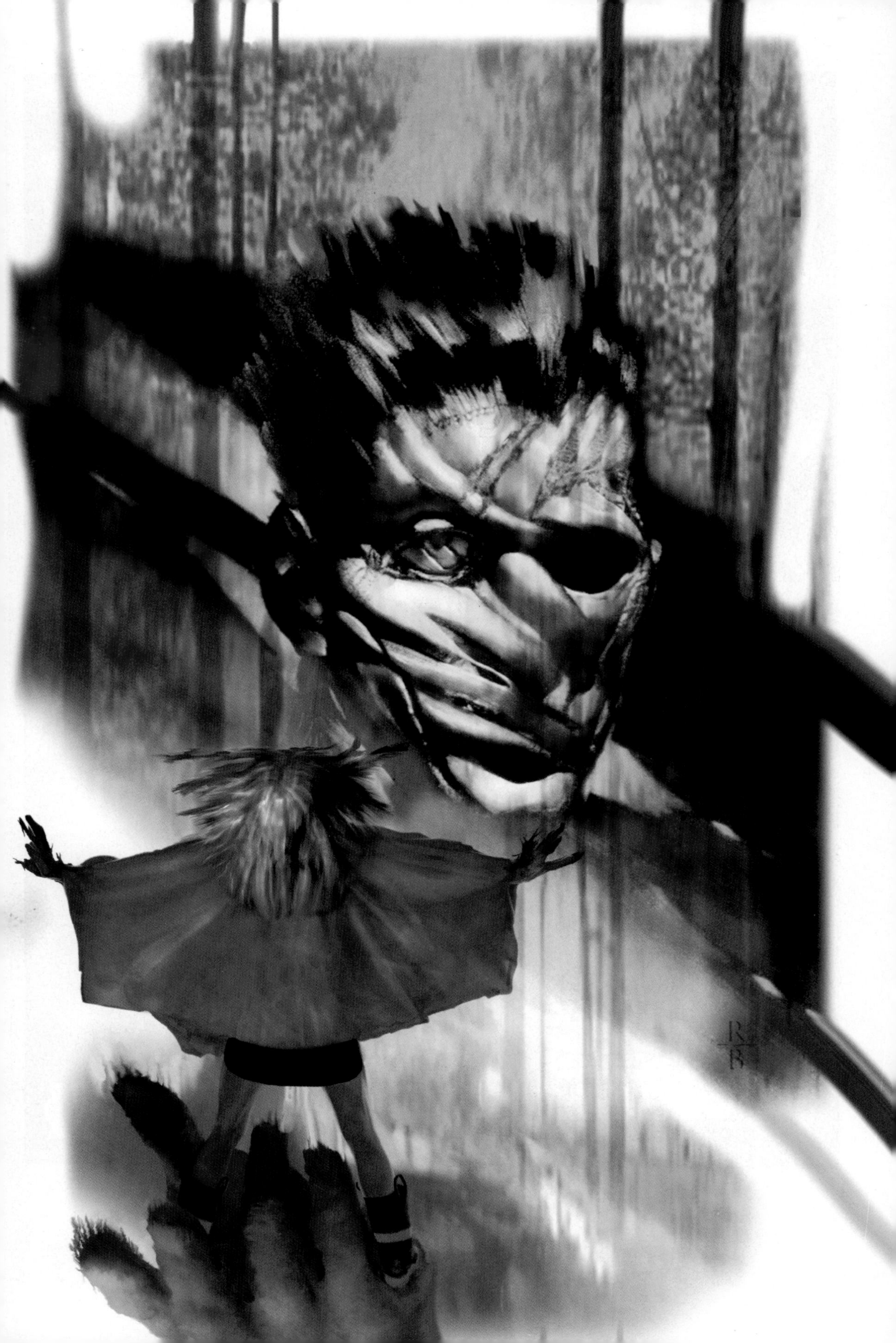

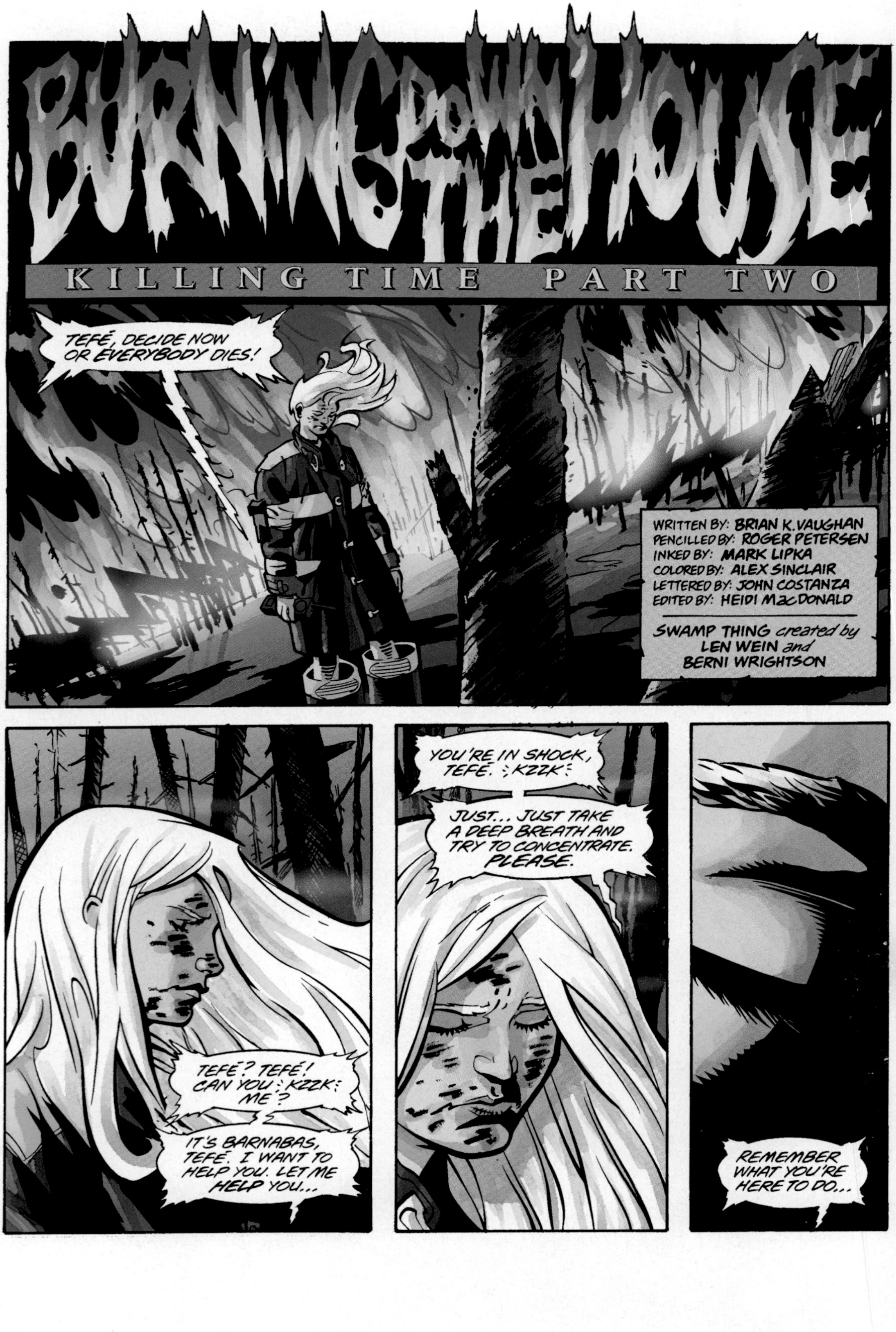

BURNING DOWN THE HOUSE
KILLING TIME PART TWO
TEFÉ, DECIDE NOW OR EVERYBODY DIES!
WRITTEN BY: BRIAN K. VAUGHAN
PENCILLED BY: ROGER PETERSEN
INKED BY: MARK LIPKA
COLORED BY: ALEX SINCLAIR
LETTERED BY: JOHN COSTANZA
EDITED BY: HEIDI MacDONALD
SWAMP THING created by LEN WEIN and BERNI WRIGHTSON
TEFÉ? TEFÉ! CAN YOU :KZZK: ME?
IT'S BARNABAS, TEFÉ. I WANT TO HELP YOU. LET ME HELP YOU...
YOU'RE IN SHOCK, TEFÉ. :KZZK:
JUST... JUST TAKE A DEEP BREATH AND TRY TO CONCENTRATE. PLEASE.
REMEMBER WHAT YOU'RE HERE TO DO...

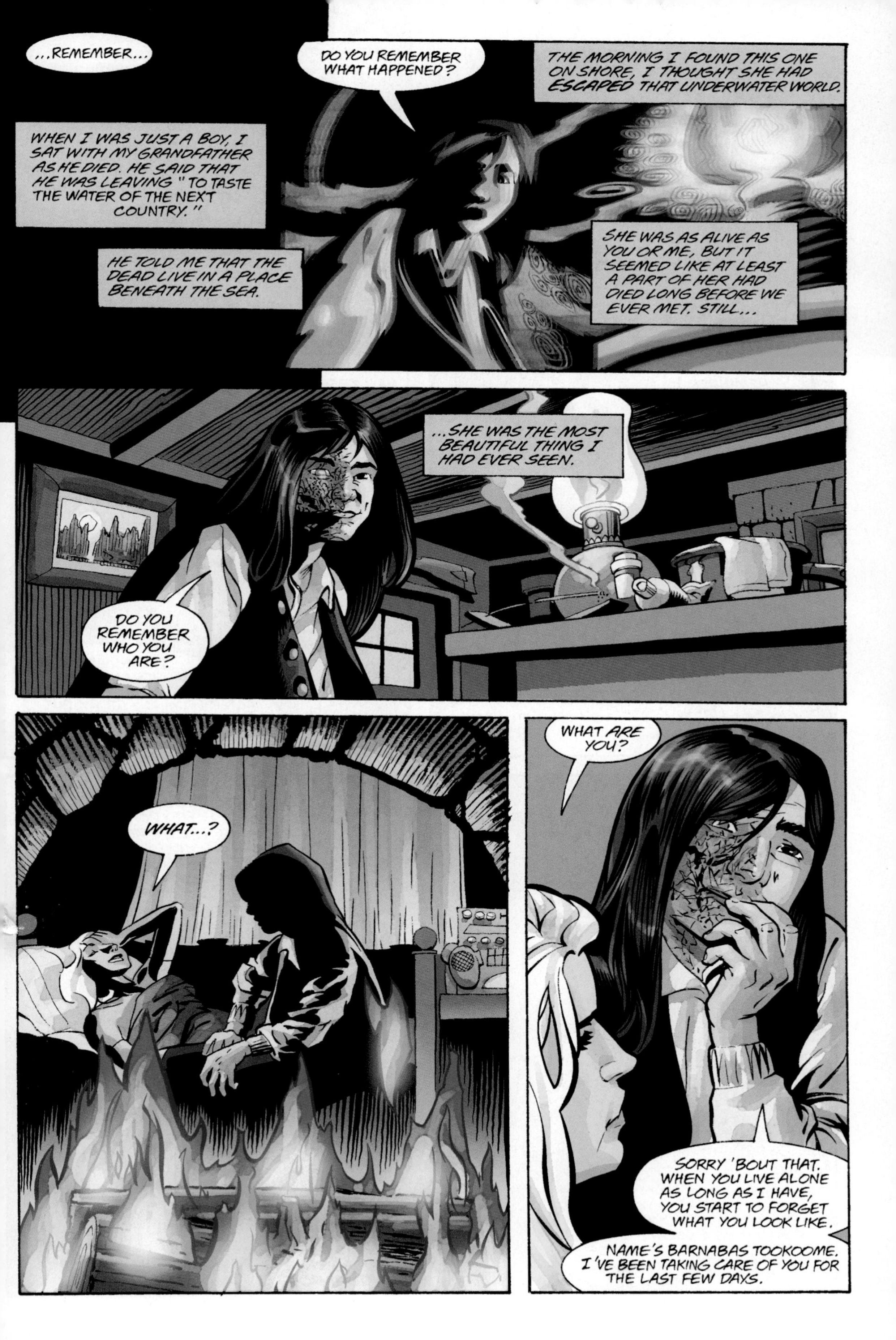

...REMEMBER...
DO YOU REMEMBER WHAT HAPPENED?
THE MORNING I FOUND THIS ONE ON SHORE, I THOUGHT SHE HAD ESCAPED THAT UNDERWATER WORLD.
WHEN I WAS JUST A BOY, I SAT WITH MY GRANDFATHER AS HE DIED. HE SAID THAT HE WAS LEAVING "TO TASTE THE WATER OF THE NEXT COUNTRY."
HE TOLD ME THAT THE DEAD LIVE IN A PLACE BENEATH THE SEA.
SHE WAS AS ALIVE AS YOU OR ME, BUT IT SEEMED LIKE AT LEAST A PART OF HER HAD DIED LONG BEFORE WE EVER MET. STILL...
...SHE WAS THE MOST BEAUTIFUL THING I HAD EVER SEEN.
DO YOU REMEMBER WHO YOU ARE?
WHAT...?
WHAT ARE YOU?
SORRY 'BOUT THAT. WHEN YOU LIVE ALONE AS LONG AS I HAVE, YOU START TO FORGET WHAT YOU LOOK LIKE.
NAME'S BARNABAS TOOKOOME. I'VE BEEN TAKING CARE OF YOU FOR THE LAST FEW DAYS.

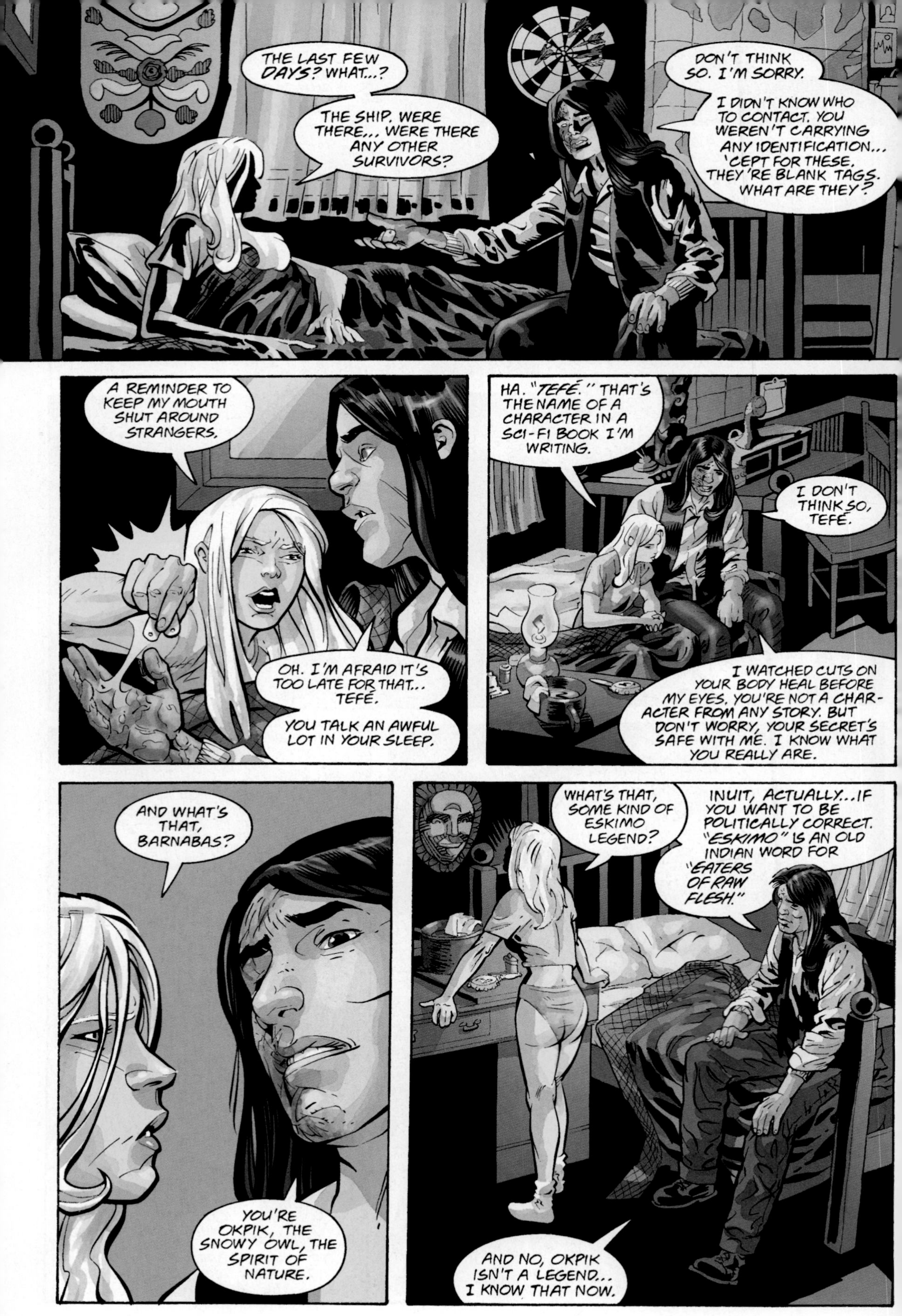
THE LAST FEW DAYS? WHAT...?
THE SHIP. WERE THERE... WERE THERE ANY OTHER SURVIVORS?
DON'T THINK SO. I'M SORRY.
I DIDN'T KNOW WHO TO CONTACT. YOU WEREN'T CARRYING ANY IDENTIFICATION... 'CEPT FOR THESE. THEY'RE BLANK TAGS. WHAT ARE THEY?
A REMINDER TO KEEP MY MOUTH SHUT AROUND STRANGERS.
OH. I'M AFRAID IT'S TOO LATE FOR THAT... TEFÉ.
YOU TALK AN AWFUL LOT IN YOUR SLEEP.
HA. "TEFÉ." THAT'S THE NAME OF A CHARACTER IN A SCI-FI BOOK I'M WRITING.
I DON'T THINK SO, TEFÉ.
I WATCHED CUTS ON YOUR BODY HEAL BEFORE MY EYES. YOU'RE NOT A CHARACTER FROM ANY STORY. BUT DON'T WORRY, YOUR SECRET'S SAFE WITH ME. I KNOW WHAT YOU REALLY ARE.
AND WHAT'S THAT, BARNABAS?
YOU'RE OKPIK, THE SNOWY OWL, THE SPIRIT OF NATURE.
WHAT'S THAT, SOME KIND OF ESKIMO LEGEND?
INUIT, ACTUALLY... IF YOU WANT TO BE POLITICALLY CORRECT. "ESKIMO" IS AN OLD INDIAN WORD FOR "EATERS OF RAW FLESH."
AND NO, OKPIK ISN'T A LEGEND... I KNOW THAT NOW.

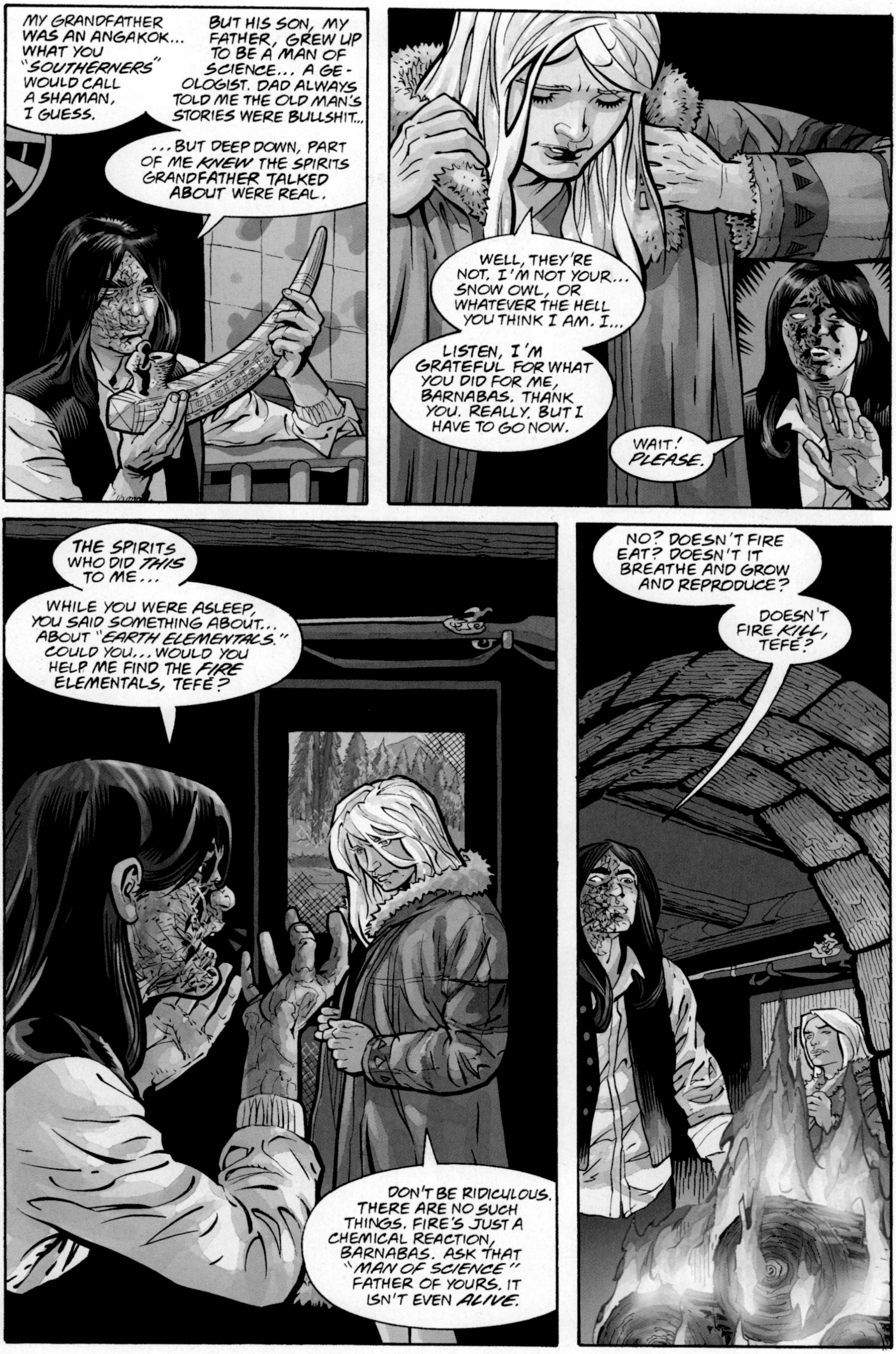
MY GRANDFATHER WAS AN ANGAKOK... WHAT YOU "SOUTHERNERS" WOULD CALL A SHAMAN, I GUESS.
BUT HIS SON, MY FATHER, GREW UP TO BE A MAN OF SCIENCE... A GE-OLOGIST. DAD ALWAYS TOLD ME THE OLD MAN'S STORIES WERE BULLSHIT...
...BUT DEEP DOWN, PART OF ME KNEW THE SPIRITS GRANDFATHER TALKED ABOUT WERE REAL.
WELL, THEY'RE NOT. I'M NOT YOUR... SNOW OWL, OR WHATEVER THE HELL YOU THINK I AM. I...
LISTEN, I'M GRATEFUL FOR WHAT YOU DID FOR ME, BARNABAS. THANK YOU. REALLY. BUT I HAVE TO GO NOW.
WAIT! PLEASE.
THE SPIRITS WHO DID THIS TO ME...
WHILE YOU WERE ASLEEP, YOU SAID SOMETHING ABOUT... ABOUT "EARTH ELEMENTALS." COULD YOU... WOULD YOU HELP ME FIND THE FIRE ELEMENTALS, TEFÉ?
DON'T BE RIDICULOUS. THERE ARE NO SUCH THINGS. FIRE'S JUST A CHEMICAL REACTION, BARNABAS. ASK THAT "MAN OF SCIENCE" FATHER OF YOURS. IT ISN'T EVEN ALIVE.
NO? DOESN'T FIRE EAT? DOESN'T IT BREATHE AND GROW AND REPRODUCE?
DOESN'T FIRE KILL, TEFÉ?

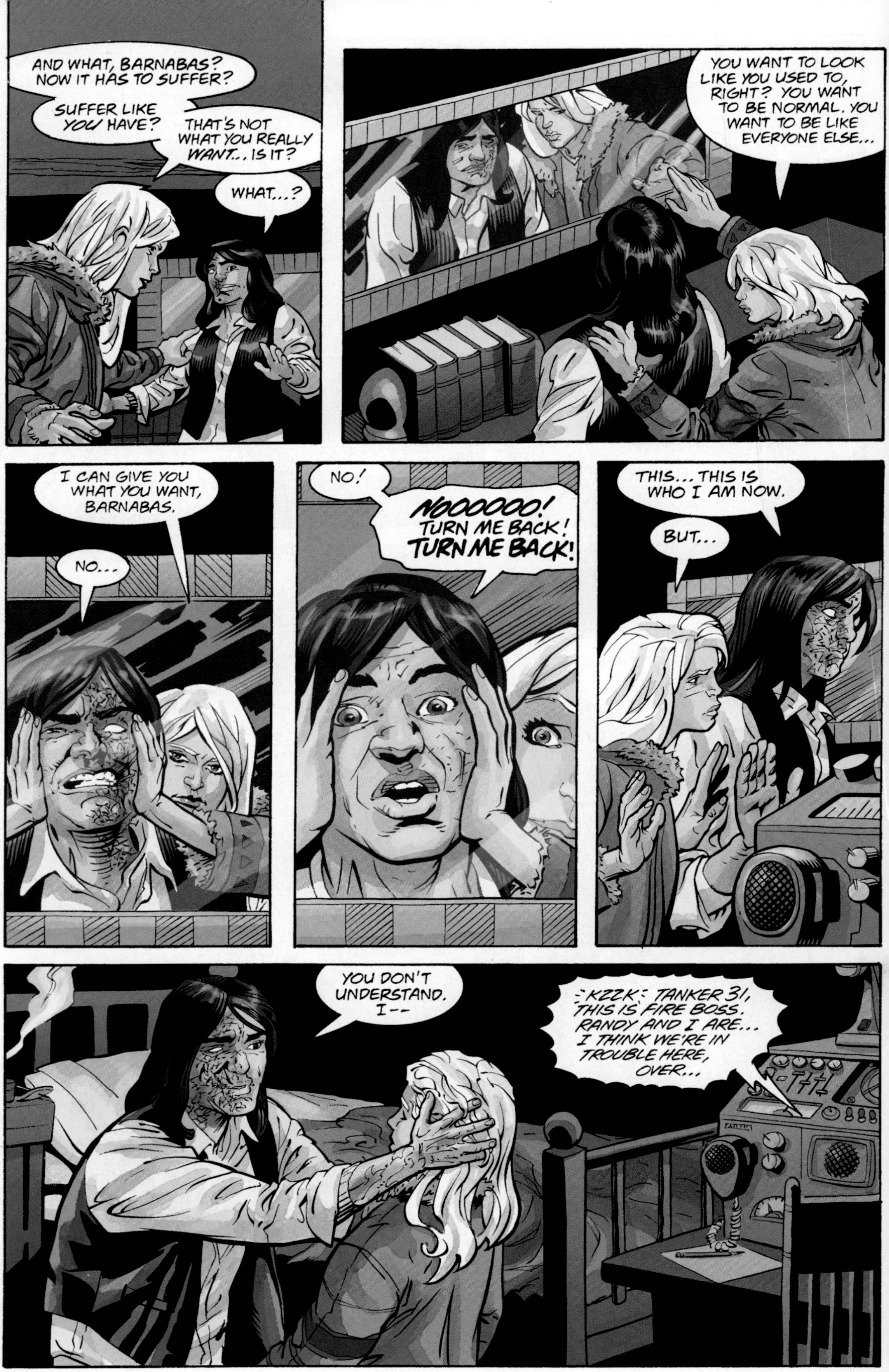
AND WHAT, BARNABAS? NOW IT HAS TO SUFFER?
SUFFER LIKE YOU HAVE?
THAT'S NOT WHAT YOU REALLY WANT... IS IT?
WHAT...?
YOU WANT TO LOOK LIKE YOU USED TO, RIGHT? YOU WANT TO BE NORMAL. YOU WANT TO BE LIKE EVERYONE ELSE...
I CAN GIVE YOU WHAT YOU WANT, BARNABAS.
NO...
NO!
NOOOOOO! TURN ME BACK! TURN ME BACK!
THIS... THIS IS WHO I AM NOW.
BUT...
YOU DON'T UNDERSTAND. I--
:KZZK: TANKER 31, THIS IS FIRE BOSS. RANDY AND I ARE... I THINK WE'RE IN TROUBLE HERE, OVER...

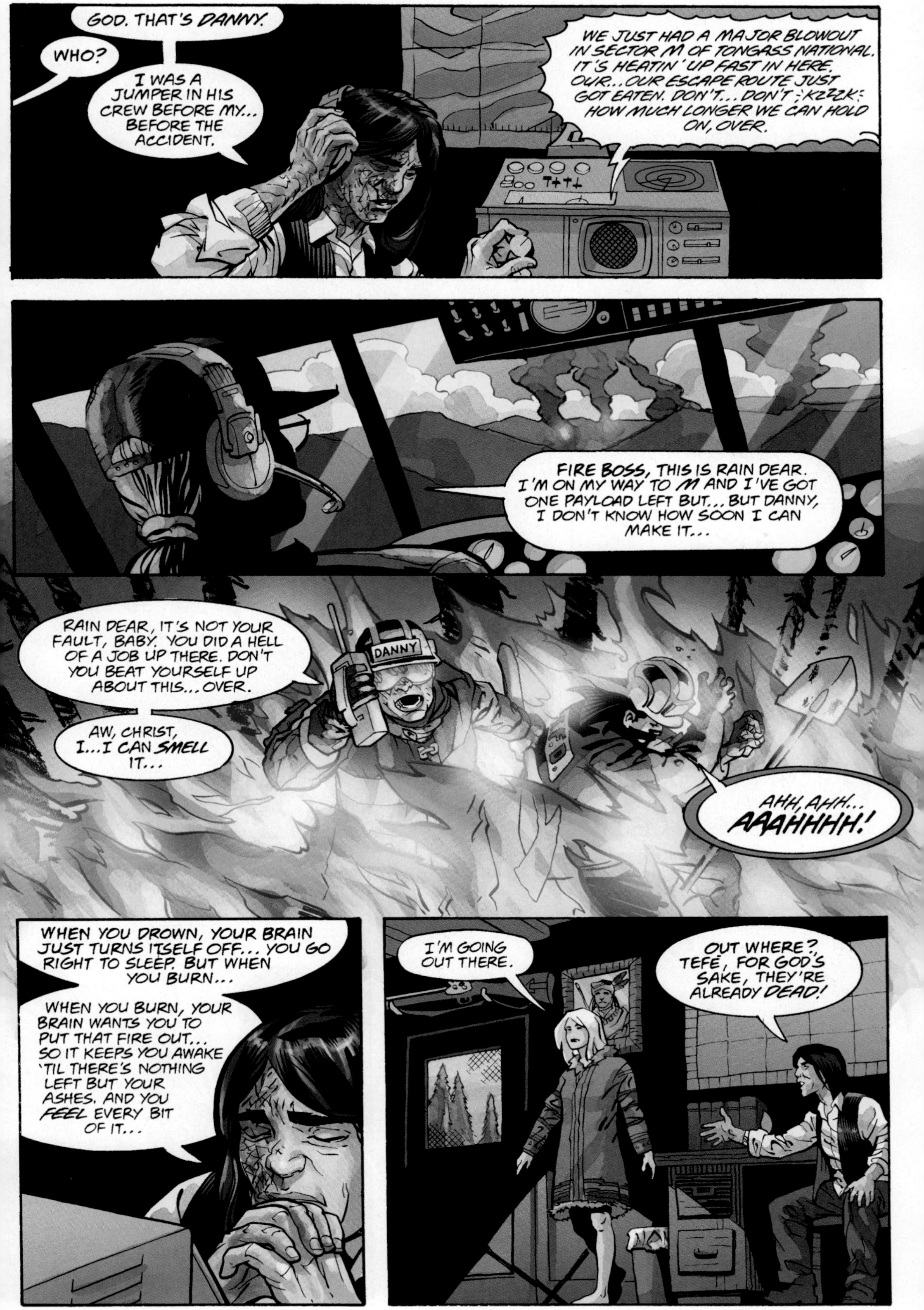
GOD. THAT'S DANNY.
WHO?
I WAS A JUMPER IN HIS CREW BEFORE MY... BEFORE THE ACCIDENT.
WE JUST HAD A MAJOR BLOWOUT IN SECTOR M OF TONGASS NATIONAL. IT'S HEATIN' UP FAST IN HERE. OUR... OUR ESCAPE ROUTE JUST GOT EATEN. DON'T... DON'T -KZZZK- HOW MUCH LONGER WE CAN HOLD ON, OVER.
FIRE BOSS, THIS IS RAIN DEAR. I'M ON MY WAY TO M AND I'VE GOT ONE PAYLOAD LEFT BUT... BUT DANNY, I DON'T KNOW HOW SOON I CAN MAKE IT...
RAIN DEAR, IT'S NOT YOUR FAULT, BABY. YOU DID A HELL OF A JOB UP THERE. DON'T YOU BEAT YOURSELF UP ABOUT THIS... OVER.
AW, CHRIST, I... I CAN SMELL IT...
DANNY
AHH, AHH... AAAHHHH!
WHEN YOU DROWN, YOUR BRAIN JUST TURNS ITSELF OFF... YOU GO RIGHT TO SLEEP. BUT WHEN YOU BURN...
WHEN YOU BURN, YOUR BRAIN WANTS YOU TO PUT THAT FIRE OUT... SO IT KEEPS YOU AWAKE 'TIL THERE'S NOTHING LEFT BUT YOUR ASHES. AND YOU FEEL EVERY BIT OF IT...
I'M GOING OUT THERE.
OUT WHERE? TEFÉ, FOR GOD'S SAKE, THEY'RE ALREADY DEAD!

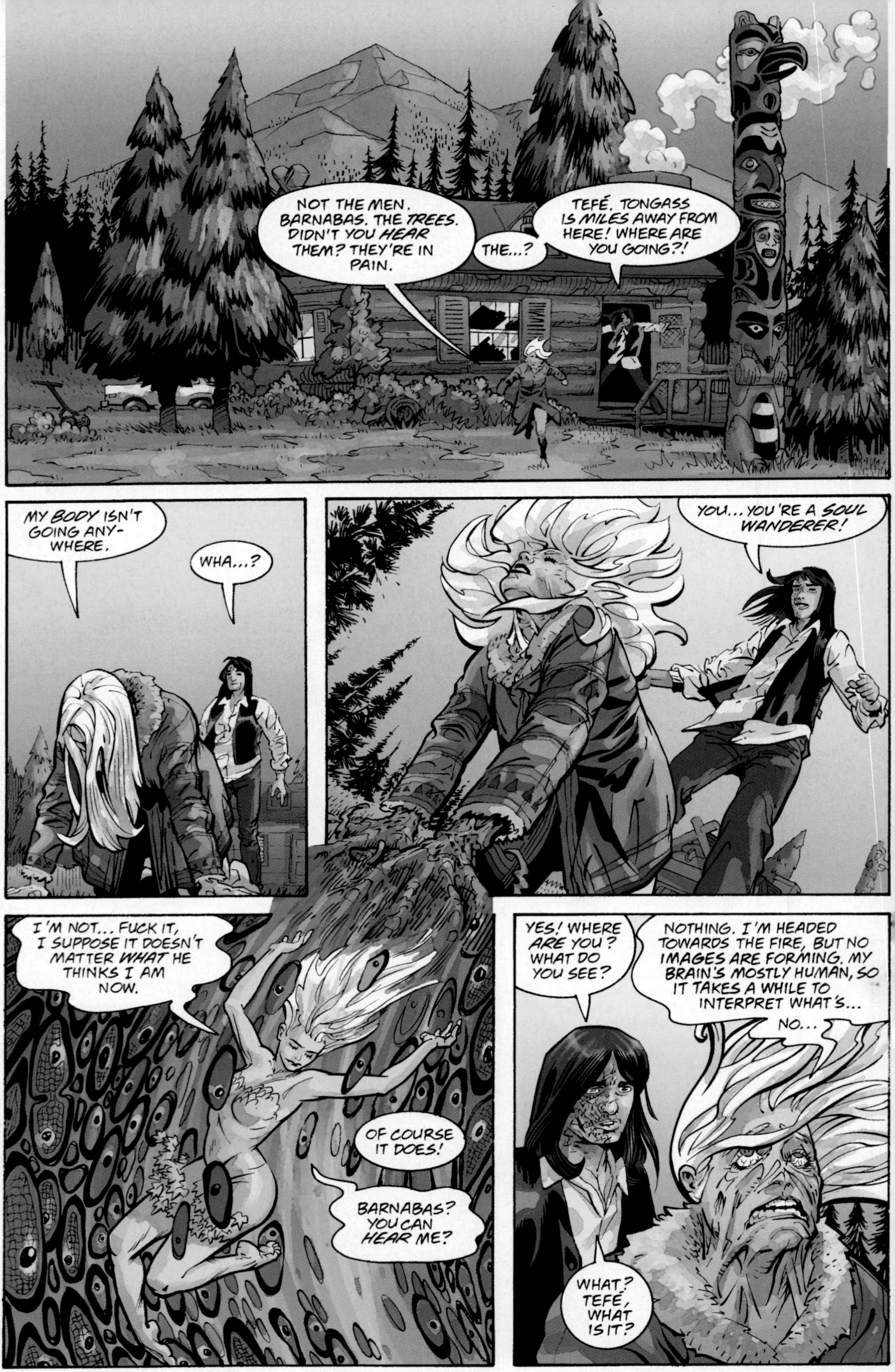
NOT THE MEN. BARNABAS. THE TREES. DIDN'T YOU HEAR THEM? THEY'RE IN PAIN.
THE...?
TEFÉ. TONGASS IS MILES AWAY FROM HERE! WHERE ARE YOU GOING?!
MY BODY ISN'T GOING ANY-WHERE.
WHA...?
YOU... YOU'RE A SOUL WANDERER!
I'M NOT... FUCK IT, I SUPPOSE IT DOESN'T MATTER WHAT HE THINKS I AM NOW.
OF COURSE IT DOES!
BARNABAS? YOU CAN HEAR ME?
YES! WHERE ARE YOU? WHAT DO YOU SEE?
NOTHING. I'M HEADED TOWARDS THE FIRE, BUT NO IMAGES ARE FORMING. MY BRAIN'S MOSTLY HUMAN, SO IT TAKES A WHILE TO INTERPRET WHAT'S...
NO...
WHAT? TEFÉ, WHAT IS IT?

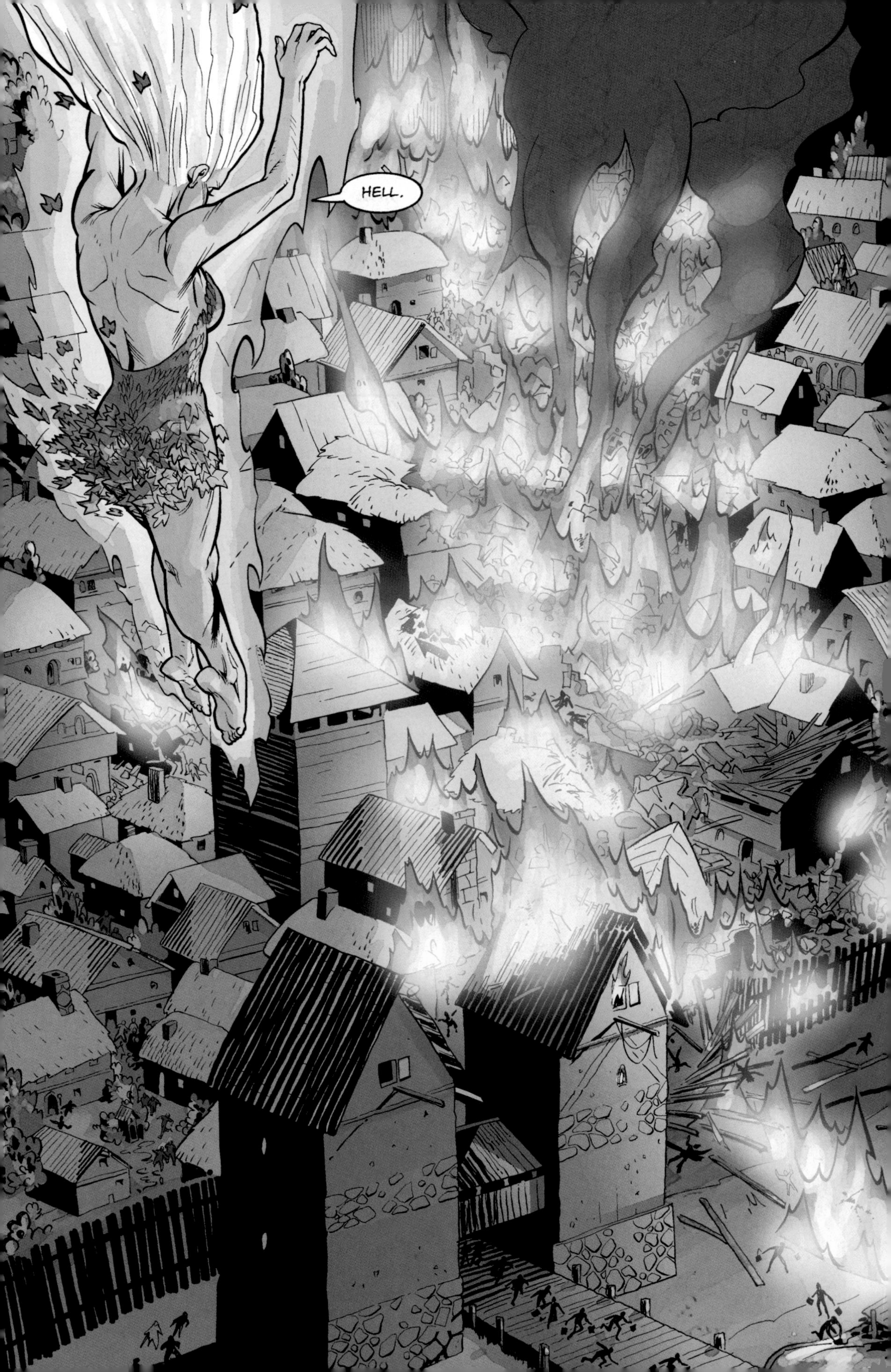
HELL.

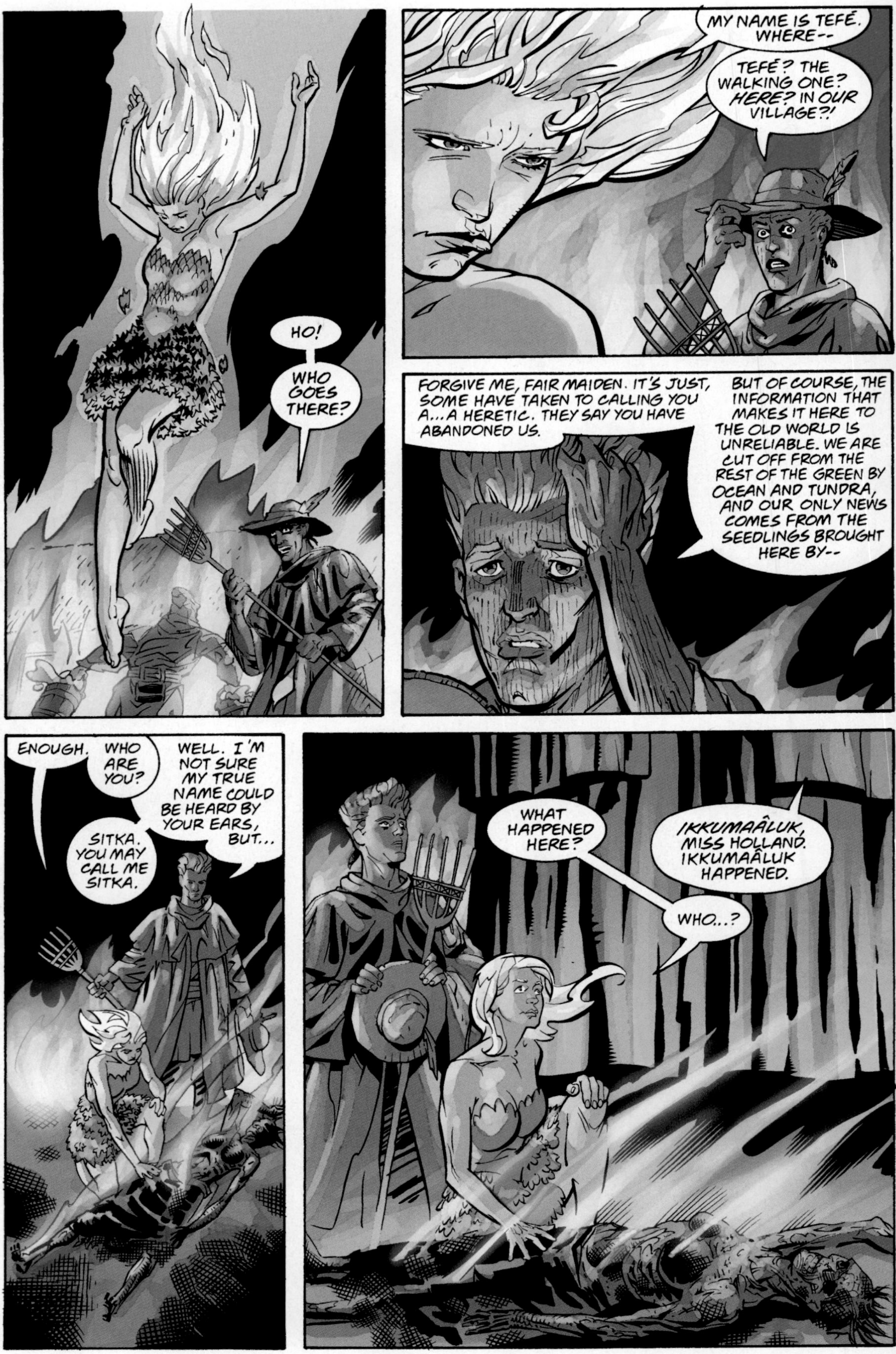

HO!
WHO GOES THERE?
MY NAME IS TEFÉ. WHERE--
TEFÉ? THE WALKING ONE? HERE? IN OUR VILLAGE?!
FORGIVE ME, FAIR MAIDEN. IT'S JUST, SOME HAVE TAKEN TO CALLING YOU A... A HERETIC. THEY SAY YOU HAVE ABANDONED US.
BUT OF COURSE, THE INFORMATION THAT MAKES IT HERE TO THE OLD WORLD IS UNRELIABLE. WE ARE CUT OFF FROM THE REST OF THE GREEN BY OCEAN AND TUNDRA, AND OUR ONLY NEWS COMES FROM THE SEEDLINGS BROUGHT HERE BY--
ENOUGH.
WHO ARE YOU?
WELL. I'M NOT SURE MY TRUE NAME COULD BE HEARD BY YOUR EARS, BUT...
SITKA. YOU MAY CALL ME SITKA.
WHAT HAPPENED HERE?
IKKUMAÂLUK, MISS HOLLAND. IKKUMAÂLUK HAPPENED.
WHO...?

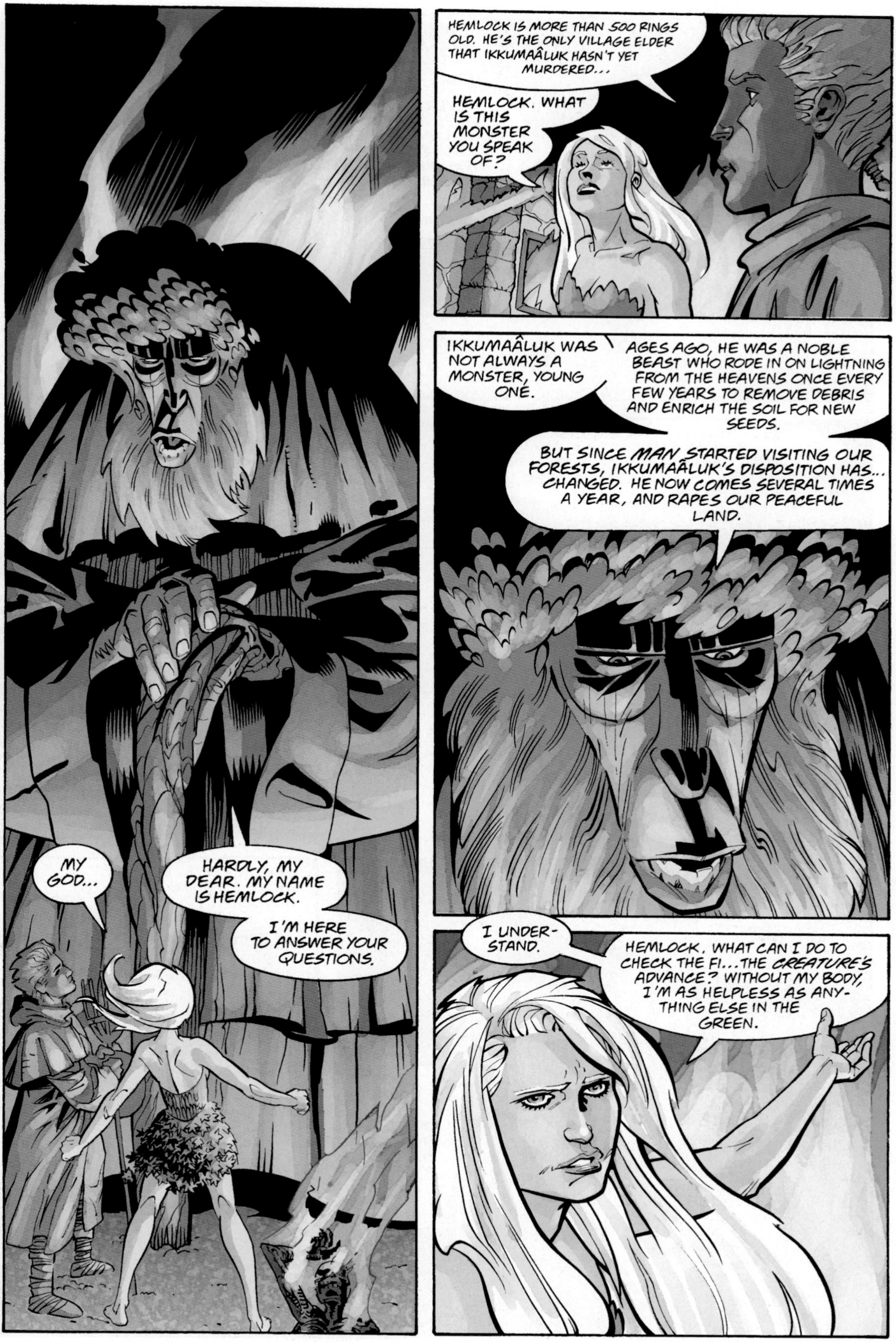
MY GOD...
HARDLY, MY DEAR. MY NAME IS HEMLOCK.
I'M HERE TO ANSWER YOUR QUESTIONS.
HEMLOCK IS MORE THAN 500 RINGS OLD. HE'S THE ONLY VILLAGE ELDER THAT IKKUMAÂLUK HASN'T YET MURDERED...
HEMLOCK. WHAT IS THIS MONSTER YOU SPEAK OF?
IKKUMAÂLUK WAS NOT ALWAYS A MONSTER, YOUNG ONE.
AGES AGO, HE WAS A NOBLE BEAST WHO RODE IN ON LIGHTNING FROM THE HEAVENS ONCE EVERY FEW YEARS TO REMOVE DEBRIS AND ENRICH THE SOIL FOR NEW SEEDS.
BUT SINCE MAN STARTED VISITING OUR FORESTS, IKKUMAÂLUK'S DISPOSITION HAS... CHANGED. HE NOW COMES SEVERAL TIMES A YEAR, AND RAPES OUR PEACEFUL LAND.
I UNDER-STAND.
HEMLOCK, WHAT CAN I DO TO CHECK THE FI... THE CREATURE'S ADVANCE? WITHOUT MY BODY, I'M AS HELPLESS AS ANY-THING ELSE IN THE GREEN.

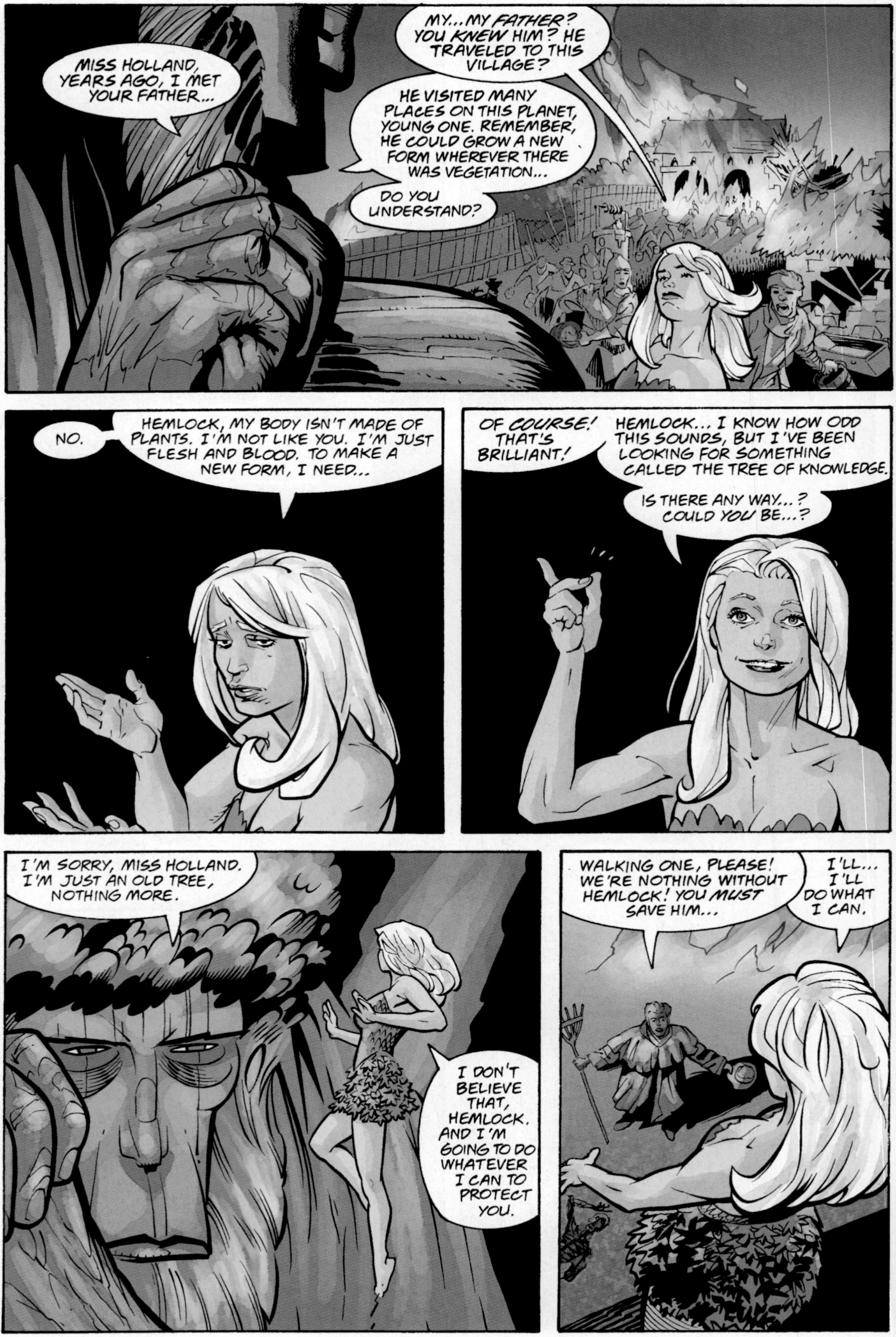
MISS HOLLAND, YEARS AGO, I MET YOUR FATHER...
MY... MY FATHER? YOU KNEW HIM? HE TRAVELED TO THIS VILLAGE?
HE VISITED MANY PLACES ON THIS PLANET, YOUNG ONE. REMEMBER, HE COULD GROW A NEW FORM WHEREVER THERE WAS VEGETATION...
DO YOU UNDERSTAND?
NO.
HEMLOCK, MY BODY ISN'T MADE OF PLANTS. I'M NOT LIKE YOU. I'M JUST FLESH AND BLOOD. TO MAKE A NEW FORM, I NEED...
OF COURSE! THAT'S BRILLIANT!
HEMLOCK... I KNOW HOW ODD THIS SOUNDS, BUT I'VE BEEN LOOKING FOR SOMETHING CALLED THE TREE OF KNOWLEDGE.
IS THERE ANY WAY...? COULD YOU BE...?
I'M SORRY, MISS HOLLAND. I'M JUST AN OLD TREE, NOTHING MORE.
I DON'T BELIEVE THAT, HEMLOCK. AND I'M GOING TO DO WHATEVER I CAN TO PROTECT YOU.
WALKING ONE, PLEASE! WE'RE NOTHING WITHOUT HEMLOCK! YOU MUST SAVE HIM...
I'LL... I'LL DO WHAT I CAN.

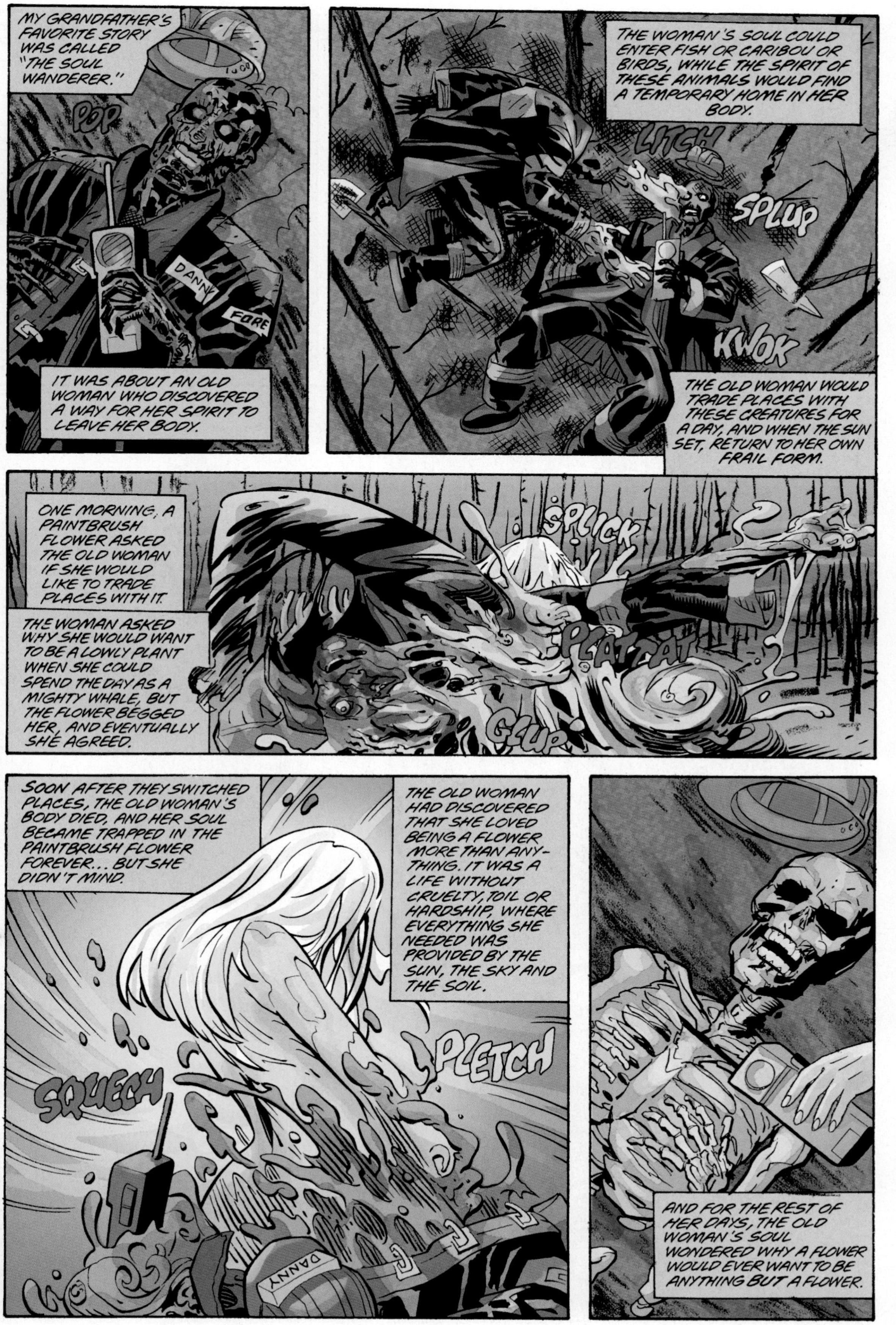

MY GRANDFATHER'S FAVORITE STORY WAS CALLED "THE SOUL WANDERER."
POP
DANN
FORE
IT WAS ABOUT AN OLD WOMAN WHO DISCOVERED A WAY FOR HER SPIRIT TO LEAVE HER BODY.
THE WOMAN'S SOUL COULD ENTER FISH OR CARIBOU OR BIRDS, WHILE THE SPIRIT OF THESE ANIMALS WOULD FIND A TEMPORARY HOME IN HER BODY.
LITCH
SPLUP
KWOK
THE OLD WOMAN WOULD TRADE PLACES WITH THESE CREATURES FOR A DAY, AND WHEN THE SUN SET, RETURN TO HER OWN FRAIL FORM.
ONE MORNING, A PAINTBRUSH FLOWER ASKED THE OLD WOMAN IF SHE WOULD LIKE TO TRADE PLACES WITH IT.
THE WOMAN ASKED WHY SHE WOULD WANT TO BE A LOWLY PLANT WHEN SHE COULD SPEND THE DAY AS A MIGHTY WHALE, BUT THE FLOWER BEGGED HER, AND EVENTUALLY SHE AGREED.
SPLICK
PLATTAT
GLUP
SOON AFTER THEY SWITCHED PLACES, THE OLD WOMAN'S BODY DIED, AND HER SOUL BECAME TRAPPED IN THE PAINTBRUSH FLOWER FOREVER... BUT SHE DIDN'T MIND.
THE OLD WOMAN HAD DISCOVERED THAT SHE LOVED BEING A FLOWER MORE THAN ANY-THING. IT WAS A LIFE WITHOUT CRUELTY, TOIL OR HARDSHIP, WHERE EVERYTHING SHE NEEDED WAS PROVIDED BY THE SUN, THE SKY AND THE SOIL.
PLETCH
SQUECH
DANNY
AND FOR THE REST OF HER DAYS, THE OLD WOMAN'S SOUL WONDERED WHY A FLOWER WOULD EVER WANT TO BE ANYTHING BUT A FLOWER.

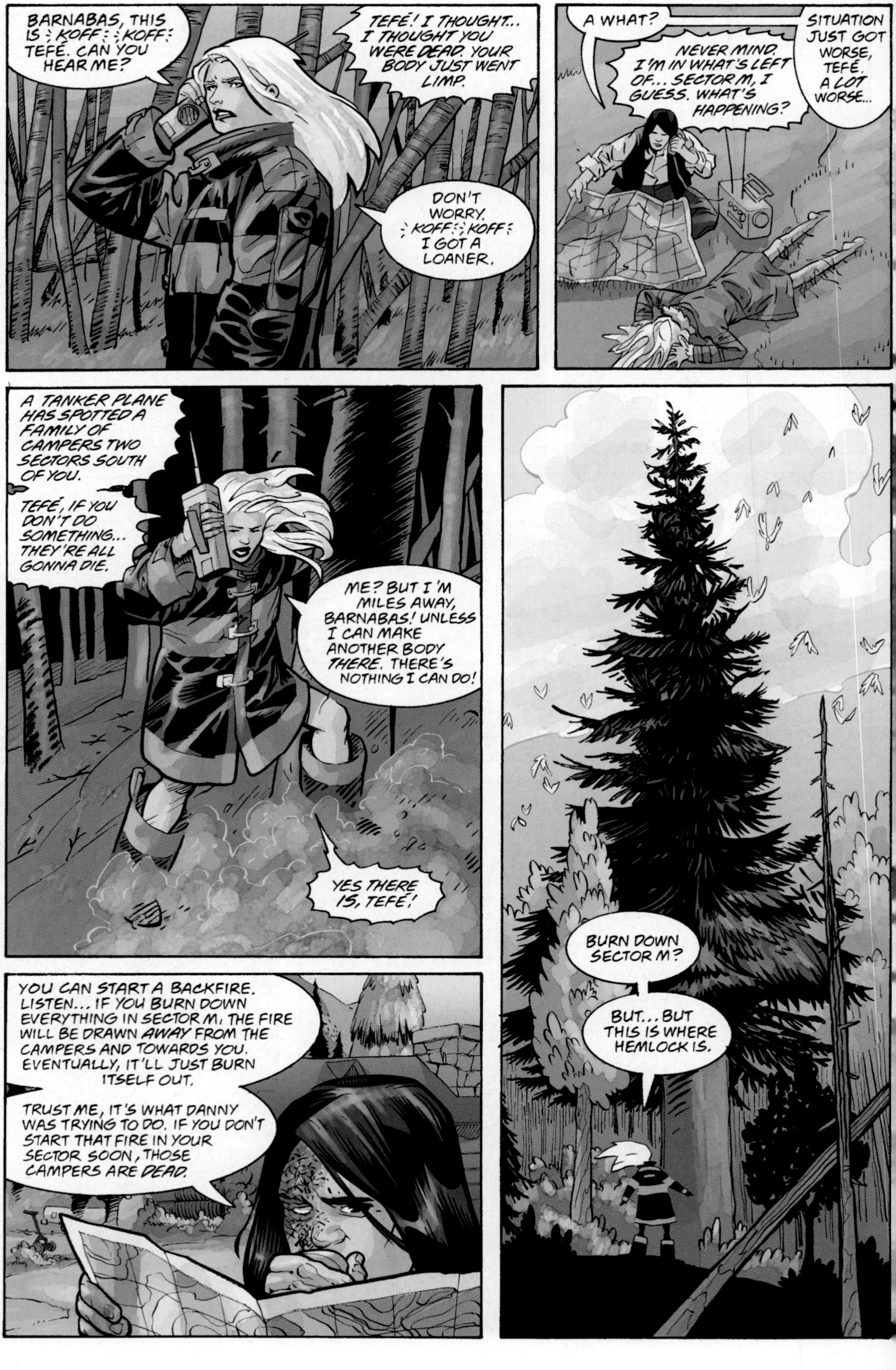
BARNABAS, THIS IS ⁝KOFF⁝ ⁝KOFF⁝ TEFÉ. CAN YOU HEAR ME?
TEFÉ! I THOUGHT... I THOUGHT YOU WERE DEAD. YOUR BODY JUST WENT LIMP.
DON'T WORRY. ⁝KOFF⁝ ⁝KOFF⁝ I GOT A LOANER.
A WHAT?
NEVER MIND. I'M IN WHAT'S LEFT OF... SECTOR M, I GUESS. WHAT'S HAPPENING?
SITUATION JUST GOT WORSE, TEFÉ. A LOT WORSE...
A TANKER PLANE HAS SPOTTED A FAMILY OF CAMPERS TWO SECTORS SOUTH OF YOU.
TEFÉ, IF YOU DON'T DO SOMETHING... THEY'RE ALL GONNA DIE.
ME? BUT I'M MILES AWAY, BARNABAS! UNLESS I CAN MAKE ANOTHER BODY THERE, THERE'S NOTHING I CAN DO!
YES THERE IS, TEFÉ!
YOU CAN START A BACKFIRE. LISTEN... IF YOU BURN DOWN EVERYTHING IN SECTOR M, THE FIRE WILL BE DRAWN AWAY FROM THE CAMPERS AND TOWARDS YOU. EVENTUALLY, IT'LL JUST BURN ITSELF OUT.
TRUST ME, IT'S WHAT DANNY WAS TRYING TO DO. IF YOU DON'T START THAT FIRE IN YOUR SECTOR SOON, THOSE CAMPERS ARE DEAD.
BURN DOWN SECTOR M?
BUT... BUT THIS IS WHERE HEMLOCK IS.

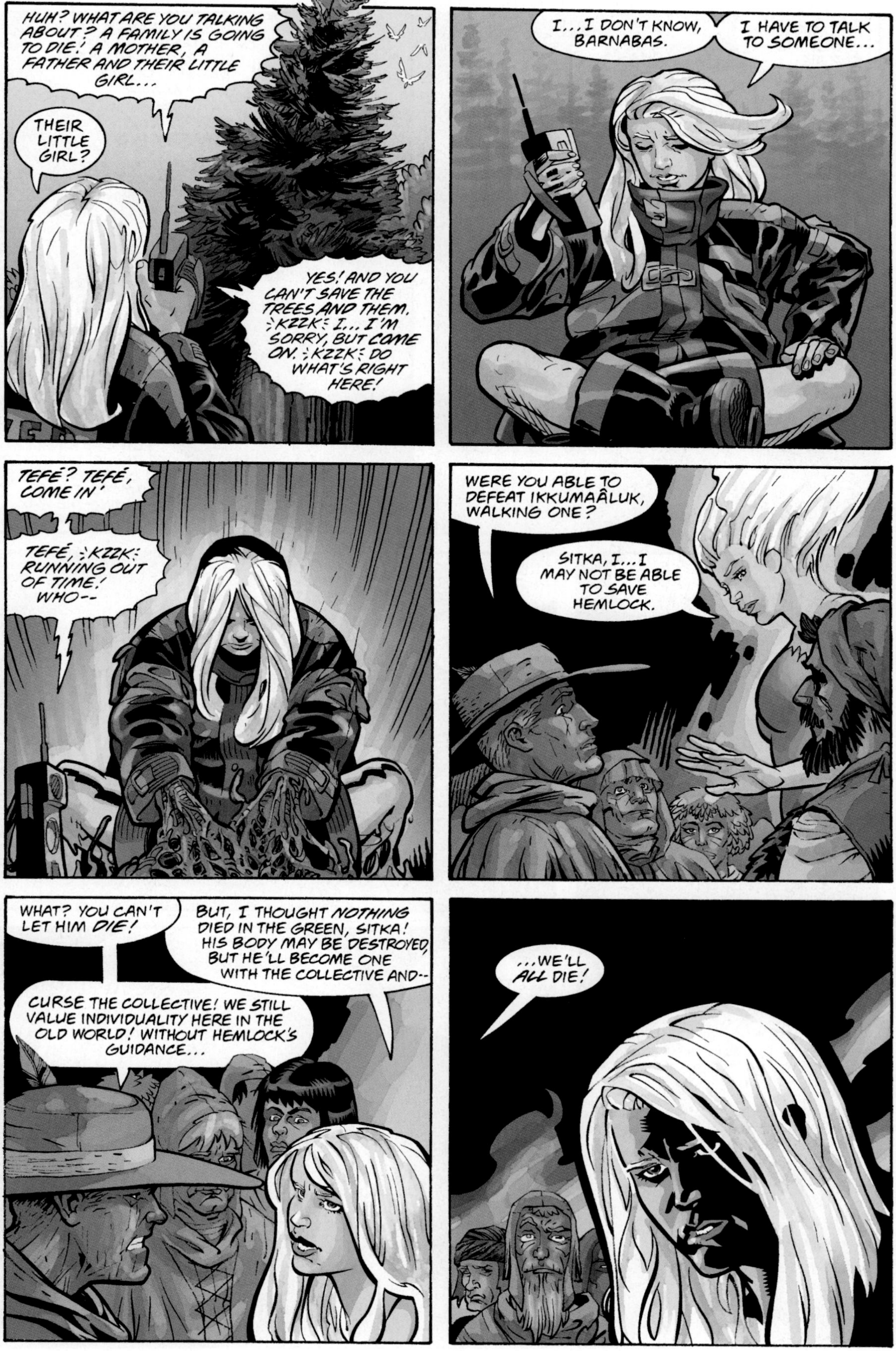
HUH? WHAT ARE YOU TALKING ABOUT? A FAMILY IS GOING TO DIE! A MOTHER, A FATHER AND THEIR LITTLE GIRL...
THEIR LITTLE GIRL?
YES! AND YOU CAN'T SAVE THE TREES AND THEM. KZZK I... I'M SORRY, BUT COME ON. KZZK DO WHAT'S RIGHT HERE!
I... I DON'T KNOW, BARNABAS.
I HAVE TO TALK TO SOMEONE...
TEFÉ? TEFÉ, COME IN!
TEFÉ, KZZK RUNNING OUT OF TIME! WHO--
WERE YOU ABLE TO DEFEAT IKKUMAÂLUK, WALKING ONE?
SITKA, I... I MAY NOT BE ABLE TO SAVE HEMLOCK.
WHAT? YOU CAN'T LET HIM DIE!
BUT, I THOUGHT NOTHING DIED IN THE GREEN, SITKA! HIS BODY MAY BE DESTROYED, BUT HE'LL BECOME ONE WITH THE COLLECTIVE AND--
CURSE THE COLLECTIVE! WE STILL VALUE INDIVIDUALITY HERE IN THE OLD WORLD! WITHOUT HEMLOCK'S GUIDANCE...
...WE'LL ALL DIE!

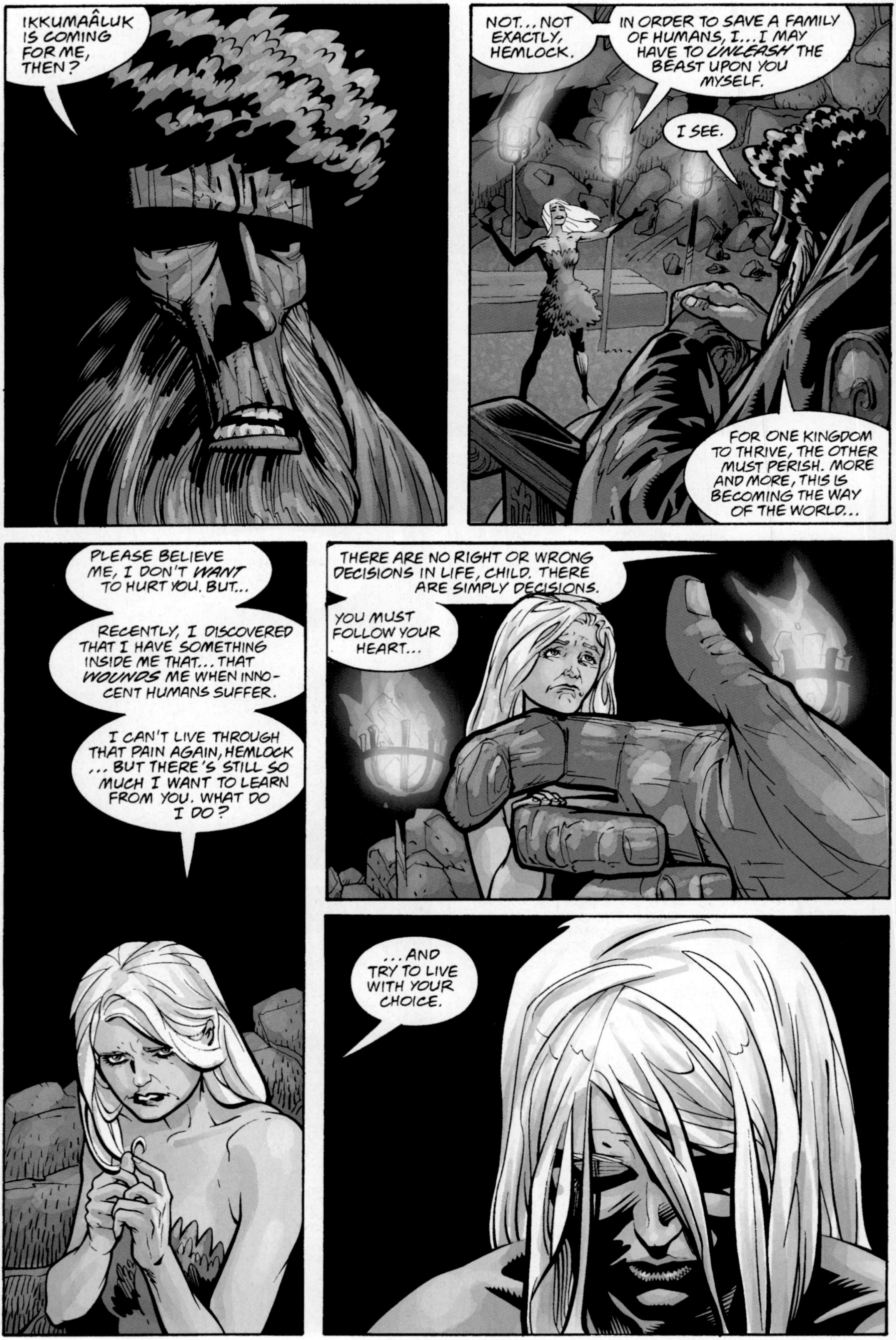
IKKUMAÂLUK IS COMING FOR ME, THEN?
NOT... NOT EXACTLY, HEMLOCK.
IN ORDER TO SAVE A FAMILY OF HUMANS, I... I MAY HAVE TO UNLEASH THE BEAST UPON YOU MYSELF.
I SEE.
FOR ONE KINGDOM TO THRIVE, THE OTHER MUST PERISH. MORE AND MORE, THIS IS BECOMING THE WAY OF THE WORLD...
PLEASE BELIEVE ME, I DON'T WANT TO HURT YOU. BUT...
RECENTLY, I DISCOVERED THAT I HAVE SOMETHING INSIDE ME THAT... THAT WOUNDS ME WHEN INNOCENT HUMANS SUFFER.
I CAN'T LIVE THROUGH THAT PAIN AGAIN, HEMLOCK ... BUT THERE'S STILL SO MUCH I WANT TO LEARN FROM YOU. WHAT DO I DO?
THERE ARE NO RIGHT OR WRONG DECISIONS IN LIFE, CHILD. THERE ARE SIMPLY DECISIONS.
YOU MUST FOLLOW YOUR HEART...
...AND TRY TO LIVE WITH YOUR CHOICE.

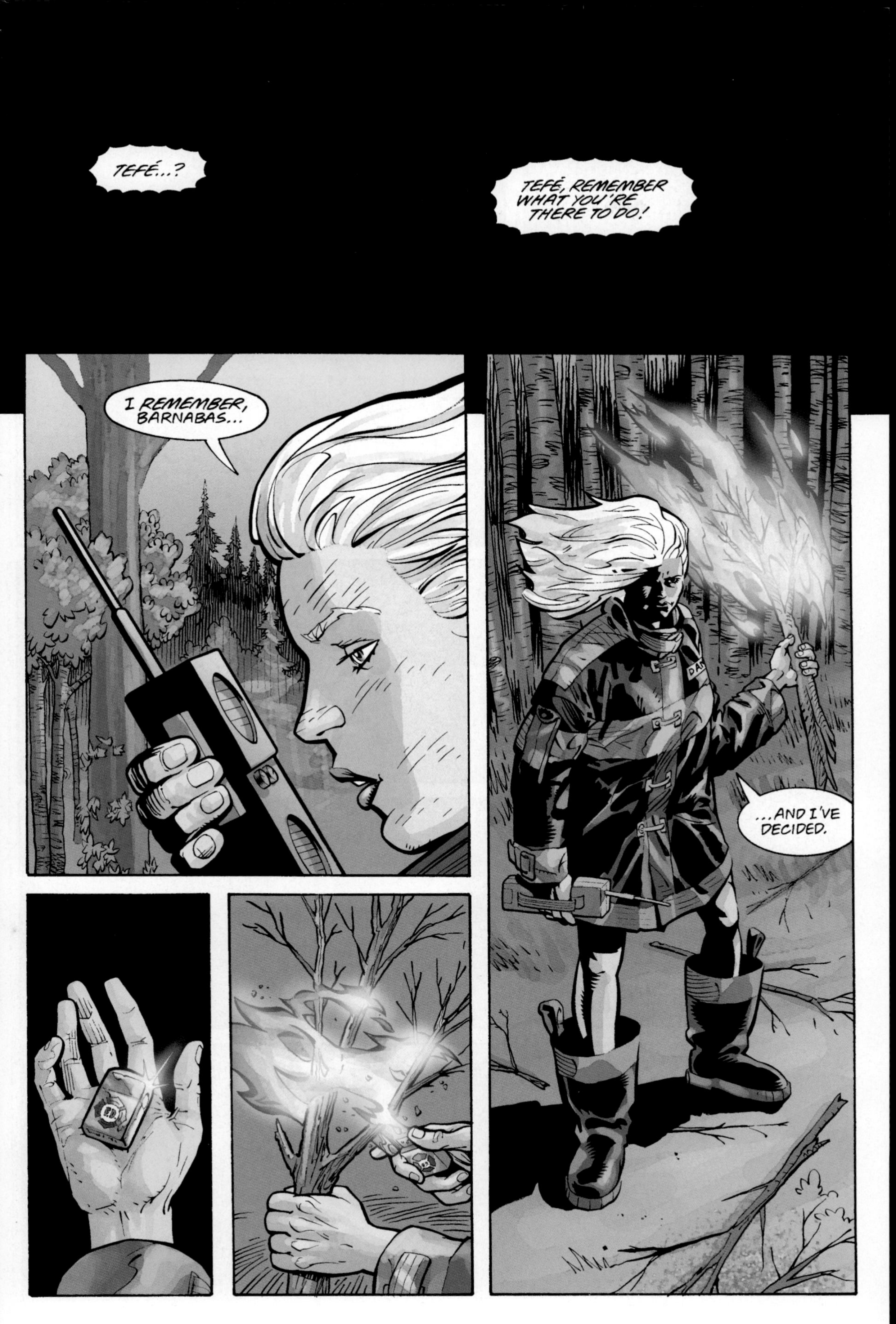
TEFÉ...?
TEFÉ, REMEMBER WHAT YOU'RE THERE TO DO!
I REMEMBER, BARNABAS...
...AND I'VE DECIDED.

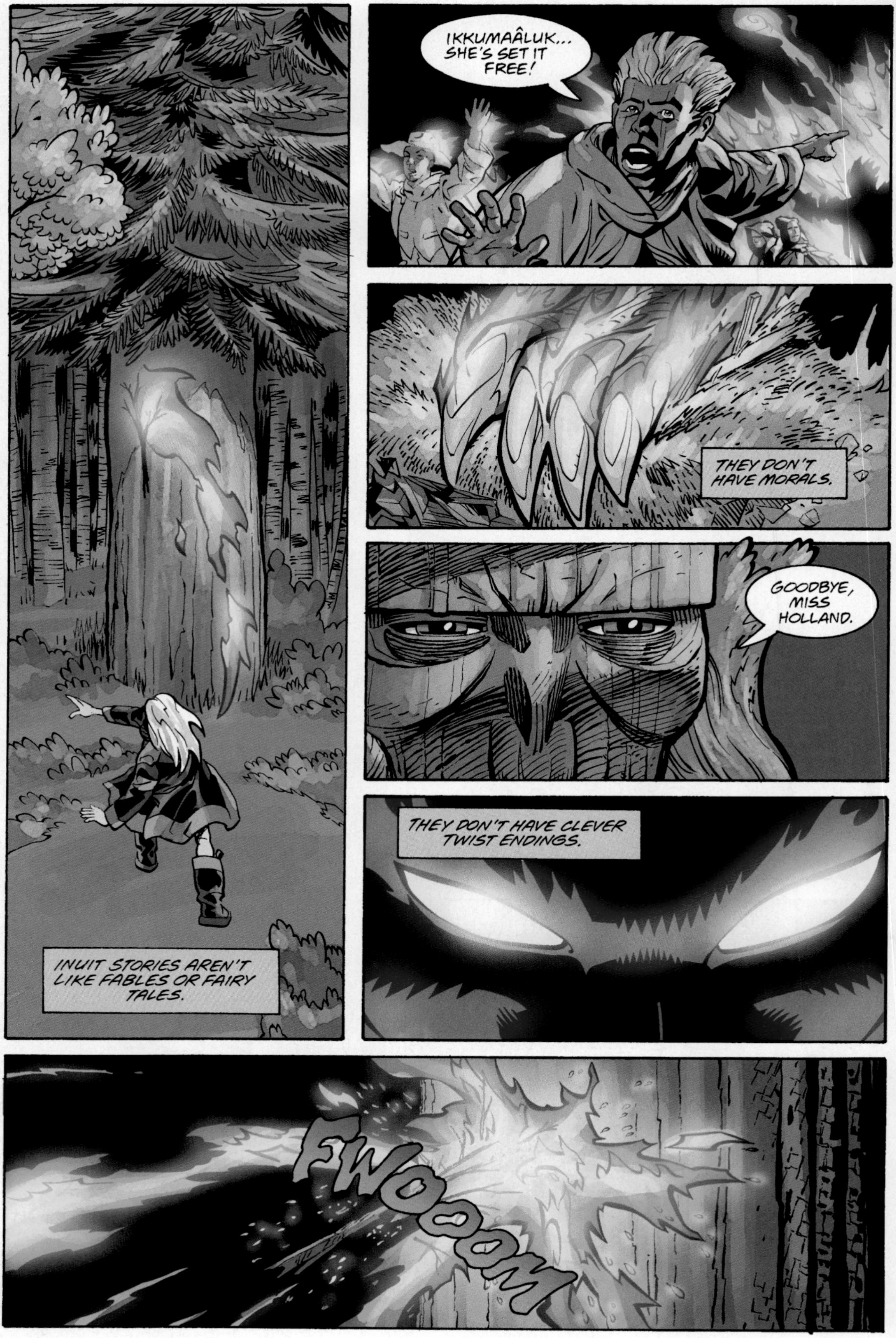
IKKUMAÂLUK... SHE'S SET IT FREE!
INUIT STORIES AREN'T LIKE FABLES OR FAIRY TALES.
THEY DON'T HAVE MORALS.
GOODBYE, MISS HOLLAND.
THEY DON'T HAVE CLEVER TWIST ENDINGS.
FWOOOOM

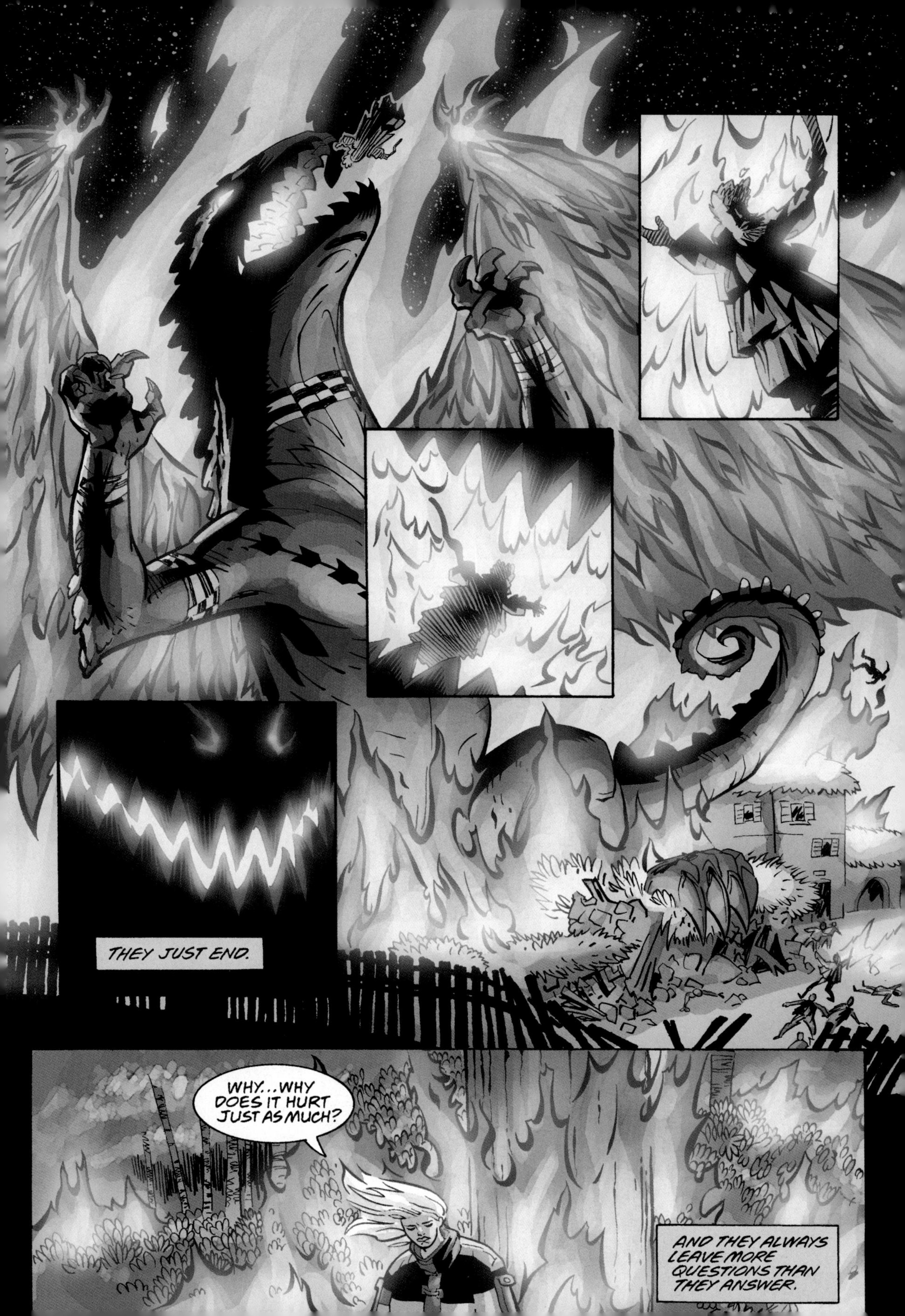
THEY JUST END.
WHY...WHY DOES IT HURT JUST AS MUCH?
AND THEY ALWAYS LEAVE MORE QUESTIONS THAN THEY ANSWER.

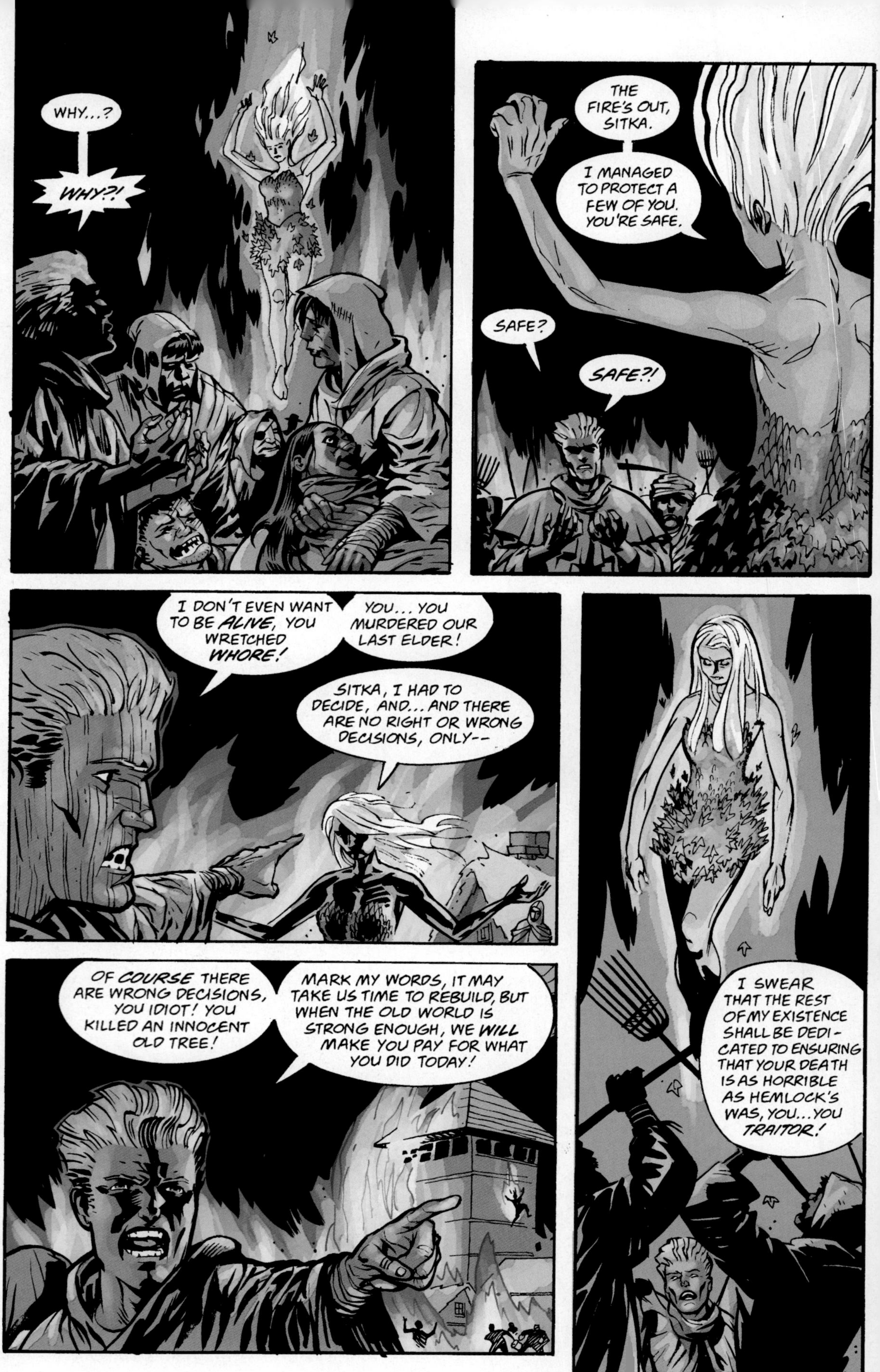
WHY...?
WHY?!
THE FIRE'S OUT, SITKA.
I MANAGED TO PROTECT A FEW OF YOU. YOU'RE SAFE.
SAFE?
SAFE?!
I DON'T EVEN WANT TO BE ALIVE, YOU WRETCHED WHORE!
YOU... YOU MURDERED OUR LAST ELDER!
SITKA, I HAD TO DECIDE, AND... AND THERE ARE NO RIGHT OR WRONG DECISIONS, ONLY--
OF COURSE THERE ARE WRONG DECISIONS, YOU IDIOT! YOU KILLED AN INNOCENT OLD TREE!
MARK MY WORDS, IT MAY TAKE US TIME TO REBUILD, BUT WHEN THE OLD WORLD IS STRONG ENOUGH, WE WILL MAKE YOU PAY FOR WHAT YOU DID TODAY!
I SWEAR THAT THE REST OF MY EXISTENCE SHALL BE DEDI-CATED TO ENSURING THAT YOUR DEATH IS AS HORRIBLE AS HEMLOCK'S WAS, YOU...YOU TRAITOR!

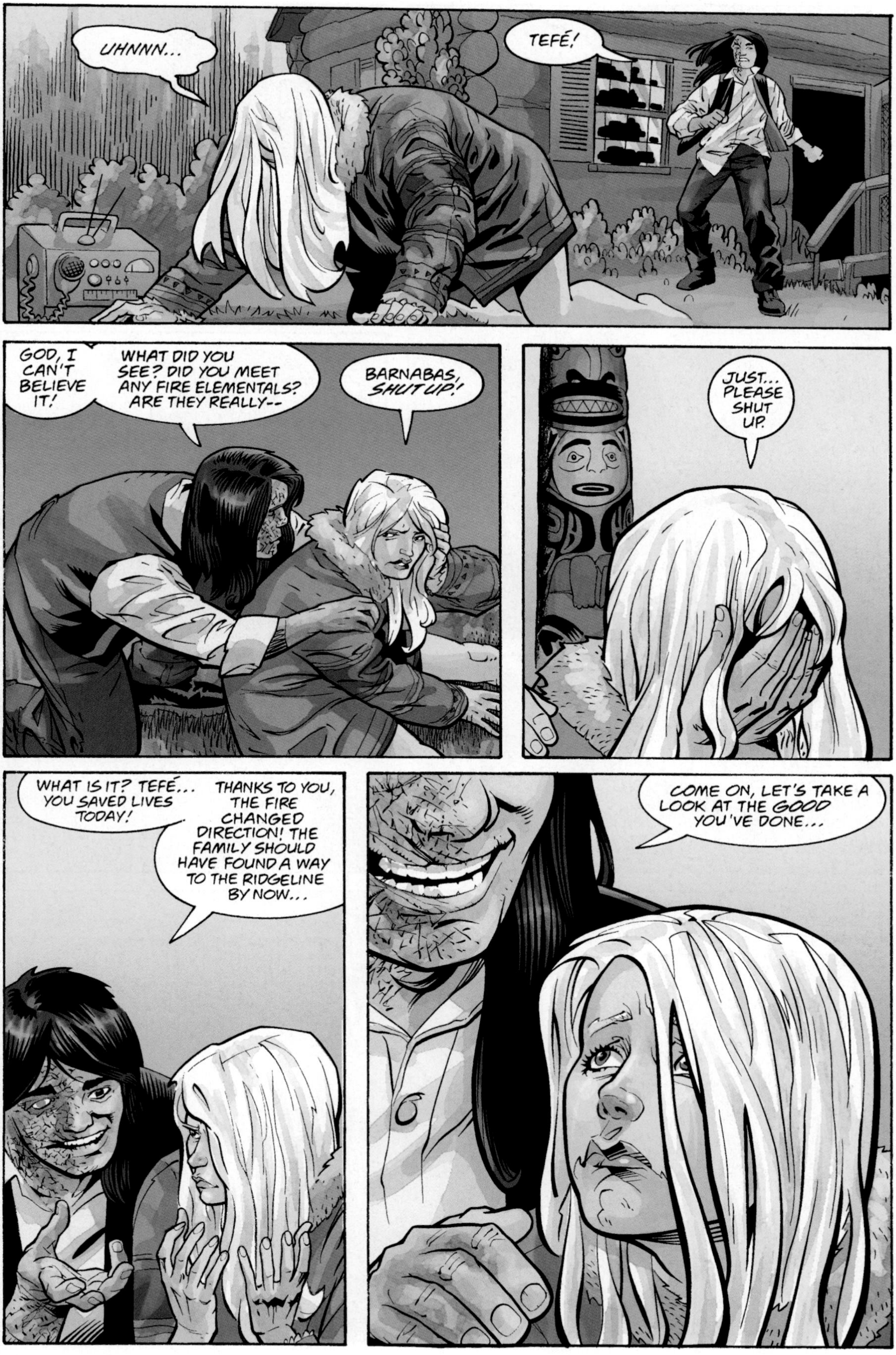
UHNNN...
TEFÉ!
GOD, I CAN'T BELIEVE IT!
WHAT DID YOU SEE? DID YOU MEET ANY FIRE ELEMENTALS? ARE THEY REALLY--
BARNABAS, *SHUT UP!*
JUST... PLEASE SHUT UP.
WHAT IS IT? TEFÉ... YOU SAVED LIVES TODAY!
THANKS TO YOU, THE FIRE CHANGED DIRECTION! THE FAMILY SHOULD HAVE FOUND A WAY TO THE RIDGELINE BY NOW...
COME ON, LET'S TAKE A LOOK AT THE *GOOD* YOU'VE DONE...

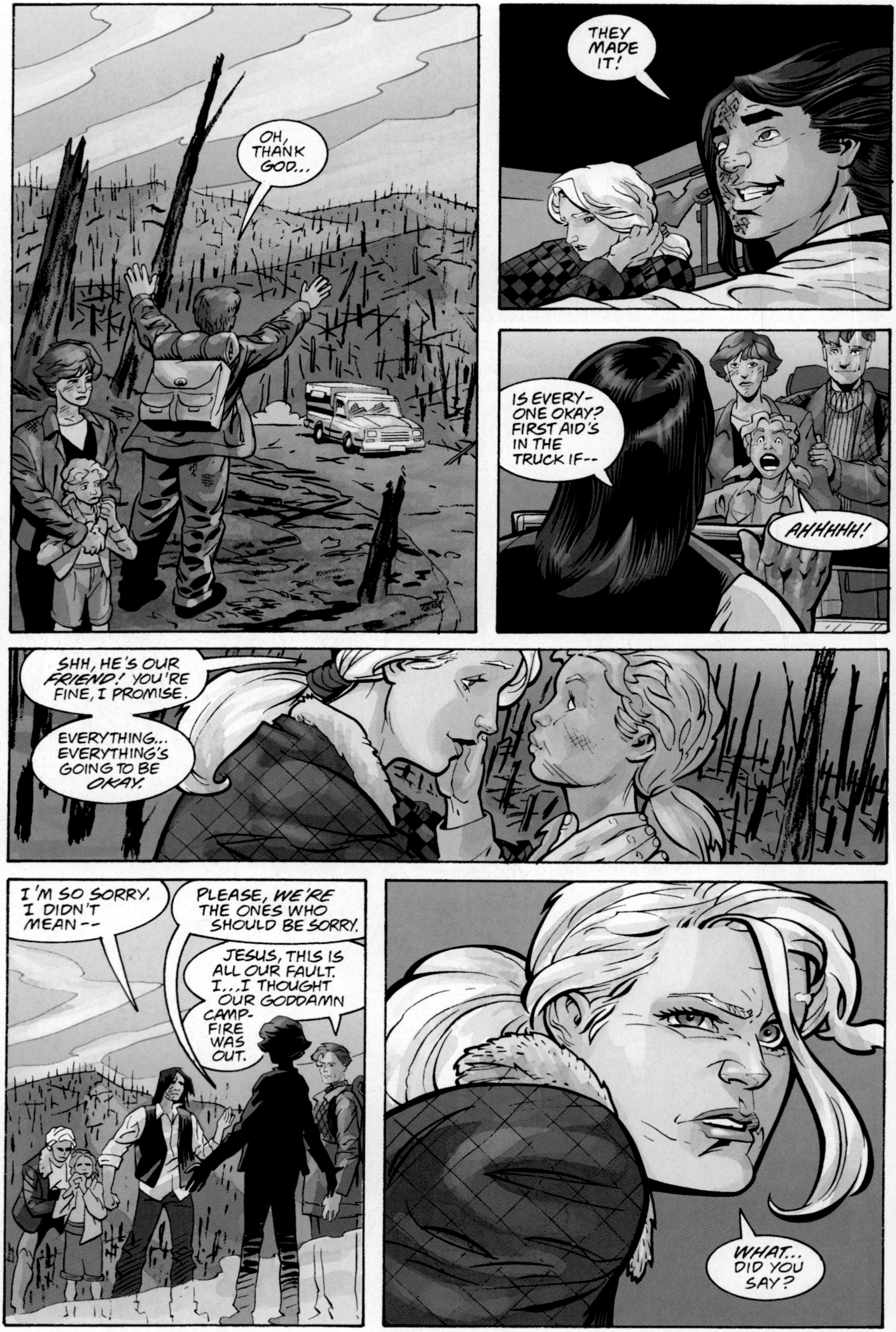
OH, THANK GOD...
THEY MADE IT!
IS EVERY-ONE OKAY? FIRST AID'S IN THE TRUCK IF--
AHHHHH!
SHH, HE'S OUR FRIEND! YOU'RE FINE, I PROMISE.
EVERYTHING... EVERYTHING'S GOING TO BE OKAY.
I'M SO SORRY. I DIDN'T MEAN--
PLEASE, WE'RE THE ONES WHO SHOULD BE SORRY.
JESUS, THIS IS ALL OUR FAULT. I...I THOUGHT OUR GODDAMN CAMP-FIRE WAS OUT.
WHAT... DID YOU SAY?

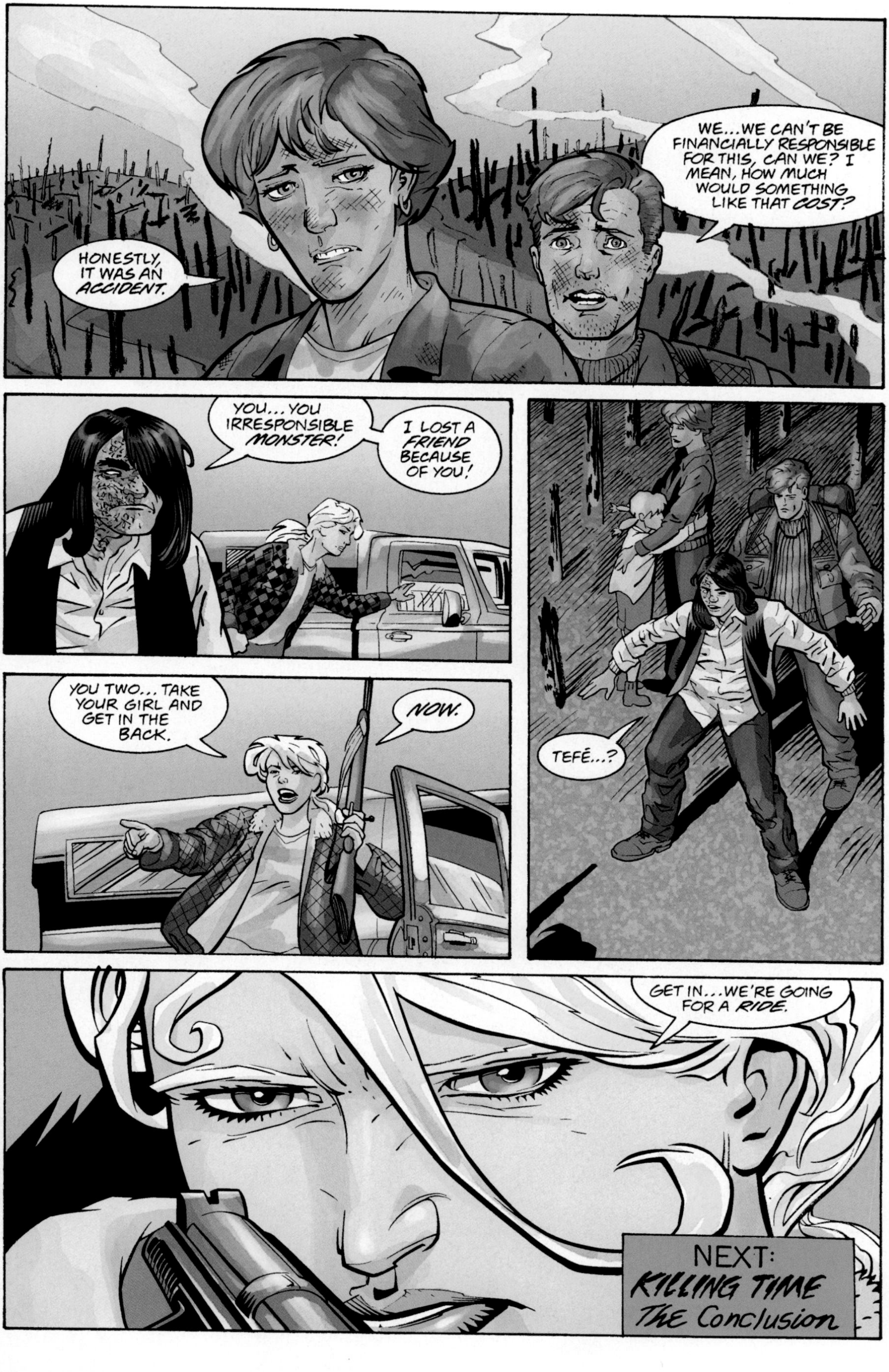
WE...WE CAN'T BE FINANCIALLY RESPONSIBLE FOR THIS, CAN WE? I MEAN, HOW MUCH WOULD SOMETHING LIKE THAT COST?
HONESTLY, IT WAS AN ACCIDENT.
YOU...YOU IRRESPONSIBLE MONSTER!
I LOST A FRIEND BECAUSE OF YOU!
TEFÊ...?
YOU TWO...TAKE YOUR GIRL AND GET IN THE BACK.
NOW.
GET IN...WE'RE GOING FOR A RIDE.
NEXT:
KILLING TIME
The Conclusion

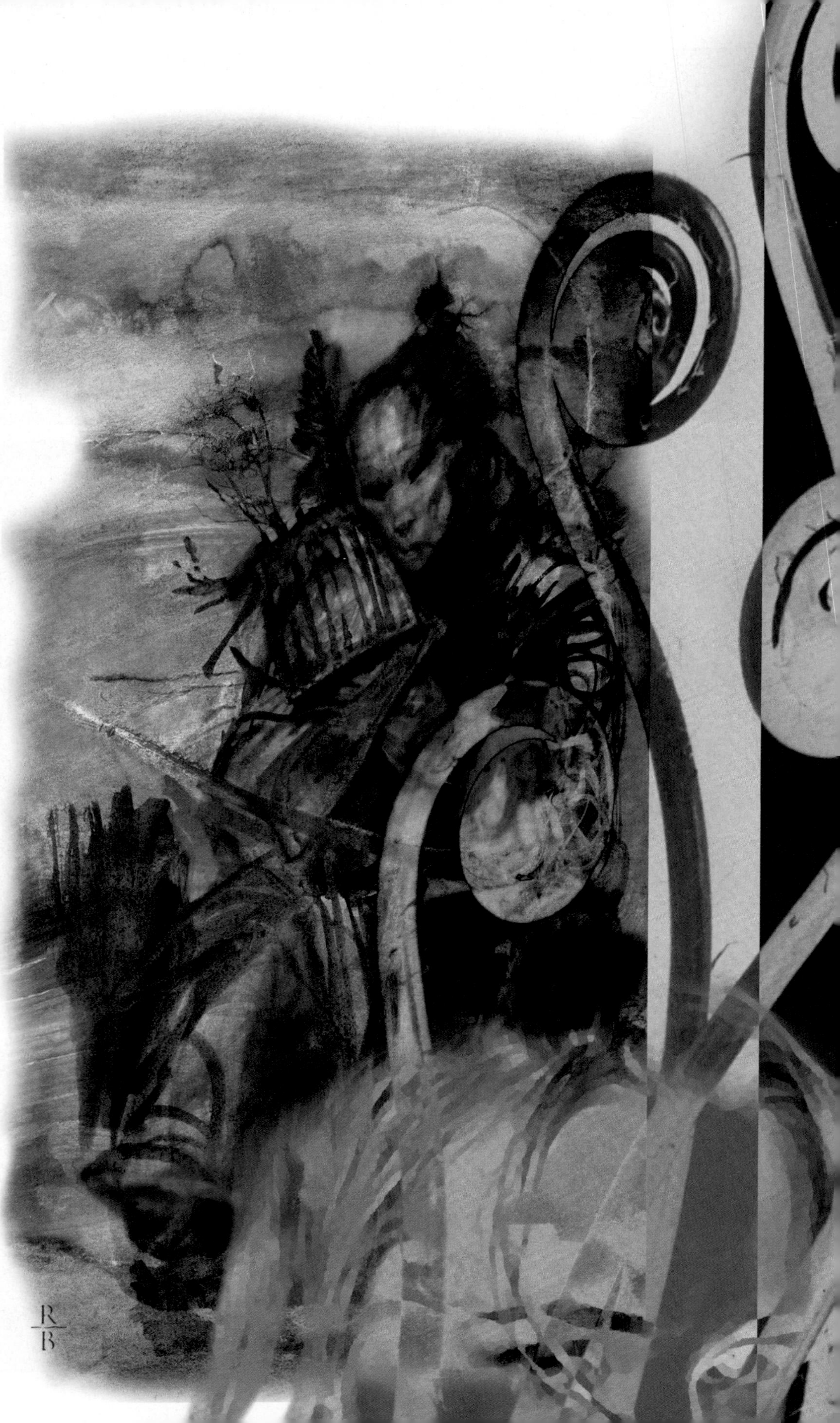

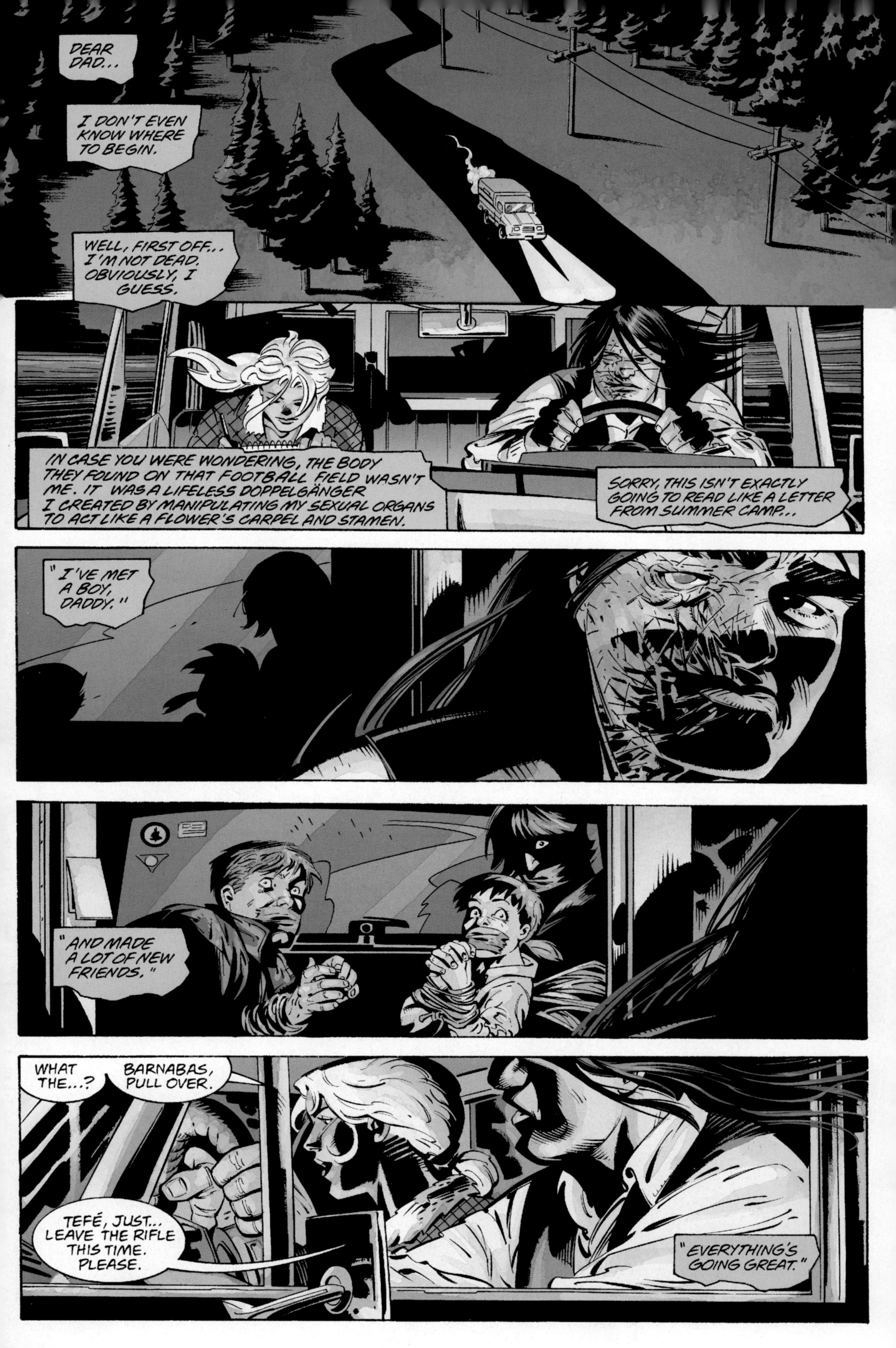
DEAR DAD...
I DON'T EVEN KNOW WHERE TO BEGIN.
WELL, FIRST OFF... I'M NOT DEAD. OBVIOUSLY, I GUESS.
IN CASE YOU WERE WONDERING, THE BODY THEY FOUND ON THAT FOOTBALL FIELD WASN'T ME. IT WAS A LIFELESS DOPPELGÄNGER I CREATED BY MANIPULATING MY SEXUAL ORGANS TO ACT LIKE A FLOWER'S CARPEL AND STAMEN.
SORRY, THIS ISN'T EXACTLY GOING TO READ LIKE A LETTER FROM SUMMER CAMP...
"I'VE MET A BOY, DADDY."
"AND MADE A LOT OF NEW FRIENDS."
WHAT THE...?
BARNABAS, PULL OVER.
TEFÉ, JUST... LEAVE THE RIFLE THIS TIME. PLEASE.
"EVERYTHING'S GOING GREAT."

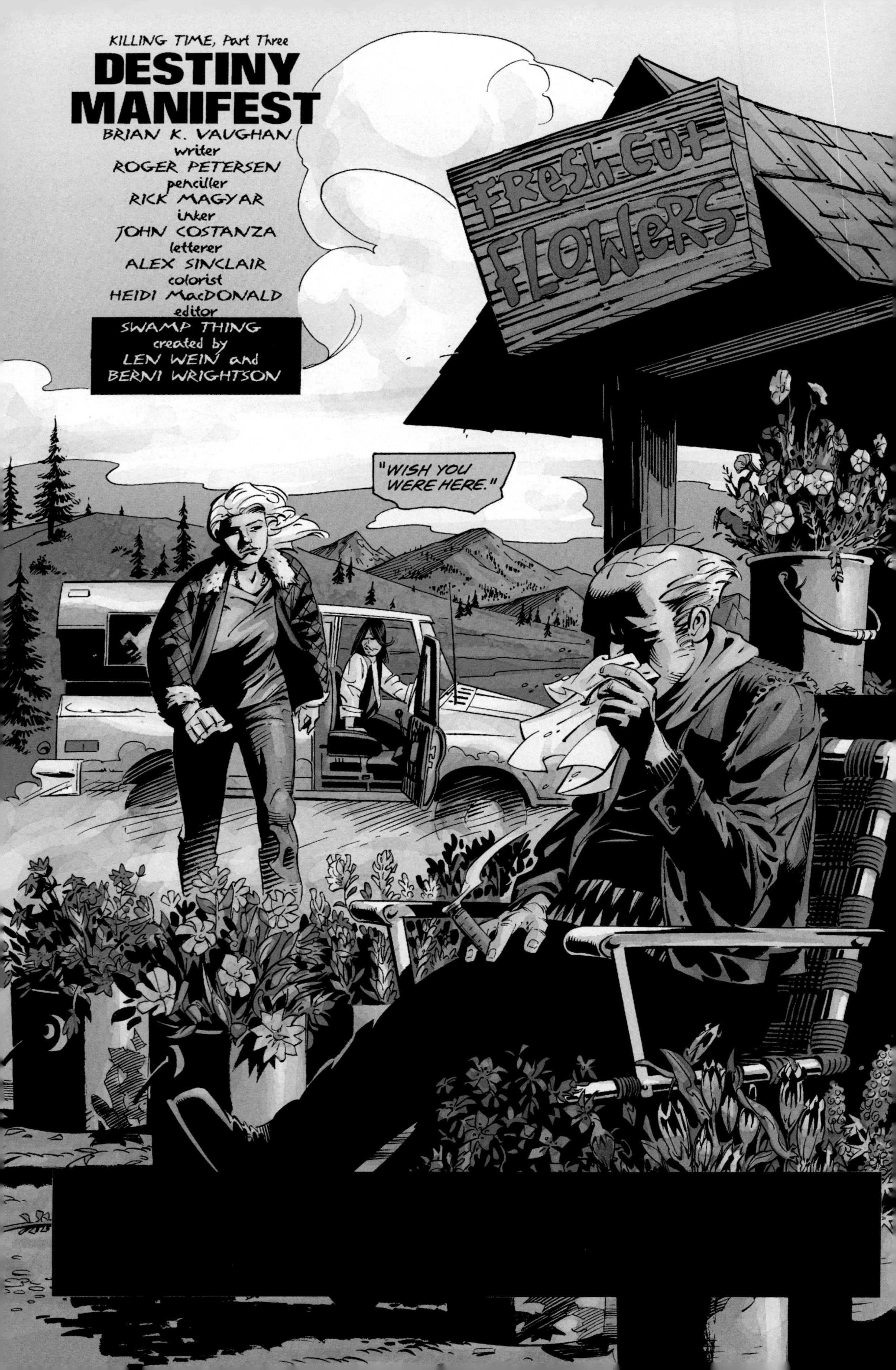

KILLING TIME, Part Three
DESTINY MANIFEST
BRIAN K. VAUGHAN writer
ROGER PETERSEN penciller
RICK MAGYAR inker
JOHN COSTANZA letterer
ALEX SINCLAIR colorist
HEIDI MacDONALD editor
SWAMP THING created by LEN WEIN and BERNI WRIGHTSON
FRESH CUT FLOWERS
"WISH YOU WERE HERE."
[redacted]

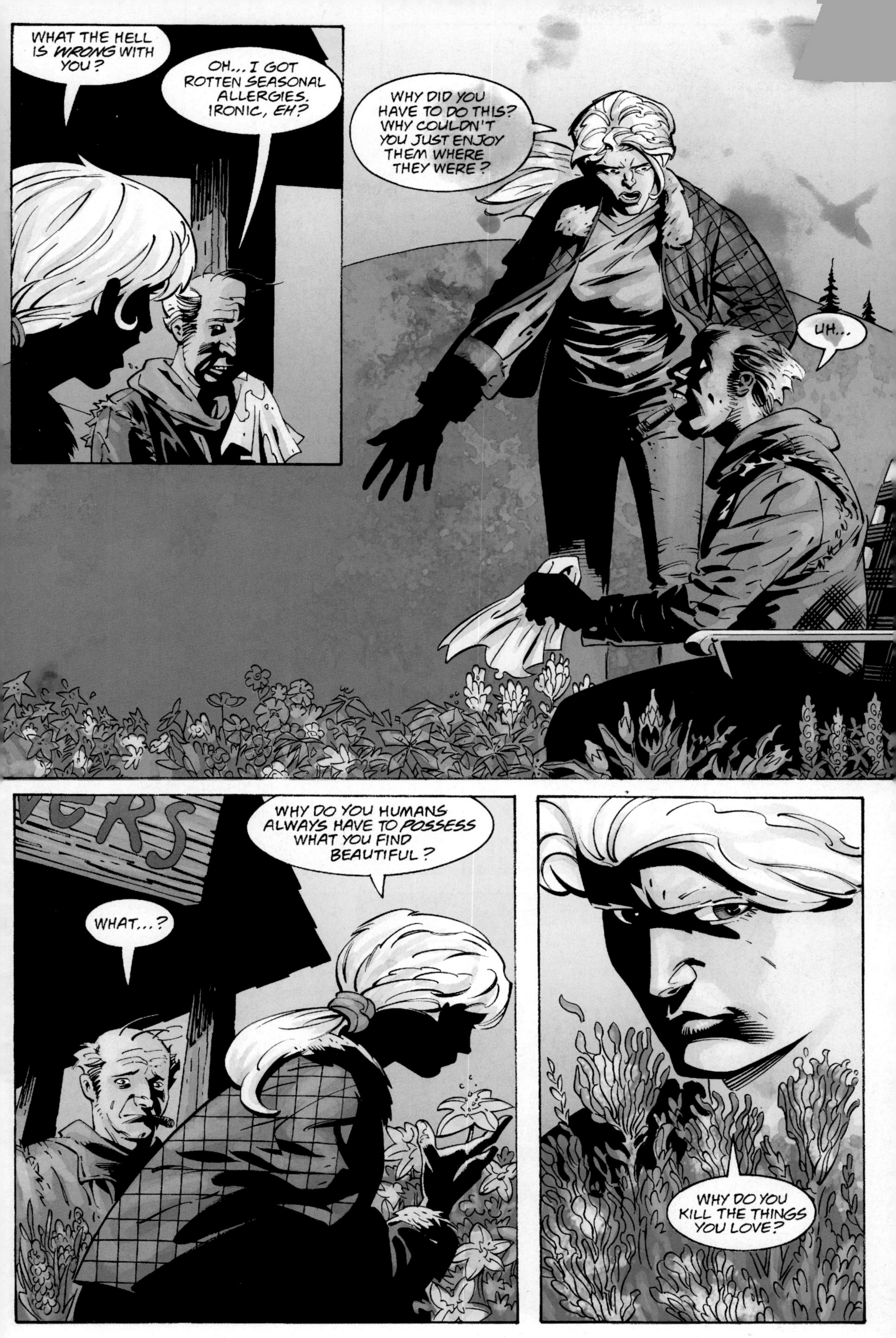
WHAT THE HELL IS WRONG WITH YOU?
OH... I GOT ROTTEN SEASONAL ALLERGIES. IRONIC, EH?
WHY DID YOU HAVE TO DO THIS? WHY COULDN'T YOU JUST ENJOY THEM WHERE THEY WERE?
UH...
ERS
WHY DO YOU HUMANS ALWAYS HAVE TO POSSESS WHAT YOU FIND BEAUTIFUL?
WHAT...?
WHY DO YOU KILL THE THINGS YOU LOVE?

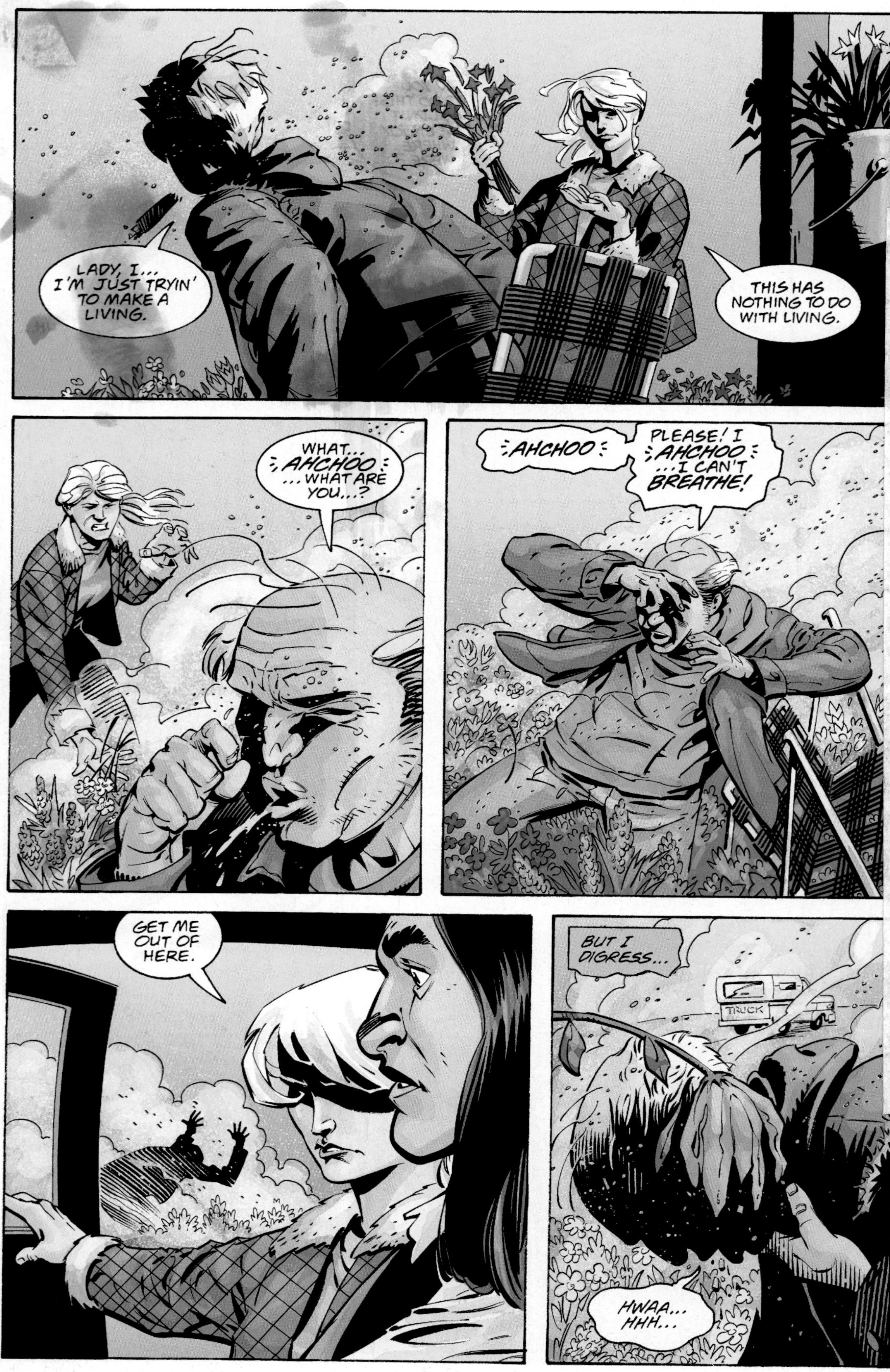
LADY, I... I'M JUST TRYIN' TO MAKE A LIVING.
THIS HAS NOTHING TO DO WITH LIVING.
WHAT... AHCHOO ...WHAT ARE YOU...?
AHCHOO
PLEASE! I AHCHOO ...I CAN'T BREATHE!
GET ME OUT OF HERE.
BUT I DIGRESS...
TRUCK
HWAA... HHH...

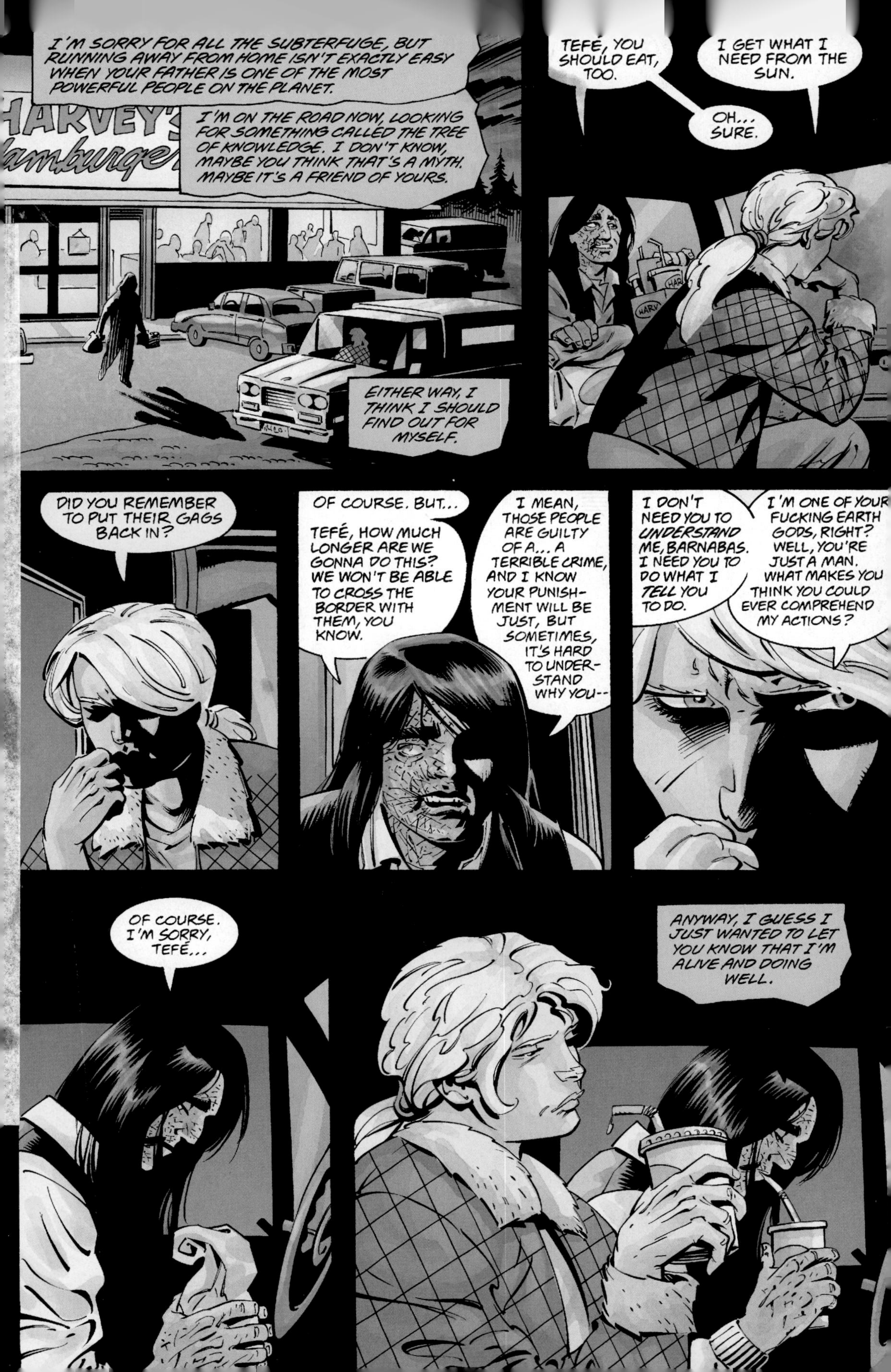
I'M SORRY FOR ALL THE SUBTERFUGE, BUT RUNNING AWAY FROM HOME ISN'T EXACTLY EASY WHEN YOUR FATHER IS ONE OF THE MOST POWERFUL PEOPLE ON THE PLANET.
HARVEY'S Hamburgers
I'M ON THE ROAD NOW, LOOKING FOR SOMETHING CALLED THE TREE OF KNOWLEDGE. I DON'T KNOW, MAYBE YOU THINK THAT'S A MYTH. MAYBE IT'S A FRIEND OF YOURS.
EITHER WAY, I THINK I SHOULD FIND OUT FOR MYSELF.
TEFÉ, YOU SHOULD EAT, TOO.
I GET WHAT I NEED FROM THE SUN.
OH... SURE.
DID YOU REMEMBER TO PUT THEIR GAGS BACK IN?
OF COURSE. BUT...
TEFÉ, HOW MUCH LONGER ARE WE GONNA DO THIS? WE WON'T BE ABLE TO CROSS THE BORDER WITH THEM, YOU KNOW.
I MEAN, THOSE PEOPLE ARE GUILTY OF A... A TERRIBLE CRIME, AND I KNOW YOUR PUNISHMENT WILL BE JUST, BUT SOMETIMES, IT'S HARD TO UNDERSTAND WHY YOU--
I DON'T NEED YOU TO UNDERSTAND ME, BARNABAS. I NEED YOU TO DO WHAT I TELL YOU TO DO.
I'M ONE OF YOUR FUCKING EARTH GODS, RIGHT? WELL, YOU'RE JUST A MAN. WHAT MAKES YOU THINK YOU COULD EVER COMPREHEND MY ACTIONS?
OF COURSE. I'M SORRY, TEFÉ...
ANYWAY, I GUESS I JUST WANTED TO LET YOU KNOW THAT I'M ALIVE AND DOING WELL.

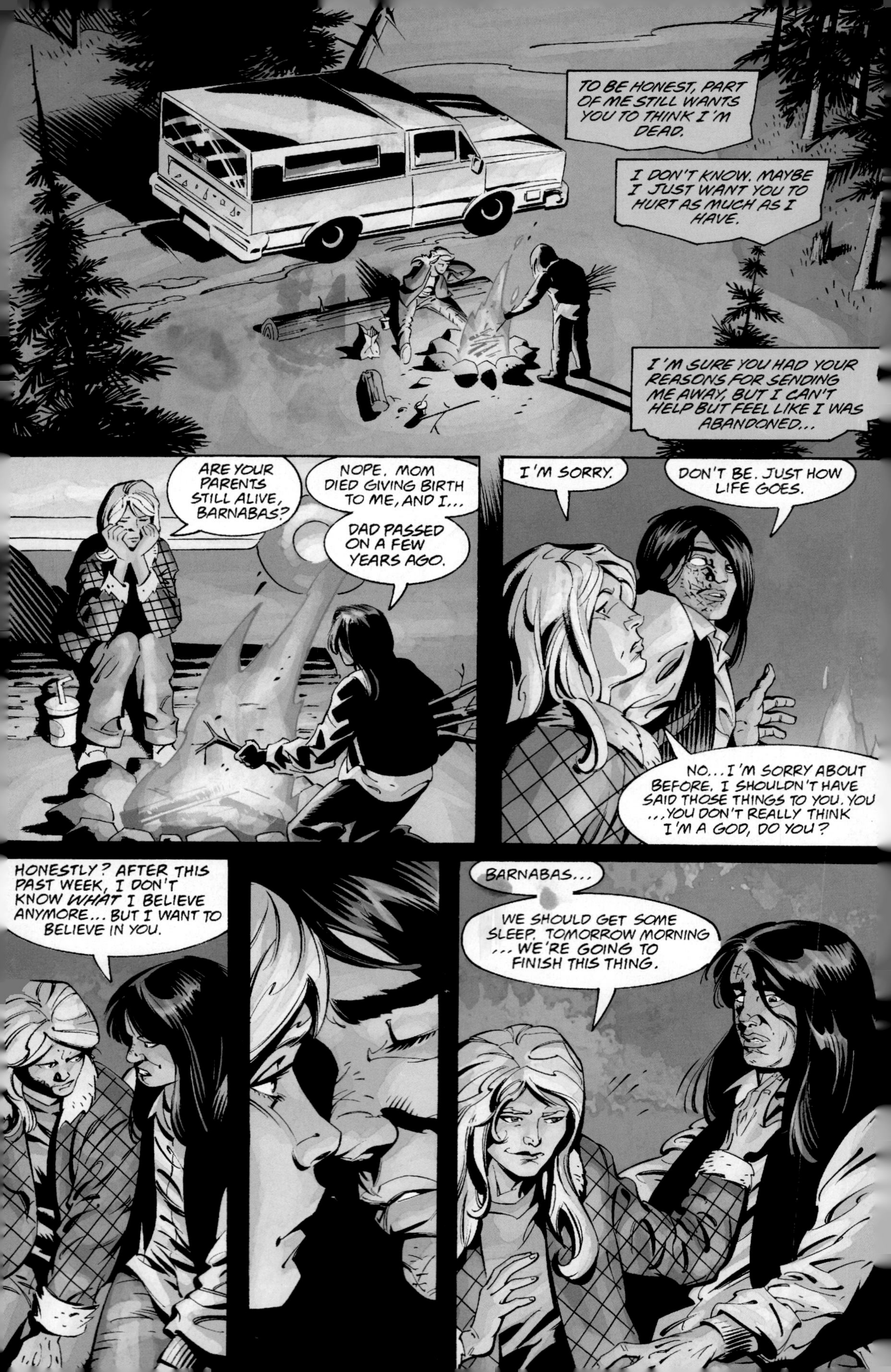
TO BE HONEST, PART OF ME STILL WANTS YOU TO THINK I'M DEAD.
I DON'T KNOW. MAYBE I JUST WANT YOU TO HURT AS MUCH AS I HAVE.
I'M SURE YOU HAD YOUR REASONS FOR SENDING ME AWAY, BUT I CAN'T HELP BUT FEEL LIKE I WAS ABANDONED...
ARE YOUR PARENTS STILL ALIVE, BARNABAS?
NOPE. MOM DIED GIVING BIRTH TO ME, AND I...
DAD PASSED ON A FEW YEARS AGO.
I'M SORRY.
DON'T BE. JUST HOW LIFE GOES.
NO... I'M SORRY ABOUT BEFORE. I SHOULDN'T HAVE SAID THOSE THINGS TO YOU. YOU ...YOU DON'T REALLY THINK I'M A GOD, DO YOU?
HONESTLY? AFTER THIS PAST WEEK, I DON'T KNOW WHAT I BELIEVE ANYMORE... BUT I WANT TO BELIEVE IN YOU.
BARNABAS...
WE SHOULD GET SOME SLEEP. TOMORROW MORNING ...WE'RE GOING TO FINISH THIS THING.

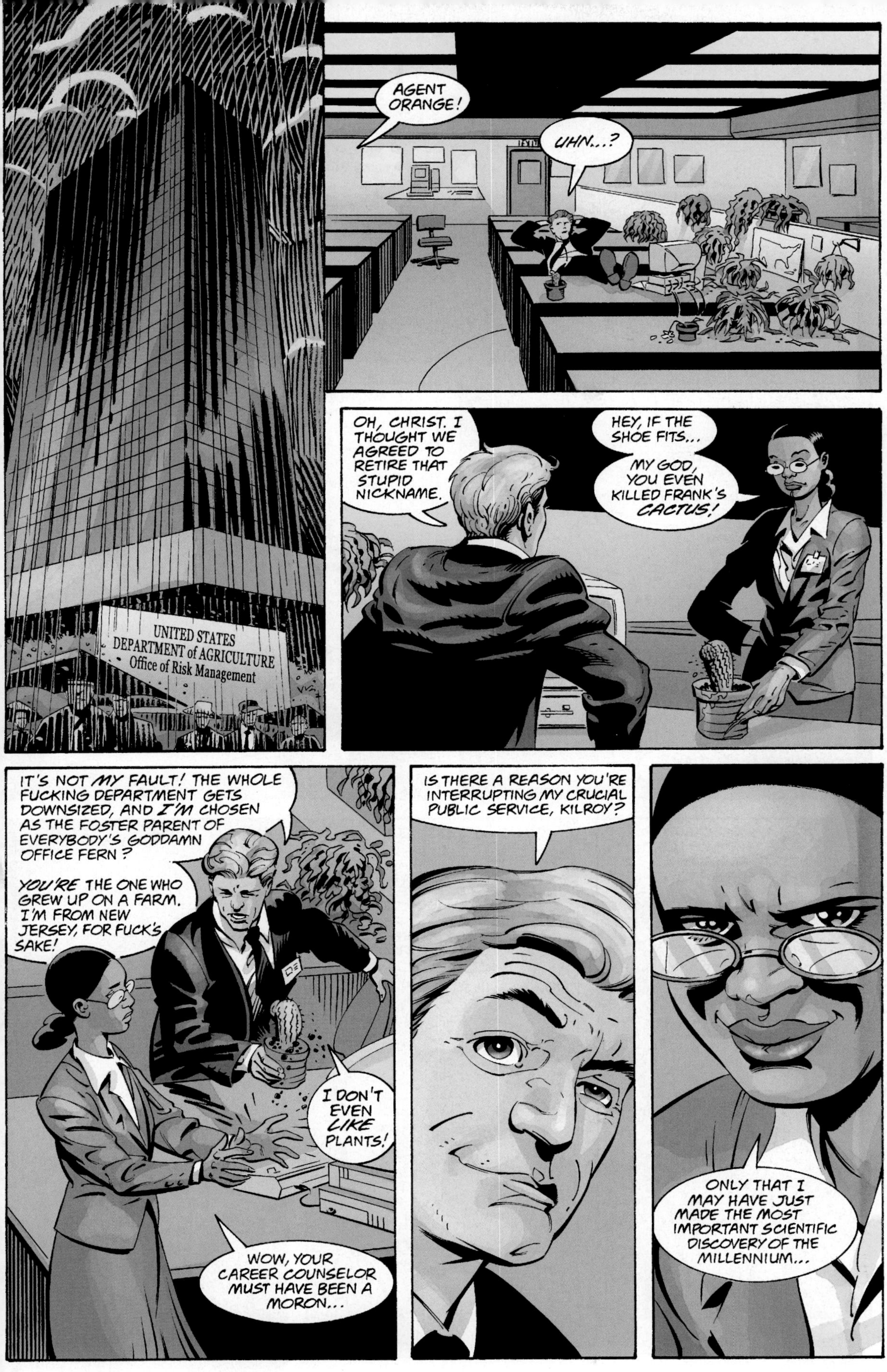

UNITED STATES
DEPARTMENT of AGRICULTURE
Office of Risk Management
AGENT ORANGE!
UHN...?
OH, CHRIST. I THOUGHT WE AGREED TO RETIRE THAT STUPID NICKNAME.
HEY, IF THE SHOE FITS...
MY GOD, YOU EVEN KILLED FRANK'S CACTUS!
IT'S NOT MY FAULT! THE WHOLE FUCKING DEPARTMENT GETS DOWNSIZED, AND I'M CHOSEN AS THE FOSTER PARENT OF EVERYBODY'S GODDAMN OFFICE FERN?
YOU'RE THE ONE WHO GREW UP ON A FARM. I'M FROM NEW JERSEY, FOR FUCK'S SAKE!
I DON'T EVEN LIKE PLANTS!
WOW, YOUR CAREER COUNSELOR MUST HAVE BEEN A MORON...
IS THERE A REASON YOU'RE INTERRUPTING MY CRUCIAL PUBLIC SERVICE, KILROY?
ONLY THAT I MAY HAVE JUST MADE THE MOST IMPORTANT SCIENTIFIC DISCOVERY OF THE MILLENNIUM...

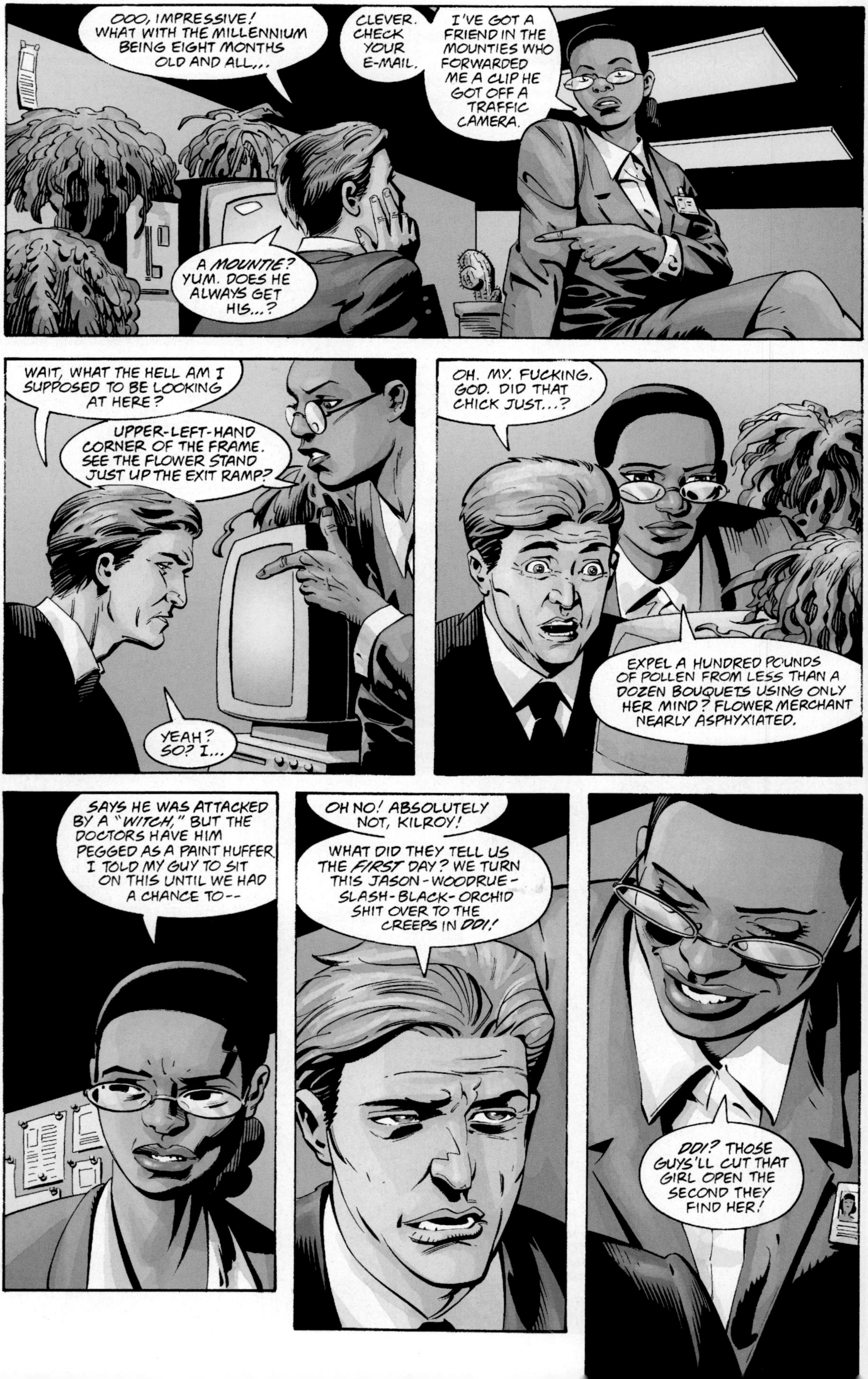
OOO, IMPRESSIVE! WHAT WITH THE MILLENNIUM BEING EIGHT MONTHS OLD AND ALL...
CLEVER. CHECK YOUR E-MAIL.
I'VE GOT A FRIEND IN THE MOUNTIES WHO FORWARDED ME A CLIP HE GOT OFF A TRAFFIC CAMERA.
A MOUNTIE? YUM. DOES HE ALWAYS GET HIS...?
WAIT, WHAT THE HELL AM I SUPPOSED TO BE LOOKING AT HERE?
UPPER-LEFT-HAND CORNER OF THE FRAME. SEE THE FLOWER STAND JUST UP THE EXIT RAMP?
YEAH? SO? I...
OH. MY. FUCKING. GOD. DID THAT CHICK JUST...?
EXPEL A HUNDRED POUNDS OF POLLEN FROM LESS THAN A DOZEN BOUQUETS USING ONLY HER MIND? FLOWER MERCHANT NEARLY ASPHYXIATED.
SAYS HE WAS ATTACKED BY A "WITCH," BUT THE DOCTORS HAVE HIM PEGGED AS A PAINT HUFFER. I TOLD MY GUY TO SIT ON THIS UNTIL WE HAD A CHANCE TO--
OH NO! ABSOLUTELY NOT, KILROY!
WHAT DID THEY TELL US THE FIRST DAY? WE TURN THIS JASON-WOODRUE-SLASH-BLACK-ORCHID SHIT OVER TO THE CREEPS IN DDI!
DDI? THOSE GUYS'LL CUT THAT GIRL OPEN THE SECOND THEY FIND HER!

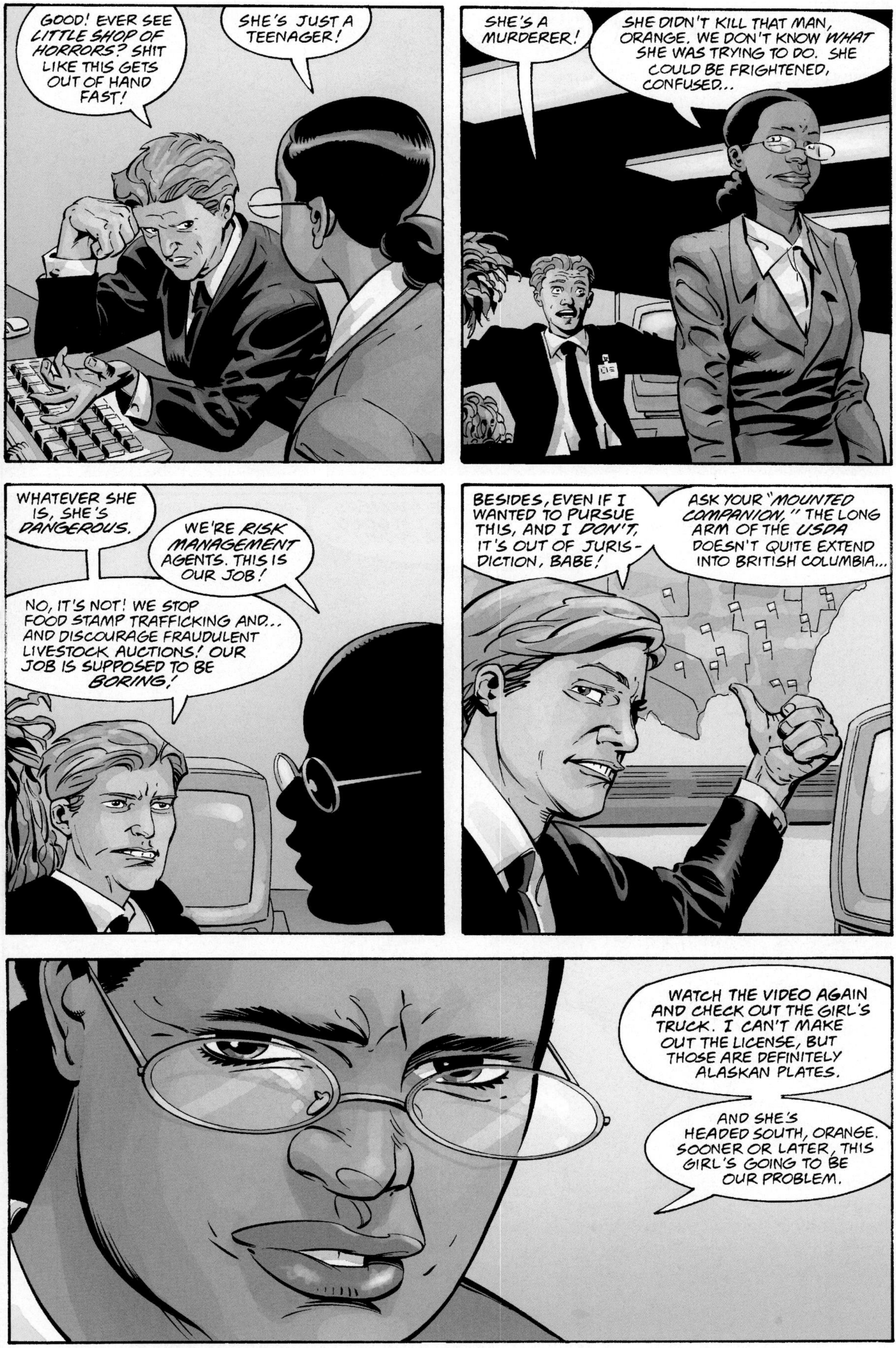
GOOD! EVER SEE LITTLE SHOP OF HORRORS? SHIT LIKE THIS GETS OUT OF HAND FAST!
SHE'S JUST A TEENAGER!
SHE'S A MURDERER!
SHE DIDN'T KILL THAT MAN, ORANGE. WE DON'T KNOW WHAT SHE WAS TRYING TO DO. SHE COULD BE FRIGHTENED, CONFUSED...
WHATEVER SHE IS, SHE'S DANGEROUS.
WE'RE RISK MANAGEMENT AGENTS. THIS IS OUR JOB!
NO, IT'S NOT! WE STOP FOOD STAMP TRAFFICKING AND... AND DISCOURAGE FRAUDULENT LIVESTOCK AUCTIONS! OUR JOB IS SUPPOSED TO BE BORING!
BESIDES, EVEN IF I WANTED TO PURSUE THIS, AND I DON'T, IT'S OUT OF JURIS-DICTION, BABE!
ASK YOUR "MOUNTED COMPANION," THE LONG ARM OF THE USDA DOESN'T QUITE EXTEND INTO BRITISH COLUMBIA...
WATCH THE VIDEO AGAIN AND CHECK OUT THE GIRL'S TRUCK. I CAN'T MAKE OUT THE LICENSE, BUT THOSE ARE DEFINITELY ALASKAN PLATES.
AND SHE'S HEADED SOUTH, ORANGE. SOONER OR LATER, THIS GIRL'S GOING TO BE OUR PROBLEM.

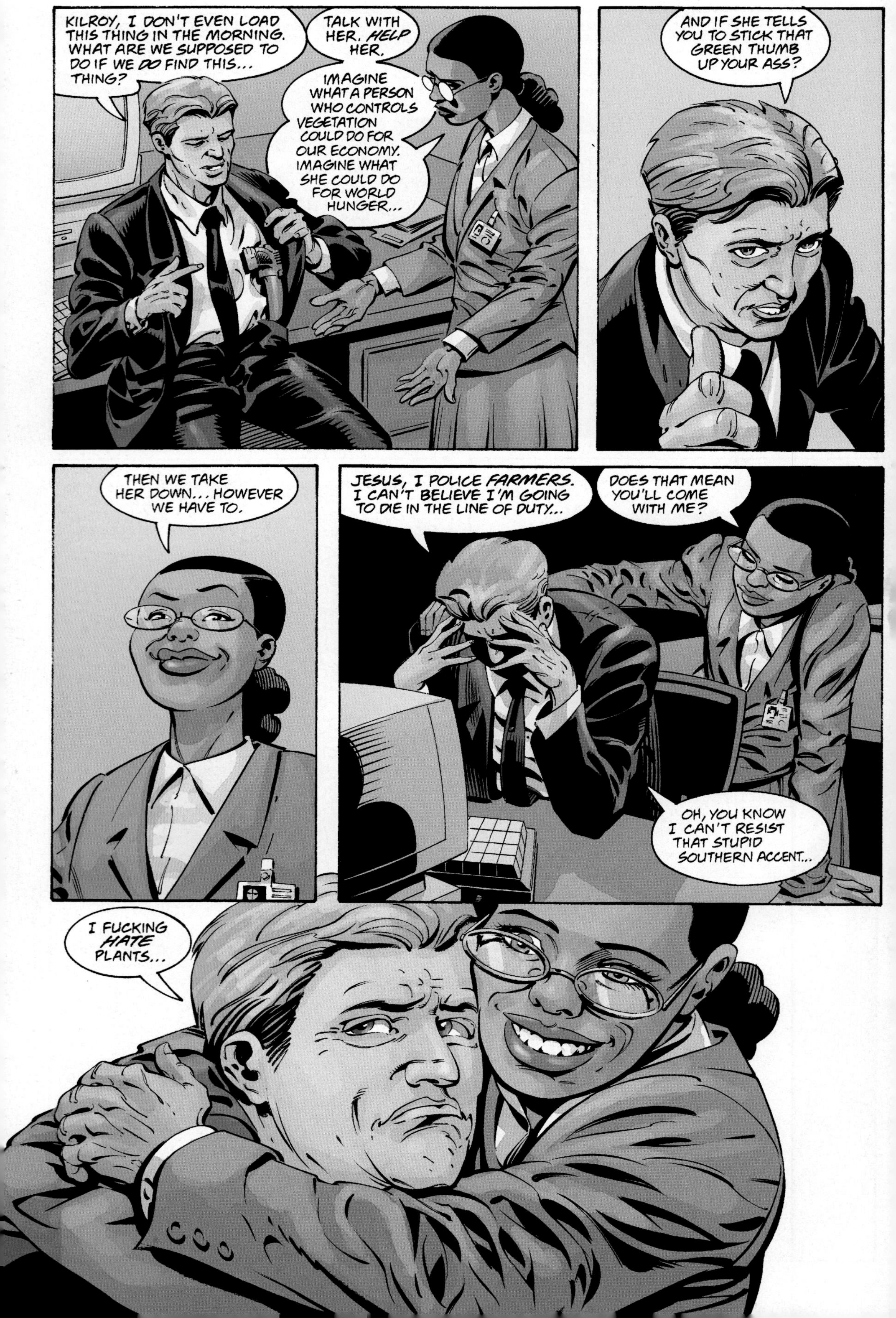
KILROY, I DON'T EVEN LOAD THIS THING IN THE MORNING. WHAT ARE WE SUPPOSED TO DO IF WE *DO* FIND THIS... THING?
TALK WITH HER. *HELP* HER.
IMAGINE WHAT A PERSON WHO CONTROLS VEGETATION COULD DO FOR OUR ECONOMY. IMAGINE WHAT SHE COULD DO FOR WORLD HUNGER...
AND IF SHE TELLS YOU TO STICK THAT GREEN THUMB UP YOUR ASS?
THEN WE TAKE HER DOWN... HOWEVER WE HAVE TO.
JESUS, I POLICE *FARMERS*. I CAN'T BELIEVE I'M GOING TO DIE IN THE LINE OF DUTY...
DOES THAT MEAN YOU'LL COME WITH ME?
OH, YOU KNOW I CAN'T RESIST THAT STUPID SOUTHERN ACCENT...
I FUCKING *HATE* PLANTS...

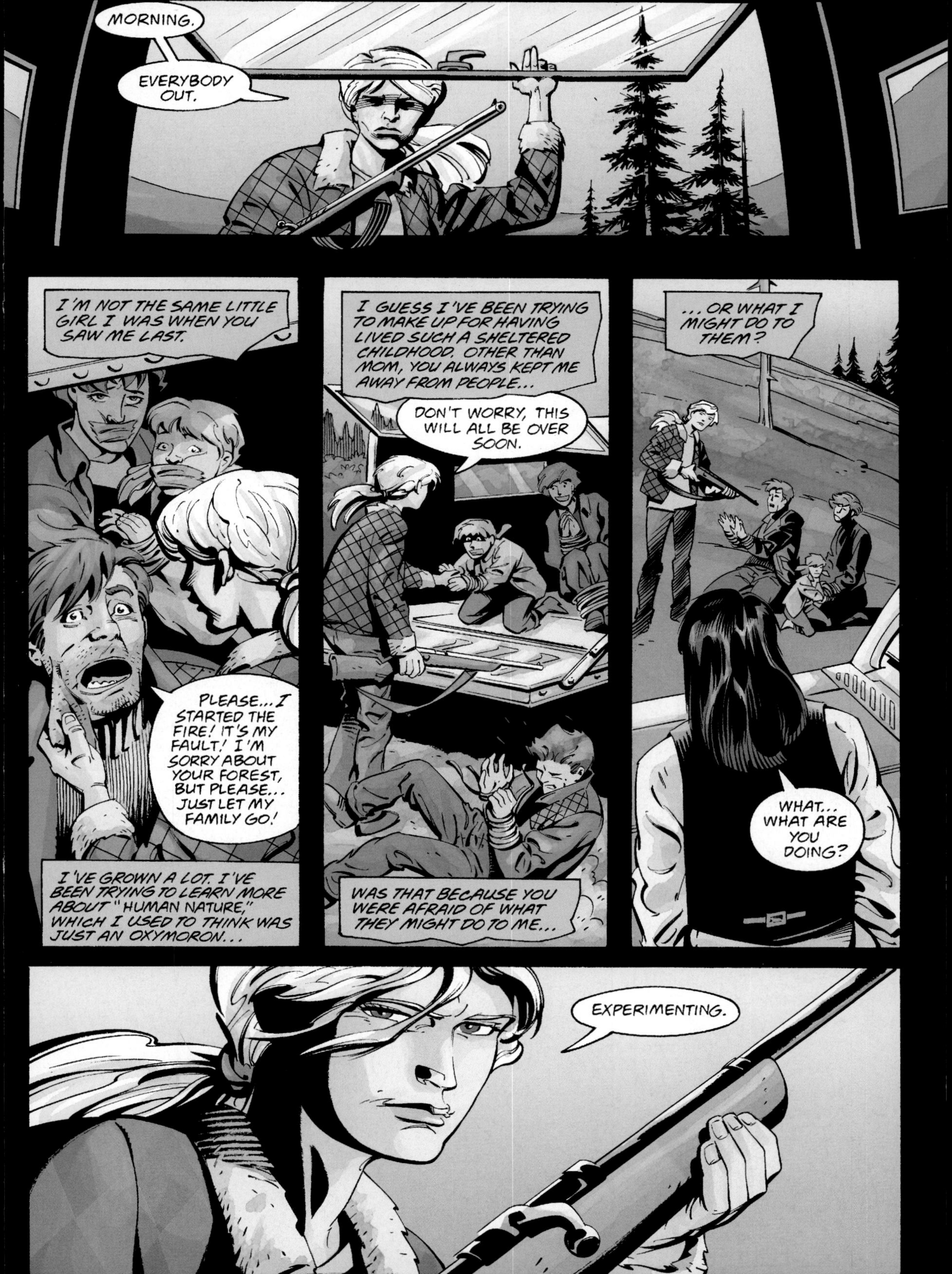
MORNING.
EVERYBODY OUT.
I'M NOT THE SAME LITTLE GIRL I WAS WHEN YOU SAW ME LAST.
PLEASE... I STARTED THE FIRE! IT'S MY FAULT! I'M SORRY ABOUT YOUR FOREST, BUT PLEASE... JUST LET MY FAMILY GO!
I'VE GROWN A LOT. I'VE BEEN TRYING TO LEARN MORE ABOUT "HUMAN NATURE," WHICH I USED TO THINK WAS JUST AN OXYMORON...
I GUESS I'VE BEEN TRYING TO MAKE UP FOR HAVING LIVED SUCH A SHELTERED CHILDHOOD. OTHER THAN MOM, YOU ALWAYS KEPT ME AWAY FROM PEOPLE...
DON'T WORRY, THIS WILL ALL BE OVER SOON.
WAS THAT BECAUSE YOU WERE AFRAID OF WHAT THEY MIGHT DO TO ME...
...OR WHAT I MIGHT DO TO THEM?
WHAT... WHAT ARE YOU DOING?
EXPERIMENTING.

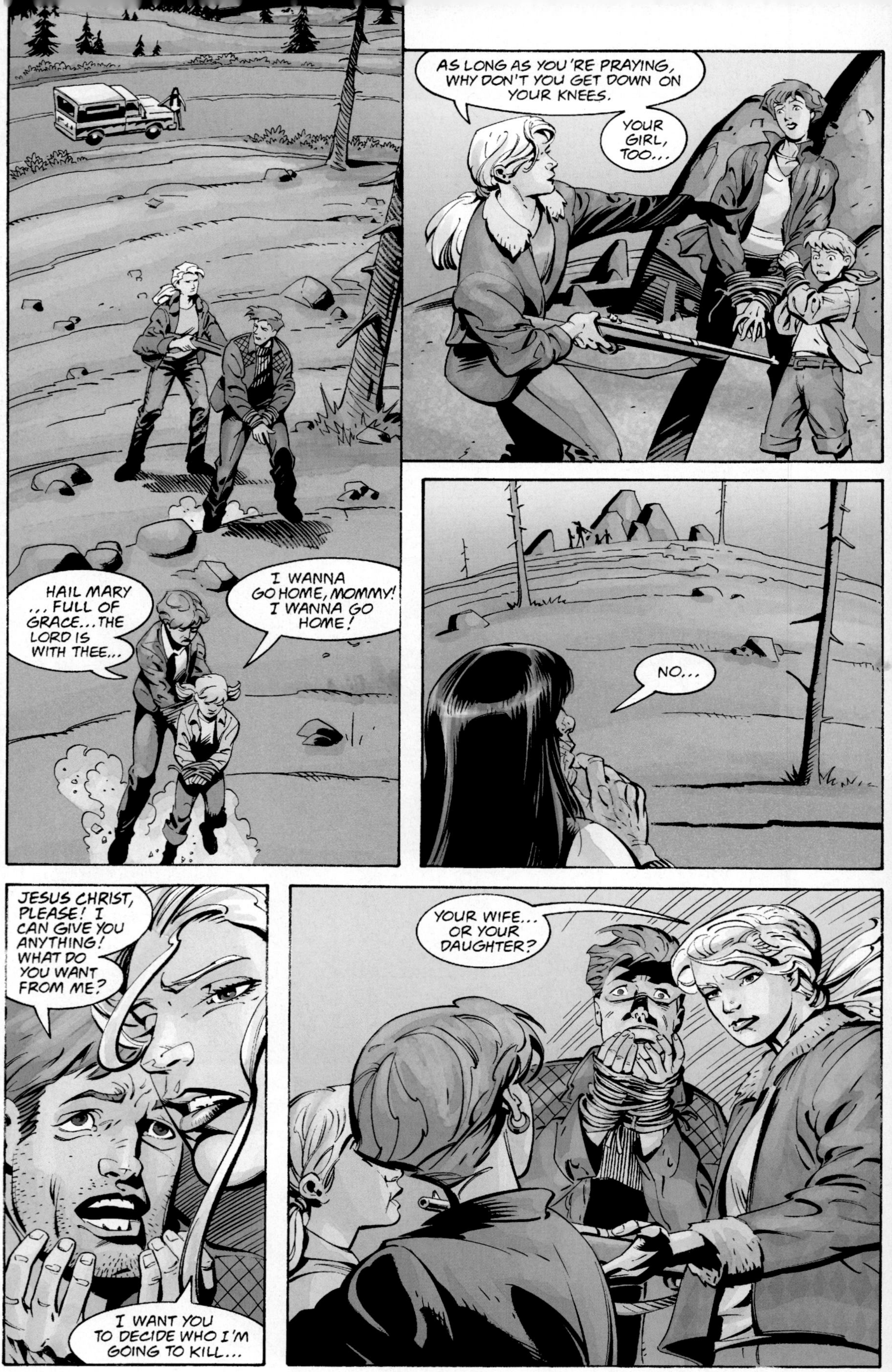
HAIL MARY ... FULL OF GRACE... THE LORD IS WITH THEE...
I WANNA GO HOME, MOMMY! I WANNA GO HOME!
AS LONG AS YOU'RE PRAYING, WHY DON'T YOU GET DOWN ON YOUR KNEES.
YOUR GIRL, TOO...
NO...
JESUS CHRIST, PLEASE! I CAN GIVE YOU ANYTHING! WHAT DO YOU WANT FROM ME?
I WANT YOU TO DECIDE WHO I'M GOING TO KILL...
YOUR WIFE... OR YOUR DAUGHTER?

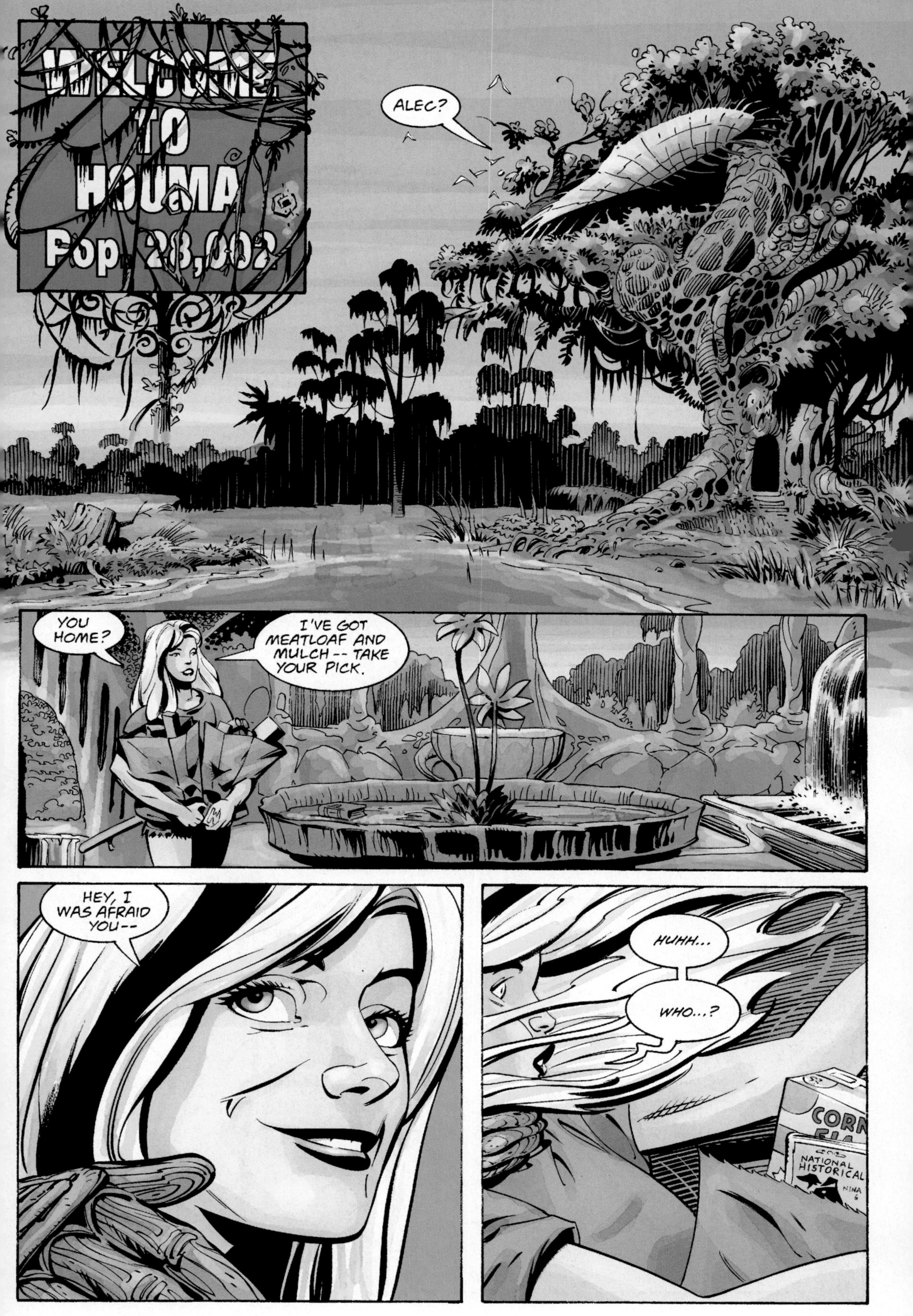
WELCOME TO HOUMA Pop. 28,002
ALEC?
YOU HOME?
I'VE GOT MEATLOAF AND MULCH -- TAKE YOUR PICK.
HEY, I WAS AFRAID YOU--
HUHH...
WHO...?
CORN
NATIONAL HISTORICAL
NINA 6

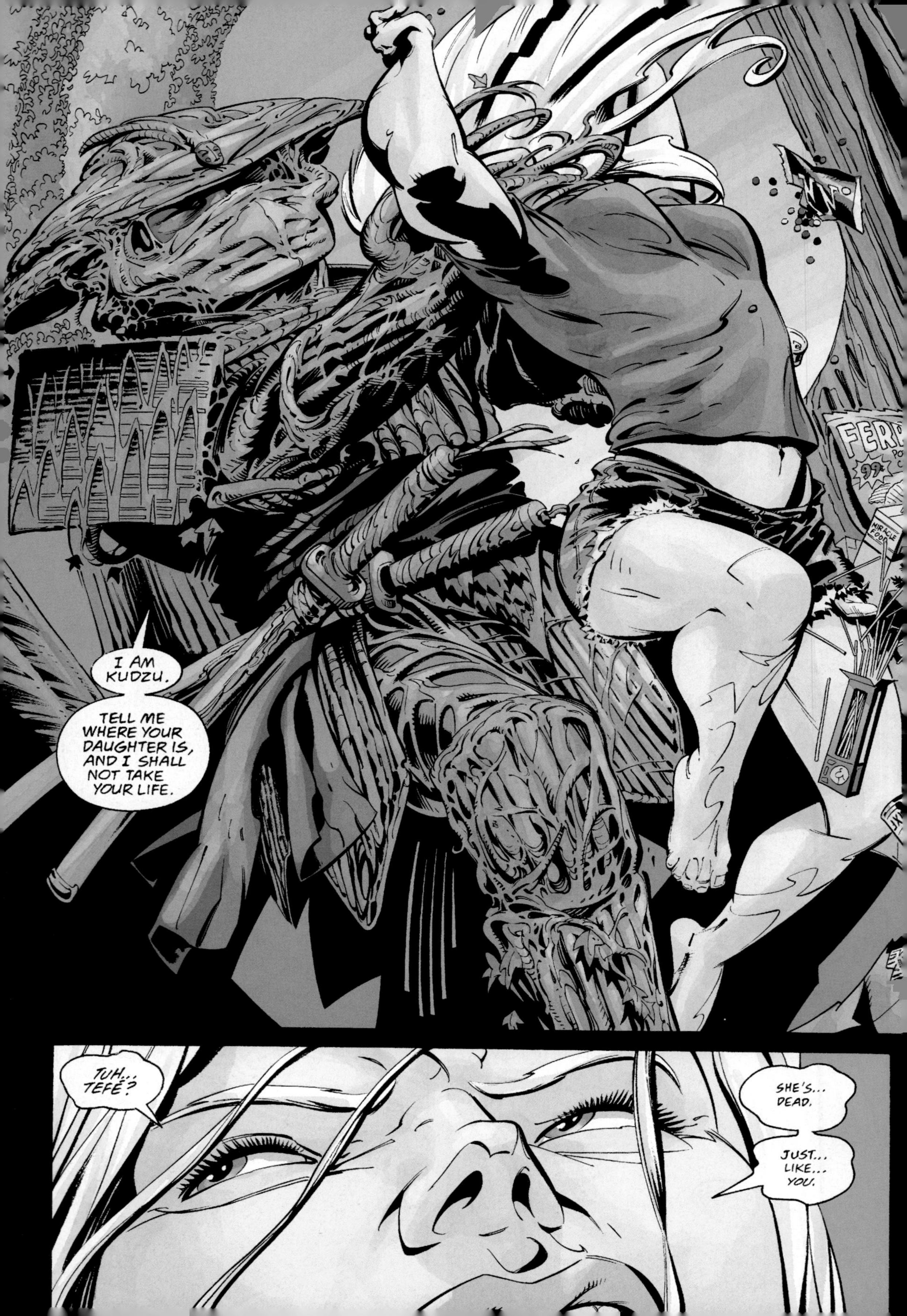
I AM KUDZU.
TELL ME WHERE YOUR DAUGHTER IS, AND I SHALL NOT TAKE YOUR LIFE.
TUH... TEFÉ?
SHE'S... DEAD.
JUST... LIKE... YOU.

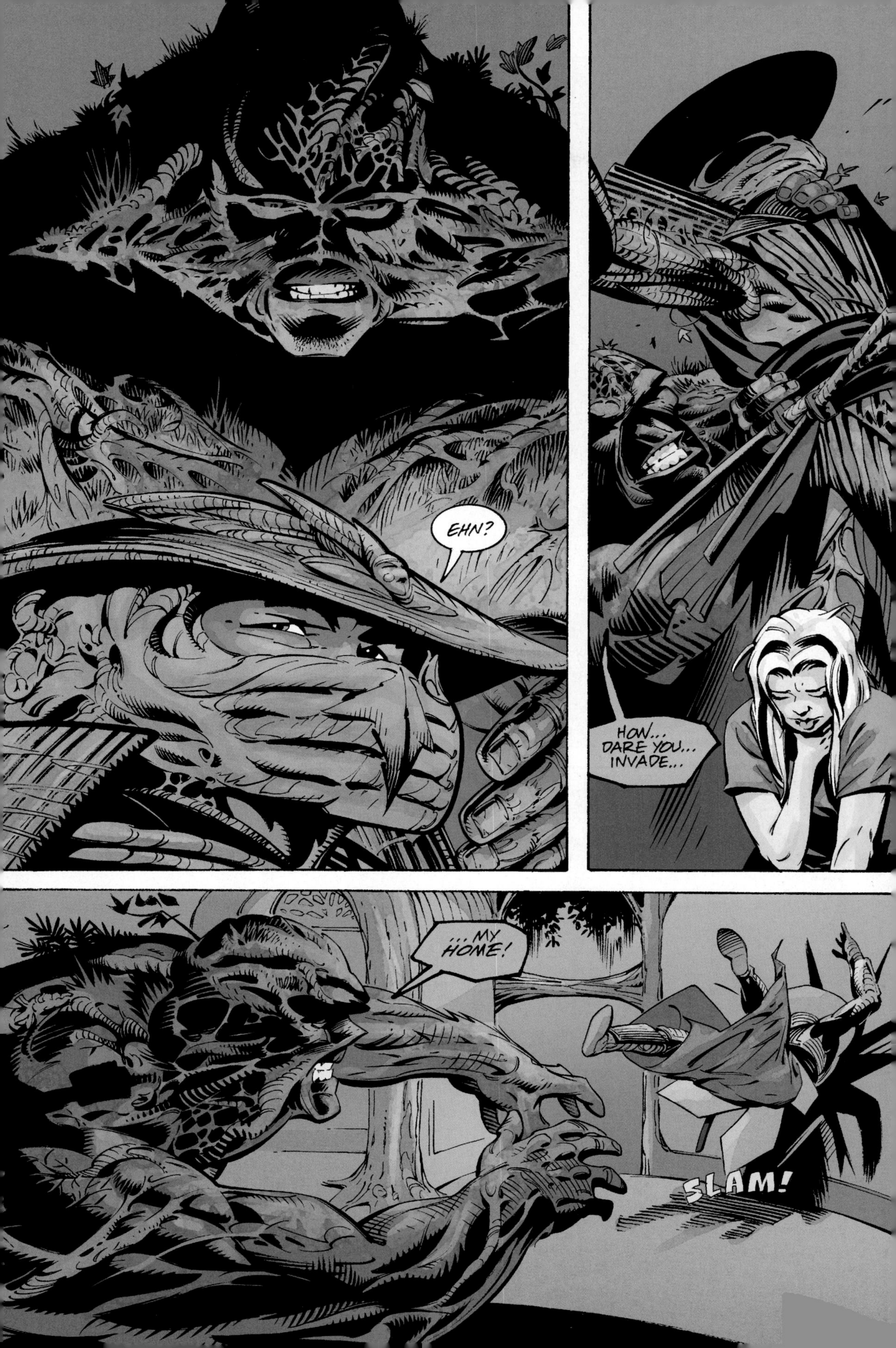
EHN?
HOW... DARE YOU... INVADE...
...MY HOME!
SLAM!

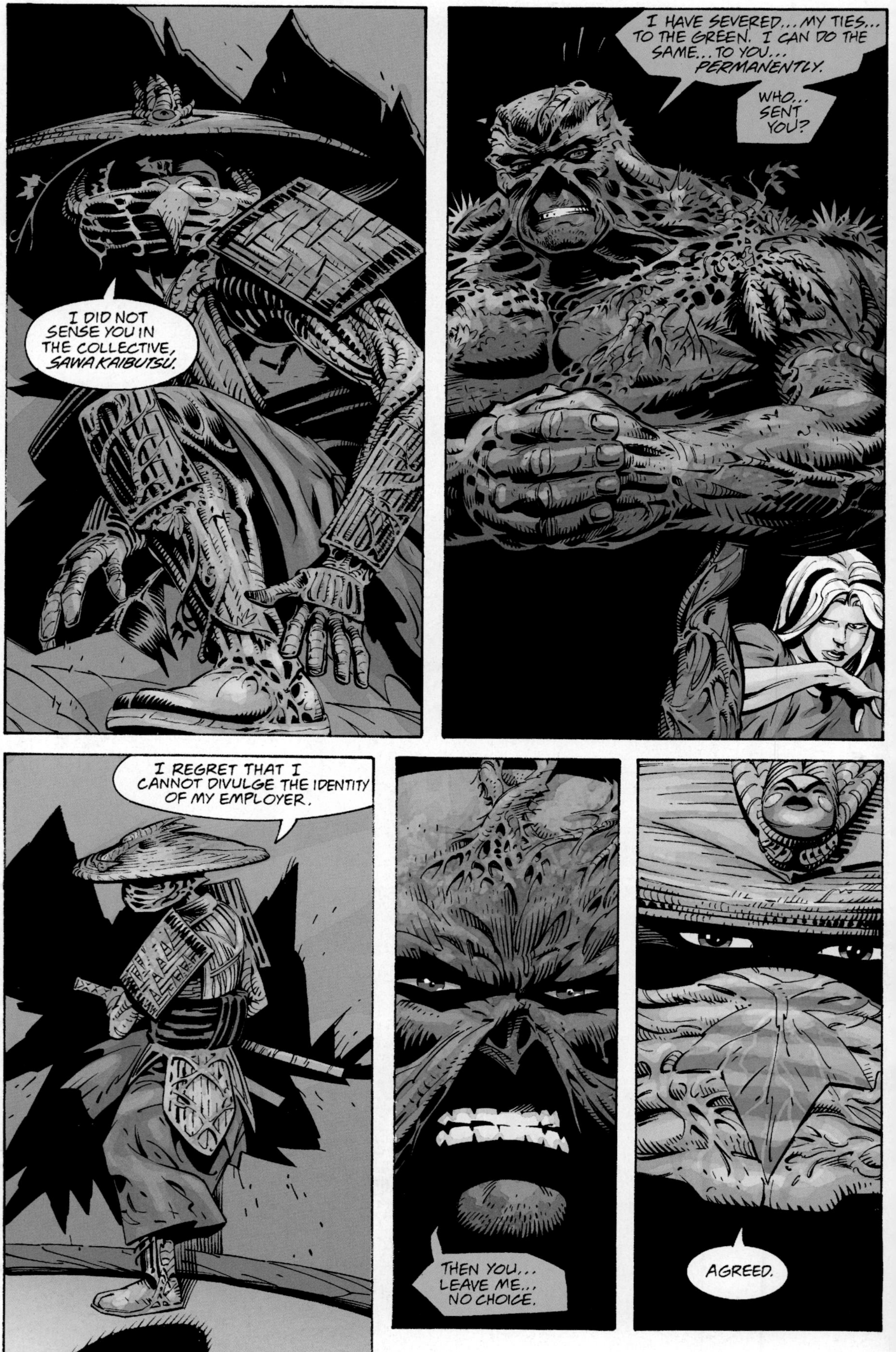
I DID NOT SENSE YOU IN THE COLLECTIVE, SAWA KAIBUTSU.
I HAVE SEVERED... MY TIES... TO THE GREEN. I CAN DO THE SAME... TO YOU... PERMANENTLY.
WHO... SENT YOU?
I REGRET THAT I CANNOT DIVULGE THE IDENTITY OF MY EMPLOYER.
THEN YOU... LEAVE ME... NO CHOICE.
AGREED.

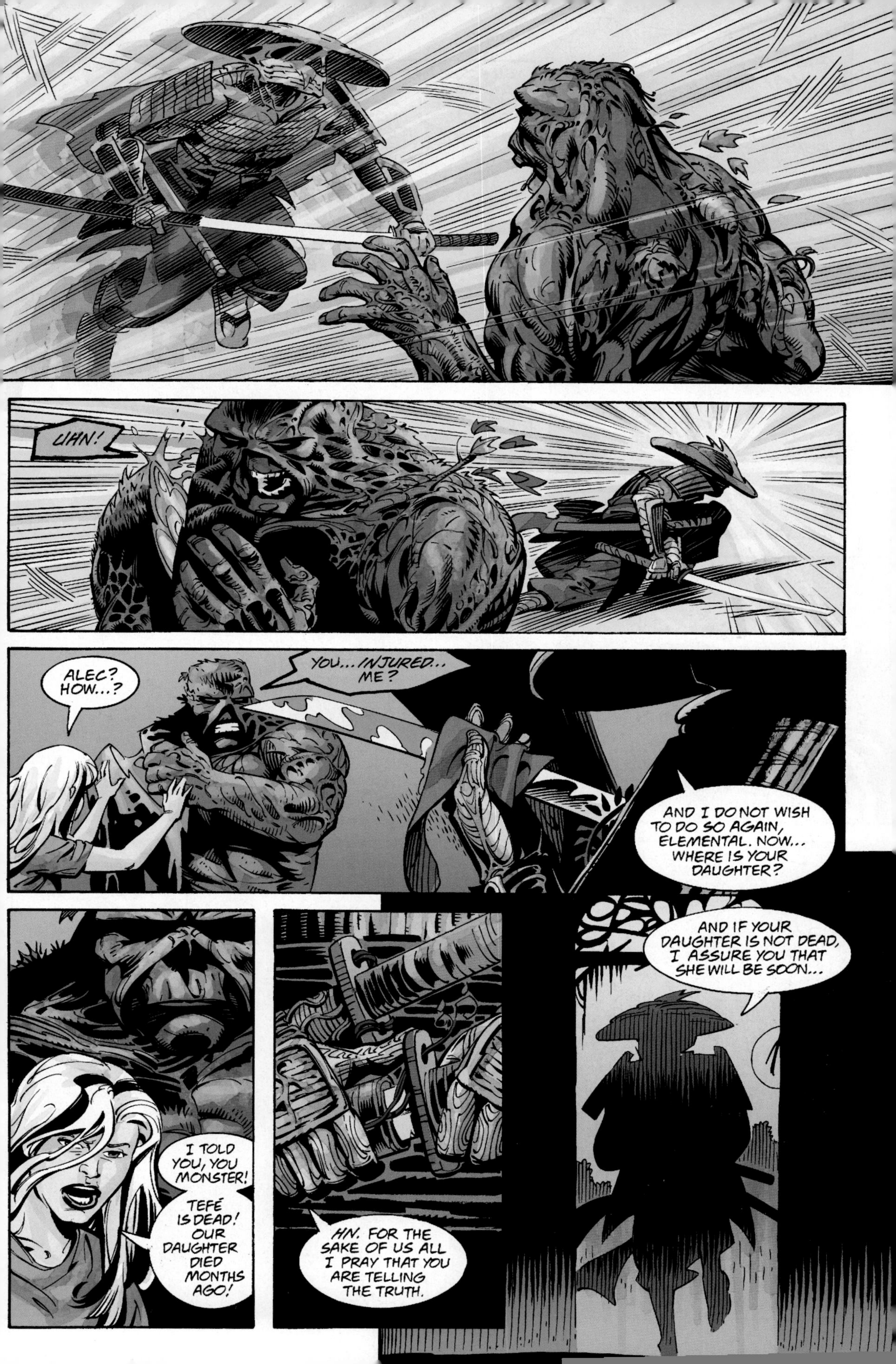

UHN!
ALEC? HOW...?
YOU... INJURED... ME?
AND I DO NOT WISH TO DO SO AGAIN, ELEMENTAL. NOW... WHERE IS YOUR DAUGHTER?
I TOLD YOU, YOU MONSTER!
TEFÉ IS DEAD! OUR DAUGHTER DIED MONTHS AGO!
HN. FOR THE SAKE OF US ALL I PRAY THAT YOU ARE TELLING THE TRUTH.
AND IF YOUR DAUGHTER IS NOT DEAD, I ASSURE YOU THAT SHE WILL BE SOON...

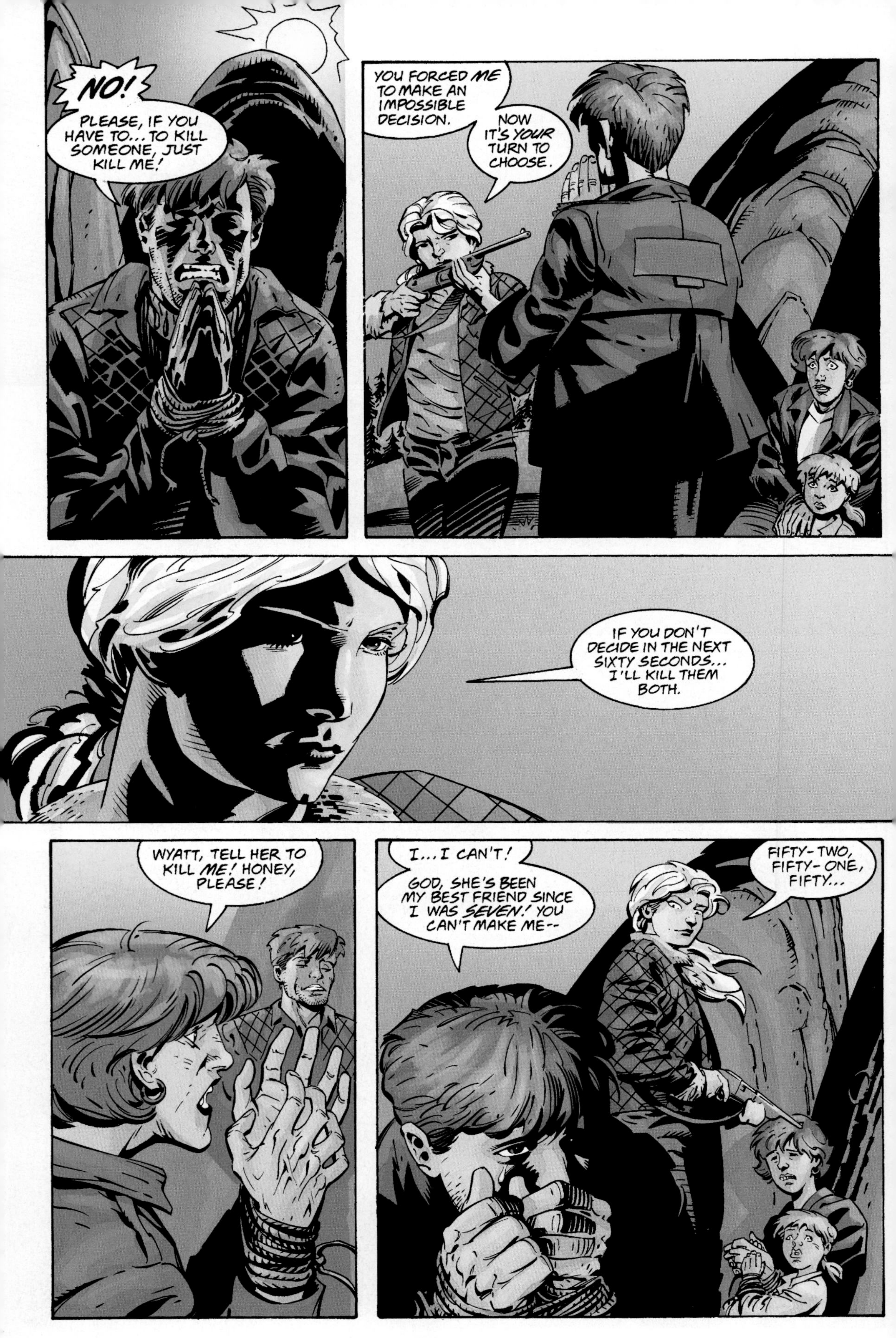
NO!
PLEASE, IF YOU HAVE TO... TO KILL SOMEONE, JUST KILL ME!
YOU FORCED ME TO MAKE AN IMPOSSIBLE DECISION.
NOW IT'S YOUR TURN TO CHOOSE.
IF YOU DON'T DECIDE IN THE NEXT SIXTY SECONDS... I'LL KILL THEM BOTH.
WYATT, TELL HER TO KILL ME! HONEY, PLEASE!
I... I CAN'T!
GOD, SHE'S BEEN MY BEST FRIEND SINCE I WAS SEVEN! YOU CAN'T MAKE ME--
FIFTY-TWO, FIFTY-ONE, FIFTY...

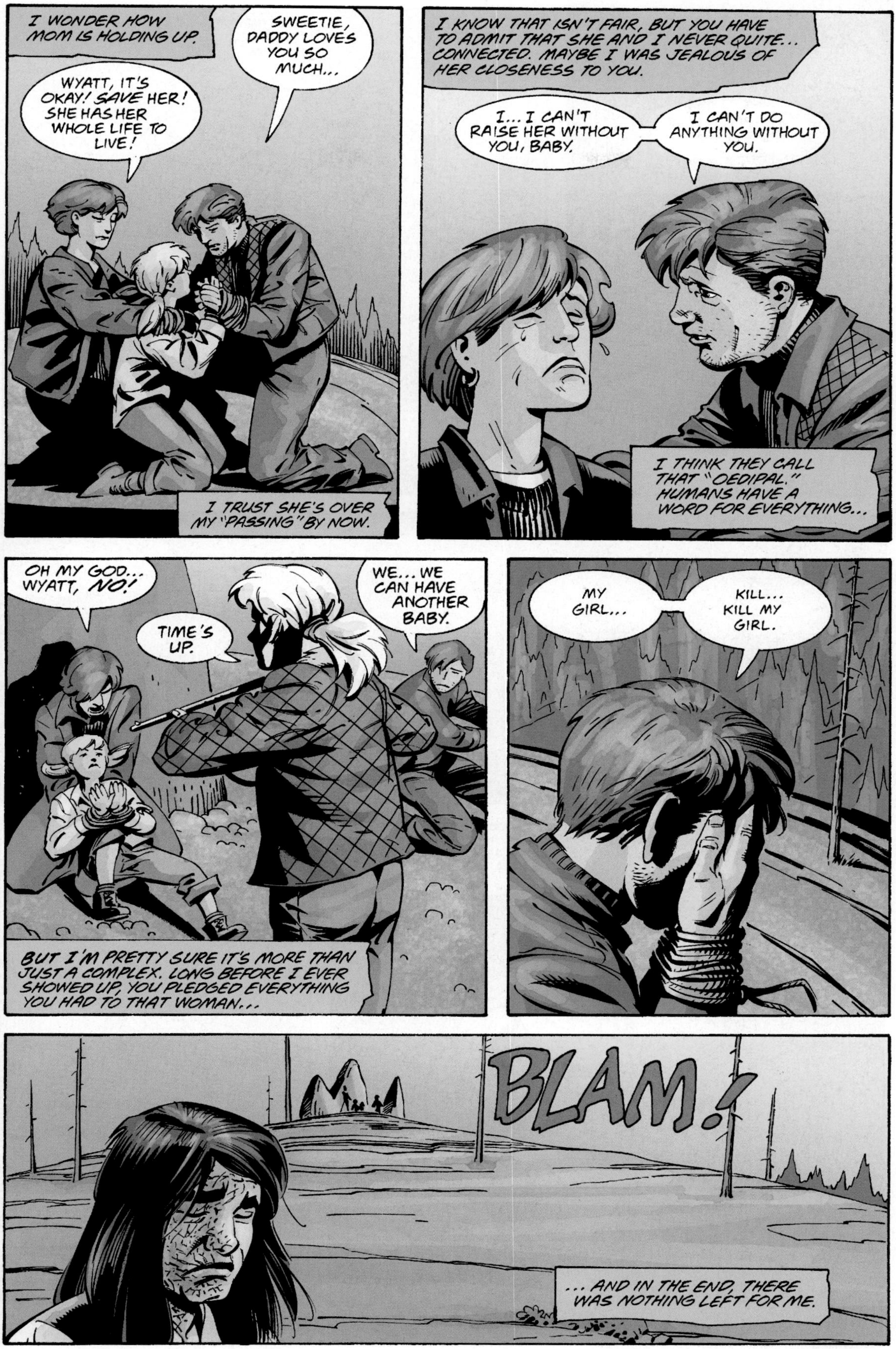

I WONDER HOW MOM IS HOLDING UP.
SWEETIE, DADDY LOVES YOU SO MUCH...
WYATT, IT'S OKAY! SAVE HER! SHE HAS HER WHOLE LIFE TO LIVE!
I TRUST SHE'S OVER MY "PASSING" BY NOW.
I KNOW THAT ISN'T FAIR, BUT YOU HAVE TO ADMIT THAT SHE AND I NEVER QUITE... CONNECTED. MAYBE I WAS JEALOUS OF HER CLOSENESS TO YOU.
I... I CAN'T RAISE HER WITHOUT YOU, BABY.
I CAN'T DO ANYTHING WITHOUT YOU.
I THINK THEY CALL THAT "OEDIPAL." HUMANS HAVE A WORD FOR EVERYTHING...
OH MY GOD... WYATT, NO!
TIME'S UP.
WE... WE CAN HAVE ANOTHER BABY.
BUT I'M PRETTY SURE IT'S MORE THAN JUST A COMPLEX. LONG BEFORE I EVER SHOWED UP, YOU PLEDGED EVERYTHING YOU HAD TO THAT WOMAN...
MY GIRL...
KILL... KILL MY GIRL.
BLAM!
...AND IN THE END, THERE WAS NOTHING LEFT FOR ME.

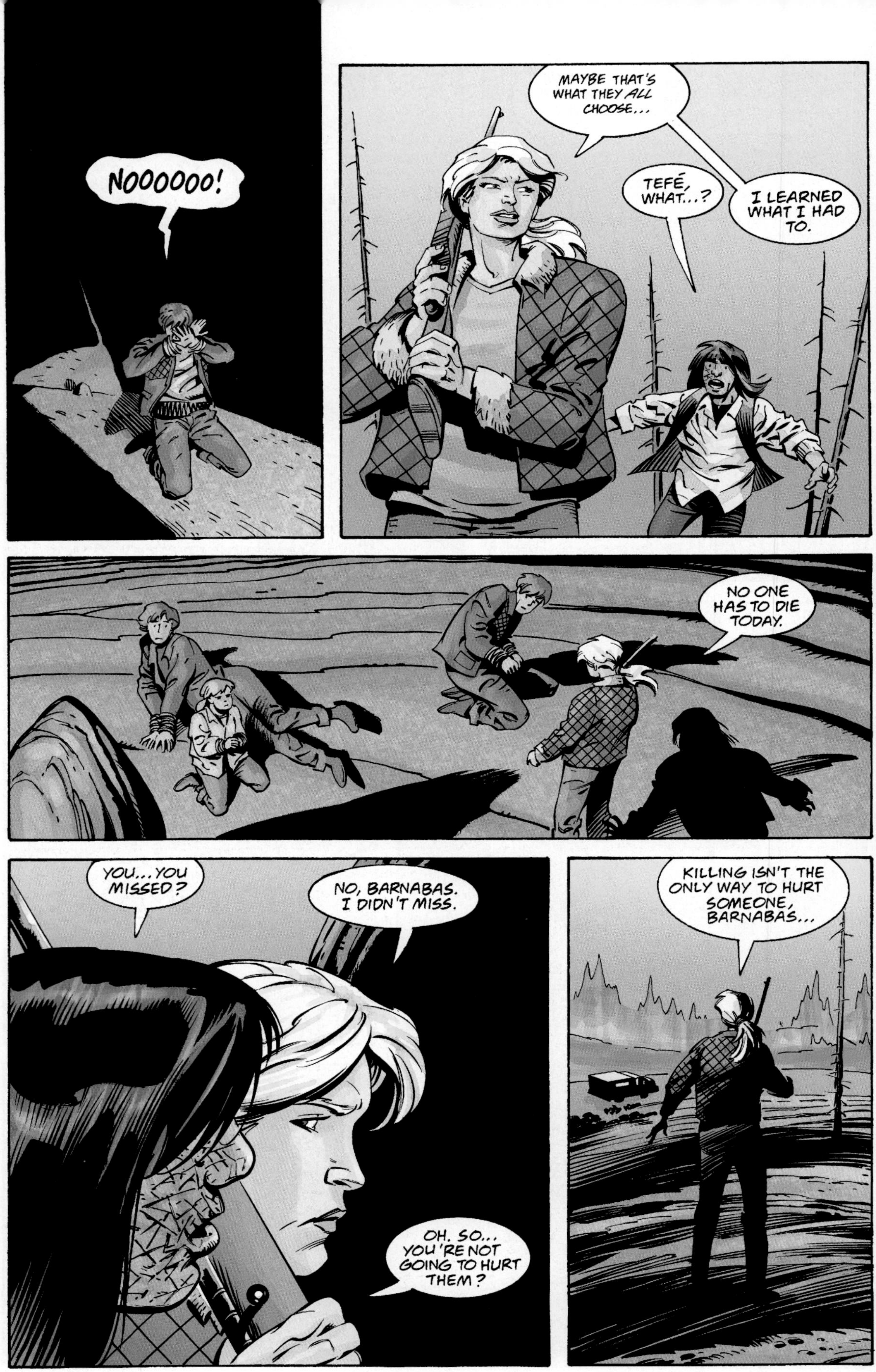
NOOOOOO!
MAYBE THAT'S WHAT THEY ALL CHOOSE...
TEFÉ, WHAT...?
I LEARNED WHAT I HAD TO.
NO ONE HAS TO DIE TODAY.
YOU... YOU MISSED?
NO, BARNABAS. I DIDN'T MISS.
OH. SO... YOU'RE NOT GOING TO HURT THEM?
KILLING ISN'T THE ONLY WAY TO HURT SOMEONE, BARNABAS...

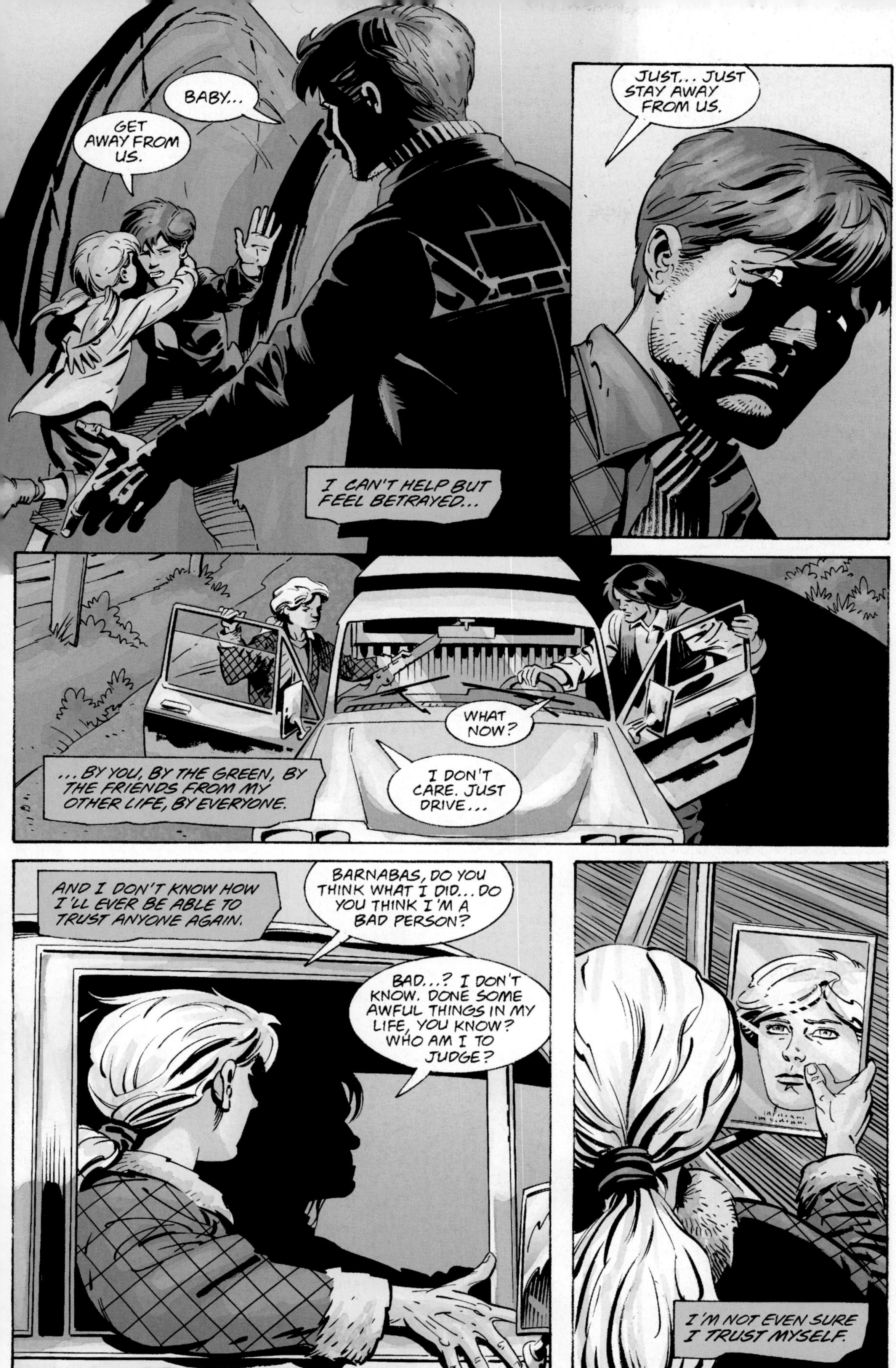
BABY...
GET AWAY FROM US.
I CAN'T HELP BUT FEEL BETRAYED...
JUST... JUST STAY AWAY FROM US.
...BY YOU, BY THE GREEN, BY THE FRIENDS FROM MY OTHER LIFE, BY EVERYONE.
WHAT NOW?
I DON'T CARE. JUST DRIVE...
AND I DON'T KNOW HOW I'LL EVER BE ABLE TO TRUST ANYONE AGAIN.
BARNABAS, DO YOU THINK WHAT I DID... DO YOU THINK I'M A BAD PERSON?
BAD...? I DON'T KNOW. DONE SOME AWFUL THINGS IN MY LIFE, YOU KNOW? WHO AM I TO JUDGE?
I'M NOT EVEN SURE I TRUST MYSELF.

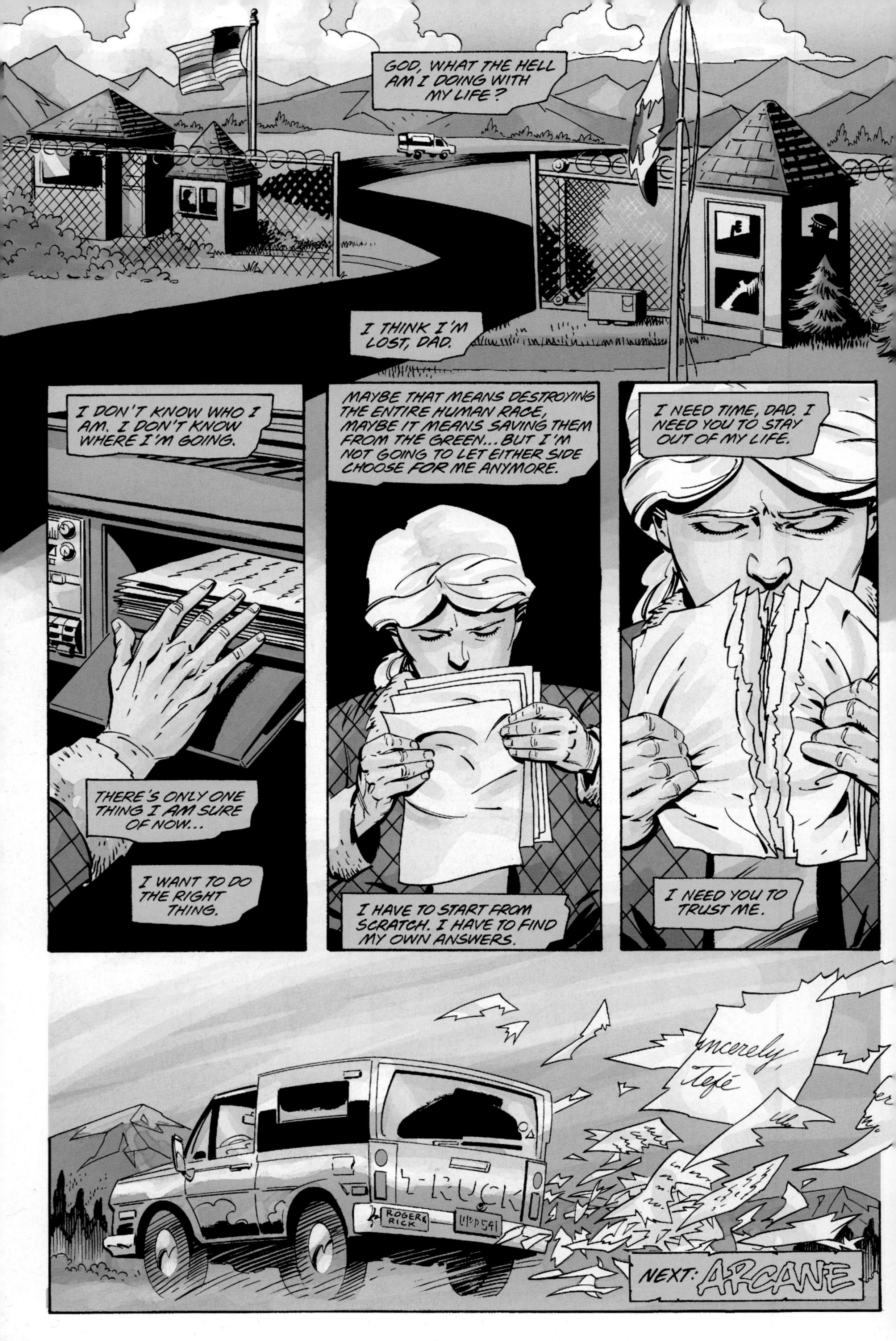
GOD, WHAT THE HELL AM I DOING WITH MY LIFE?
I THINK I'M LOST, DAD.
I DON'T KNOW WHO I AM. I DON'T KNOW WHERE I'M GOING.
THERE'S ONLY ONE THING I AM SURE OF NOW...
I WANT TO DO THE RIGHT THING.
MAYBE THAT MEANS DESTROYING THE ENTIRE HUMAN RACE, MAYBE IT MEANS SAVING THEM FROM THE GREEN... BUT I'M NOT GOING TO LET EITHER SIDE CHOOSE FOR ME ANYMORE.
I HAVE TO START FROM SCRATCH. I HAVE TO FIND MY OWN ANSWERS.
I NEED TIME, DAD. I NEED YOU TO STAY OUT OF MY LIFE.
I NEED YOU TO TRUST ME.
ncerely,
Tefé
T-RUCK
ROGER & RICK
NEXT: ARCANE

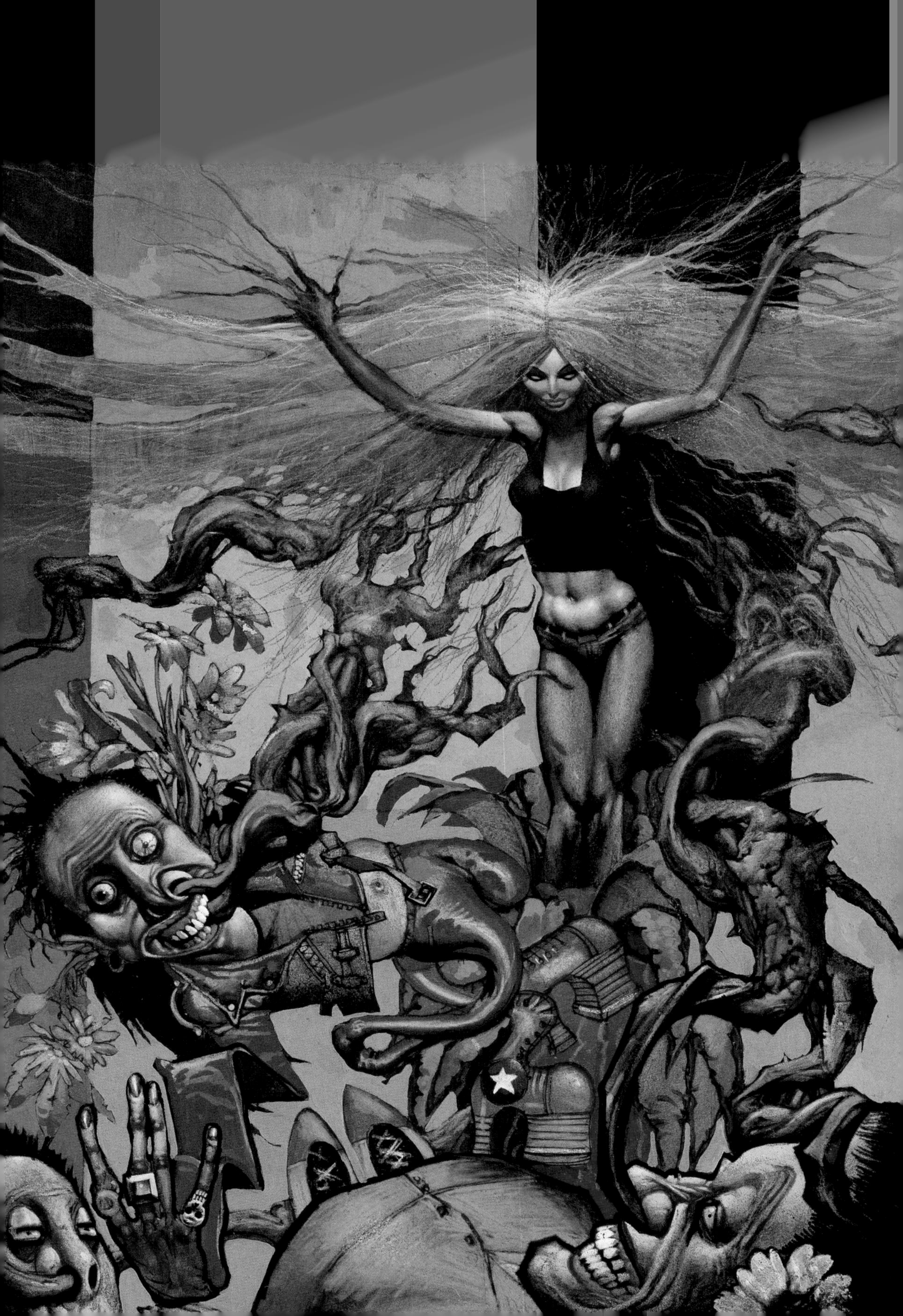

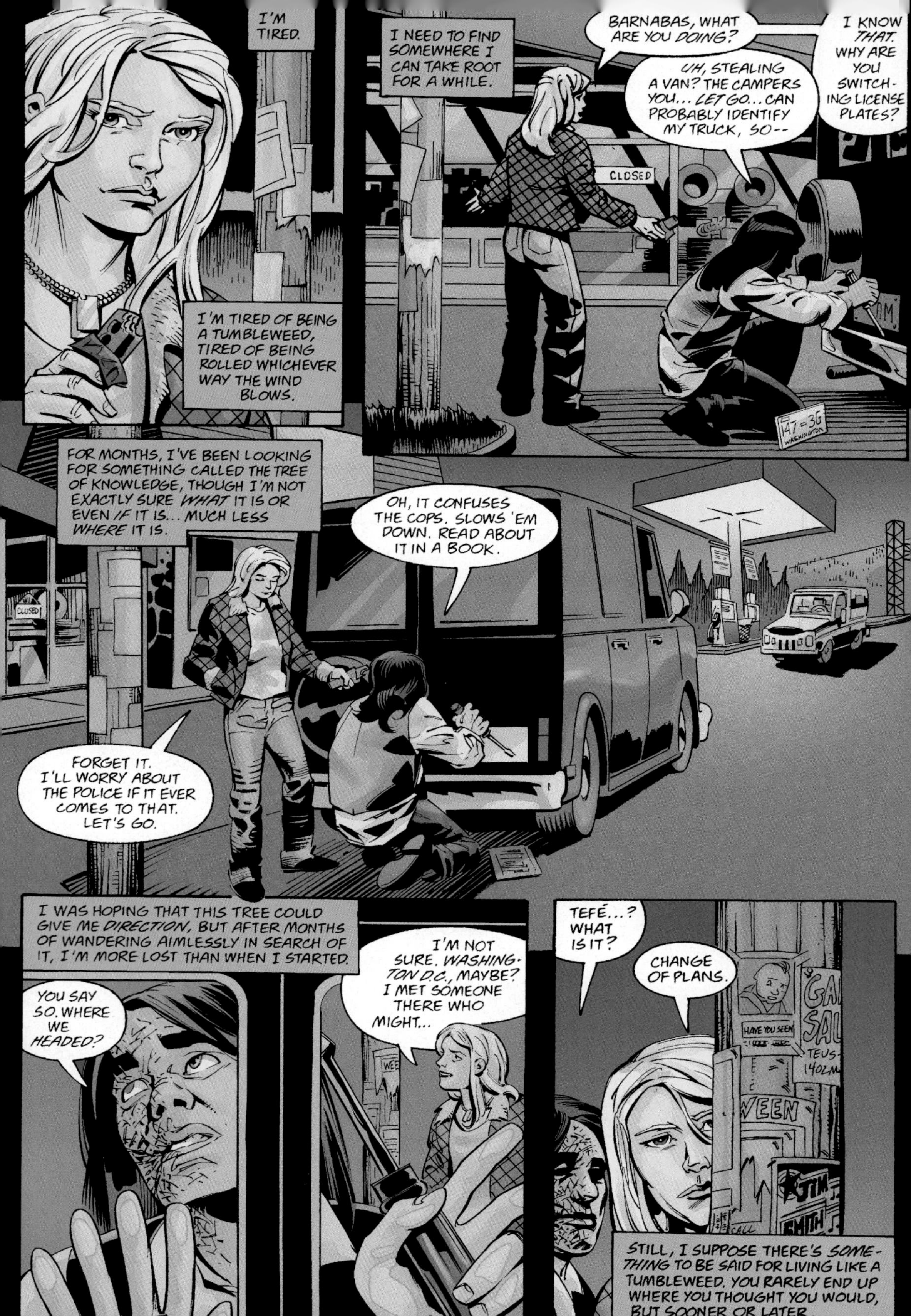
I'M TIRED.
I'M TIRED OF BEING A TUMBLEWEED, TIRED OF BEING ROLLED WHICHEVER WAY THE WIND BLOWS.
I NEED TO FIND SOMEWHERE I CAN TAKE ROOT FOR A WHILE.
BARNABAS, WHAT ARE YOU DOING?
UH, STEALING A VAN? THE CAMPERS YOU... LET GO... CAN PROBABLY IDENTIFY MY TRUCK, SO--
I KNOW THAT. WHY ARE YOU SWITCHING LICENSE PLATES?
CLOSED
147-3G WASHINGTON
FOR MONTHS, I'VE BEEN LOOKING FOR SOMETHING CALLED THE TREE OF KNOWLEDGE, THOUGH I'M NOT EXACTLY SURE WHAT IT IS OR EVEN IF IT IS... MUCH LESS WHERE IT IS.
OH, IT CONFUSES THE COPS. SLOWS 'EM DOWN. READ ABOUT IT IN A BOOK.
CLOSED
FORGET IT. I'LL WORRY ABOUT THE POLICE IF IT EVER COMES TO THAT. LET'S GO.
I WAS HOPING THAT THIS TREE COULD GIVE ME DIRECTION, BUT AFTER MONTHS OF WANDERING AIMLESSLY IN SEARCH OF IT, I'M MORE LOST THAN WHEN I STARTED.
YOU SAY SO. WHERE WE HEADED?
I'M NOT SURE. WASHINGTON D.C., MAYBE? I MET SOMEONE THERE WHO MIGHT...
TEFÉ...? WHAT IS IT?
CHANGE OF PLANS.
HAVE YOU SEEN
WEEN
JIM SMITH
STILL, I SUPPOSE THERE'S SOMETHING TO BE SAID FOR LIVING LIKE A TUMBLEWEED. YOU RARELY END UP WHERE YOU THOUGHT YOU WOULD, BUT SOONER OR LATER...

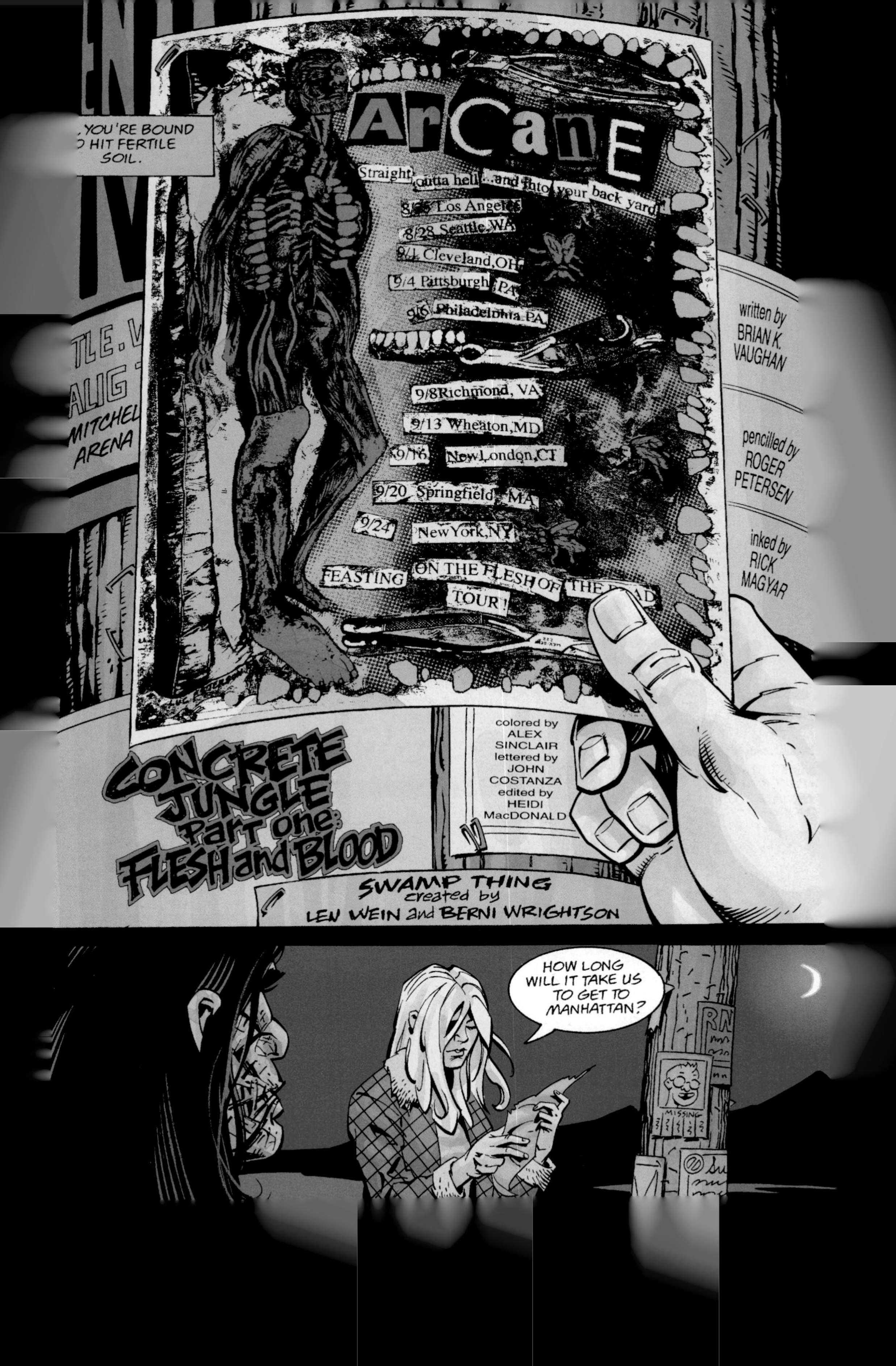
YOU'RE BOUND
O HIT FERTILE
SOIL.
ArCanE
Straight outta hell... and into your back yard!
Los Angel
8/28 Seattle, WA
Cleveland, OH
9/4 Pittsburgh, PA
Philadelphia, PA
9/8 Richmond, VA
9/13 Wheaton, MD
New London, CT
9/20 Springfield, MA
9/24 New York, NY
FEASTING ON THE FLESH OF THE
TOUR!
MITCHEL
ARENA
written by
BRIAN K.
VAUGHAN
pencilled by
ROGER
PETERSEN
inked by
RICK
MAGYAR
colored by
ALEX
SINCLAIR
lettered by
JOHN
COSTANZA
edited by
HEIDI
MacDONALD
CONCRETE JUNGLE Part one: FLESH and BLOOD
SWAMP THING
created by
LEN WEIN and BERNI WRIGHTSON
HOW LONG WILL IT TAKE US TO GET TO MANHATTAN?
MISSING

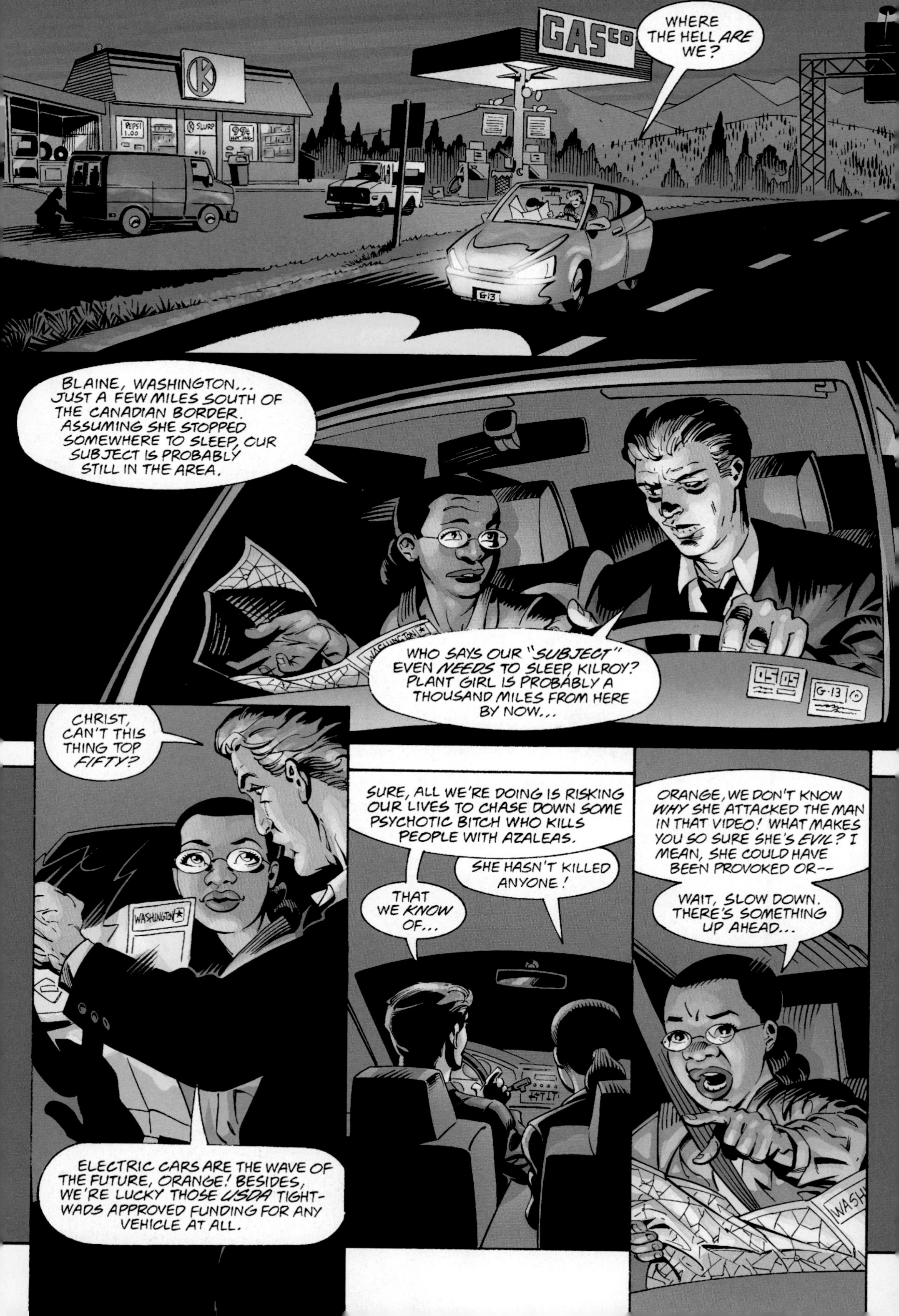
GASco
PEPSI 1.00
SLURP
99¢ HOT DOGS
WHERE THE HELL *ARE* WE?
G-13
BLAINE, WASHINGTON... JUST A FEW MILES SOUTH OF THE CANADIAN BORDER. ASSUMING SHE STOPPED SOMEWHERE TO SLEEP, OUR SUBJECT IS PROBABLY STILL IN THE AREA.
WHO SAYS OUR "*SUBJECT*" EVEN *NEEDS* TO SLEEP, KILROY? PLANT GIRL IS PROBABLY A THOUSAND MILES FROM HERE BY NOW...
WASHINGTON
05 05
G-13
CHRIST, CAN'T THIS THING TOP *FIFTY*?
WASHINGTON
ELECTRIC CARS ARE THE WAVE OF THE FUTURE, ORANGE! BESIDES, WE'RE LUCKY THOSE *USDA* TIGHT-WADS APPROVED FUNDING FOR ANY VEHICLE AT ALL.
SURE, ALL WE'RE DOING IS RISKING OUR LIVES TO CHASE DOWN *SOME* PSYCHOTIC BITCH WHO KILLS PEOPLE WITH AZALEAS.
SHE HASN'T KILLED ANYONE!
THAT WE *KNOW* OF...
ORANGE, WE DON'T KNOW *WHY* SHE ATTACKED THE MAN IN THAT VIDEO! WHAT MAKES YOU SO SURE SHE'S *EVIL*? I MEAN, SHE COULD HAVE BEEN PROVOKED OR--
WAIT, SLOW DOWN. THERE'S SOMETHING UP AHEAD...
WASH

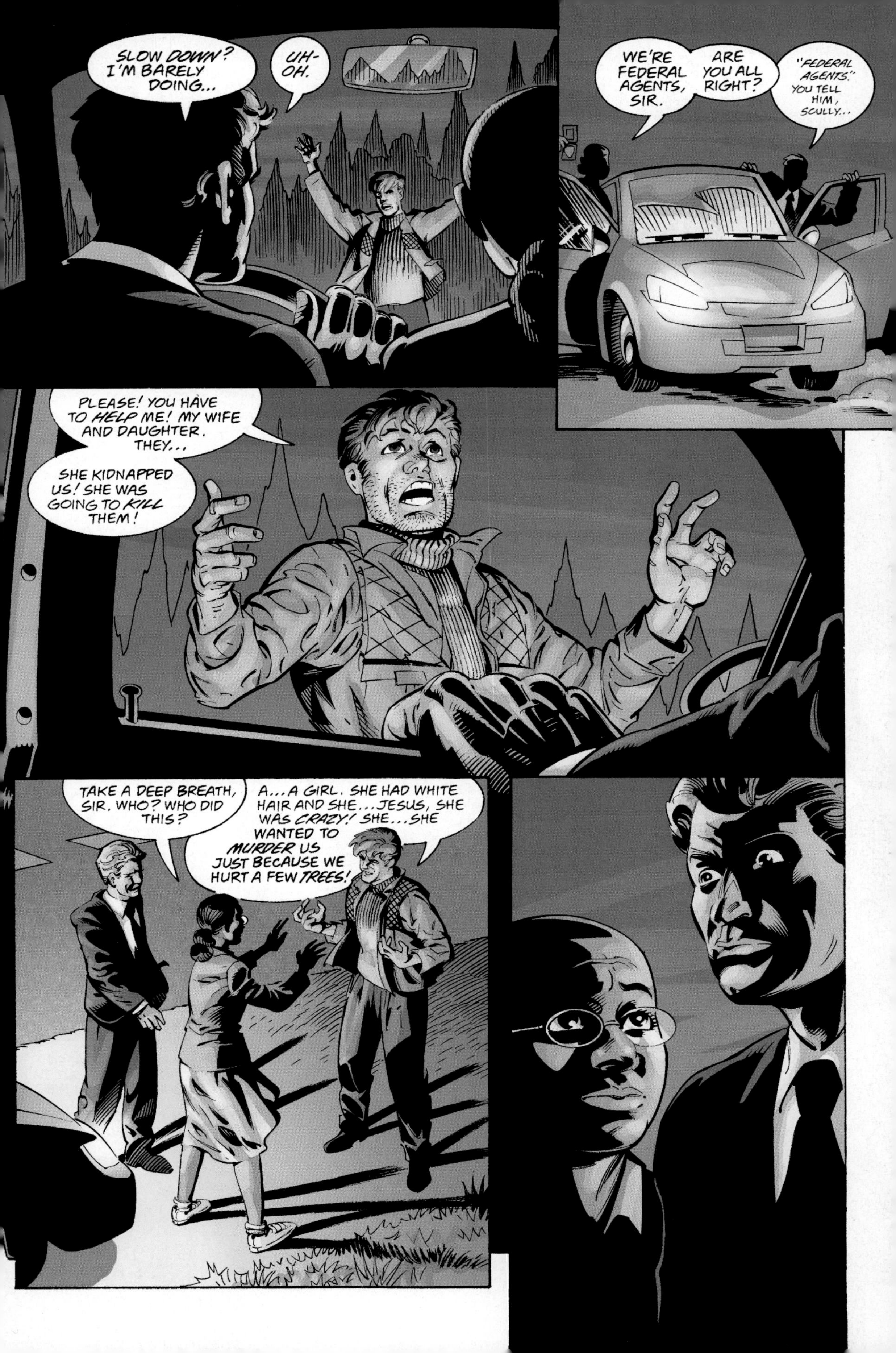
SLOW DOWN? I'M BARELY DOING...
UH-OH.
WE'RE FEDERAL AGENTS, SIR.
ARE YOU ALL RIGHT?
"FEDERAL AGENTS." YOU TELL HIM, SCULLY...
PLEASE! YOU HAVE TO HELP ME! MY WIFE AND DAUGHTER. THEY...
SHE KIDNAPPED US! SHE WAS GOING TO KILL THEM!
TAKE A DEEP BREATH, SIR. WHO? WHO DID THIS?
A...A GIRL. SHE HAD WHITE HAIR AND SHE...JESUS, SHE WAS CRAZY! SHE...SHE WANTED TO MURDER US JUST BECAUSE WE HURT A FEW TREES!

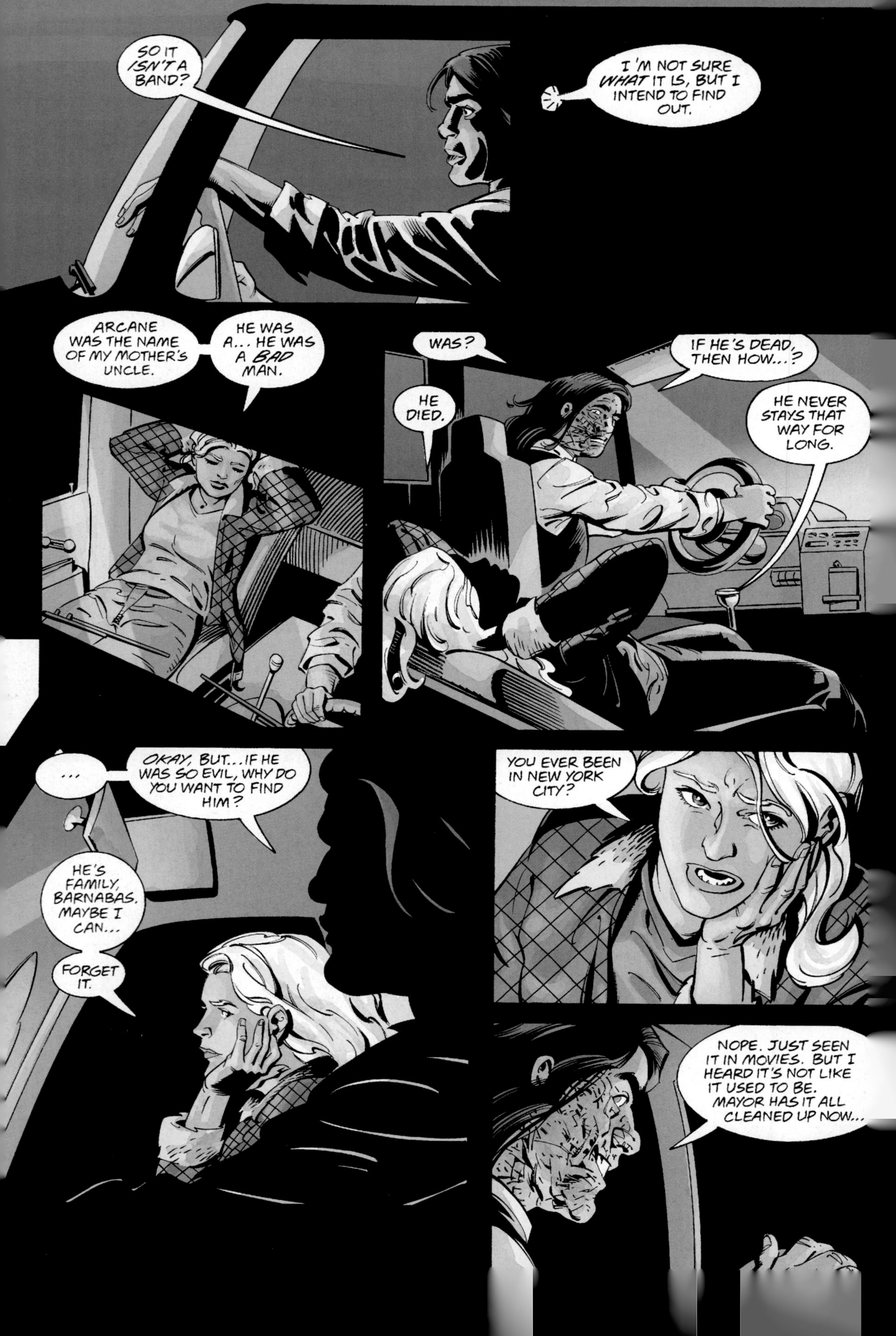
SO IT ISN'T A BAND?
I'M NOT SURE WHAT IT IS, BUT I INTEND TO FIND OUT.
ARCANE WAS THE NAME OF MY MOTHER'S UNCLE.
HE WAS A... HE WAS A BAD MAN.
WAS?
HE DIED.
IF HE'S DEAD, THEN HOW...?
HE NEVER STAYS THAT WAY FOR LONG.
...
OKAY, BUT...IF HE WAS SO EVIL, WHY DO YOU WANT TO FIND HIM?
HE'S FAMILY, BARNABAS. MAYBE I CAN...
FORGET IT.
YOU EVER BEEN IN NEW YORK CITY?
NOPE. JUST SEEN IT IN MOVIES. BUT I HEARD IT'S NOT LIKE IT USED TO BE. MAYOR HAS IT ALL CLEANED UP NOW...

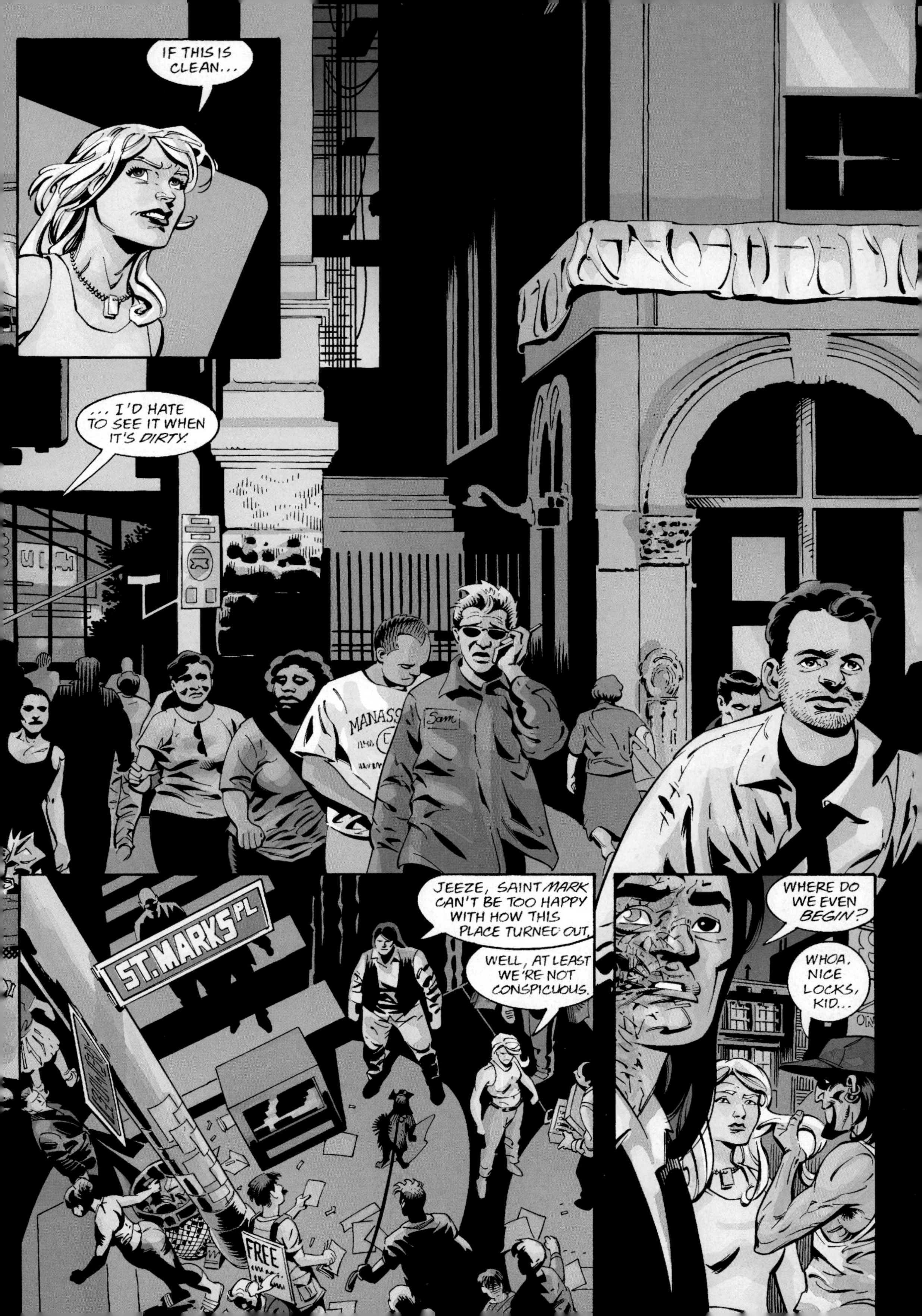
IF THIS IS CLEAN...
... I'D HATE TO SEE IT WHEN IT'S *DIRTY.*
MANASS
Sam
ST. MARKS PL
JEEZE, SAINT *MARK* CAN'T BE TOO HAPPY WITH HOW THIS PLACE TURNED OUT.
WELL, AT LEAST WE'RE NOT CONSPICUOUS.
FREE
WHERE DO WE EVEN *BEGIN?*
WHOA. NICE LOCKS, KID...

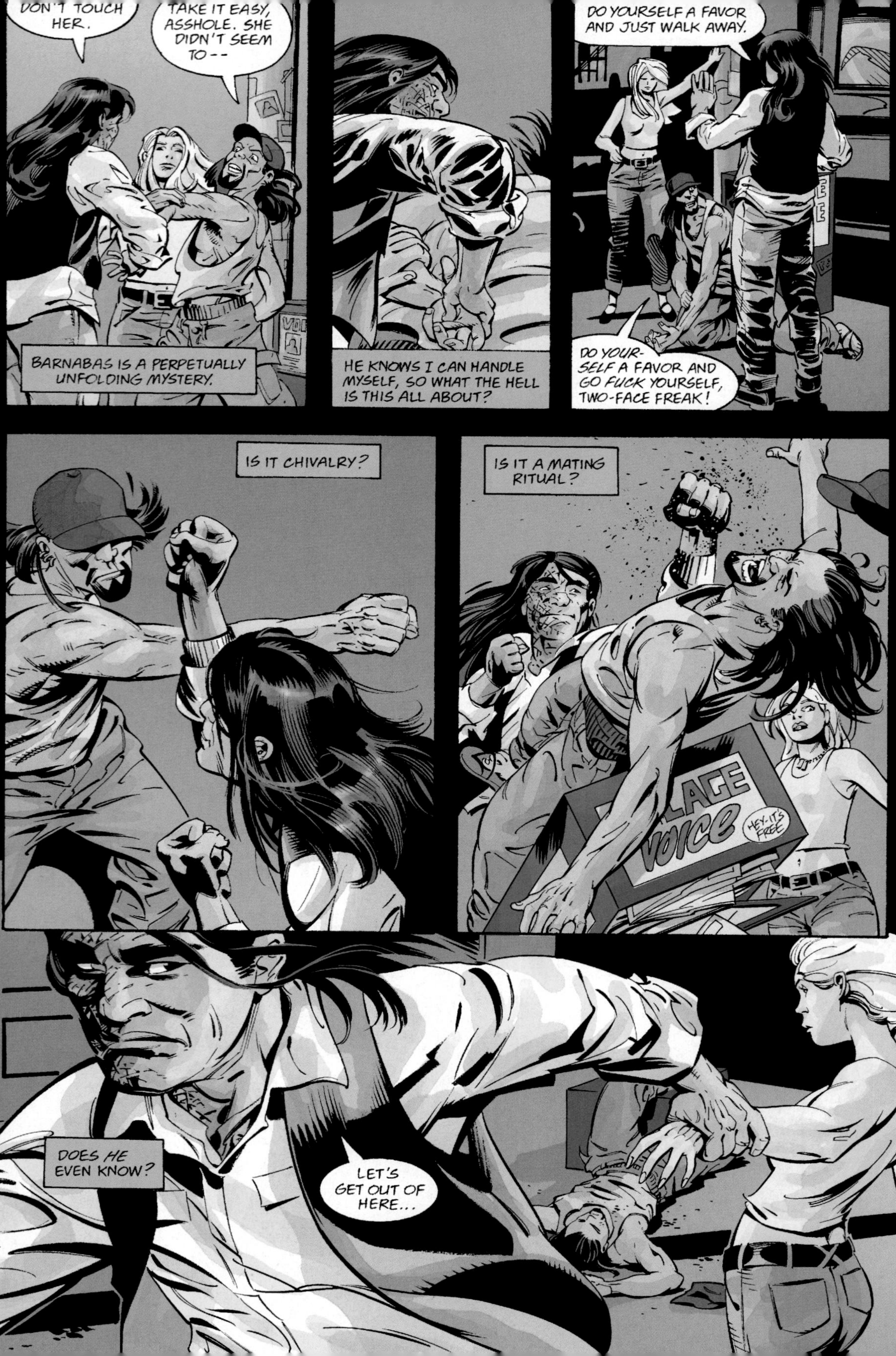
DON'T TOUCH HER.
TAKE IT EASY, ASSHOLE. SHE DIDN'T SEEM TO --
BARNABAS IS A PERPETUALLY UNFOLDING MYSTERY.
HE KNOWS I CAN HANDLE MYSELF, SO WHAT THE HELL IS THIS ALL ABOUT?
DO YOURSELF A FAVOR AND JUST WALK AWAY.
DO YOURSELF A FAVOR AND GO FUCK YOURSELF, TWO-FACE FREAK!
IS IT CHIVALRY?
IS IT A MATING RITUAL?
VOICE
HEY-IT'S FREE
DOES HE EVEN KNOW?
LET'S GET OUT OF HERE...

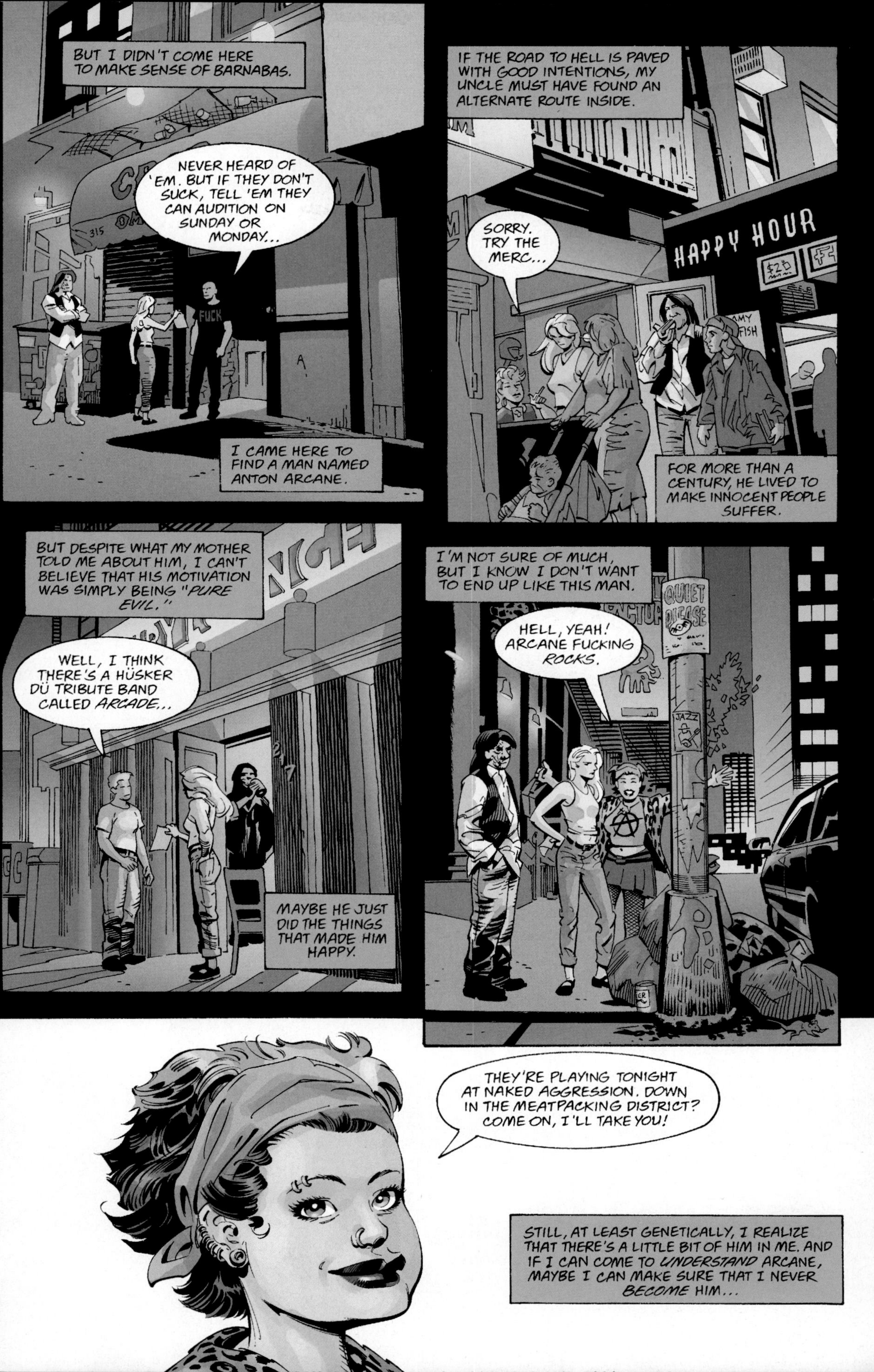

BUT I DIDN'T COME HERE TO MAKE SENSE OF BARNABAS.
NEVER HEARD OF 'EM. BUT IF THEY DON'T SUCK, TELL 'EM THEY CAN AUDITION ON SUNDAY OR MONDAY...
FUCK
I CAME HERE TO FIND A MAN NAMED ANTON ARCANE.
IF THE ROAD TO HELL IS PAVED WITH GOOD INTENTIONS, MY UNCLE MUST HAVE FOUND AN ALTERNATE ROUTE INSIDE.
SORRY. TRY THE MERC...
HAPPY HOUR
FOR MORE THAN A CENTURY, HE LIVED TO MAKE INNOCENT PEOPLE SUFFER.
BUT DESPITE WHAT MY MOTHER TOLD ME ABOUT HIM, I CAN'T BELIEVE THAT HIS MOTIVATION WAS SIMPLY BEING "PURE EVIL."
WELL, I THINK THERE'S A HÜSKER DÜ TRIBUTE BAND CALLED ARCADE...
MAYBE HE JUST DID THE THINGS THAT MADE HIM HAPPY.
I'M NOT SURE OF MUCH, BUT I KNOW I DON'T WANT TO END UP LIKE THIS MAN.
QUIET PLEASE
HELL, YEAH! ARCANE FUCKING ROCKS.
JAZZ
THEY'RE PLAYING TONIGHT AT NAKED AGGRESSION. DOWN IN THE MEATPACKING DISTRICT? COME ON, I'LL TAKE YOU!
STILL, AT LEAST GENETICALLY, I REALIZE THAT THERE'S A LITTLE BIT OF HIM IN ME. AND IF I CAN COME TO UNDERSTAND ARCANE, MAYBE I CAN MAKE SURE THAT I NEVER BECOME HIM...

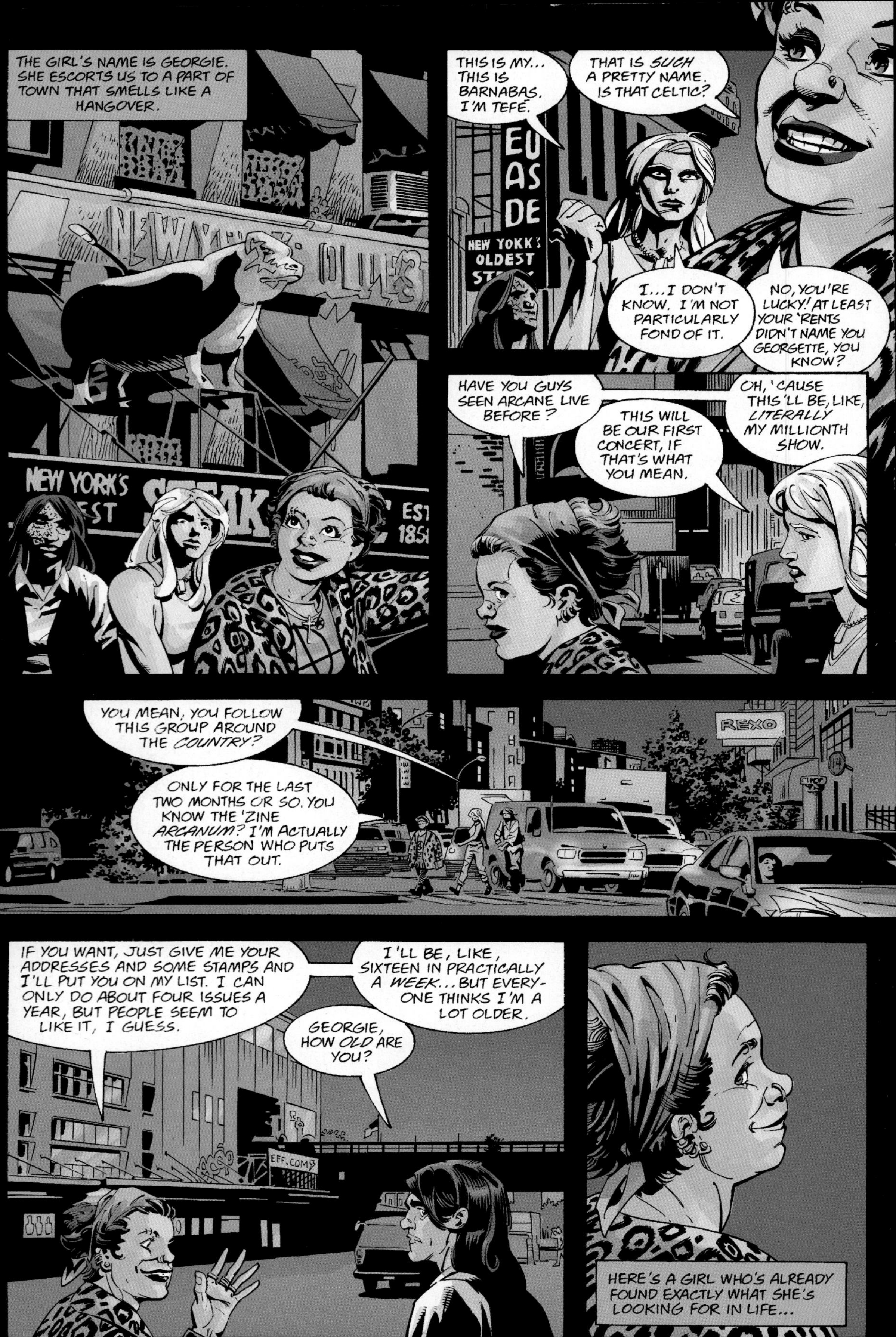
THE GIRL'S NAME IS GEORGIE. SHE ESCORTS US TO A PART OF TOWN THAT SMELLS LIKE A HANGOVER.
NEW YORK'S
STEAK
EST 185
THIS IS MY... THIS IS BARNABAS. I'M TEFÉ.
THAT IS SUCH A PRETTY NAME. IS THAT CELTIC?
NEW YORK'S OLDEST
I... I DON'T KNOW. I'M NOT PARTICULARLY FOND OF IT.
NO, YOU'RE LUCKY! AT LEAST YOUR 'RENTS DIDN'T NAME YOU GEORGETTE, YOU KNOW?
HAVE YOU GUYS SEEN ARCANE LIVE BEFORE?
THIS WILL BE OUR FIRST CONCERT, IF THAT'S WHAT YOU MEAN.
OH, 'CAUSE THIS'LL BE, LIKE, LITERALLY MY MILLIONTH SHOW.
YOU MEAN, YOU FOLLOW THIS GROUP AROUND THE COUNTRY?
ONLY FOR THE LAST TWO MONTHS OR SO. YOU KNOW THE 'ZINE ARCANUM? I'M ACTUALLY THE PERSON WHO PUTS THAT OUT.
REXO
IF YOU WANT, JUST GIVE ME YOUR ADDRESSES AND SOME STAMPS AND I'LL PUT YOU ON MY LIST. I CAN ONLY DO ABOUT FOUR ISSUES A YEAR, BUT PEOPLE SEEM TO LIKE IT, I GUESS.
GEORGIE, HOW OLD ARE YOU?
I'LL BE, LIKE, SIXTEEN IN PRACTICALLY A WEEK... BUT EVERYONE THINKS I'M A LOT OLDER.
EFF.COM
HERE'S A GIRL WHO'S ALREADY FOUND EXACTLY WHAT SHE'S LOOKING FOR IN LIFE...

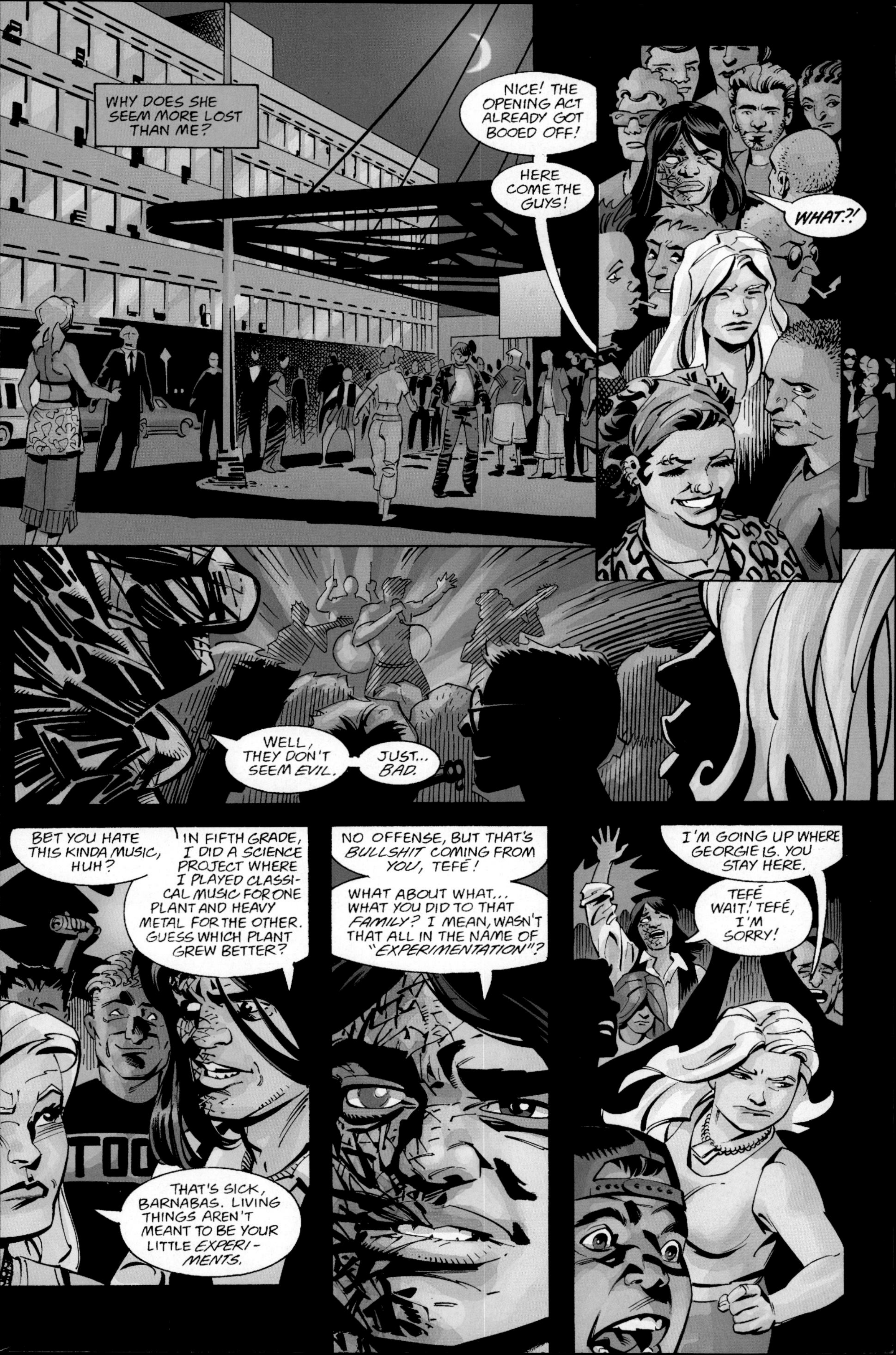
WHY DOES SHE SEEM MORE LOST THAN ME?
NICE! THE OPENING ACT ALREADY GOT BOOED OFF!
HERE COME THE GUYS!
WHAT?!
WELL, THEY DON'T SEEM EVIL.
JUST... BAD.
BET YOU HATE THIS KINDA MUSIC, HUH?
IN FIFTH GRADE, I DID A SCIENCE PROJECT WHERE I PLAYED CLASSICAL MUSIC FOR ONE PLANT AND HEAVY METAL FOR THE OTHER. GUESS WHICH PLANT GREW BETTER?
THAT'S SICK, BARNABAS. LIVING THINGS AREN'T MEANT TO BE YOUR LITTLE EXPERIMENTS.
NO OFFENSE, BUT THAT'S BULLSHIT COMING FROM YOU, TEFÉ!
WHAT ABOUT WHAT... WHAT YOU DID TO THAT FAMILY? I MEAN, WASN'T THAT ALL IN THE NAME OF "EXPERIMENTATION"?
I'M GOING UP WHERE GEORGIE IS. YOU STAY HERE.
TEFÉ WAIT! TEFÉ, I'M SORRY!
TOO

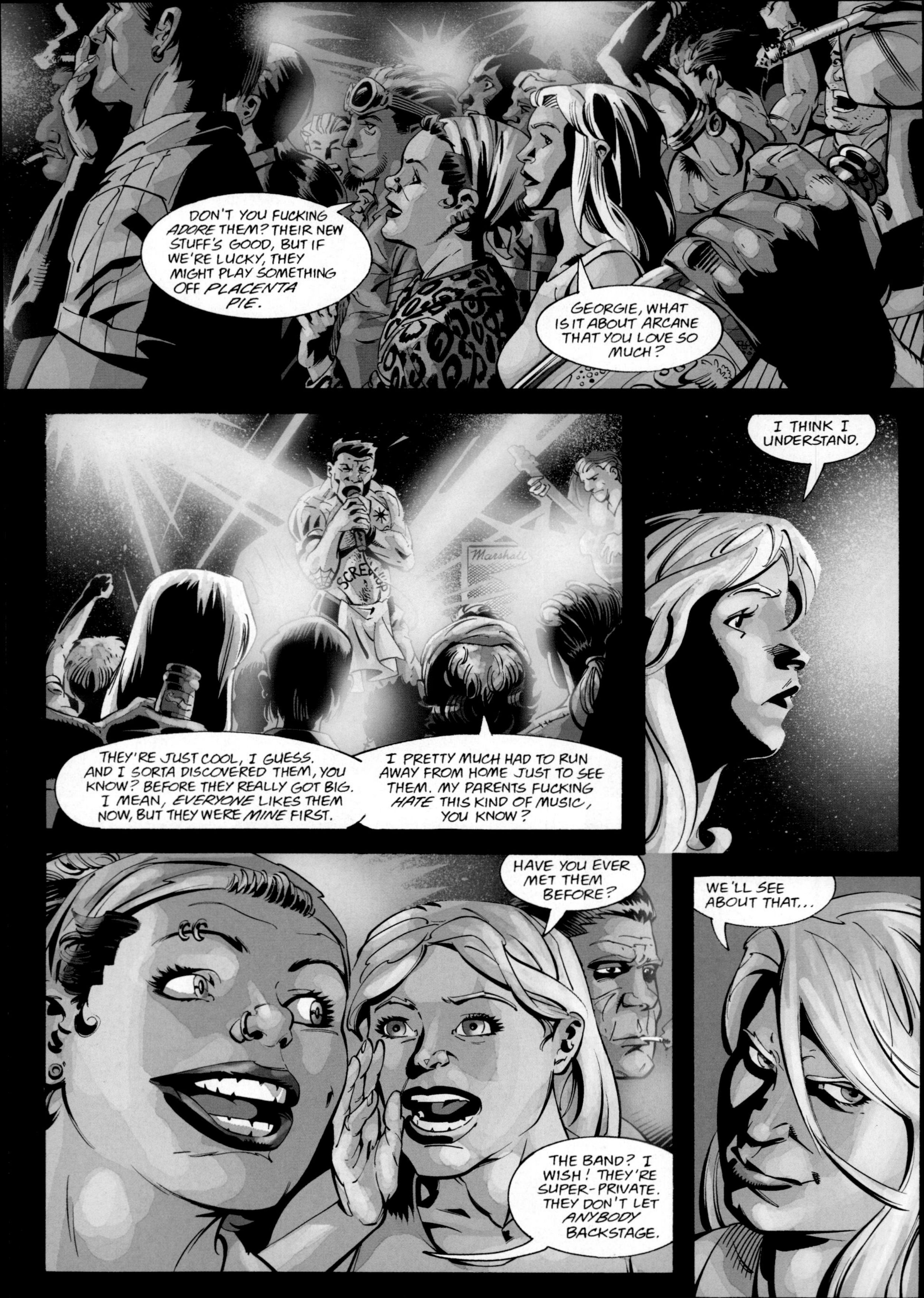
DON'T YOU FUCKING ADORE THEM? THEIR NEW STUFF'S GOOD, BUT IF WE'RE LUCKY, THEY MIGHT PLAY SOMETHING OFF PLACENTA PIE.
GEORGIE, WHAT IS IT ABOUT ARCANE THAT YOU LOVE SO MUCH?
Marshall
SCREAM
THEY'RE JUST COOL, I GUESS. AND I SORTA DISCOVERED THEM, YOU KNOW? BEFORE THEY REALLY GOT BIG. I MEAN, EVERYONE LIKES THEM NOW, BUT THEY WERE MINE FIRST.
I PRETTY MUCH HAD TO RUN AWAY FROM HOME JUST TO SEE THEM. MY PARENTS FUCKING HATE THIS KIND OF MUSIC, YOU KNOW?
I THINK I UNDERSTAND.
HAVE YOU EVER MET THEM BEFORE?
THE BAND? I WISH! THEY'RE SUPER-PRIVATE. THEY DON'T LET ANYBODY BACKSTAGE.
WE'LL SEE ABOUT THAT...

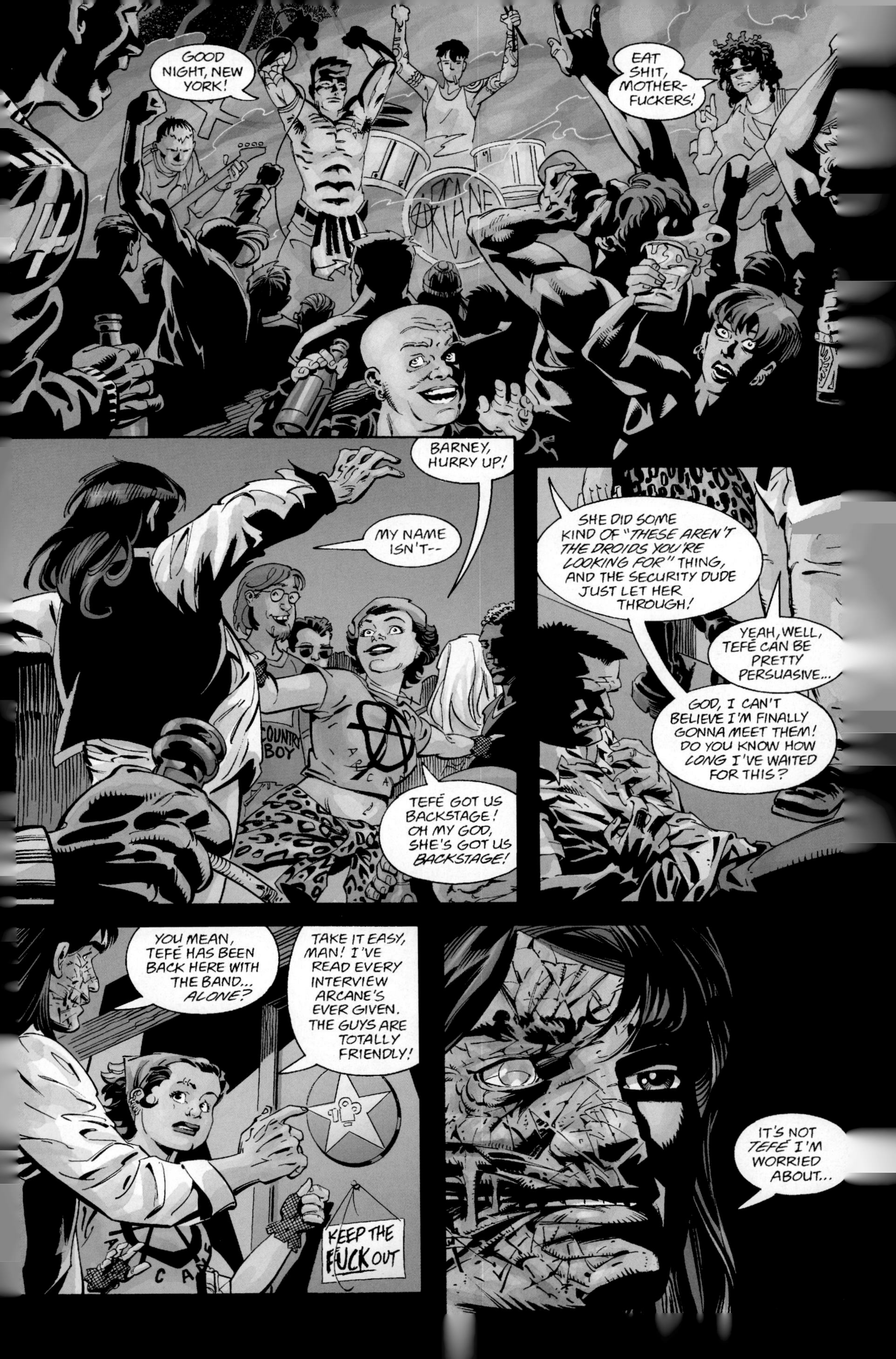
GOOD NIGHT, NEW YORK!
EAT SHIT, MOTHER-FUCKERS!
BARNEY, HURRY UP!
MY NAME ISN'T--
TEFÉ GOT US BACKSTAGE! OH MY GOD, SHE'S GOT US BACKSTAGE!
SHE DID SOME KIND OF "THESE AREN'T THE DROIDS YOU'RE LOOKING FOR" THING, AND THE SECURITY DUDE JUST LET HER THROUGH!
YEAH, WELL, TEFÉ CAN BE PRETTY PERSUASIVE...
GOD, I CAN'T BELIEVE I'M FINALLY GONNA MEET THEM! DO YOU KNOW HOW LONG I'VE WAITED FOR THIS?
YOU MEAN, TEFÉ HAS BEEN BACK HERE WITH THE BAND... ALONE?
TAKE IT EASY, MAN! I'VE READ EVERY INTERVIEW ARCANE'S EVER GIVEN. THE GUYS ARE TOTALLY FRIENDLY!
KEEP THE FUCK OUT
IT'S NOT TEFÉ I'M WORRIED ABOUT...

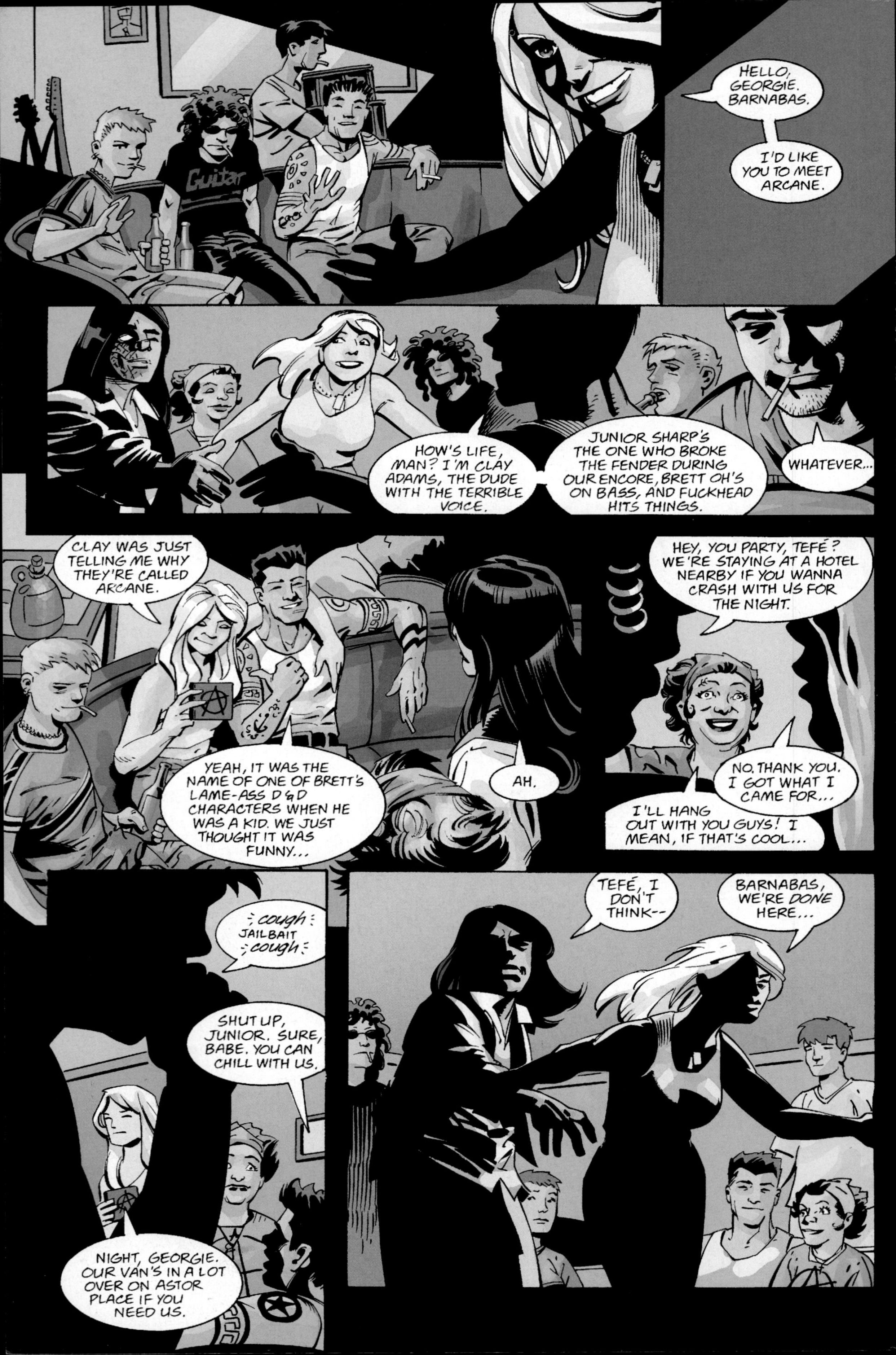
HELLO, GEORGIE. BARNABAS.
I'D LIKE YOU TO MEET ARCANE.
HOW'S LIFE, MAN? I'M CLAY ADAMS, THE DUDE WITH THE TERRIBLE VOICE.
JUNIOR SHARP'S THE ONE WHO BROKE THE FENDER DURING OUR ENCORE, BRETT OH'S ON BASS, AND FUCKHEAD HITS THINGS.
WHATEVER...
CLAY WAS JUST TELLING ME WHY THEY'RE CALLED ARCANE.
YEAH, IT WAS THE NAME OF ONE OF BRETT'S LAME-ASS D&D CHARACTERS WHEN HE WAS A KID. WE JUST THOUGHT IT WAS FUNNY...
AH.
HEY, YOU PARTY, TEFÉ? WE'RE STAYING AT A HOTEL NEARBY IF YOU WANNA CRASH WITH US FOR THE NIGHT.
NO. THANK YOU. I GOT WHAT I CAME FOR...
I'LL HANG OUT WITH YOU GUYS! I MEAN, IF THAT'S COOL...
:cough: JAILBAIT :cough:
SHUT UP, JUNIOR. SURE, BABE. YOU CAN CHILL WITH US.
NIGHT, GEORGIE. OUR VAN'S IN A LOT OVER ON ASTOR PLACE IF YOU NEED US.
TEFÉ, I DON'T THINK--
BARNABAS, WE'RE DONE HERE...

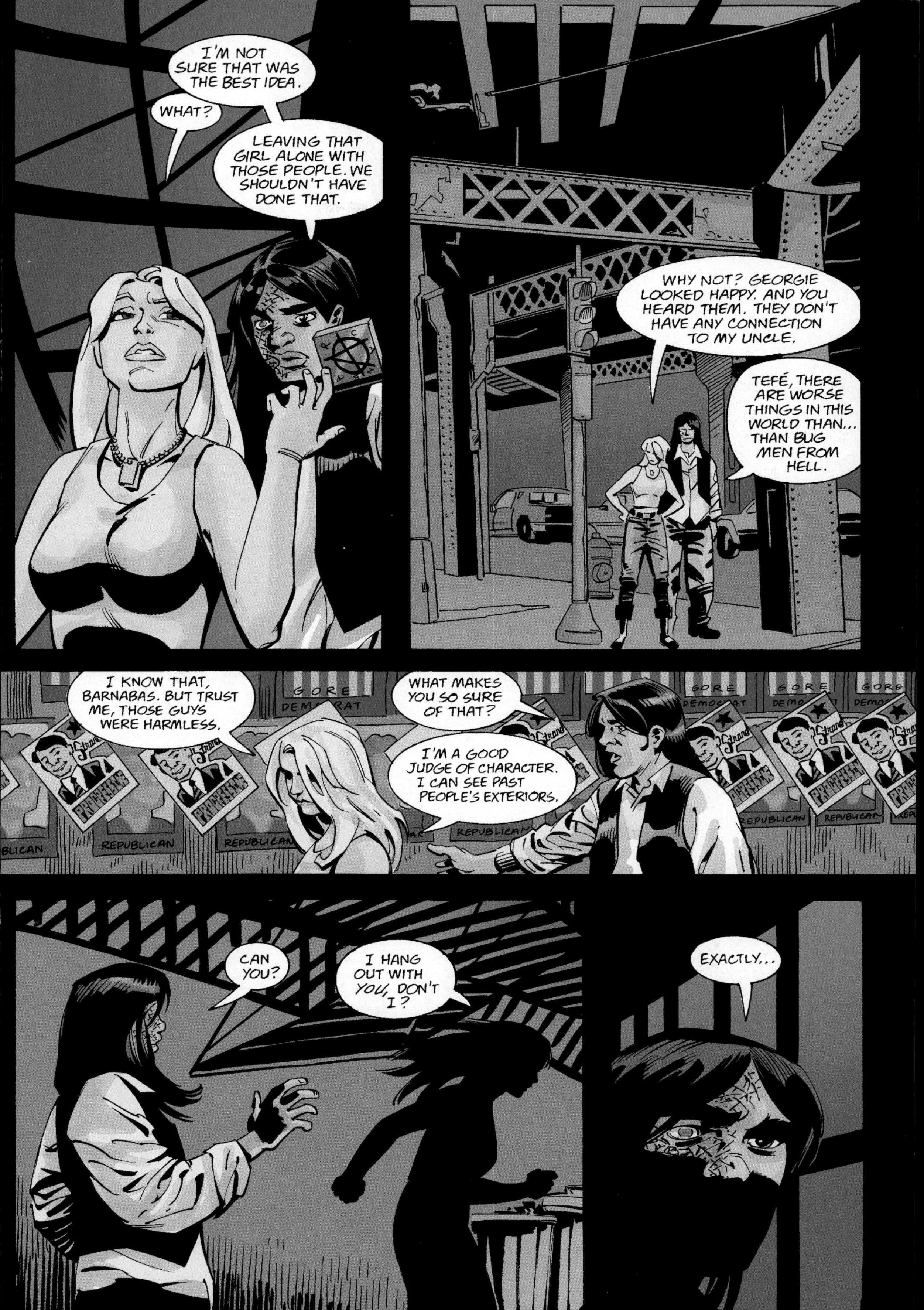
I'M NOT SURE THAT WAS THE BEST IDEA.
WHAT?
LEAVING THAT GIRL ALONE WITH THOSE PEOPLE. WE SHOULDN'T HAVE DONE THAT.
WHY NOT? GEORGIE LOOKED HAPPY. AND YOU HEARD THEM. THEY DON'T HAVE ANY CONNECTION TO MY UNCLE.
TEFÉ, THERE ARE WORSE THINGS IN THIS WORLD THAN... THAN BUG MEN FROM HELL.
I KNOW THAT, BARNABAS. BUT TRUST ME, THOSE GUYS WERE HARMLESS.
WHAT MAKES YOU SO SURE OF THAT?
I'M A GOOD JUDGE OF CHARACTER. I CAN SEE PAST PEOPLE'S EXTERIORS.
CAN YOU?
I HANG OUT WITH YOU, DON'T I?
EXACTLY...

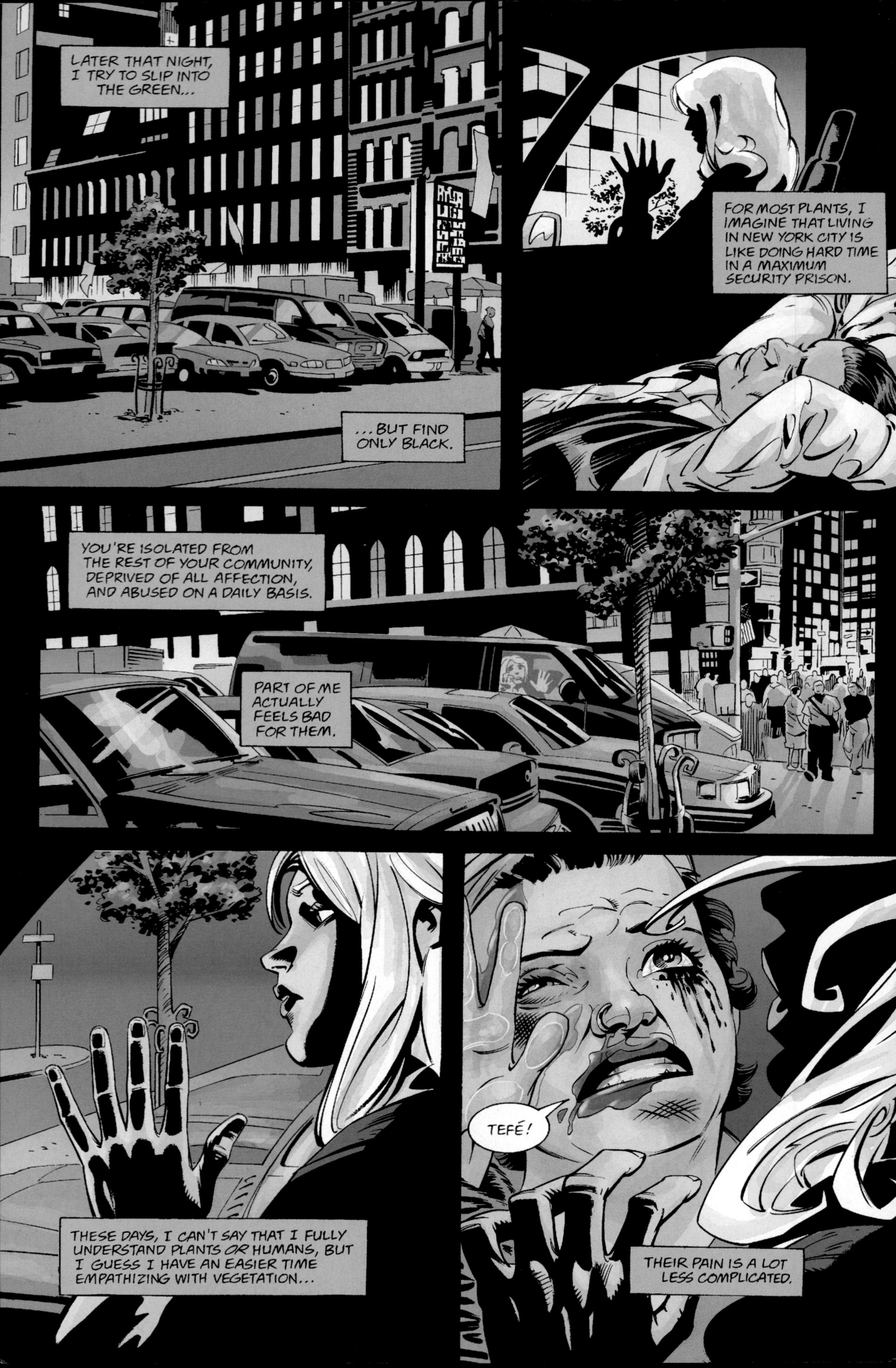
LATER THAT NIGHT, I TRY TO SLIP INTO THE GREEN...
...BUT FIND ONLY BLACK.
FOR MOST PLANTS, I IMAGINE THAT LIVING IN NEW YORK CITY IS LIKE DOING HARD TIME IN A MAXIMUM SECURITY PRISON.
YOU'RE ISOLATED FROM THE REST OF YOUR COMMUNITY, DEPRIVED OF ALL AFFECTION, AND ABUSED ON A DAILY BASIS.
PART OF ME ACTUALLY FEELS BAD FOR THEM.
THESE DAYS, I CAN'T SAY THAT I FULLY UNDERSTAND PLANTS *OR* HUMANS, BUT I GUESS I HAVE AN EASIER TIME EMPATHIZING WITH VEGETATION...
TEFÉ!
THEIR PAIN IS A LOT LESS COMPLICATED.

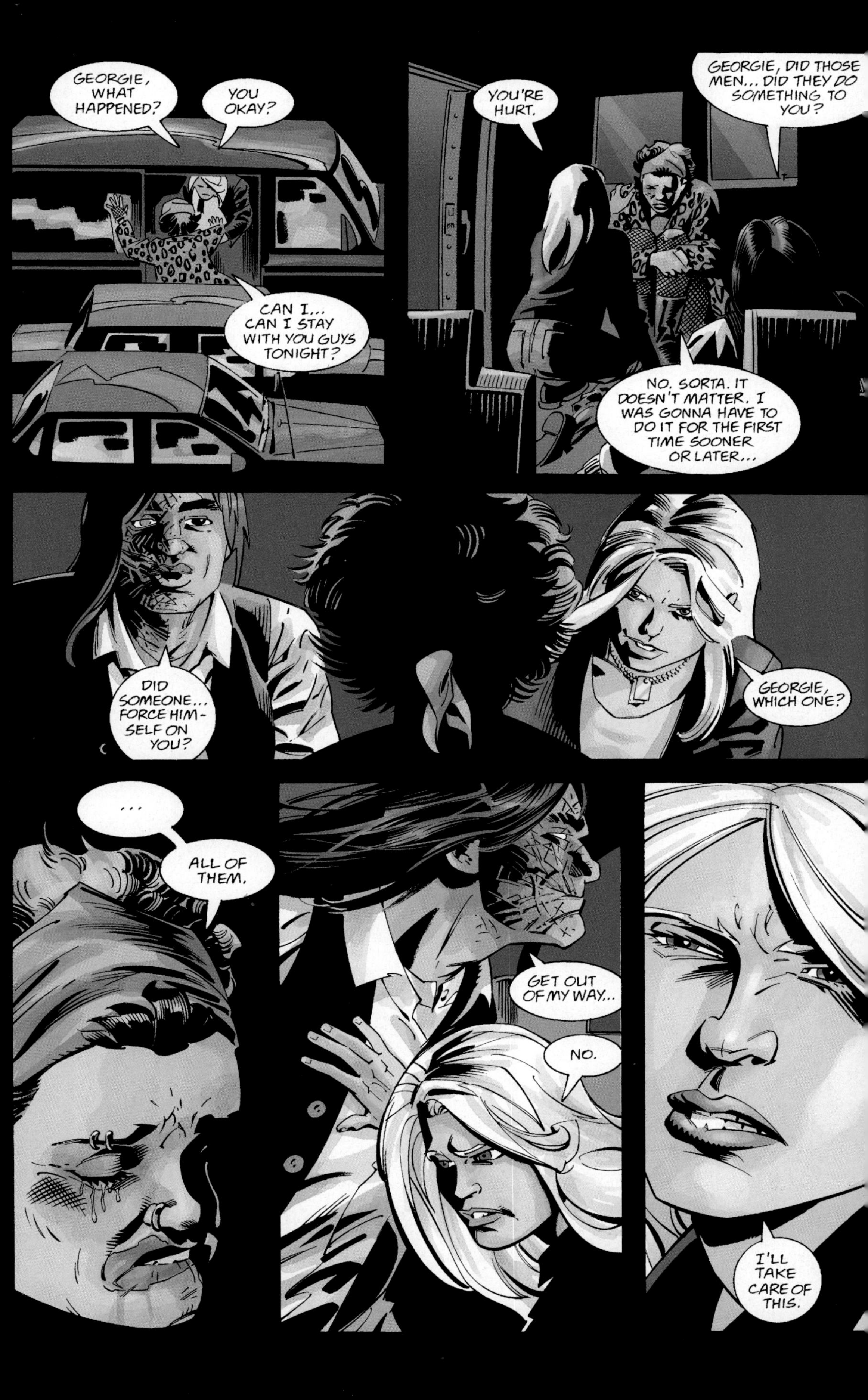
GEORGIE, WHAT HAPPENED?
YOU OKAY?
CAN I... CAN I STAY WITH YOU GUYS TONIGHT?
YOU'RE HURT.
GEORGIE, DID THOSE MEN... DID THEY DO SOMETHING TO YOU?
NO. SORTA. IT DOESN'T MATTER. I WAS GONNA HAVE TO DO IT FOR THE FIRST TIME SOONER OR LATER...
DID SOMEONE... FORCE HIM-SELF ON YOU?
GEORGIE, WHICH ONE?
...
ALL OF THEM.
GET OUT OF MY WAY...
NO.
I'LL TAKE CARE OF THIS.

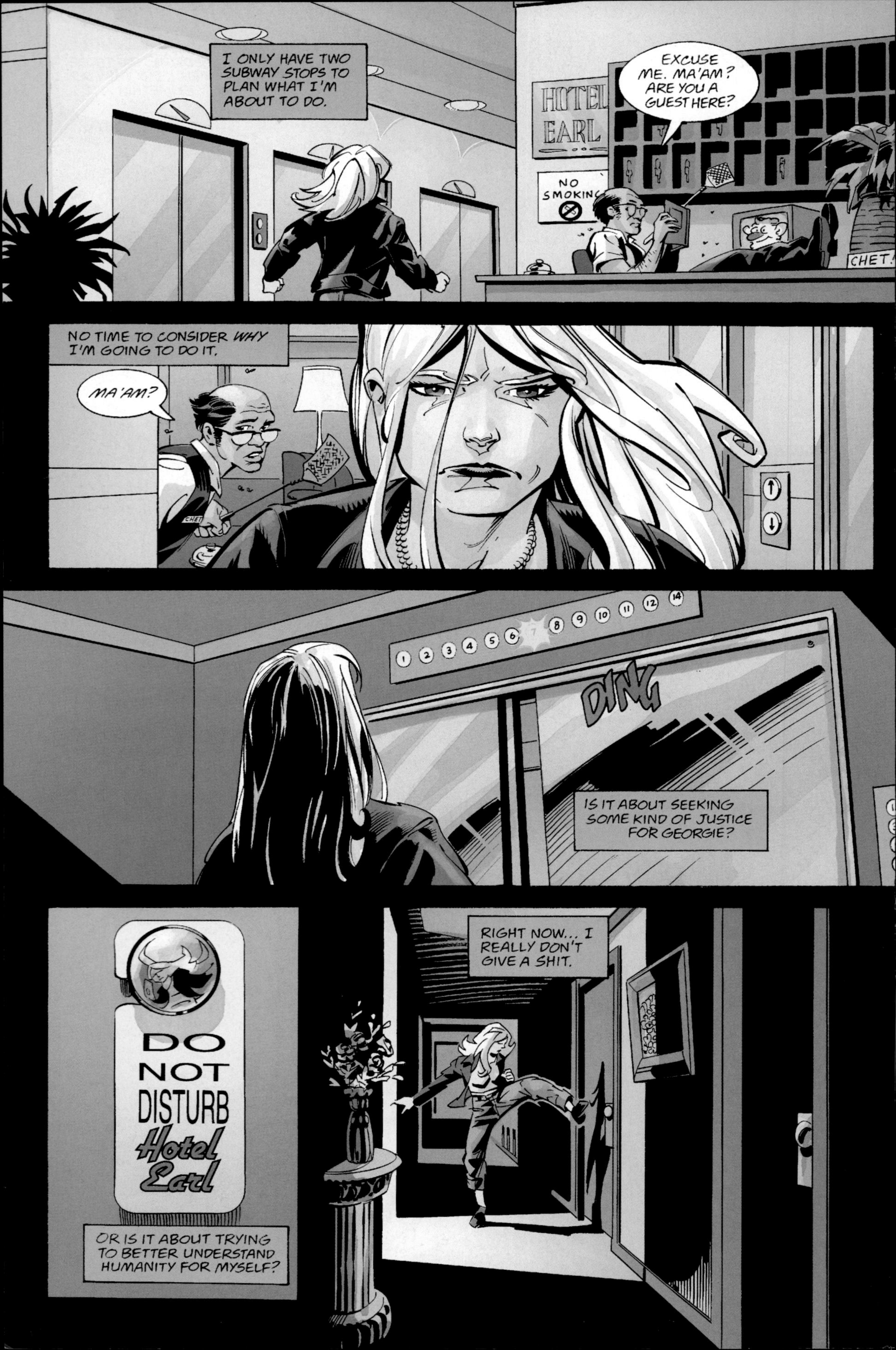
I ONLY HAVE TWO SUBWAY STOPS TO PLAN WHAT I'M ABOUT TO DO.
HOTEL EARL
NO SMOKING
EXCUSE ME. MA'AM? ARE YOU A GUEST HERE?
CHET
NO TIME TO CONSIDER WHY I'M GOING TO DO IT.
MA'AM?
CHET
1 2 3 4 5 6 7 8 9 10 11 12 14
DING
IS IT ABOUT SEEKING SOME KIND OF JUSTICE FOR GEORGIE?
DO NOT DISTURB Hotel Earl
OR IS IT ABOUT TRYING TO BETTER UNDERSTAND HUMANITY FOR MYSELF?
RIGHT NOW... I REALLY DON'T GIVE A SHIT.

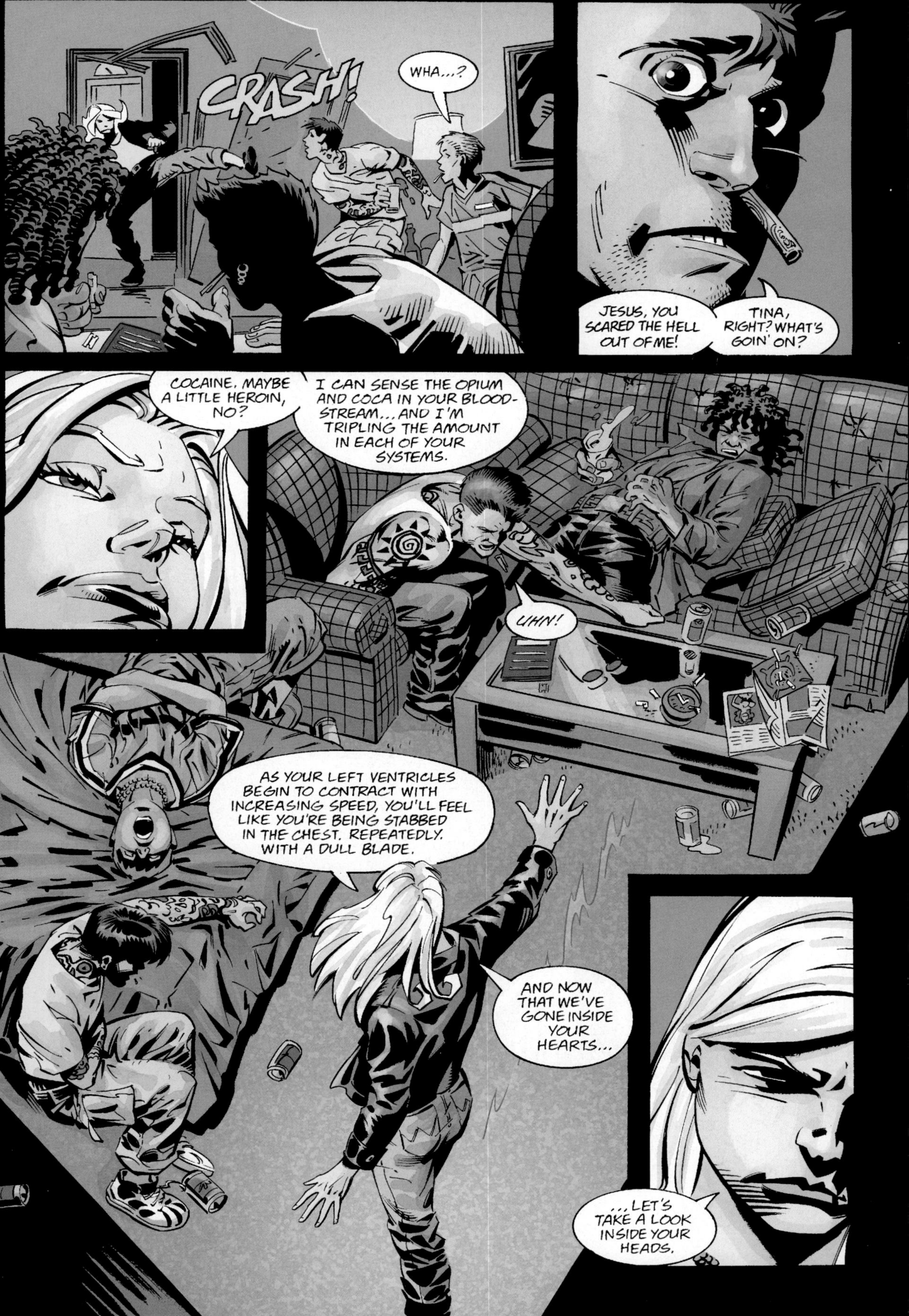
CRASH!
WHA...?
JESUS, YOU SCARED THE HELL OUT OF ME!
TINA, RIGHT? WHAT'S GOIN' ON?
COCAINE. MAYBE A LITTLE HEROIN, NO?
I CAN SENSE THE OPIUM AND COCA IN YOUR BLOOD-STREAM... AND I'M TRIPLING THE AMOUNT IN EACH OF YOUR SYSTEMS.
UHN!
AS YOUR LEFT VENTRICLES BEGIN TO CONTRACT WITH INCREASING SPEED, YOU'LL FEEL LIKE YOU'RE BEING STABBED IN THE CHEST. REPEATEDLY. WITH A DULL BLADE.
AND NOW THAT WE'VE GONE INSIDE YOUR HEARTS...
...LET'S TAKE A LOOK INSIDE YOUR HEADS.

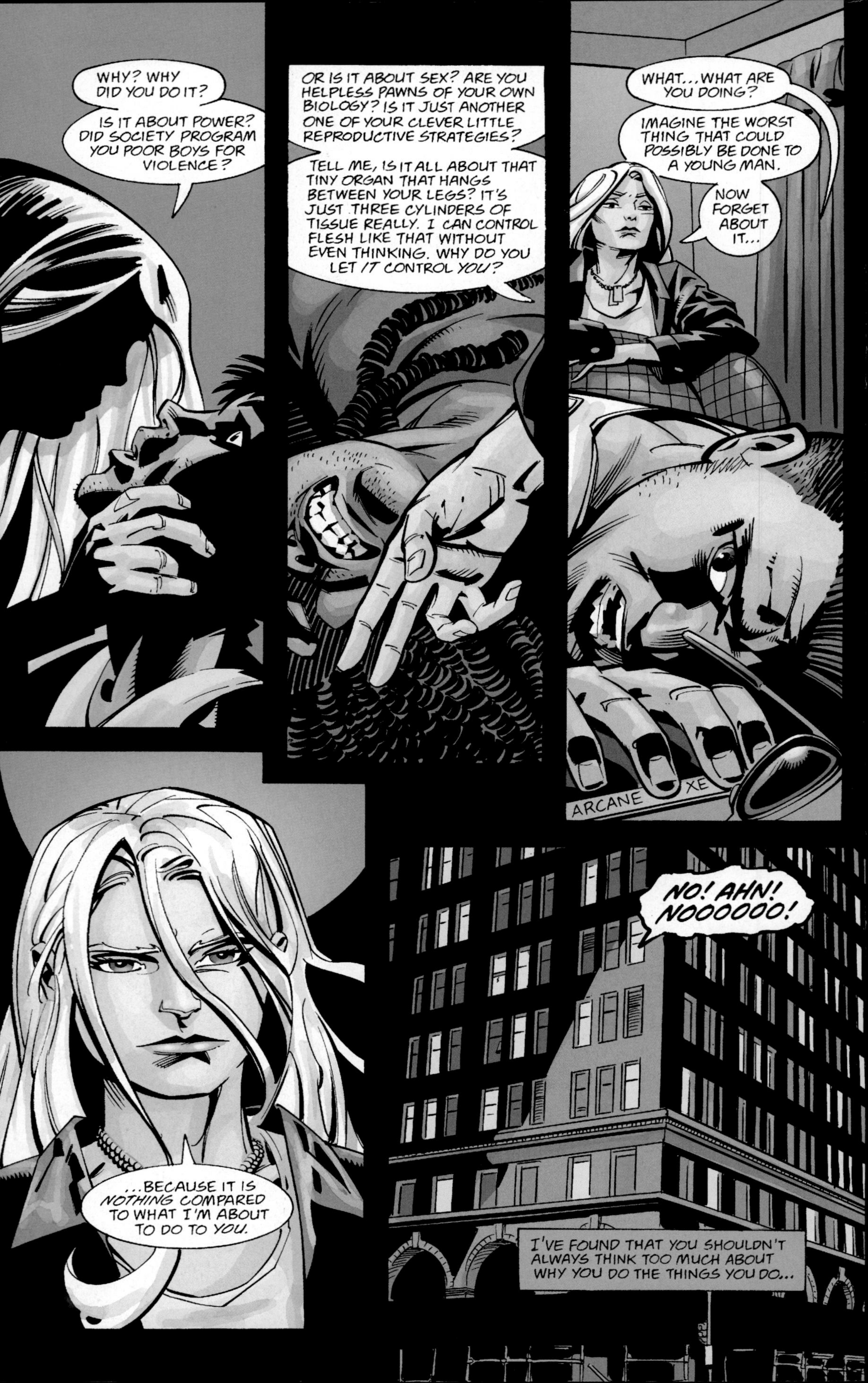
WHY? WHY DID YOU DO IT?
IS IT ABOUT POWER? DID SOCIETY PROGRAM YOU POOR BOYS FOR VIOLENCE?
OR IS IT ABOUT SEX? ARE YOU HELPLESS PAWNS OF YOUR OWN BIOLOGY? IS IT JUST ANOTHER ONE OF YOUR CLEVER LITTLE REPRODUCTIVE STRATEGIES?
TELL ME, IS IT ALL ABOUT THAT TINY ORGAN THAT HANGS BETWEEN YOUR LEGS? IT'S JUST THREE CYLINDERS OF TISSUE REALLY. I CAN CONTROL FLESH LIKE THAT WITHOUT EVEN THINKING. WHY DO YOU LET *IT* CONTROL *YOU*?
WHAT...WHAT ARE YOU DOING?
IMAGINE THE WORST THING THAT COULD POSSIBLY BE DONE TO A YOUNG MAN.
NOW FORGET ABOUT IT...
ARCANE
XE
...BECAUSE IT IS *NOTHING* COMPARED TO WHAT I'M ABOUT TO DO TO *YOU*.
NO! AHN! NOOOOOO!
I'VE FOUND THAT YOU SHOULDN'T ALWAYS THINK TOO MUCH ABOUT WHY YOU DO THE THINGS YOU DO...

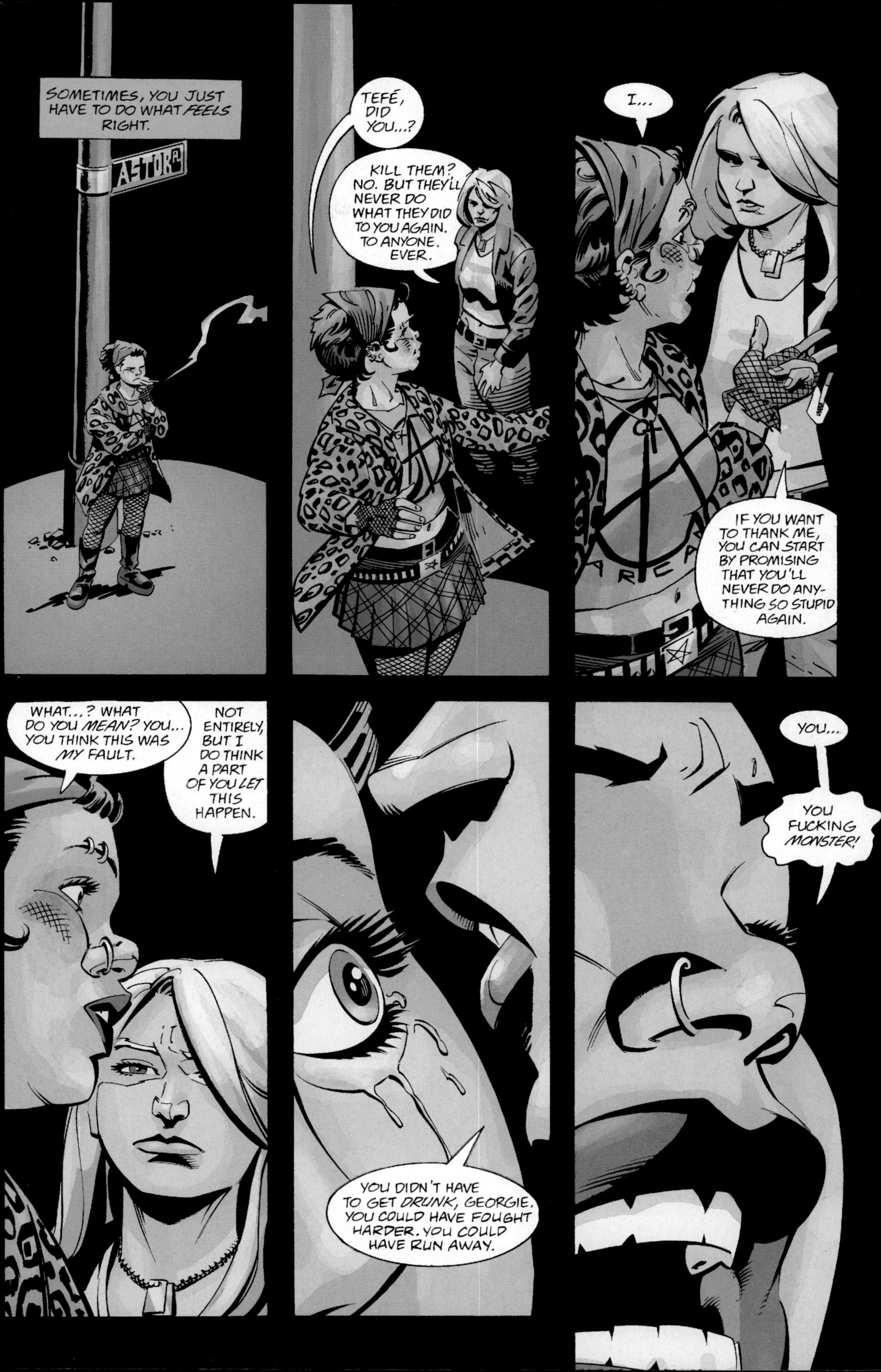
SOMETIMES, YOU JUST HAVE TO DO WHAT *FEELS* RIGHT.
ASTOR PL
TEFÉ, DID YOU...?
KILL THEM? NO. BUT THEY'LL NEVER DO WHAT THEY DID TO YOU AGAIN. TO ANYONE. EVER.
I...
IF YOU WANT TO THANK ME, YOU CAN START BY PROMISING THAT YOU'LL NEVER DO ANYTHING SO STUPID AGAIN.
WHAT...? WHAT DO YOU *MEAN*? YOU... YOU THINK THIS WAS *MY* FAULT.
NOT ENTIRELY, BUT I DO THINK A PART OF YOU *LET* THIS HAPPEN.
YOU DIDN'T HAVE TO GET *DRUNK*, GEORGIE. YOU COULD HAVE FOUGHT HARDER. YOU COULD HAVE RUN AWAY.
YOU...
YOU FUCKING *MONSTER!*

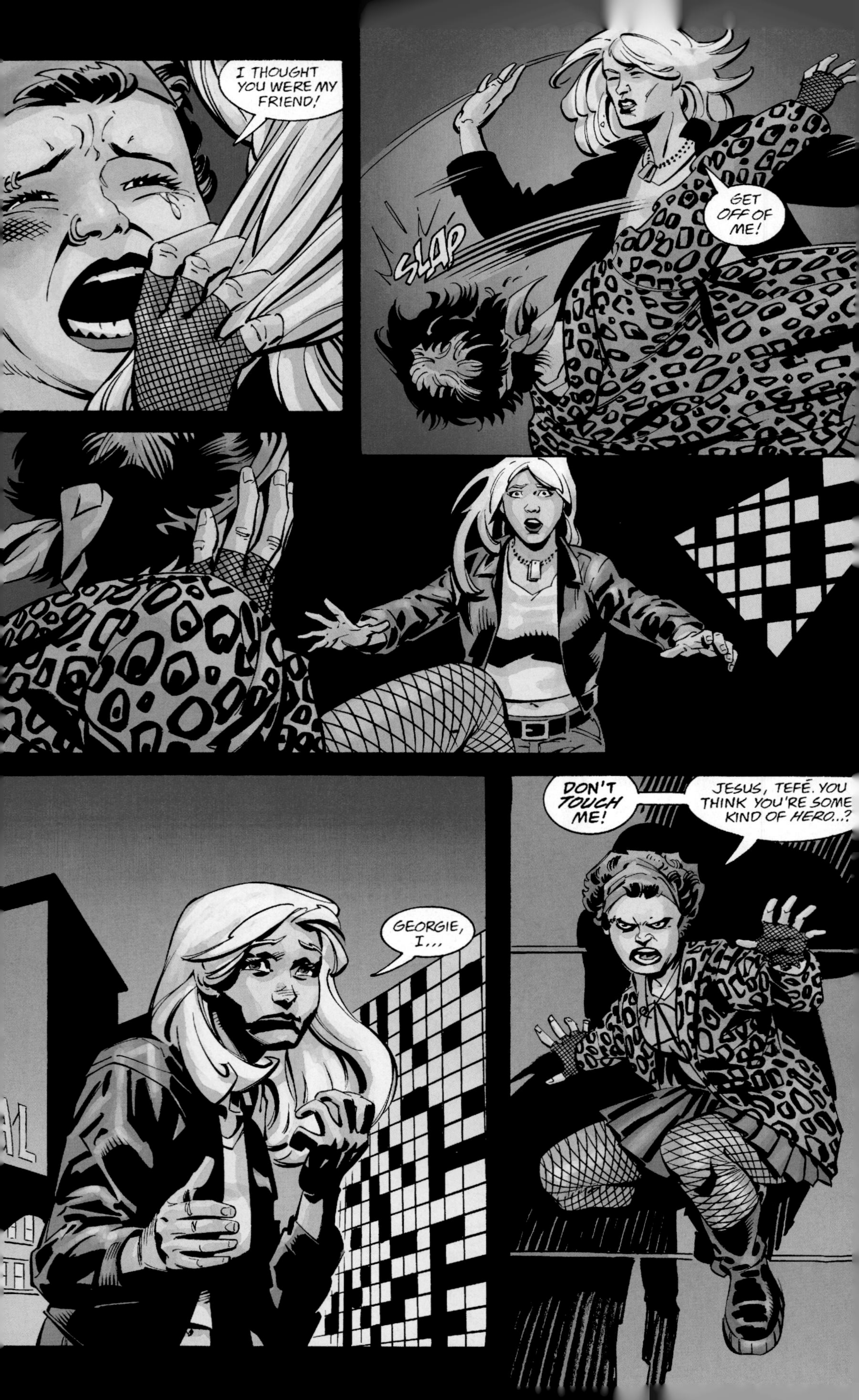
I THOUGHT YOU WERE MY FRIEND!
SLAP
GET OFF OF ME!
GEORGIE, I...
DON'T TOUCH ME!
JESUS, TEFÉ. YOU THINK YOU'RE SOME KIND OF HERO...?

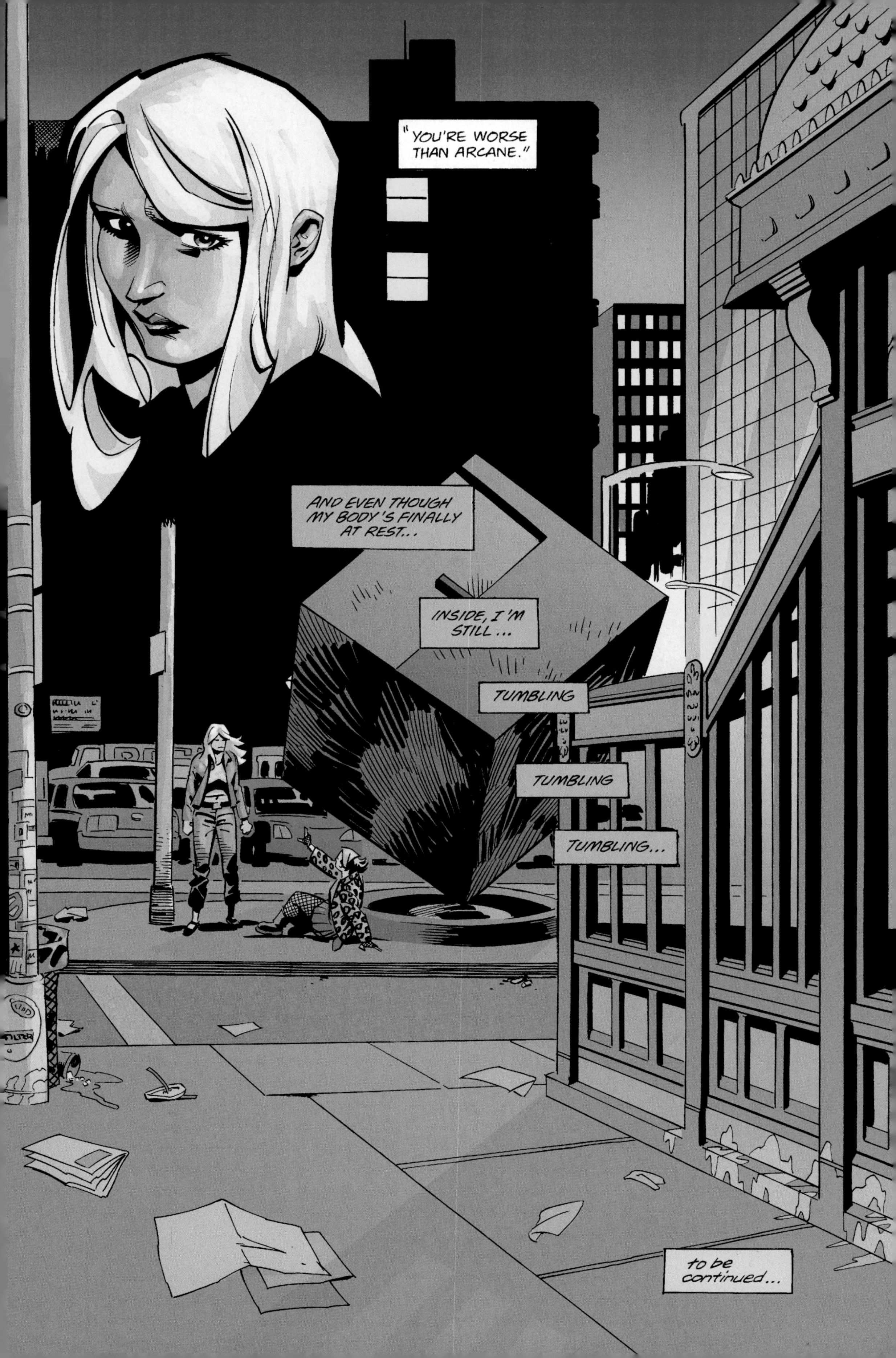
"YOU'RE WORSE THAN ARCANE."
AND EVEN THOUGH MY BODY'S FINALLY AT REST...
INSIDE, I'M STILL...
TUMBLING
TUMBLING
TUMBLING...
to be continued...

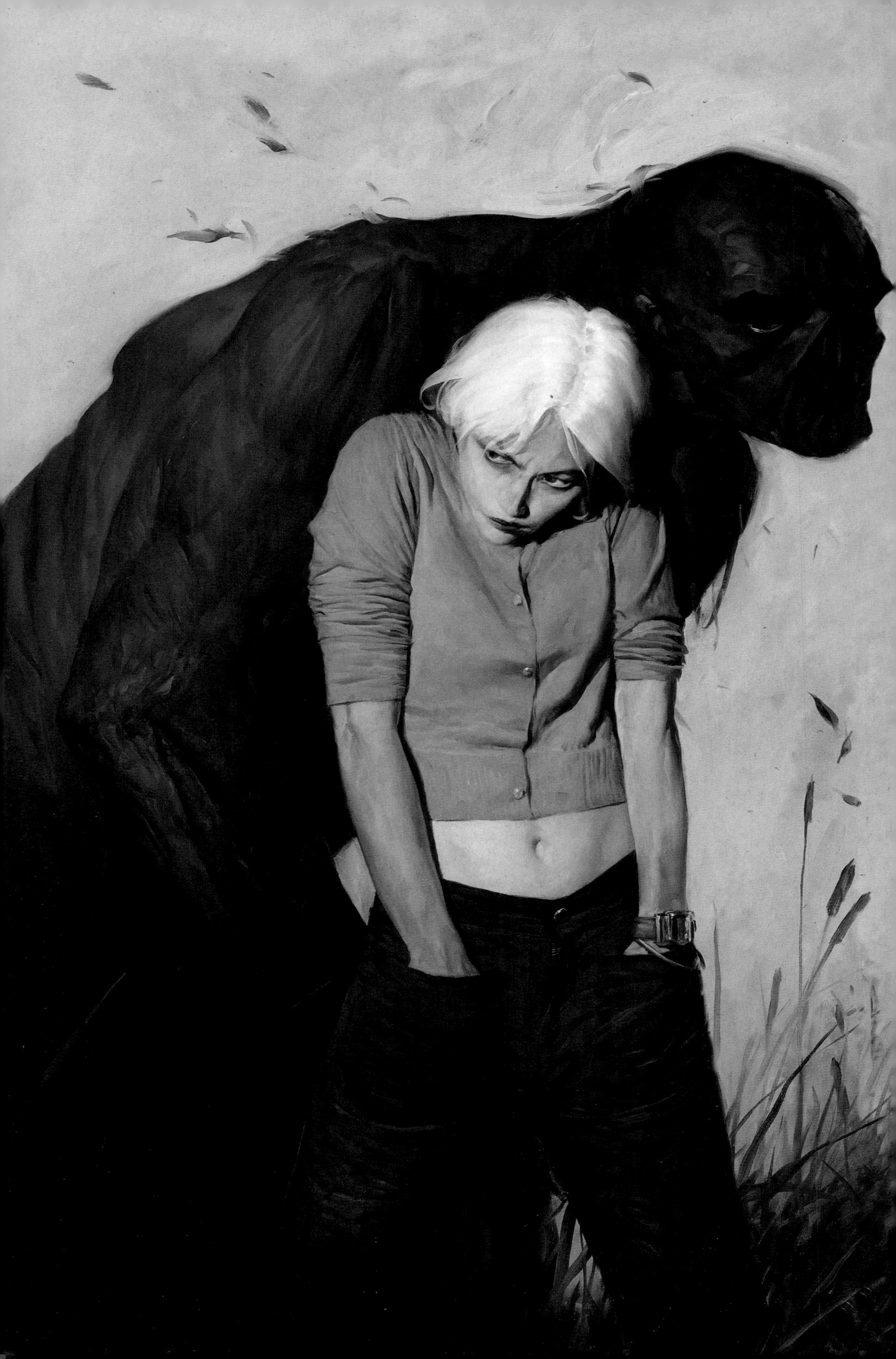

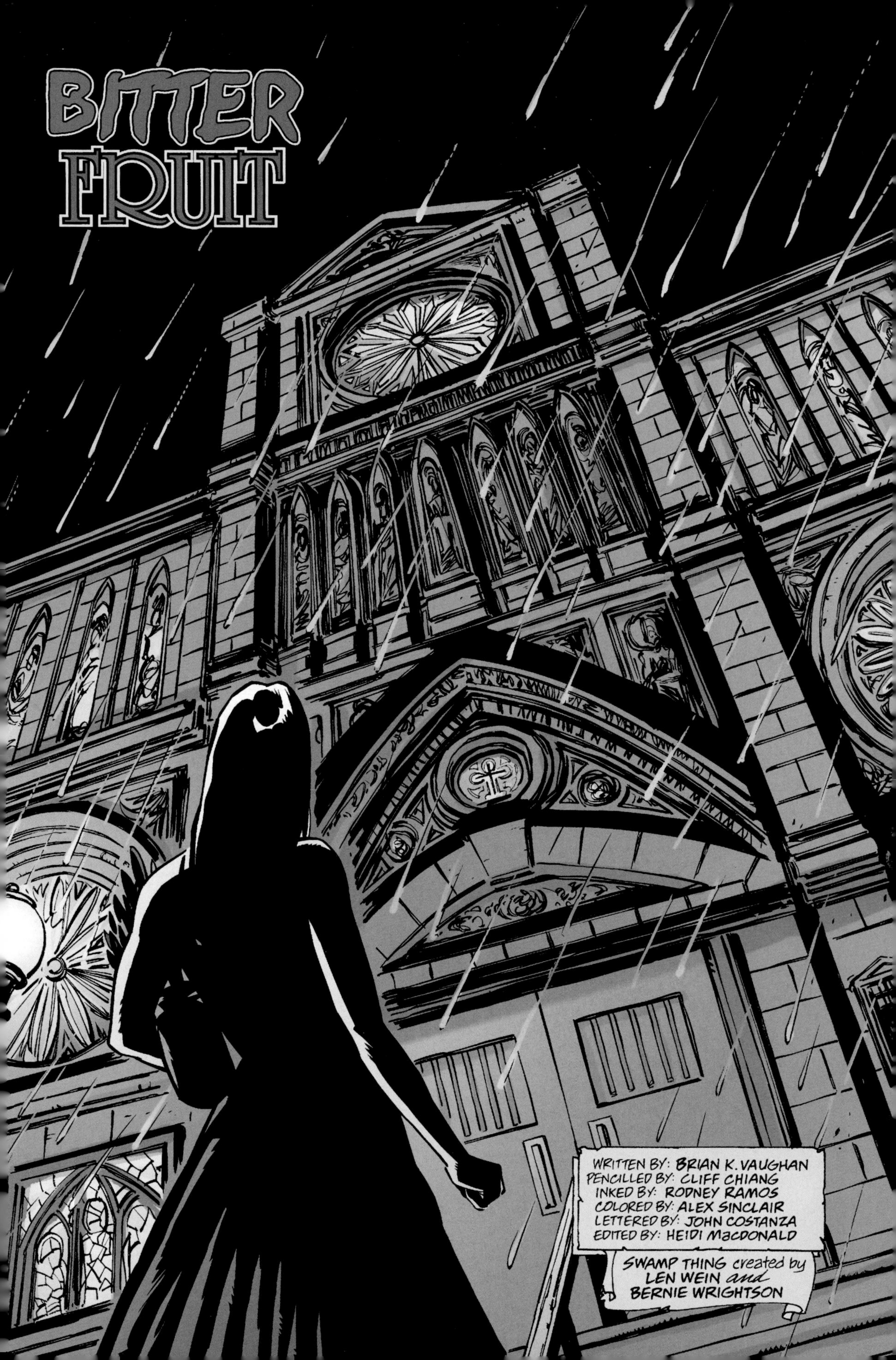
BITTER FRUIT
WRITTEN BY: BRIAN K. VAUGHAN
PENCILLED BY: CLIFF CHIANG
INKED BY: RODNEY RAMOS
COLORED BY: ALEX SINCLAIR
LETTERED BY: JOHN COSTANZA
EDITED BY: HEIDI MacDONALD
SWAMP THING created by LEN WEIN and BERNIE WRIGHTSON

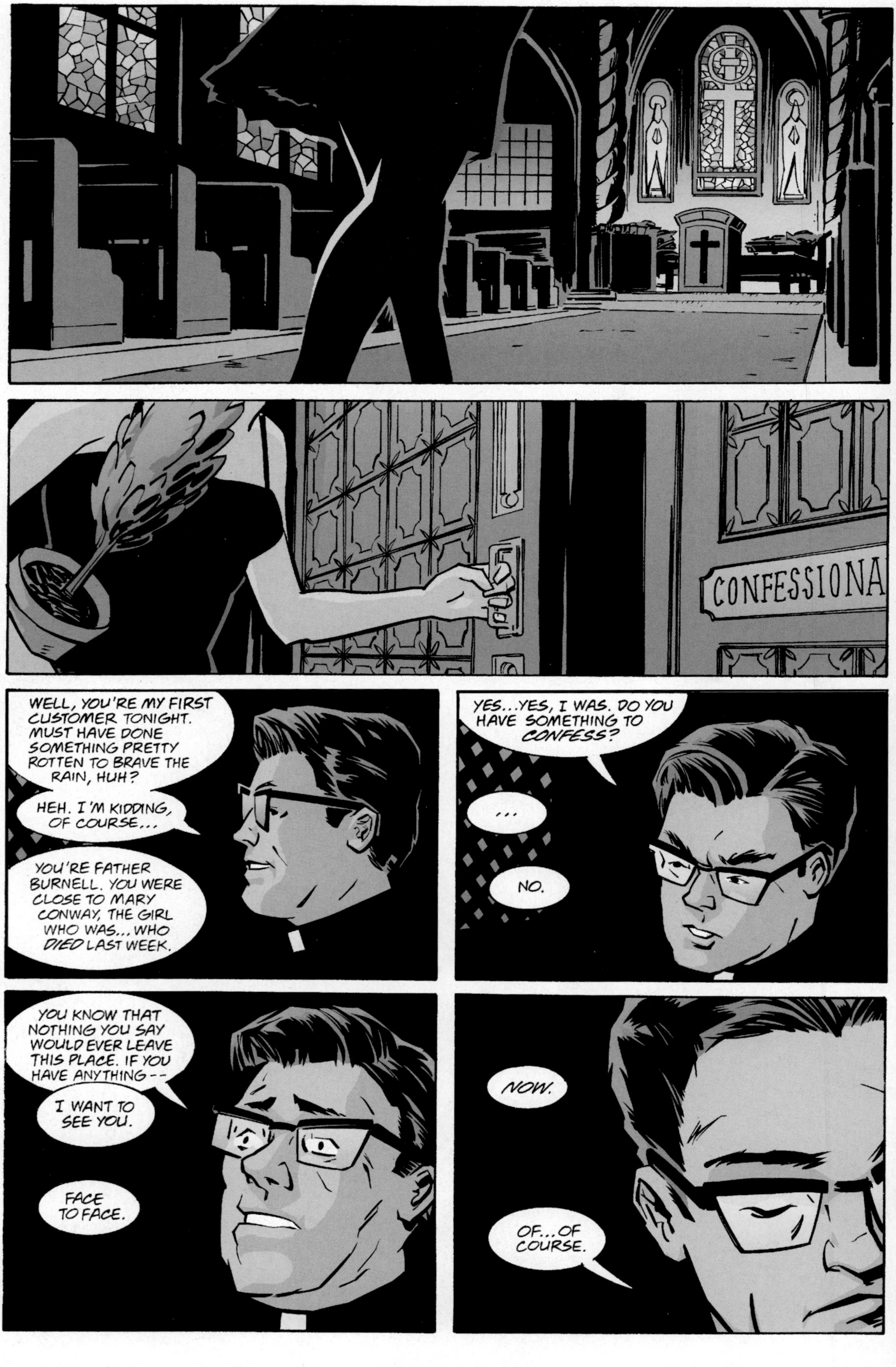
CONFESSIONAL
WELL, YOU'RE MY FIRST CUSTOMER TONIGHT. MUST HAVE DONE SOMETHING PRETTY ROTTEN TO BRAVE THE RAIN, HUH?
HEH. I'M KIDDING, OF COURSE...
YOU'RE FATHER BURNELL. YOU WERE CLOSE TO MARY CONWAY, THE GIRL WHO WAS... WHO DIED LAST WEEK.
YES...YES, I WAS. DO YOU HAVE SOMETHING TO CONFESS?
...
NO.
YOU KNOW THAT NOTHING YOU SAY WOULD EVER LEAVE THIS PLACE. IF YOU HAVE ANYTHING--
I WANT TO SEE YOU.
FACE TO FACE.
NOW.
OF...OF COURSE.

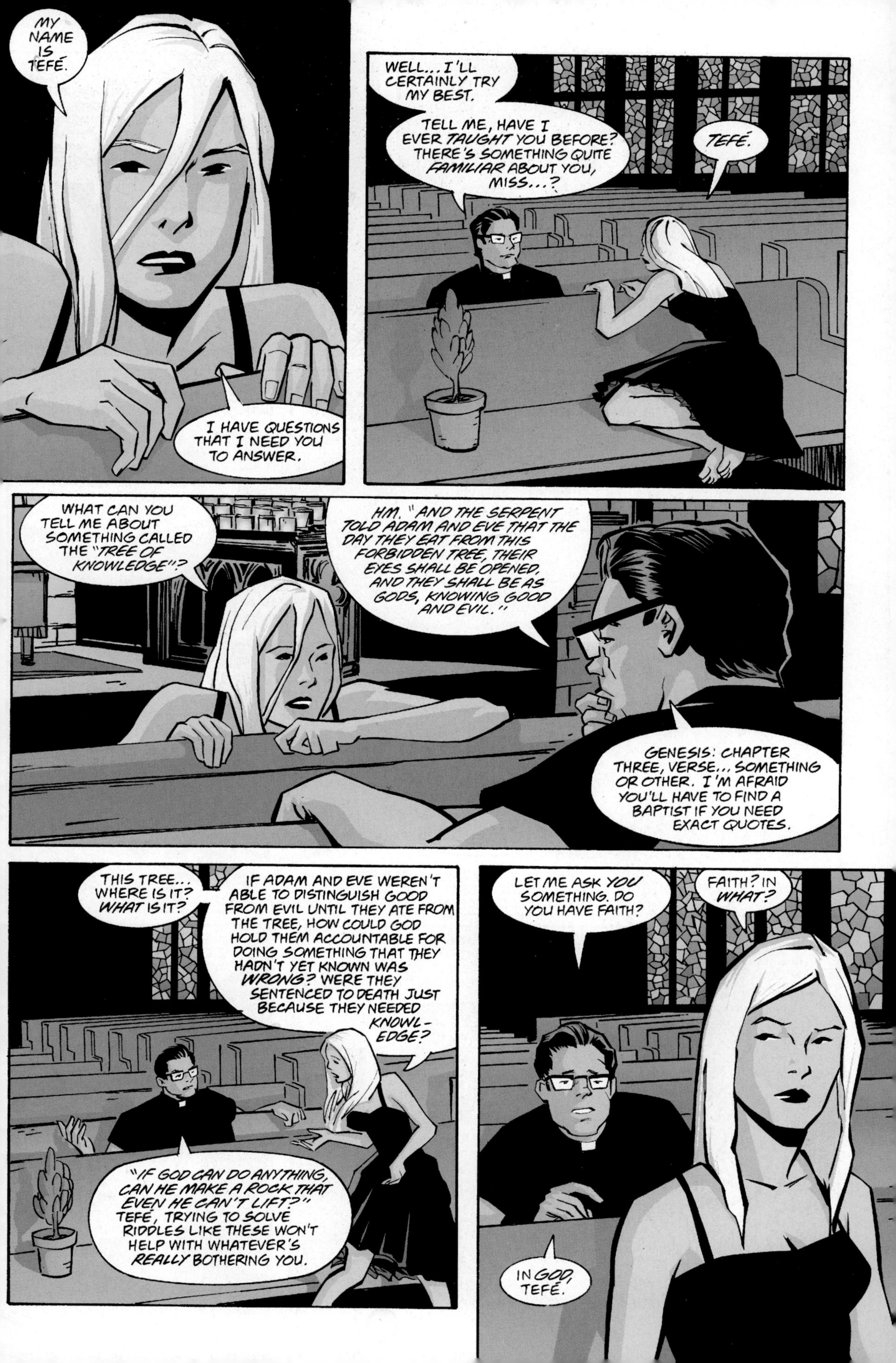
MY NAME IS TEFÉ.
I HAVE QUESTIONS THAT I NEED YOU TO ANSWER.
WELL... I'LL CERTAINLY TRY MY BEST.
TELL ME, HAVE I EVER TAUGHT YOU BEFORE? THERE'S SOMETHING QUITE FAMILIAR ABOUT YOU, MISS...?
TEFÉ.
WHAT CAN YOU TELL ME ABOUT SOMETHING CALLED THE "TREE OF KNOWLEDGE"?
HM. "AND THE SERPENT TOLD ADAM AND EVE THAT THE DAY THEY EAT FROM THIS FORBIDDEN TREE, THEIR EYES SHALL BE OPENED, AND THEY SHALL BE AS GODS, KNOWING GOOD AND EVIL."
GENESIS: CHAPTER THREE, VERSE... SOMETHING OR OTHER. I'M AFRAID YOU'LL HAVE TO FIND A BAPTIST IF YOU NEED EXACT QUOTES.
THIS TREE... WHERE IS IT? WHAT IS IT?
IF ADAM AND EVE WEREN'T ABLE TO DISTINGUISH GOOD FROM EVIL UNTIL THEY ATE FROM THE TREE, HOW COULD GOD HOLD THEM ACCOUNTABLE FOR DOING SOMETHING THAT THEY HADN'T YET KNOWN WAS WRONG? WERE THEY SENTENCED TO DEATH JUST BECAUSE THEY NEEDED KNOWL-EDGE?
"IF GOD CAN DO ANYTHING, CAN HE MAKE A ROCK THAT EVEN HE CAN'T LIFT?" TEFÉ, TRYING TO SOLVE RIDDLES LIKE THESE WON'T HELP WITH WHATEVER'S REALLY BOTHERING YOU.
LET ME ASK YOU SOMETHING. DO YOU HAVE FAITH?
FAITH? IN WHAT?
IN GOD, TEFÉ.

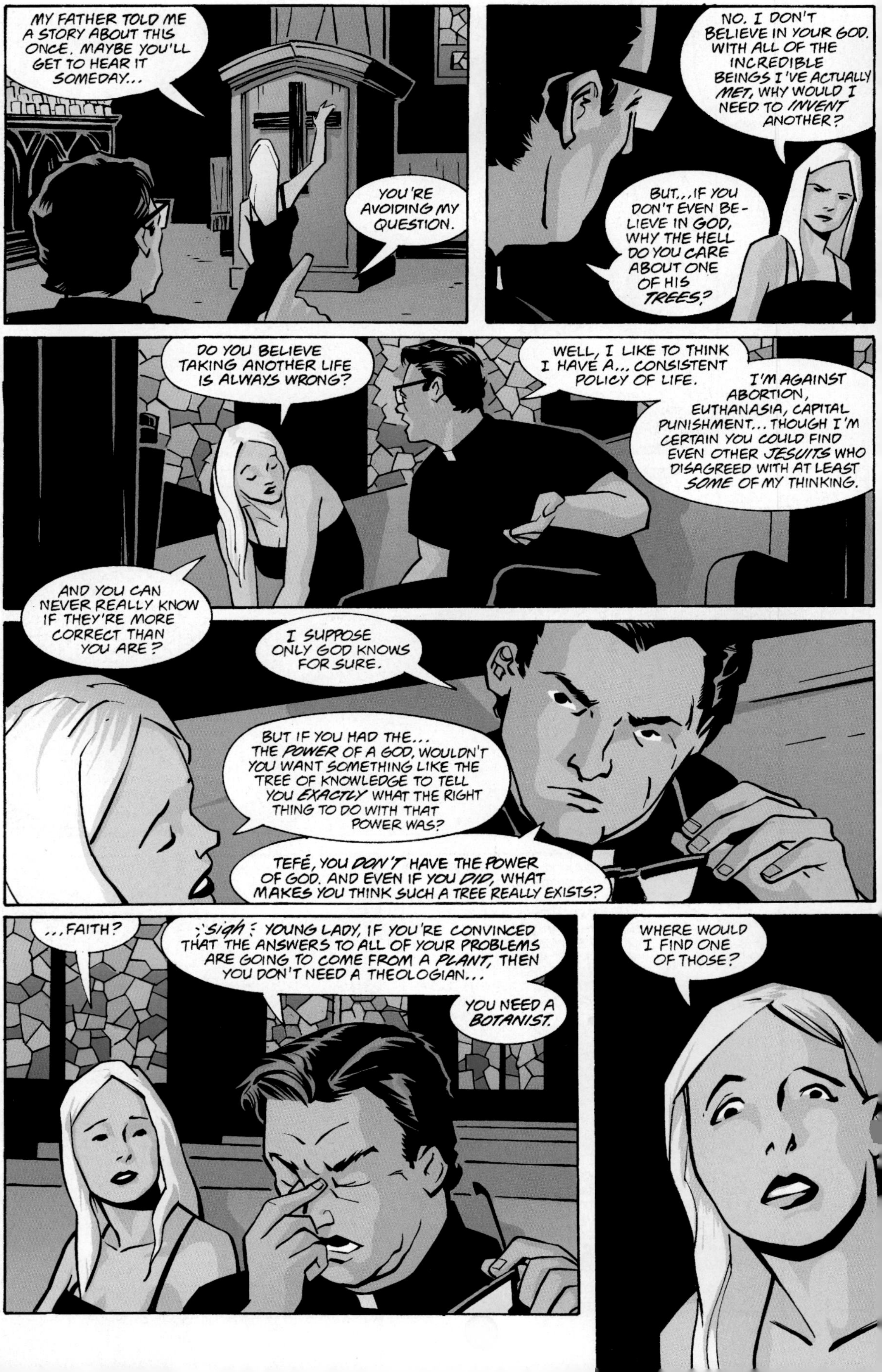
MY FATHER TOLD ME A STORY ABOUT THIS ONCE. MAYBE YOU'LL GET TO HEAR IT SOMEDAY...
YOU'RE AVOIDING MY QUESTION.
NO. I DON'T BELIEVE IN YOUR GOD. WITH ALL OF THE INCREDIBLE BEINGS I'VE ACTUALLY MET, WHY WOULD I NEED TO INVENT ANOTHER?
BUT... IF YOU DON'T EVEN BE-LIEVE IN GOD, WHY THE HELL DO YOU CARE ABOUT ONE OF HIS TREES?
DO YOU BELIEVE TAKING ANOTHER LIFE IS ALWAYS WRONG?
WELL, I LIKE TO THINK I HAVE A... CONSISTENT POLICY OF LIFE.
I'M AGAINST ABORTION, EUTHANASIA, CAPITAL PUNISHMENT... THOUGH I'M CERTAIN YOU COULD FIND EVEN OTHER JESUITS WHO DISAGREED WITH AT LEAST SOME OF MY THINKING.
AND YOU CAN NEVER REALLY KNOW IF THEY'RE MORE CORRECT THAN YOU ARE?
I SUPPOSE ONLY GOD KNOWS FOR SURE.
BUT IF YOU HAD THE... THE POWER OF A GOD, WOULDN'T YOU WANT SOMETHING LIKE THE TREE OF KNOWLEDGE TO TELL YOU EXACTLY WHAT THE RIGHT THING TO DO WITH THAT POWER WAS?
TEFÉ, YOU DON'T HAVE THE POWER OF GOD. AND EVEN IF YOU DID, WHAT MAKES YOU THINK SUCH A TREE REALLY EXISTS?
...FAITH?
:sigh: YOUNG LADY, IF YOU'RE CONVINCED THAT THE ANSWERS TO ALL OF YOUR PROBLEMS ARE GOING TO COME FROM A PLANT, THEN YOU DON'T NEED A THEOLOGIAN...
YOU NEED A BOTANIST.
WHERE WOULD I FIND ONE OF THOSE?

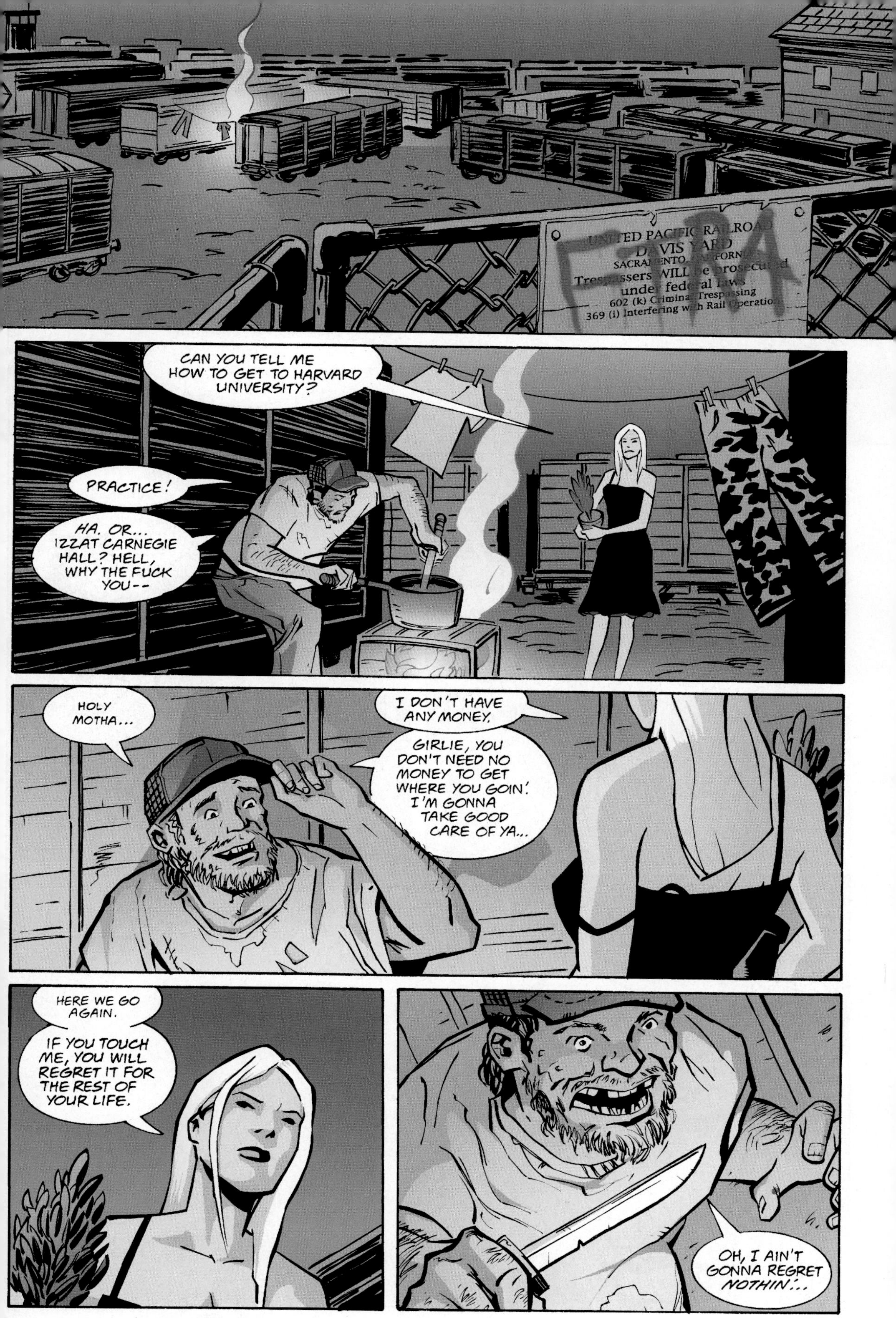

UNITED PACIFIC RAILROAD
DAVIS YARD
SACRAMENTO, CALIFORNI
Trespassers WILL be prosecuted
under federal laws
602 (k) Criminal Trespassing
369 (i) Interfering with Rail Operation
FTRA
CAN YOU TELL ME HOW TO GET TO HARVARD UNIVERSITY?
PRACTICE!
HA. OR... IZZAT CARNEGIE HALL? HELL, WHY THE FUCK YOU--
HOLY MOTHA...
I DON'T HAVE ANY MONEY.
GIRLIE, YOU DON'T NEED NO MONEY TO GET WHERE YOU GOIN'. I'M GONNA TAKE GOOD CARE OF YA...
HERE WE GO AGAIN.
IF YOU TOUCH ME, YOU WILL REGRET IT FOR THE REST OF YOUR LIFE.
OH, I AIN'T GONNA REGRET NOTHIN'...

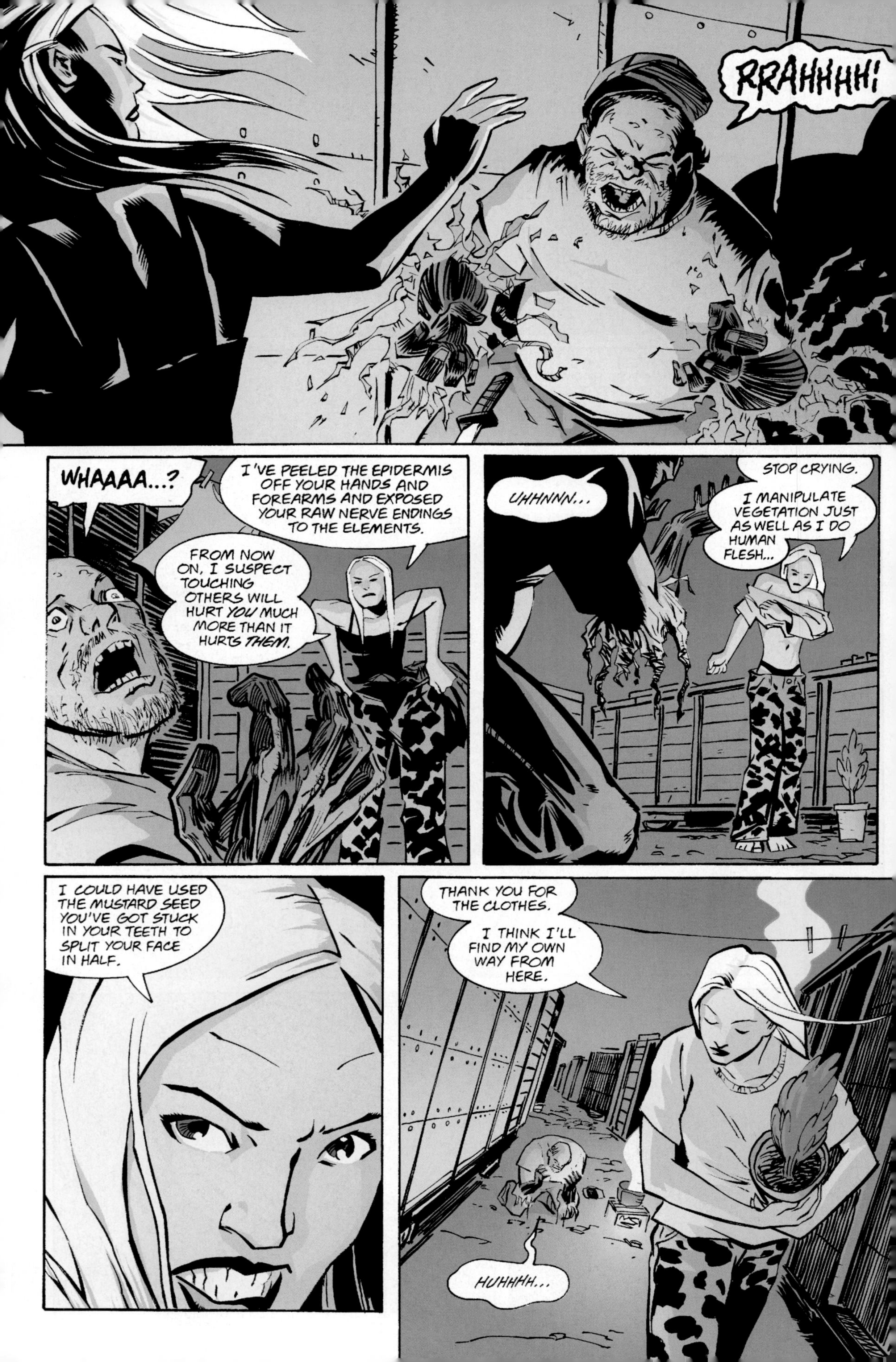
RRAHHHH!
WHAAAA...?
I'VE PEELED THE EPIDERMIS OFF YOUR HANDS AND FOREARMS AND EXPOSED YOUR RAW NERVE ENDINGS TO THE ELEMENTS.
FROM NOW ON, I SUSPECT TOUCHING OTHERS WILL HURT YOU MUCH MORE THAN IT HURTS THEM.
UHHNNN...
STOP CRYING.
I MANIPULATE VEGETATION JUST AS WELL AS I DO HUMAN FLESH...
I COULD HAVE USED THE MUSTARD SEED YOU'VE GOT STUCK IN YOUR TEETH TO SPLIT YOUR FACE IN HALF.
THANK YOU FOR THE CLOTHES.
I THINK I'LL FIND MY OWN WAY FROM HERE.
HUHHHH...

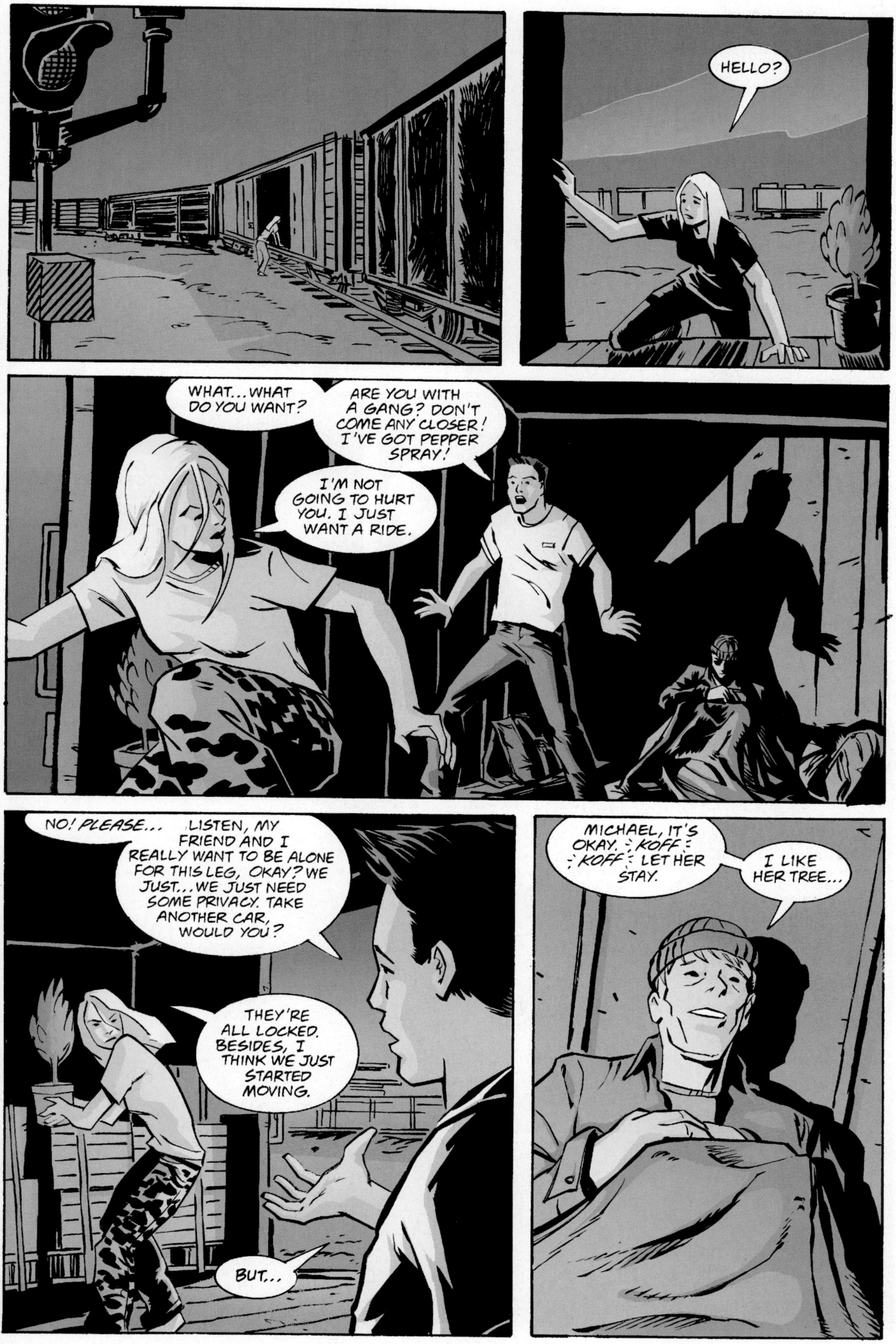
HELLO?
WHAT... WHAT DO YOU WANT?
ARE YOU WITH A GANG? DON'T COME ANY CLOSER! I'VE GOT PEPPER SPRAY!
I'M NOT GOING TO HURT YOU. I JUST WANT A RIDE.
NO! PLEASE... LISTEN, MY FRIEND AND I REALLY WANT TO BE ALONE FOR THIS LEG, OKAY? WE JUST... WE JUST NEED SOME PRIVACY. TAKE ANOTHER CAR, WOULD YOU?
THEY'RE ALL LOCKED. BESIDES, I THINK WE JUST STARTED MOVING.
BUT...
MICHAEL, IT'S OKAY. KOFF KOFF LET HER STAY.
I LIKE HER TREE...

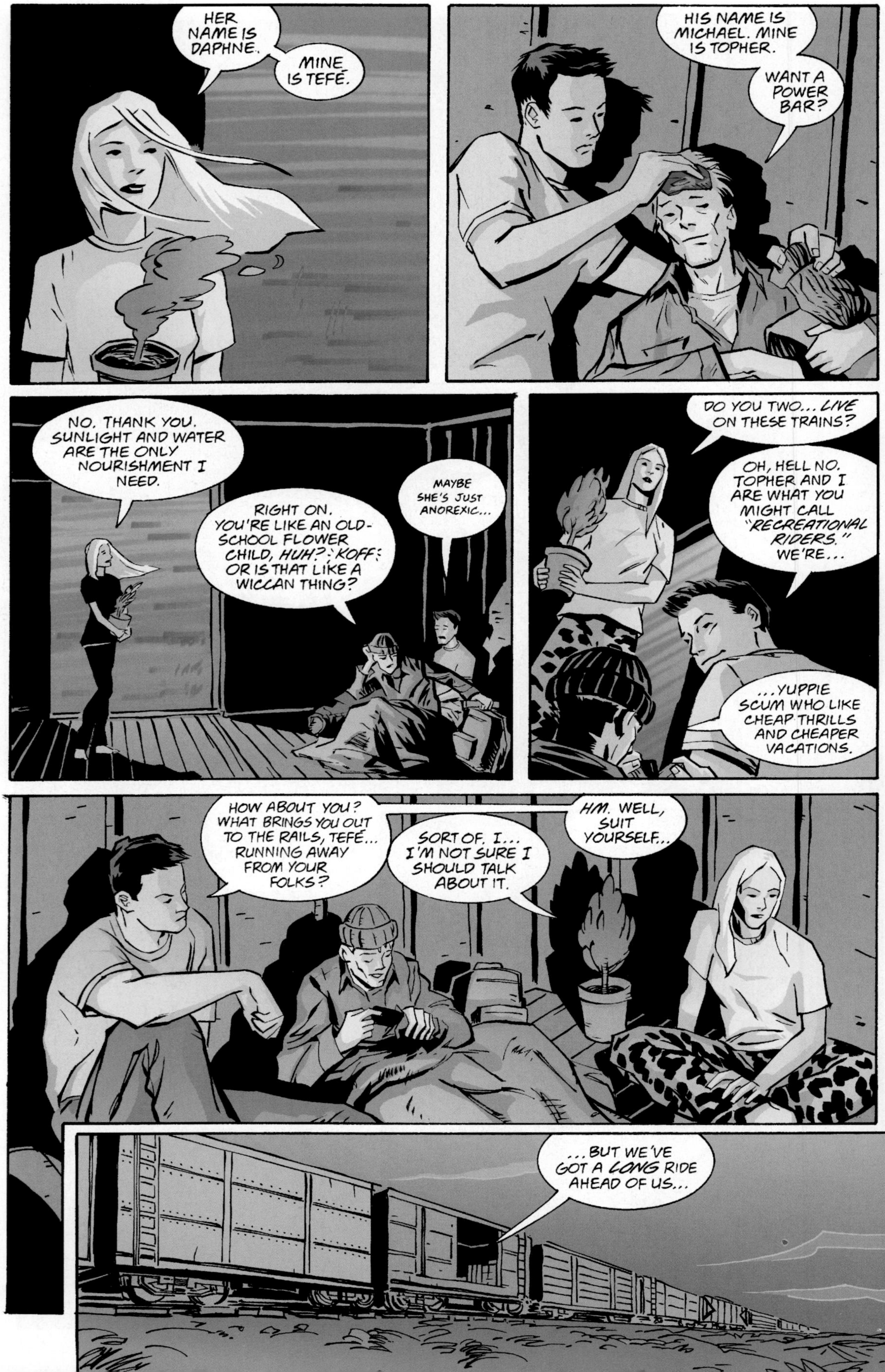
HER NAME IS DAPHNE.
MINE IS TEFÉ.
HIS NAME IS MICHAEL. MINE IS TOPHER.
WANT A POWER BAR?
NO, THANK YOU. SUNLIGHT AND WATER ARE THE ONLY NOURISHMENT I NEED.
RIGHT ON. YOU'RE LIKE AN OLD-SCHOOL FLOWER CHILD, *HUH?* :KOFF: OR IS THAT LIKE A WICCAN THING?
MAYBE SHE'S JUST ANOREXIC...
DO YOU TWO... *LIVE* ON THESE TRAINS?
OH, HELL NO. TOPHER AND I ARE WHAT YOU MIGHT CALL *"RECREATIONAL RIDERS."* WE'RE...
...YUPPIE SCUM WHO LIKE CHEAP THRILLS AND CHEAPER VACATIONS.
HOW ABOUT YOU? WHAT BRINGS YOU OUT TO THE RAILS, TEFÉ... RUNNING AWAY FROM YOUR FOLKS?
SORT OF. I... I'M NOT SURE I SHOULD TALK ABOUT IT.
HM. WELL, SUIT YOURSELF...
...BUT WE'VE GOT A *LONG* RIDE AHEAD OF US...

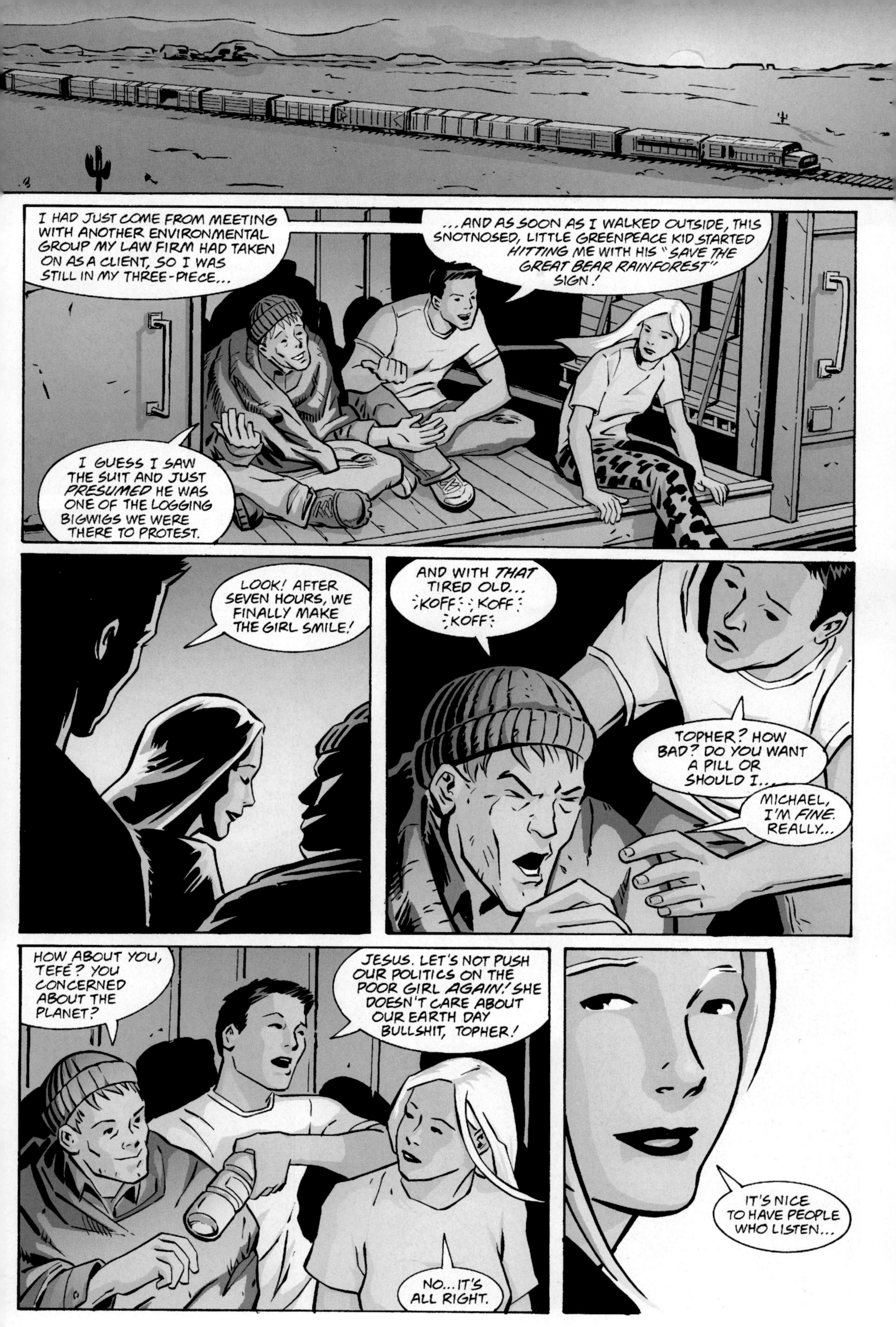
I HAD JUST COME FROM MEETING WITH ANOTHER ENVIRONMENTAL GROUP MY LAW FIRM HAD TAKEN ON AS A CLIENT, SO I WAS STILL IN MY THREE-PIECE...
...AND AS SOON AS I WALKED OUTSIDE, THIS SNOTNOSED, LITTLE GREENPEACE KID STARTED *HITTING* ME WITH HIS "*SAVE THE GREAT BEAR RAINFOREST*" SIGN!
I GUESS I SAW THE SUIT AND JUST *PRESUMED* HE WAS ONE OF THE LOGGING BIGWIGS WE WERE THERE TO PROTEST.
LOOK! AFTER SEVEN HOURS, WE FINALLY MAKE THE GIRL SMILE!
AND WITH *THAT* TIRED OLD... KOFF KOFF KOFF
TOPHER? HOW BAD? DO YOU WANT A PILL OR SHOULD I...
MICHAEL, I'M *FINE*. REALLY...
HOW ABOUT YOU, TEFÉ? YOU CONCERNED ABOUT THE PLANET?
JESUS. LET'S NOT PUSH OUR POLITICS ON THE POOR GIRL *AGAIN*! SHE DOESN'T CARE ABOUT OUR EARTH DAY BULLSHIT, TOPHER!
NO... IT'S ALL RIGHT.
IT'S NICE TO HAVE PEOPLE WHO LISTEN...

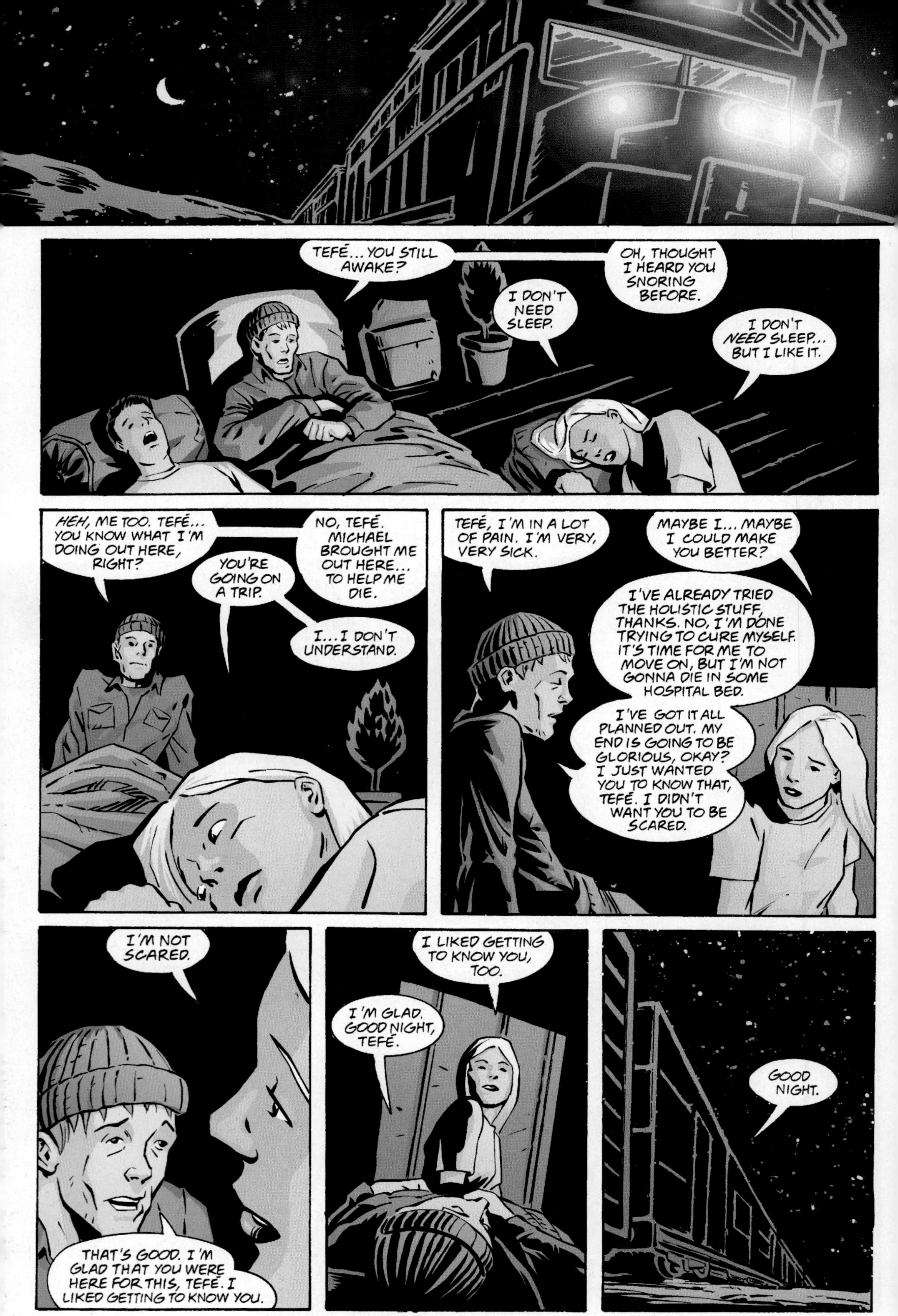
TEFÉ... YOU STILL AWAKE?
I DON'T NEED SLEEP.
OH, THOUGHT I HEARD YOU SNORING BEFORE.
I DON'T NEED SLEEP... BUT I LIKE IT.
HEH, ME TOO. TEFÉ... YOU KNOW WHAT I'M DOING OUT HERE, RIGHT?
YOU'RE GOING ON A TRIP.
NO, TEFÉ. MICHAEL BROUGHT ME OUT HERE... TO HELP ME DIE.
I... I DON'T UNDERSTAND.
TEFÉ, I'M IN A LOT OF PAIN. I'M VERY, VERY SICK.
MAYBE I... MAYBE I COULD MAKE YOU BETTER?
I'VE ALREADY TRIED THE HOLISTIC STUFF, THANKS. NO, I'M DONE TRYING TO CURE MYSELF. IT'S TIME FOR ME TO MOVE ON, BUT I'M NOT GONNA DIE IN SOME HOSPITAL BED.
I'VE GOT IT ALL PLANNED OUT. MY END IS GOING TO BE GLORIOUS, OKAY? I JUST WANTED YOU TO KNOW THAT, TEFÉ. I DIDN'T WANT YOU TO BE SCARED.
I'M NOT SCARED.
THAT'S GOOD. I'M GLAD THAT YOU WERE HERE FOR THIS, TEFÉ. I LIKED GETTING TO KNOW YOU.
I LIKED GETTING TO KNOW YOU, TOO.
I'M GLAD. GOOD NIGHT, TEFÉ.
GOOD NIGHT.

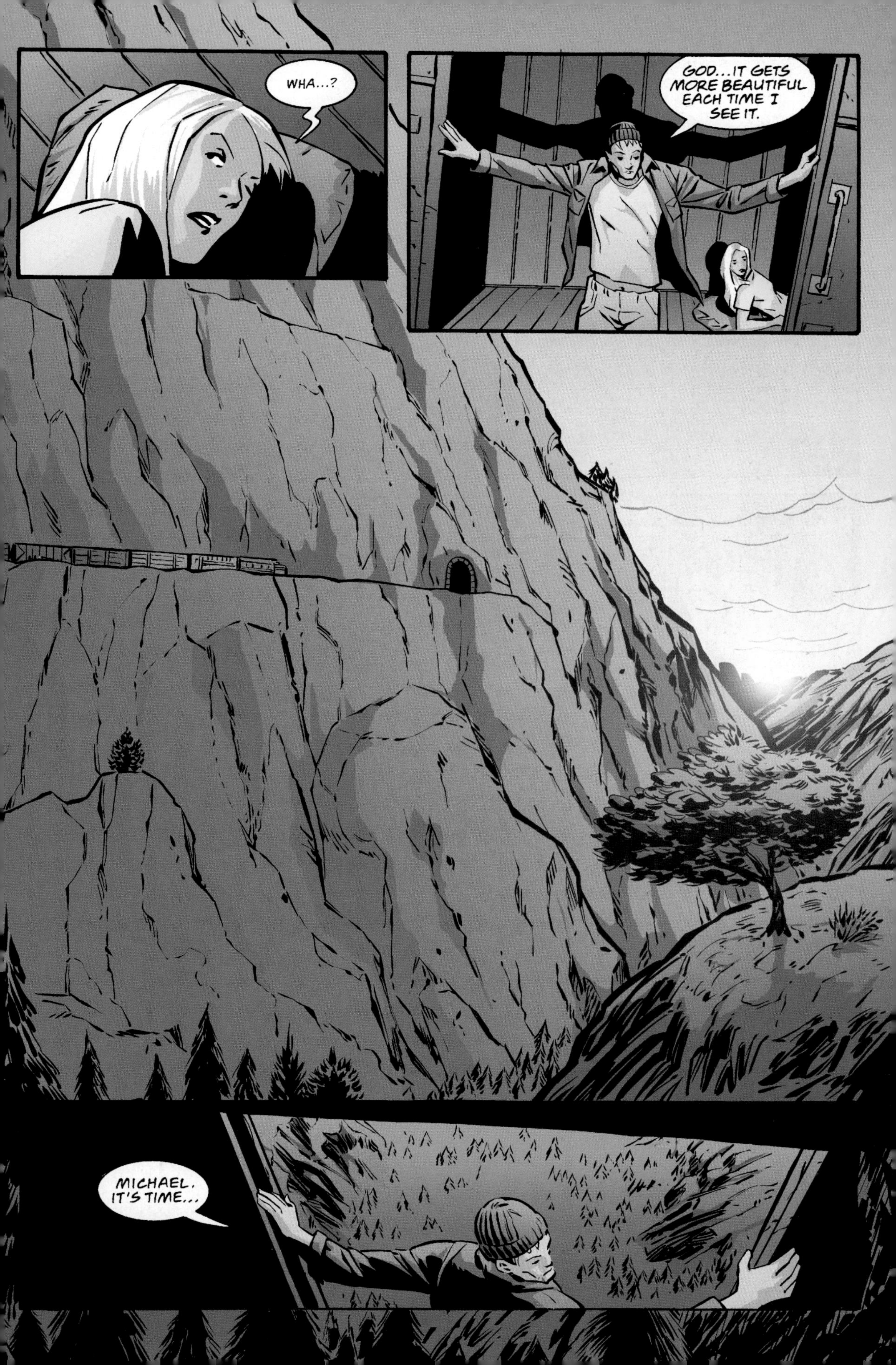
WHA...?
GOD...IT GETS MORE BEAUTIFUL EACH TIME I SEE IT.
MICHAEL. IT'S TIME...

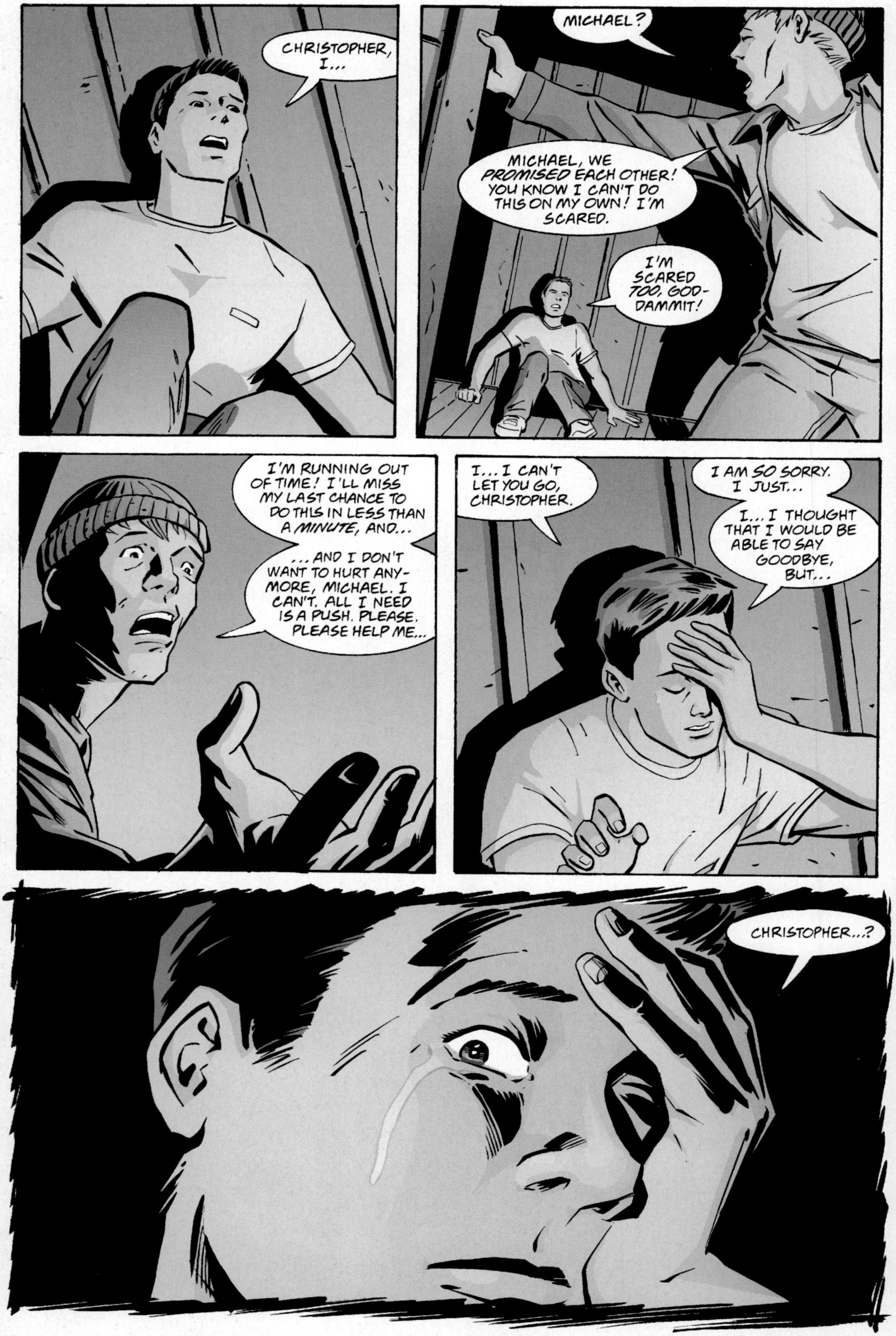
CHRISTOPHER, I...
MICHAEL?
MICHAEL, WE *PROMISED* EACH OTHER! YOU KNOW I CAN'T DO THIS ON MY OWN! I'M SCARED.
I'M SCARED *TOO*, GOD-DAMMIT!
I'M RUNNING OUT OF TIME! I'LL MISS MY LAST CHANCE TO DO THIS IN LESS THAN A *MINUTE*, AND...
...AND I DON'T WANT TO HURT ANY-MORE, MICHAEL. I CAN'T. ALL I NEED IS A PUSH. PLEASE. PLEASE HELP ME...
I... I CAN'T LET YOU GO, CHRISTOPHER.
I AM *SO* SORRY. I JUST...
I... I THOUGHT THAT I WOULD BE ABLE TO SAY GOODBYE, BUT...
CHRISTOPHER...?

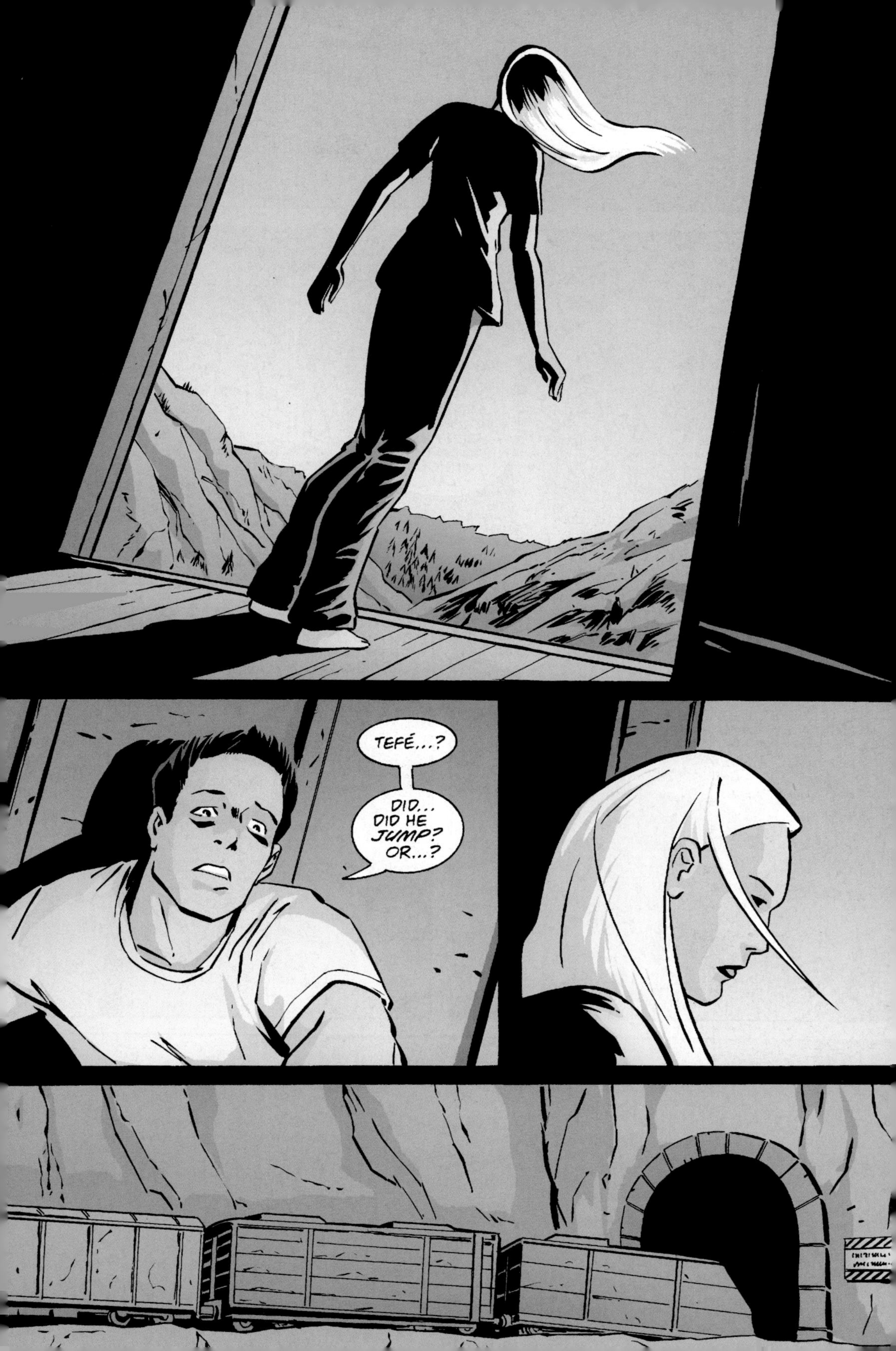
TEFÉ...?
DID... DID HE JUMP? OR...?

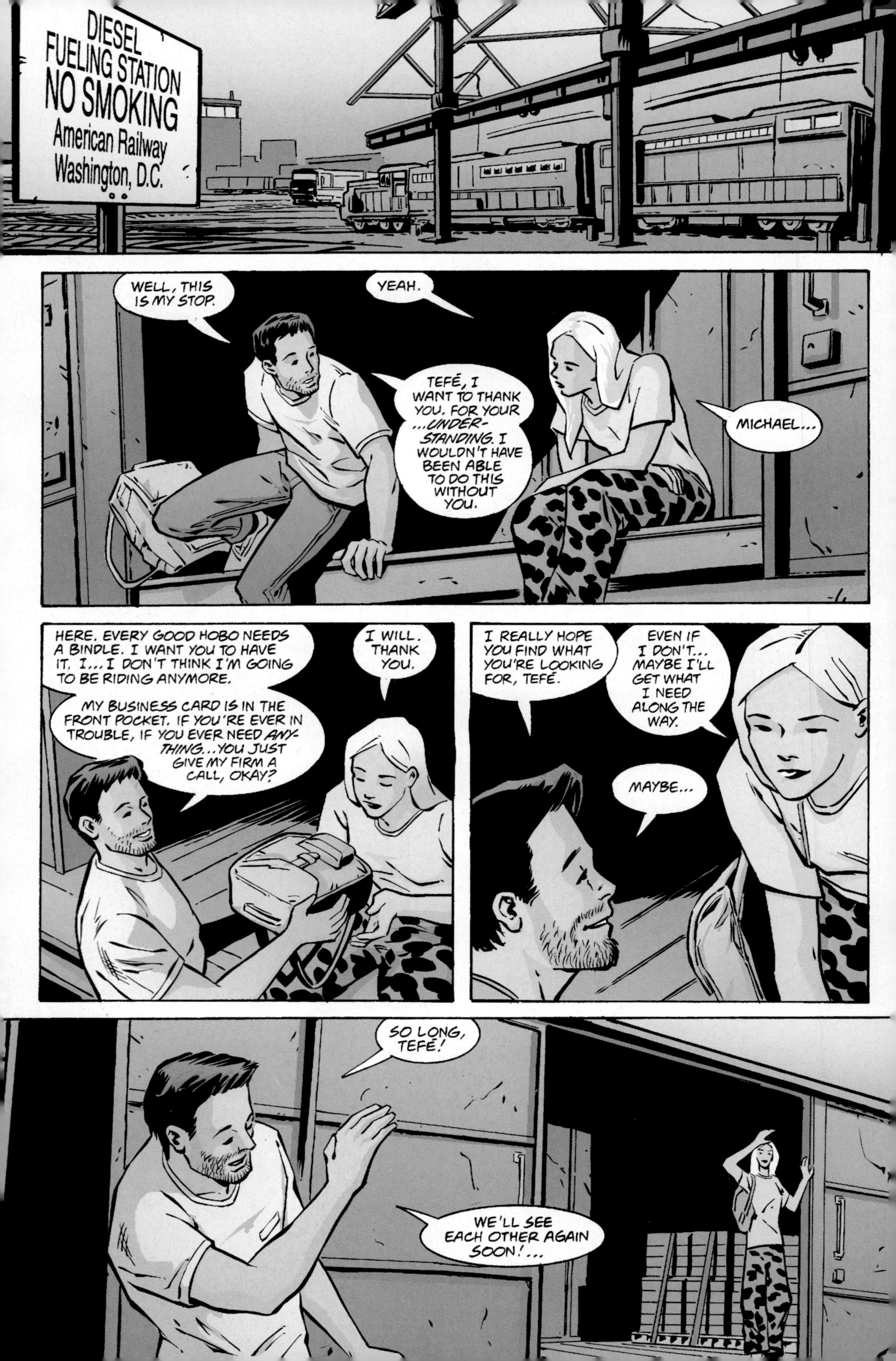
DIESEL
FUELING STATION
NO SMOKING
American Railway
Washington, D.C.
WELL, THIS IS MY STOP.
YEAH.
TEFÉ, I WANT TO THANK YOU. FOR YOUR ...UNDER-STANDING. I WOULDN'T HAVE BEEN ABLE TO DO THIS WITHOUT YOU.
MICHAEL...
HERE. EVERY GOOD HOBO NEEDS A BINDLE. I WANT YOU TO HAVE IT. I... I DON'T THINK I'M GOING TO BE RIDING ANYMORE.
MY BUSINESS CARD IS IN THE FRONT POCKET. IF YOU'RE EVER IN TROUBLE, IF YOU EVER NEED ANY-THING...YOU JUST GIVE MY FIRM A CALL, OKAY?
I WILL. THANK YOU.
I REALLY HOPE YOU FIND WHAT YOU'RE LOOKING FOR, TEFÉ.
EVEN IF I DON'T... MAYBE I'LL GET WHAT I NEED ALONG THE WAY.
MAYBE...
SO LONG, TEFÉ!
WE'LL SEE EACH OTHER AGAIN SOON!...

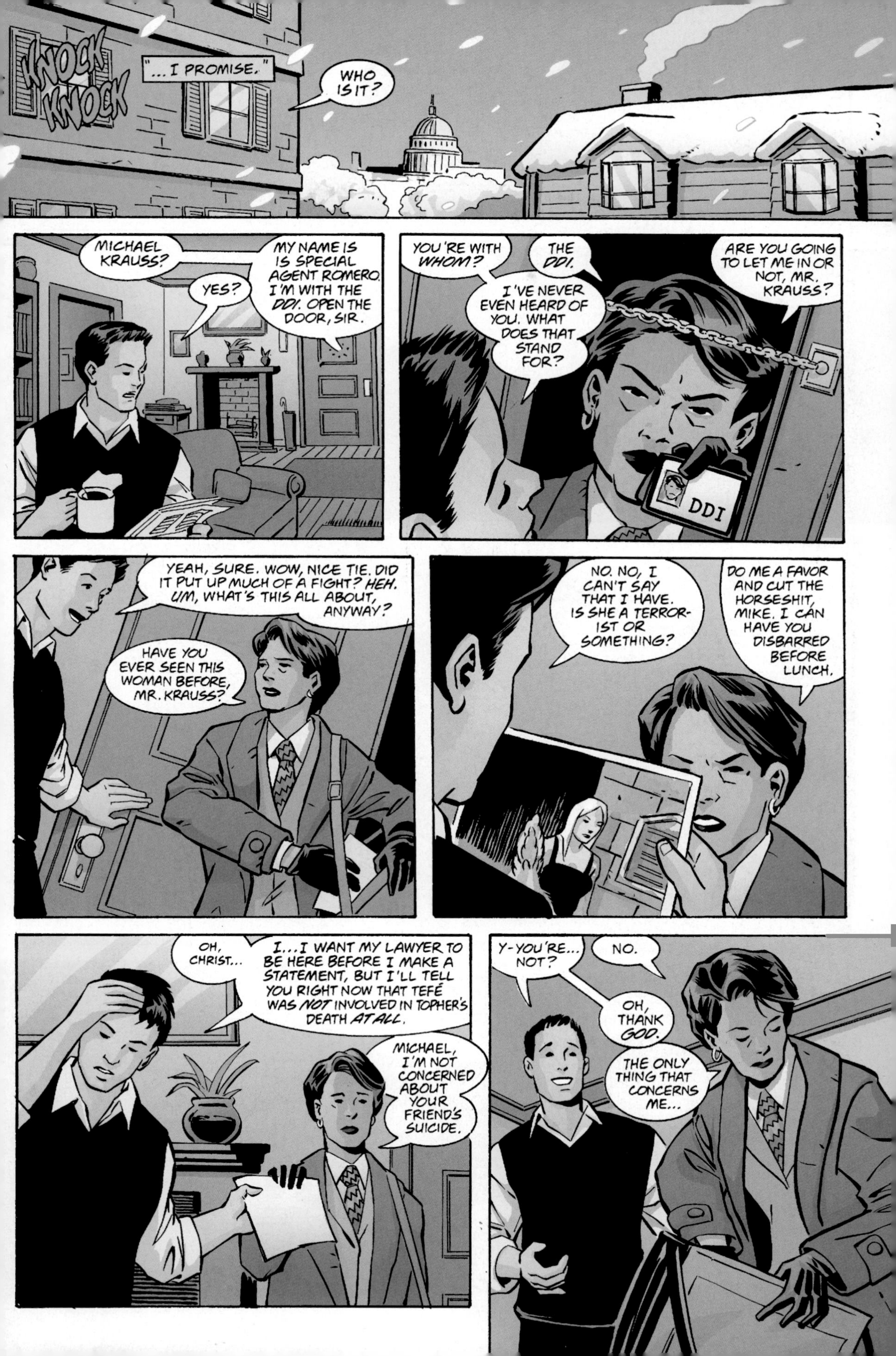
KNOCK KNOCK
"...I PROMISE."
WHO IS IT?
MICHAEL KRAUSS?
YES?
MY NAME IS IS SPECIAL AGENT ROMERO. I'M WITH THE DDI. OPEN THE DOOR, SIR.
YOU'RE WITH WHOM?
THE DDI.
I'VE NEVER EVEN HEARD OF YOU. WHAT DOES THAT STAND FOR?
ARE YOU GOING TO LET ME IN OR NOT, MR. KRAUSS?
DDI
YEAH, SURE. WOW, NICE TIE. DID IT PUT UP MUCH OF A FIGHT? HEH. UM, WHAT'S THIS ALL ABOUT, ANYWAY?
HAVE YOU EVER SEEN THIS WOMAN BEFORE, MR. KRAUSS?
NO. NO, I CAN'T SAY THAT I HAVE. IS SHE A TERRORIST OR SOMETHING?
DO ME A FAVOR AND CUT THE HORSESHIT, MIKE. I CAN HAVE YOU DISBARRED BEFORE LUNCH.
OH, CHRIST...
I... I WANT MY LAWYER TO BE HERE BEFORE I MAKE A STATEMENT, BUT I'LL TELL YOU RIGHT NOW THAT TEFÉ WAS NOT INVOLVED IN TOPHER'S DEATH AT ALL.
MICHAEL, I'M NOT CONCERNED ABOUT YOUR FRIEND'S SUICIDE.
Y-YOU'RE... NOT?
NO.
OH, THANK GOD.
THE ONLY THING THAT CONCERNS ME...

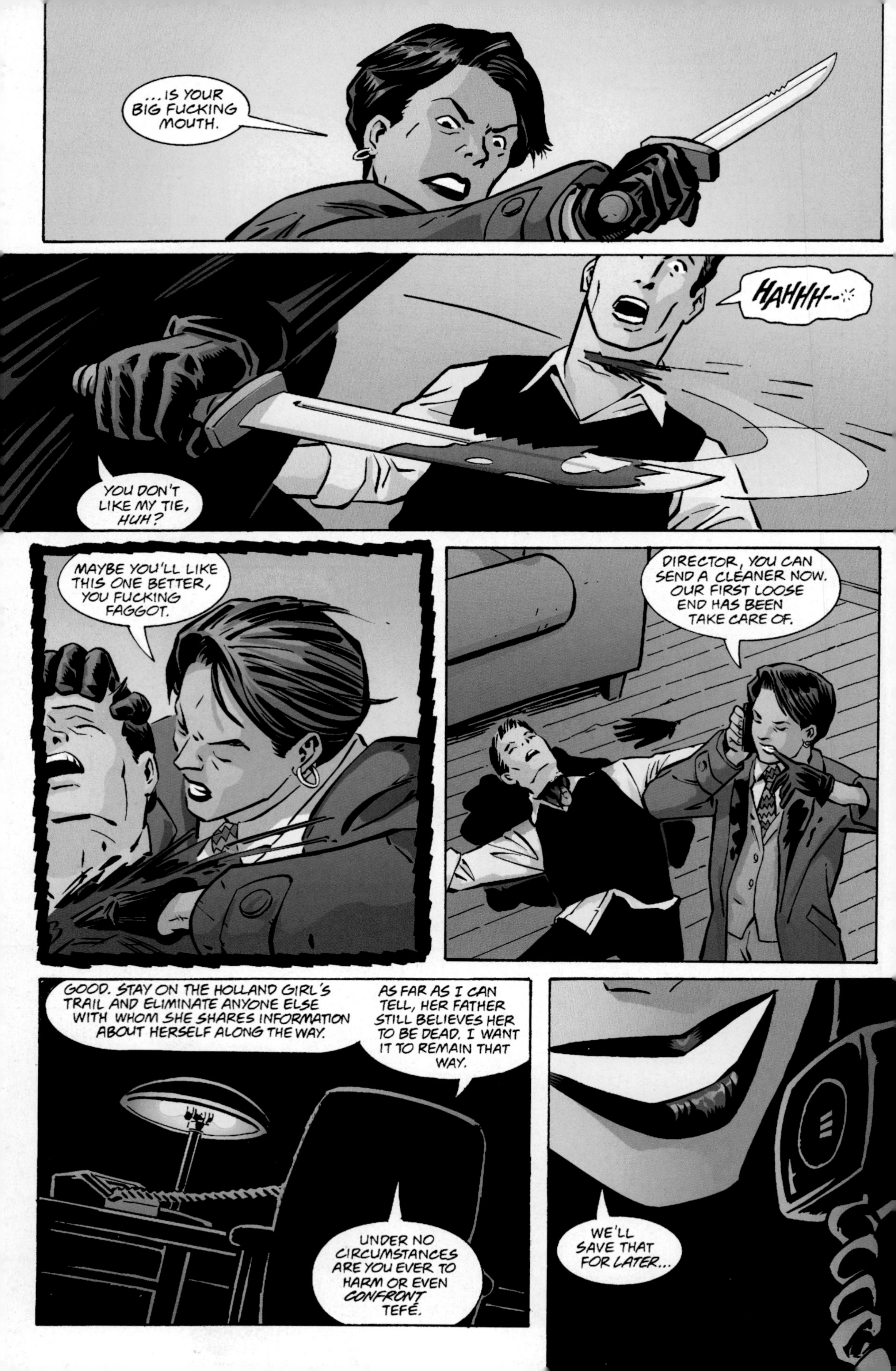
...IS YOUR BIG FUCKING MOUTH.
HAHHH--
YOU DON'T LIKE MY TIE, HUH?
MAYBE YOU'LL LIKE THIS ONE BETTER, YOU FUCKING FAGGOT.
DIRECTOR, YOU CAN SEND A CLEANER NOW. OUR FIRST LOOSE END HAS BEEN TAKE CARE OF.
GOOD. STAY ON THE HOLLAND GIRL'S TRAIL AND ELIMINATE ANYONE ELSE WITH WHOM SHE SHARES INFORMATION ABOUT HERSELF ALONG THE WAY.
AS FAR AS I CAN TELL, HER FATHER STILL BELIEVES HER TO BE DEAD. I WANT IT TO REMAIN THAT WAY.
UNDER NO CIRCUMSTANCES ARE YOU EVER TO HARM OR EVEN CONFRONT TEFÉ.
WE'LL SAVE THAT FOR LATER...

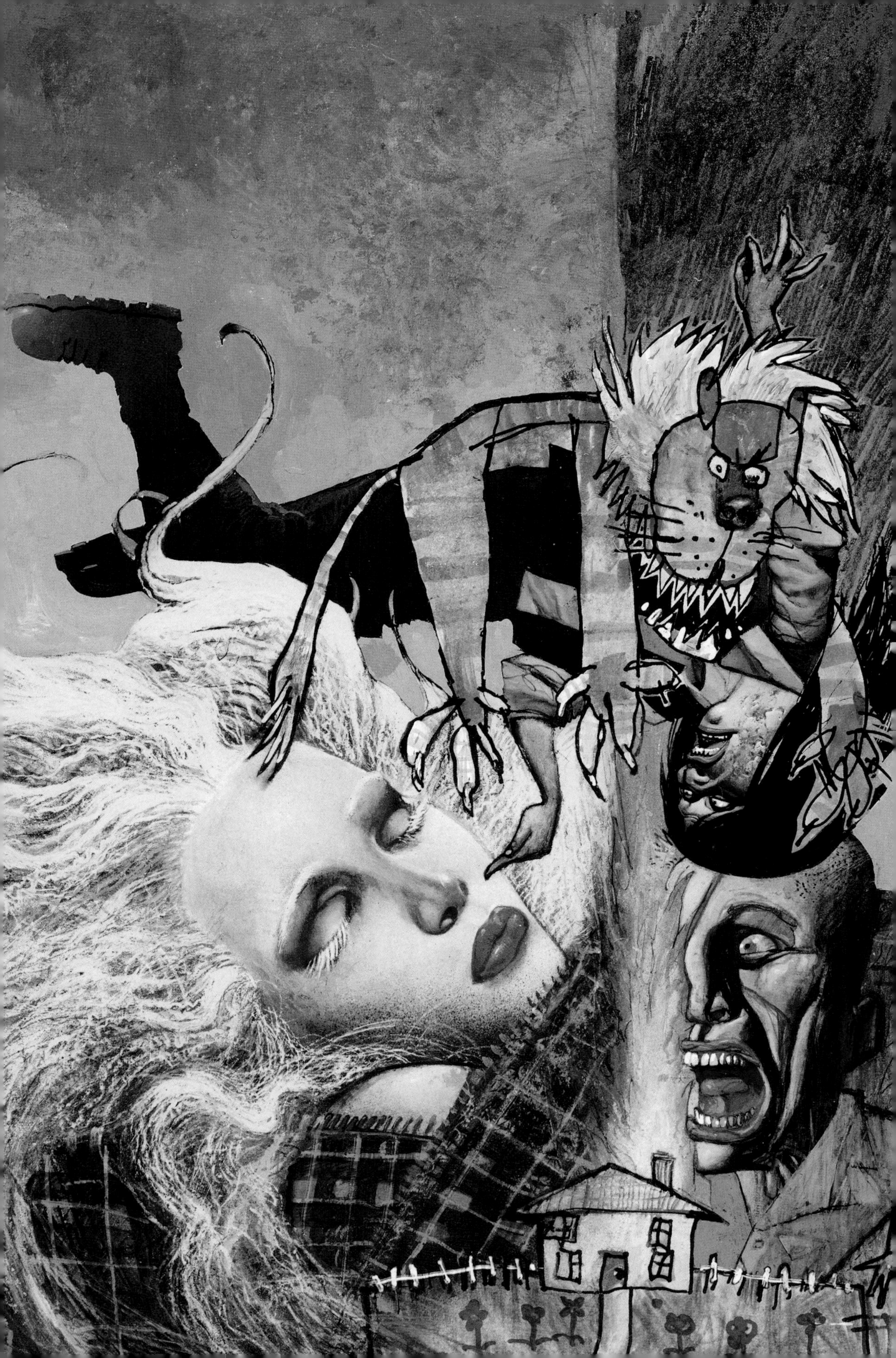

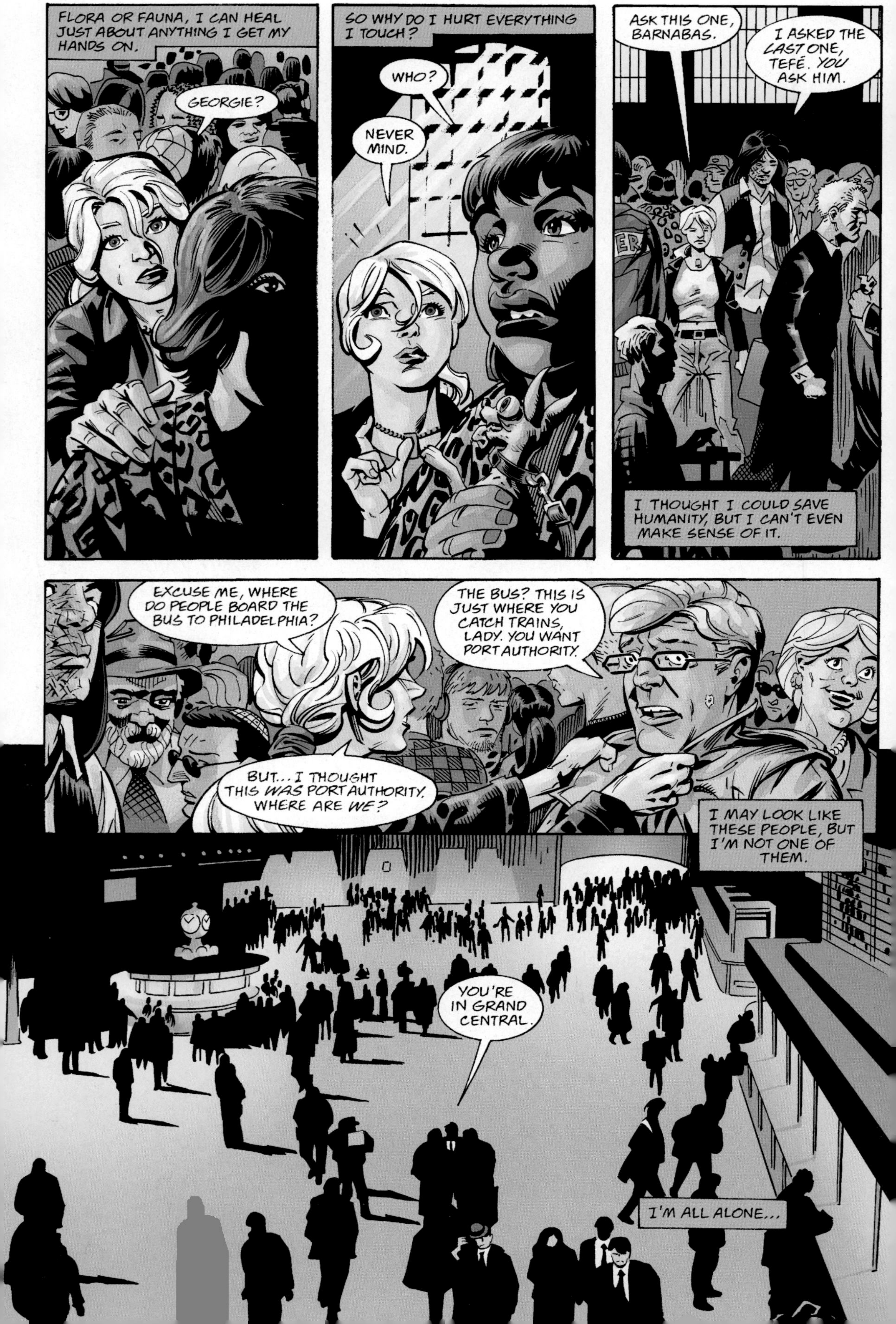
FLORA OR FAUNA, I CAN HEAL JUST ABOUT ANYTHING I GET MY HANDS ON.
GEORGIE?
SO WHY DO I HURT EVERYTHING I TOUCH?
WHO?
NEVER MIND.
ASK THIS ONE, BARNABAS.
I ASKED THE LAST ONE, TEFÉ. YOU ASK HIM.
I THOUGHT I COULD SAVE HUMANITY, BUT I CAN'T EVEN MAKE SENSE OF IT.
EXCUSE ME, WHERE DO PEOPLE BOARD THE BUS TO PHILADELPHIA?
THE BUS? THIS IS JUST WHERE YOU CATCH TRAINS, LADY. YOU WANT PORT AUTHORITY.
BUT... I THOUGHT THIS WAS PORT AUTHORITY. WHERE ARE WE?
I MAY LOOK LIKE THESE PEOPLE, BUT I'M NOT ONE OF THEM.
YOU'RE IN GRAND CENTRAL.
I'M ALL ALONE...

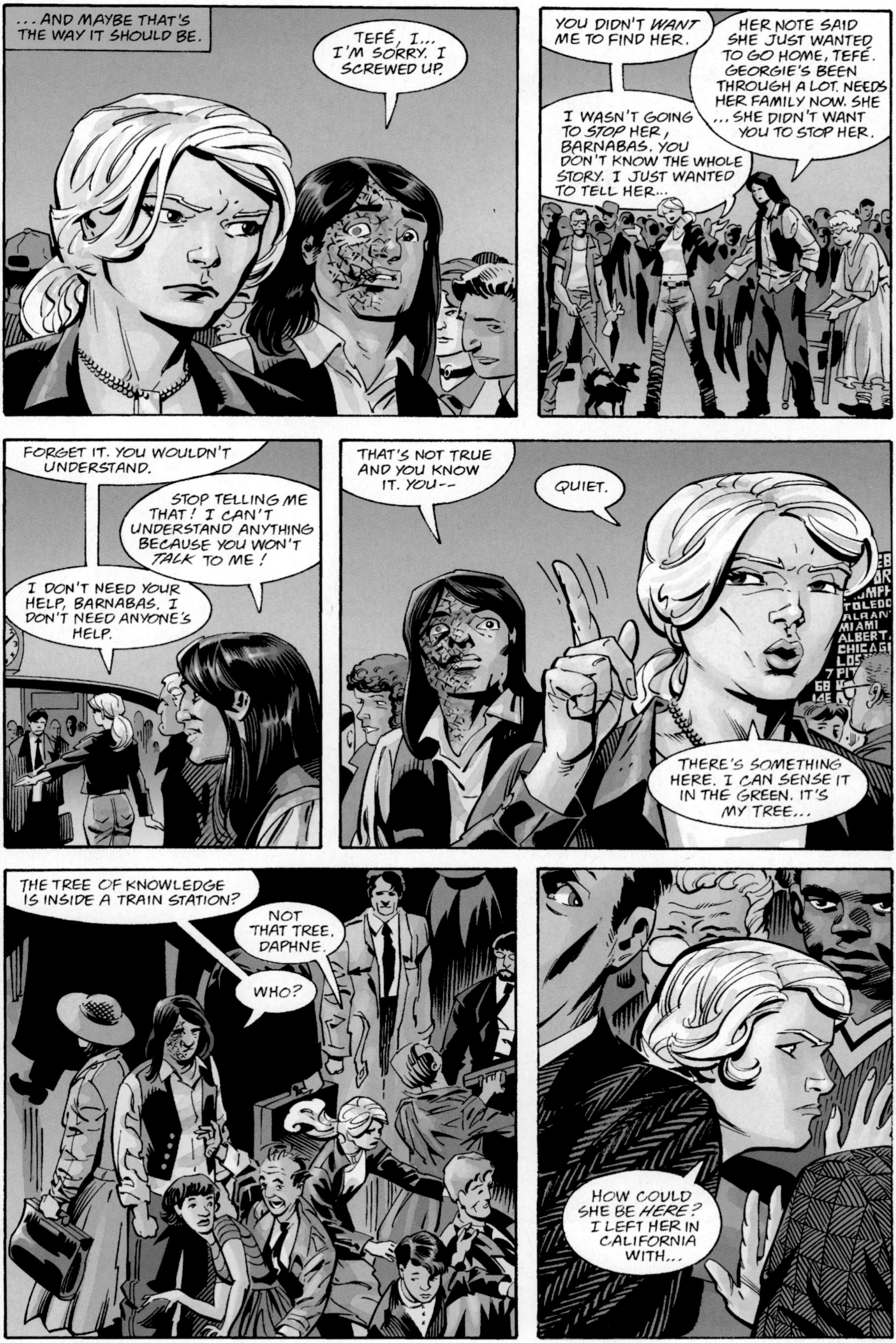
. . . AND MAYBE THAT'S THE WAY IT SHOULD BE.
TEFÉ, I... I'M SORRY. I SCREWED UP.
YOU DIDN'T WANT ME TO FIND HER.
I WASN'T GOING TO STOP HER, BARNABAS. YOU DON'T KNOW THE WHOLE STORY. I JUST WANTED TO TELL HER...
HER NOTE SAID SHE JUST WANTED TO GO HOME, TEFÉ. GEORGIE'S BEEN THROUGH A LOT. NEEDS HER FAMILY NOW. SHE ... SHE DIDN'T WANT YOU TO STOP HER.
FORGET IT. YOU WOULDN'T UNDERSTAND.
STOP TELLING ME THAT! I CAN'T UNDERSTAND ANYTHING BECAUSE YOU WON'T TALK TO ME!
I DON'T NEED YOUR HELP, BARNABAS. I DON'T NEED ANYONE'S HELP.
THAT'S NOT TRUE AND YOU KNOW IT. YOU--
QUIET.
THERE'S SOMETHING HERE. I CAN SENSE IT IN THE GREEN. IT'S MY TREE...
THE TREE OF KNOWLEDGE IS INSIDE A TRAIN STATION?
NOT THAT TREE, DAPHNE.
WHO?
HOW COULD SHE BE HERE? I LEFT HER IN CALIFORNIA WITH...

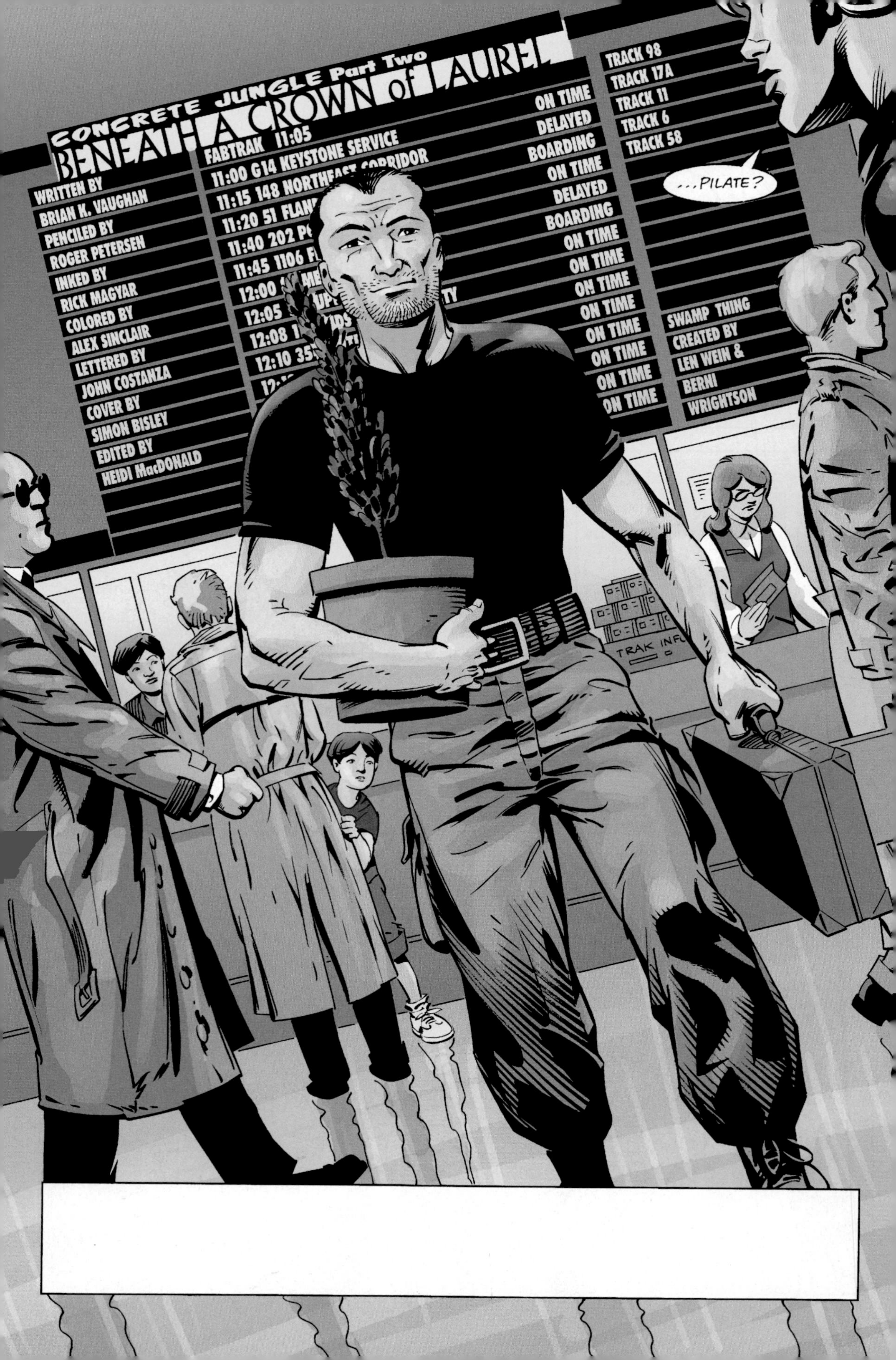
CONCRETE JUNGLE Part Two
BENEATH A CROWN of LAUREL
WRITTEN BY
BRIAN K. VAUGHAN
PENCILED BY
ROGER PETERSEN
INKED BY
RICK MAGYAR
COLORED BY
ALEX SINCLAIR
LETTERED BY
JOHN COSTANZA
COVER BY
SIMON BISLEY
EDITED BY
HEIDI MacDONALD
FABTRAK 11:05
11:00 G14 KEYSTONE SERVICE
ON TIME
DELAYED
BOARDING
ON TIME
DELAYED
BOARDING
ON TIME
ON TIME
ON TIME
ON TIME
ON TIME
ON TIME
ON TIME
ON TIME
TRACK 98
TRACK 17A
TRACK 11
TRACK 6
TRACK 58
...PILATE?
SWAMP THING
CREATED BY
LEN WEIN &
BERNI
WRIGHTSON
TRAK INFO

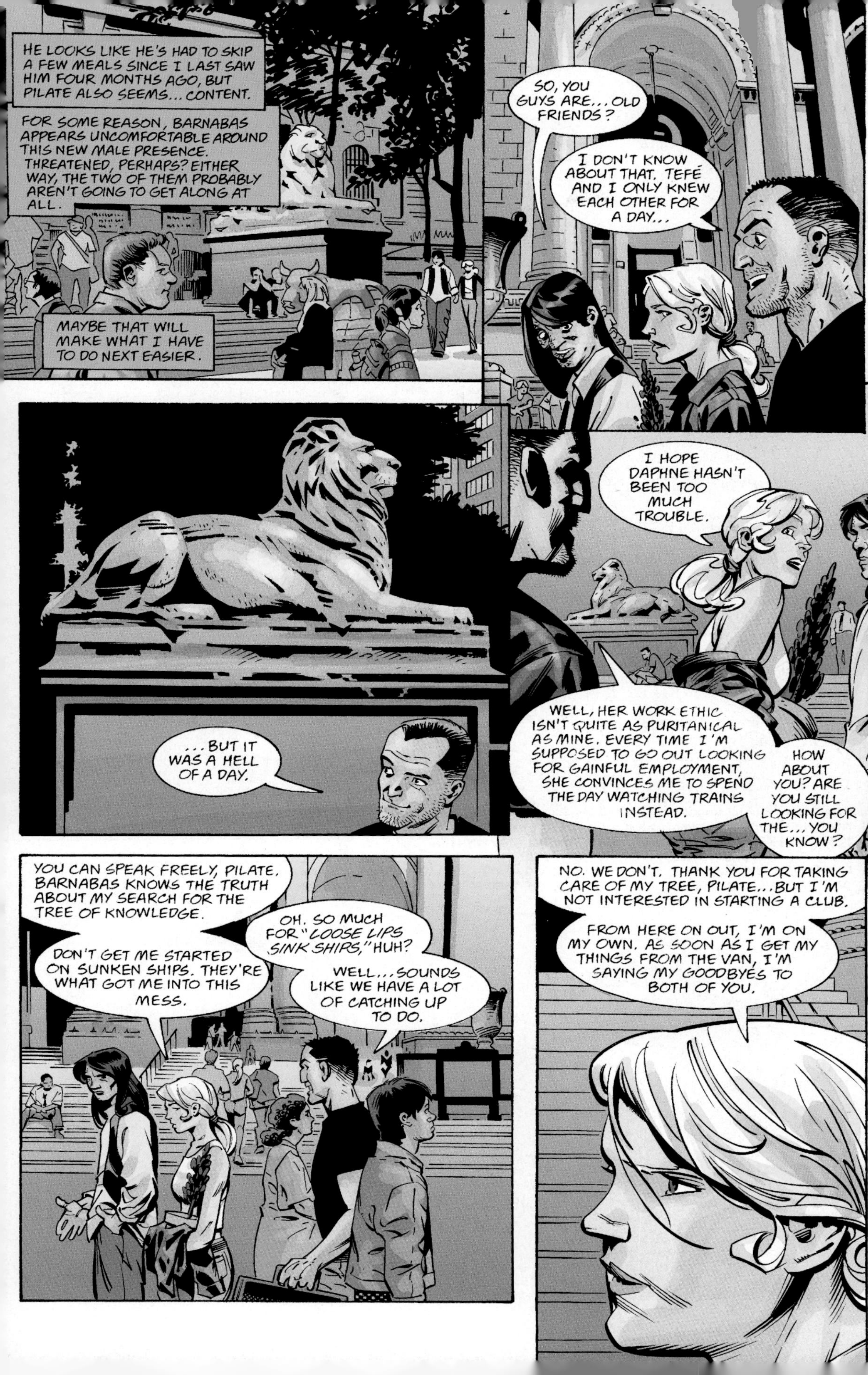
HE LOOKS LIKE HE'S HAD TO SKIP A FEW MEALS SINCE I LAST SAW HIM FOUR MONTHS AGO, BUT PILATE ALSO SEEMS... CONTENT.
FOR SOME REASON, BARNABAS APPEARS UNCOMFORTABLE AROUND THIS NEW MALE PRESENCE. THREATENED, PERHAPS? EITHER WAY, THE TWO OF THEM PROBABLY AREN'T GOING TO GET ALONG AT ALL.
MAYBE THAT WILL MAKE WHAT I HAVE TO DO NEXT EASIER.
SO, YOU GUYS ARE... OLD FRIENDS?
I DON'T KNOW ABOUT THAT. TEFÉ AND I ONLY KNEW EACH OTHER FOR A DAY...
...BUT IT WAS A HELL OF A DAY.
I HOPE DAPHNE HASN'T BEEN TOO MUCH TROUBLE.
WELL, HER WORK ETHIC ISN'T QUITE AS PURITANICAL AS MINE. EVERY TIME I'M SUPPOSED TO GO OUT LOOKING FOR GAINFUL EMPLOYMENT, SHE CONVINCES ME TO SPEND THE DAY WATCHING TRAINS INSTEAD.
HOW ABOUT YOU? ARE YOU STILL LOOKING FOR THE... YOU KNOW?
YOU CAN SPEAK FREELY, PILATE. BARNABAS KNOWS THE TRUTH ABOUT MY SEARCH FOR THE TREE OF KNOWLEDGE.
DON'T GET ME STARTED ON SUNKEN SHIPS. THEY'RE WHAT GOT ME INTO THIS MESS.
OH. SO MUCH FOR "LOOSE LIPS SINK SHIPS," HUH?
WELL... SOUNDS LIKE WE HAVE A LOT OF CATCHING UP TO DO.
NO. WE DON'T. THANK YOU FOR TAKING CARE OF MY TREE, PILATE... BUT I'M NOT INTERESTED IN STARTING A CLUB.
FROM HERE ON OUT, I'M ON MY OWN. AS SOON AS I GET MY THINGS FROM THE VAN, I'M SAYING MY GOODBYES TO BOTH OF YOU.

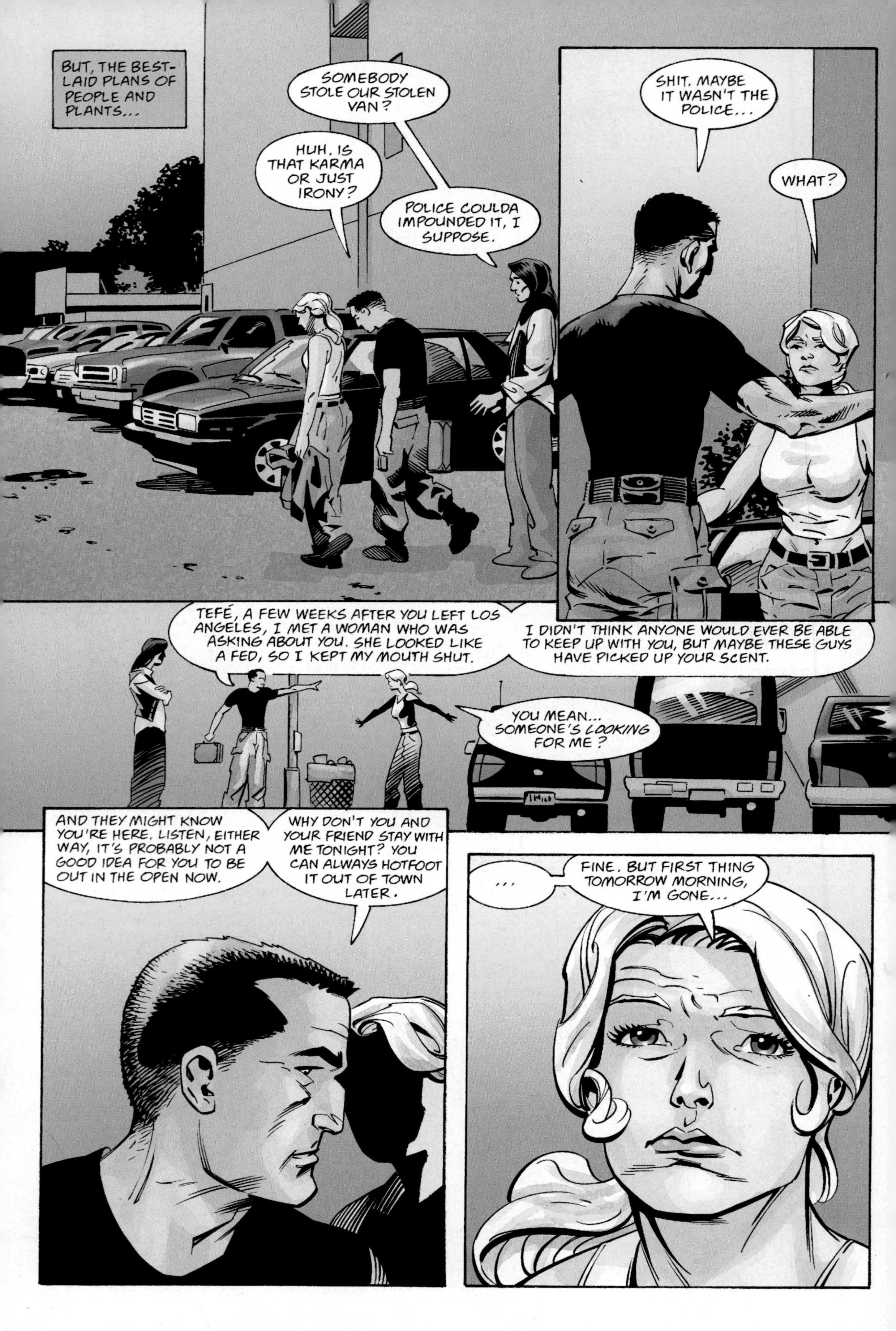

BUT, THE BEST-LAID PLANS OF PEOPLE AND PLANTS...
SOMEBODY STOLE OUR STOLEN VAN?
HUH. IS THAT KARMA OR JUST IRONY?
POLICE COULDA IMPOUNDED IT, I SUPPOSE.
SHIT. MAYBE IT WASN'T THE POLICE...
WHAT?
TEFÉ, A FEW WEEKS AFTER YOU LEFT LOS ANGELES, I MET A WOMAN WHO WAS ASKING ABOUT YOU. SHE LOOKED LIKE A FED, SO I KEPT MY MOUTH SHUT.
I DIDN'T THINK ANYONE WOULD EVER BE ABLE TO KEEP UP WITH YOU, BUT MAYBE THESE GUYS HAVE PICKED UP YOUR SCENT.
YOU MEAN... SOMEONE'S LOOKING FOR ME?
AND THEY MIGHT KNOW YOU'RE HERE. LISTEN, EITHER WAY, IT'S PROBABLY NOT A GOOD IDEA FOR YOU TO BE OUT IN THE OPEN NOW.
WHY DON'T YOU AND YOUR FRIEND STAY WITH ME TONIGHT? YOU CAN ALWAYS HOTFOOT IT OUT OF TOWN LATER.
...
FINE. BUT FIRST THING TOMORROW MORNING, I'M GONE...

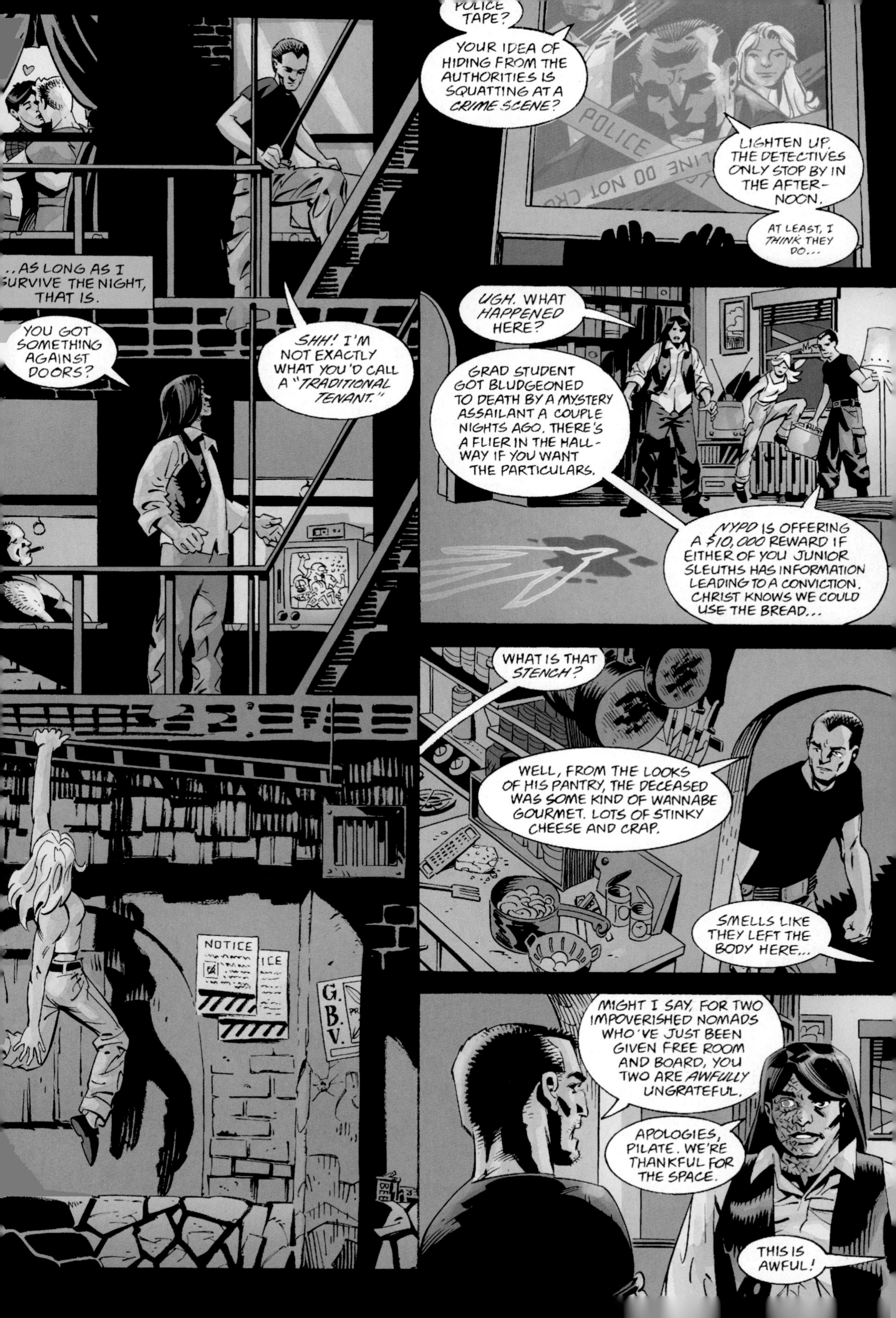

..AS LONG AS I SURVIVE THE NIGHT, THAT IS.
YOU GOT SOMETHING AGAINST DOORS?
SHH! I'M NOT EXACTLY WHAT YOU'D CALL A "TRADITIONAL TENANT."
NOTICE
POLICE TAPE?
YOUR IDEA OF HIDING FROM THE AUTHORITIES IS SQUATTING AT A CRIME SCENE?
POLICE
LIGHTEN UP. THE DETECTIVES ONLY STOP BY IN THE AFTER-NOON.
AT LEAST, I THINK THEY DO...
UGH. WHAT HAPPENED HERE?
GRAD STUDENT GOT BLUDGEONED TO DEATH BY A MYSTERY ASSAILANT A COUPLE NIGHTS AGO. THERE'S A FLIER IN THE HALL-WAY IF YOU WANT THE PARTICULARS.
NYPD IS OFFERING A $10,000 REWARD IF EITHER OF YOU JUNIOR SLEUTHS HAS INFORMATION LEADING TO A CONVICTION. CHRIST KNOWS WE COULD USE THE BREAD...
WHAT IS THAT STENCH?
WELL, FROM THE LOOKS OF HIS PANTRY, THE DECEASED WAS SOME KIND OF WANNABE GOURMET. LOTS OF STINKY CHEESE AND CRAP.
SMELLS LIKE THEY LEFT THE BODY HERE...
MIGHT I SAY, FOR TWO IMPOVERISHED NOMADS WHO'VE JUST BEEN GIVEN FREE ROOM AND BOARD, YOU TWO ARE AWFULLY UNGRATEFUL.
APOLOGIES, PILATE. WE'RE THANKFUL FOR THE SPACE.
THIS IS AWFUL!

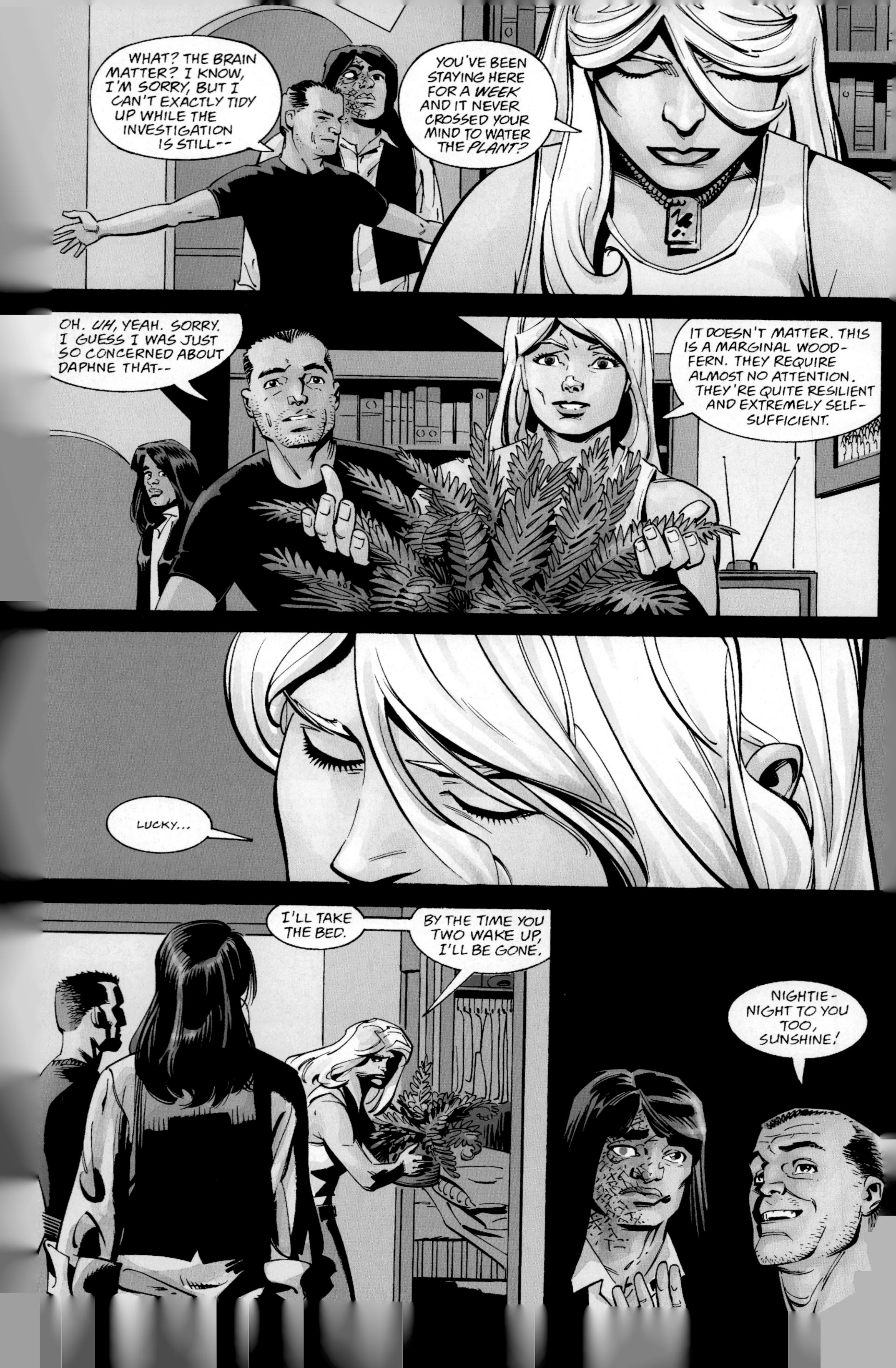
WHAT? THE BRAIN MATTER? I KNOW, I'M SORRY, BUT I CAN'T EXACTLY TIDY UP WHILE THE INVESTIGATION IS STILL--
YOU'VE BEEN STAYING HERE FOR A WEEK AND IT NEVER CROSSED YOUR MIND TO WATER THE PLANT?
OH. UH, YEAH. SORRY. I GUESS I WAS JUST SO CONCERNED ABOUT DAPHNE THAT--
IT DOESN'T MATTER. THIS IS A MARGINAL WOOD-FERN. THEY REQUIRE ALMOST NO ATTENTION. THEY'RE QUITE RESILIENT AND EXTREMELY SELF-SUFFICIENT.
LUCKY...
I'LL TAKE THE BED.
BY THE TIME YOU TWO WAKE UP, I'LL BE GONE.
NIGHTIE-NIGHT TO YOU TOO, SUNSHINE!

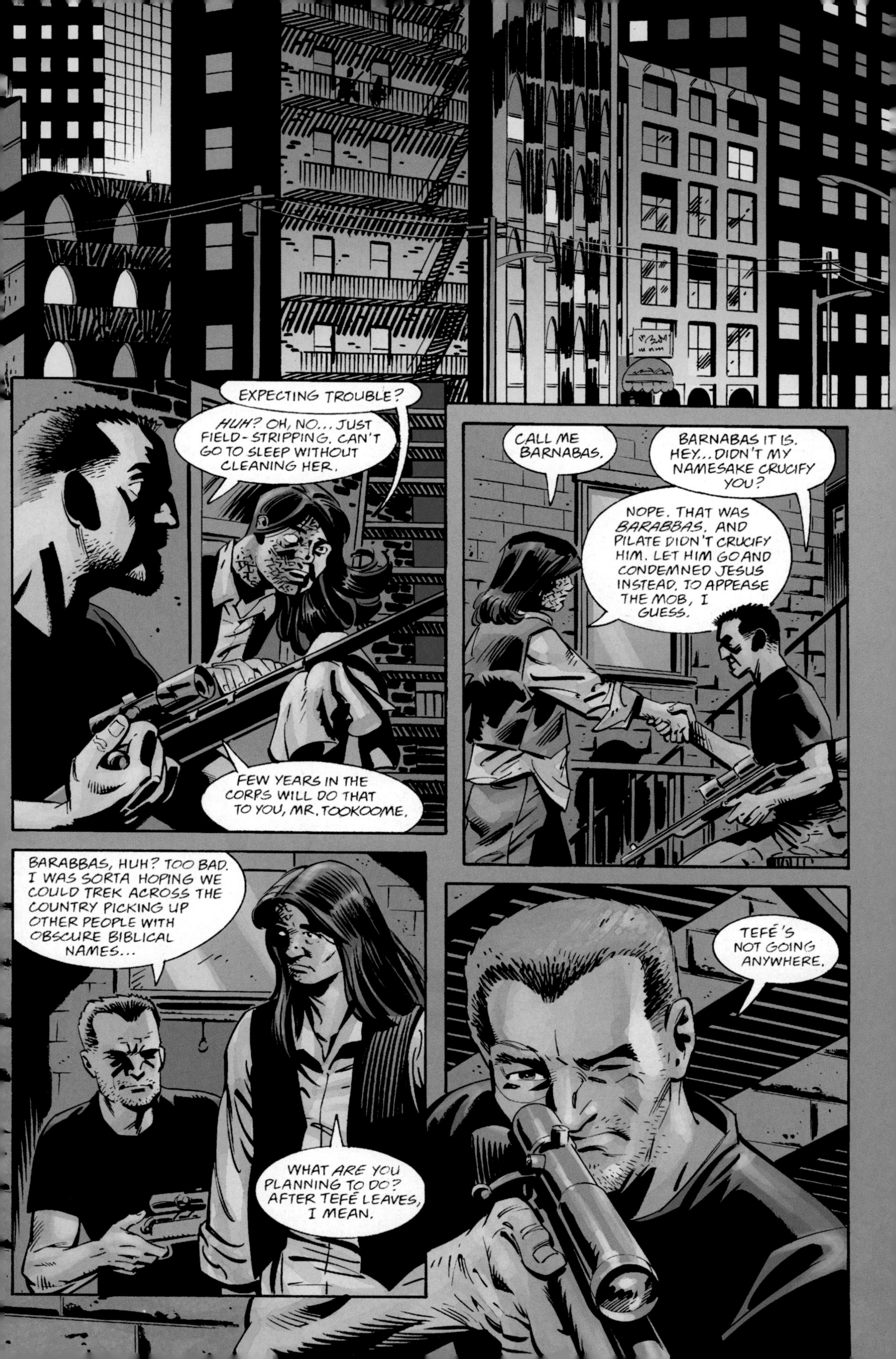
EXPECTING TROUBLE?
HUH? OH, NO... JUST FIELD-STRIPPING. CAN'T GO TO SLEEP WITHOUT CLEANING HER.
FEW YEARS IN THE CORPS WILL DO THAT TO YOU, MR. TOOKOOME.
CALL ME BARNABAS.
BARNABAS IT IS. HEY... DIDN'T MY NAMESAKE CRUCIFY YOU?
NOPE. THAT WAS BARABBAS, AND PILATE DIDN'T CRUCIFY HIM. LET HIM GO AND CONDEMNED JESUS INSTEAD, TO APPEASE THE MOB, I GUESS.
BARABBAS, HUH? TOO BAD. I WAS SORTA HOPING WE COULD TREK ACROSS THE COUNTRY PICKING UP OTHER PEOPLE WITH OBSCURE BIBLICAL NAMES...
WHAT ARE YOU PLANNING TO DO? AFTER TEFÉ LEAVES, I MEAN.
TEFÉ'S NOT GOING ANYWHERE.

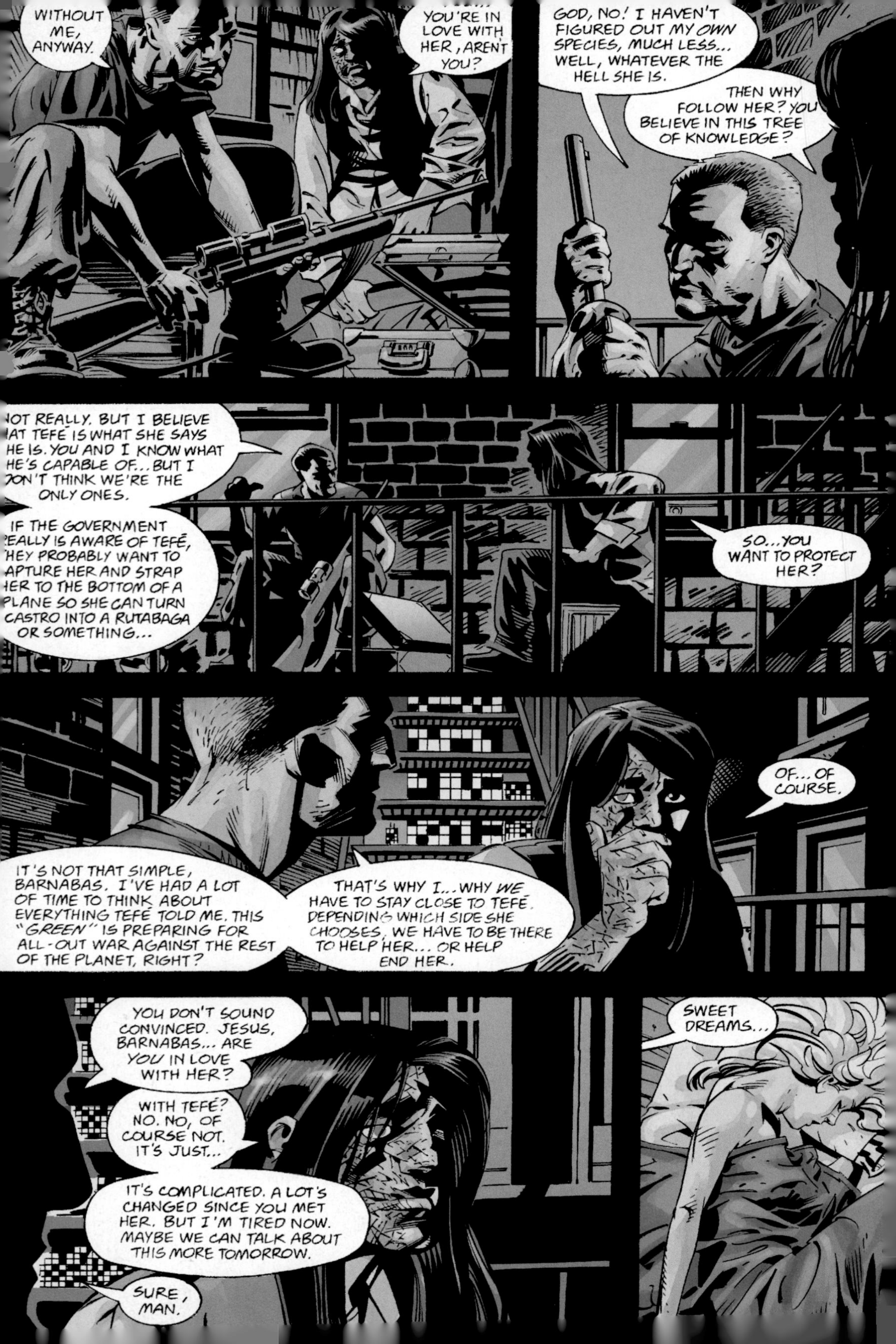
WITHOUT ME, ANYWAY.
YOU'RE IN LOVE WITH HER, AREN'T YOU?
GOD, NO! I HAVEN'T FIGURED OUT MY OWN SPECIES, MUCH LESS... WELL, WHATEVER THE HELL SHE IS.
THEN WHY FOLLOW HER? YOU BELIEVE IN THIS TREE OF KNOWLEDGE?
NOT REALLY. BUT I BELIEVE THAT TEFÉ IS WHAT SHE SAYS SHE IS. YOU AND I KNOW WHAT SHE'S CAPABLE OF... BUT I DON'T THINK WE'RE THE ONLY ONES.
IF THE GOVERNMENT REALLY IS AWARE OF TEFÉ, THEY PROBABLY WANT TO CAPTURE HER AND STRAP HER TO THE BOTTOM OF A PLANE SO SHE CAN TURN CASTRO INTO A RUTABAGA OR SOMETHING...
SO...YOU WANT TO PROTECT HER?
OF... OF COURSE.
IT'S NOT THAT SIMPLE, BARNABAS. I'VE HAD A LOT OF TIME TO THINK ABOUT EVERYTHING TEFÉ TOLD ME. THIS "GREEN" IS PREPARING FOR ALL-OUT WAR AGAINST THE REST OF THE PLANET, RIGHT?
THAT'S WHY I... WHY WE HAVE TO STAY CLOSE TO TEFÉ. DEPENDING WHICH SIDE SHE CHOOSES, WE HAVE TO BE THERE TO HELP HER... OR HELP END HER.
YOU DON'T SOUND CONVINCED. JESUS, BARNABAS... ARE YOU IN LOVE WITH HER?
WITH TEFÉ? NO. NO, OF COURSE NOT. IT'S JUST...
IT'S COMPLICATED. A LOT'S CHANGED SINCE YOU MET HER. BUT I'M TIRED NOW. MAYBE WE CAN TALK ABOUT THIS MORE TOMORROW.
SURE, MAN.
SWEET DREAMS...

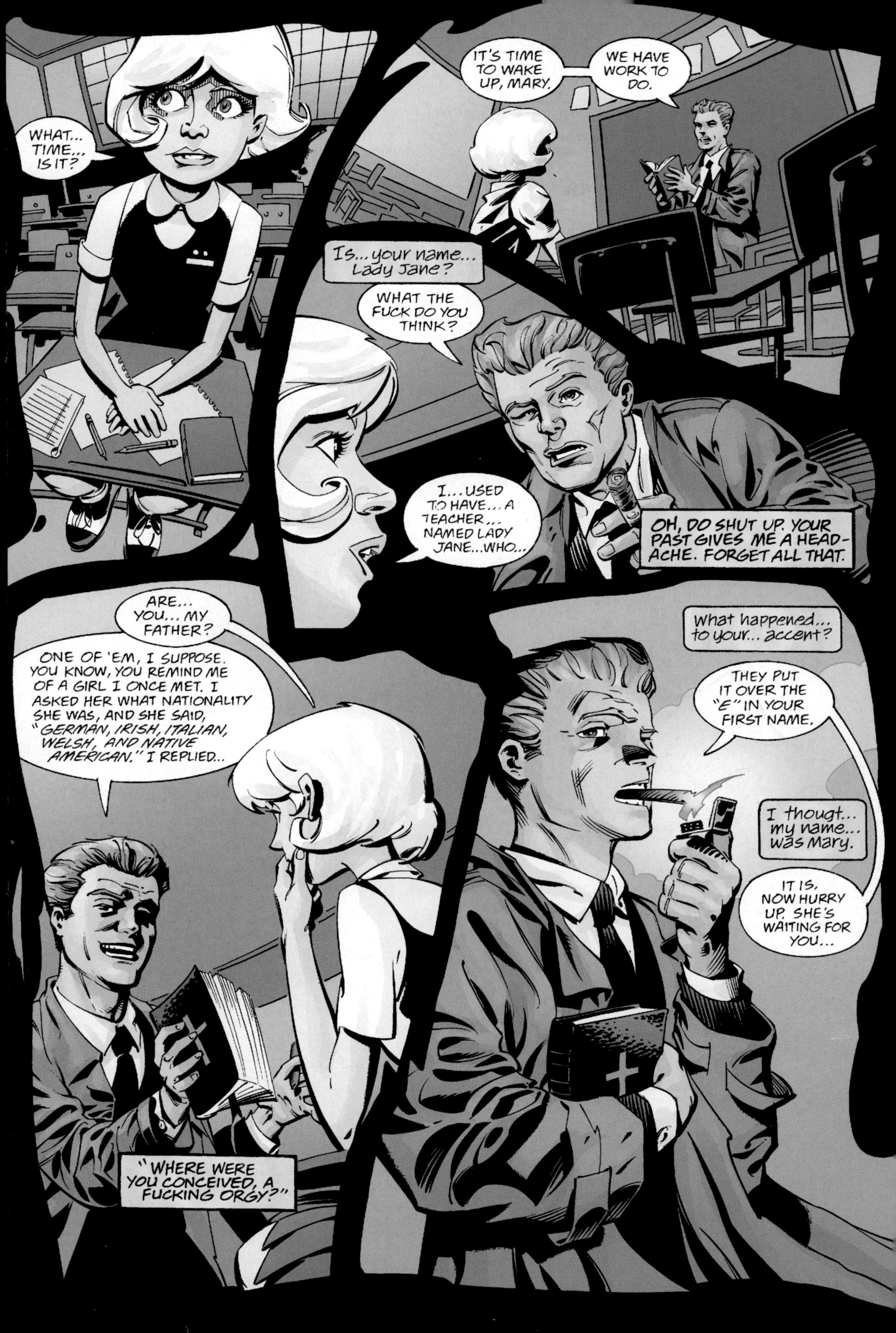
WHAT... TIME... IS IT?
IT'S TIME TO WAKE UP, MARY.
WE HAVE WORK TO DO.
Is... your name... Lady Jane?
WHAT THE FUCK DO YOU THINK?
I... USED TO HAVE... A TEACHER... NAMED LADY JANE... WHO...
OH, DO SHUT UP. YOUR PAST GIVES ME A HEAD-ACHE. FORGET ALL THAT.
ARE... YOU... MY FATHER?
ONE OF 'EM, I SUPPOSE. YOU KNOW, YOU REMIND ME OF A GIRL I ONCE MET. I ASKED HER WHAT NATIONALITY SHE WAS, AND SHE SAID, "GERMAN, IRISH, ITALIAN, WELSH, AND NATIVE AMERICAN." I REPLIED...
"WHERE WERE YOU CONCEIVED, A FUCKING ORGY?"
What happened... to your... accent?
THEY PUT IT OVER THE "E" IN YOUR FIRST NAME.
I thougt... my name... was Mary.
IT IS. NOW HURRY UP. SHE'S WAITING FOR YOU...

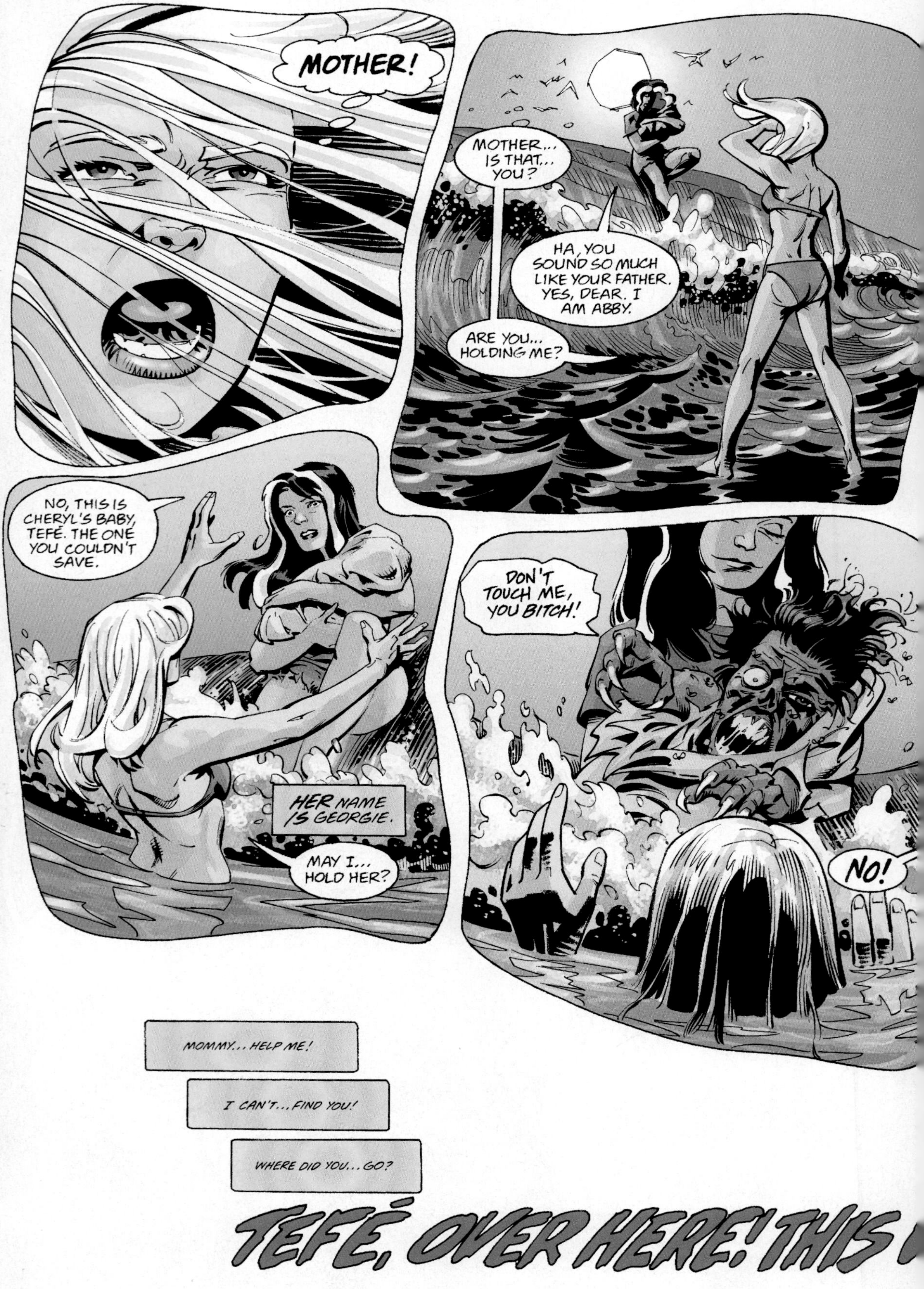
MOTHER!
MOTHER... IS THAT... YOU?
HA, YOU SOUND SO MUCH LIKE YOUR FATHER. YES, DEAR. I AM ABBY.
ARE YOU... HOLDING ME?
NO, THIS IS CHERYL'S BABY, TEFÉ. THE ONE YOU COULDN'T SAVE.
HER NAME IS GEORGIE.
MAY I... HOLD HER?
DON'T TOUCH ME, YOU BITCH!
NO!
MOMMY... HELP ME!
I CAN'T... FIND YOU!
WHERE DID YOU... GO?
TEFÉ, OVER HERE! THIS

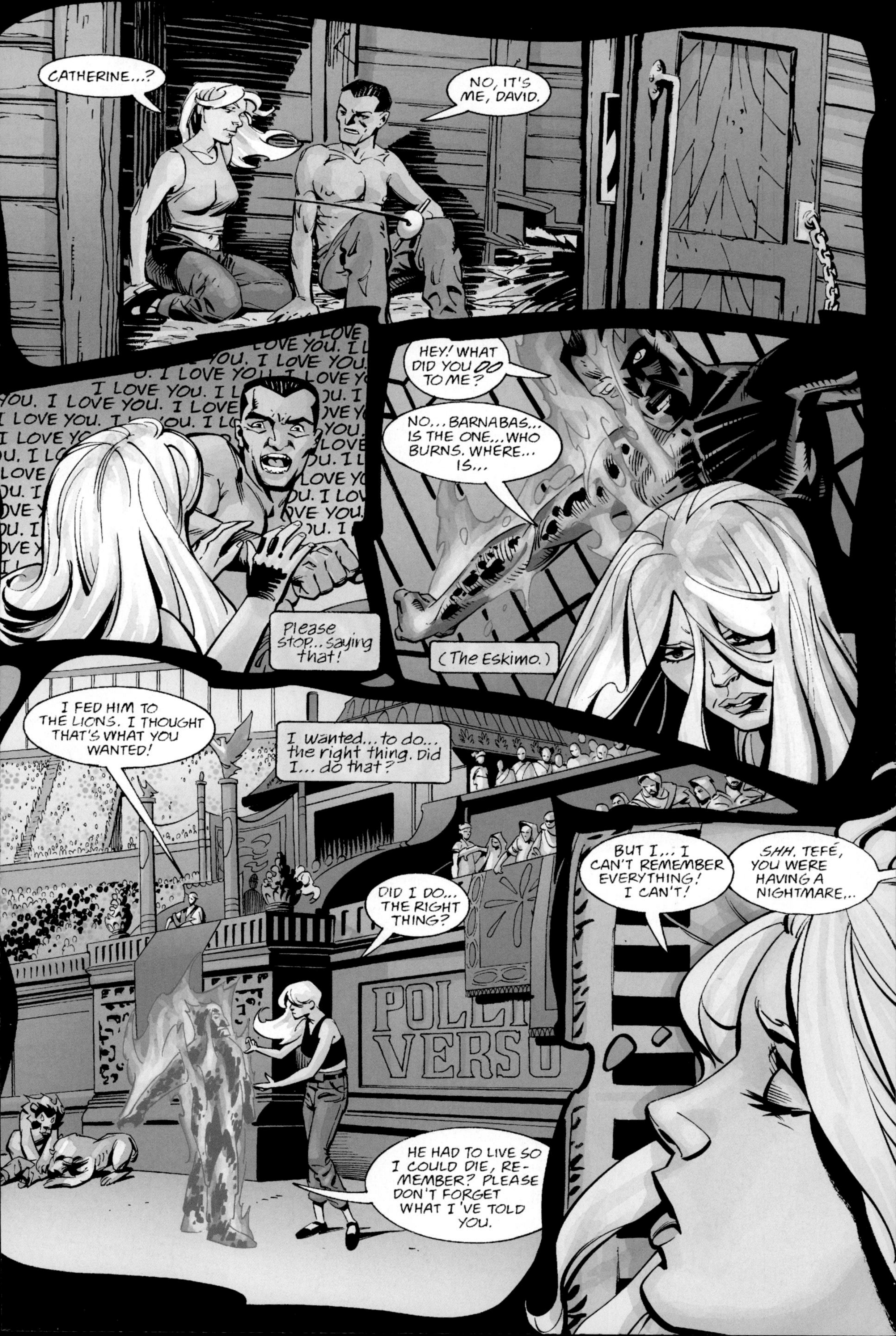
CATHERINE...?
NO, IT'S ME, DAVID.
I LOVE YOU. I LOVE YOU. I LOVE YOU. I LOVE YOU.
Please stop... saying that!
HEY! WHAT DID YOU DO TO ME?
NO... BARNABAS... IS THE ONE... WHO BURNS. WHERE... IS...
(The Eskimo.)
I FED HIM TO THE LIONS. I THOUGHT THAT'S WHAT YOU WANTED!
I wanted... to do... the right thing. Did I... do that?
DID I DO... THE RIGHT THING?
POLLI VERSO
HE HAD TO LIVE SO I COULD DIE, REMEMBER? PLEASE DON'T FORGET WHAT I'VE TOLD YOU.
BUT I... I CAN'T REMEMBER EVERYTHING! I CAN'T!
SHH. TEFÉ, YOU WERE HAVING A NIGHTMARE...

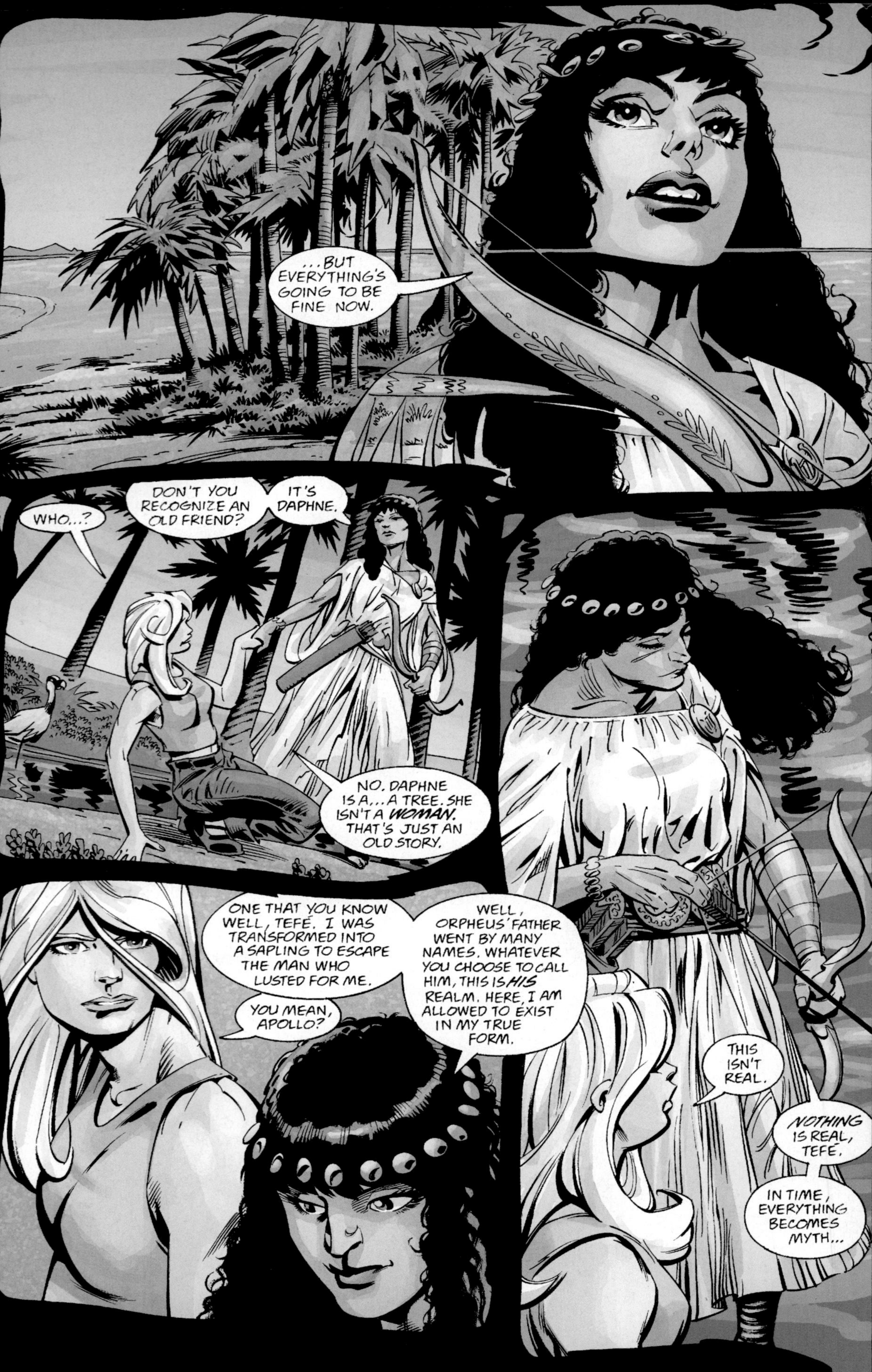
...BUT EVERYTHING'S GOING TO BE FINE NOW.
WHO...?
DON'T YOU RECOGNIZE AN OLD FRIEND?
IT'S DAPHNE.
NO. DAPHNE IS A... A TREE. SHE ISN'T A *WOMAN.* THAT'S JUST AN OLD STORY.
ONE THAT YOU KNOW WELL, TEFÉ. I WAS TRANSFORMED INTO A SAPLING TO ESCAPE THE MAN WHO LUSTED FOR ME.
YOU MEAN, APOLLO?
WELL, ORPHEUS' FATHER WENT BY MANY NAMES. WHATEVER YOU CHOOSE TO CALL HIM, THIS IS *HIS* REALM. HERE, I AM ALLOWED TO EXIST IN MY TRUE FORM.
THIS ISN'T REAL.
NOTHING IS REAL, TEFÉ.
IN TIME, EVERYTHING BECOMES MYTH...

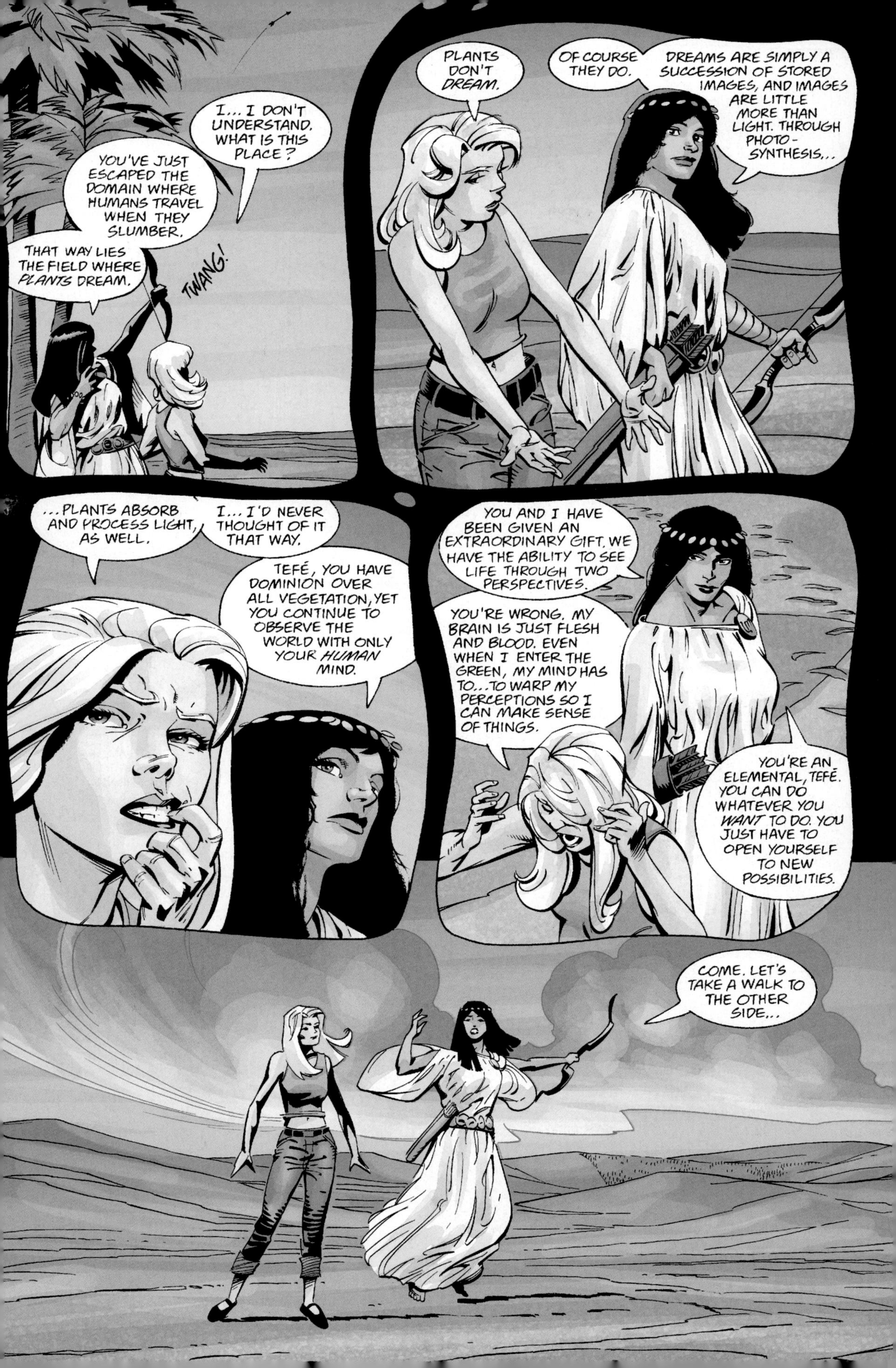

I... I DON'T UNDERSTAND. WHAT IS THIS PLACE?
YOU'VE JUST ESCAPED THE DOMAIN WHERE HUMANS TRAVEL WHEN THEY SLUMBER.
THAT WAY LIES THE FIELD WHERE PLANTS DREAM.
TWANG!
PLANTS DON'T DREAM.
OF COURSE THEY DO.
DREAMS ARE SIMPLY A SUCCESSION OF STORED IMAGES, AND IMAGES ARE LITTLE MORE THAN LIGHT. THROUGH PHOTO-SYNTHESIS...
...PLANTS ABSORB AND PROCESS LIGHT, AS WELL.
I... I'D NEVER THOUGHT OF IT THAT WAY.
TEFÉ, YOU HAVE DOMINION OVER ALL VEGETATION, YET YOU CONTINUE TO OBSERVE THE WORLD WITH ONLY YOUR HUMAN MIND.
YOU AND I HAVE BEEN GIVEN AN EXTRAORDINARY GIFT. WE HAVE THE ABILITY TO SEE LIFE THROUGH TWO PERSPECTIVES.
YOU'RE WRONG. MY BRAIN IS JUST FLESH AND BLOOD. EVEN WHEN I ENTER THE GREEN, MY MIND HAS TO... TO WARP MY PERCEPTIONS SO I CAN MAKE SENSE OF THINGS.
YOU'RE AN ELEMENTAL, TEFÉ. YOU CAN DO WHATEVER YOU WANT TO DO. YOU JUST HAVE TO OPEN YOURSELF TO NEW POSSIBILITIES.
COME. LET'S TAKE A WALK TO THE OTHER SIDE...

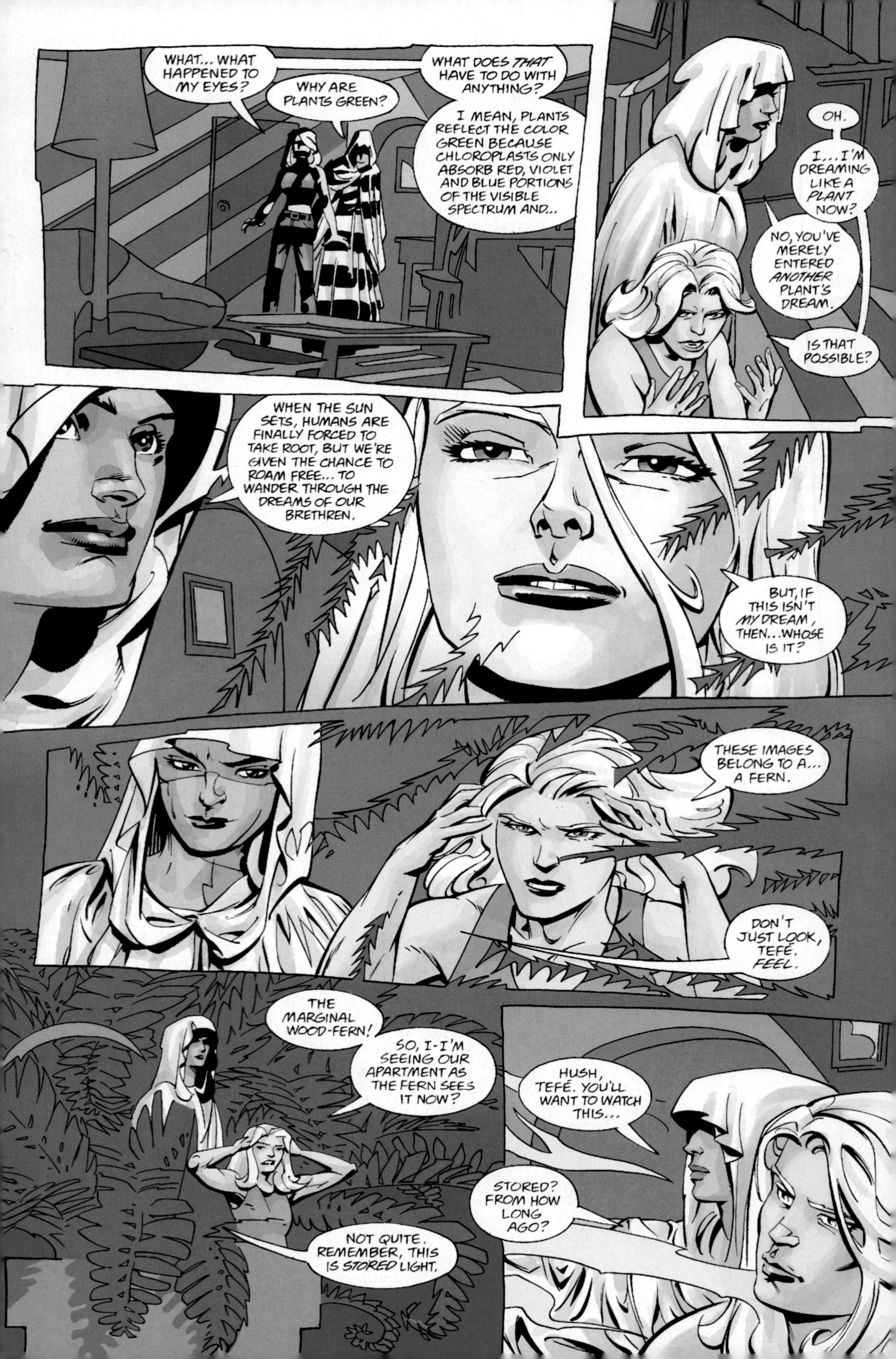
WHAT... WHAT HAPPENED TO MY EYES?
WHY ARE PLANTS GREEN?
WHAT DOES *THAT* HAVE TO DO WITH ANYTHING?
I MEAN, PLANTS REFLECT THE COLOR GREEN BECAUSE CHLOROPLASTS ONLY ABSORB RED, VIOLET AND BLUE PORTIONS OF THE VISIBLE SPECTRUM AND...
OH.
I... I'M DREAMING LIKE A *PLANT* NOW?
NO, YOU'VE MERELY ENTERED *ANOTHER* PLANT'S DREAM.
IS THAT POSSIBLE?
WHEN THE SUN SETS, HUMANS ARE FINALLY FORCED TO TAKE ROOT, BUT WE'RE GIVEN THE CHANCE TO ROAM FREE... TO WANDER THROUGH THE DREAMS OF OUR BRETHREN.
BUT, IF THIS ISN'T *MY DREAM*, THEN... WHOSE IS IT?
THESE IMAGES BELONG TO A... A FERN.
DON'T JUST LOOK, TEFÉ. *FEEL.*
THE MARGINAL WOOD-FERN!
SO, I-I'M SEEING OUR APARTMENT AS THE FERN SEES IT NOW?
NOT QUITE. REMEMBER, THIS IS *STORED* LIGHT.
STORED? FROM HOW LONG AGO?
HUSH, TEFÉ. YOU'LL WANT TO WATCH THIS...

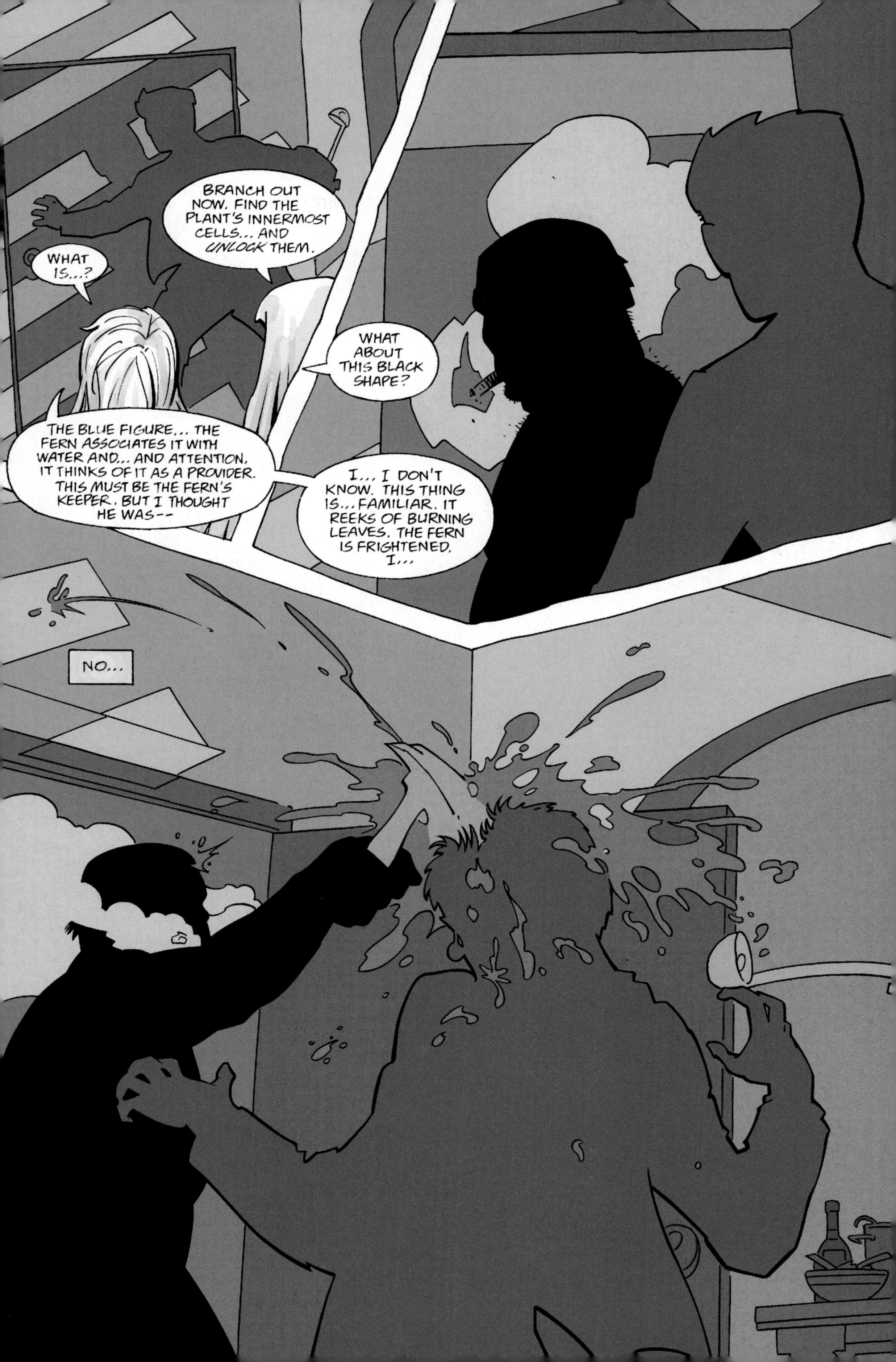
BRANCH OUT NOW. FIND THE PLANT'S INNERMOST CELLS... AND *UNLOCK* THEM.
WHAT IS...?
WHAT ABOUT THIS BLACK SHAPE?
THE BLUE FIGURE... THE FERN ASSOCIATES IT WITH WATER AND... AND ATTENTION. IT THINKS OF IT AS A PROVIDER. THIS MUST BE THE FERN'S KEEPER. BUT I THOUGHT HE WAS--
I... I DON'T KNOW. THIS THING IS... FAMILIAR. IT REEKS OF BURNING LEAVES. THE FERN IS FRIGHTENED. I...
NO...

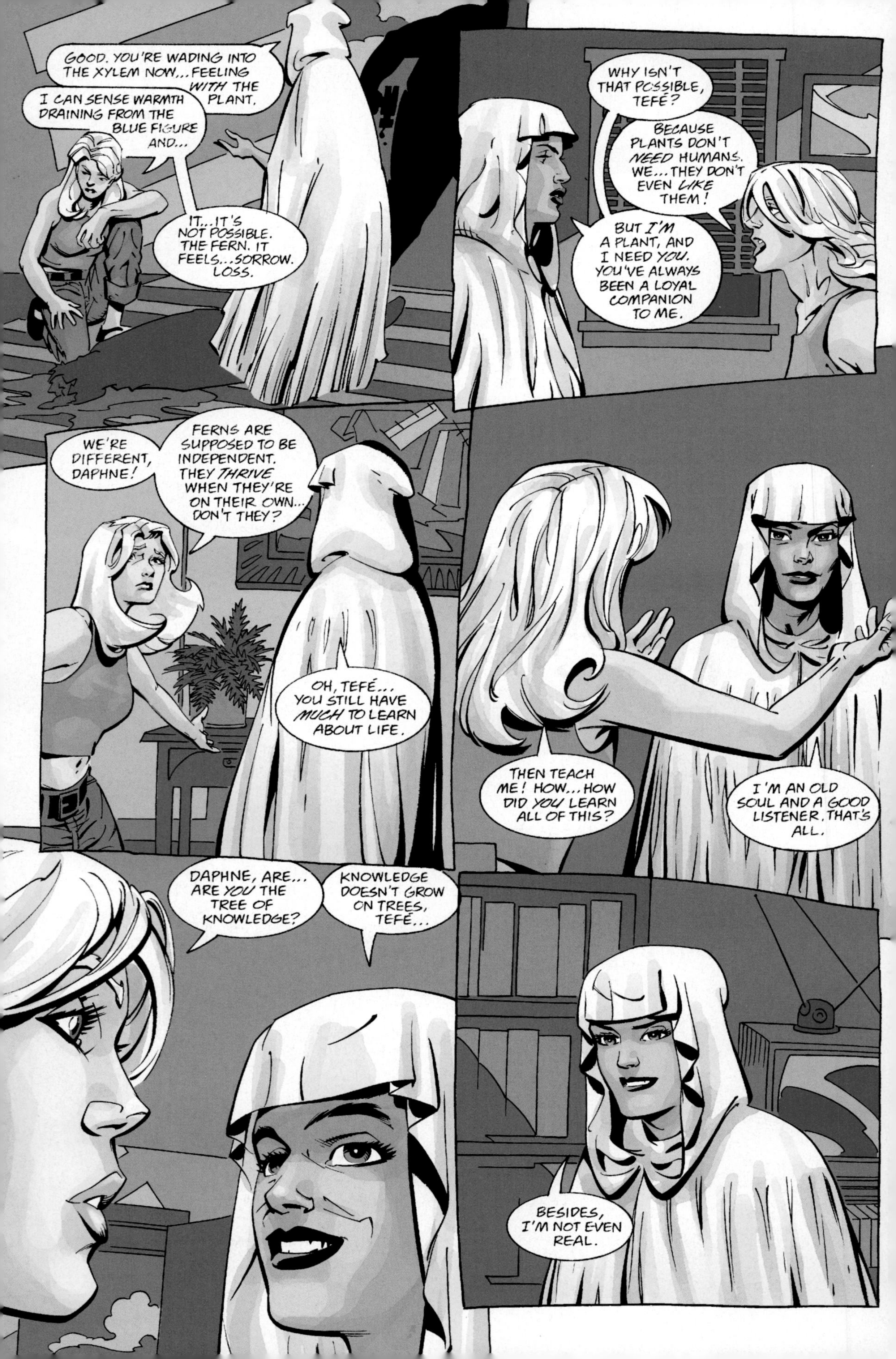
GOOD. YOU'RE WADING INTO THE XYLEM NOW... FEELING *WITH* THE PLANT.
I CAN SENSE WARMTH DRAINING FROM THE BLUE FIGURE AND...
IT...IT'S NOT POSSIBLE. THE FERN. IT FEELS...SORROW. LOSS.
WHY ISN'T THAT POSSIBLE, TEFÉ?
BECAUSE PLANTS DON'T *NEED* HUMANS. WE... THEY DON'T EVEN *LIKE* THEM!
BUT *I'M* A PLANT, AND I NEED *YOU*. YOU'VE ALWAYS BEEN A LOYAL COMPANION TO ME.
WE'RE DIFFERENT, DAPHNE!
FERNS ARE SUPPOSED TO BE INDEPENDENT. THEY *THRIVE* WHEN THEY'RE ON THEIR OWN... DON'T THEY?
OH, TEFÉ... YOU STILL HAVE *MUCH* TO LEARN ABOUT LIFE.
THEN TEACH ME! HOW... HOW DID *YOU* LEARN ALL OF THIS?
I'M AN OLD SOUL AND A GOOD LISTENER, THAT'S ALL.
DAPHNE, ARE... ARE *YOU* THE TREE OF KNOWLEDGE?
KNOWLEDGE DOESN'T GROW ON TREES, TEFÉ...
BESIDES, I'M NOT EVEN REAL.

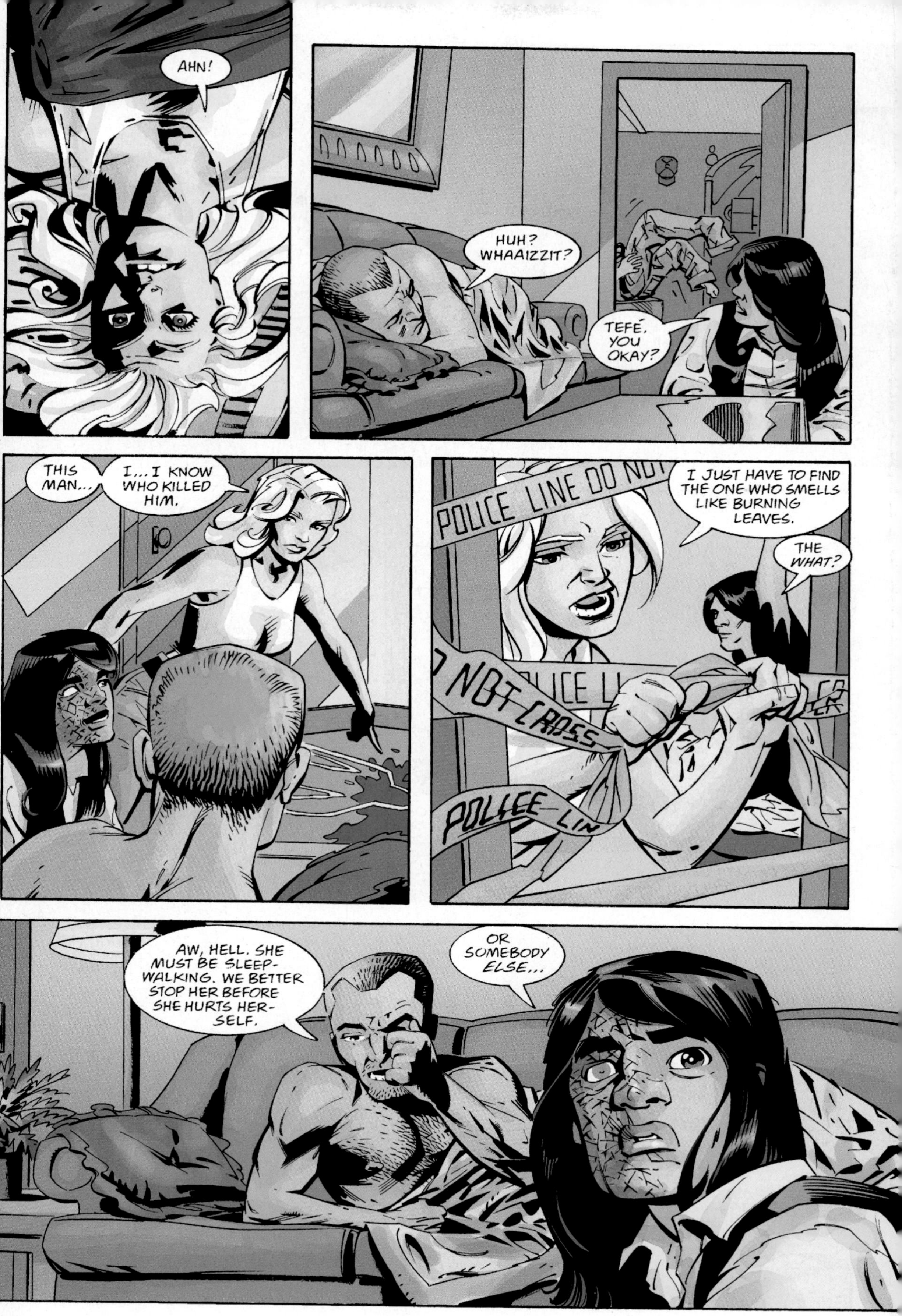
AHN!
HUH? WHAAIZZIT?
TEFÉ, YOU OKAY?
THIS MAN...
I... I KNOW WHO KILLED HIM.
POLICE LINE DO NOT
I JUST HAVE TO FIND THE ONE WHO SMELLS LIKE BURNING LEAVES.
THE WHAT?
O NOT CROSS
POLICE LI
POLICE LIN
AW, HELL. SHE MUST BE SLEEP-WALKING. WE BETTER STOP HER BEFORE SHE HURTS HER-SELF.
OR SOMEBODY ELSE...

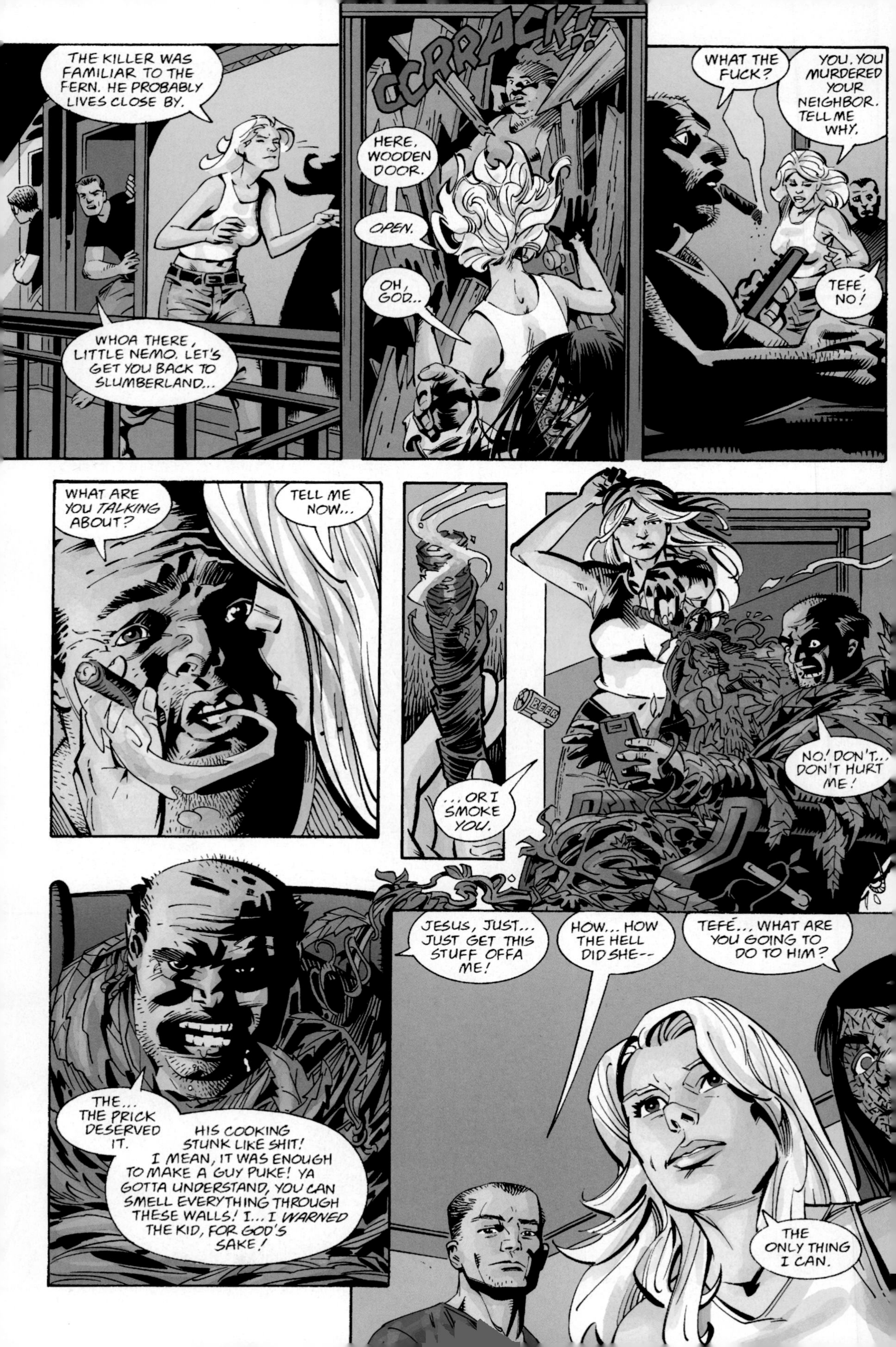
THE KILLER WAS FAMILIAR TO THE FERN. HE PROBABLY LIVES CLOSE BY.
WHOA THERE, LITTLE NEMO. LET'S GET YOU BACK TO SLUMBERLAND...
CCRRACK!!
HERE, WOODEN DOOR.
OPEN.
OH, GOD...
WHAT THE FUCK?
YOU. YOU MURDERED YOUR NEIGHBOR. TELL ME WHY.
TEFÉ, NO!
WHAT ARE YOU *TALKING* ABOUT?
TELL ME NOW...
...OR I SMOKE *YOU*.
BEER
NO! DON'T... DON'T HURT ME!
THE... THE PRICK DESERVED IT.
HIS COOKING STUNK LIKE SHIT! I MEAN, IT WAS ENOUGH TO MAKE A GUY PUKE! YA GOTTA UNDERSTAND, YOU CAN SMELL EVERYTHING THROUGH THESE WALLS! I... I *WARNED* THE KID, FOR GOD'S SAKE!
JESUS, JUST... JUST GET THIS STUFF OFFA ME!
HOW... HOW THE HELL DID SHE--
TEFÉ... WHAT ARE YOU GOING TO DO TO HIM?
THE ONLY THING I CAN.

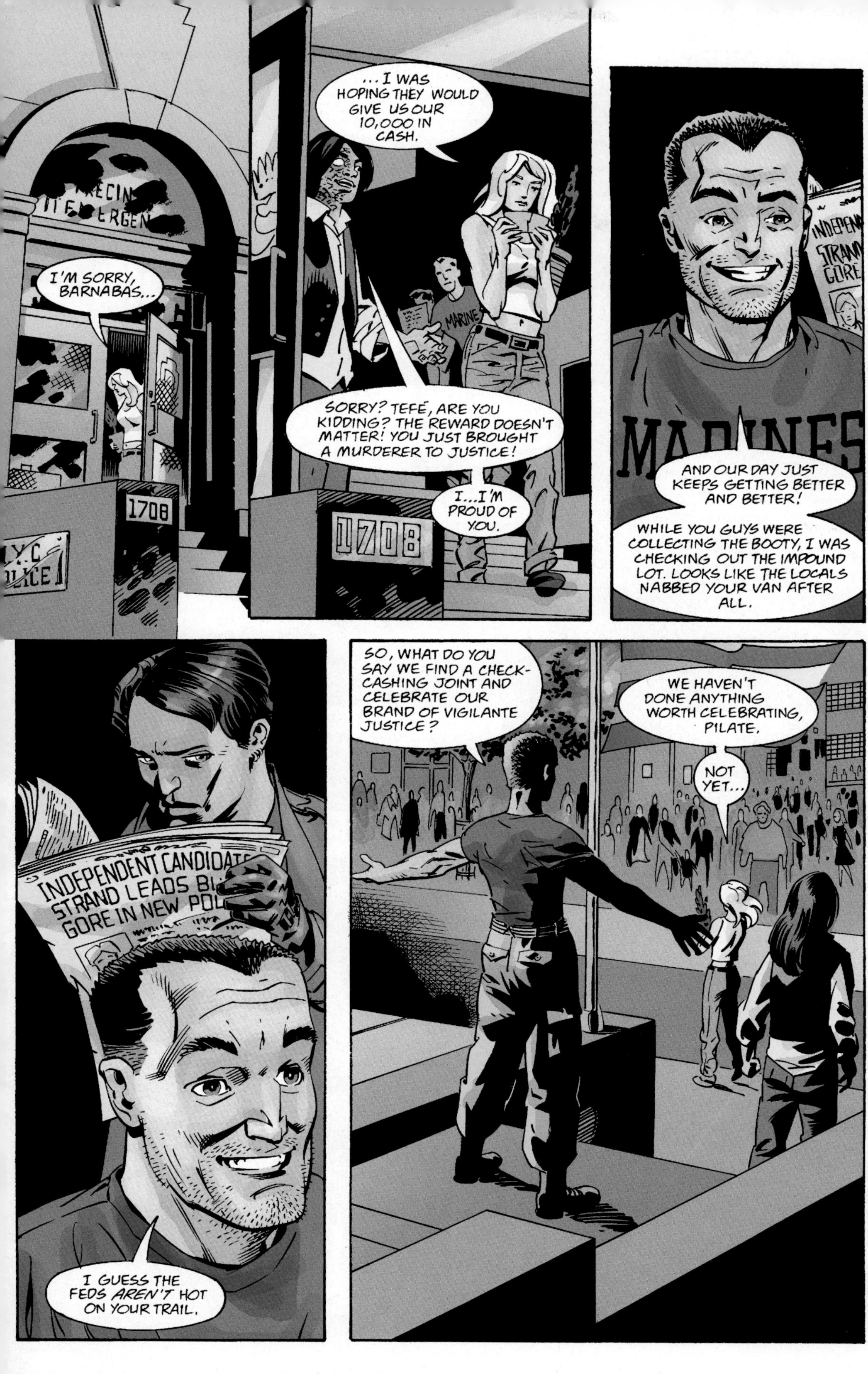

I'M SORRY, BARNABAS...
...I WAS HOPING THEY WOULD GIVE US OUR 10,000 IN CASH.
SORRY? TEFÉ, ARE YOU KIDDING? THE REWARD DOESN'T MATTER! YOU JUST BROUGHT A MURDERER TO JUSTICE!
I...I'M PROUD OF YOU.
1708
MARINES
AND OUR DAY JUST KEEPS GETTING BETTER AND BETTER!
WHILE YOU GUYS WERE COLLECTING THE BOOTY, I WAS CHECKING OUT THE IMPOUND LOT. LOOKS LIKE THE LOCALS NABBED YOUR VAN AFTER ALL.
INDEPENDENT CANDIDATE STRAND LEADS BL GORE IN NEW PO
I GUESS THE FEDS *AREN'T* HOT ON YOUR TRAIL.
SO, WHAT DO YOU SAY WE FIND A CHECK-CASHING JOINT AND CELEBRATE OUR BRAND OF VIGILANTE JUSTICE?
WE HAVEN'T DONE ANYTHING WORTH CELEBRATING, PILATE.
NOT YET...

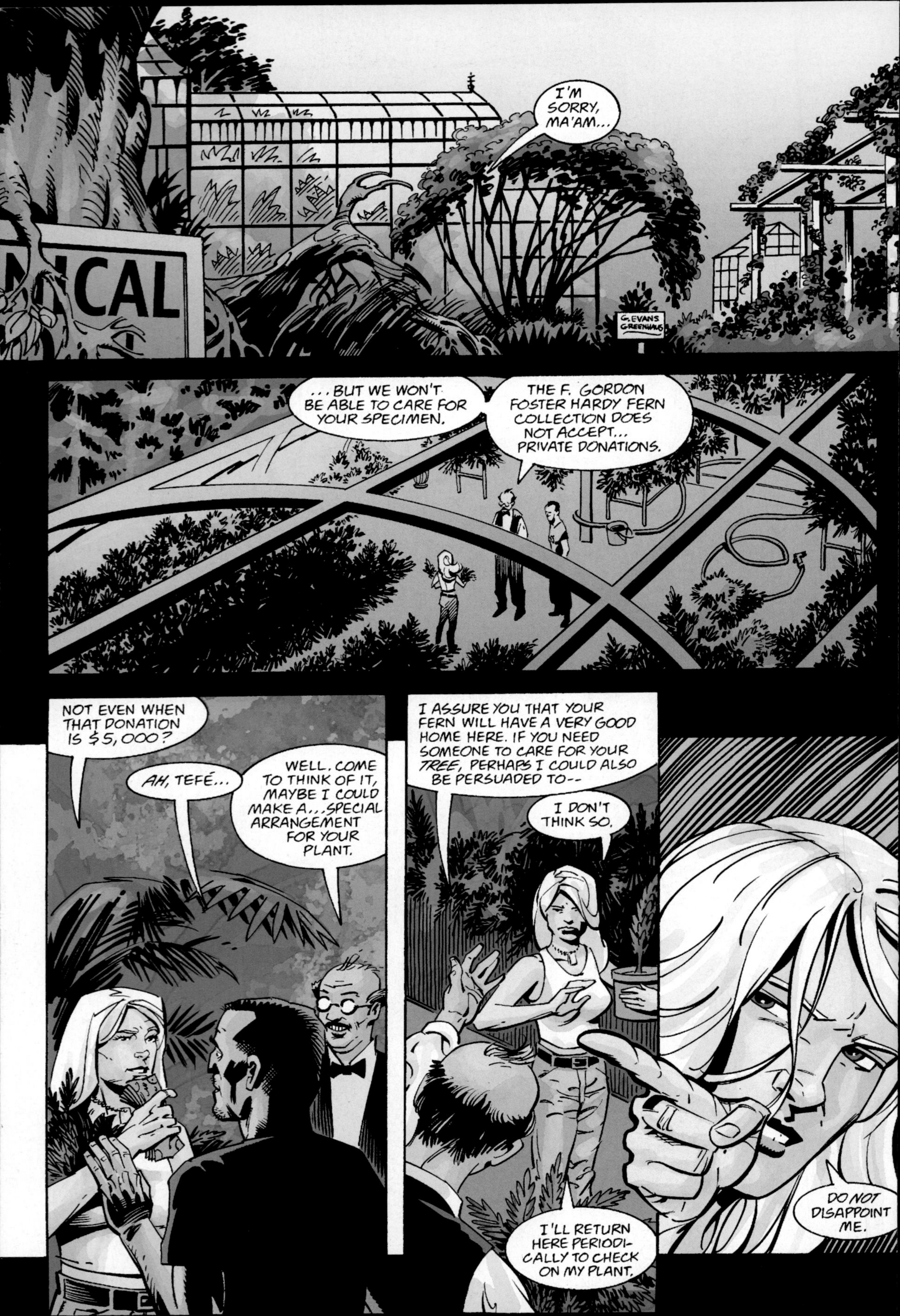

NCAL
I'M SORRY, MA'AM...
G. EVANS GREENHAUS
...BUT WE WON'T BE ABLE TO CARE FOR YOUR SPECIMEN.
THE F. GORDON FOSTER HARDY FERN COLLECTION DOES NOT ACCEPT... PRIVATE DONATIONS.
NOT EVEN WHEN THAT DONATION IS $5,000?
AH, TEFÉ...
WELL, COME TO THINK OF IT, MAYBE I COULD MAKE A...SPECIAL ARRANGEMENT FOR YOUR PLANT.
I ASSURE YOU THAT YOUR FERN WILL HAVE A VERY GOOD HOME HERE. IF YOU NEED SOMEONE TO CARE FOR YOUR *TREE*, PERHAPS I COULD ALSO BE PERSUADED TO--
I DON'T THINK SO.
I'LL RETURN HERE PERIODI-CALLY TO CHECK ON MY PLANT.
DO NOT DISAPPOINT ME.

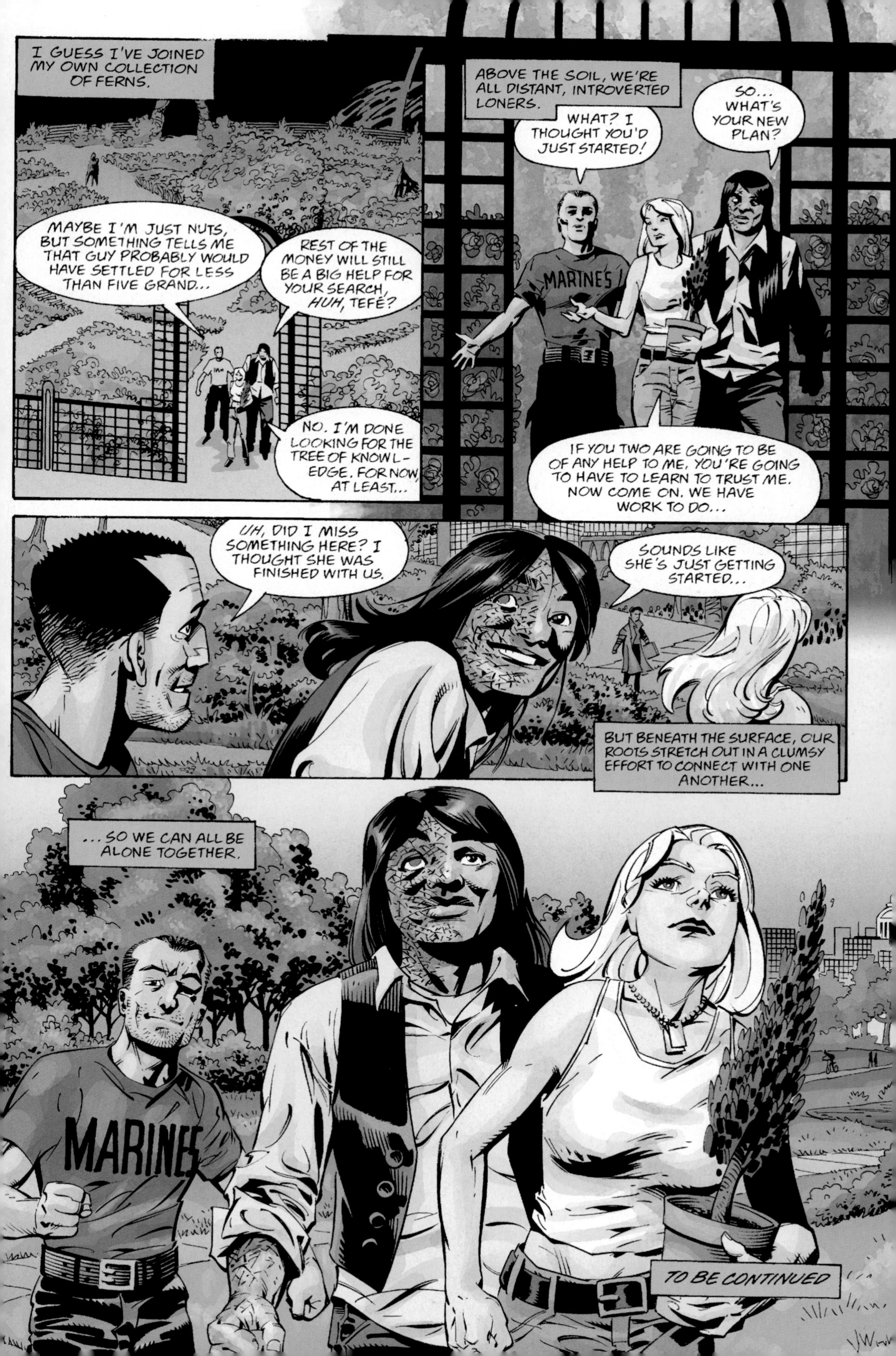

I GUESS I'VE JOINED MY OWN COLLECTION OF FERNS.
MAYBE I'M JUST NUTS, BUT SOMETHING TELLS ME THAT GUY PROBABLY WOULD HAVE SETTLED FOR LESS THAN FIVE GRAND...
REST OF THE MONEY WILL STILL BE A BIG HELP FOR YOUR SEARCH, HUH, TEFÉ?
NO. I'M DONE LOOKING FOR THE TREE OF KNOWL-EDGE. FOR NOW, AT LEAST...
ABOVE THE SOIL, WE'RE ALL DISTANT, INTROVERTED LONERS.
WHAT? I THOUGHT YOU'D JUST STARTED!
SO... WHAT'S YOUR NEW PLAN?
MARINES
IF YOU TWO ARE GOING TO BE OF ANY HELP TO ME, YOU'RE GOING TO HAVE TO LEARN TO TRUST ME. NOW COME ON. WE HAVE WORK TO DO...
UH, DID I MISS SOMETHING HERE? I THOUGHT SHE WAS FINISHED WITH US.
SOUNDS LIKE SHE'S JUST GETTING STARTED...
BUT BENEATH THE SURFACE, OUR ROOTS STRETCH OUT IN A CLUMSY EFFORT TO CONNECT WITH ONE ANOTHER...
...SO WE CAN ALL BE ALONE TOGETHER.
MARINES
TO BE CONTINUED

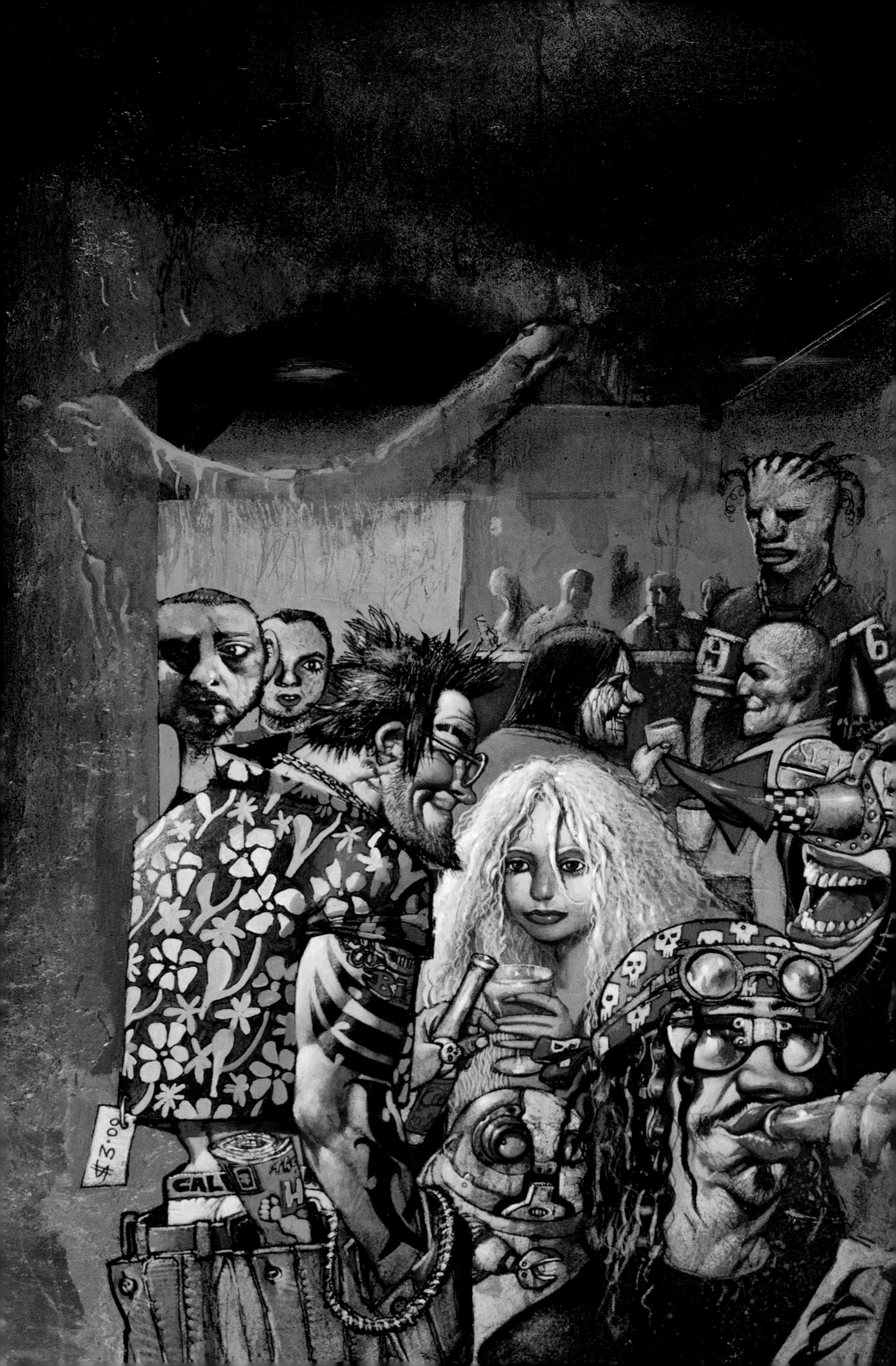
$3.00

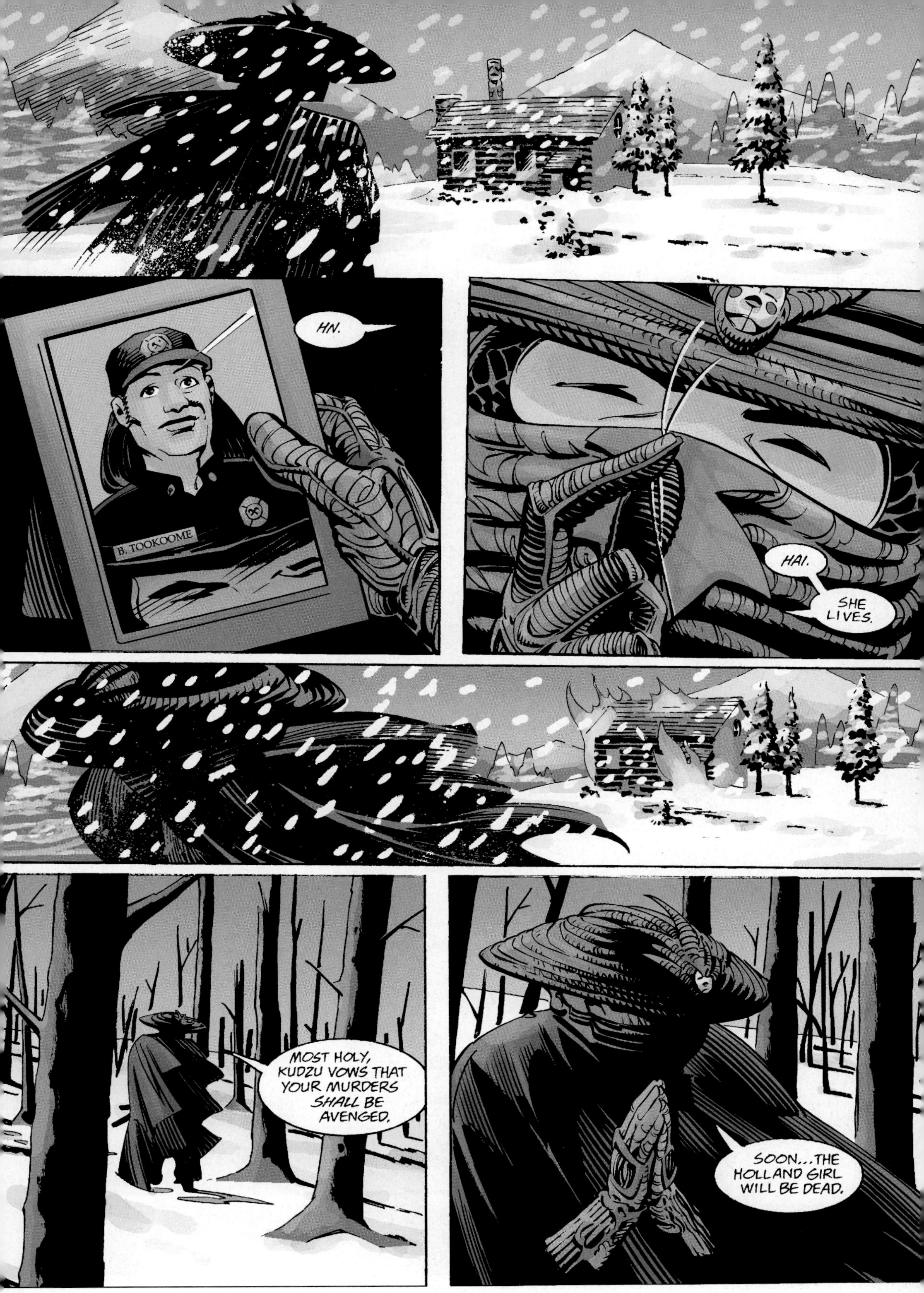
B. TOOKOOME
HN.
HAI.
SHE LIVES.
MOST HOLY, KUDZU VOWS THAT YOUR MURDERS SHALL BE AVENGED.
SOON...THE HOLLAND GIRL WILL BE DEAD.

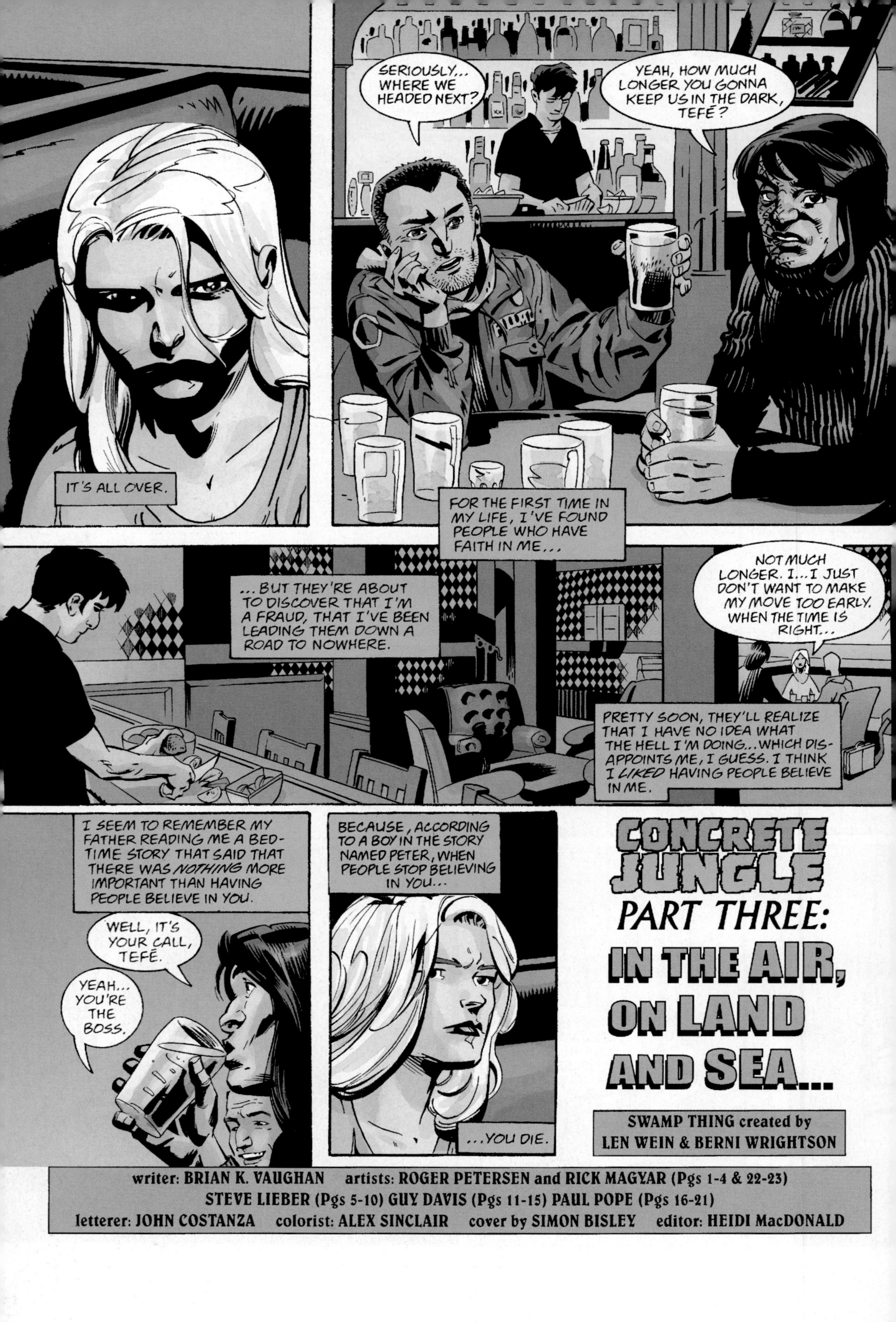
SERIOUSLY... WHERE WE HEADED NEXT?
YEAH, HOW MUCH LONGER YOU GONNA KEEP US IN THE DARK, TEFÉ?
IT'S ALL OVER.
FOR THE FIRST TIME IN MY LIFE, I'VE FOUND PEOPLE WHO HAVE FAITH IN ME...
...BUT THEY'RE ABOUT TO DISCOVER THAT I'M A FRAUD, THAT I'VE BEEN LEADING THEM DOWN A ROAD TO NOWHERE.
NOT MUCH LONGER. I...I JUST DON'T WANT TO MAKE MY MOVE TOO EARLY. WHEN THE TIME IS RIGHT...
PRETTY SOON, THEY'LL REALIZE THAT I HAVE NO IDEA WHAT THE HELL I'M DOING...WHICH DISAPPOINTS ME, I GUESS. I THINK I *LIKED* HAVING PEOPLE BELIEVE IN ME.
I SEEM TO REMEMBER MY FATHER READING ME A BEDTIME STORY THAT SAID THAT THERE WAS *NOTHING* MORE IMPORTANT THAN HAVING PEOPLE BELIEVE IN YOU.
WELL, IT'S YOUR CALL, TEFÉ.
YEAH... YOU'RE THE BOSS.
BECAUSE, ACCORDING TO A BOY IN THE STORY NAMED PETER, WHEN PEOPLE STOP BELIEVING IN YOU...
...YOU DIE.
CONCRETE JUNGLE
PART THREE:
IN THE AIR, ON LAND AND SEA...
SWAMP THING created by LEN WEIN & BERNI WRIGHTSON

writer: BRIAN K. VAUGHAN artists: ROGER PETERSEN and RICK MAGYAR (Pgs 1-4 & 22-23)
STEVE LIEBER (Pgs 5-10) GUY DAVIS (Pgs 11-15) PAUL POPE (Pgs 16-21)
letterer: JOHN COSTANZA colorist: ALEX SINCLAIR cover by SIMON BISLEY editor: HEIDI MacDONALD

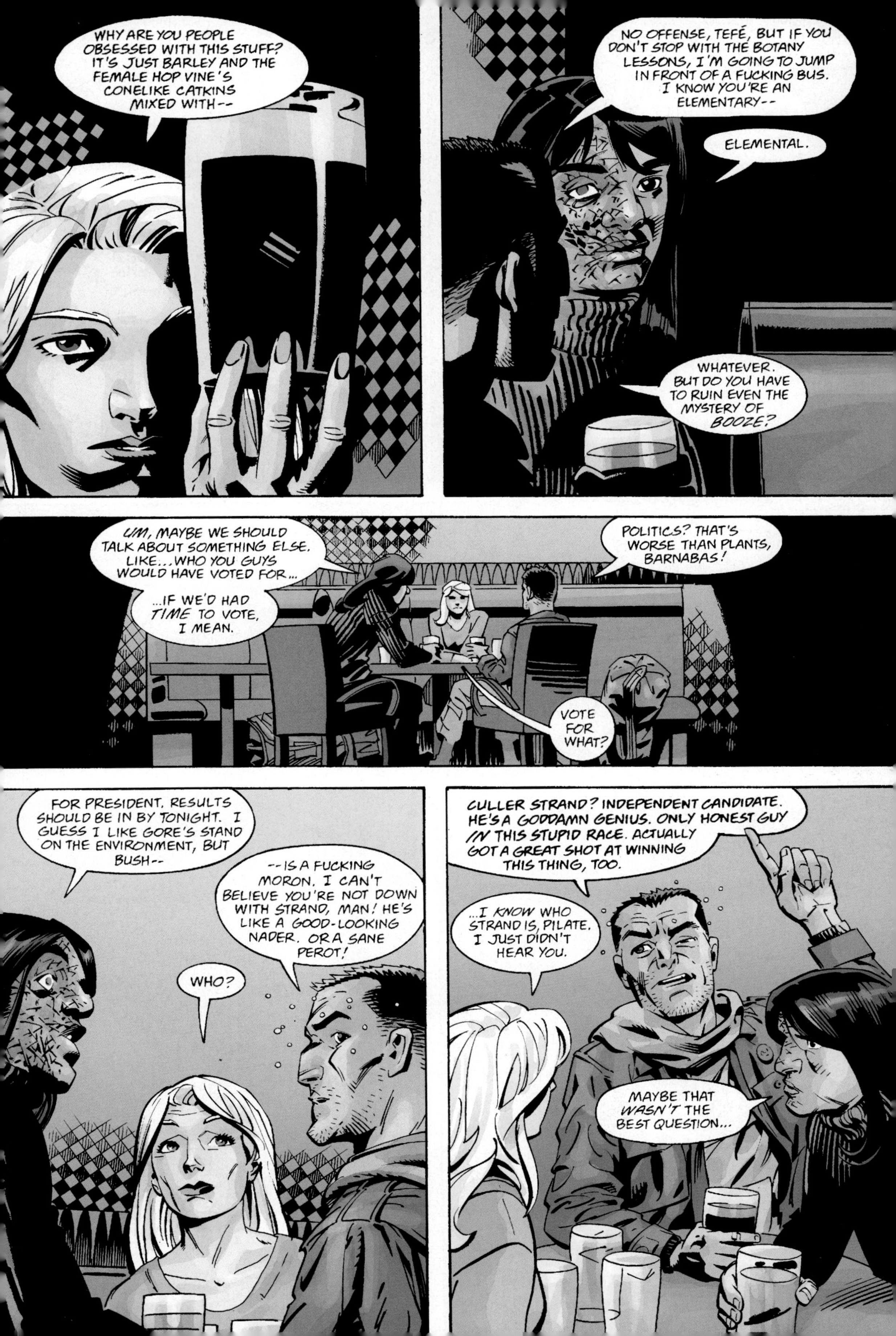
WHY ARE YOU PEOPLE OBSESSED WITH THIS STUFF? IT'S JUST BARLEY AND THE FEMALE HOP VINE'S CONELIKE CATKINS MIXED WITH--
NO OFFENSE, TEFÉ, BUT IF YOU DON'T STOP WITH THE BOTANY LESSONS, I'M GOING TO JUMP IN FRONT OF A FUCKING BUS. I KNOW YOU'RE AN ELEMENTARY--
ELEMENTAL.
WHATEVER. BUT DO YOU HAVE TO RUIN EVEN THE MYSTERY OF BOOZE?
UM, MAYBE WE SHOULD TALK ABOUT SOMETHING ELSE. LIKE... WHO YOU GUYS WOULD HAVE VOTED FOR...
...IF WE'D HAD TIME TO VOTE, I MEAN.
POLITICS? THAT'S WORSE THAN PLANTS, BARNABAS!
VOTE FOR WHAT?
FOR PRESIDENT. RESULTS SHOULD BE IN BY TONIGHT. I GUESS I LIKE GORE'S STAND ON THE ENVIRONMENT, BUT BUSH--
--IS A FUCKING MORON. I CAN'T BELIEVE YOU'RE NOT DOWN WITH STRAND, MAN! HE'S LIKE A GOOD-LOOKING NADER. OR A SANE PEROT!
WHO?
CULLER STRAND? INDEPENDENT CANDIDATE. HE'S A GODDAMN GENIUS. ONLY HONEST GUY IN THIS STUPID RACE. ACTUALLY GOT A GREAT SHOT AT WINNING THIS THING, TOO.
...I KNOW WHO STRAND IS, PILATE. I JUST DIDN'T HEAR YOU.
MAYBE THAT WASN'T THE BEST QUESTION...

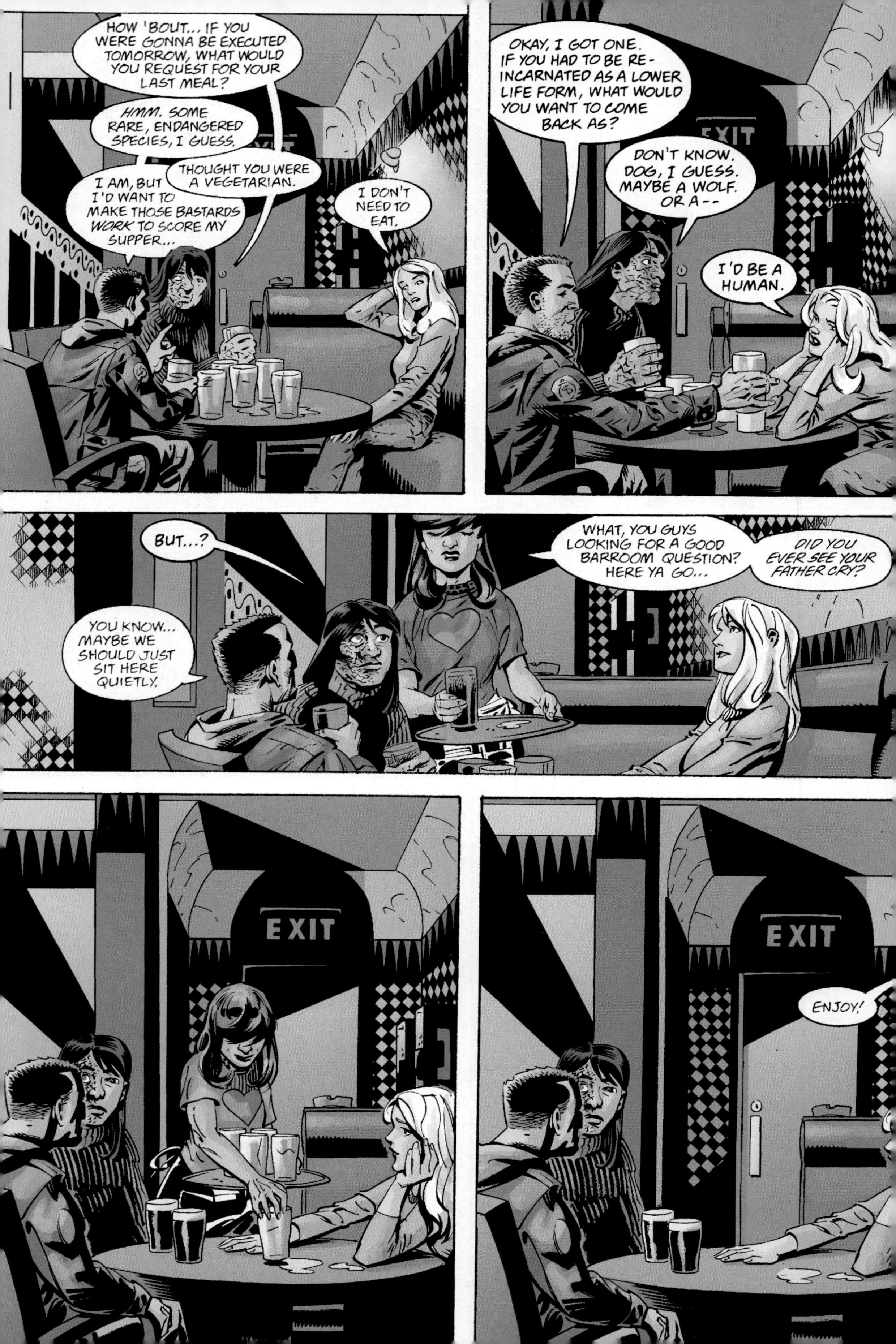
HOW 'BOUT... IF YOU WERE GONNA BE EXECUTED TOMORROW, WHAT WOULD YOU REQUEST FOR YOUR LAST MEAL?
HMM. SOME RARE, ENDANGERED SPECIES, I GUESS.
THOUGHT YOU WERE A VEGETARIAN.
I AM, BUT I'D WANT TO MAKE THOSE BASTARDS WORK TO SCORE MY SUPPER...
I DON'T NEED TO EAT.
OKAY, I GOT ONE. IF YOU HAD TO BE RE-INCARNATED AS A LOWER LIFE FORM, WHAT WOULD YOU WANT TO COME BACK AS?
EXIT
DON'T KNOW. DOG, I GUESS. MAYBE A WOLF. OR A--
I'D BE A HUMAN.
BUT...?
YOU KNOW... MAYBE WE SHOULD JUST SIT HERE QUIETLY.
WHAT, YOU GUYS LOOKING FOR A GOOD BARROOM QUESTION? HERE YA GO...
DID YOU EVER SEE YOUR FATHER CRY?
EXIT
EXIT
ENJOY!

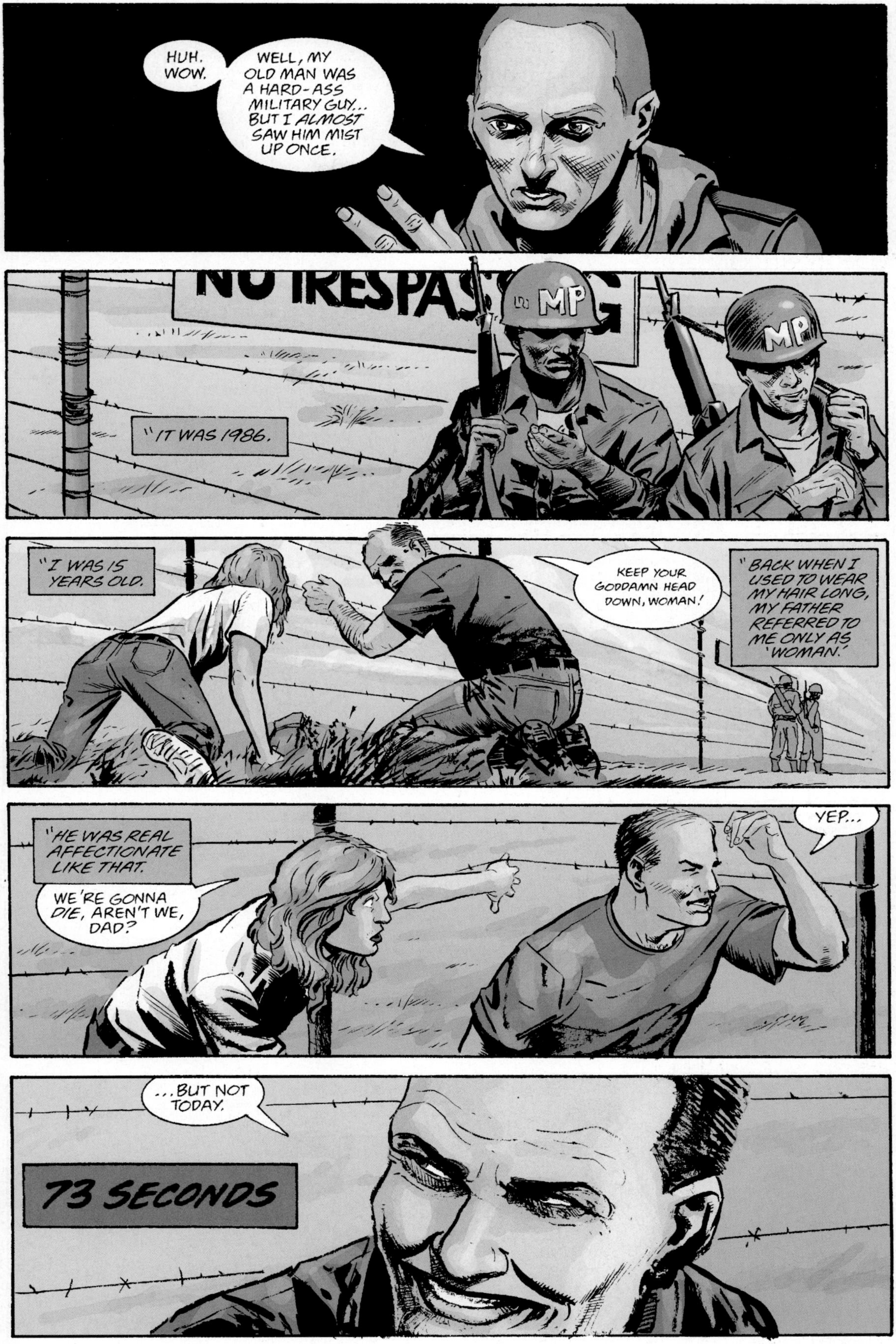
HUH. WOW.
WELL, MY OLD MAN WAS A HARD-ASS MILITARY GUY... BUT I *ALMOST* SAW HIM MIST UP ONCE.
NO TRESPAS
MP
MP
"IT WAS 1986.
"I WAS 15 YEARS OLD.
KEEP YOUR GODDAMN HEAD DOWN, WOMAN!
"BACK WHEN I USED TO WEAR MY HAIR LONG, MY FATHER REFERRED TO ME ONLY AS 'WOMAN.'
"HE WAS REAL AFFECTIONATE LIKE THAT.
WE'RE GONNA *DIE*, AREN'T WE, DAD?
YEP...
...BUT NOT TODAY.
73 SECONDS

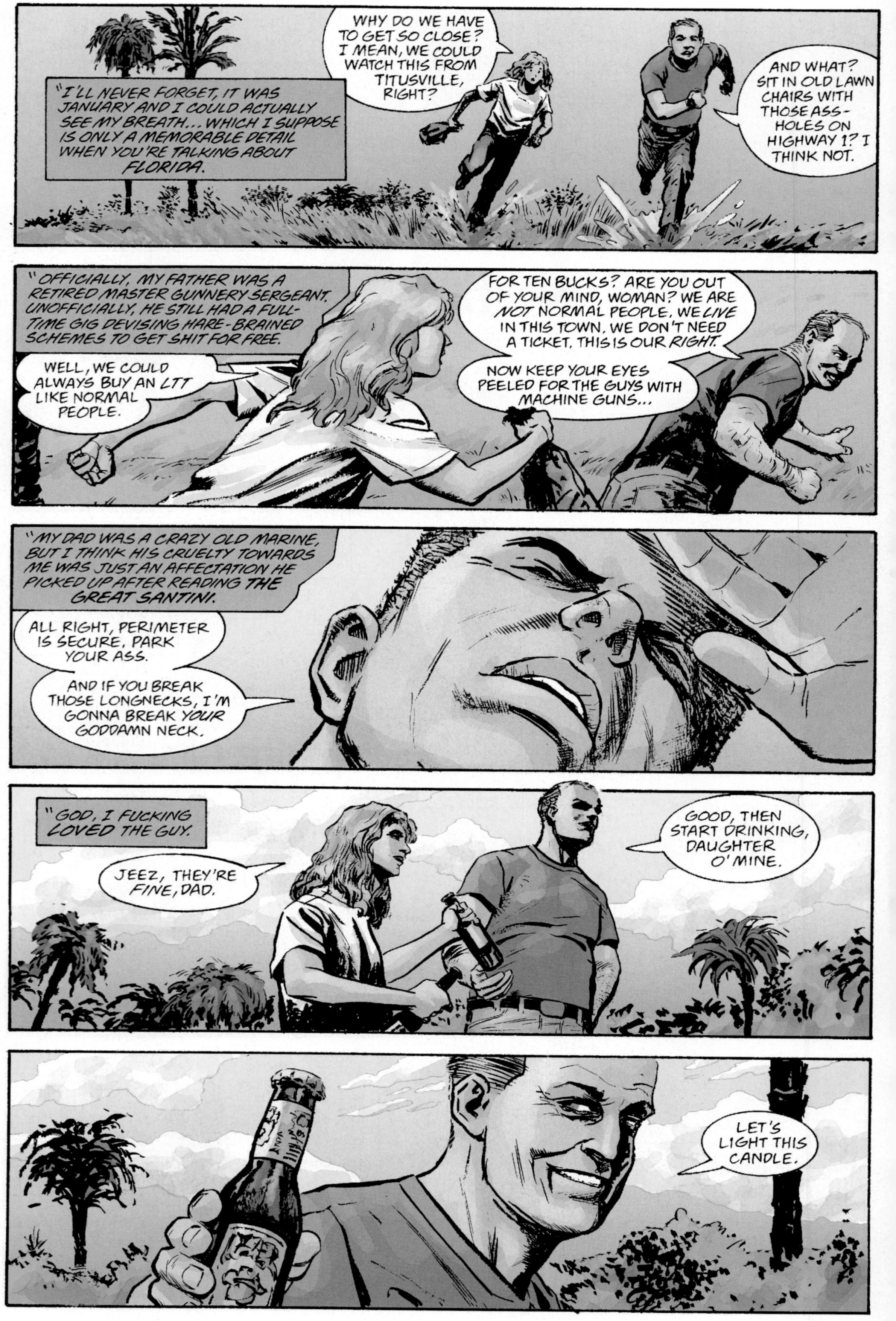
"I'LL NEVER FORGET, IT WAS JANUARY AND I COULD ACTUALLY SEE MY BREATH... WHICH I SUPPOSE IS ONLY A MEMORABLE DETAIL WHEN YOU'RE TALKING ABOUT FLORIDA.
WHY DO WE HAVE TO GET SO CLOSE? I MEAN, WE COULD WATCH THIS FROM TITUSVILLE, RIGHT?
AND WHAT? SIT IN OLD LAWN CHAIRS WITH THOSE ASS-HOLES ON HIGHWAY 1? I THINK NOT.
"OFFICIALLY, MY FATHER WAS A RETIRED MASTER GUNNERY SERGEANT. UNOFFICIALLY, HE STILL HAD A FULL-TIME GIG DEVISING HARE-BRAINED SCHEMES TO GET SHIT FOR FREE.
WELL, WE COULD ALWAYS BUY AN LTT LIKE NORMAL PEOPLE.
FOR TEN BUCKS? ARE YOU OUT OF YOUR MIND, WOMAN? WE ARE NOT NORMAL PEOPLE. WE LIVE IN THIS TOWN. WE DON'T NEED A TICKET. THIS IS OUR RIGHT.
NOW KEEP YOUR EYES PEELED FOR THE GUYS WITH MACHINE GUNS...
"MY DAD WAS A CRAZY OLD MARINE, BUT I THINK HIS CRUELTY TOWARDS ME WAS JUST AN AFFECTATION HE PICKED UP AFTER READING THE GREAT SANTINI.
ALL RIGHT, PERIMETER IS SECURE. PARK YOUR ASS.
AND IF YOU BREAK THOSE LONGNECKS, I'M GONNA BREAK YOUR GODDAMN NECK.
"GOD, I FUCKING LOVED THE GUY.
JEEZ, THEY'RE FINE, DAD.
GOOD, THEN START DRINKING, DAUGHTER O'MINE.
LET'S LIGHT THIS CANDLE.

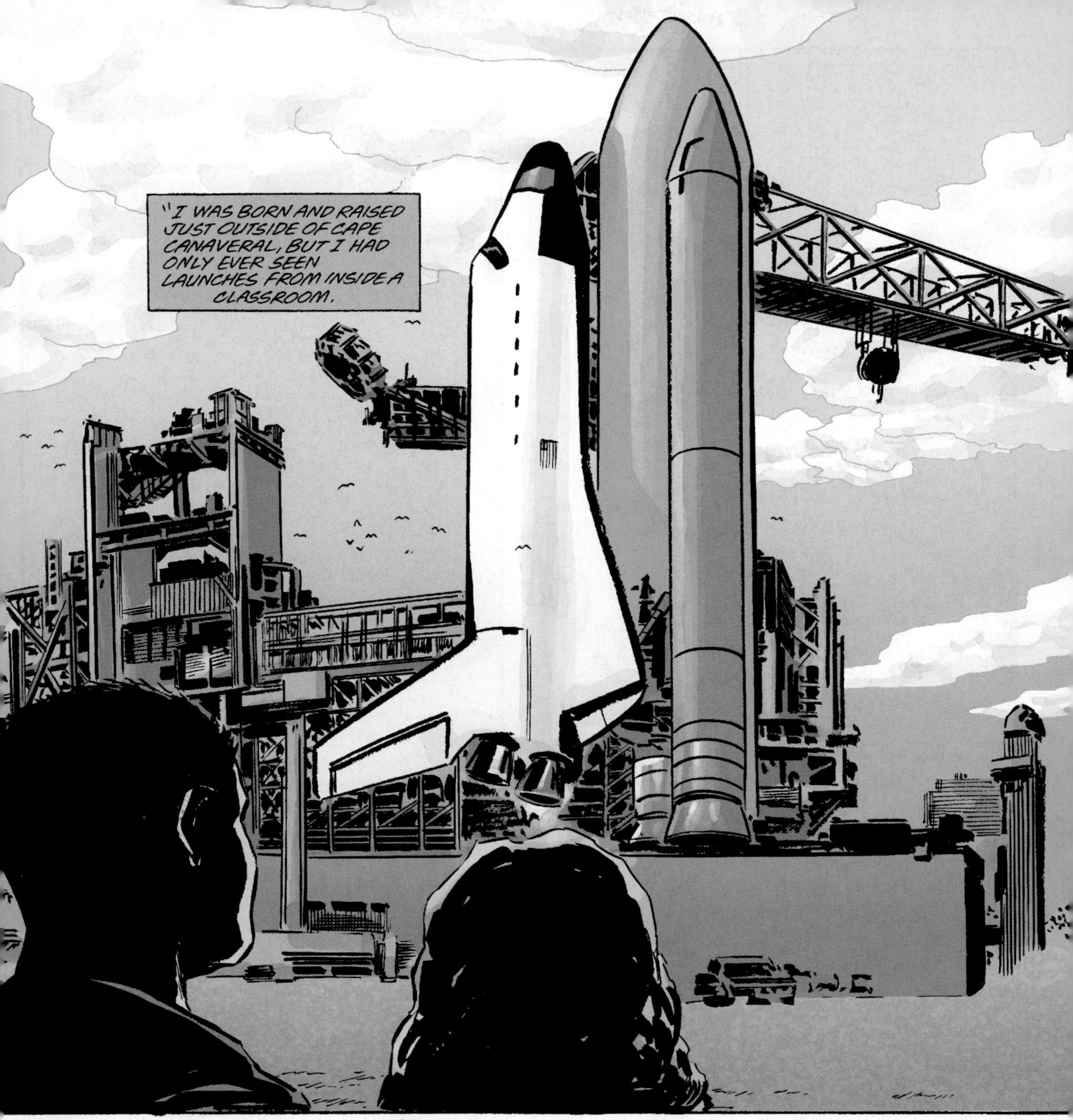
"I WAS BORN AND RAISED JUST OUTSIDE OF CAPE CANAVERAL, BUT I HAD ONLY EVER SEEN LAUNCHES FROM INSIDE A CLASSROOM.

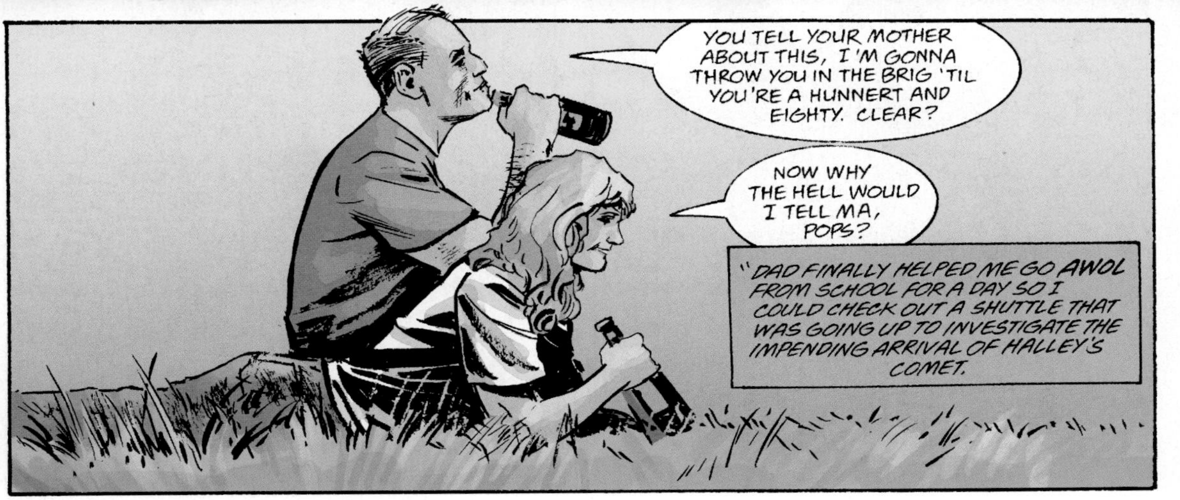
YOU TELL YOUR MOTHER ABOUT THIS, I'M GONNA THROW YOU IN THE BRIG 'TIL YOU'RE A HUNNERT AND EIGHTY. CLEAR?
NOW WHY THE HELL WOULD I TELL MA, POPS?
"DAD FINALLY HELPED ME GO AWOL FROM SCHOOL FOR A DAY SO I COULD CHECK OUT A SHUTTLE THAT WAS GOING UP TO INVESTIGATE THE IMPENDING ARRIVAL OF HALLEY'S COMET.

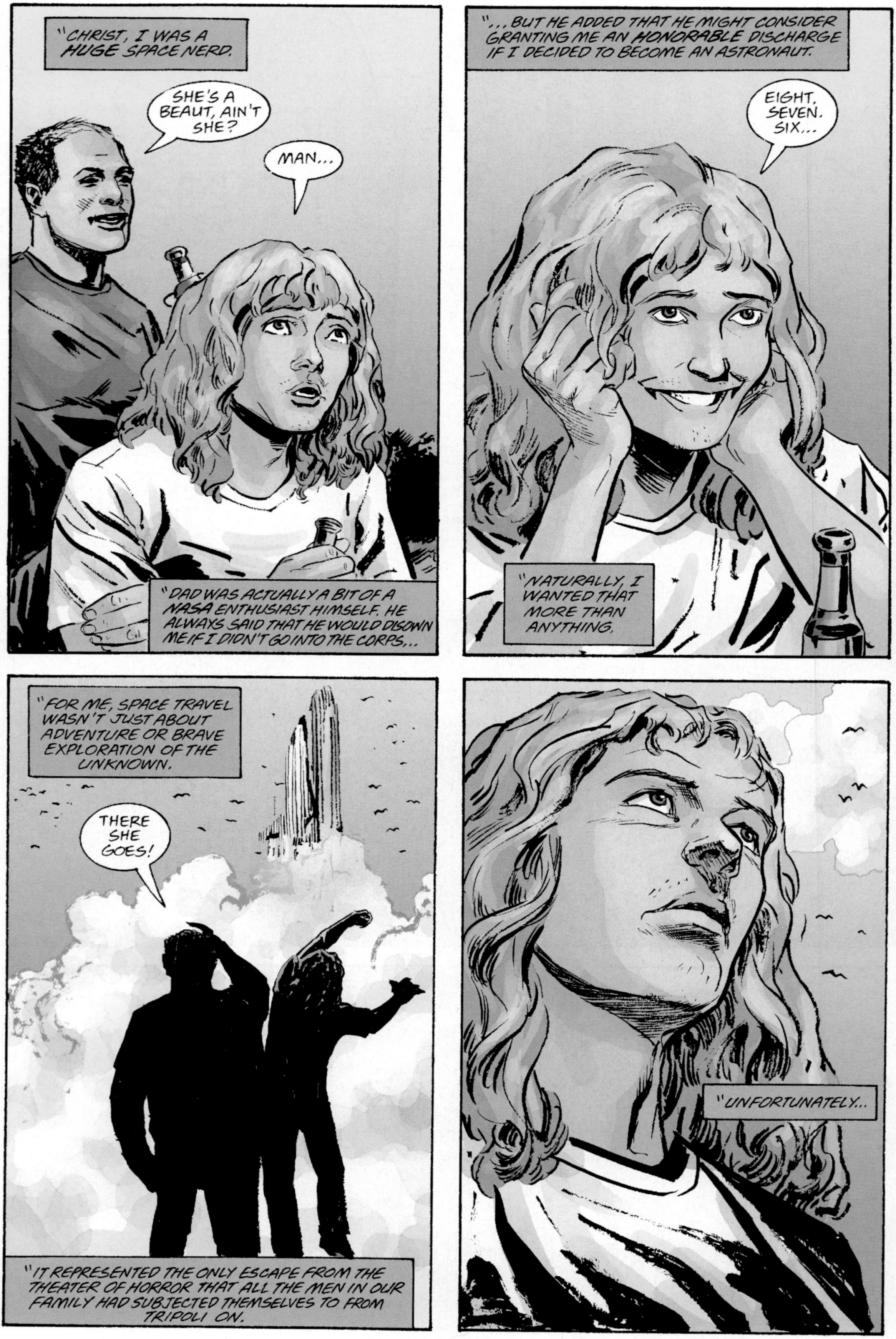
"CHRIST, I WAS A HUGE SPACE NERD.
SHE'S A BEAUT, AIN'T SHE?
MAN...
"DAD WAS ACTUALLY A BIT OF A NASA ENTHUSIAST HIMSELF. HE ALWAYS SAID THAT HE WOULD DISOWN ME IF I DIDN'T GO INTO THE CORPS...
"...BUT HE ADDED THAT HE MIGHT CONSIDER GRANTING ME AN HONORABLE DISCHARGE IF I DECIDED TO BECOME AN ASTRONAUT.
EIGHT, SEVEN. SIX...
"NATURALLY, I WANTED THAT MORE THAN ANYTHING.
"FOR ME, SPACE TRAVEL WASN'T JUST ABOUT ADVENTURE OR BRAVE EXPLORATION OF THE UNKNOWN.
THERE SHE GOES!
"IT REPRESENTED THE ONLY ESCAPE FROM THE THEATER OF HORROR THAT ALL THE MEN IN OUR FAMILY HAD SUBJECTED THEMSELVES TO FROM TRIPOLI ON.
"UNFORTUNATELY...

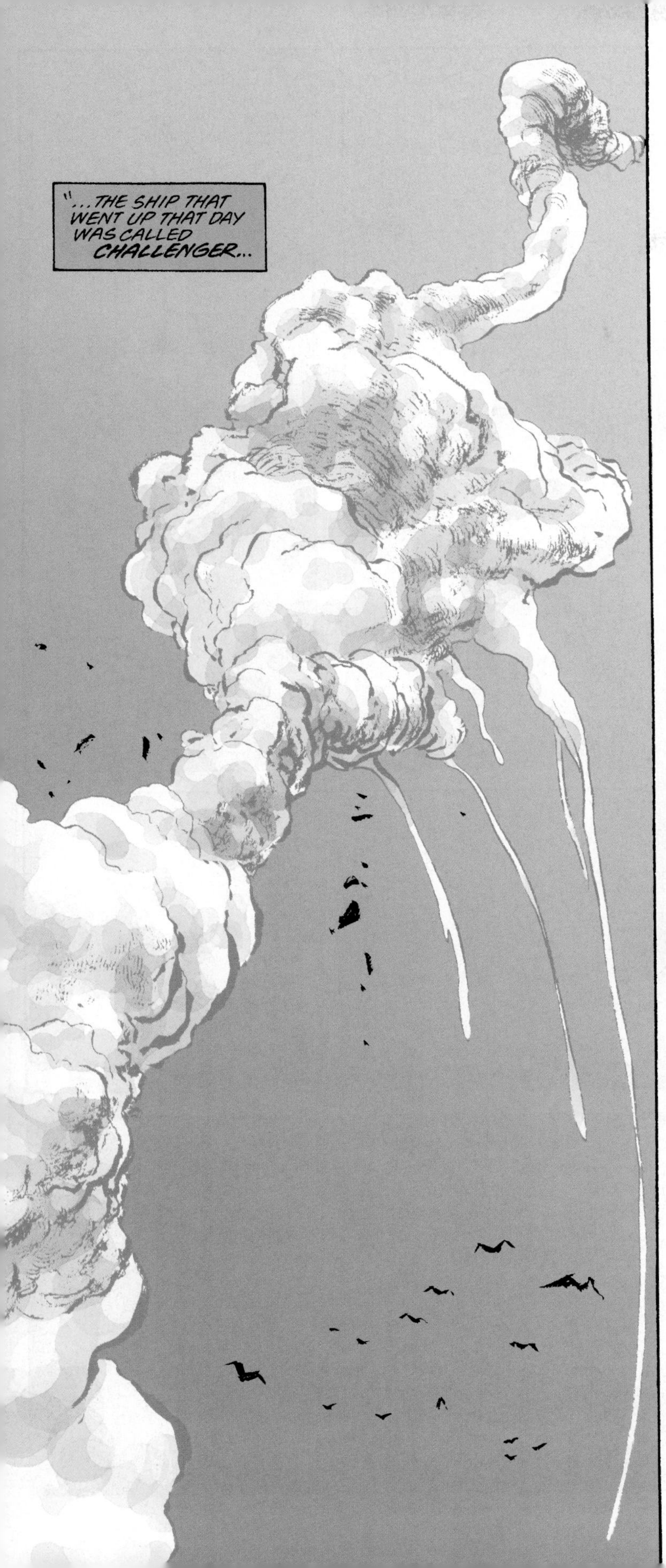
"...THE SHIP THAT WENT UP THAT DAY WAS CALLED CHALLENGER...

"...AND ONE MINUTE AND THIRTEEN SECONDS LATER, MY DREAMS WERE BLASTED LIKE THIN SHIT AGAINST A PINE-BOARD FENCE.

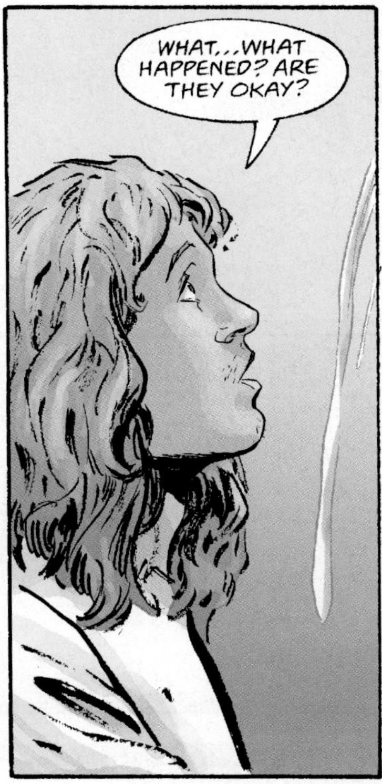
WHAT...WHAT HAPPENED? ARE THEY OKAY?

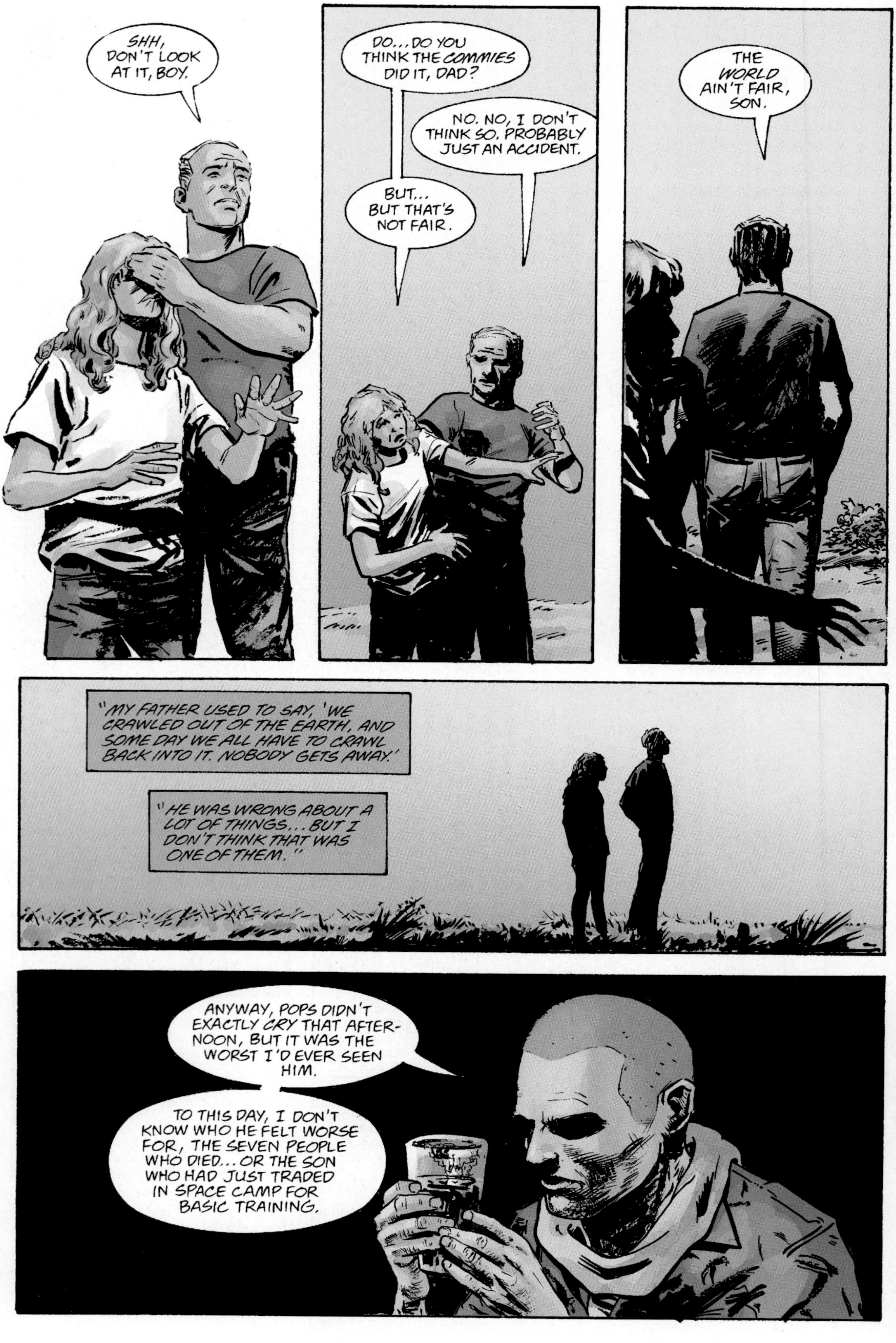

SHH, DON'T LOOK AT IT, BOY.
DO... DO YOU THINK THE *COMMIES* DID IT, DAD?
NO. NO, I DON'T THINK SO. PROBABLY JUST AN ACCIDENT.
BUT... BUT THAT'S NOT FAIR.
THE *WORLD* AIN'T FAIR, SON.
"MY FATHER USED TO SAY, 'WE CRAWLED OUT OF THE EARTH, AND SOME DAY WE ALL HAVE TO CRAWL BACK INTO IT. NOBODY GETS AWAY.'
"HE WAS WRONG ABOUT A LOT OF THINGS... BUT I DON'T THINK THAT WAS ONE OF THEM."
ANYWAY, POPS DIDN'T EXACTLY *CRY* THAT AFTER-NOON, BUT IT WAS THE WORST I'D EVER SEEN HIM.
TO THIS DAY, I DON'T KNOW WHO HE FELT WORSE FOR, THE SEVEN PEOPLE WHO DIED... OR THE SON WHO HAD JUST TRADED IN SPACE CAMP FOR BASIC TRAINING.

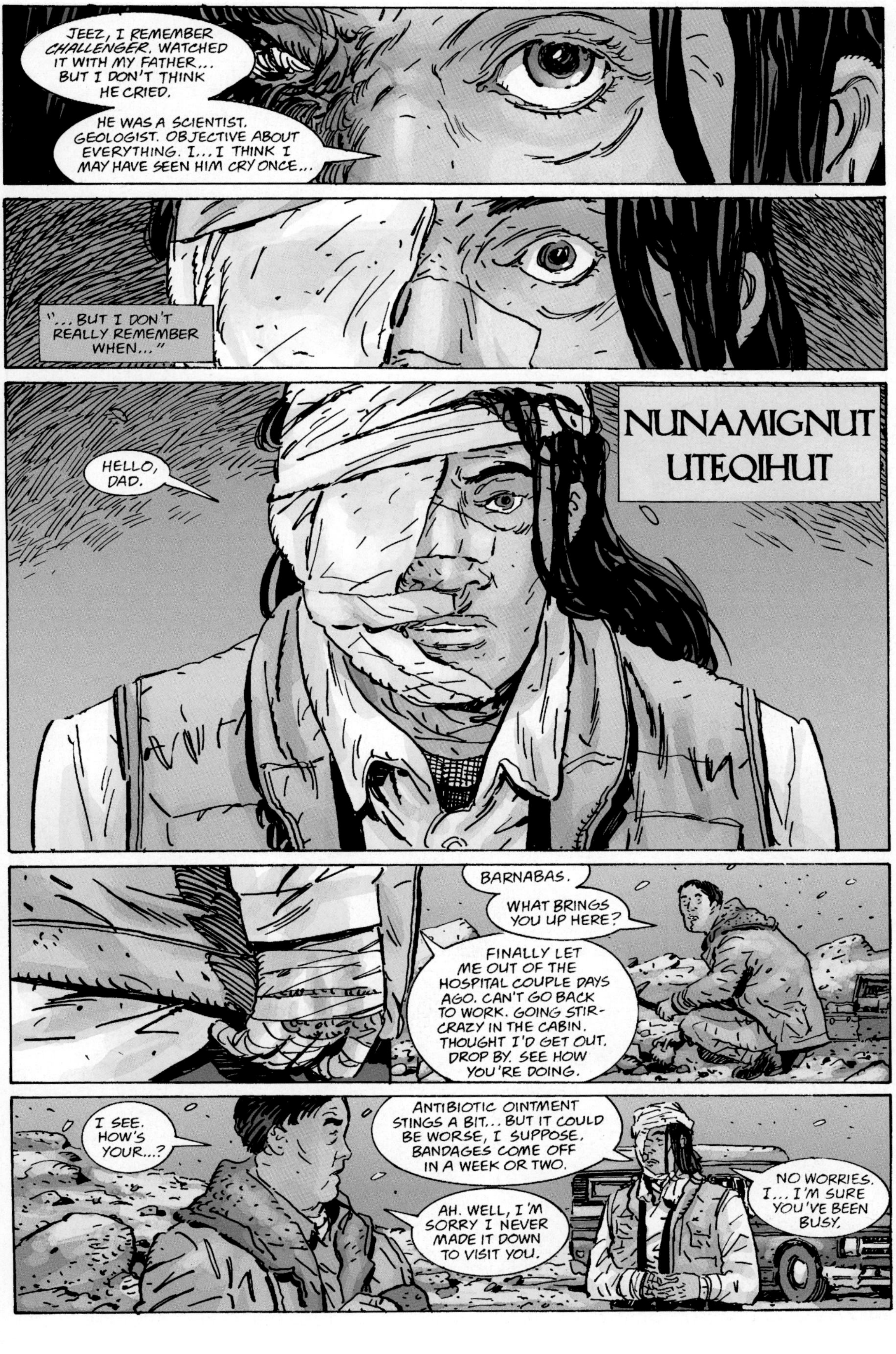
JEEZ, I REMEMBER CHALLENGER. WATCHED IT WITH MY FATHER... BUT I DON'T THINK HE CRIED.
HE WAS A SCIENTIST. GEOLOGIST. OBJECTIVE ABOUT EVERYTHING. I... I THINK I MAY HAVE SEEN HIM CRY ONCE...
"...BUT I DON'T REALLY REMEMBER WHEN..."
NUNAMIGNUT UTEQIHUT
HELLO, DAD.
BARNABAS.
WHAT BRINGS YOU UP HERE?
FINALLY LET ME OUT OF THE HOSPITAL COUPLE DAYS AGO. CAN'T GO BACK TO WORK. GOING STIR-CRAZY IN THE CABIN. THOUGHT I'D GET OUT. DROP BY. SEE HOW YOU'RE DOING.
I SEE. HOW'S YOUR...?
ANTIBIOTIC OINTMENT STINGS A BIT... BUT IT COULD BE WORSE, I SUPPOSE. BANDAGES COME OFF IN A WEEK OR TWO.
AH. WELL, I'M SORRY I NEVER MADE IT DOWN TO VISIT YOU.
NO WORRIES. I... I'M SURE YOU'VE BEEN BUSY.

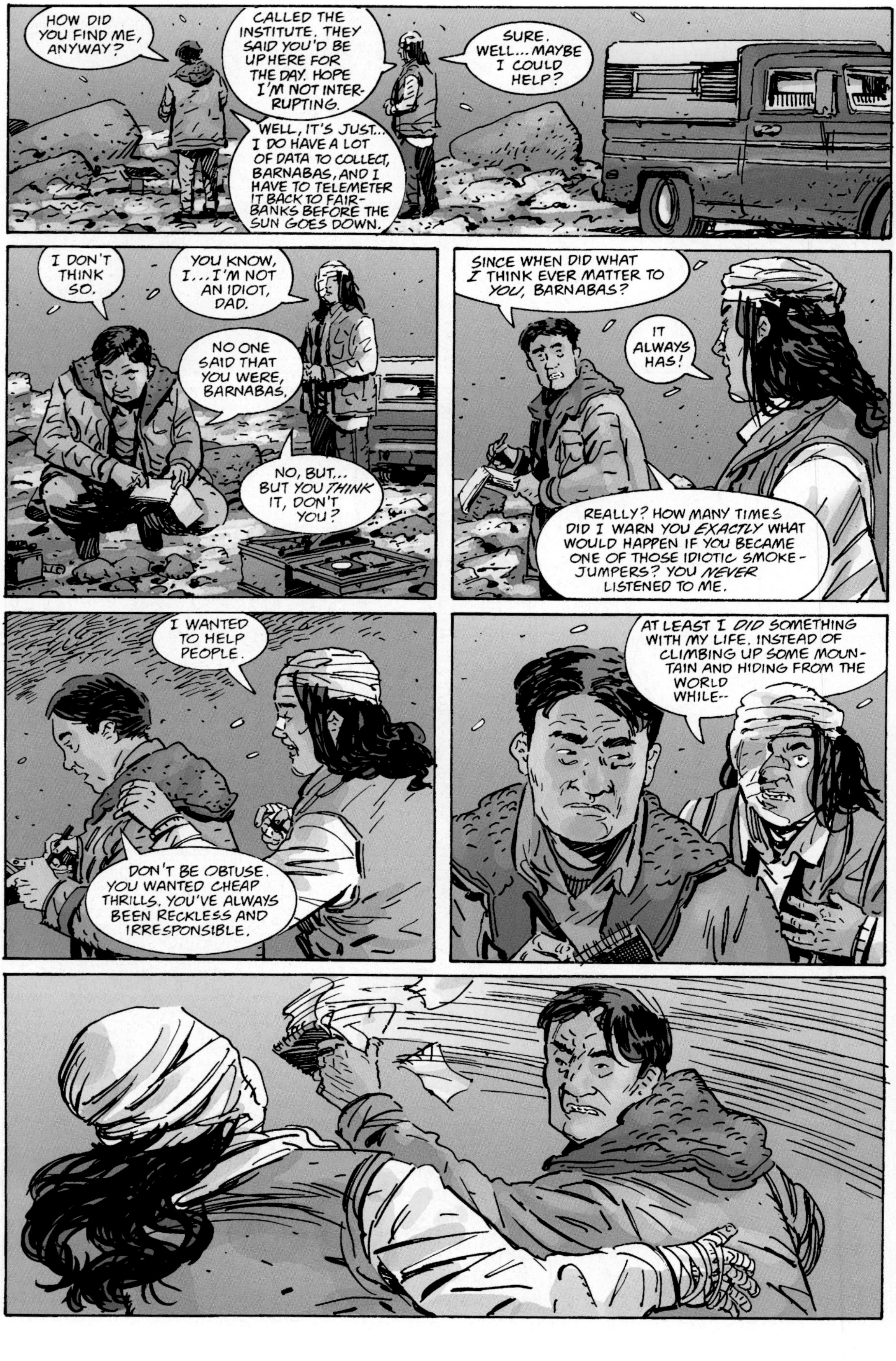
HOW DID YOU FIND ME, ANYWAY?
CALLED THE INSTITUTE. THEY SAID YOU'D BE UP HERE FOR THE DAY. HOPE I'M NOT INTER-RUPTING.
SURE. WELL... MAYBE I COULD HELP?
WELL, IT'S JUST... I DO HAVE A LOT OF DATA TO COLLECT, BARNABAS, AND I HAVE TO TELEMETER IT BACK TO FAIR-BANKS BEFORE THE SUN GOES DOWN.
I DON'T THINK SO.
YOU KNOW, I... I'M NOT AN IDIOT, DAD.
NO ONE SAID THAT YOU WERE, BARNABAS.
NO, BUT... BUT YOU THINK IT, DON'T YOU?
SINCE WHEN DID WHAT I THINK EVER MATTER TO YOU, BARNABAS?
IT ALWAYS HAS!
REALLY? HOW MANY TIMES DID I WARN YOU EXACTLY WHAT WOULD HAPPEN IF YOU BECAME ONE OF THOSE IDIOTIC SMOKE-JUMPERS? YOU NEVER LISTENED TO ME.
I WANTED TO HELP PEOPLE.
DON'T BE OBTUSE. YOU WANTED CHEAP THRILLS. YOU'VE ALWAYS BEEN RECKLESS AND IRRESPONSIBLE.
AT LEAST I DID SOMETHING WITH MY LIFE. INSTEAD OF CLIMBING UP SOME MOUN-TAIN AND HIDING FROM THE WORLD WHILE--

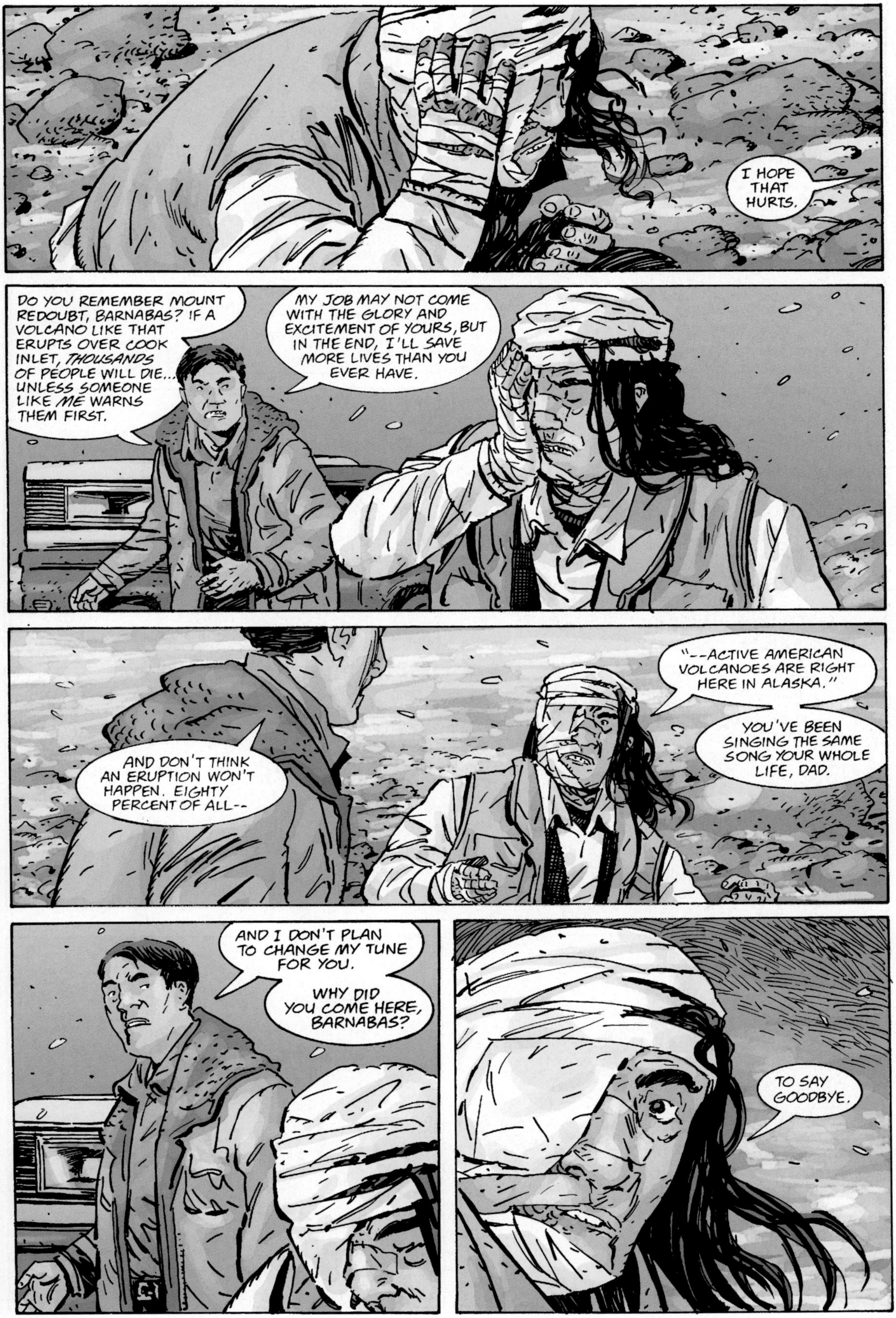
I HOPE THAT HURTS.
DO YOU REMEMBER MOUNT REDOUBT, BARNABAS? IF A VOLCANO LIKE THAT ERUPTS OVER COOK INLET, *THOUSANDS* OF PEOPLE WILL DIE... UNLESS SOMEONE LIKE *ME* WARNS THEM FIRST.
MY JOB MAY NOT COME WITH THE GLORY AND EXCITEMENT OF YOURS, BUT IN THE END, I'LL SAVE MORE LIVES THAN YOU EVER HAVE.
AND DON'T THINK AN ERUPTION WON'T HAPPEN. EIGHTY PERCENT OF ALL--
"--ACTIVE AMERICAN VOLCANOES ARE RIGHT HERE IN ALASKA."
YOU'VE BEEN SINGING THE SAME SONG YOUR WHOLE LIFE, DAD.
AND I DON'T PLAN TO CHANGE MY TUNE FOR YOU.
WHY DID YOU COME HERE, BARNABAS?
TO SAY GOODBYE.

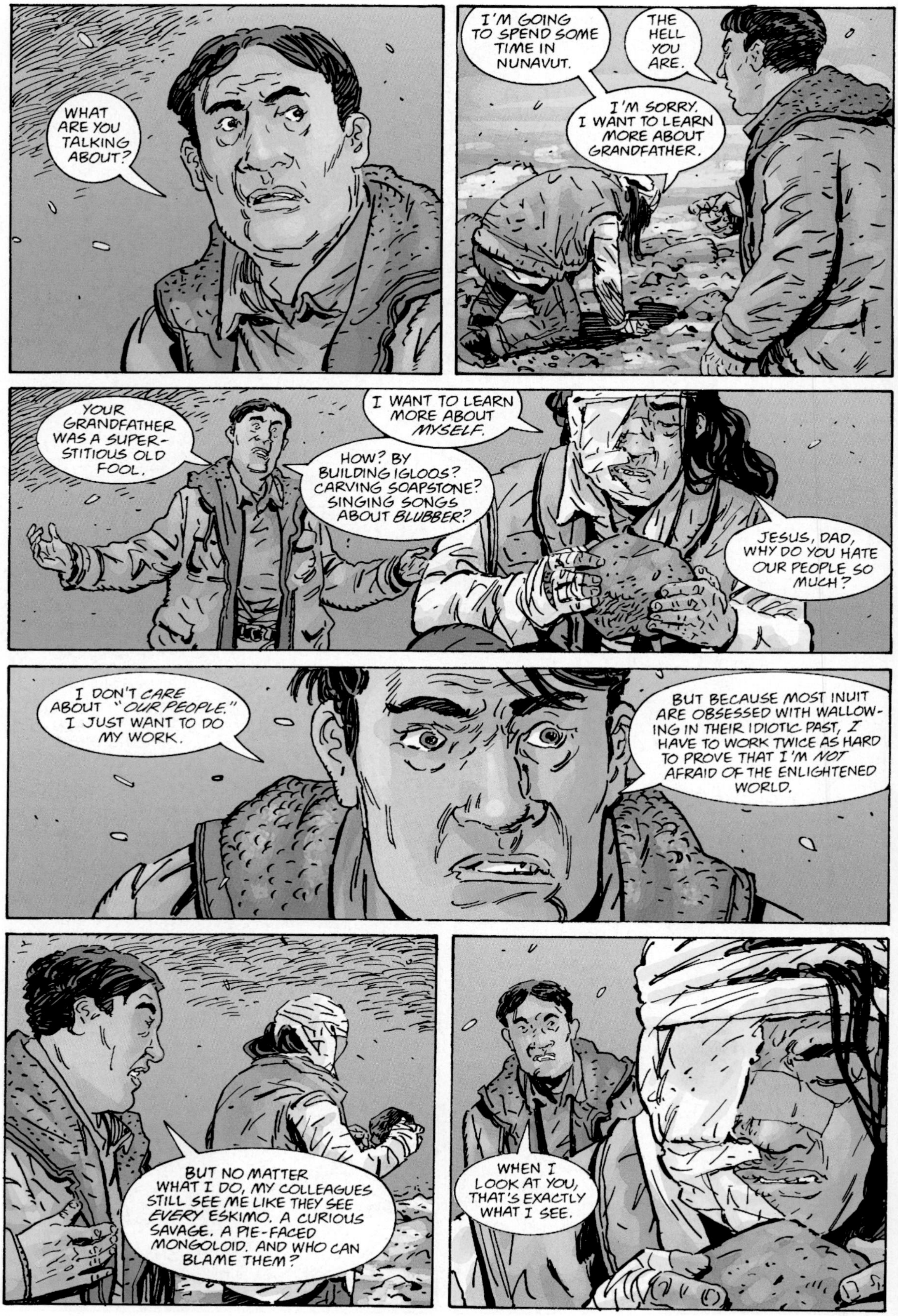
WHAT ARE YOU TALKING ABOUT?
I'M GOING TO SPEND SOME TIME IN NUNAVUT.
THE HELL YOU ARE.
I'M SORRY. I WANT TO LEARN MORE ABOUT GRANDFATHER.
YOUR GRANDFATHER WAS A SUPER-STITIOUS OLD FOOL.
I WANT TO LEARN MORE ABOUT MYSELF.
HOW? BY BUILDING IGLOOS? CARVING SOAPSTONE? SINGING SONGS ABOUT BLUBBER?
JESUS, DAD, WHY DO YOU HATE OUR PEOPLE SO MUCH?
I DON'T CARE ABOUT "OUR PEOPLE." I JUST WANT TO DO MY WORK.
BUT BECAUSE MOST INUIT ARE OBSESSED WITH WALLOW-ING IN THEIR IDIOTIC PAST, I HAVE TO WORK TWICE AS HARD TO PROVE THAT I'M NOT AFRAID OF THE ENLIGHTENED WORLD.
BUT NO MATTER WHAT I DO, MY COLLEAGUES STILL SEE ME LIKE THEY SEE EVERY ESKIMO. A CURIOUS SAVAGE. A PIE-FACED MONGOLOID. AND WHO CAN BLAME THEM?
WHEN I LOOK AT YOU, THAT'S EXACTLY WHAT I SEE.

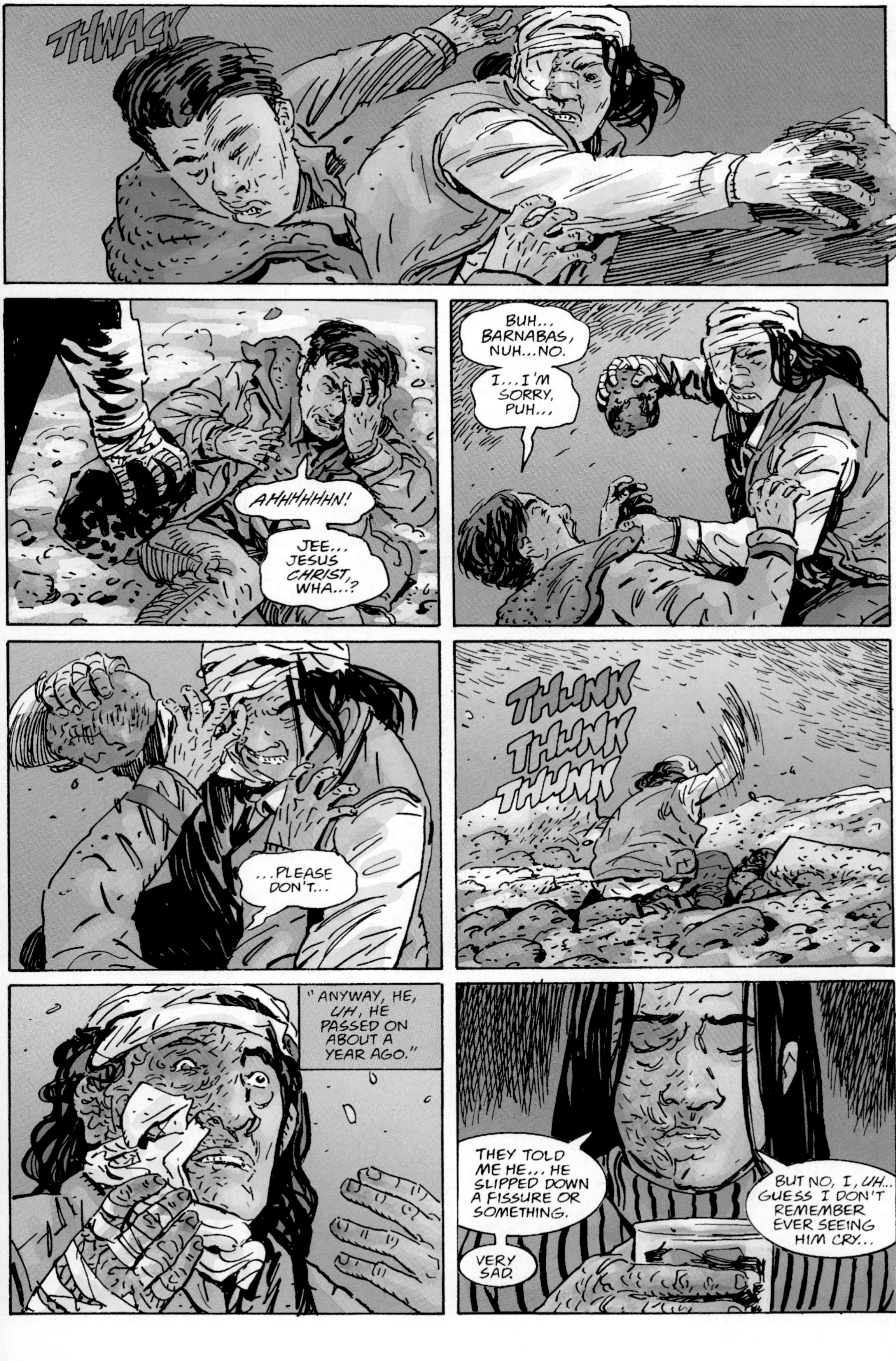
THWACK
AHHHHHHN!
JEE... JESUS CHRIST, WHA...?
BUH... BARNABAS, NUH...NO.
I...I'M SORRY, PUH...
...PLEASE DON'T...
THUNK
THUNK
THUNK
"ANYWAY, HE, UH, HE PASSED ON ABOUT A YEAR AGO."
THEY TOLD ME HE... HE SLIPPED DOWN A FISSURE OR SOMETHING.
VERY SAD.
BUT NO, I, UH... GUESS I DON'T REMEMBER EVER SEEING HIM CRY...

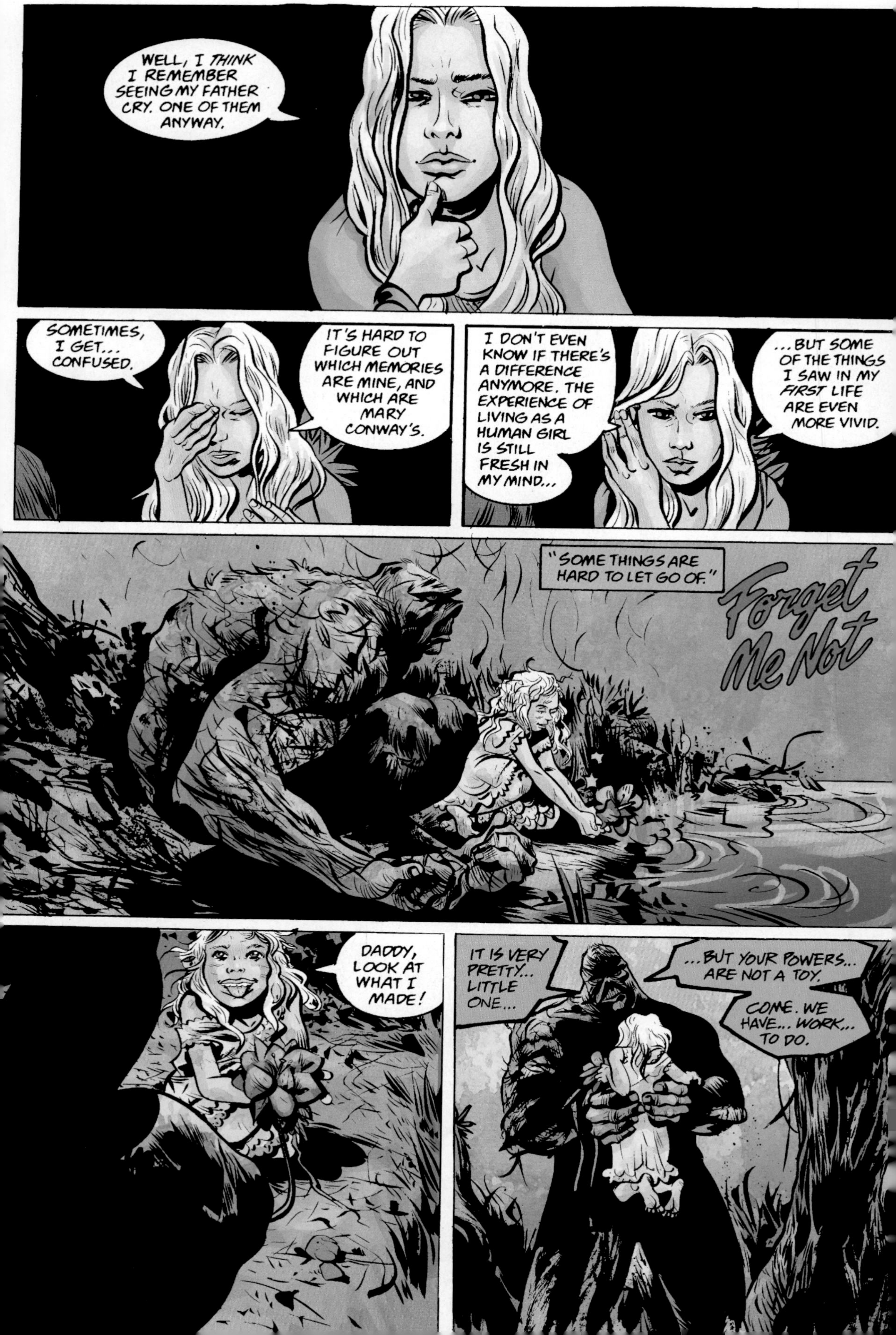
WELL, I *THINK* I REMEMBER SEEING MY FATHER CRY. ONE OF THEM ANYWAY.
SOMETIMES, I GET... CONFUSED.
IT'S HARD TO FIGURE OUT WHICH MEMORIES ARE MINE, AND WHICH ARE MARY CONWAY'S.
I DON'T EVEN KNOW IF THERE'S A DIFFERENCE ANYMORE. THE EXPERIENCE OF LIVING AS A HUMAN GIRL IS STILL FRESH IN MY MIND...
...BUT SOME OF THE THINGS I SAW IN MY *FIRST* LIFE ARE EVEN MORE VIVID.
"SOME THINGS ARE HARD TO LET GO OF."
Forget Me Not
DADDY, LOOK AT WHAT I MADE!
IT IS VERY PRETTY... LITTLE ONE...
...BUT YOUR POWERS... ARE NOT A TOY.
COME. WE HAVE... WORK... TO DO.

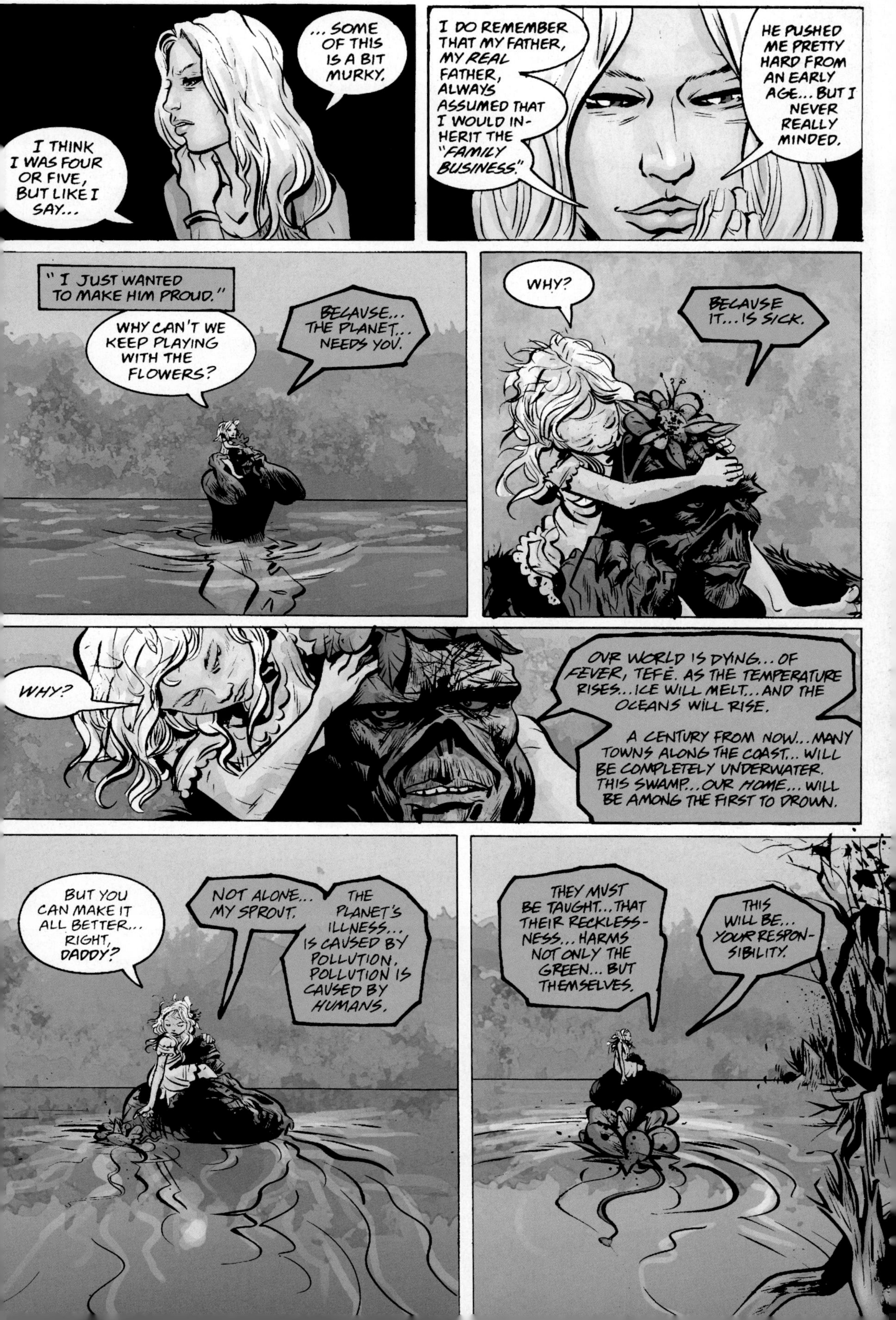
I THINK I WAS FOUR OR FIVE, BUT LIKE I SAY...
...SOME OF THIS IS A BIT MURKY.
I DO REMEMBER THAT MY FATHER, MY REAL FATHER, ALWAYS ASSUMED THAT I WOULD INHERIT THE "FAMILY BUSINESS."
HE PUSHED ME PRETTY HARD FROM AN EARLY AGE... BUT I NEVER REALLY MINDED.
"I JUST WANTED TO MAKE HIM PROUD."
WHY CAN'T WE KEEP PLAYING WITH THE FLOWERS?
BECAUSE... THE PLANET... NEEDS YOU.
WHY?
BECAUSE IT... IS SICK.
WHY?
OUR WORLD IS DYING... OF FEVER, TEFÉ. AS THE TEMPERATURE RISES...ICE WILL MELT... AND THE OCEANS WILL RISE.
A CENTURY FROM NOW... MANY TOWNS ALONG THE COAST... WILL BE COMPLETELY UNDERWATER. THIS SWAMP... OUR HOME... WILL BE AMONG THE FIRST TO DROWN.
BUT YOU CAN MAKE IT ALL BETTER... RIGHT, DADDY?
NOT ALONE... MY SPROUT.
THE PLANET'S ILLNESS... IS CAUSED BY POLLUTION. POLLUTION IS CAUSED BY HUMANS.
THEY MUST BE TAUGHT... THAT THEIR RECKLESSNESS... HARMS NOT ONLY THE GREEN... BUT THEMSELVES.
THIS WILL BE... YOUR RESPONSIBILITY.

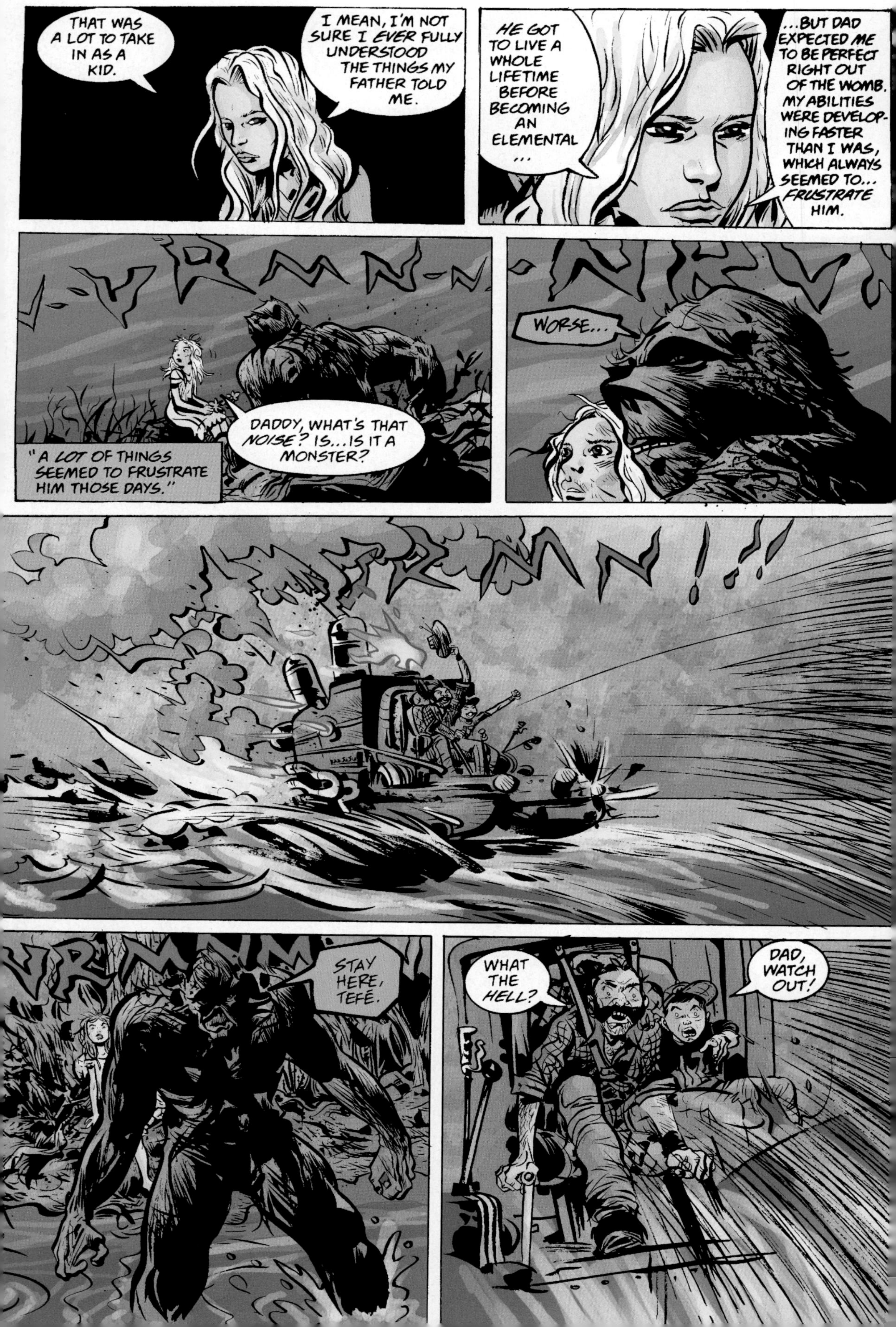
THAT WAS A LOT TO TAKE IN AS A KID.
I MEAN, I'M NOT SURE I EVER FULLY UNDERSTOOD THE THINGS MY FATHER TOLD ME.
HE GOT TO LIVE A WHOLE LIFETIME BEFORE BECOMING AN ELEMENTAL ...
...BUT DAD EXPECTED ME TO BE PERFECT RIGHT OUT OF THE WOMB. MY ABILITIES WERE DEVELOPING FASTER THAN I WAS, WHICH ALWAYS SEEMED TO... FRUSTRATE HIM.
-VRMN-N-
"A LOT OF THINGS SEEMED TO FRUSTRATE HIM THOSE DAYS."
DADDY, WHAT'S THAT NOISE? IS...IS IT A MONSTER?
-NRVN
WORSE...
VRRMN!!!
VRMNM
STAY HERE, TEFÉ.
WHAT THE HELL?
DAD, WATCH OUT!

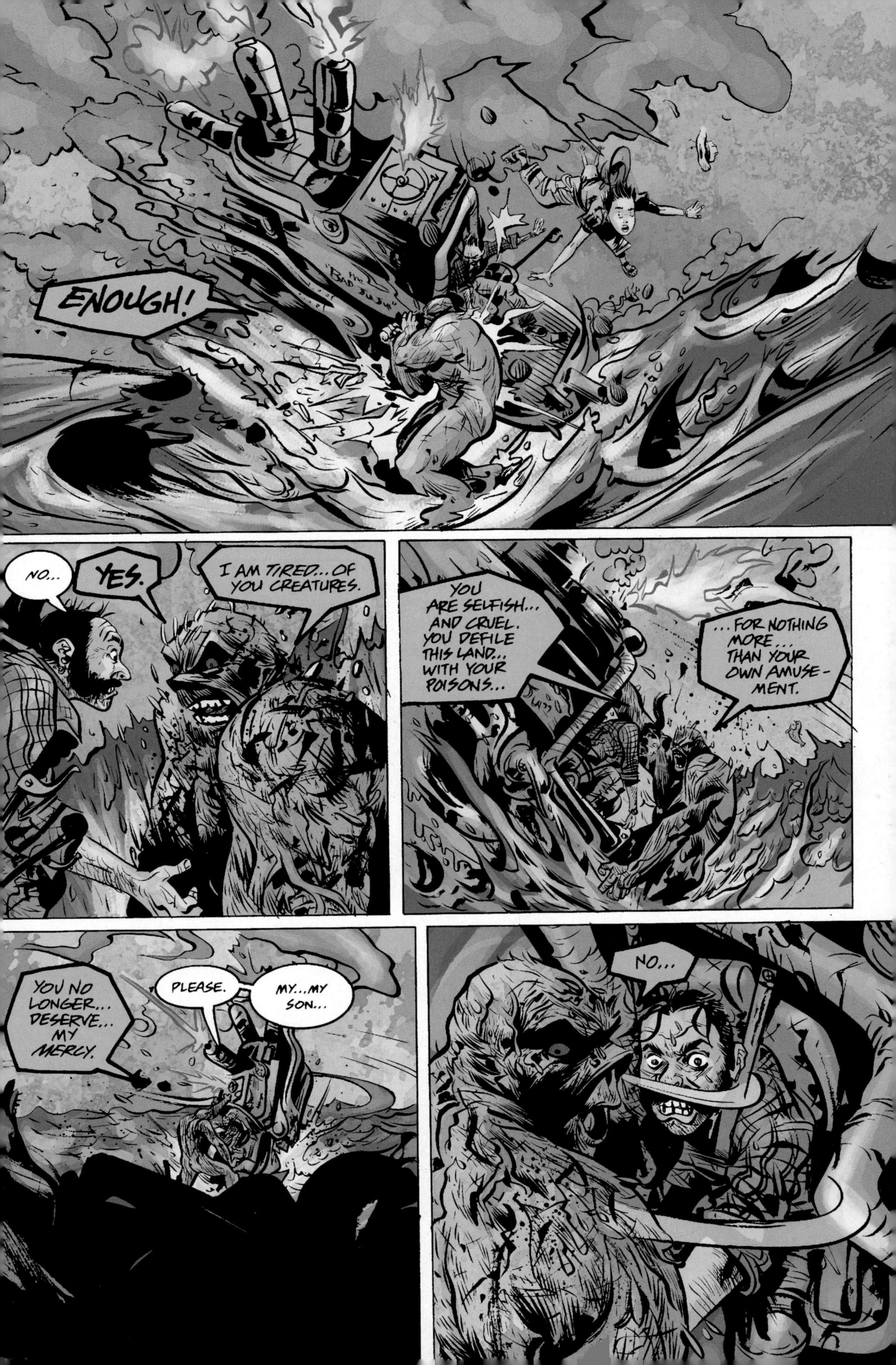
ENOUGH!
NO...
YES.
I AM TIRED... OF YOU CREATURES.
YOU ARE SELFISH... AND CRUEL. YOU DEFILE THIS LAND... WITH YOUR POISONS...
...FOR NOTHING MORE... THAN YOUR OWN AMUSE-MENT.
YOU NO LONGER... DESERVE... MY MERCY.
PLEASE.
MY...MY SON...
NO...

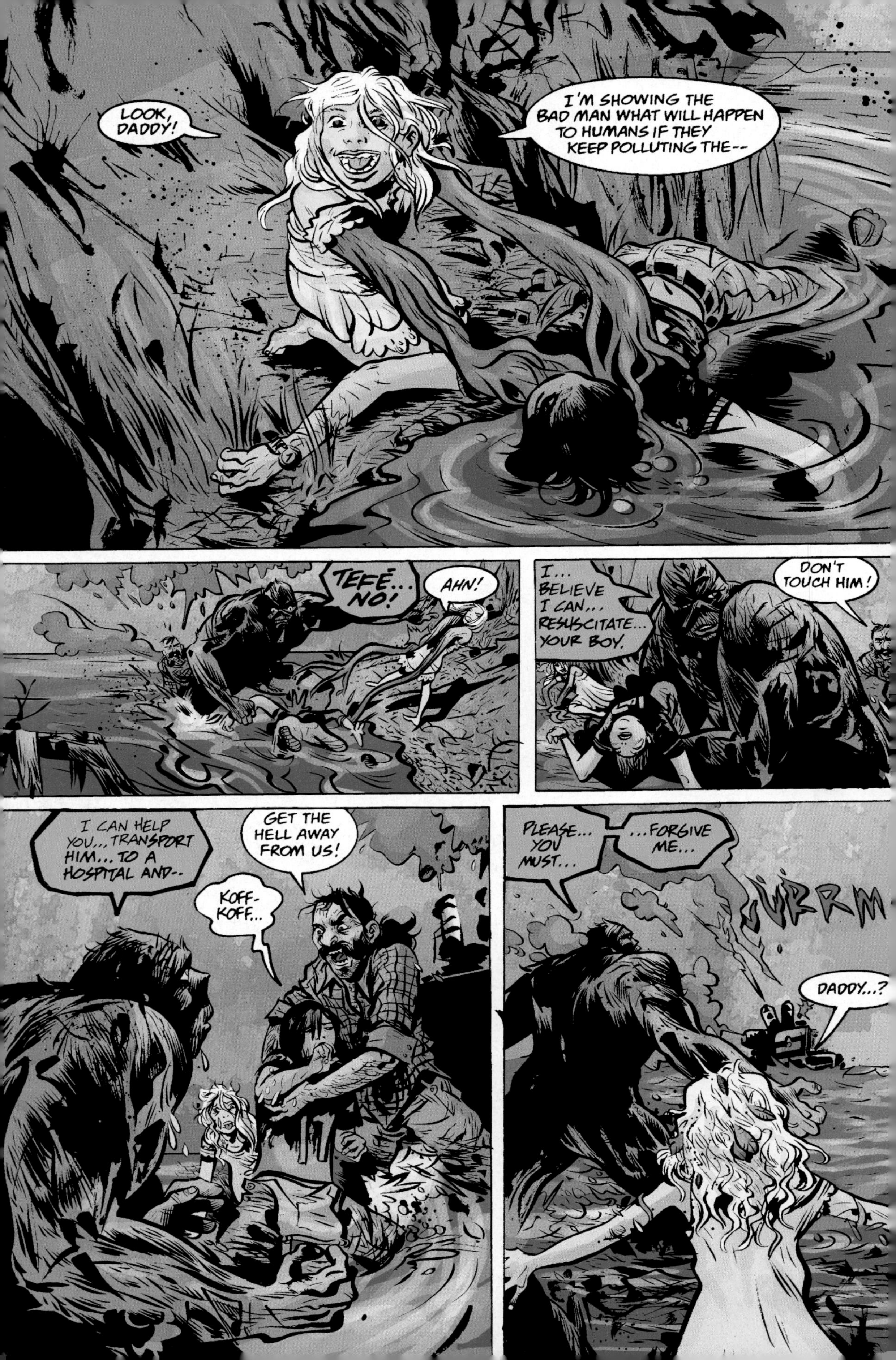
LOOK, DADDY!
I'M SHOWING THE BAD MAN WHAT WILL HAPPEN TO HUMANS IF THEY KEEP POLLUTING THE--
TEFÉ... NO!
AHN!
I... BELIEVE I CAN... RESUSCITATE... YOUR BOY.
DON'T TOUCH HIM!
I CAN HELP YOU... TRANSPORT HIM... TO A HOSPITAL AND--
GET THE HELL AWAY FROM US!
KOFF-KOFF...
PLEASE... YOU MUST...
...FORGIVE ME...
VRRM
DADDY...?

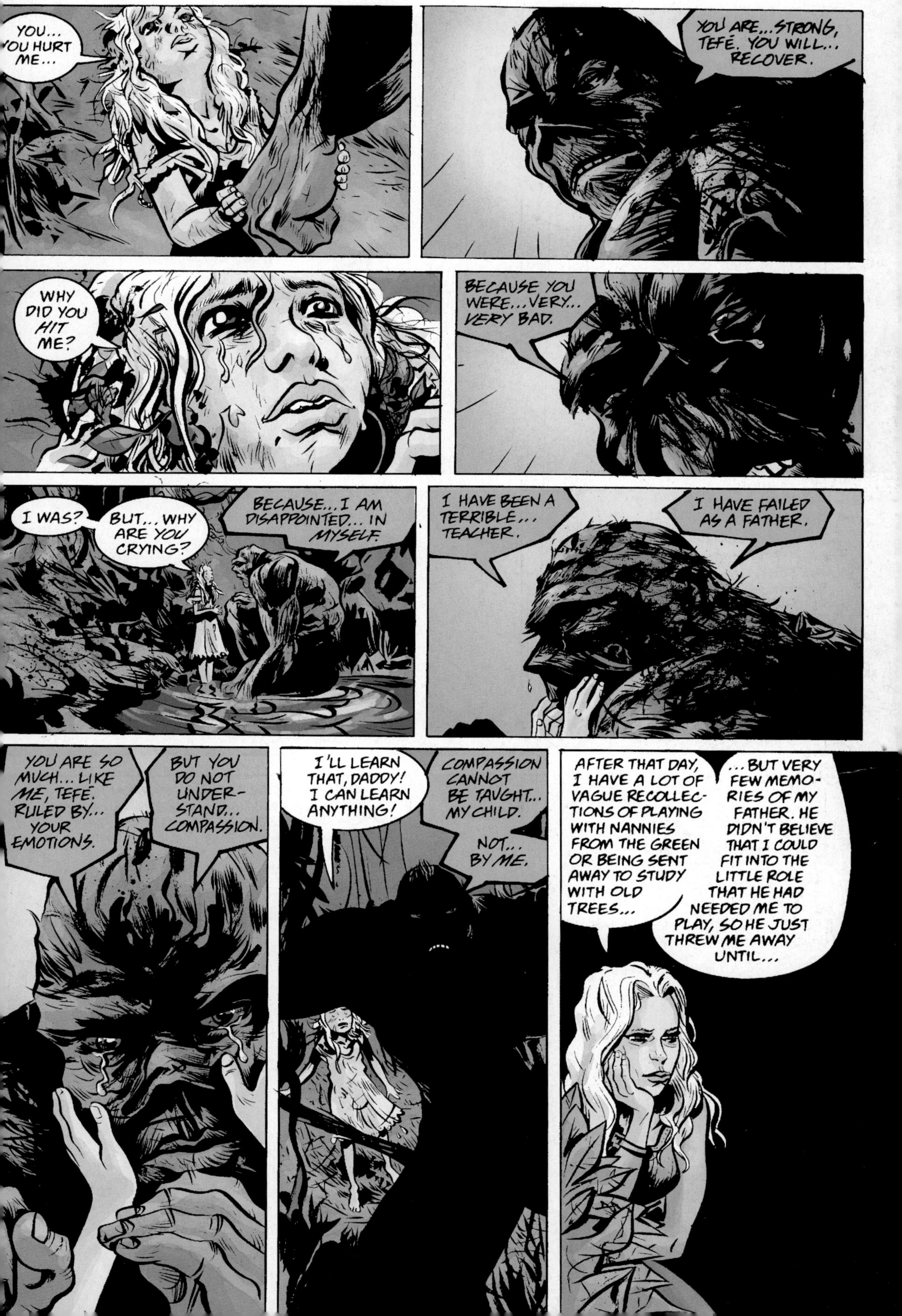
YOU... YOU HURT ME...
YOU ARE... STRONG, TEFÉ. YOU WILL... RECOVER.
WHY DID YOU HIT ME?
BECAUSE YOU WERE... VERY... VERY BAD.
I WAS?
BUT... WHY ARE YOU CRYING?
BECAUSE... I AM DISAPPOINTED... IN MYSELF.
I HAVE BEEN A TERRIBLE... TEACHER.
I HAVE FAILED AS A FATHER.
YOU ARE SO MUCH... LIKE ME, TEFÉ. RULED BY... YOUR EMOTIONS.
BUT YOU DO NOT UNDER-STAND... COMPASSION.
I'LL LEARN THAT, DADDY! I CAN LEARN ANYTHING!
COMPASSION CANNOT BE TAUGHT... MY CHILD.
NOT... BY ME.
AFTER THAT DAY, I HAVE A LOT OF VAGUE RECOLLEC-TIONS OF PLAYING WITH NANNIES FROM THE GREEN OR BEING SENT AWAY TO STUDY WITH OLD TREES...
...BUT VERY FEW MEMO-RIES OF MY FATHER. HE DIDN'T BELIEVE THAT I COULD FIT INTO THE LITTLE ROLE THAT HE HAD NEEDED ME TO PLAY, SO HE JUST THREW ME AWAY UNTIL...

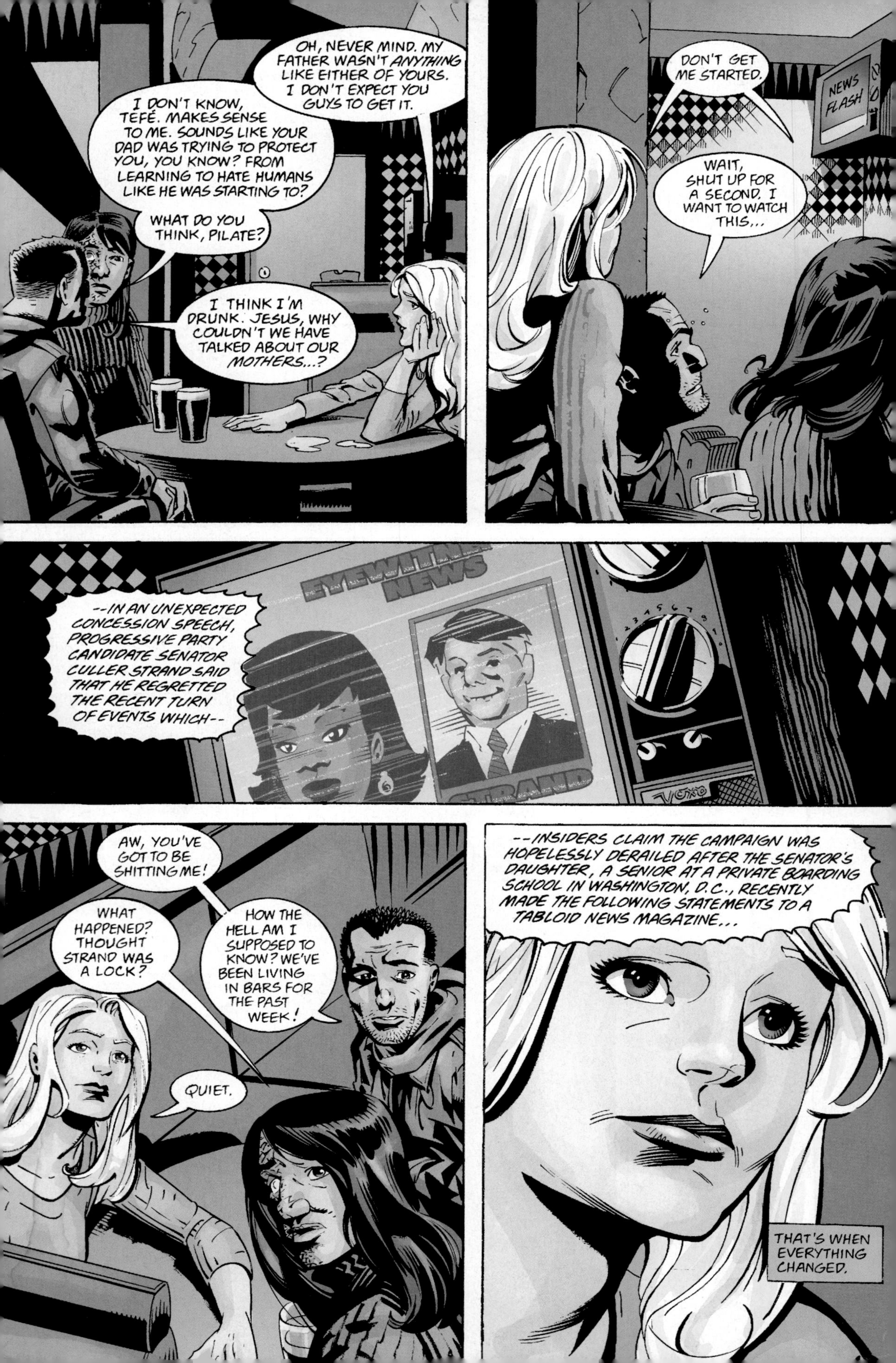
OH, NEVER MIND. MY FATHER WASN'T ANYTHING LIKE EITHER OF YOURS. I DON'T EXPECT YOU GUYS TO GET IT.
I DON'T KNOW, TEFÉ. MAKES SENSE TO ME. SOUNDS LIKE YOUR DAD WAS TRYING TO PROTECT YOU, YOU KNOW? FROM LEARNING TO HATE HUMANS LIKE HE WAS STARTING TO?
WHAT DO YOU THINK, PILATE?
I THINK I'M DRUNK. JESUS, WHY COULDN'T WE HAVE TALKED ABOUT OUR MOTHERS...?
DON'T GET ME STARTED.
NEWS FLASH
WAIT, SHUT UP FOR A SECOND. I WANT TO WATCH THIS...
NEWS
--IN AN UNEXPECTED CONCESSION SPEECH, PROGRESSIVE PARTY CANDIDATE SENATOR CULLER STRAND SAID THAT HE REGRETTED THE RECENT TURN OF EVENTS WHICH--
STRAND
AW, YOU'VE GOT TO BE SHITTING ME!
WHAT HAPPENED? THOUGHT STRAND WAS A LOCK?
HOW THE HELL AM I SUPPOSED TO KNOW? WE'VE BEEN LIVING IN BARS FOR THE PAST WEEK!
QUIET.
--INSIDERS CLAIM THE CAMPAIGN WAS HOPELESSLY DERAILED AFTER THE SENATOR'S DAUGHTER, A SENIOR AT A PRIVATE BOARDING SCHOOL IN WASHINGTON, D.C., RECENTLY MADE THE FOLLOWING STATEMENTS TO A TABLOID NEWS MAGAZINE...
THAT'S WHEN EVERYTHING CHANGED.

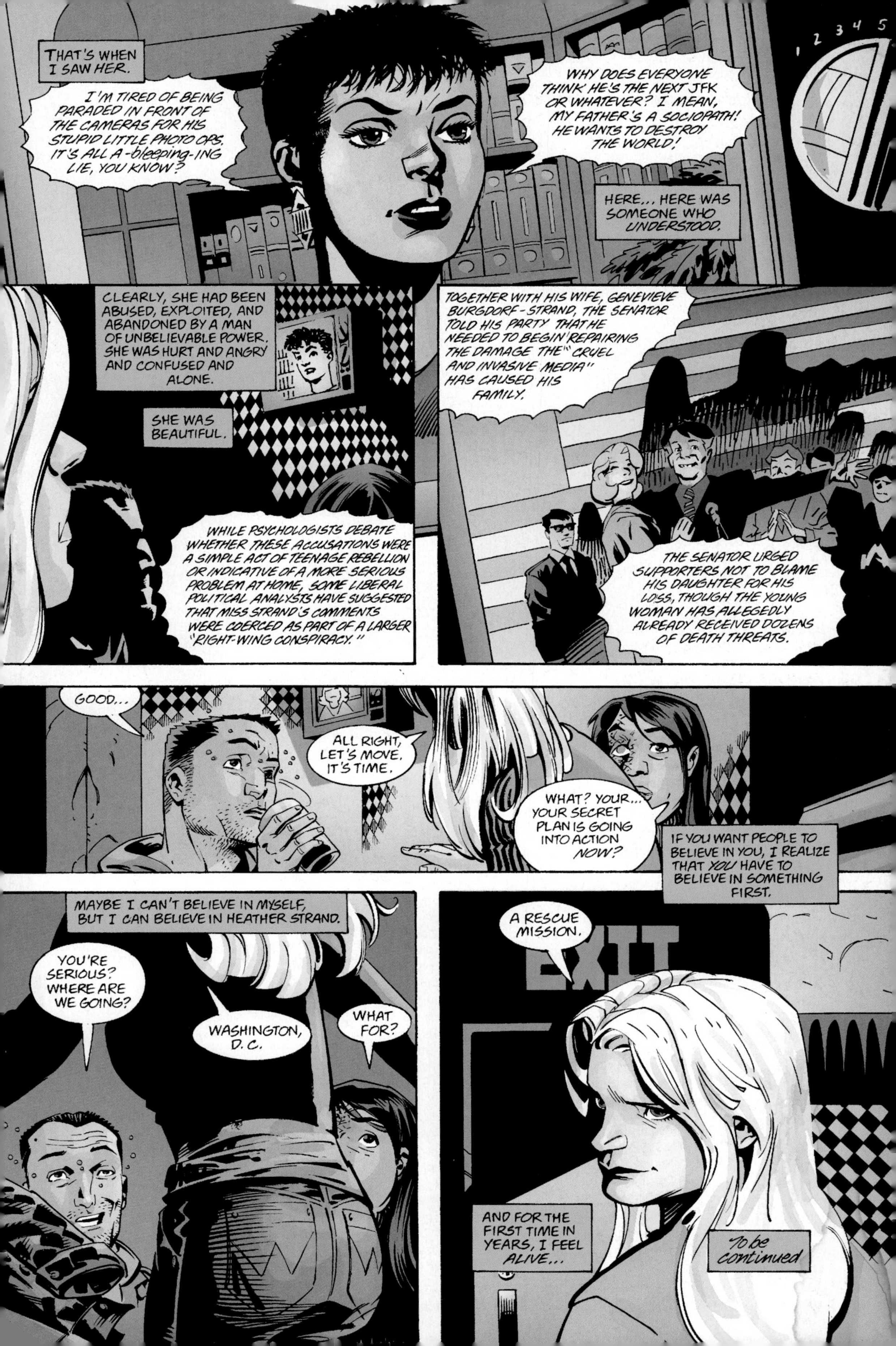
THAT'S WHEN I SAW HER.
I'M TIRED OF BEING PARADED IN FRONT OF THE CAMERAS FOR HIS STUPID LITTLE PHOTO OPS. IT'S ALL A -bleeping-ING LIE, YOU KNOW?
WHY DOES EVERYONE THINK HE'S THE NEXT JFK OR WHATEVER? I MEAN, MY FATHER'S A SOCIOPATH! HE WANTS TO DESTROY THE WORLD!
HERE... HERE WAS SOMEONE WHO UNDERSTOOD.
1 2 3 4 5
CLEARLY, SHE HAD BEEN ABUSED, EXPLOITED, AND ABANDONED BY A MAN OF UNBELIEVABLE POWER. SHE WAS HURT AND ANGRY AND CONFUSED AND ALONE.
SHE WAS BEAUTIFUL.
WHILE PSYCHOLOGISTS DEBATE WHETHER THESE ACCUSATIONS WERE A SIMPLE ACT OF TEENAGE REBELLION OR INDICATIVE OF A MORE SERIOUS PROBLEM AT HOME, SOME LIBERAL POLITICAL ANALYSTS HAVE SUGGESTED THAT MISS STRAND'S COMMENTS WERE COERCED AS PART OF A LARGER "RIGHT-WING CONSPIRACY."
TOGETHER WITH HIS WIFE, GENEVIEVE BURGDORF-STRAND, THE SENATOR TOLD HIS PARTY THAT HE NEEDED TO BEGIN REPAIRING THE DAMAGE THE "CRUEL AND INVASIVE MEDIA" HAS CAUSED HIS FAMILY.
THE SENATOR URGED SUPPORTERS NOT TO BLAME HIS DAUGHTER FOR HIS LOSS, THOUGH THE YOUNG WOMAN HAS ALLEGEDLY ALREADY RECEIVED DOZENS OF DEATH THREATS.
GOOD...
ALL RIGHT, LET'S MOVE. IT'S TIME.
WHAT? YOUR... YOUR SECRET PLAN IS GOING INTO ACTION NOW?
IF YOU WANT PEOPLE TO BELIEVE IN YOU, I REALIZE THAT YOU HAVE TO BELIEVE IN SOMETHING FIRST.
MAYBE I CAN'T BELIEVE IN MYSELF, BUT I CAN BELIEVE IN HEATHER STRAND.
YOU'RE SERIOUS? WHERE ARE WE GOING?
WASHINGTON, D.C.
WHAT FOR?
A RESCUE MISSION.
EXIT
AND FOR THE FIRST TIME IN YEARS, I FEEL ALIVE...
To be continued

TEFÉ

Legal Name: Tefé Holland
Base of Operations: Mobile
Height: 5'6"*
Eyes: Green*
First Sighting:

Occupation: Earth Elemental
Marital Status: Single
Weight: 125 lbs.*
Hair: White*

(as Sprout) October, 1987 [FILE: ST-VOL 2- 65]
(as infant) December, 1989 [FILE: ST-VOL 2-90]
(as teenager) May, 2000 [FILE: ST-VOL 3-1]

*Tefé may be able to use her Elemental abilities to alter her own appearance.

Madam Director, I realize you know this subject's history better than anyone, but please indulge me for this brief synopsis of her life so far. It still confuses the hell out of me, and I would appreciate the opportunity to again attempt to make sense of it in my own head.

Believing Alec Holland, the Earth Elemental known as "Swamp Thing," to be dead, the collective consciousness of nature known as the Green created a new protector in the form of a young Sprout. When the Green discovered that Holland was still alive, they ordered this now-redundant Sprout executed. A reprieve came in the form of hellbound magician John Constantine. Alec inhabited his body to impregnate his human wife, Abigail Arcane Cable Holland, with the "seed" of this Sprout. Cloaked in the flesh and blood of an infant child, this first human Elemental was given the name Tefé (after the river of the same name, I presume). With the ability to manipulate both vegetation and flesh on an Elemental scale, she may be the most powerful creature who has ever existed.

Though her parents hoped that Tefé would heal the growing rift between the plant kingdom and humanity, the Green tried to convince the girl that her actual destiny was to save "their" ailing planet by destroying mankind. Frightened and confused, a runaway Tefé took several human lives before eventually being found by her parents. Knowing that their wayward child was too powerful to simply be destroyed, Alec and Abby attempted to "deprogram" Tefé by placing her far from the swamps. They placed her with a loving human family that believed her to be their own gravely ill daughter, Mary Conway.

Apparently, Tefé's true nature was recently reawakened, as she murdered two of the Conway girl's friends and used her powers to create a lifeless simulacrum of Mary herself, presumably to convince Alec and Abby that their daughter is dead. Refusing to pay blind allegiance to the Green or humanity, Tefé, I suspect, is now looking for something she can trust to tell her what her true purpose is... and it's become very clear to this agent that she's willing to destroy anything that gets in her way.

DAPHNE

Legal Name: N/A

Occupation: Potted Plant

Base of Operations: Mobile

Height: 16 inches

Weight: 3 lbs.

First Sighting: May, 2000 [FILE: ST-VOL 3-1]

I've written a lot of reports in my career, but this is a first...

This small evergreen laurel tree (Laurus nobilis) appears to be the Holland girl's closest companion. Doubtlessly named after the nymph from classical mythology who became a laurel tree to escape the lustful pursuit of the god Apollo, Daphne is the only remnant of Tefé's life as Mary Conway that she still carries with her.

Strange as it sounds, I believe she definitely shares some kind of bond with this tree. Because Tefé seems to have significantly less affection for most humans, threatening the plant may ultimately prove the best way to exploit and manipulate the girl.

Though I never saw Tefé without this potted tree during their first trek across America, I have not seen Daphne since the girl's return to the Los Angeles area. Perhaps she left her precious plant with someone before stowing away on an oil tanker bound for Alaska, but I have no idea who Tefé trusts that much...

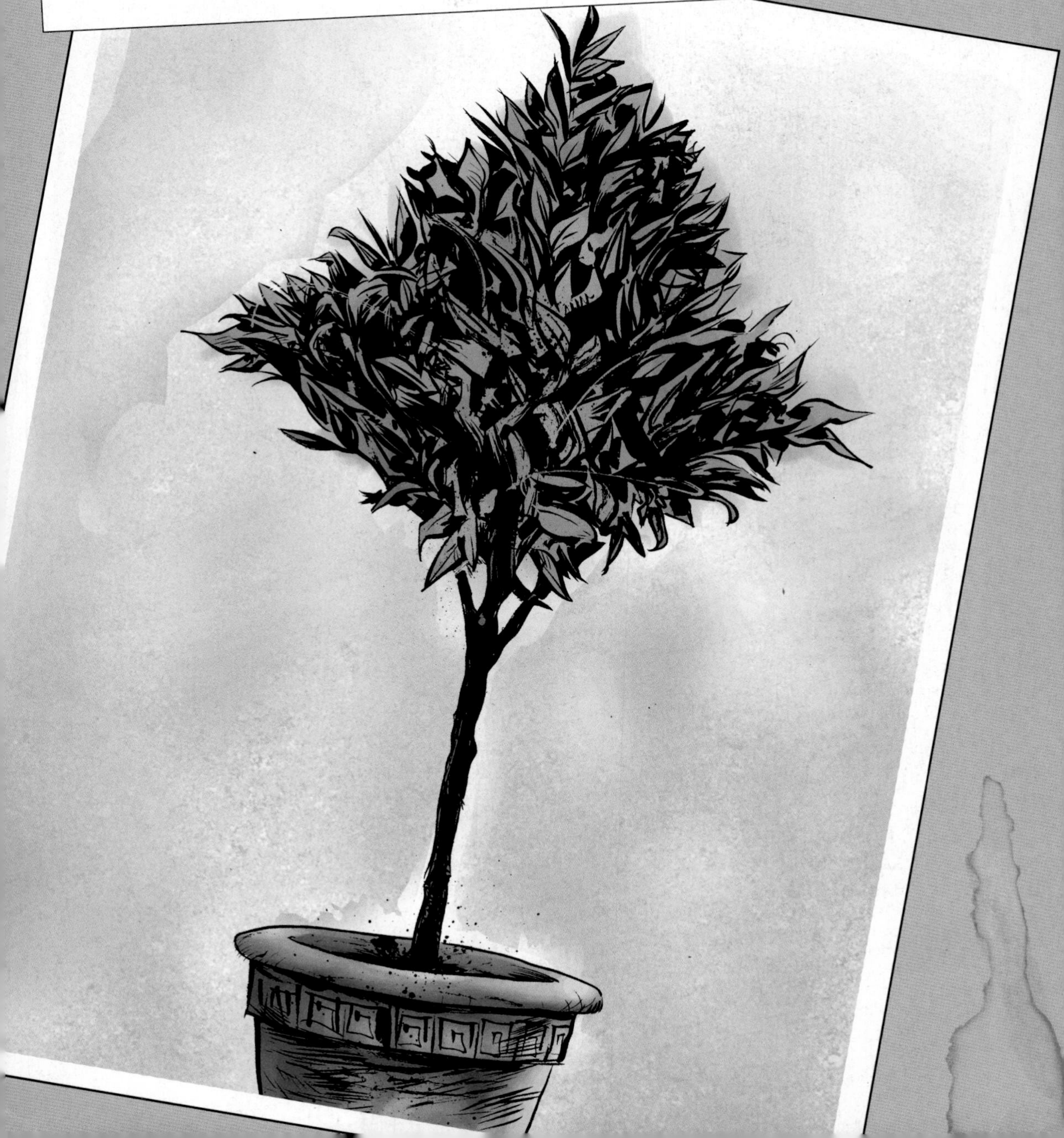

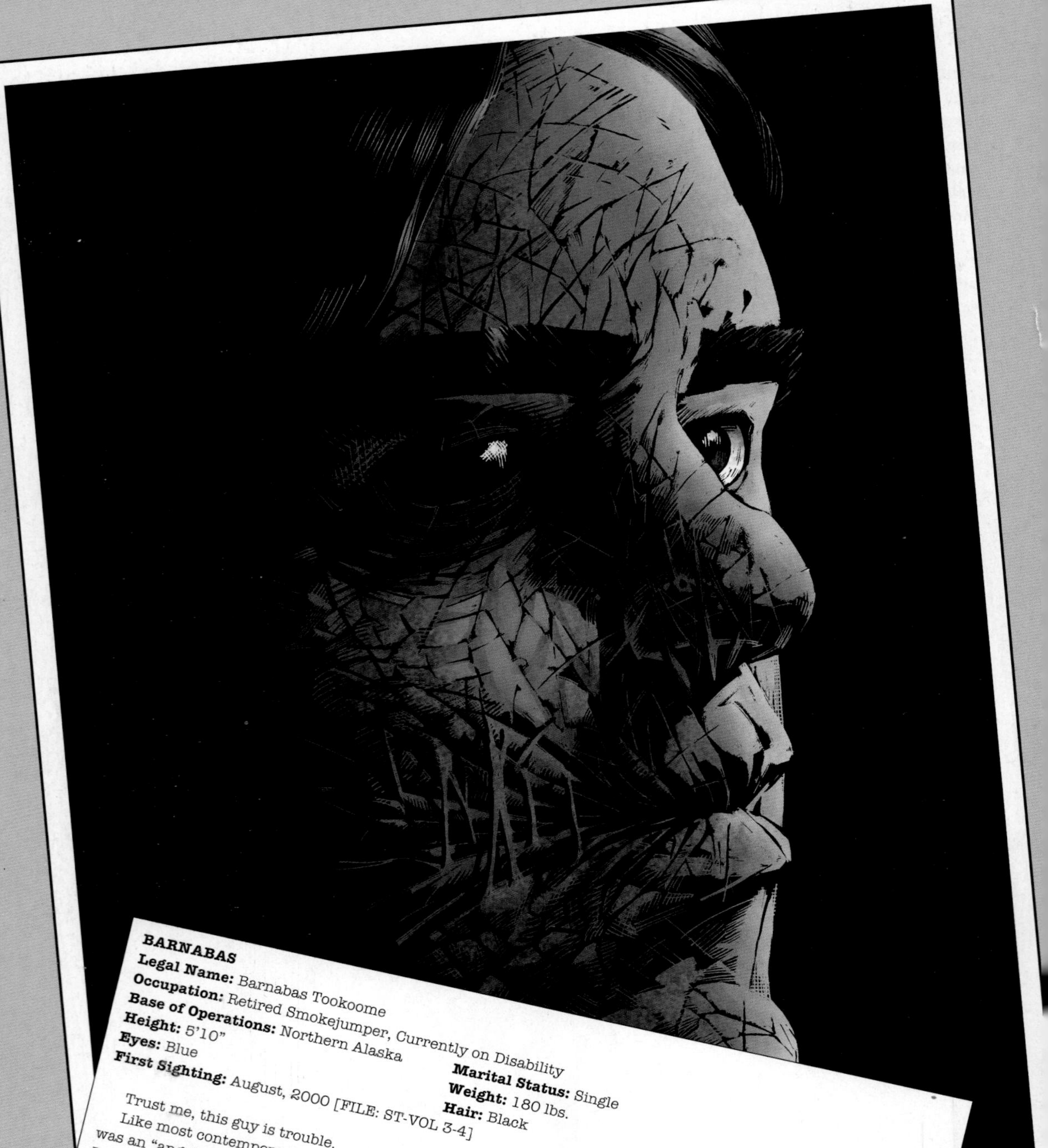

BARNABAS
Legal Name: Barnabas Tookoome
Occupation: Retired Smokejumper, Currently on Disability
Base of Operations: Northern Alaska
Height: 5'10"
Eyes: Blue
First Sighting: August, 2000 [FILE: ST-VOL 3-4]

Marital Status: Single
Weight: 180 lbs.
Hair: Black

Trust me, this guy is trouble.

Like most contemporary Inuit, Barnabas is an amalgamation of the past and present. While his grandfather was an "angakok," a medicine man right out of Nanook of the North, his dad was a highly respected geologist. I say "was" because Barnabas' father recently died under strange circumstances, and I wouldn't be surprised if his son was involved. While he may seem perfectly harmless, there's something not quite right about this Eskimo... and I don't mean his hideously disfigured face.

According to newspaper reports, Barnabas was severely burned while serving as a fire-fighting smokejumper in the woods of Northern Alaska, an incident that his colleagues say has left him eerily obsessed with fire. Like I say, he's a bit of a creepshow.

After the fishing vessel Kelly capsized, I believe that Barnabas found Tefé (the ship's only confirmed survivor) washed up on the shoreline near his cabin. He then personally nursed her back to health, though I suspect the Elemental would have done just fine without him. Barnabas now follows her around like a puppy dog, but because of your edict for me to keep my distance from Tefé at all times, I have been unable to ascertain the exact nature of their relationship. Still, it seems clear that he adores, possibly even worships the young woman.

At the end of the day, I'm not sure if Barnabas will be a bad influence on Tefé, or if she'll be a worse influence on him.